Fodor's 2002

South Florida

Fodor's Travel Publications • New York, Toronto, London, Sydney, Auckland
www.fodors.com

CONTENTS

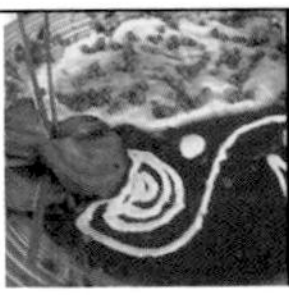

MAPS

Circled letters in text correspond to letters on the photographs. For more information on the sights pictured, turn to the indicated page number (A)> on each photograph.

DESTINATION SOUTH FLORIDA

Consider the sizzling salsa culture in South Beach and the preppy chic of Palm Beach. The coexistence of these two wildly different styles is just one example of the region's great diversity. The landscape ranges from the coral reefs of the Keys and the amazing water-based prairies of the Everglades to Atlantic-pounded beaches, which stretch from Miami to Palm Beach and on up the Treasure Coast. When you meet the people who call the area home, you encounter a veritable United Nations. Bahamian conch divers, European boutique owners, Cuban cigar rollers, and Yankee blue bloods. Meanwhile, foodies love South Florida. Culinary invention makes headlines at new restaurants, fresh-caught seafood still sings of the sea, and ethnic cuisine—especially Latin—spices up menus. The texture of the region richly rewards those who take the time to know it better.

MIAMI AND MIAMI BEACH

Ⓐ 39

To get the most out of Miami and its neighbor, Miami Beach, it helps to be a bit of a hedonist. By day, many local pleasures revolve around water and sunshine, as at the Ⓐ **Venetian Pool,** perhaps the most whimsical municipal swimming hole anywhere, complete with gondola moorings and Italian architecture. You can also learn to enjoy life with a Latin rhythm. Practical seminars are on view daily at Little Havana's Ⓑ**Domino Park,** on Southwest 15th Avenue, where Cuban-American retirees spend long afternoons indulging their passion. Forget about joining them, even if you

Ⓑ 34

Ⓒ 82

think of yourself as a pretty fair domino player—these guys will clean your clock. Instead, watch and wait for the subtropical sunset to turn the tempo way up: After nightfall, Miami is playland for party animals. Street musicians rule on

Ⓔ **Calle Ocho** (Southwest 8th Street), not far from Domino Park. The area around the Ⓒ**Bayside Marketplace** offers live music and cuisines of the world until late, as well as till-you-drop shopping until 11 on weekends. The pastels that brighten Miami's days give way to hot neon hues at bars like Ⓓ**The Clevelander.** Spend an hour strolling in superhip Ⓕ**South Beach,** home to hundreds of historic Art Deco buildings, where even the lifeguard stations have a retro look. If you know how to have fun, Miami is for you. If you're not sure how, well, *practice.* You've come to the right place.

To visit the Everglades is to see South Florida as it has been for millennia, since long before the coastal swamps were drained and long before Miami rose a short heron's flight to the east. This wilderness of almost otherworldly beauty stands in perfect, fragile counterpoint to Miami's throbbing Latin energy, offering refuge not only to hundreds of species of plants and animals but also to humans in need of communion with the natural world.

THE EVERGLADES

Ⓐ 115

On guided day trips, by walkway or boat, you'll see things of ineffable beauty, like snowy egrets feeding among the mangrove trees, in zones where no discernible boundary exists between the sea and the land. You're likely to come upon alligators, too, key players in the delicate Everglades ecosystem—strikingly on display at attractions such as the **ⒸEverglades Gator Park.** (The vast majority of a gator's facial muscles are devoted to snapping its jaws shut. The opposing muscles, which open the jaws, are few and weak. In theory—mind you, in *theory*—a headlock applied to an alligator's jaws can keep them from opening. If a gator comes at you with jaws wide open, run.) To properly see the River of Grass preserved by the **ⒺEverglades National Park,** rent a canoe for a multi-

Ⓑ 115

day paddle. Or climb into an airboat for a ride through similar terrain nearby. (Mosquito repellent is mandatory.) Or drive on down to Ⓓ**Smallwood's Store** in Chokoloskee Bay near Everglades City, built as a trading post in 1906 by an undauntable Everglades pioneer. When the din of the cicadas palls, try snorkeling among the reefs or canoeing through the mangroves that edge the shore of ⒶⒷ**Biscayne National Park.** The northern extremity of Florida's living reef, with 180,000 acres of coral and cays in Biscayne Bay, this, too, is Florida at its wild, gorgeous best, and its beauty puts description to shame.

FORT LAUDERDALE AND BROWARD COUNTY

Ⓐ 133

Fort Lauderdale has undergone a renaissance in the past decade. Once the premier spring-break spot to party hearty, the city has been transformed as officials have put the squeeze on student revelers and massively renovated the downtown and beach areas. In fact the Ⓐ**Fort Lauderdale beachfront** is looking better than ever. Yachts are spiffily tied up next to humbler craft at Pier Sixty-Six and along the city's characteristic canals, which edge the backyards along residential streets such as Ⓑ**Gordon Drive.** If you're yachtless, not to worry: Grab a water taxi to tour the city's 300 miles of navigable waterways. Downtown, along Las Olas Boulevard, musicians and crowds of strollers bring the night alive. At the Riverwalk, cafés and gazebos line the New River promenade. If you want to take a break from window-shopping, play 18 holes on one of the area's championship links. Students are still welcome in Fort Lauderdale, of course, but *Animal House* behavior is a thing of the past.

Ⓑ 126

PALM BEACH AND THE TREASURE COAST

Ⓐ 162

Palm Beach was built by—and exclusively for—the very wealthy. The stage was set by Whitehall, now the Ⓐ**Henry Morrison Flagler Museum,** named after the Standard Oil cofounder and railroad baron, who spared no expense in its construction. During ensuing decades Flagler's trains ferried other plutocrats, who created yet other trophy retreats, and today Rolls-Royces jostle Bentleys for parking spaces on Ⓒ**Worth Avenue.** Other towns above and below Palm Beach have their own affluent populations. But even in elegant communities such as Boca Raton, places like the Ⓑ**Gumbo Limbo Nature Center** let you get away from it all—and back to nature.

Ⓑ 183

Ⓒ 165

No other place in America, much less Florida, resembles the Keys. For starters, the largest portion of the continental United States' only living coral reef is here. Protecting the reef and the fragile

THE FLORIDA KEYS

Ⓐ 222

ecosystems it supports is a matter of critical concern. Appreciate the reef when you drive the Overseas Highway; it may not be with us forever. The beauty of the Keys would be reason enough to visit. A bonus is the Keys lifestyle. This is where America goes Caribbean. Your wristwatch starts to chafe, and napping at midday feels obligatory (though not much else does). Welcome to the Land That Stress Forgot. As you roll westward, leave the highway now and again to marvel at sun and sea or lay your head in places like Ⓐ**The Moorings** on Islamorada, as charming a lodging as you'll find, or the Ⓑ**Hawk's Cay Resort,** with its own movie-set appeal. The end of the road, literally, is Key West, a capital of High Quirk and, regrettably to admirers, no longer

Ⓑ 227

Ⓒ 240

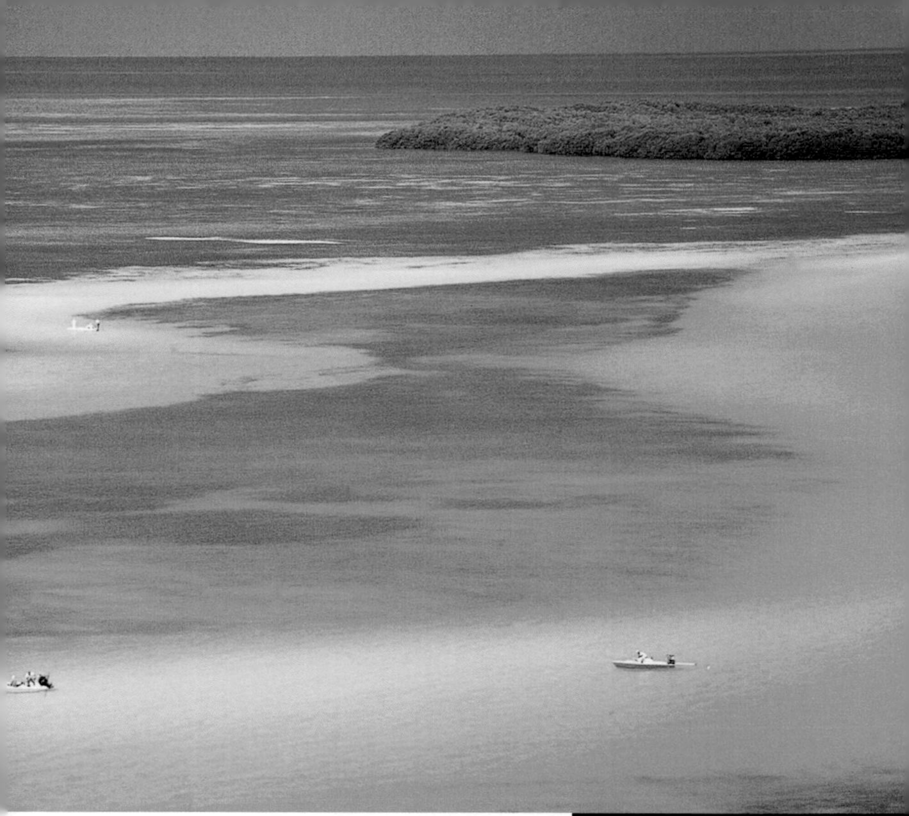

off the beaten track. No matter. If the crowds that gather daily at ©**Key West's Mallory Square** to watch the sunsets are bigger than ever, well, that just makes for a better street party afterward (and a party it is). Following your own sun worship, repair to Ⓓ**Duval Street** for pure living theater. There is *nothing* you might not see here. On the way back to America proper, stop at Ⓔ**John Pennekamp Coral Reef State Park** on Key Largo. As you snorkel or scuba dive among the vivid coral reefs swarming with bewitchingly bright fish, time stands still, which might just make your vacation feel a little longer.

Ⓓ〉242

Ⓔ〉211

FODOR'S CHOICE

Even with so many special places in South Florida, Fodor's writers and editors have their favorites. Here are a few that stand out.

BEACHES

Bahia Honda State Park, Bahia Honda Key. The natural sandy beach here, unusual in the Keys, extends on both gulf and ocean sides, and activities in the park abound, from hawk-watching to hiking. ☞ p. 233

Ⓓ **Bill Baggs Cape Florida State Recreation Area, Key Biscayne.** The beach is constantly buffeted by warm breezes and boasts a plethora of facilities, a historic lighthouse, and great views of sunsets and the Miami skyline. ☞ p. 43

Fort Lauderdale Beach. The area along Route A1A between Las Olas and Sunrise boulevards is a hot spot again, thanks to a pedestrian-friendly promenade and the absence of spring breakers. ☞ p. 132

South Beach, Miami. At this beach, which is as much a social experience as a sun-worshipping spot, there are volleyball nets, chickee huts for shade, and the most vibrantly painted lifeguard stands you'll ever see. Separating the sand from the traffic of Ocean Drive is palm-fringed Lummus Park. ☞ p. 22

Spanish River Park, Boca Raton. The renourished beach is connected to a large park by pedestrian tunnels under Route A1A. Filled with native vegetation, the park has nature trails and plenty of picnic tables and grills. ☞ p. 183

COMFORTS

Banyan Marina Apartments, Ft. Lauderdale. For high-end amenities and a water view at a bargain price, this gem can't be beat. *$$–$$$* ☞ p. 138

The Breakers, Palm Beach. The building, originally built over a century ago to resemble an opulent Italian Renaissance palace, is remarkable, as is the resort's ability to balance old-world luxury with modern conveniences. *$$$$* ☞ p. 167

Ⓙ **Delano Hotel, Miami Beach.** An air of surrealism hangs about this much-talked-about SoBe hotel, *the* hot spot for celebrities and other well-to-do visitors. *$$$$* ☞ p. 66

Ⓒ **Little Palm Island.** On its own palm-fringed island 3 mi off the shores of Little Torch Key, this dazzling resort of thatch-roof villas on stilts provides a secluded, one-of-a-kind experience. *$$$$* ☞ p. 236

The Moorings, Islamorada. This onetime coconut plantation has romantic cottages and houses tucked into a tropical forest that opens onto a private beach. *$$$–$$$$* ☞ p. 222

FLAVORS

Ⓖ **Norman's, Coral Gables.** Chef Norman Van Aken turns out artful masterpieces of New World cuisine, combining bold tastes from Latin, American, Caribbean, and Asian traditions. *$$$$* ☞ p. 45

Ⓑ **Café des Artistes, Key West.** Chef Andrew Berman's brilliant tropical version of French cuisine is served in a series of intimate dining rooms filled with tropical art and an upstairs outdoor patio. *$$$–$$$$* ☞ p. 247

Café L'Europe, Palm Beach. One of the area's most popular restaurants, noted for its European fine-dining experience and mood-setting atmosphere. *$$$–$$$$* ☞ p. 165

Mark's Las Olas, Fort Lauderdale. Chef/owner Mark Militello offers dazzling Florida-style creations, adding flavors from the Mediterranean, Caribbean, and Southwest. *$$–$$$* ☞ p. 135

Tom's Place, Boca Raton. Tom Wright serves up legendary barbecue ribs, friendly service, and moderate prices at this local landmark. *$* ☞ p. 186

MOMENTS

Everglades National Park from the tower on Shark Valley Loop. This 50-ft observation tower yields a splendid panorama of the wide River of Grass as it sweeps southward toward the Gulf of Mexico. ☞ p. 107

Ⓘ **Ocean Drive in the Art Deco District, Miami Beach.** Feast your eyes on the brilliantly restored vintage art deco hotels and the glorious palm-lined beachfront. ☞ p. 24

Seven Mile Bridge, Marathon. One of the world's longest, this Middle Keys bridge lifts you above the shimmering waters of ocean and bay, providing a spectacular blend of color and light. ☞ p. 232

Sunset scene at Mallory Square, Key West. Here sunset draws street performers, vendors, and thousands of onlookers to Mallory Dock and the eponymous square nearby. ☞ p. 240

PLACES

Flagler Museum, Palm Beach. Henry Flagler, the Standard Oil magnate, built Whitehall in 1901 as a gift for his wife. The building has been restored, and visitors can now get a glimpse of Palm Beach's gilded age. ☞ p. 162

Ⓔ **Hemingway House, Key West.** The home where Ernest Hemingway wrote several of his famous novels remains Key West's most popular attraction. ☞ p. 243

Ⓗ **Morikami Museum and Japanese Gardens, Delray Beach.** The leading U.S. center for Japanese and American cultural exchange is housed in a model of a Japanese imperial villa. ☞ p. 181

Ⓕ **Museum of Discovery and Science, Fort Lauderdale.** Providing hands-on experiences, this playground for kids (and adults) contains fun, interactive exhibits on ecology, health, and other sciences. ☞ p. 131

Ⓐ **Vizcaya Museum and Gardens, Coconut Grove.** The estate of industrialist James Deering, overlooking Biscayne Bay, has an Italian Renaissance–style villa containing Baroque, Rococo, and Neoclassical art and furniture. ☞ p. 42

1 MIAMI AND MIAMI BEACH

Miami is arguably the most exotic city that Americans can visit without a passport. On a typical evening in South Beach, you'll witness the energy and passion of Rio, Monte Carlo, Havana, and Hemingway's Paris. Other neighborhoods also bring the world into clearer focus through diverse architecture, dining, and customs, sparking a renaissance for Miami and its sultry sister, Miami Beach, that's reminiscent of the cities' glory days in the 1920s.

Updated by Kathy Foster, Jen Karetnick, Martha Limner, Tiffany Madera, Gretchen Schmidt, Lisa Simundson, Matthew Windsor

MIAMI IS DIFFERENT from any other city in America—or any city in Latin America for that matter, although it has a distinctly Latin flavor. Both logically and geologically, Miami shouldn't even be here. Resting on a paved swamp between the Everglades and the Atlantic Ocean, the city is subject to periodic flooding, riots, hurricanes, and the onslaught of swallow-size mosquitoes. Despite the downsides, however, Miami is a vibrant city that works and plays with vigor.

The Tequesta Indians called this area home long before Spain's gold-laden treasure ships sailed along the Gulf Stream a few miles offshore. Foreshadowing 20th-century corporations, they traded with mainland neighbors to the north and island brethren to the south. Today their descendants are the 150-plus U.S. and multinational companies whose Latin American headquarters are based in Greater Miami. For fans of international business and random statistics, Greater Miami is home to more than 40 foreign bank agencies, 11 Edge Act banks, 23 foreign trade offices, 31 binational chambers of commerce, and 53 foreign consulates.

The city has seen a decade of big changes. In the late 1980s Miami Beach was an ocean-side geriatric ward. Today's South Beach residents have the kind of hip that doesn't break. The average age dropped from the mid-sixties in 1980 to a youthful early forties today. Toned young men outnumber svelte young women 2 to 1, and hormones are as plentiful as pierced tongues. At night the revitalized Lincoln Road Mall is in full swing with cafés, galleries, and theaters, but it is also suffering vacancies due to rapidly rising rents. The bloom may not be off the rose, but cash-crazy entrepreneurs hoping to strike it rich on Miami's popularity are finding the pie isn't large enough to feed their financial fantasies. Those who have seen how high rents can crush a dream are heading to North Beach and the southern neighborhoods of South Beach, whose derelict buildings are a flashback to the pre-renaissance days of the 1980s. Perhaps this is where the next revival will take place (file this under insider information).

As you plan your trip, know that winter *is* the best time to visit, but if money is an issue, come in the off-season—after Easter and before October. You'll find plenty to do, and room rates are considerably lower. Summer brings many European and Latin American vacationers, who find Miami congenial despite the heat, humidity, and intense afternoon thunderstorms.

Regardless of when you arrive, once you're here, you'll suspect that you've entered Cuban air space. No matter where you spin your radio dial, virtually every announcer punctuates each sentence with an emphatic "COO-BAH!" Look around, and you'll see Spanish on billboards, hear it on elevators, and pick it up on the streets. But Miami sways to more than just a Latin beat. *Newsweek* called the city "America's Casablanca," and it may be right. In addition to populations from Brazil, Colombia, El Salvador, Haiti, Jamaica, Nicaragua, Panama, Puerto Rico, Venezuela, and of course Cuba, there are also representatives from China, Germany, Greece, Iran, Israel, Italy, Lebanon, Malaysia, Russia, and Sweden—all speaking a veritable babel of tongues. Miami has accepted its montage of nationalities, and it now celebrates this cultural diversity through languages, festivals, world-beat music, and a wealth of exotic restaurants.

If you're concerned about Miami crime, you'll be glad to know that criminals are off the street—and seem to be running for public office.

Forget about D.C. If you want weird politics, spread out a blanket and enjoy the show. Ex-mayor Xavier Suarez was removed from office in March 1998 after a judge threw out absentee ballots that included votes from dead people. The Miami City Commission chairman was also removed following a voter fraud conviction, and a state senator was re-elected despite being under indictment for pocketing profits from sham home-health-care companies. Oddly enough, Miami-Dade County came out fairly unscathed in the 2000 Florida presidential race, perhaps overshadowed by the well-publicized ballot woes of Palm Beach County to the north.

Corrupt politicians aside, Miami has its share of the same crimes that plague any major city. However, the widely publicized crimes against tourists of the early 1990s led to stepped-up and effective visitor-safety programs. Highway direction signs with red-sunburst logos are installed at ¼-mi intervals on major roads and lead directly to such tourist hot spots as Coconut Grove, Coral Gables, South Beach, and the Port of Miami. Patrol cars bearing the sunburst logo are driven by TOP (Tourist Oriented Police) Cops, who cruise heavily touristed areas and add a sense of safety. Identification that made rental cars conspicuous to would-be criminals has been removed, and multilingual pamphlets on avoiding crime are widely distributed. The precautions have had a positive impact. From 1992 to 1998 the number of tourist robberies in Greater Miami decreased more than 80%.

What *is* on the increase is Miami's film profile. In recent years Arnold Schwarzenegger and Jamie Lee Curtis filmed *True Lies* here, Al Pacino and Johnny Depp dropped by to shoot scenes for *Donnie Brasco,* Jim Carrey rose to stardom through the Miami-based *Ace Ventura: Pet Detective,* Robin Williams and Nathan Lane used two Deco buildings on Ocean Drive as their nightclub in *The Birdcage,* and Cameron Diaz discovered a new brand of hair gel in *There's Something About Mary.* All in all, it's a far cry from when Esther Williams used to perform water ballet in Coral Gables's Venetian Pool. Add to this mix daily fashion-magazine and TV shoots, and you'll see that Miami is made for the media.

Five major-league sports franchises call Miami home, along with the Doral-Ryder Open Tournament, the Lipton Championships, Genuity Classic in golf, the Ericsson Open, and the culture-contributing Miami City Ballet and Florida Grand Opera. Miami played host to the Summit of the Americas in 1994 and to the Super Bowl in 1999. Nearly 10 million tourists arrive annually to see what's shaking in Miami-Dade County and discover a multicultural metropolis that invites the world to celebrate its diversity.

New and Noteworthy

There's so much construction going on in Miami, you'd suspect they're trying to tear down the town and put up a city. Tool belts are nearly as prevalent as bikinis, and building sounds echo everywhere.

Up Biscayne Boulevard, the **Freedom Tower,** one of downtown's most prominent landmarks, is being restored by the Cuban American National Foundation to house its museum. **Parrot Jungle** is destined to give up its South Miami location for digs near Watson Island by the Port of Miami. At press time (summer 2001) the move was scheduled to be completed by May 2002.

Three new **Ritz-Carlton** properties are in the works, in Coconut Grove, Key Biscayne, and on South Beach, where $95 million will be poured into the less-than-impressive DiLido to bring it up to Ritz standards.

Pleasures and Pastimes

Beaches

Greater Miami has numerous free beaches to fit every style. A sandy, 300-ft-wide beach with several distinct sections extends for 10 mi from the foot of Miami Beach north to Haulover Beach Park. Amazingly, it's all man-made. Seriously eroded during the mid-1970s, the beach was restored in a $51.5 million project between 1977 and 1981 and remains an ongoing project for environmental engineers, who spiff up the sands every few years. Between 23rd and 44th streets, Miami Beach built boardwalks and protective walkways atop a dune landscaped with sea oats, sea grape, and other native plants whose roots keep the sand from blowing away. Farther north there's even a nude beach, and Key Biscayne adds more great strands to Miami's collection. Even if the Deco District didn't exist, the area's beaches would be enough to satisfy tourists.

Boating

It's not uncommon for traffic to jam at boat ramps, especially on weekend mornings, but the waters are worth the wait. If you have the opportunity to sail, do so. Blue skies, calm seas, and a view of the city skyline make for a pleasurable outing—especially at twilight, when the fabled "moon over Miami" casts a soft glow on the water. Key Biscayne's calm waves and strong breezes are perfect for sailing and windsurfing, and although Dinner Key and the Coconut Grove waterfront remain the center of sailing in Greater Miami, sailboat moorings and rentals sit along other parts of the bay and up the Miami River.

Miami's idle rich prefer attacking the water in sleek, fast, and nicotine-free cigarette boats, but there's plenty of less powerful powerboating to enjoy as well. Greater Miami has numerous marinas, and dockmasters can provide information on any marine services you may need. Ask for *Teall's Tides and Guides, Miami-Dade County,* and other nautical publications.

Dining

Miami cuisine is what mouths were made for. The city serves up a veritable United Nations of dining experiences, including dishes native to Spain, Cuba, and Nicaragua as well as China, India, Thailand, Vietnam, and other Asian cultures. Chefs from the tropics combine fresh, natural foods—especially seafood—with classic island-style dishes, creating a new American cuisine that is sometimes called Floribbean. Another style finding its way around U.S. restaurants is the Miami-born New World cuisine. The title comes from chefs who realized their latest creations were based on ingredients found along the trade routes discovered by early explorers of the "New World."

Nightlife

Miami has more clubs than a deck of cards, but the ones that command the most attention are those where people pose with less expression than Mona Lisa and where mirrored balls salvaged from the set of *Saturday Night Fever* spin as fast as the techno-pop CDs.

The heaviest concentration of these nightspots is in South Beach along Ocean Drive, Washington Avenue, and Lincoln Road Mall. Other nightlife centers on Little Havana, Coconut Grove, and the fringes of downtown Miami. Clubs offer jazz, reggae, salsa, various forms of rock, disco, and Top 40 sounds on different nights of the week—most played at a body-thumping, ear-throbbing volume. If you prefer to hear what people are saying, look for small lobby bars in art deco hotels. Throughout Greater Miami, bars and cocktail lounges in larger hotels operate nightly discos with live weekend entertainment. Many hotels extend their bars into open-air courtyards, where patrons dine and dance under the stars throughout the year. Some clubs refuse entrance to anyone under 21, others to those under 25, so if that is a concern, call ahead. It's also a good idea to ask in advance about cover charges; policies change frequently. And be warned: Even the most popular club can fall out of favor quickly. Ask your hotel's concierge, check Friday's *Miami Herald,* or grab a copy of *New Times,* an entertainment tabloid that includes listings of alternative clubs and live bands. With this and some insider info from locals, you should be able to tell what's hot and what's just a dying ember.

Spectator Sports

Greater Miami has franchises in NBA and WNBA basketball, football, hockey, and baseball. Thanks to Dan Marino's record-breaking accomplishments, fans still turn out en masse for the Dolphins, as they do for basketball's Heat and the 1997 World Series champion Marlins. Miami also hosts top-rated events in NASCAR racing, boat racing, jai alai, and tennis, and it's home to the high-ranking University of Miami Hurricanes football team. Generally you can find daily listings of local events in the sports section of the *Miami Herald,* while Friday's "Weekend" section carries more detailed schedules and coverage.

Activities of the annual Orange Bowl and Junior Orange Bowl Festival take place from early November until well into the new year. Best known for its King Orange Jamboree Parade and the Federal Express/Orange Bowl Football Classic, the festival also includes two tennis tournaments. The Junior Orange Bowl Festival is the world's largest youth festival, with more than 20 events between November and January, including sports, cultural, and performing-arts activities held throughout Miami-Dade County.

EXPLORING MIAMI AND MIAMI BEACH

If you had arrived here 40 years ago with Fodor's guide in hand, chances are you'd be thumbing through listings looking for alligator wrestlers and u-pick citrus groves. Well, things have changed. While Disney sidetracked families in Orlando, Miami was developing a grown-up attitude courtesy of *Miami Vice,* European fashion photographers, and historic preservationists. Nowadays the wildest ride is the city itself.

Climb aboard and check out the different sides of Greater Miami. Miami, on the mainland, is South Florida's commercial hub, while its sultry sister, Miami Beach (America's Riviera), encompasses 17 islands in Biscayne Bay. Seducing winter refugees with its warm sunshine, sandy beaches, shady palms, and ever-rocking nightlife, this is what most people envision when planning a trip to what they think of as Miami. These same visitors fail to realize that there's more to Miami Beach than the bustle of South Beach and its Deco District. Indeed there are quieter areas to the north, with names like Sunny Isles, Surfside, and Bal Harbour.

During the day downtown Miami has become the lively hub of the mainland city, now more accessible thanks to the Metromover extension. Other major attractions include Coconut Grove, Coral Gables, Little Havana, and, of course, the South Beach/Art Deco District, but since these areas are spread out beyond the reach of public transportation, you'll have to drive. Rent a convertible if you can. There's nothing quite like wearing cool shades and feeling the wind in your hair as you drive across one of the causeways en route to Miami Beach. Take precautions if you wear a rug.

You're in luck: finding your way around Greater Miami is easy if you know how the numbering system works—just as quantum mechanics is easy for physicists. Miami is laid out on a grid with four quadrants—northeast, northwest, southeast, and southwest—which meet at Miami Avenue and Flagler Street. Miami Avenue separates east from west, and Flagler Street separates north from south. Avenues and courts run north–south; streets, terraces, and ways run east–west. Roads run diagonally, northwest–southeast. But other districts—Miami Beach, Coral Gables, and Hialeah—may or may not follow this system, and along the curve of Biscayne Bay, the symmetrical grid may shift diagonally. It's best to buy a detailed map, stick to the major roads, and ask directions early and often. However, make sure you're in a safe neighborhood or public place when you seek guidance; cabbies and cops are good resources.

Numbers in the text correspond to numbers in the margin and on the Miami Beach; Downtown Miami; Miami, Coral Gables, Coconut Grove, and Key Biscayne; and South Dade maps.

Great Itineraries

IF YOU HAVE 3 DAYS

To recuperate from your journey, grab your lotion and head to the ocean, more specifically Ocean Drive on South Beach, where you can catch some rays while relaxing on the white sands. Afterward, take a guided or self-guided tour of the Art Deco District to see what all the fuss is about. Keep the evening free to socialize at Ocean Drive cafés. The following day drive through Little Havana to witness the heartbeat of Miami's Cuban culture (and snag a stogie) on your way south to Coconut Grove's Vizcaya. Wrap up the evening a few blocks away in downtown Coconut Grove, enjoying its partylike atmosphere and many nightspots. On the last day head over to Coral Gables to take in the eye-popping display of 1920s Mediterranean revival architecture in the neighborhoods surrounding the city center and the majestic Biltmore Hotel; then take a dip in the fantastic thematic Venetian Pool. That night indulge in an evening of fine dining at your choice of gourmet restaurants in Coral Gables.

IF YOU HAVE 5 DAYS

Follow the suggested three-day itinerary, and on day four add a visit to the beaches of Virginia Key and Key Biscayne, where you can take a diving trip or fishing excursion, learn to windsurf, or do absolutely nothing but watch the water. On day five step back to the 1950s with a cruise up Collins Avenue to some of the monolithic hotels, such as the Fontainebleau Hilton and Eden Roc; continue north to the elegant shops of Bal Harbour; and return to South Beach for an evening of shopping, drinking, and outdoor dining at Lincoln Road Mall.

IF YOU HAVE 7 DAYS

A week gives you just enough time to experience fully the multicultural, cosmopolitan, tropical mélange that is Greater Miami and its beaches. On day six see where it all began. Use the Miami Metromover to ride above downtown Miami before touring the streets (if possible, on a tour with historian Dr. Paul George). Take time to visit the Miami-Dade Cultural Center, home of art and history museums. In the evening check out the shops and clubs at Bayside Marketplace. The final day can be used to visit South Miami, site of Parrot Jungle (for now), Fairchild Tropical Garden, and the Shops at Sunset Place. Keep the evening free to revisit your favorite nightspots.

South Beach/Miami Beach

The hub of Miami Beach is South Beach (SoBe, to anyone but locals), and the hub of South Beach is the 1-square-mi Art Deco District, fronted on the east by Ocean Drive and on the west by Alton Road. The story of South Beach has become the story of Miami. In the early 1980s South Beach's vintage hotels were badly run down, catering mostly to infirm retirees. But a group of visionaries led by the late Barbara Baer Capitman, a spirited New York transplant, saw this collection of buildings as an architectural treasure to be salvaged from a sea of mindless urban renewal. It was, and is, a peerless grouping of art deco architecture from the 1920s to 1950s, whose forms and decorative details are drawn from nature, the streamlined shapes of modern transportation and industrial machinery, and human extravagance.

Investors started fixing up the interiors of these hotels and repainting their exteriors with a vibrant pastel palette—a look made famous by *Miami Vice*. International bistro operators sensed the potential for a new café society. Fashion photographers and the media took note, and celebrities like singer Gloria Estefan; the late designer Gianni Versace, whose fashions captured the feel of the awakening city; and record executive Chris Blackwell bought a piece of the action.

As a result, South Beach now holds the distinction of being the nation's first 20th-century district on the National Register of Historic Places, with more than 800 significant buildings making the roll. New high-rises and hotels spring up, areas like SoFi (south of Fifth) blossom, and clubs open (and close) with dizzying speed. Photographers pose beautiful models for shoots, tanned skaters zip past palm trees, and tourists flock to see the action.

Yet Miami Beach is more than just SoBe. (The northern edge of South Beach is generally considered to be around 24th–28th streets, while Miami Beach itself extends well north.) It also consists of a collection of quiet neighborhoods where Little Leaguers play ball, senior citizens stand at bus stops, and locals do their shopping away from the prying eyes of visitors. Surprisingly, Miami Beach is a great walking town in the middle of a great city.

Several things are plentiful in SoBe: pierced body parts, cell phones, and meter maids. Tickets are given freely when meters expire, and towing charges are high. Check the meter to see when parking fees are required; times vary by district. From mid-morning on, parking is scarce along Ocean Drive. You'll do better on Collins or Washington avenues, the next two streets to the west. Fortunately, there are several surface parking lots south and west of the Jackie Gleason Theater, on 17th Street, and parking garages on Collins Avenue at 7th and 13th streets, on Washington Avenue at 12th Street, and west of Washington at 17th Street. Keep these sites in mind, especially at night, when cruising traffic makes it best to park your car and see SoBe on foot. Better yet, catch the colorful Electrowave shuttle buses that cover South Beach well into the wee hours—for 25¢, they're the best deal in town.

A Good Walk

The stretch of Ocean Drive from 1st to 23rd streets—primarily the 10-block stretch from 5th to 15th streets—has become the most talked-about beachfront in America. A bevy of art deco jewels hugs the drive, while across the street lies palm-fringed **Lummus Park** ①, whose south end is a good starting point for a walk. Beginning early (at 8) gives you the pleasure of watching the awakening city without distraction. Sanitation men hose down dirty streets, merchants prepare window displays, bakers bake, and construction workers change the skyline one brick at a time. Cross to the west side of Ocean Drive, where there are many sidewalk cafés, and walk north, taking note of the Park Central Hotel, built in 1937 by Deco architect Henry Hohauser.

At 10th Street recross Ocean Drive to the beach side and visit the **Art Deco District Welcome Center** ② in the 1950s-era Oceanfront Auditorium. Here you can rent tapes or hire a guide for a Deco District tour.

Look back across Ocean Drive and take a look at the wonderful flying-saucer architecture of the Clevelander, at No. 1020. On the next block you'll see the late Gianni Versace's Spanish Mediterranean **Casa Casuarina** ③, once known as Amsterdam Palace. Graceful fluted columns stand guard at the Leslie (No. 1244) and **The Carlyle** ④.

Walk two blocks west (away from the ocean) on 13th Street to Washington Avenue, where a mix of chic restaurants, avant-garde shops, delicatessens, produce markets, and nightclubs have spiced up a once-derelict neighborhood. Turn left on Washington and walk 2½ blocks south to **Wolfsonian–Florida International University** ⑤, which showcases artistic movements from 1885 to 1945.

Provided you haven't spent too long in the museum, return north on Washington Avenue past 14th Street, and turn left on **Espanola Way** ⑥, a narrow street of Mediterranean revival buildings, eclectic shops, and a weekend market. Continue west to Meridian Avenue and turn right. Three blocks north of Espanola Way is the redesigned **Lincoln Road Mall** ⑦, which is often paired with Ocean Drive as part of must-see South Beach.

The next main street north of Lincoln Road is 17th Street, and to the east is the Miami Beach Convention Center. Walk behind the massive building to the corner of Meridian Avenue and 19th Street to see the chilling **Holocaust Memorial** ⑧, a monumental record honoring the 6 million Jewish victims of the Holocaust.

Head east to the **Bass Museum of Art** ⑨, a Maya-inspired temple filled with European splendors. Return to Ocean Drive in time to pull up a chair at an outdoor café, order an espresso, and settle down for an evening of people-watching, SoBe's most popular pastime. If you've seen enough people, grab some late rays at one of the area's beaches, which offer different sands for different tans. You can go back to Lummus Park (*the* beach) or head north, where there's a boardwalk for walking but no allowance for skates and bicycles.

TIMING

To see only the art deco buildings on Ocean Drive, allow one hour minimum. Depending on your interests, schedule at least five hours and include a drink or meal at a café and browsing time in the shops on Ocean Drive, along Espanola Way, and at Lincoln Road Mall.

Start your walking tour as early in the day as possible. In winter the street becomes crowded as the day wears on, and in summer, afternoon heat and humidity can be unbearable, wilting even the hardiest soul. Finishing by mid-afternoon also enables you to hit the beach and cool your heels in the warm sand.

Sights to See

❷ **Art Deco District Welcome Center.** Run by the Miami Design Preservation League, this clearinghouse in the Oceanfront Auditorium provides information about the buildings in the Art Deco District. A well-stocked gift shop sells 1930s–50s art deco memorabilia, posters, and books on Miami's history. Several tours—covering Lincoln Road, Espanola Way, North Beach, the entire Art Deco District, and more—start here. You can choose to rent audiotapes for a self-guided tour, join the regular Saturday-morning or Thursday-evening walking tour, or take a bicycle tour, all providing detailed histories of the Deco hotels. ✉ *1001 Ocean Dr., at Barbara Capitman Way,* ☎ *305/531–3484.* 🎫 *Free.* ⏲ *Sun.–Thurs. 10–10, Fri.–Sat. 10–midnight.*

Art Deco District Welcome Center 2
Bass Museum of Art . . .9
The Carlyle 4
Casa Casuarina 3
Espanola Way 6
Holocaust Memorial 8
Lincoln Road Mall 7
Lummus Park 1
The Wolfsonian–Florida International University 5

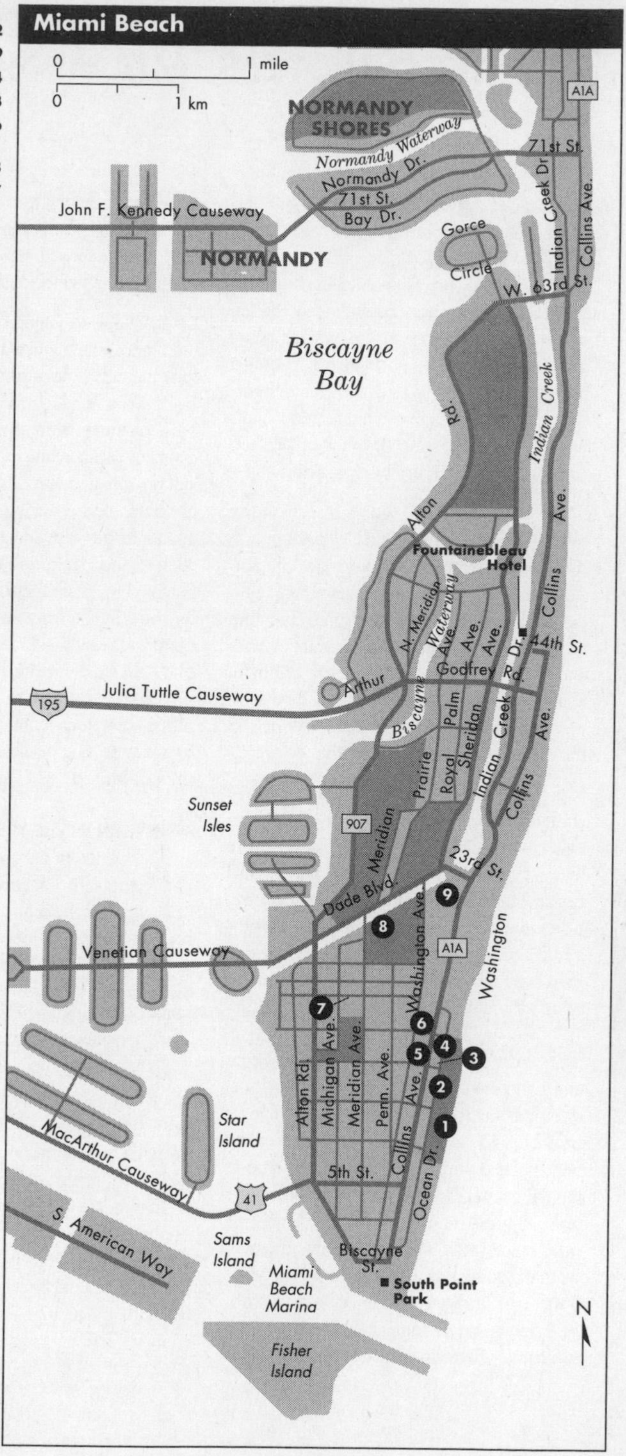

Close-Up

ART DECO HOTELS: MIAMI NICE

WITH APOLOGIES TO the flamingo, Miami's most recognizable icons are now the art deco hotels of South Beach. Their story begins in the 1920s, when Miami Beach was a winter playground of the rich, and grand, themed hotels ruled. By the late '20s, however, shipping problems and a hurricane turned the boom to bust, and another approach to attract vacationers was needed.

In the early 1930s it was the turn of the middle class, which was drawn south by a more affordable version of paradise. New hotels were needed, and the architectural motif of choice became what we call Deco (for purists, Moderne), based on a sleek and cheerful look with geometric designs and creative colors. It was introduced in Paris in the '20s and later crossed the Atlantic.

In South Beach, architects added other shapes brought to America by industrial designers: streamlined, aerodynamic forms based on trains, ocean liners, and automobiles. Using a steel-and-concrete box as a foundation, architects dipped into this new grab bag of styles to accessorize their hotels. Pylons, spheres, cylinders, and cubes thrust out from facades and roofs. "Eyebrows," small ledges topping window frames, popped out of buildings like concrete caps. To soften sharp edges, designers added wraparound windows and curved corners, many ornamented with racing stripes. To reflect the beach locale, nautical elements were added: portholes appeared in sets of three. Small images of seaweed, starfish, and rolling waves were plastered, painted, or etched on walls. Buildings looked ready to go to sea. Also taking advantage of the environment, sunlight, an abundant commodity, was brought indoors through glass blocks. But because there was no air-conditioning, coolness was achieved by planting shady palms and laying terrazzo tile.

Of course, everything has a life span, and the Deco hotels were no exception. Eventually, bold colors and creative accents became cliché, and ensuing decades saw owners hide their hotels beneath coats of plain white or beige paint. Deco still had its proponents, inspiring later architects, most notably Morris Lapidus, to create larger-than-life 1950s Deco hotels, such as the Fontainebleau and Eden Roc. But the days of small Deco hotels had passed. By the 1970s they were no longer welcoming tourists . . . or welcoming to look at. Most had matured into flophouses or dirt-cheap homes for retirees. Various plans ranging from leveling the buildings to legalizing gambling were proposed—and defeated.

THEN IN THE 1980S, an unusual confluence of people and events proved the area's salvation. The hyperactive cop show *Miami Vice*, set against the newly painted pastel facades of Ocean Drive, portrayed an exotic tropical appeal. European fashion photographers, restaurateurs, and entrepreneurs started using the area as a backdrop for models, cafés, and resurrected hotels. Above all, there was Barbara Baer Capitman, a senior citizen who reviewed South Beach's buildings and proposed it for the National Register of Historic Places. Thanks to her efforts and the ongoing drive of others to rescue, maintain, and improve these historic jewels, a new generation (yourself included) can experience the same tropical pleasures enjoyed by travelers of the 1930s.

Bal Harbour. This affluent community, known for its upscale shops, has a stretch of prime beach real estate, where wealthy condominium owners cluster during the winter. Look close, and you may spy Bob Dole sunning himself outside his condo. ✉ *Collins Ave. between 96th and 103rd Sts.*

❾ **Bass Museum of Art.** A diverse collection of European art is the focus of this fortresslike museum made of keystone, a short drive north of SoBe's key sights. Works on display include *The Holy Family,* a painting by Peter Paul Rubens; *The Tournament,* one of several 16th-century Flemish tapestries; and works by Albrecht Dürer and Henri de Toulouse-Lautrec. An $8 million, three-phase expansion by architect Arata Isozaki added a new wing, cafeteria, and theater, doubling the museum's size to nearly 40,000 square ft. ✉ *2121 Park Ave.,* ☎ *305/673–7530,* WEB *www.bassmuseum.org.* 🎫 *$5.* ⏲ *Tues.–Sat. 10–5, except 1–9 the 2nd and 4th Wed. of each month; Sun. 1–5.*

❹ **The Carlyle.** Built in 1941, this empty Deco building no longer functions as a hotel, but it's still popular as a movie location. Fans will recognize it and its neighbor, the Leslie, as the nightclub from *The Birdcage,* starring Robin Williams and Nathan Lane. ✉ *1250 Ocean Dr.*

❸ **Casa Casuarina.** In the early 1980s, before South Beach became the hotbed of chicness, the late Italian designer Gianni Versace purchased this run-down Spanish Mediterranean residence, built before the arrival of Deco. Today the home is an ornate three-story palazzo with a guest house and a copper-dome rooftop observatory and pool that were added at the expense of a 1950s hotel, the Revere. Its loss and the razing of the fabled Deco Senator became a rallying point for preservationists, who like to point out that although they lost a few, they saved 40. In July 1997 Versace was tragically shot and killed in front of his home. Like a tropical Ford's Theatre, this now attracts picture-taking tourists. Eerie. ✉ *1114 Ocean Dr.*

★ ❻ **Espanola Way.** The Mediterranean revival buildings along this road were constructed in 1925 and frequented through the years by artists and writers. In the 1930s future bandleader Desi Arnaz strapped on a conga drum and started beating out a rumba rhythm at a nightclub that is now the Clay Hotel, a youth hostel. Since high rents have pushed some merchants out and vacant storefronts have resulted, try to visit this quaint avenue on a Sunday afternoon, when itinerant dealers and craftspeople set up shop to sell everything from garage-sale items to handcrafted bongo drums. Between Washington and Drexel avenues, the road has been narrowed to a single lane, and Miami Beach's trademark pink sidewalks have been widened to accommodate sidewalk cafés and shops selling imaginative clothing, jewelry, and art.

★ **Fontainebleau Hilton Resort and Towers.** For a sense of what Miami was like during the Fabulous '50s, take a drive north to see the finest example of Miami Beach's grandiose architecture. By the 1950s smaller Deco-era hotels were passé, and architects like Morris Lapidus got busy designing free-flowing hotels that affirmed the American attitude of "bigger is better." Even if you're not a guest, wander through the lobby and spectacular pool area just to feel the energy generated by an army of bellhops, clerks, concierges, and travelers. ✉ *4441 Collins Ave.,* ☎ *305/538–2000.*

Haulover Beach Park. At this county park, far from the action of SoBe, you can see the Miami of 30 years ago. Pack a picnic, use the barbecue grills, or grab a snack at the concession stand. If you're into fitness, you may like the tennis and volleyball courts or paths designed for exercise, walking, and bicycling. If you're into cleanliness, take advantage of the shower facilities. The beach is nice for those who want water without long marches across hot sand, and a popular clothing-optional section at the north end of the beach lures people who want to tan every nook and cranny. Other offerings are kite rentals, kayak rentals, charter fishing excursions, and a par-3, nine-hole golf course. ✉ *10800 Collins Ave., Sunny Isles,* ☎ *305/947–3525,* WEB *co.miami-dade.fl.us/parks.* 🎫 *$4 per vehicle.* ⏲ *Daily sunrise–sunset.*

❽ **Holocaust Memorial.** The focus of the memorial is a 42-ft-high bronze arm rising from the ground, with sculptured people climbing the arm seeking escape. Don't stare from the street. Enter the courtyard to see the chilling memorial wall and hear the eerie songs that seem to give voice to the victims. ✉ *1933–1945 Meridian Ave.,* ☎ *305/538–1663,* WEB *www.holocaustmmb.org.* 🎫 *Donation welcome.* ⏲ *Daily 9–9.*

NEED A BREAK? If your feet are still holding up, head to the **Delano Hotel** (✉ 1685 Collins Ave., ☎ 305/674–6400) for a drink. This surrealistic hotel, like a Calvin Klein ad come to life, delivers fabulousness every step of the way. It's popular among SoBe's fashion models and hepcats.

★ ❼ **Lincoln Road Mall.** A playful redesign of this grande dame of Miami Beach overran its original $16 million budget, but the results were worth the extra bucks. The renovation spruced up the futuristic 1950s vision of Fontainebleau designer Morris Lapidus and added a grove of 20 towering date palms and five linear pools. The best times to hit the road are during Sunday-morning farmers' markets and on weekend evenings, when cafés are bustling; art galleries, like Romero Britto's Britto Central, schedule openings; street performers take the stage; and bookstores, import shops, and clothing stores are open for late-night purchases. ✉ *Lincoln Rd. between Collins Ave. and Alton Rd.*

❶ **Lummus Park.** Once part of a turn-of-the-last-century plantation owned by brothers John and James Lummus, this palm-shaded oasis on the beach side of Ocean Drive attracts beach-going families with its children's play area. Senior citizens predominate early in the day. Volleyball, in-line skating along the wide and winding sidewalk, and a lot of posing go on here. Gays like the beach between 11th and 13th streets. The lush foliage is a pleasing, natural counterpoint to the ultrachic atmosphere just across the street, where endless sidewalk cafés make it easy to come ashore for everything from burgers to quiche. Like New York's Central Park, this is a natural venue for big-name public concerts by such performers as Luciano Pavarotti and past art deco Weekend stars Cab Calloway and Lionel Hampton. ✉ *East of Ocean Dr. between 5th and 15th Sts.*

North Beach. Families and those who like things quiet prefer this section of beach. Metered parking is ample right behind the dune and a block behind Collins Avenue along a pleasant, old shopping street. With high prices discouraging developers from SoBe, this area will no doubt see some redevelopment in years to come. However, without the cafés or 300-ft-wide beach to lure tourists, it may never match SoBe's appeal. ✉ *Ocean Terr. between 73rd and 75th Sts.*

OFF THE BEATEN PATH **OLETA RIVER STATE RECREATION AREA** – At nearly 1,000 acres, this is the largest urban park in Florida. It's backed by lush tropical growth rather than hotels and offers group and youth camping, 14 log cabins, kayak and canoe rentals, mountain-bike trails, and a fishing pier. Popular with outdoors enthusiasts, it also attracts dolphins, ospreys, and manatees, who arrive for the winter. ✉ *3400 N.E. 163rd St., North Miami,*

☎ 305/919–1846, WEB www.dep.state.fl.us/parks. $4 per vehicle with up to 8 people, $1 for pedestrians. ⏲ Daily 8–sunset.

Sanford L. Ziff Jewish Museum of Florida. This museum chronicles 230 years of the Jewish experience in Florida through lectures, films, storytelling, walking tours, and special events. If you've never seen a crate of kosher citrus, drop in. From the photo of a party girl in a seashell dress to ark ornaments from a Florida synagogue to a snapshot of Miss Florida 1885 (Mena Williams), exhibits reflect all things Jewish. Even the building is the former Congregation Beth Jacob Synagogue. ✉ *301 Washington Ave., ☎ 305/672–5044, WEB www.jewishmuseum.com. $5. ⏲ Tues.–Sun. 10–5.*

South Pointe Park. From the 50-yard Sunshine Pier, which adjoins the 1-mi-long jetty at the mouth of Government Cut, you can fish while watching huge ships pass. No bait or tackle is available in the park. Facilities include two observation towers, rest rooms, and volleyball courts. ✉ *1 Washington Ave.*

Surfside. *Parlez-vous français?* If you do, you'll feel quite comfortable in and around this community, a French Canadian enclave. Many folks have spent their winters along this stretch of beach (and elsewhere down to 72nd Street) for years. ✉ *Collins Ave. between 88th and 96th Sts.*

5 **Wolfsonian–Florida International University.** An elegantly renovated 1927 storage facility is now both a research center and home to the 70,000-plus-item collection of modern design and "propaganda arts" amassed by Miami native Mitchell Wolfson, Jr., a world traveler and connoisseur. Included in the museum's eclectic holdings, representing Art Moderne, Art Nouveau, Arts and Crafts, and other artistic movements, is a 1930s braille edition of Hitler's *Mein Kampf*. Exhibitions such as World's Fair designs and the architectural heritage of S. H. Kress add to the appeal. ✉ *1001 Washington Ave., ☎ 305/531–1001, WEB www.wolfsonian.fiu.edu. $5. ⏲ Mon.–Tues. and Fri.–Sat. 11–6, Thurs. 11–9, Sun. noon–5.*

Downtown Miami

Although steel-and-glass buildings have sprung up around downtown, the heart of the city hasn't changed much since the 1960s—except that it's a little seedier. Not surprising for a city that, although one of the country's greatest, has its share of political corruption, cronyism, nepotism, shortsightedness, and insensitivity. In 1997 a proposal to disband the city actually reached voters, but they voted overwhelmingly to keep it, flaws and all.

Nevertheless, by day there's plenty of activity downtown, as office workers and motorists crowd the area. Staid, suited lawyers and bankers share the sidewalks with Latino merchants wearing open-neck, intricately embroidered shirts called guayaberas. Fruit merchants sell their wares from pushcarts, young European travelers with backpacks stroll the streets, and foreign businesspeople haggle over prices in import-export shops, including more electronics and camera shops than you'd see in Tokyo. You hear Arabic, Chinese, Creole, French, German, Hebrew, Hindi, Japanese, Portuguese, Spanish, Yiddish, and even a little English now and then. But what's best in the heart of downtown Miami is its Latinization and the sheer energy of Latino shoppers.

At night, however, downtown is sorely neglected. Except for Bayside Marketplace and the new AmericanAirlines Arena, the area is deserted, and arena patrons rarely linger. Visitors spend little time here since most tourist attractions are in other neighborhoods, but there is a movement afoot to bring a renaissance to downtown. A huge new performing-arts center within the next few years may revitalize the area yet.

Thanks to the Metromover, which has inner and outer loops through downtown plus north and south extensions, this is an excellent tour to take by rail, and it's only 25¢ to boot. Attractions are conveniently located within about two blocks of the nearest station. Parking downtown is no less convenient or more expensive than in any other city, but the best idea is to park near Bayside Marketplace or leave your car at an outlying Metrorail station and take the train downtown.

A Good Tour

A smart place to start is at the Bayfront Park Metromover stop. There's plenty of parking in lots in the median of Biscayne Boulevard and slightly more expensive covered parking at the Bayfront Marketplace. If you want, you can wait until you return to walk through the **Mildred and Claude Pepper Bayfront Park** ⑩, but look south of the park and you'll see the Hotel Inter-Continental Miami, which displays *The Spindle,* a huge sculpture by Henry Moore, in its lobby. West of Bayfront Park Station stands the tallest building in Florida, the **First Union Financial Center** ⑪.

Now it's time to board the Metromover northbound and take in the fine view of Bayfront Park's greenery, the bay beyond, the stunning new AmericanAirlines Arena, the Port of Miami in the bay, and Miami Beach across the water. The next stop, College/Bayside, serves the downtown campus of **Miami-Dade Community College** ⑫, which has two fine galleries.

As the Metromover rounds the curve after the College/Bayside station, look northeast for a view of the vacant **Freedom Tower** ⑬, an important milepost in the history of Cuban immigration, now being renovated as a Cuban museum. You'll also catch a view of the *Miami Herald* building.

Survey the city as the train works its way toward Government Center station. Look off to your right (north) as you round the northwest corner of the loop to see the round, windowless, pink Miami Arena.

Now it's time to see the city on foot. Get off at Government Center, a large station with small shops, restaurants, and a hair salon, in case you're looking shaggy. It's also where the 21-mi elevated Metrorail commuter system connects with the Metromover, so this is a good place to start your tour if you're coming downtown by train. Walk out the east doors to Northwest 1st Street and head a block south to the **Miami-Dade Cultural Center** ⑭, which contains the city's main art museum, historical museum, and library and made an appearance in the movie *There's Something About Mary.*

After sopping up some culture, hoof it east down Flagler Street. On the corner is the **Dade County Courthouse** ⑮, whose pinnacle is accented by circling vultures. Now you're in the heart of downtown, where the smells range from pleasant (hot dog carts) to rancid (hot dog carts). If you cleaned up the streets and put a shine on the city, you'd see Miami circa 1950. Still thriving today, the downtown area is a far cry from what it was in 1896, when it was being carved out of pine woods and palmetto scrub to make room for Flagler's railroad. If you're in the market for jewelry, avoid the street peddlers and duck into the Seybold Building, at 36 Northeast 1st Street; it comprises 10 stories with 250 jewelers hawking watches, rings, bracelets, etc.

Just a few blocks from your starting point at the Bayfront Park Metromover station, stop in at the **Gusman Center for the Performing Arts** ⑯, a stunningly beautiful movie palace that now serves as downtown Miami's concert hall. If there's a show on—even a bad one—get tickets. It's worth it just to sit in here.

When you get back to your car and the entrance to the Bayfront Marketplace, you can opt to hit the road, go shopping, or grab a brew at a bay-front bar.

TIMING
To walk and ride to the various points of interest, allow two hours. If you want to spend additional time eating and shopping at Bayside, allow at least four hours. To include museum visits, allow six hours.

Sights to See

AmericanAirlines Arena. The stylish new bay-front home of the NBA's Miami Heat includes Gloria and Emilio Estefan's Bongos restaurant, shops, and a pedestrian bridge to Bayside Marketplace. *Biscayne Blvd., between N.E. 8th and 9th Sts., ☎ 305/577–4328, WEB www.aaarena.com.*

American Police Hall of Fame and Museum. This museum exhibits more than 11,000 law enforcement–related items, including weapons, a jail cell, and an electric chair, as well as a 400-ton marble memorial listing the names of more than 6,000 police officers killed in the line of duty since 1960. ✉ *3801 Biscayne Blvd., ☎ 305/573–0070, WEB www.aphf.org.* *$6.* *Daily 10–5:30.*

⓯ **Dade County Courthouse.** Built in 1928, this was once the tallest building south of Washington, D.C. Unlike Capistrano, turkey vultures—not swallows—return to roost here in winter. ✉ *73 W. Flagler St.*

⓫ **First Union Financial Center.** The tallest building in Florida is this 55-story structure. Unfortunately, there's no observation deck, but a 1-acre plaza graced by towering palms can be a nice place to rest your feet. ✉ *200 S. Biscayne Blvd.*

⓭ **Freedom Tower.** In the 1960s this imposing Spanish Baroque structure was used by the Cuban Refugee Center to process more than 500,000 Cubans who entered the United States after fleeing Fidel Castro's regime. Built in 1925 for the *Miami Daily News,* it was inspired by the Giralda, an 800-year-old bell tower in Seville, Spain. Preservationists were pleased to see the tower restored to its original grandeur in 1988, and the building is being renovated to make way for a Cuban museum. At press time (summer 2001) Freedom Tower was scheduled to open in May 2002. ✉ *600 Biscayne Blvd.*

★ ⓰ **Gusman Center for the Performing Arts.** Carry an extra pair of socks when you come here; the beauty of this former movie palace will knock yours clean off. Restored as a concert hall, it resembles a Moorish courtyard on the inside, with twinkling stars in the sky. You can catch performances by the Florida Philharmonic and movies of the Miami Film Festival. If the hall is closed, call the office and they may let you in. ✉ *174 E. Flagler St., ☎ 305/374–2444 administration; 305/372–0925 box office.*

⓬ **Miami-Dade Community College.** The campus houses two fine galleries: the larger, third-floor **Centre Gallery** hosts various photography, painting, and sculpture exhibitions, and the fifth-floor **Frances Wolfson Art Gallery** houses smaller photo exhibits. ✉ *300 N.E. 2nd Ave., ☎ 305/237–3278.* *Free.* *Mon.–Thurs. 9–4:30.*

★ ⓮ **Miami-Dade Cultural Center.** Containing three important cultural resources, this 3-acre complex is one of the focal points of downtown. From books to paintings to history, you'll find it all right here. The **Miami Art Museum** (☎ 305/375–3000, WEB www.miamiartmuseum.org)

Downtown Miami

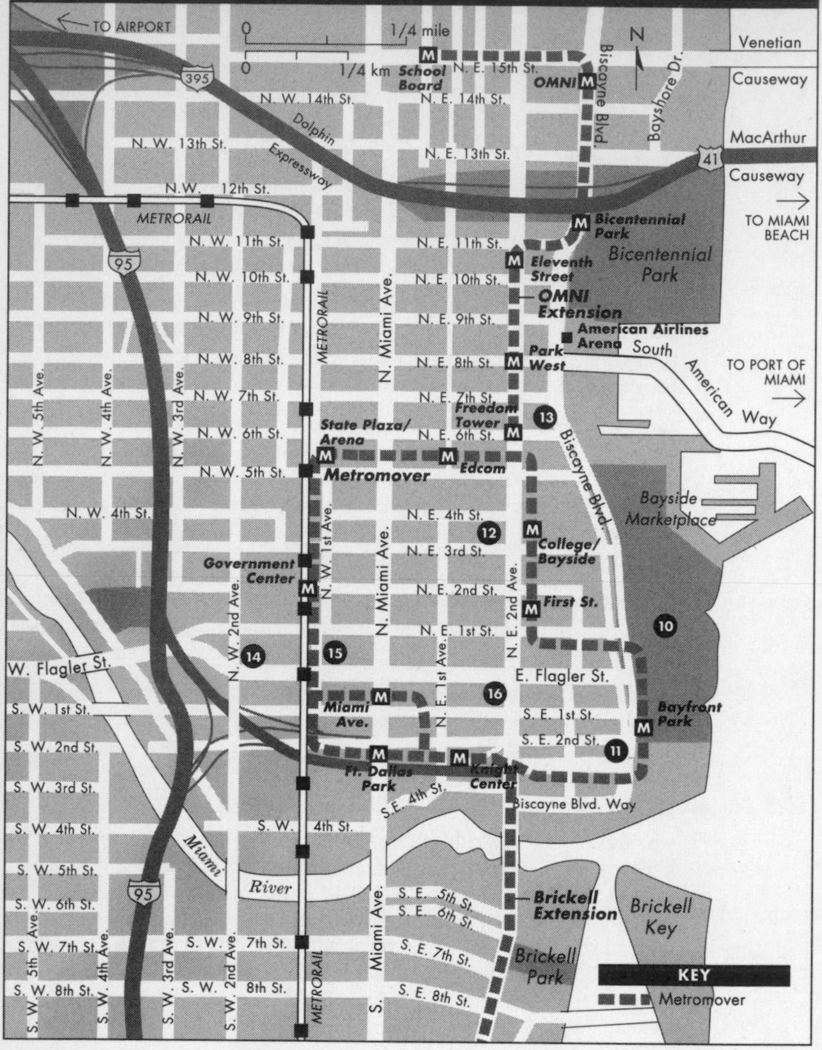

Dade County Courthouse 15
First Union Financial Center . . . 11
Freedom Tower 13
Gusman Center for the Performing Arts 16
Miami-Dade Community College 12
Miami-Dade Cultural Center 14
Mildred and Claude Pepper Bayfront Park 10

displays a permanent collection as well as putting on major touring exhibitions of work by international artists, focusing on work completed since 1945. Open Tuesday–Friday 10–5 and weekends noon–5, the museum charges $5 admission ($6 including the Historical Museum). At the **Historical Museum of Southern Florida** (☎ 305/375–1492, WEB www.historical-museum.org), visitors are treated to pure Floridiana, including an old Miami streetcar, cigar labels, and a railroad exhibit as well as a display on prehistoric Miami. Admission is $5 ($6 including the Miami Art Museum), and hours are Monday–Wednesday and Friday–Saturday 10–5, Thursday 10–9, and Sunday noon–5. The **Main Public Library** (☎ 305/375–2665), which is open Monday–Wednesday and Friday–Saturday 9–6, Thursday 9–9, and Sunday 1–5, contains nearly 4 million holdings and offers art exhibits in the auditorium and second-floor lobby. ✉ *101 W. Flagler St.*

⑩ **Mildred and Claude Pepper Bayfront Park.** This oasis among the skyscrapers borders the Bayfront Marketplace, making it a natural place for a pre- or post-shopping walk. An urban landfill in the 1920s, it became the site of a World War II memorial in 1943, which was revised in 1980 to include the names of victims of later wars. Japanese sculptor Isamu Noguchi redesigned the park before his death in 1989 to include two amphitheaters, a memorial to the *Challenger* astronauts, and a fountain honoring the late Florida congressman Claude Pepper and his wife. At the park's north end, the Friendship Torch was erected to honor JFK during his presidency and was dedicated in 1964. ✉ *Biscayne Blvd. between 2nd and 3rd Sts.*

Little Havana

More than 40 years ago the tidal wave of Cubans fleeing the Castro regime flooded into an older neighborhood west of downtown Miami. Don't expect a sparkling and lively reflection of 1950s Havana, however. What you will find are ramshackle motels and cluttered storefronts. With a million Cubans and other Latinos—who make up more than half the metropolitan population—dispersed throughout Greater Miami, Little Havana and neighboring East Little Havana remain magnets for Hispanics and Anglos alike, who come to experience the flavor of traditional Cuban culture. That culture, of course, functions in Spanish. Many Little Havana residents and shopkeepers speak little or no English.

A Good Tour

From downtown go west on Flagler Street across the Miami River to Teddy Roosevelt Avenue (Southwest 17th Avenue) and pause at **Plaza de la Cubanidad** ⑰, on the southwest corner. The plaza's monument is indicative of the prominent role of Cuban history and culture here.

Turn left at Douglas Road (Southwest 37th Avenue), drive south to **Calle Ocho** ⑱ (Southwest 8th Street), and turn left again. You are now on the main commercial thoroughfare of Little Havana. After you cross Unity Boulevard (Southwest 27th Avenue), Calle Ocho becomes a one-way street eastbound through the heart of Little Havana.

At Avenida Luis Muñoz Marín (Southwest 15th Avenue), stop at **Domino Park** ⑲, where elderly Cuban men pass the day with their black-and-white tiles. The **Brigade 2506 Memorial** ⑳, commemorating the victims of the unsuccessful 1961 Bay of Pigs invasion, stands at Memorial Boulevard (Southwest 13th Avenue). A block south are several other monuments relevant to Cuban history, including a bas-relief of and quotations by José Martí.

TIMING

If the history hidden in the monuments is your only interest, set aside one hour. Allow more time to stop along Calle Ocho for a strong cup of Cuban coffee or to shop for a cigar made of Honduran tobacco hand-rolled in the United States by Cubans.

Sights to See

20 **Brigade 2506 Memorial.** To honor those who died in the Bay of Pigs invasion, an eternal flame burns atop a simple stone monument with the inscription CUBA—A LOS MARTIRES DE LA BRIGADA DE ASALTO ABRIL 17 DE 1961. The monument also bears a shield with the Brigade 2506 emblem, a Cuban flag superimposed on a cross. ✉ *S.W. 8th St. and S.W. 13th Ave.*

18 **Calle Ocho.** In Little Havana's commercial heart, experience such Cuban customs as hand-rolled cigars or sandwiches piled with meats and cheeses. Although it all deserves exploring, if time is limited, try the stretch from Southwest 14th to 11th avenues. ✉ *S.W. 8th St.*

19 **Domino Park.** Officially known as Maximo Gomez Park, this is a major gathering place for elderly, guayabera-clad Cuban males, who, after 40 years, still pass the day playing dominoes while arguing anti-Castro politics. ✉ *S.W. 8th St. and S.W. 15th Ave.* ⏲ *Daily 9–6.*

17 **Plaza de la Cubanidad.** Redbrick sidewalks surround a fountain and monument with the words of José Martí, a leader in Cuba's struggle for independence from Spain and a hero to Cuban refugees and immigrants in Miami. The quotation, LAS PALMAS SON NOVIAS QUE ESPERAN (The palm trees are waiting brides), counsels hope and fortitude to the Cubans. ✉ *W. Flagler St. and S.W. 17th Ave.*

Coral Gables

If not for George E. Merrick, Coral Gables would be just another suburb. Merrick envisioned an American Venice, with canals and gracious homes spreading across the community. In 1911 his minister father died, and Merrick inherited 1,600 acres of citrus and avocado groves; by 1921 he had upped that to 3,000 acres. Using this as a foundation, Merrick began designing a city based on centuries-old prototypes from Mediterranean countries. He began planning lush landscaping, magnificent entrances, and broad boulevards named for Spanish explorers, cities, and provinces. His uncle, Denman Fink, helped Merrick crystallize his artistic vision, and he hired architects trained abroad to create themed neighborhood villages, such as Florida pioneer, Chinese, French city, Dutch South African, and French Normandy. The result was a planned community with Spanish Mediterranean architecture that justifiably calls itself the City Beautiful—a moniker it acquired by following the Garden City method of urban planning in the 1920s.

Unfortunately for Merrick, the devastating no-name hurricane of 1926 and the Great Depression prevented him from fulfilling many of his plans. He died at 54, working for the post office. His city languished until after World War II but then grew rapidly. Today Coral Gables has a population of about 41,000. In its bustling downtown, more than 140 multinational companies maintain headquarters or regional offices, and the University of Miami campus in the southern part of Coral Gables brings a youthful vibrancy: the median age of residents is 36.

Like much of Miami, Coral Gables has realized the aesthetic and economic importance of historic preservation and has passed a Mediterranean design ordinance, rewarding businesses for maintaining their building's architectural style. Even the street signs (ground-level markers that are hard to see in daylight, impossible at night) are preserved due to their historical value. They're worth the inconvenience, if only to honor the memory of Merrick.

A Good Tour

Heading south on downtown's Brickell Avenue, turn right onto Coral Way—also marked as Southwest 13th Street—and stay on Coral Way even as it turns into Southwest 3rd and Southwest 22nd avenues. An arch of banyan trees prepares you for the grand entrance onto **Miracle Mile** ㉑, the heart of downtown Coral Gables. Park your car and take time to explore on foot.

When you've seen enough, continue driving west, passing the 1930s Miracle Theater on your left, which now serves as home of the Actors' Playhouse. Keep heading west, cross LeJeune Road, and bear right onto Coral Way, catching an eyeful of the ornate Spanish Renaissance **Coral Gables City Hall** ㉒.

Continue a few blocks until you see Toledo Street, and make a left. A few blocks up on your left, you'll see the gates surrounding the exotic and unusual Merrick-designed **Venetian Pool** ㉓, created from an old coral quarry. There's parking on your right. Immediately ahead of you is the Merrick-designed **De Soto Plaza and Fountain** ㉔.

As in many areas of Coral Gables, there's a traffic circle surrounding the fountain. Head to 12 o'clock (the opposite side of the fountain) and stay on De Soto for a magnificent vista and entrance to the, yes, Merrick-designed and reborn **Biltmore Hotel** ㉕. On your right, before you reach the hotel, you'll see the **Coral Gables Congregational Church** ㉖, one of the first churches in this planned community. After visiting the hotel, double back to the fountain, this time circling to 9 o'clock and Granada Boulevard. Several blocks away you'll arrive at the Granada Golf Course, where you turn left onto North Greenway. As you cruise up the street, notice the stand of banyan trees that separates the fairways. At the end of the course the road makes a horseshoe bend, but instead cross Alhambra to loop around the restored **Alhambra Water Tower** ㉗, a city landmark dating from 1924. By the way, it's Merrick designed.

Return to Alhambra and follow it straight to the next light (Coral Way), where you can turn left and ogle beautifully maintained Spanish homes from the 1920s. Although there's only a small sign to announce it, the **Coral Gables Merrick House and Gardens** ㉘, Merrick's boyhood home, is at Coral Way and Toledo Street. It's a charming glimpse into old-time Florida. Parking is behind the house.

Afterward, take a right on Coral Way, followed by a left on Granada, which winds south past Bird Road and eventually to Ponce de León Boulevard. Turn right and follow it to the entrance of the main campus of the **University of Miami** ㉙. Turn right at the first stoplight (Stanford Drive) to enter the campus, and park in the lot on your right designated for visitors to the Lowe Art Museum.

You may have noticed that this tour contains some backtracking. Unfortunately, no matter how you navigate Coral Gables, directions get confusing. This tour takes in the highlights first and lets you fill out the balance of your day as you see fit. Now bow to your partner, and bow to your corner, and promenade home.

TIMING

Strolling Miracle Mile should take slightly more than an hour—unless you plan to shop. In that case, allow four hours. Save time for a refreshing dip at the Venetian Pool, and plan to spend at least an hour

Miami, Coral Gables, Coconut Grove, and Key Biscayne

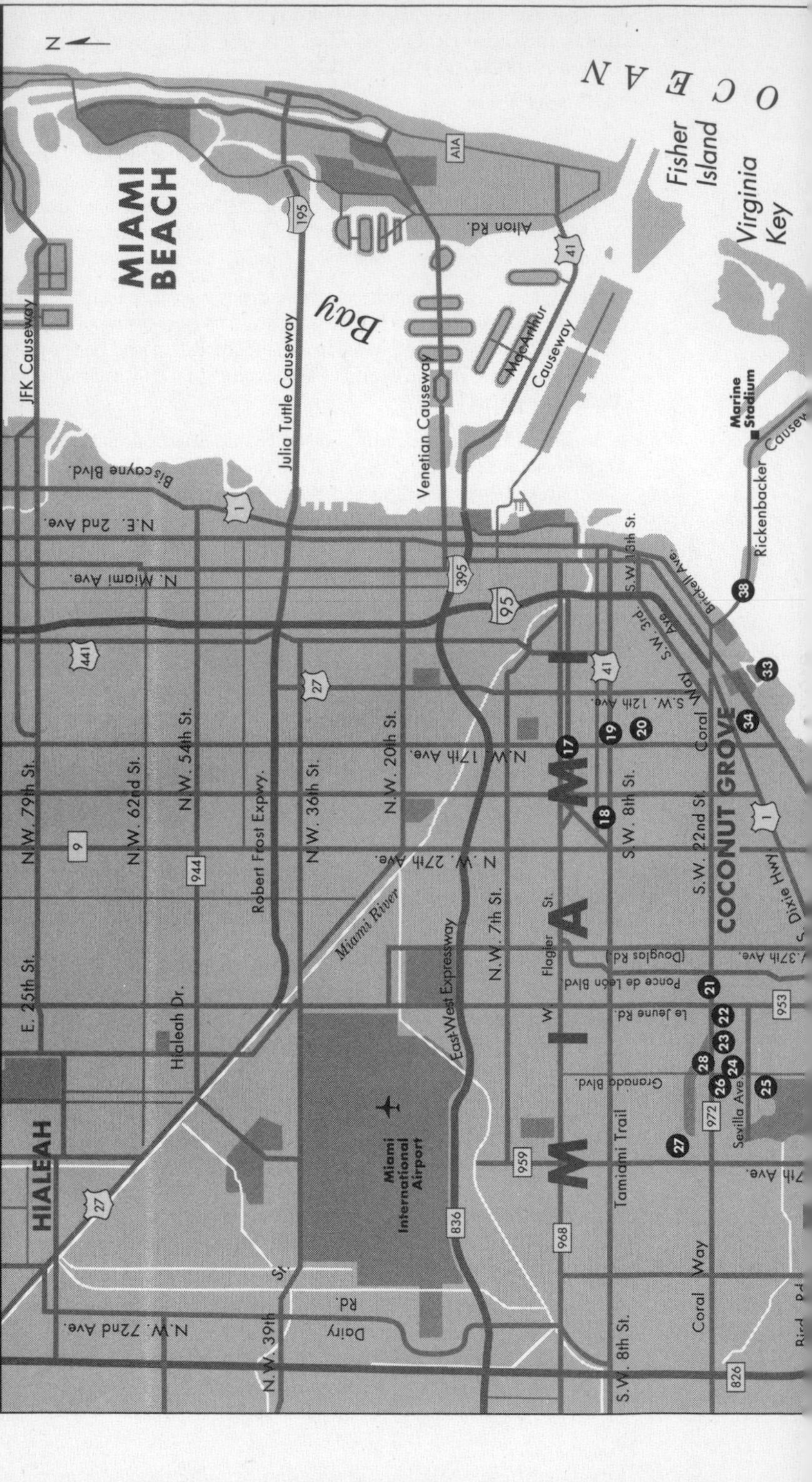

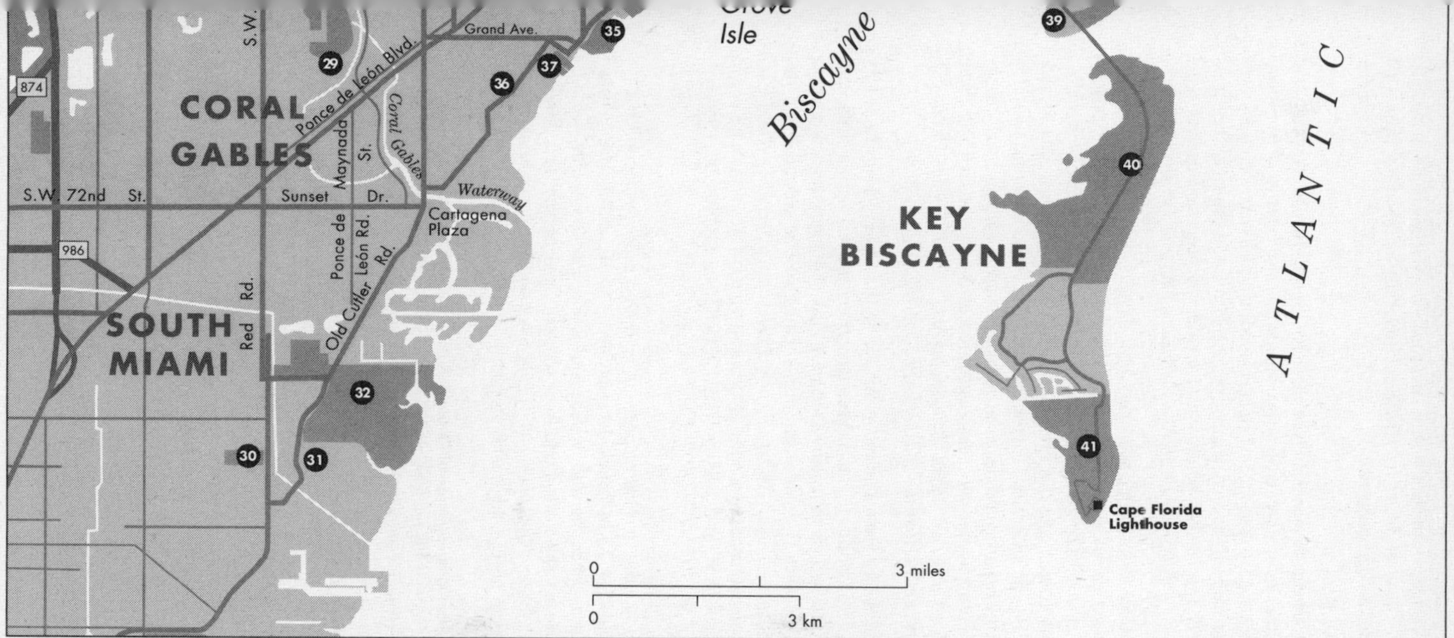

Alhambra Water Tower	27
Barnacle State Historic Site	37
Bill Baggs Cape Florida State Recreation Area	41
Biltmore Hotel	25
Brigade 2506 Memorial	20
Calle Ocho	18
Coral Gables City Hall	22
Coral Gables Congregational Church	26
Coral Gables Merrick House and Gardens	28
Crandon Park	40
De Soto Plaza and Fountain	24
Domino Park	19
Fairchild Tropical Garden	31
Matheson Hammock Park	32
Miami City Hall	35
Miami Museum of Science and Space Transit Planetarium	34
Miami Seaquarium	39
Miracle Mile	21
Old Rickenbacker Causeway Bridge	38
Parrot Jungle	30
Plaza de la Cubanidad	17
Plymouth Congregational Church	36
University of Miami	29
Venetian Pool	23
Vizcaya Museum and Gardens	33

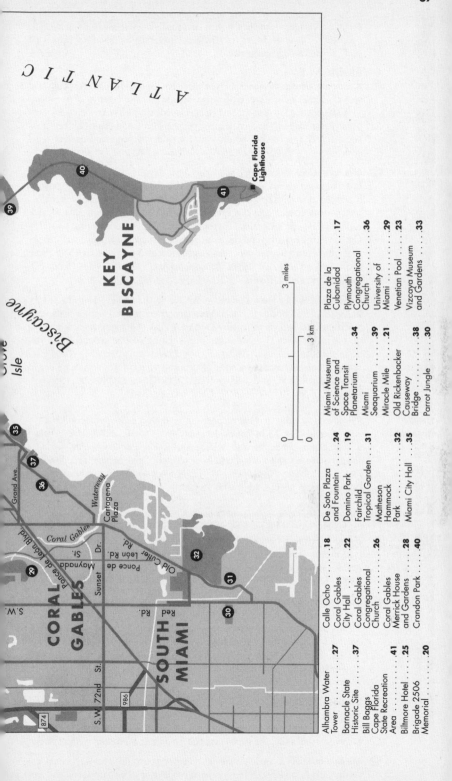

getting acquainted with the Biltmore—longer if you'd like to order a drink and linger poolside. If you can pull yourself away from the lap of luxury, allow an hour to visit the University of Miami campus (if you're into college campuses).

Sights to See

27 **Alhambra Water Tower.** In 1924 this city landmark stored water and was clad in a decorative Moresque, lighthouselike exterior. After more than 50 years of disuse and neglect, the windmill-like tower was completely restored in 1993 with a copper-rib dome and multicolored frescoes. Pretty impressive when you consider its peers are merely steel containers. ✉ *Alhambra Circle, Greenway Ct., and Ferdinand St.*

25 **Biltmore Hotel.** Bouncing back from dark days as an army hospital, this hotel has become the jewel of Coral Gables. After extensive renovations it reopened in 1992 and hosted the Summit of the Americas in 1994. Its 16-story tower, like the Freedom Tower in downtown Miami, is a replica of Seville's Giralda Tower. To the west is the Biltmore Country Club, a richly ornamented beaux arts–style structure with a superb colonnade and courtyard; it was reincorporated into the hotel in 1989. Free tours are offered. ✉ *1200 Anastasia Ave.,* ☎ *305/445–1926,* WEB *www.biltmorehotel.com.* ⏲ *Tours Sun. 1:30, 2:30, and 3:30.*

22 **Coral Gables City Hall.** Far more attractive than today's modular city halls, this 1928 building has a three-tier tower topped with a clock and a 500-pound bell. A mural by Denman Fink (George Merrick's uncle and artistic adviser), inside the dome ceiling on the second floor, depicts the four seasons. (Although not as well known as Maxfield Parrish, Fink demonstrated a similar utopian vision.) Also on display are paintings, photos, and ads touting 1920s Coral Gables. ✉ *405 Biltmore Way,* ☎ *305/446–6800.* ⏲ *Weekdays 8–5.*

NEED A BREAK? Whether you want to relax or grab an on-the-go snack, you can't miss with **Wrapido** (✉ 2334 Ponce de León Blvd., ☎ 305/443–1884). The funky, upbeat atmosphere shows signs of SoHo, and the healthy wraps, soups, and smoothies are made from scratch. Strawberry Fields, the restaurant's best-selling smoothie, is prepared with fresh bananas, strawberries, apple juice, and low-fat yogurt.

26 **Coral Gables Congregational Church.** The parish was organized in 1923, and with George Merrick as a charter member (and donor of the land), this small church became the first in the city. Rumor has it Merrick built it in honor of his father, a Congregational minister. The original interiors are still in magnificent condition. ✉ *3010 De Soto Blvd.,* ☎ *305/448–7421.* ⏲ *Weekdays 8:30–4:30, services Sun. 9:15 and 10:45.*

28 **Coral Gables Merrick House and Gardens.** In 1976 the city of Coral Gables acquired George Merrick's boyhood home. Restored to its 1920s appearance, it contains Merrick family furnishings and artwork. The lush and lazy tropical atmosphere suggests the inspiration for George's masterpiece: Coral Gables. ✉ *907 Coral Way,* ☎ *305/460–5361.* 🎟 *House $2, grounds free.* ⏲ *House Wed. and Sun. 1–4, grounds daily 8–sunset, also by appointment.*

24 **De Soto Plaza and Fountain.** Water flows from the mouths of four sculpted faces on a classical column on a pedestal in this Denman Fink–designed fountain from the early 1920s. The closed eyes of the face looking west symbolize the day's end. ✉ *Granada Blvd. and Sevilla Ave.*

21 **Miracle Mile.** This upscale yet neighborly stretch of retail stores is actually only ½ mi long. After years of neglect, it's been updated and upgraded, and now offers a delightful mix of owner-operated shops and

chain stores, bridal shops, art galleries and bistros, and enough late-night hot spots to keep things hopping. ✉ *Coral Way between S.W. 37th Ave. (Douglas Rd.) and S.W. 42nd Ave. (LeJeune Rd.).*

㉙ **University of Miami.** With almost 14,000 full-time, part-time, and noncredit students, UM is the largest private research university in the southeast. Walk around campus and visit the **Lowe Art Museum,** which has a permanent collection of 8,000 works that include Renaissance and Baroque art, American paintings, Latin American art, and Navajo and Pueblo Indian textiles and baskets. The museum also hosts traveling exhibitions and the popular beaux arts Festival in January. ✉ *1301 Stanford Dr.,* ☎ *305/284–3535 or 305/284–3536,* WEB *www.miami.edu.* 🎟 *$5.* ⏲ *Tues.–Wed. and Fri.–Sat. 10–5, Thurs. noon–7, Sun. noon–5.*

★ ㉓ **Venetian Pool.** Sculpted from a rock quarry in 1923 and fed by artesian wells, this 825,000-gallon municipal pool remains quite popular due to its themed architecture—a fantasized version of a waterfront Italian village—created by Denman Fink. The pool has earned a place on the National Register of Historic Places and showcases a nice collection of vintage photos depicting 1920s beauty pageants and swank soirees held long ago. Paul Whiteman played here, Johnny Weissmuller and Esther Williams swam here, and you should, too (but no kids under 3). A snack bar, lockers, and showers make this must-see user-friendly as well. ✉ *2701 De Soto Blvd.,* ☎ *305/460–5356,* WEB *www.venetianpool.com.* 🎟 *$8, free parking across De Soto Blvd.* ⏲ *Weekends 10–4:30; plus June–Aug., weekdays 11–7:30; Sept.–Oct. and Apr.–May, Tues.–Fri. 11–5:30; and Nov.–Mar., Tues.–Fri. 10–4:30.*

South Miami

South of Miami and Coral Gables is a city called South Miami, which is not to be confused with the region known as South Dade. A pioneer farm community, it grew into a suburb but retains its small-town charm. Fine old homes and stately trees line Sunset Drive, a city-designated Historic and Scenic Road to and through the town. The pace in this friendly suburb has picked up steam since the arrival of the Shops at Sunset Place, a retail complex larger than Coconut Grove's CocoWalk—big digs for a quiet town.

A Good Tour

Drive south from Sunset Drive on Red Road (watching for the plentiful orchid merchants), and turn right just before Killian Drive (Southwest 112th Street) into the 13-acre grounds of **Parrot Jungle** ㉚, one of Greater Miami's oldest and most popular commercial tourist attractions.

From Parrot Jungle follow Red Road ⅓ mi south and turn left on scenic Old Cutler Road, which curves north along the uplands of southern Florida's coastal ridge toward the 83-acre **Fairchild Tropical Garden** ㉛. Just north of the gardens, Old Cutler Road traverses Dade County's lovely **Matheson Hammock Park** ㉜. From here you can follow the road back to U.S. 1, heading north to Miami.

TIMING

Most people should allow at least half a day to see these three natural attractions, but dedicated ornithologists and botanists will want to leave a full day. Driving from SoBe should take only 25 minutes—longer during afternoon rush hour.

Sights to See

㉛ **Fairchild Tropical Garden.** Comprising 83 acres, this is the largest tropical botanical garden in the continental United States. Eleven lakes, a rain forest, and lots of palm trees, cycads, and flowers, including orchids, mountain roses, bellflowers, coral trees, and bougainvillea, make it a garden for the senses—and there's special assistance for deaf guests. Take the free guided tram tour, which leaves on the hour. Spicing up the social calendar are garden sales (don't miss the Ramble in November or the International Mango Festival in July), moonlight strolls, and symphony concerts. A combination bookstore–gift shop is a popular source for books on gardening and horticulture, ordered by botanists the world over. ✉ *10901 Old Cutler Rd.,* ☎ *305/667–1651,* WEB *www.fairchildgarden.org.* 🎫 *$8.* ⏲ *Daily 9:30–4:30.*

32 **Matheson Hammock Park.** In the 1930s the Civilian Conservation Corps developed this 100-acre tract of upland and mangrove swamp on land donated by a local pioneer, Commodore J. W. Matheson. The park, Miami-Dade County's oldest and most scenic, features a bathing beach and changing facilities. In 1997 the marina was expanded to include 243 slips, 71 dry-storage spaces, a bait-and-tackle shop, and a restaurant. Noticeably absent are fishing and diving charters, although there is a sailing school. ✉ *9610 Old Cutler Rd., Coral Gables,* ☎ *305/665–5475,* WEB *www.co.miami-dade.fl.us/parks.* 🎫 *Parking for beach and marina $3.50 per car, $8 per car with trailer, $6 per bus and RV; limited free upland parking.* ⏲ *Daily 6–sunset; pool lifeguards winter, daily 8:30–5; summer, weekends 8:30–6.*

30 **Parrot Jungle.** One of South Florida's original tourist attractions, Parrot Jungle opened in 1936 and is now home to more than 1,100 exotic birds, who look for handouts from visitors. The tone is kitschy (in the tradition of Florida favorites Silver Springs and Cypress Gardens) but oddly peaceful and exotic after you've experienced the urban jungle. Once you've photographed the postcard-perfect Caribbean flamingos and watched a trained-bird show, stroll among orchids and other flowering plants nestled in ferns, bald cypress, and massive live oaks. An imminent move (sometime in 2002) will take the birds to a new home on Watson Island, across from the Port of Miami, but this park will be preserved as some type of wildlife sanctuary. ✉ *11000 S.W. 57th Ave.,* ☎ *305/666–7834,* WEB *www.parrotjungle.com.* 🎫 *$14.95.* ⏲ *Daily 9:30–6, last admission 4:30; café daily 8–5.*

Coconut Grove

South Florida's oldest settlement, the Grove was inhabited as early as 1834 and established by 1873, two decades before Miami. Its early settlers included Bahamian blacks, "Conchs" (white Key Westers, many originally from the Bahamas), and New England intellectuals. They built a community that attracted artists, writers, and scientists to establish winter homes. By the end of World War I more people listed in *Who's Who* gave addresses in Coconut Grove than any other place in the country.

To this day Coconut Grove reflects its pioneers' eclectic origins. Posh estates mingle with rustic cottages, modest frame homes, and stark modern dwellings, often on the same block. To keep Coconut Grove a village in a jungle, residents lavish affection on exotic plantings while battling to protect remaining native vegetation.

The historic center of the Village of Coconut Grove went through a hippie period in the 1960s, a laid-back funkiness in the 1970s, and a teenybopper invasion in the early 1980s. Today the tone is upscale and urban, with a mix of galleries, boutiques, restaurants, bars, and sidewalk cafés. On weekends the Grove is jam-packed with both locals and tourists—especially teenagers—shopping at the Streets of Mayfair, CocoWalk, and small boutiques. Parking can be a problem, especially on weekend evenings, when police direct traffic and prohibit turns at some intersections to prevent gridlock. Be prepared to walk several blocks from the periphery into the heart of the Grove.

A Good Tour

From downtown Miami take Brickell Avenue south and follow the signs pointing to Vizcaya and Coconut Grove. If you're interested in seeing celeb estates, turn left at Southeast 32nd Road and follow the loop—Sylvester Stallone's former estate is the one with the huge gates on the right at the turn, and Madonna's past abode is the one at 3029 Brickell. Turn left back on South Miami Avenue.

Immediately on your left you'll see the entrance to the don't-miss **Vizcaya Museum and Gardens** ㉝, an estate with an Italian Renaissance–style villa. Less than 100 yards down the road on your right is the **Miami Museum of Science and Space Transit Planetarium** ㉞, a participatory museum with animated displays for all ages.

The road switches from four lanes to two and back again as you approach downtown Coconut Grove. With 28 waterfront acres of Australian pine, lush lawns, and walking and jogging paths, the bay-side David T. Kennedy Park makes a pleasant stop. If you're interested in the history of air travel, take a quick detour down Pan American Drive to see the 1930s art deco Pan Am terminal, which has been horribly renovated inside to become **Miami City Hall** ㉟. You'll also see the Coconut Grove Convention Center, where antiques, boat, and home shows are held, and Dinner Key Marina, where seabirds soar and sailboats ride at anchor.

South Miami Avenue, now known as South Bayshore Drive, heads directly into McFarlane Road, which takes a sharp right into the center of the action. If you can forsake instant gratification, turn left on Main Highway and drive less than ½ mi to Devon Road and the interesting **Plymouth Congregational Church** ㊱ and its gardens.

Return to Main Highway and travel northeast toward the historic Village of Coconut Grove. As you reenter the village center, note on your left the Coconut Grove Playhouse. On your right, beyond the benches and shelter, is the entrance to the **Barnacle State Historic Site** ㊲, a pioneer residence built by Commodore Ralph Munroe in 1891. After getting your fill of history, relax and spend the evening mingling with Coconut Grove's eccentrics.

TIMING

Plan on devoting from six to eight hours to enjoy Vizcaya, other bayfront sights, and the village's shops, restaurants, and nightlife.

Sights to See

㊲ **Barnacle State Historic Site.** The oldest Miami home still on its original foundation rests in the middle of 5 acres of native hardwood and landscaped lawns surrounded by flashy Coconut Grove. Built by Florida's first snowbird—New Yorker Commodore Ralph Munroe—the home features many original furnishings, a broad sloping roof, and deeply recessed verandas that channel sea breezes into the house. If your timing is right, you may catch one of the monthly Moonlight Concerts. ✉ *3485 Main Hwy.,* ☎ *305/448–9445,* WEB *www.gate.net/~barnacle.* *$1, concerts $5.* ⏲ *Fri.–Sun. 9–4; tours 10, 11:30, 1, and 2:30, but call ahead; group tours (10 or more) Mon.–Thurs. by reservation; call ahead for concert times.*

㉟ **Miami City Hall.** Built in 1934 as the terminal for the Pan American Airways seaplane base at Dinner Key, the building retains its nautical-style art deco trim. Sadly, the interior is generic government, but a 1938

Pan Am menu on display (with filet mignon, *petit pois au beurre,* and Jenny Lind pudding) lets you know Miami officials appreciate from whence they came. ✉ *3500 Pan American Dr.,* ☎ *305/250–5400.* ⏲ *Weekdays 8–5.*

34 **Miami Museum of Science and Space Transit Planetarium.** This museum is chock-full of hands-on sound, gravity, and electricity displays for children and adults alike. A wildlife center houses native Florida snakes, turtles, tortoises, and birds of prey. Outstanding traveling exhibits appear throughout the year, and virtual-reality, life-science demonstrations, and Internet technology are on hand every day. A new affiliation with the Smithsonian Institution means top-notch exhibitions, and development of a waterfront Science Center of the Americas a few years down the road. Stick around after dark on Friday and Saturday nights for the laser-light rock-and-roll shows presented in the planetarium. ✉ *3280 S. Miami Ave.,* ☎ *305/854–4247 museum; 305/854–2222 planetarium information,* WEB *www.miamisci.org.* 🎟 *Museum exhibits, planetarium shows, and wildlife center $8–10; laser show $6.* ⏲ *Daily 10–6.*

36 **Plymouth Congregational Church.** Opened in 1917, this handsome coral-rock structure resembles a Mexican mission church. The front door, made of hand-carved walnut and oak with original wrought-iron fittings, came from an early 17th-century monastery in the Pyrenees. Also on the 11-acre grounds are the first schoolhouse in Miami-Dade County (one room), which was moved to this property, and the site of the original Coconut Grove water and electric works. ✉ *3400 Devon Rd.,* ☎ *305/444–6521.* ⏲ *Weekdays 9–4:30, Sun. service at 10 AM.*

★ 33 **Vizcaya Museum and Gardens.** Of the 10,000 people living in Miami between 1912 and 1916, about 1,000 of them were gainfully employed by Chicago industrialist James Deering to build this $20 million Italian Renaissance–style winter residence. Once comprising 180 acres, the grounds now cover a still-substantial 30-acre tract, including a native hammock and more than 10 acres of formal gardens and fountains overlooking Biscayne Bay. The house, open to the public, contains 70 rooms, 34 of which are filled with paintings, sculpture, antique furniture, and other decorative arts dating from the 15th through the 19th centuries and representing the Renaissance, Baroque, rococo, and neoclassical styles. So unusual and impressive is Vizcaya, its guest list has included Ronald Reagan, Pope John Paul II, Queen Elizabeth II, Bill Clinton, and Boris Yeltsin. It's a shame the guided tour can be far less impressive and interesting than the home's guest list and surroundings. ✉ *3251 S. Miami Ave.,* ☎ *305/250–9133,* WEB *www.co.miami-dade.fl.us/parks.* 🎟 *$10.* ⏲ *House and ticket booth daily 9:30–4:30, garden daily 9:30–5:30.*

Virginia Key and Key Biscayne

Government Cut and the Port of Miami separate the city's dense urban fabric from two of its playground islands, Virginia Key and Key Biscayne. Parks occupy much of both keys, providing facilities for golf, tennis, softball, picnicking, and sunbathing, plus uninviting but ecologically valuable stretches of dense mangrove swamp. Key Biscayne's long and winding roads are great for rollerblading and bicycling, and its lush, lazy setting provides a respite from the buzz-saw tempo of SoBe.

A Good Tour

To reach Virginia Key and Key Biscayne take the Rickenbacker Causeway ($1 per car) across Biscayne Bay from the mainland at Brickell Avenue and Southwest 26th Road, about 2 mi south of downtown Miami. The causeway links several islands in the bay.

The William M. Powell Bridge rises 75 ft above the water to eliminate the need for a draw span. The panoramic view from the top encompasses the bay, keys, port, and downtown skyscrapers, with Miami Beach and the Atlantic Ocean in the distance. Just south of the Powell Bridge, a stub of the **Old Rickenbacker Causeway Bridge** ㊳, built in 1947, is now a fishing pier with a nice view.

Immediately after crossing the Rickenbacker Causeway onto Virginia Key, you'll see a long strip of bay front popular with windsurfers and jet skiers. Nearby rest rooms and a great view of the curving shoreline make this an ideal place to park and have your own tailgate party. Look for the gold dome of the **Miami Seaquarium** ㊴, one of the country's first marine attractions. Opposite the causeway from the Seaquarium, a road leads north to Virginia Key Beach and the adjacent Virginia Key Critical Wildlife Area, which is often closed to the public to protect nesting birds.

From Virginia Key the causeway crosses Bear Cut to the north end of Key Biscayne and becomes Crandon Boulevard. The boulevard bisects 1,211-acre **Crandon Park** ㊵, which has a popular Atlantic Ocean beach and nature center. On your right are entrances to the Crandon Park Golf Course and the Tennis Center at Crandon Park, home of the Ericsson Open (formerly known as the Lipton Championships). Keep your eyes open for pure Miami icons: coconut palms and iguana-crossing signs.

From the traffic circle at the south end of Crandon Park, Crandon Boulevard continues to the **Bill Baggs Cape Florida State Recreation Area** ㊶, a 460-acre park containing, among other things, the brick Cape Florida Lighthouse and light keeper's cottage.

Follow Crandon Boulevard back to Crandon Park through Key Biscayne's downtown village, where shops and a 10-acre village green cater mainly to local residents. On your way back to the mainland, pause as you approach the Powell Bridge to admire the Miami skyline. At night the brightly lighted NationsBank Tower looks like a clipper ship running under full sail before the breeze.

TIMING

Set aside the better part of a day for this tour, and double that if you're into beaches, fishing, and water sports.

Sights to See

★ ❹❶ **Bill Baggs Cape Florida State Recreation Area.** Thanks to great beaches, blue-green waters, amenities, sunsets, and a lighthouse, this park at Key Biscayne's southern tip is well worth the drive. Since Hurricane Andrew, it has returned better than ever, with new boardwalks, 18 picnic shelters, and a café that serves beer, wine, and meals ranging from hot dogs to lobster. An additional 54 acres of wetlands were acquired in 1997, and a marina is on the drawing board. A stroll or ride along walking and bicycle paths and boardwalks provides wonderful views of Miami's dramatic skyline. Also on site are bicycle and skate rentals, a playground, fishing piers, and kayak rental. Guided tours of the cultural complex and the **Cape Florida Lighthouse,** South Florida's oldest structure, are offered, but call for availability. The lighthouse was erected in 1845 to replace an earlier one destroyed in an 1836 Seminole attack, in which the keeper's helper was killed. ✉ *1200 S. Crandon Blvd.,* ☎ *305/361–5811 or 305/361–8779,* WEB *www.dep.state.fl.us/parks.* 🎫 *$4 per vehicle with up to 8 people; $1 per person on bicycle, bus, motorcycle, or foot.* ⏲ *Daily 8–sunset, tours Thurs.–Mon. 10 and 1 (sign up ½ hr beforehand).*

40 **Crandon Park.** This laid-back park in northern Key Biscayne is popular with families, and many educated beach enthusiasts rate the 3½-mi county beach here among the top 10 beaches in North America. The sand is soft, there's a great view of the Atlantic, and parking is both inexpensive and plentiful. So large is this park that it includes a marina, a golf course, a tennis center, and ball fields. There's also a kids' section with a restored carousel, a playground, and a splash pool. At the north end of the beach is the free **Marjory Stoneman Douglas Biscayne Nature Center** (☎ 305/642–9600). Explore a variety of natural habitats by taking a tour that includes dragging nets through sea-grass beds to catch, study, and release such marine creatures as sea cucumbers, seahorses, crabs, and shrimp. Nature center hours vary, so call ahead. ✉ *4000 Crandon Blvd.,* ☎ *305/361–5421,* WEB *www.co.miami-dade.fl.us/parks.* *$4 per vehicle.* ⏲ *Daily 8–sunset.*

39 **Miami Seaquarium.** This old-fashioned attraction has six daily shows featuring sea lions, dolphins, and Lolita, a killer whale. (Lolita's tank is small for seaquariums—just three times her length—and so some wildlife advocates are trying to get her back to sea.) Exhibits include a shark pool, a 235,000-gallon tropical-reef aquarium, and manatees. Glass-bottom boats take tours of Biscayne Bay. Want to get your feet (and everything else) wet? The Water and Dolphin Exploration program (WADE) enables you to swim with dolphins during a two-hour session. Reservations are required. ✉ *4400 Rickenbacker Causeway,* ☎ *305/361–5705,* WEB *www.miamiseaquarium.com.* *$24.45, WADE $125, parking $4.* ⏲ *Daily 9:30–6, last admission 4:30; WADE Wed.–Sun. 8:30 and noon.*

38 **Old Rickenbacker Causeway Bridge.** Here you can watch boat traffic pass through the channel, pelicans and other seabirds soar and dive, and dolphins cavort in the bay. Park at its entrance, about a mile from the tollgate, and walk past anglers tending their lines to the gap where the center draw span across Biscayne Bay was removed. *South of Powell Bridge.*

DINING

Revised by Jen Karetnick

Restaurants listed here have passed the test of time, but you might double-check by phone before you set out for the evening. At many of the hottest spots, you'll need a reservation to avoid a long wait for a table. And when you get your check, note whether a gratuity is already included; most restaurants add 15% (ostensibly for the convenience of and protection from the many Latin-American and European tourists who are used to this practice in their homelands), but you can reduce or supplement it depending on your opinion of the service.

Coconut Grove

Contemporary

$$$–$$$$ ✕ **Mayfair Grill and Orchids Champagne and Wine Bar.** This long-running dining room in the Mayfair House Hotel can seem old world, thanks to its muffled atmosphere and carpeted elegance, but the cooking is more innovative than the decor would suggest. Executive chef Frank Liberoni, who draws on Asian, Caribbean, and French influences, prepares some stunning dishes: Thai crab cakes with panko crumbs and a sesame-chili glaze; Colorado buffalo loin carpaccio splashed with white truffle oil; roulade of free-range chicken stuffed with spinach and goat cheese; and barbecued rack of lamb with apple and ancho chili notes. If it all sounds a bit too filling, head instead for the outdoor courtyard at Orchids, the only champagne bar in town, where bubbly personalities can feel free to be themselves. ✉ *3000 Florida Ave.,* ☎ *305/441–0000. AE, D, DC, MC, V. No lunch.*

$$–$$$$ ✕ **Baleen.** The ballyhooed location of private Grove Isle finally gets a restaurant worthy of the hype. Culinary director and consultant Robbin Haas earned his New World stripes at a variety of South Beach restaurants, and was awarded the Best New Chef prize from *Food & Wine* magazine a few years ago for his efforts. Some of his signature dishes, like his tangy Caesar salad or salmon tartare with Thai spices and citron caviar, have carried over from eatery to eatery, but others are reinvented: hummus-parsley-crusted salmon with tahini butter, for instance, or Roquefort-crusted filet mignon with red-wine sauce. Main plates are à la carte, with steak house–type side dishes padding the bill a bit. ✉ *4 Grove Isle Dr.,* ☏ *305/858–8300. Reservations essential. AE, D, DC, MC, V.*

Indian

$–$$$ ✕ **Anokha.** "There is no doubt that all Indians love food," the menu says at Anokha, and there's also no doubt that all Miamians love this Indian food: shrimp cooked in pungent mustard sauce; fish soothed with an almond-cream curry; chicken wrapped in spinach and cilantro. The fare is at once home style and upscale, served over flaming Bunsen burners in order to keep it warm throughout the meal. The wait between starters such as the Anokha roll, a combo of chicken and coriander enclosed in an egg-battered roti, and main courses like the Kashmiri *rogan josh,* lamb in red curry sauce, can seem as long as a cab ride in Manhattan during rush hour. Don't fret—there's only one cook in the kitchen, and she's worth the delay. The pause is good for digestion, anyway, allowing you to consume more naan and chutney while you relax. ✉ *3195 Commodore Plaza,* ☏ *786/552–1030. AE, MC, V. Closed Mon.*

Coral Gables

Austrian

$$–$$$ ✕ **Mozart Stube.** It's Oktoberfest year-round at this Austrian *Schnitzelhaus.* The Bitburger flows early and often as you peruse a menu loaded down with heavy but scrumptious food. Start with a light garlic soup or maybe some snails in a lagoon of butter and garlic. A terrific side of German potato salad, homemade slaw, and more precedes ultrameaty entrées like veal shank, roast duckling, medallions of filet mignon in peppercorn-mushroom sauce, and of course wurst and schnitzel. The Black Forest cake is as legendary as the woods themselves. ✉ *325 Alcazar Ave.,* ☏ *305/446–1600. AE, D, DC, MC, V.*

Caribbean

$$–$$$$ ✕ **Ortanique on the Mile.** Named after an exotic citrus fruit, this restaurant screams "island," from the breezy interior decorated like a Jamaican terraced garden to the exquisite pan-Caribbean cuisine. Proprietor Delius Shirley and chef-proprietor Cindy Hutson used to run Norma's on the Beach, an erstwhile staple on Lincoln Road. They've improved upon themselves with their new eatery, offering old favorites like pumpkin soup or fried calamari salad, and new ones such as *escovitched* (a spicy Jamaican preparation) whole yellowtail snapper or jerk pork loin. Dessert doesn't get better than drunken banana fritters, unless you accompany it with a press pot of Blue Mountain coffee, direct from Jamaica and practically vibrating with caffeine. ✉ *278 Miracle Mile,* ☏ *305/446–7710. AE, MC, V. No lunch weekends.*

Contemporary

$$$–$$$$ ★ ✕ **Norman's.** This premier destination restaurant, which has won as many awards as it has customers, turns out some of Miami's most imaginative cuisine. Chef Norman Van Aken has created an international buzz by perfecting the art of New World cuisine—a combination

N
ATLANTIC OCEAN
MIAMI BEACH
NORTH MIAMI BEACH
NORTH MIAMI
Collins Ave.
Broad Causeway
Biscayne Blvd.
JFK Causeway
Julia Tuttle Causeway
Miami Gdns. Dr.
N. Miami Beach Blvd.
N.E. 6th Ave.
N.E. 2nd Ave.
N. Miami Ave.
Florida's Turnpike
N.E. 135th St.
N.E. 103rd St.
N.E. 95th St.
N.W. 7th Ave.
N.W. Gratigny Rd.
N.W. 135th St.
N.W. 27th Ave.
N.W. 103rd St.
N.W. 95th St.
N.W. 79th St.
N.W. 62nd St.
N.W. 54th St.
Robert Frost Expwy.
N.W. 36th St.
N.W. 20th St.
Palmetto Expwy.
N.W. 8th Ave.
E. 49th St.
E. 25th St.
Hialeah Dr.
Miami River
Red Rd.
W. 4th Ave.
W. 49th St.
N.W. 72nd Ave.
Dairy Rd.
N.W. 39th St.
N.W. 58th St.
N.W. 87th Ave.
Okeechobee Rd.
Miami

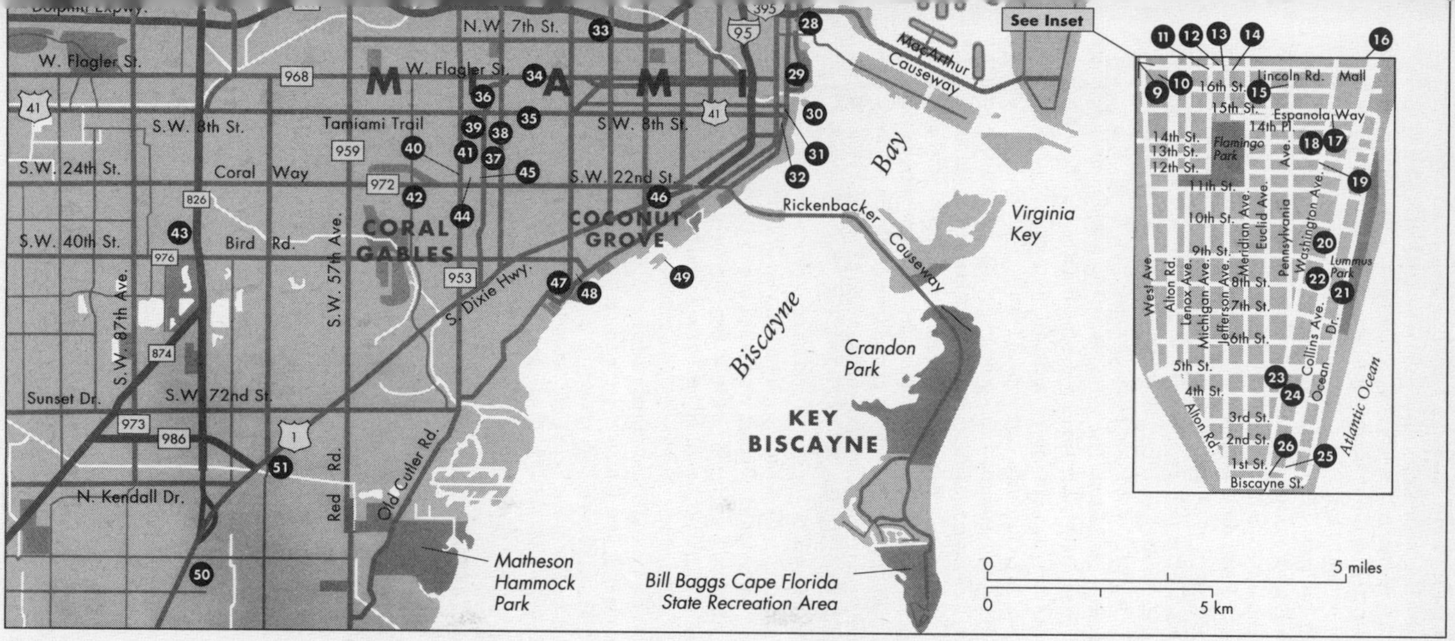

Anokha	47
Arnie and Richie's	5
Azul	30
Baleen	49
Bambú	13
Blue Door at Delano	16
Café Prima Pasta	4
Caffe Abbracci	45
Caffè Sambuca	10
Captain's Tavern	43
Cheeky Monkey	20
Chef Allen's	1
China Grill	23
Crystal Café	7
Daily Bread Marketplace	46
Donna's Bistro	42
El Bodegon Gallego	33
El Rancho Grande	15
Fishbone Grill	31
The Forge	6
Gaucho Room	18
Hy-Vong Vietnamese Cuisine	39
Indigo	29
Joe Allen	9
Joe's Stone Crab Restaurant	26
La Dorada	37
Las Nuevas Culebrinas	34
Los Ranchos	28
Mayfair Grill	48
Mozart Stube	36
Nemo	25
News Café	21
Norman's	40
Oasis Café	8
Ortanique on the Mile	44
Osteria del Teatro	17
Pacific Time	12
Paramount Grill	2
Pascal's on Ponce	38
Perricone's Marketplace	32
Restaurant St. Michel	41
Shula's Steak House	52
Spiga	19
Sushi Republic	3
Tony Chan's Water Club	27
Touch	11
Tropical Chinese Restaurant	50
Tuscan Steak	24
Two Chefs	51
Van Dyke Café	14
Versailles	35
Wish	22

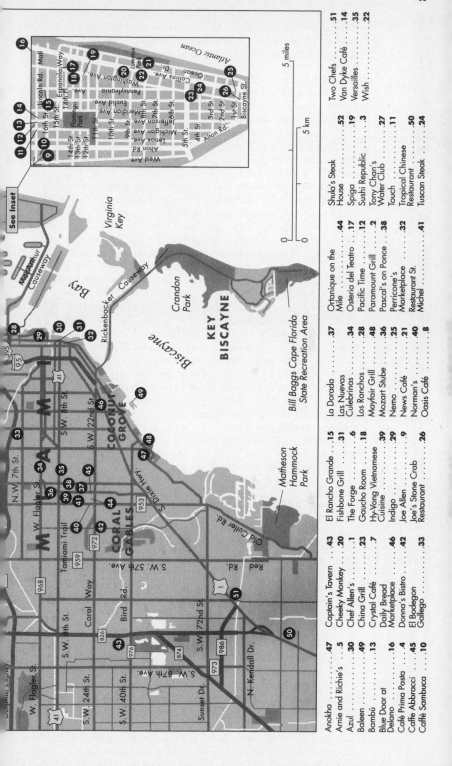

rooted in Latin, North American, Caribbean, and Asian influences. Bold tastes are delivered in every dish, from a simple black-and-white bean soup with sour cream, chorizo, and tortillas to a rum-and-pepper–painted grouper on a mango-habañero sauce. The sophisticated decor includes plenty of wrought iron, vaunted ceilings, railings, interior balconies, and open kitchens. The emphasis here is on service, and the ultragracious staff never seems harried, even when all seats are filled (usually every minute between opening and closing). Norman's captures the essence of Miami dining. Here's a fair warning: you'll be asked for a credit-card number when you make reservations (shoot for a month in advance); if you pull a no-show, you'll be charged a set fee per head anyway. ✉ *21 Almeria Ave.,* ☎ *305/446–6767. Reservations essential. AE, DC, MC, V. Closed Sun. No lunch.*

$$–$$$$ ✕ **Restaurant St. Michel.** The setting is utterly French, the little hotel it's in evokes the Mediterranean, the town has a very Spanish aura, and the cuisine is modern American. Stuart Bornstein's window on Coral Gables is a lace-curtained café with sidewalk tables that would be at home across from a railroad station in Avignon or Bordeaux. A sculpted bust here, a circus poster there, Deco chandeliers, and a mirrored, palm frond–shape mosaic all create a whimsical feel. Lighter dishes include moist couscous chicken and pasta primavera. Among the heartier entrées are a plum-, soy-, and lemon-glazed fillet of salmon; sesame-coated loin of tuna; and local yellowtail snapper. ✉ *162 Alcazar Ave.,* ☎ *305/444–1666. AE, DC, MC, V.*

$$–$$$ ✕ **Donna's Bistro.** A gourmet market and dining room, this cheerful, cozy bistro is exactly what the intimate David William Hotel needed. Executive chef Donna Wynter, who was born in Jamaica and trained in New York and France, plies guests with her blend of Asian, Caribbean, French, and local cuisines. Both her heritage and her influences are apparent in dishes such as sautéed baby calamari with lime and ancho chili; Florida avocado and hearts-of-palm salad with ruby-red grapefruit vinaigrette; and Jamaican jerked free-range chicken with savory potato timbale. Not yet well known by the community, Donna's is just waiting to be discovered; consider yourself Ponce de Léon. ✉ *700 Biltmore Way,* ☎ *305/445–7821. AE, MC, V.*

French

$$–$$$ ✕ **Pascal's on Ponce.** Stream-lined French cuisine disdains trends and discounts flash. Instead, diners are supplied with substantive delicacies like sautéed sea bass wrapped in a crispy potato crust with braised leeks, veal rib eye au jus, and tenderloin of beef sautéed with snails and wild mushrooms. Service is proper, textures are perfect, and wines ideally complementary. The only dilemma is deciding between the tarte Tatin or a cheese course for dessert. ✉ *2611 Ponce de Léon Blvd., Coral Gables,* ☎ *305/444–2024. Reservations required. AE, D, DC, MC, V. No lunch weekends.*

Italian

$$–$$$ ✕ **Caffe Abbracci.** Although the kitchen closes at midnight, the last wave of weekend customers—usually Brazilians—is still partying to flamenco or salsa music at 2 AM. The gracious Deco setting overflows with flowers, and the light above each table operates on an individual dimmer. After the cold and hot antipasti—various carpaccios, porcini mushrooms, calamari, grilled goat cheese, shrimps, mussels—come festive entrées. Most pasta is made fresh, so consider sampling two or three, maybe with pesto sauce, Gorgonzola, and fresh tomatoes. Since this place is more like a club than like a restaurant, patrons tend to fare better when they're recognized, so go with a local or pretend you've been there before. ✉ *318 Aragon Ave.,* ☎ *305/441–0700. Reservations essential. AE, DC, MC, V. No lunch weekends.*

Spanish

$$$–$$$$ ✕ **La Dorada.** This roomy, two-story eatery sets the standard for fine Spanish cuisine in the city. Named after the royal sea bream, the restaurant brings in fresh fish daily from the Bay of Biscay, rather than Biscayne Bay. Preparations are both classic and excellent: scallops sautéed with grapes, monkfish stuffed with shrimp, whole fish baked in rock salt. Not a lot of English is spoken here, thanks to an all-Spanish staff, so service can be a little off. But they do make an effort to please, catering to those whims that get across language barriers. ✉ *177 Giralda Ave.,* ☎ *305/446–2002. Closed Mon. AE, MC, V.*

Downtown Miami

Chinese

$$ ✕ **Tony Chan's Water Club.** One of a pair of outstanding Chinese restaurants, this beautiful dining room just off the lobby of the high-rise DoubleTree Grand Hotel looks onto a bay-side marina. Filled with art and detailed with chrome, the long room is modern rather than stereotypically Chinese. On the menu of more than 200 appetizers and entrées are minced quail tossed with bamboo shoots and mushrooms wrapped in lettuce leaves. Indulge in a seafood spectacular of shrimp, conch, scallops, fish cakes, and crabmeat tossed with broccoli in a bird's nest, or go for pork chops sprinkled with green pepper in a black bean–garlic sauce. A lighter favorite is steamed sea bass with ginger and garlic. Don't let the delicate flavors fool you—this restaurant is not just for the nosher, but for the power-hungry power-luncher as well. ✉ *1717 N. Bayshore Dr.,* ☎ *305/374–8888. AE, D, DC, MC, V.*

Contemporary

$$–$$$$ ✕ **Azul.** Located in the new Mandarin Oriental hotel on Brickell Key, this sumptuous restaurant has conquered the devil in the details. Along with locally—and soon-to-be-nationally—famous executive chef Michelle Bernstein's exotically rendered French-Caribbean cuisine, the restaurant offers complete and utter elegance. Too cold to properly appreciate the poached eggs with lobster knuckle hollandaise? Ask for one of the house pashminas, available in a variety of fashionable colors. Forgot your reading glasses and can't decipher the hanger steak with foie gras sauce? Request a pair from the host. Want to see how the other half lives? Descend the interior staircase to Cafe Sambal, the all-day casual restaurant downstairs. And if you have the stomach—or the head—for it, the martini bar offers up to 250 different concoctions. ✉ *500 Brickell Key Dr.,* ☎ *305/913–8288. Reservations essential. AE, MC, V. Closed Sun.*

$$–$$$ ✕ **Indigo.** When the Hotel Inter-Continental decided to redo its lobby restaurants, it didn't fool around. Now the entire lobby is one big, open-wall eatery, where diners can watch tourists get ready to depart for the cruise ships while they sup on the globally influenced cuisine. The menu's a trifle too cutesy for serious gourmets, with categories like "salappzs and ladles" featuring stone crab *croquetas* to start, and "dare 2 share" offering Moroccan tagine. And some items can be overly ambitious, while service doesn't try hard enough. However, a great wine list includes New Zealand and South African vintages, and moderately priced brunches, lunch buffets, and happy-hour spreads suit the suits who work in nearby downtown. ✉ *100 Chopin Plaza,* ☎ *305/854–9550. AE, D, DC, MC, V.*

Italian

$–$$ ✕ **Perricone's Marketplace.** The emerging neighborhood along Brickell Avenue south of the Miami River seems to be swelling with Italian restaurants. This one, housed in a 120-year-old barn brought down from Vermont by the owner, is the biggest and most popular among them. The recipes are ancient, too, handed down grandmother to mother to daughter, and the cooking is simple and good. Next door, a deli carries a selection of wine and beer that you can bring to the table for a small corkage fee. Enjoy a glass with homemade minestrone; a generous antipasto; linguine with a sauté of jumbo shrimp, fresh asparagus, and chopped tomatoes; or gnocchi with four cheeses. The homemade tiramisu and fruit tart are top-notch. ✉ *15 S.E. 10th St.,* ☎ *305/374–9449. AE, MC, V. Closed Sun. No lunch Sat.*

Latin

$–$$$ ✕ **Los Ranchos.** Owner Carlos Somoza, nephew of Nicaragua's late president Anastasio Somoza, sustains the tradition of Managua's original Los Ranchos by serving Argentine-style beef—lean, grass-fed tenderloin with chimichurri at this, for now, unique-to-Miami chain. Nicaraguan sauces include a tomato-based marinara and a fiery *cebollitas encurtidas,* with jalapeño and pickled onion. Specialties include chorizo and *cuajada con maduro* (skim cheese with fried bananas). Don't look for veggies or brewed decaf, but there is live entertainment. ✉ *Bayside Marketplace, 401 Biscayne Blvd.,* ☎ *305/375–8188 or 305/375–0666;* ✉ *2728 Ponce de León Blvd., Coral Gables,* ☎ *305/446–0050;* ✉ *Kendall Town & Country, 8505 Mills Dr., Kendall (South Miami),* ☎ *305/596–5353;* ✉ *The Falls, 8888 S.W. 136th St., Suite 303, South Miami,* ☎ *305/238–6867;* ✉ *125 S.W. 107th Ave., Little Managua (West Dade),* ☎ *305/221–9367. AE, DC, MC, V.*

Middle-Eastern

$ ✕ **Daily Bread Marketplace.** Essentially a marketplace run by an Israeli family, the fare here actually comes under the heading pan–Middle Eastern. Falafel and gyro pita pockets, some of the most tempting in the county, counter Arabic meat pies and Greek spinach pies. Desserts are uniformly sticky with honey, drenched with butter, and encrusted with nuts—not a bad way to go out, whether you eat in at the self-service tables or opt for takeout. ✉ *2400 S.W. 27th St.,* ☎ *305/856–5893. MC, V.*

Seafood

$–$$ ✕ **Fishbone Grill.** The artsy humor of this place is evident in the campy decor, but the fish here is artful, no-nonsense, globally influenced, and impeccably fresh. Start with cakelike jalapeño corn bread served alongside a small salad with homemade tomato-basil dressing. Then order your fish from a blackboard and have it grilled, blackened, sautéed, baked, française, or Asian. Pizzas are available, too, as is a mean cioppino, the San Francisco–style fish stew in a tomato base. Fishbone serves beer and wine only, and justifiably prides itself on a reasonably priced, varied selection. Watch for wine makers' dinners, when superb vintages are paired with the chef's whims. ✉ *650 S. Miami Ave.,* ☎ *305/530–1915. AE, MC, V. No dinner Sun.*

Spanish

$ ✕ **El Bodegon Gallego.** Ridiculously cheap and relentlessly craving-inducing, this shabby little Spanish-only storefront serves tasty tapas and hefty main courses. While the menu may escape the monolingual, sign language will get you an absurdly large order of chickpeas sautéed with chorizo, or lusty seafood soup, or yellow rice with chicken and shrimp. Consider the wrought iron on the windows not an indication of how bad the neighborhood is, but how good the creamy desserts flavored with alcohol are—most customers will willingly put themselves behind bars for just a single spoonful. ✉ *3174 N.W. 7th Ave.,* ☎ *305/649–0801. No credit cards.*

Little Havana

Cuban

$–$$ ✕ **Versailles.** Cubans meet to dine on Calle Ocho in quite possibly the most ornate budget restaurant you'll ever see, all mirrors and candelabras and hairdos and tuxedoed waiters, overflowing with hundreds of seats and accompanied by a tremendous din. And the royal treatment isn't just limited to the atmosphere in this veritable institution. The food is terrific, especially classics like *ropa vieja* (shredded beef), *arroz con pollo* (chicken and rice), *palomilla* (thin, boneless) steak, *sopa de platanos* (plantain soup), ham shank, and roast pork. To complete the experience, have the town's strongest Cuban coffee and terrific flan or sweet *tres leches* ("three milks," a creamy Latin dessert) to finish. ✉ *3555 S.W. 8th St.,* ☎ *305/444–0240. AE, D, DC, MC, V.*

Spanish

$–$$ ✕ **Las Nuevas Culebrinas.** A Spanish *tapacería* ("house of little plates") is a place to live each meal as if it were your last, although you may wait for it as long as some inmates do for an appeal. Tapas are not small at all; some are entrée size, such as a succulent mix of garbanzos with ham, sausage, red peppers, and oil, or the Spanish tortilla, a giant round omelet. Indulge in a tender fillet of crocodile, fresh fish, grilled pork, or the kicker, goat in Coca-Cola sauce. For dessert, there's a bit of drama—*crema Catalana,* caramelized right at the table with a blowtorch. This is a good time to remind your kids not to touch. ✉ *4700 W. Flagler St.,* ☎ *305/445–2337. AE, MC, V.*

Vietnamese

$$ ★ ✕ **Hy-Vong Vietnamese Cuisine.** This plain little restaurant is an anomaly on Calle Ocho, and also a novelty—come before 7 to avoid a wait. Spring springs forth with spring rolls, ground pork, cellophane noodles, and black mushrooms wrapped in homemade rice paper. Folks mill about on the sidewalk for hours to sample the whole fish panfried with *nuoc man,* a garlic-lime fish sauce, not to mention the thinly sliced pork barbecued with sesame seeds, almonds, and peanuts. Beer-savvy proprietor Kathy Manning serves a half dozen top brews (Double Grimbergen, Moretti, and Spaten, among them) to further inoculate the experience against the ordinary. ✉ *3458 S.W. 8th St.,* ☎ *305/446–3674. No credit cards. Closed Mon. and 2 wks in Aug. No lunch.*

Miami Beach North of South Beach

Contemporary

$$–$$$ ✕ **Crystal Café.** As cozy as Grandma's dining room, this New Continental restaurant takes the classics and lightens 'em up. Beef Stroganoff and chicken paprikash are two such updated stars; and osso buco literally falls off the bone. More contemporary items include chicken Kiev, stuffed with goat cheese and topped with a tricolor salad, and pan-seared duck breast served with raspberry sauce. Macedonian and multiple Golden Spoon award-winning chef-proprietor Klime Kovaceski, who strolls around the art deco restaurant frequently to greet both regulars and newcomers, takes pride in serving more food than you can possibly manage—the watercress-mushroom salad with homemade honey-mustard dressing is big enough for four to share, and three side dishes garnish every main course. Regardless, home-baked rhubarb pie, courtesy of Kovaceski's mother-in-law, is a sweet-tart absolute. ✉ *726 41st St.,* ☎ *305/673–8266. AE, D, MC, V. Closed Mon. No lunch.*

Continental

$$$–$$$$ ✕ **The Forge.** Often compared to a museum, this landmark bills itself as "the Versailles of steak." Behind a mansionlike facade, each intimate dining salon has its own historical artifacts, including a chandelier that hung in James Madison's White House. The wine cellar contains 380,000 bottles—including more than 500 dating from 1822 (and costing as much as $35,000). In addition to steak, specialties include Norwegian salmon served over fresh garden vegetables with spinach vinaigrette and free-range Wisconsin duck roasted with black currants. For dessert try the blacksmith pie. This place is a hot party spot on Wednesday night, and the adjoining club, Café Nostalgia, is very popular with the "I remember Cuba" crowd. ✉ *432 Arthur Godfrey Rd.,* ☎ *305/538–8533. AE, DC, MC, V. No lunch.*

Delicatessens

$–$$ ✕ **Arnie and Richie's.** Take a deep whiff when you walk in, and you'll know what you're in for: onion rolls, smoked whitefish salad, half-sour pickles, herring in sour cream sauce, chopped liver, corned beef, pastrami. Deli doesn't get more delicious than in this family-run operation. Casual to the extreme, most customers are regulars and seat themselves at tables that have baskets of plastic knives and forks; if you request a menu, it's a clear sign you're a newcomer. If you want to be inconspicuous, peruse the deli cases first so you know what the place offers, then take a seat and put on a good front. Service can be brusque, but it sure is quick. ✉ *525 41st St.,* ☎ *305/531–7691. AE, MC, V.*

Italian

$–$$ ★ ✕ **Café Prima Pasta.** One of Miami's many signatures is its Argentine-Italian cuisine. This exemplary spot, run by Gerardo Cea, whose dad, Arturo, cooks, rules the emerging North Beach neighborhood. Consistently intense flavors, high-quality ingredients, and on-the-spot preparation are the keys to its success. Service can be disjointed and erratic, but you forget it all upon delivery of fresh-made bread with a bowl of spiced olive oil. Tender carpaccio and plentiful antipasti are a delight to share, but the real treat here is the hand-rolled pasta, which can range from crab-stuffed ravioli to simple fettuccine with seafood. Try the legendary tiramisu to add espresso notes to your unavoidable garlic breath. ✉ *414 71st St.,* ☎ *305/867–0106. No credit cards.*

Japanese

$–$$ ✕ **Sushi Republic.** A long and narrow storefront with sponge-painted walls, this eatery prides itself on making customers feel welcome. So don't be surprised when the sushi chefs say "Hi!" when you walk in. Nor should you expect anything but the freshest sashimi, which is elegantly presented and perfectly succulent. As far as cooked fare goes, the Republic is more like a democracy—everything is even and consistent. *Shumai,* soft shrimp dumplings with ponzu dipping sauce; whole fried soft-shell crab; and salmon teriyaki are particularly noteworthy. Among rolls, the Tiger Woods roll—tuna rolled with cream cheese and topped with avocado and salmon—is a hole in one. Cool nights call for a steaming noodle soup like *nabeyaki udon,* a broth laden with udon noodles, eggs, mushrooms, and big pieces of shrimp tempura. ✉ *9583 Harding Ave., Surfside,* ☎ *305/867–8036. AE, D, DC, MC, V. Closed Mon. No lunch Sun.*

Mediterranean

$–$$ ✕ **Oasis Café.** The emphasis in Mediterranean cuisine is on healthy cooking, and at Oasis, a coolly tiled spot with breezy decor, the tradition continues—the chefs here stuff grape leaves, not arteries. In other words, natural-food aficionados feel right at home, with delicacies like eggplant salads, hummus, grilled sesame tofu and sautéed garlic spinach for starters, and for entrées, pan-seared turkey chop, roasted vegetable lasagna, grilled fresh fish on focaccia, or penne with turkey, tomato, saffron, and pine nuts. The homemade rum cake is a superb way to drink dessert. ✉ *976 41st St.,* ☎ *305/674–7676. AE, D, DC, MC, V.*

North Miami Beach and North Dade

Contemporary

$$$–$$$$ ★ ✕ **Chef Allen's.** James Beard Award–winning chef and cookbook author Allen Susser, a member of the original, self-designated Mango Gang, presents his global cuisine in this art gallery of a dining room. Susser not only created a new type of regional cuisine, he also designed the decor that it's presented in, including a picture window into the kitchen, so you can watch him create his contemporary American masterpieces from a menu that changes nightly. After a salad of baby greens and warm wild mushrooms or a rock-shrimp hash with roasted corn, consider swordfish with conch-citrus couscous, macadamia nuts, and lemon, or grilled lamb chops with eggplant timbale and a three-nut salsa. Few serious diners can resist finishing the meal with a nightly soufflé; order this when you receive your appetizers to eliminate a mouthwatering wait. ✉ *19088 N.E. 29th Ave., Aventura,* ☎ *305/935–2900. AE, DC, MC, V.*

$–$$$ ✕ **Paramount Grill.** Yes, it's located on the second story of the Aventura Mall. True, there's a kids' menu. Indeed, the place doesn't take reservations, and there may be a wait. So what? When it comes to this handsomely appointed, bistro-style eatery, owned by the venerated Allen Susser of Chef Allen's, diners don't quibble. They simply enjoy Susser's creative innovations—pizza topped with smoked salmon and citrus cream cheese; rock shrimp cakes with lemon aioli; Caribe-crusted skirt steak; or key lime chicken with yuca fries—for half the dough they'd spend at Chef Allen's. Sit under the flickering gaslights, lean against a red-brick column, and raise a toast to the master chef for coming up with this casual concept. ✉ *19501 Biscayne Blvd., Aventura,* ☎ *305/466–1466. AE, MC, V.*

Steak

$$$–$$$$ ✕ **Shula's Steak House.** Prime rib, fish, and steaks displayed on a cart along with live, 3-pound lobsters are almost an afterthought to the objets de sports in this shrine for the NFL-obsessed. Dine in a manly wood-lined setting with a fireplace, surrounded by memorabilia of retired coach Don Shula's perfect 1972 season with the Miami Dolphins. Gaze upon game footballs, assistant coach Howard Schnellenberger's pipe, and a playbook autographed by President Richard Nixon while munching on your salad. Polish off the 48-ounce porterhouse steak and achieve a sort of immortality—your name on a plaque, and an autographed picture of Shula to take home. Do be aware, though, that you'll pay a whole lot more for the baked potato than the average couch potato spends on chips. Also for fans, there's shula's steak 2 (lowercase borrowed from espn2), a sports celebrity hangout in the Don Shula hotel. ✉ *Don Shula Golf Club, 7601 N.W. 154th St., Miami Lakes,* ☎ *305/820–8102. AE, DC, MC, V.*

South Beach

American

$$ ✕ **Joe Allen.** Hidden away in an exploding neighborhood of condos, town houses, and a huge supermarket, this casual, upscale eatery is a hangout for locals who crave a good martini along with a terrific burger. Owner Joe Allen, reared in the kitchens and dining rooms of Manhattan, wants to feel at home in his own place, and he does it by serving meat loaf as well as grilled fish over mesclun greens. The eclectic crowd includes kids and grandparents, and the menu has everything from pizzas to calves' liver to steaks. Always start with an innovative salad, such as arugula with pear, prosciutto, and a Gorgonzola dressing, or roast beef salad on greens with Parmesan. Desserts are home style as well, including banana cream pie and ice cream sandwiched with cookies. ✉ *1787 Purdy Ave.,* ☎ *305/531–7007. MC, V.*

Café

$$ ★ ✕ **News Café.** An Ocean Drive landmark, this 24-hour café attracts a big crowd around the clock with snacks, light meals, drinks, and the sidewalk people parade. There's a bar with 12 stools in back, but most diners prefer sitting outside, where they can feel the salt breeze and gawk at the human scenery. Offering a little of this and a little of that—bagels, pâtés, chocolate fondue, sandwiches, and a terrific wine list—this joint has something for everyone. In 1997 the café spawned a new location—twice as large—in Coconut Grove; although service can be indifferent to the point of laissez-faire, the café remains a scene. ✉ *800 Ocean Dr.,* ☎ *305/538–6397; 2901 Florida Ave., Coconut Grove,* ☎ *305/774–6397. AE, DC, MC, V.*

$–$$ ✕ **Van Dyke Café.** Just as its parent News Café draws the fashion crowd, this offshoot attracts the artsy crowd. In the restored 1924 Van Dyke Hotel, this place seems even livelier than its Ocean Drive counterpart, with pedestrians passing by on the Lincoln Road Mall and live jazz playing upstairs every evening—or, more to the point, every early morning. The kitchen serves dishes from mammoth omelets with home fries to soups and grilled dolphin sandwiches to basil-grilled lamb and pasta dishes, although it's best to stick to basics. There's an enticing list of gourmet drinks like Bellinis and kir royales. ✉ *846 Lincoln Rd.,* ☎ *305/534–3600. AE, DC, MC, V.*

Contemporary

$$$–$$$$ ★ ✕ **Blue Door at Delano.** In a hotel where style reigns supreme, acclaimed consulting chef Claude Troisgros and his executive chef Elizabeth Barlow combine the flavors of classic French cuisine with South American influences to create dishes like the Big Ravioli, filled with crab-and-scallop mousseline, and osso buco in Thai curry sauce with caramelized pineapple and bananas. The menu changes quarterly, but look for peppermint mousse in a chocolate crust for dessert. Equally pleasing is dining with the crème de la crème of Miami (and New York, and Paris) society. Don't worry if you don't recognize some apparent bigwig next to you—eavesdrop on the cell phone conversation and you'll no doubt be filled in pronto. ✉ *1685 Collins Ave.,* ☎ *305/674–6400. Reservations essential. AE, D, DC, MC, V.*

$$$–$$$$ ✕ **Touch.** Five million bucks later, what was formerly Michael Caine's South Beach Brasserie is now a sensually designed restaurant, perched among the more mundane Lincoln Road eateries like a diva. Executive chef Sean Brasel wraps his dishes in a haze of acceptable sins—Sonoma quail stuffed with wild rice, foie gras, and black plums with plum-vanilla glacé is just one example of his brand of decadence. Decor elements include tufted silk on the walls and lambskin cushions, not to mention the palm trees literally growing out of the corners of the bar. If the red curry–crusted ahi tuna or the veal chop marinated Tahitian style doesn't entice you, perhaps the hip crowd that dallies here will. But if you don't have a reservation, don't expect to be welcomed beyond the velvet ropes. ✉ *910 Lincoln Rd.,* ☎ *305/532–8003. Reservations essential. AE, MC, V. No lunch.*

$$–$$$$ ★ ✕ **Nemo.** A SoFi pioneer, Nemo receives raves from gourmets in a neighborhood that has emerged as South Beach's next hot spot. The open-air atmosphere, bright colors, copper fixtures, and tree-shaded courtyard lend casual comfort, and a menu that blends Caribbean, Asian, Mediterranean, and Middle Eastern influences promises an explosion of cultures in each bite. Popular appetizers include garlic-cured salmon rolls with tabiko caviar and wasabi mayo, and crispy prawns with spicy salsa cruda. Main courses are works-in-progress now that founding chef–proprietor, Michael Schwartz, who trained under Wolfgang Puck, is back in the kitchen, but a typical option would be the wok-charred salmon or the grilled Indian-spiced pork chop. Nemo also serves up a terrific Sunday brunch, and Hedy Goldsmith's funky pastries are exquisitely sinful. A sibling sushi bar is next door. ✉ *100 Collins Ave.,* ☎ *305/532–4550. Reservations essential. AE, MC, V.*

$$–$$$$ ✕ **Wish.** It's easy to get what you wish for in this eatery if what you wish for is stupendous cuisine served in a designer-Deco environment. Fashion designer Todd Oldham, a part-time resident of South Beach, redesigned the former Tiffany Hotel, the art deco gem that houses this fresh, youthful restaurant. His whimsical, colorful design (you'll marvel at the creative use of something like 50 hanging light fixtures) provides an apt setting for young, up-and-coming chef Andrea Curto's imaginative dishes. Her fusion fare—yellow-eye snapper with grilled shrimp and poblano chile risotto; pan-roasted chicken with Brie polenta; or center-cut pork chop stuffed with rabbit sausage and Granny Smith apples—makes even more of a statement than the dining room. ✉ *801 Collins Ave. Miami Beach,* ☎ *305/674–9474. AE, D, DC, MC, V.*

$$$ ✕ **Cheeky Monkey.** An old British expression, meaning "you fresh thing," Cheeky Monkey lives up to its implied reputation. Located in Merv Griffin's Blue Moon Hotel, the chimp is outfitted in animal prints and oil paintings of hairy relatives. Fare is globally influenced; indeed, dishes like the Turkish fig wrapped in phyllo with *prosciutto di Carpegna,* Danish blue cheese, toasted pignoli cream, and a port wine–balsamic glaze seem to want to gather as many countries on one plate as possible. Chimichurri-grilled lamb riblets are toothsome little starters; almond-crusted wild catfish meunière also has a loyal fan base. The Monkey frequently throws private shindigs and closes the restaurant to the public, so it's best to call first and find out if there's a do. ✉ *944 Collins Ave.,* ☎ *305/534–2650. AE, MC, V.*

Italian

$$–$$$$ ★ ✕ **Tuscan Steak.** Dark wood, mirrors, and green upholstery define this masculine, chic, expensive place, where big platters of meats and fish are served family-style, but as if your family were a royal one. Part of the restaurant empire run by China Grill Management, Tuscan can be busy as a subway stop and still the staff will be gracious and giving. Executive chef Dewey LoSasso takes his cues from the Tuscan countryside, where pasta is rich with truffles and main plates are simply but deliciously grilled. Sip a deep red Barolo with any of the house specialties: three-mushroom risotto with white truffle oil; gnocchi with Gorgonzola cream; Florentine T-bone with roasted garlic puree; whole yellowtail snapper with braised garlic; or the filet mignon with a Gorgonzola crust in red wine sauce. ✉ *431 Washington Ave.,* ☎ *305/534–2233. AE, DC, MC, V.*

$$–$$$ ✕ **Caffè Sambuca.** Carpeted, quiet, and softly lighted—is this really South Beach? You betcha. Hidden in a corner of the Lincoln Road walking mall that most visitors don't frequent, locals consider this place their private Italian refuge. Proprietors Ernesto Soler and Eduardo Gaguine call everyone from babies to elders "family," and wink as they serve you huge portions of traditional Caesar salad. Gnocchi in pesto sauce works delightfully as a second course or as the entire meal, depending on your appetite, but it'd be a shame to miss out on chicken stuffed with goat cheese and glazed with a sun-dried tomato reduction. For a quick trip to Europe, choose a bottle of wine from the extensive list, sit out on the sidewalk under an umbrella, and fantasize about Florence. ✉ *1233 Lincoln Rd.,* ☎ *305/532–2800. AE, MC, V. No lunch.*

$$–$$$ ★ ✕ **Osteria del Teatro.** Thanks to word of mouth, this northern Italian restaurant is constantly full. Orchids grace the tables in the intimate gray-on-gray room with a low, laced-canvas ceiling, deco lamps, and the most refined clink and clatter along Washington Avenue. Regulars know not to order off the printed menu, however. A tremendous variety of daily specials offers the best grub, and it's plenty of fun to see if your waiter forgets any. A representative appetizer is poached asparagus served over polenta triangles with a Gorgonzola sauce. Stuffed pastas, including the spinach crepes overflowing with ricotta, might sound heavy but taste light; fish dishes yield a rosemary-marinated tuna or salmon in pink peppercorn-citrus sauce. Just don't eat too much—this cornerstone eatery is a tight squeeze, and patrons are stuffed in like ground veal in ravioli. ✉ *1443 Washington Ave.,* ☎ *305/538–7850. AE, DC, MC, V. Closed Tues. No lunch.*

$–$$ ✕ **Spiga.** When you need a break from Miami's abundant exotic fare, savor the modestly priced Italian standards that are served with flair in this small, pretty place. Homemade is the hallmark here, and pastas and breads are fresh daily. Carpaccio *di salmone* (thinly sliced salmon with mixed greens) is a typical appetizer, and the *zuppa di pesce* (fish soup) is unparalleled. Entrées include ravioli *di vitello ai funghi shitaki,* homemade ravioli stuffed with veal and sautéed with shiitake mushrooms. The cozy restaurant has become a neighborhood favorite where customers sometimes bring in CDs for their personal enjoyment. ✉ *1228 Collins Ave.,* ☎ *305/534–0079. AE, D, DC, MC, V.*

Mexican

$$ ✕ **El Rancho Grande.** The location (just off Lincoln Road) and the menu (mainstream Mexican) have made this neighborhood restaurant so popular it's won a slew of "best" awards in area dining polls. Prices are reasonable and service is casual and laid-back. Beef flautas, chicken enchiladas, taquitas, and more are served in a cantina-style setting, which was recently expanded to include a second dining room, a bar, and an outdoor terrace. Don't look for frills, but do watch out for some tangy *cochinita pibil,* or marinated pork, and some hefty California-style burritos. Even vegetarians can't gripe—they get a page of the menu all to themselves. ✉ *1626 Pennsylvania Ave.,* ☎ *305/673–0480. AE, MC, V.*

Pan-Asian

$$$–$$$$ ✕ **Bambú.** Don't expect marquee proprietor Cameron Diaz to be waiting tables here. She's really an in-name owner only. But do anticipate glam surroundings and customers who are (or think they are) equal to her status. The second eatery from Astor Place hotelier and restaurateur Karim Masri and his partner, Hubert Baudoin, Bambú's muted khaki colors, woven raffia drapes, bars formed from river rocks and coconut wood, and spectacular 14-ft granite waterfall provide some Zen for the world-weary. But the real beauty here lies in executive chef Rob Boone's fare: tuna hand rolls with avocado, cilantro, and pickled eggplant; soy-lacquered cod with tempura chrysanthemum leaves; and Kobe beef with tiny Asian vegetables and lotus root. ✉ *1661 Meridian Ave. Miami Beach,* ☎ *305/531–4800. Reservations essential. AE, MC, V. No lunch.*

$$$–$$$$ ✕ **China Grill.** This crowded, noisy place has no view, but that doesn't detract from its popularity. Chef Ephraim Kadish turns out not Chinese food but rather "world cuisine," in portions large and meant for sharing. Crispy duck with caramelized black vinegar sauce and scallion pancakes is a nice surprise, as is pork and beans with green apple and balsamic mojo marinade. Mechanical service will provide an ac-

ceptable broccoli rabe dumpling starter, the wild mushroom pasta entrée, or the flash-fried crispy spinach that shatters like a good martini glass thrown into a fireplace. Unless you're frequent diners Boris Becker or George Clooney, don't expect your drinks to arrive before your food. ✉ *404 Washington Ave.,* ☎ *305/534–2211. Reservations essential. AE, DC, MC, V. No lunch Sat.*

$$$–$$$$ ★ ✕ **Pacific Time.** Packed nearly every night, this superb eatery owned by chef Jonathan Eismann has a high blue ceiling and banquettes, accents of mahogany and brass, plank floors, and an open-window kitchen. The brilliant American-Asian cuisine includes such entrées as cedar-roasted salmon, rosemary-roasted chicken, and dry-aged Colorado beef grilled with shiitake mushrooms. The cuttlefish appetizer and the Florida pompano entrée are masterpieces. Rice dishes, potatoes, and vegetables are à la carte; however, a pre-theater prix-fixe dinner ($20), served 6–7, comes with a noodle dish, Szechuan mixed grill, and grilled ginger chicken. Desserts (around $7) include a fresh pear-pecan spring roll. There's an extensive California wine list. Pacific Time/Next Door, a casual satellite restaurant a door to the west, has the same excellent food and service for a bit less. ✉ *915 Lincoln Rd.,* ☎ *305/534–5979. AE, DC, MC, V.*

Seafood

$–$$$$ ✕ **Joe's Stone Crab Restaurant.** Joe's attracts phenomenal crowds despite stubbornly refusing reservations, so go prepared to wait—up to an hour to register for a table, perhaps another *three* to sit down. Depending on the crowd, the wait can be convivial or contentious. The centerpiece of the menu is, of course, stone crab: about a ton of claws are served daily with drawn butter, lemon wedges, and piquant mustard sauce. Save room for dessert—key lime pie or apple pie with a crumb-pecan topping. If you can't stand loitering hungrily while self-important patrons try to grease the maître d's palm, go next door for Joe's takeout. ✉ *227 Biscayne St.,* ☎ *305/673–0365; 305/673–4611 for takeout; 800/780–2722 for overnight shipping. Reservations not accepted. AE, D, DC, MC, V. Closed Sept. 1–Oct. 15. No lunch Sun.–Mon.*

Steak

$$$–$$$$ ✕ **Gaucho Room.** Granted, you'll never bite down on a more succulent steak anywhere than in this Argentine-cowboy-themed room, located in the convention-friendly Loews hotel. But don't you dare call this a steak house. Executive chef Frank Randazzo cut his culinary teeth on fusion cuisine, and he takes the Latin beat and puts the metronome on allegro. The result is items such as a pulled duck empanada with smoked chili sauce; Chilean sea bass with ginger puree; and seared turbot with pickled beet–brown butter escabéche. Which is not to say that you shouldn't order the supple *churrasco,* a whole skirt steak that is marinated, grilled, and then sliced tableside. In fact, service may be the finest and most solicitous in South Beach—a compliment indeed. ✉ *1601 Collins Ave.,* ☎ *305/604–5290. Reservations essential. AE, D, DC, MC, V. No lunch.*

South Miami

Contemporary

$$–$$$$ ✕ **Two Chefs.** Meet the two chefs—Jan Jorgensen and Soren Bredahl—both great Danes who've been cooking together for 15 years. This restaurant, decorated like a Williams-Sonoma catalog, began as a cooking school and quickly evolved into one of few fine dining destinations in South Miami. The menu changes daily, but scan for seared foie gras with gnocchi, an unusually textured combination that features reduced boysenberries. The chefs pride themselves on the unexpected,

as a matter of fact, and think nothing of pairing goat meat with lobster or composing an escargot potpie. Sometimes an experiment will fail, but for the most part, these culinary scientists succeed in not just feeding but delighting their faithful following. ✉ *8287 S. Dixie Hwy., South Miami,* ☎ *305/663–2100. AE, D, DC, MC, V. Closed Sun.*

Seafood

$$–$$$$ ✕ **Captain's Tavern.** This family fish house has an unusually interesting menu fortified with Caribbean and South American influences. The decor may be hokey, with paneled walls and witty sayings on plaques hung here and there, but the food can fascinate. Beyond good versions of the typical fare—conch chowder and conch fritters—you'll find a Portuguese fish stew, fish with various tropical fruits, a delightful black-bean soup, and oysters in cream sauce with fresh rosemary, not to mention decadent desserts. ✉ *7495 S.E. 98th St.,* ☎ *305/661–4237. AE, MC, V.*

West Miami

Chinese

$–$$$ ✕ **Tropical Chinese Restaurant.** This big, lacquer-free room feels as open and busy as a railway station. You'll find unfamiliar items on the menu—early spring leaves of snow pea pods, for example, which are sublimely tender and flavorful. The extensive menu is filled with tofu combinations, poultry, beef, and pork, as well as tender seafood. An exuberant dim sum lunch—brunch on the weekends—is chosen from wheeled carts. In the open kitchen, 10 chefs prepare everything as if for dignitaries. ✉ *7991 S.W. 40th St.,* ☎ *305/262–7576 or 305/262–1552. AE, DC, MC, V.*

LODGING

Although some hotels (especially on the mainland) have adopted steady year-round rates, many adjust their rates to reflect seasonal demand. The peak occurs in winter, with a dip in summer (prices are often more negotiable than rate cards let on). You'll find the best values between Easter and Memorial Day (which is actually a delightful time in Miami but a difficult time for many people to travel) and in September and October (the height of hurricane season). Keep in mind that Miami hoteliers collect roughly 12.5%—ouch—for city and resort taxes; parking fees can run up to $16 per evening; and tips for bellhops, valet parkers, concierges, and housekeepers add to the expense. Some hotels actually tack on an automatic 15% gratuity. All told, you can easily spend 25% more than your room rate to sleep in Miami.

Coconut Grove

$$$$ ★ **Wyndham Grand Bay.** Combining the classical elegance of Greece, a stepped facade that looks vaguely Aztec, a hint of the South, and a brush of the tropical, this hotel is like no other in South Florida. Guest rooms are filled with superb touches, such as antique sideboards that hold house phones and matched woods variously inlaid and fluted. Whoopi Goldberg, Arnold Schwarzenegger, and Bruce Willis have all stayed here, perhaps enjoying the easterly views that look over the bay. Afternoon tea is served in the lobby. Bice, the trendy Italian restaurant, is extremely popular. ✉ *2669 S. Bayshore Dr., Coconut Grove 33133,* ☎ *305/858–9600 or 800/327–2788,* FAX *305/859–2026,* WEB *www.wyndham.com. 125 rooms, 52 suites. Restaurant, bar, pool, beauty salon, hot tub, massage, sauna, health club, concierge, parking (fee). AE, DC, MC, V.*

$$$–$$$$ **Mayfair House.** This European-style luxury hotel sits within the Streets of Mayfair, an exclusive open-air shopping mall in the heart of the Grove. Part business hotel and part romantic getaway, it has Art Nouveau public areas. Soft, flowing lines run through Tiffany windows, polished mahogany and marble accents, imported ceramics and crystal, and an impressive glassed-in elevator. The individually furnished suites have terraces facing the street, screened by vegetation and wood latticework. Each room has a small Japanese hot tub on the balcony or a Roman tub inside, and 10 have antique pianos. A rooftop recreation area is peaceful (although the miniature lap pool is odd for such a large hotel), and the Orchid Bar, a ground-floor lounge, is a quiet spot that attracts a trendy clientele. ✉ *3000 Florida Ave., Coconut Grove 33133,* ☎ *305/441–0000 or 800/433–4555,* FAX *305/447–9173,* WEB *www.mayfairhousehotel.com 179 suites. Restaurant, bar, snack bar, pool, hot tub, laundry service, concierge, business services, parking (fee). AE, D, DC, MC, V.*

Coral Gables

$$$–$$$$ ★ **Biltmore Hotel.** Miami's grand boom-time hotel has undergone two renovations since 1986 but still manages to recapture a bygone era. Now owned by the city of Coral Gables, the 1926 Biltmore rises like a sienna-color wedding cake in the heart of a residential district. The vaulted lobby has hand-painted rafters on a twinkling sky-blue background. Large guest rooms are done in a restrained Moorish style, and for slightly more than the average rate ($2,550) you can book the Everglades (aka Al Capone) Suite—President Clinton's favorite room when he was in town. The first week of each month a Michelin-rated chef is flown in from France to surprise diners and teach Biltmore chefs something new, and the Cellar Club is open for guests who wish to sample fine wines and premium cigars. Historical tours are given Sunday at 1:30, 2:30, and 3:30. ✉ *1200 Anastasia Ave., 33134,* ☎ *305/445–1926 or 800/727–1926,* FAX *305/913–3159,* WEB *www.biltmorehotel.com 237 rooms, 38 suites. Restaurant, bar, café, lobby lounge, pool, sauna, spa, golf, 10 tennis courts, health club, meeting room. AE, D, DC, MC, V.*

$$–$$$ ★ **Hotel Place St. Michel.** Art Nouveau chandeliers suspended from vaulted ceilings light the public areas of this intimate boutique hotel in the heart of downtown Coral Gables. Built in 1926, the historic low-rise was restored between 1981 and 1986 and yet again in 1995. Within easy walking distance of Miracle Mile, the inn is filled with the scent of fresh flowers, circulated by paddle fans. Its fine restaurant is an undeniable asset. Each room has its own dimensions, personality, and antiques imported from England, Scotland, and France, although plusher beds would be a welcome improvement. ✉ *162 Alcazar Ave., 33134,* ☎ *305/444–1666 or 800/848–4683,* FAX *305/529–0074,* WEB *www.hotelplacestmichel.com 24 rooms, 3 suites. Restaurant, bar, laundry service, parking (fee). AE, DC, MC, V. CP.*

Downtown Miami

$$$$ ★ **Mandarin Oriental Miami.** Miami's most luxurious business hotel, this elegant newcomer is the first South Florida foray for Mandarin Oriental, one of Asia's most celebrated brands. They certainly picked a killer location—the tip of Brickell Key in Biscayne Bay, with a panoramic view of the downtown skyline. Or, turn the other way and gaze across the bay to Miami Beach and the blue Atlantic beyond. The proprietors are fanatically picky about details, from the Bulova alarm clocks and hand-painted room numbers on rice paper to the recessed data ports on room desks that eliminate laptop cord clutter. Decor combines traditional Asian with Latin-tinged Miami: in the lobby lounge, cocktail waitresses wear cutoff silk blouses and capri pants. Although a favorite of Wall Street

Miami Area Lodging

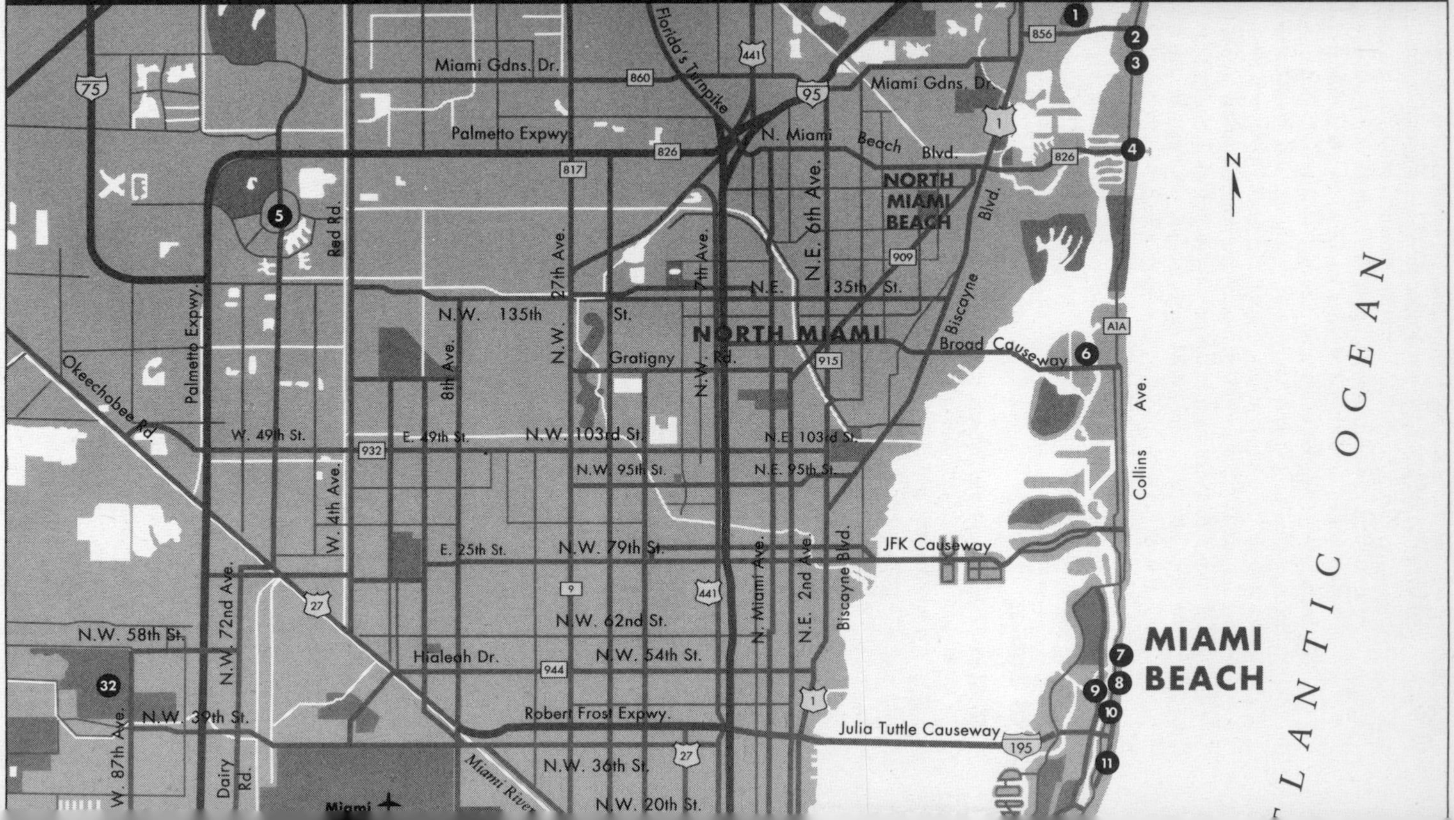

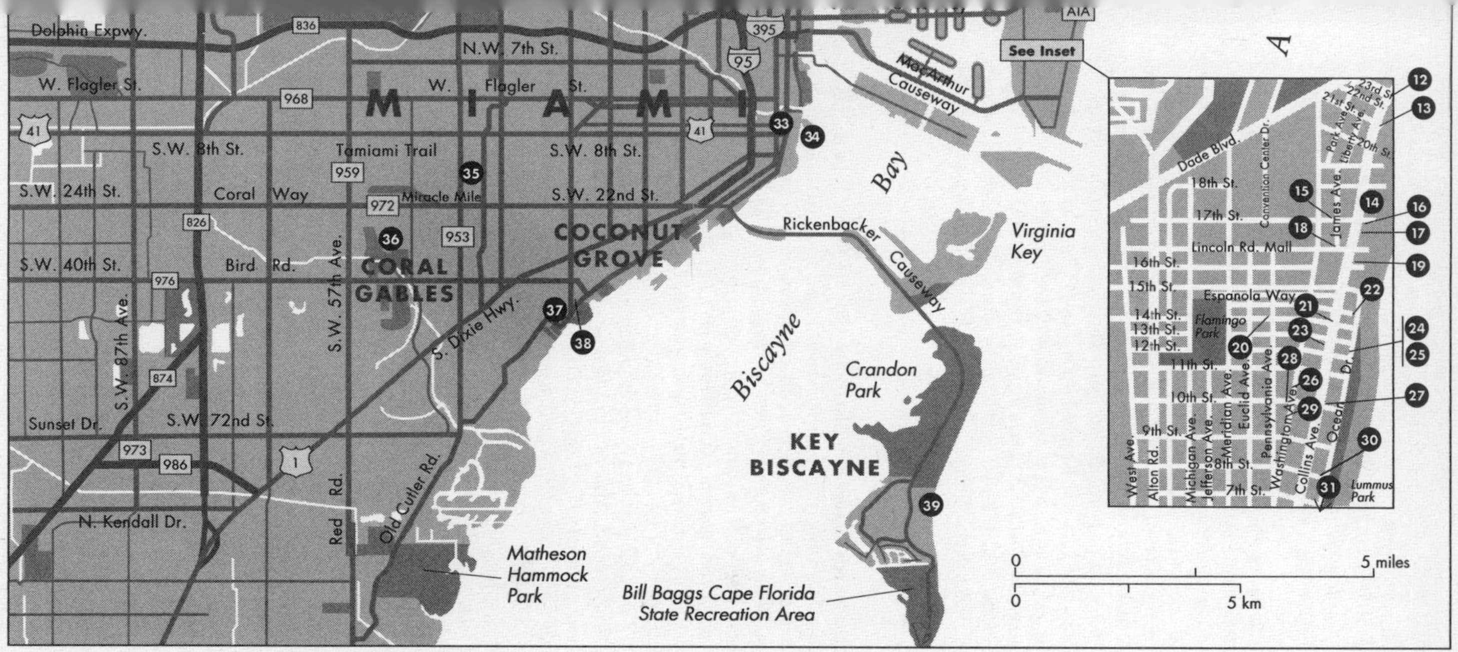

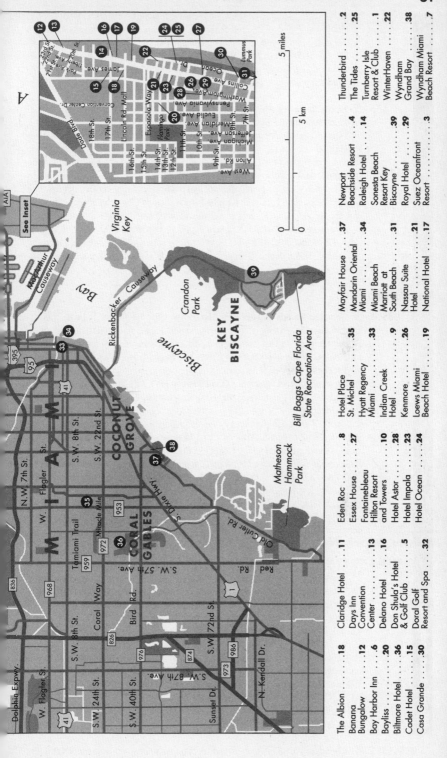

The Albion 18	Claridge Hotel 11	Eden Roc 8	Hotel Place St. Michel 35	Mayfair House 37	Newport Beachside Resort 4	Thunderbird 2
Banana Bungalow 12	Days Inn Convention Center 13	Essex House 27	Hyatt Regency Miami 33	Mandarin Oriental Miami 34	Raleigh Hotel 14	The Tides 25
Bay Harbor Inn 6	Delano Hotel 16	Fontainebleau Hilton Resort and Towers 10	Indian Creek Hotel 9	Miami Beach Marriott at South Beach 31	Sonesta Beach Resort Key Biscayne 39	Turnberry Isle Resort & Club 1
Bayliss 20	Don Shula's Hotel & Golf Club 5	Hotel Astor 28	Kenmore 26	Nassau Suite Hotel 21	Royal Hotel 29	WinterHaven 22
Biltmore Hotel 36	Doral Golf Resort and Spa 32	Hotel Impala 23	Loews Miami Beach Hotel 19	National Hotel 17	Suez Oceanfront Resort 3	Wyndham Grand Bay 38
Cadet Hotel 15		Hotel Ocean 24				Wyndham Miami Beach Resort 7
Casa Grande 30						

tycoons and Latin American CEOs doing business with the international banks lining Brickell Avenue, anyone who can afford to stay here won't regret it. ✉ *500 Brickell Key Dr., 33131,* ☎ *305/913–8288 or 866/888–6780,* FAX *305/913–8300,* WEB *www.mandarinoriental.com 329 rooms. Restaurant, 2 bars, in-room data ports, in-room safes, pool, spa, dry cleaning, laundry service, concierge, business services, meeting rooms, parking (fee). AE, D, DC, MC, V.*

$$$ **Hyatt Regency Miami.** The Hyatt is well positioned for the downtown renaissance, located near the Miami Avenue Bridge, Port of Miami, and the AmericanAirlines Arena. If your vacation is based on boats, basketball, or business, you can't do much better. The distinctive public spaces are more colorful than businesslike, and guest rooms are done in an unusual combination of avocado, beige, and blond. Rooms yield views of the river or port, and not surprisingly the best ones occupy the upper floors. The James L. Knight International Center is accessible without stepping outside, as is the downtown Metromover and its Metrorail connection. ✉ *400 S.E. 2nd Ave., 33131,* ☎ *305/358–1234 or 800/233–1234,* FAX *305/358–0529,* WEB *www.miami.hyatt.com 612 rooms, 51 suites. Restaurant, 2 bars, pool, health club, laundry service, concierge, business services, parking (fee). AE, D, DC, MC, V.*

Key Biscayne

$$$$ ★ **Sonesta Beach Resort Key Biscayne.** One of Miami's best, this resort in a great setting offers stunning sea views from east-facing units. Rooms are done in sand tones with fabrics in emerald, purple, gold, and ruby. Villas are actually three-bedroom homes with full kitchens and screened pools. The size of the property, its Olympic pool, and the range of activities make it a good family getaway, and the popular Just Us Kids program can keep the offspring creatively busy. Museum-quality modern art by prominent painters and sculptors graces public areas; the hotel's disco bar displays Andy Warhol's drawings of Mick Jagger. The 750-ft beach, one of Florida's most gorgeous, has a wide variety of recreational opportunities, including catamarans and sailing lessons. ✉ *350 Ocean Dr., Key Biscayne 33149,* ☎ *305/361–2021 or 800/766–3782,* FAX *305/361–3096,* WEB *www.sonesta.com 284 rooms, 15 suites, 3 villas. 3 restaurants, 3 bars, snack bar, pool, massage, steam room, 9 tennis courts, aerobics, health club, beach, windsurfing, parasailing, children's programs (ages 5–13). AE, D, DC, MC, V.*

Miami Beach North of South Beach

$$$$ **Eden Roc Renaissance Resort & Spa.** Who knows why this grand 1950s hotel, now owned by Marriott, designed by Morris Lapidus, is overshadowed by the larger, more prominent Fontainebleau? From the moment you enter, the free-flowing lines of the nautical-Deco architecture make you feel casual and comfortable. There's an indoor basketball court and a rock-climbing wall and the resort's yacht is available for oceangoing meetings. The 55,000-square-ft Spa of Eden usually runs full tilt, while former Dolphins coach Jimmy Johnson's beachside sports bar caters to those who prefer lifting weights 16 ounces at a time. Rooms blend a touch of the '50s with informal elegance. ✉ *4525 Collins Ave., 33140,* ☎ *305/531–0000 or 800/327–8337,* FAX *305/674–5555,* WEB *www.renaissancehotels.com 349 rooms. 2 restaurants, sports bar, 2 pools, massage, spa, basketball, squash, exercise room, racquetball, meeting room. AE, MC, V.*

$$$–$$$$ ★ **Claridge Hotel.** A cool Mediterranean breeze in a somewhat stagnant corner of Miami Beach, this is the city's most impressive renovation. The exterior has been restored to the canary-yellow glory of the 1928 original; inside, time slips back a few hundred more years.

Rich Venetian frescoed walls are hung with Peruvian oil paintings, the floors are fashioned from volcanic ash, and the whole is supported by majestic volcanic stone columns. A Moroccan terrace overlooks the soaring inner atrium, which doubles as a restaurant during meal times. Tucked away at the far end is a splash Jacuzzi. The spare but elegant rooms are equipped with dual phone lines and high-speed Internet access, as well as Gilchrest and Soames amenities. ✉ *3500 Collins Ave., 33140,* ☎ *305/604–8485 or 888/422–9111,* FAX *305/674–0881,* WEB *www.claridgefl.com 52 rooms and suites. Restaurant, in-room data ports, in-room safes, hot tub, concierge, business services, parking (fee). AE, D, DC, MC, V.*

$$$–$$$$ **Fontainebleau Hilton Resort and Towers.** This big, busy, and ornate grande dame wrapped up a complete overhaul in mid-2001. Corridors, guest rooms, suites, pools, recreation areas, and the building's exterior have been spiffed up with new carpet, wall coverings, lighting, and furnishings. Tower rooms, already luxurious, are now even more so, with upgraded amenities, a personal concierge, and Italian marble baths. Throughout the property, room themes vary from the 1950s to the contemporary—very contemporary. Even the smallest room is large by Miami standards. A 40,000-square-ft beachside spa is ideal for self-indulgence. Adult guests enjoy complimentary admission to the hotel's *Club Tropigala,* a Vegas-style floor show with a Latin twist. Children can participate in half- and full-day Kids' Corner programs, which have different daily themes, such as treasure hunts, circus days, and the Olympics. ✉ *4441 Collins Ave., 33140,* ☎ *305/538–2000 or 800/548–8886,* FAX *305/673–5351,* WEB *www.hilton.com 1,146 rooms, 60 suites. 12 restaurants, 4 bars, 3 pools, sauna, spa, 7 tennis courts, health club, volleyball, beach, windsurfing, boating, jet skiing, parasailing, nightclub, children's programs (ages 5–12), convention center. AE, D, DC, MC, V.*

$$$–$$$$ ★ **Wyndham Miami Beach Resort.** Of the great Miami Beach hotels, this 18-story glass tower remains a standout, as does its polished staff offering exceptional service, from helping you find the best shopping to bringing you an icy drink on the beach. Warm-tone accommodations are filled with attentive details: minirefrigerators, three layers of drapes (including blackout curtains), big closets, and bathrooms with high-end toiletries and a magnifying mirror. Two presidential suites were designed in consultation with the Secret Service, and a rooftop meeting room offers views of bay and ocean. A car-rental office is in the lobby. ✉ *4833 Collins Ave., 33140,* ☎ *305/532–3600 or 800/203–8368,* FAX *305/534–7409,* WEB *www.wyndham.com 378 rooms, 46 suites. 2 restaurants, 2 bars, pool, massage, tennis court, exercise room, beach, meeting room. AE, D, DC, MC, V.*

$$–$$$ **Indian Creek Hotel.** Not as grand as the North Beach behemoths or as hectic as the Ocean Drive offerings, this 1936 Pueblo Deco jewel may just be Miami's most charming and sincere lodge. Owner Marc Levin rescued the inn and filled its rooms with art deco furniture, much of it discovered in the basement. Items were cleaned, reupholstered, and put back in service, helping the hotel win the Miami Design Preservation League's award for outstanding restoration. Suites have VCR/CD players and modem capabilities. The dining room offers an eclectic and appetizing menu, which you can also enjoy outdoors by the lush pool and garden. Stay a while, and manager Zammy Migdal and his staff will have you feeling like family. ✉ *2727 Indian Creek Dr., 33140,* ☎ *305/531–2727 or 800/491–2772,* FAX *305/531–5651,* WEB *www.indiancreekhotelmb.com 55 rooms, 6 suites. Restaurant, refrigerators, pool, meeting room. AE, D, DC, MC, V.*

North Miami, North Miami Beach, and North Dade

$$$$ ★ **Turnberry Isle Resort & Club.** Finest of the grand resorts, Turnberry is a tapestry of islands and waterways on 300 superbly landscaped acres by the bay. Guests have two choices for accommodations: the 1920s Addison Mizner–designed Country Club Hotel on the Intracoastal Waterway, or the Ocean Club, which is a slightly less impressive structure, although it does have the virtue of being on the beach. Oversize rooms are decorated in light woods and earth tones and have large curving terraces and hot tubs. The marina has moorings for 117 boats that can each be up to 150 ft, there's a free shuttle to the beach club and the Aventura Mall, and Robert Trent Jones stopped by to design two tropical golf courses. For those whose vacation plans include deep-tissue stress relief, there's the three-story Spa at Turnberry Isle. ✉ *19999 W. Country Club Dr., Aventura 33180,* ☎ *305/932–6200 or 800/327–7028,* FAX *305/933–6560,* WEB *www.turnberryisle.com 354 rooms, 41 suites. 4 restaurants, 5 bars, in-room safes, minibars, 2 pools, spa, steam rooms, two 18-hole golf courses, 19 tennis courts (16 lighted), health club, jogging, racquetball, beach, docks, windsurfing, boating, helipad. AE, D, DC, MC, V.*

$$–$$$$ ★ **Newport Beachside Resort.** Built before the present crop of luxury towers started to spring up, this is still one of the nicest hotels in Sunny Isles. The combination time-share and hotel seems like the place to stay when Mom or Dad is here on business and the family needs a clean, safe place to enjoy the beach and activities. The lobby is large and bright, with macaws adding a dash of color, and the pool area is perfectly suited for enjoying the sun. There are the wading pool, a standard pool, a fishing pier, and the ocean. Kids' activities, calypso entertainment, and water sports also add to the pleasure. Back inside, rooms are tropically bright and feature king beds, minifridges, and microwaves. The one- and two-bedroom suites are similar but are much larger and include a marble bath. Downstairs, there's a big sports bar as well as a dive shop, fitness center, and travel agency. Check in here, and you'll never want to leave. ✉ *16701 Collins Ave., Sunny Isles 33160,* ☎ *305/949–1300 or 800/327–5476,* FAX *305/947–5873,* WEB *www.newportbeachsideresort.com 80 rooms, 210 suites. Restaurant, bar, pool, beach, shops, nightclub, concierge, meeting rooms. AE, D, DC, MC, V.*

$$–$$$ **Bay Harbor Inn.** The inn's not on the ocean, but the tranquil Indian Creek flowing outside is sure to soothe. Rooms with queen- and king-size beds are quite pleasant and baths are large. One of the most pleasing features is your own front porch, where you can sit with a book or drink or both and view the village of Bal Harbour a five-minute walk away. The restaurant here (Islands) is very nice, but it's also pleasant to walk around the corner to a small Italian restaurant (DaVinci's) or over the bridge to Surfside for a wider selection of neighborhood bars and eateries. The hotel staff is composed largely of hotel students from Johnson & Wales University, so the service is enthusiastic but not flawlessly professional. ✉ *9660 E. Bayshore Dr., Bal Harbour 33154,* ☎ *305/868–4141,* FAX *305/867–9094,* WEB *www.bayharborinn.com 22 rooms, 23 suites. Restaurant, bar, pool, meeting room. AE, MC, V. CP.*

$$–$$$ **Don Shula's Hotel & Golf Club.** This low-rise resort is part of Miami Lakes, a planned town about 14 mi northwest of downtown. Opened in 1962 and renovated in 1999, the golf club includes a championship course, a lighted executive course, and a golf school. All club rooms have balconies, and the theme is English traditional, rich in leather and wood. The hotel, on the other hand, has a typical Florida-tropics look—light pastels and furniture of wicker and light wood. In both locations the best rooms are near the lobby for convenient access; ask for a room away from the elevators. ✉ *6842 Main St., Miami Lakes 33014,* ☎ *305/821–1150 or 800/247–4852,* FAX *305/820–8071,* WEB *www.donshula.com 205 rooms, 22 suites. 2 restaurants, bar, 2 pools, saunas, steam rooms, 36-hole golf course, 9 tennis courts, aerobics, basketball, health club, racquetball, volleyball. AE, DC, MC, V.*

$–$$ **Suez Oceanfront Resort.** Several miles north of Miami Beach, the family-run Suez stands out from the area's pricier but nondescript motels. Look beyond the bright, striped exterior and tacky sphinx statuary to the quiet, gardenlike lounge and the landscaped palm courtyard. Rooms have tropical-style furniture and dazzling colors, offsetting generally small spaces. Those in the north wing, with parking-lot views, are the smallest and least expensive. Fresh and saltwater pools, kitchens in some rooms, and special kids' rates make this an especially good value, popular with Europeans. ✉ *18215 Collins Ave., Sunny Isles 33160,* ☎ *305/932–0661 or 800/327–5278,* FAX *305/937–0058,* WEB *www.dezerhotels.com 196 rooms. Restaurant, bar, refrigerators, 2 pools, wading pool, tennis court, shuffleboard, volleyball, beach, playground, concierge, laundry service. AE, DC, MC, V. MAP.*

$–$$ **Thunderbird Resort.** A great North Beach find, this well-priced hotel has pretty and spacious rooms that can accommodate up to four people at no extra charge. A few efficiencies are also available. Even more appealing is what you'll find outdoors. The tropical courtyard and Olympic-size pool create a miniature oasis, and the Tiki bar is a perfect place to watch the waves. This hotel provides a fair rate for a clean and neat place that makes it especially popular with the snowbird crowd. An added convenience is the supermarket across the street, a nice perk since there's a hefty charge at the ice machine. The Thunderbird, like some other small local properties, has been gobbled up by the Dezer Hotels empire, and is slated for demolition in 2003 to make way for more upscale fare. If you're interested in experiencing the last of a dying breed, catch them before they're gone. ✉ *18401 Collins Ave., Sunny Isles 33160,* ☎ *305/931–7700 or 800/327–2044,* FAX *305/932–7521,* WEB *www.dezerhotels.com 180 rooms. Restaurant, 2 bars, in-room safes, refrigerators, pool, beauty salon, hot tub, exercise room, beach, coin laundry, meeting room, parking (fee). AE, D, DC, MC, V.*

South Beach

$$$$ **The Albion.** With the South Beach boom in full swing, the Rubell Family, new owners of the Albion, hired Carlos Zapata to update this 1939 nautical-Deco building by Igor Polevitzky. The two-story lobby sweeps into a secluded courtyard and is framed by an indoor waterfall. A crowd of hip but friendly types makes up the clientele; they like to gather at the mezzanine-level pool, which has portholes that allow courtyard strollers an underwater view of the swimmers. The blond-wood Fallabella Bar recalls the styling of Heywood-Wakefield, and the Pantry offers breakfast and sandwiches overlooking the pool or the lobby. As with other Rubell properties, guest rooms are minimalist in design, although filled with what travelers expect: data ports, two-line phones, minibars, and stereos. ✉ *1650 James Ave., 33139,* ☎ *305/913–1000 or 888/665–0008,* FAX *305/674–0507,* WEB *www.rubellhotels.com 85 rooms, 9 suites. 2 restaurants, bar, in-room data ports, minibars, pool, exercise room, laundry service, concierge, meeting room. AE, D, DC, MC, V.*

$$$$ ★ **Casa Grande.** This, still one of South Beach's best, is one of Chris Blackwell's five Island Outpost hotels. The lobby's teak, tile, and recessed lighting create a warm and relaxing look. Luxurious Balinese-inspired suites are done in teak and mahogany, capturing the fashionable air of Ocean Drive yet standing out. They have dhurrie rugs, Indonesian fabrics and artifacts, two-poster beds with ziggurat turns, full electric kitchens with quality utensils, and large baths—practically unheard of in the Art Deco District. Goodies range from a daily newspaper and in-room coffee to fresh flowers, TV/VCR/CD/radio entertainment centers, and evening turndown with Italian chocolates. Insulated windows keep the noise of the Ocean Drive revelers at bay. Book well in advance for peak periods. ✉ *834 Ocean Dr., 33139,* ☎ *305/672–7003 or 800/688–7678,* FAX *305/673–3669,* WEB *www.islandoutpost.com 34 suites. Café, in-room safes, in-room VCRs, kitchenettes, refrigerators, beach, shops, laundry service, concierge, business services, travel services. AE, D, DC, MC, V.*

$$$$ ★ **Delano Hotel.** Visitors marvel at the lobby hung with massive white, billowing drapes and try to act casual while watching for Bono, Elvis Costello, George Clooney, Michael Keaton, or Spike Lee (an actual week's roster of celebrity guests). Fashion models and men of independent means gather beneath cabanas, pose by the infinity pool, and sniff the heady aromas wafting in from the popular Blue Door restaurant. Comprehensive executive services are offered for business travelers, and all guests can access 1,500 videos and have the run of a rooftop bathhouse and solarium on alternating schedules. Although the standard rooms are of average size, their stark whiteness makes them appear larger. The gift shop carries magazines you wouldn't want your parents to see. The real appeal here is the *Alice in Wonderland*–like surrealism. ✉ *1685 Collins Ave., 33139,* ☎ *305/672–2000 or 800/555–5001,* FAX *305/532–0099. 184 rooms, 24 suites. Restaurant, bar, lobby lounge, pool, spa, health club, beach, laundry service, concierge, business services. AE, D, DC, MC, V.*

$$$$ ★ **Loews Miami Beach Hotel.** Miami had been waiting for a major new beachfront luxury hotel for 30 years. Although others had been renovated, this 18-story, 800-room gem was built from the blueprints up. Not only did Loews manage to snag 99 ft of oceanfront, it took over the vacant St. Moritz next door and restored it to its original 1939 art deco splendor, adding another 100 rooms to the complex. The resort has kids' programs, a health spa, 85,000 square ft of meeting space, and an enormous ocean-view grand ballroom. Dining, too, is a pleasure, courtesy of the Argentinian-inspired Gaucho Room, Preston's South Beach Coffee Bar, and Hemisphere Lounge. ✉ *1601 Collins Ave., 33139,* ☎ *305/604–1601,* FAX *305/531–8677,* WEB *www.loewshotels.com 740 rooms, 50 suites. 4 restaurants, 2 bars, lobby lounge, pool, spa, beach, children's programs (ages 5–13), meeting room. AE, D, DC, MC, V.*

$$$$ **National Hotel.** This resurrected 1939 shorefront hotel reopened in 1997. The tropical pool, Miami Beach's longest (205 ft), is truly spectacular; in daylight it's a perfect backdrop for the film crews that often work here. With curtains closed, poolside rooms could be generic Holiday Inn, displaying little of the creativity of other recently arrived hotels. Rooms in the main building are far more appealing, however, and the interiors approach a higher level of creativity. Applause is in order for preserved pieces, such as the original chandelier and furniture in the dining room, and for such modern in-room amenities as ironing boards, safes, data ports, and robes. Another notable feature is the clubby '30s-style Press Room cigar bar and meeting room, off the lobby. ✉ *1677 Collins Ave., 33139,* ☎ *305/532–2311 or 800/327–8370,* FAX *305/534–1426,* WEB *www.nationalhotel.com 115 rooms, 5 suites. Restaurant, bar, pool, in-room data ports, in-room safes, minibars, no-smoking floor, exercise room, beach, laundry service, concierge, meeting room, parking (fee). AE, DC, MC, V.*

$$$$ ★ 🏨 **Raleigh Hotel.** Hidden behind a thick veil of greenery is one of the nicest oceanfront hotels in South Beach. Among the first Art Deco District hotels to be renovated, it added Victorian accents (hallway chandeliers and in-room oil paintings) to soften the edges. The hotel has been a consistent favorite of fashion photographers and production crews, who appreciate state-of-the-art rooms with three phones, two phone lines, and T-1 Internet access. Even standard rooms are spacious, and the suites more so. Each room or suite offers a radio/CD/cassette player and a refrigerator stocked to your taste. The gorgeous fleur-de-lis pool is the focal point year-round. If you prefer salt with your water, the 300-ft beach is yours. Other pluses: the lobby coffee bar, a romantic restaurant (Tiger Oak Room), and the old-fashioned Martini Bar. ✉ *1775 Collins Ave., 33139,* ☎ *305/534–6300 or 800/848–1775,* FAX *305/538–8140,* WEB *www.raleighhotel.com 107 rooms, 14 suites. Restaurant, bar, in-room data ports, in-room safes, in-room VCRs, refrigerators, pool, massage, exercise room, beach, laundry service, concierge, business services, meeting room, parking (fee). AE, D, DC, MC, V.*

$$$$ ★ 🏨 **The Tides.** Miami hotels like white, and this one is no exception. However, the nice twists here are the added features that Chris Blackwell introduced as part of the flawless renovation. Some touches are small—spyglasses in each room (since they all face the ocean), a blackboard for messages to maids, newspapers on request. Others are large—every room has a king-size bed, capacious closets, and generous baths, the result of turning 115 rooms into 45 suites. Elvis would have liked the blackout curtains and VIP entrance. The downstairs lobby is large and austere (and white), and facilities include a reading room, hypercool terrace dining, and an Olympic-size (the only one on Ocean Drive) mezzanine pool where women can go topless (total nudity is "undesirable"). ✉ *1220 Ocean Dr., 33139,* ☎ *305/604–5000 or 800/688–7678,* FAX *305/604–5180,* WEB *www.islandoutpost.com 45 suites. 2 restaurants, in-room data ports, in-room safes, minibars, pool, exercise room, jogging, beach, baby-sitting, dry cleaning, concierge, business services, meeting room, travel services. AE, D, DC, MC, V.*

$$$–$$$$ 🏨 **Essex House.** Already adequate before renovation, the Essex House annexed the building next door and prettied it up with 20 luxury suites, putting the hotel well above average. All the work put into the large suites has paid off: reached by crossing a tropical courtyard, each includes a wet bar, king-size bed, pull-out sofa, 100-square-ft bathroom, fridge, and hot tub. Rooms are no slouches, either. Club chairs, custom carpet and lighting, mahogany entertainment units and matching desks, marble tubs, two phone lines, computer data ports, voice mail—it's like the home office you wish you had built. You're in the heart of South Beach, only a block from the beach and busy Ocean Drive, but sound-absorbing windows keep rooms quiet; the free Continental breakfast will do the same for your stomach. ✉ *1001 Collins Ave., 33139,* ☎ *305/534–2700 or 800/553–7739,* FAX *305/532–3827,* WEB *www.essexhotel.com 59 rooms, 20 suites. Bar, in-room data ports, in-room safes, in-room VCRs, pool, spa, dry cleaning, laundry services, parking (fee). AE, D, MC, V.*

$$$–$$$$ ★ 🏨 **Hotel Astor.** Among the very best that South Beach has to offer, the Astor stands apart from the crowd by double-insulating walls against noise and offering such quiet luxuries as thick towels, down pillows, paddle fans, and a seductive pool. During its renovation, guest rooms and baths were expanded, then furnished with custom-milled French furniture, Roman shades, and sleek sound and video systems. A tasteful, muted color scheme and the most comfortable king beds imaginable make for eminently restful rooms, and excellent service eliminates any worries about practical matters. The bar off the lobby offers an exquisite view of the waterfall alongside the pool. ✉ *956 Washington*

Ave., 33139, ☏ 305/531–8081 or 800/270–4981, FAX 305/531–3193, WEB www.hotelastor.com 40 rooms. Restaurant, bar, in-room data ports, in-room safes, minibars, room service, pool, massage, laundry service, concierge, business services, parking (fee). AE, DC, MC, V.

$$$–$$$$ **Hotel Ocean.** If the street signs didn't read Ocean Drive, you might suspect you were whiling away the day on the Riviera at this hotel formerly known as the Ocean Front Hotel. The tropical French feel is evident when you enter the shaded, bougainvillea-draped courtyard and see diners enjoying a complimentary breakfast in the hotel's brasserie. Two buildings connected by this courtyard contain many pleasant surprises. The comfortable rooms (which average 425 square ft each) are highlighted by soft beds, authentic 1930s art deco pieces, large fold-out couches, and clean, spacious baths. Add to this wet bars with refrigerators, TV/VCR/CD players, and two phone lines with data-port access. Rooms have soundproof windows, praise be. ✉ *1230–38 Ocean Dr., 33139, ☏ 305/672–2579 or 800/783–1725, FAX 305/672–7665, WEB www.hotelocean.com 4 rooms, 23 suites. Restaurant, bar, in-room data ports, in-room safes, in-room VCRs, minibars, concierge. AE, D, DC, MC, V.*

$$$–$$$$ **Miami Beach Marriott at South Beach.** South Beach has become so popular that the national chains have moved in with a vengeance. But oceanfront real estate is scarce, and the Marriott entry is down at the very end of Ocean Drive, several blocks from the traditional heart of the action. Continuing the trend started by the Loews the architecture is all nouveau art deco flourishes, concealing a pragmatic beach resort designed to yield as many ocean-view rooms as possible. Those rooms are larger than most on the beach, with a liberal helping of very un-Marriott-like tropical color that proves the mega-brand really is trying to fit in. The restaurant is appealing and the mini-spa, quiet beach, and reliable service make this a safe bet for business types or families who want to experience South Beach while keeping the wildest partying at a distance. ✉ *161 Ocean Dr., 33139, ☏ 305/536–7700 or 800/228–9290, FAX 305/536–9900, WEB www.miamibeachmarriott.com 236 rooms, 7 suites. Restaurant, 2 bars, in-room data ports, in-room safes, pool, spa, beach, laundry service, concierge, business services, meeting rooms, parking (fee). AE, D, DC, MC, V.*

$$$ ★ **Hotel Impala.** One of the nicest inns in the area, this is a stunning tropical Mediterranean revival in the heart of the Art Deco District and one block from the beach. Iron, mahogany, and stone on the inside are in synch with the sporty white-trim ocher exterior and quiet courtyard. Rooms are elegant, comfortable, and complete, each with a TV/VCR/stereo and a stock of CDs and videos. It's all very European, from mineral water and orchids to the Mediterranean-style armoires, Italian fixtures, and Spanish surrealist art above triple-sheeted white-on-white modified Eastlake sleigh beds. Everything from wastebaskets to towels to toilet paper is of extraordinary quality. This place definitely has great feng shui. Families should note that the hotel doesn't welcome children under 16. ✉ *1228 Collins Ave., 33139, ☏ 305/673–2021 or 800/646–7252, FAX 305/673–5984, WEB www.hotelimpalamiamibeach.com 14 rooms, 3 suites. Restaurant, bar, in-room data ports, in-room VCRs, laundry service, concierge. AE, D, DC, MC, V. CP.*

$$$ ★ **Royal Hotel.** *Austin Powers* meets *2001* in this avant-garde offering that, thankfully, doesn't take itself too seriously. Each room really only has two pieces of furniture: a "digital chaise-longue" and a bed, both molded white plastic contortions from designer Jordan Moser. The bed sits in the middle of the room, with projecting wings that hold a phone and alarm clock. The headboard arcs back like a car spoiler, and doubles as a minibar, set up to each guest's taste. The chaise longue holds a TV/Web TV and keyboard for surfing the Net. Lest all this space-age technology make the room dull, a wild shag carpet and

rainbow-paisley bathrobes remind guests they're here to have fun. The hotel is a few blocks from the beach and Ocean Drive, but the wacky rooms make it worth the extra effort. A stay at the Royal is a wild trip indeed. ✉ *758 Washington Ave., 33139,* ☎ *305/673–9009 or 888/394–6835,* FAX *305/673–9244,* WEB *www.royalhotelsouthbeach.com. 38 rooms, 4 suites. Restaurant, in-room data ports, laundry service, business services, meeting room. AE, D, DC, MC, V.*

$$$ ★ WinterHaven. "Bright" and "airy" are not words one usually associates with South Beach hotels, but this artfully restored classic is both—in spades. Whereas most hip SoBe digs favor muted grays and whites, WinterHaven is a riot of color, from the garnet-and-aquamarine lobby lounge to the ginger-and-cream upholstery in guest rooms. In those rooms, black-and-white pictures of South Beach's former self grace the walls above custom-designed deco furniture that—surprise—doesn't strive to be a conversation piece. The two-story lobby and split-level mezzanine regularly play host to parties and fashion shoots, both of which dally at the elegant wood-and-glass bar. Take the complimentary breakfast up to the rooftop sundeck and enjoy a bird's-eye view of South Beach at dawn. ✉ *1400 Ocean Dr., 33139,* ☎ *305/531–5571 or 800/395–2322,* FAX *305/538–6387,* WEB *www.winterhavenhotelsobe.com 71 rooms. Bar, in-room safes, in-room data ports, concierge, parking (fee). AE, D, DC, MC, V.*

$$–$$$ Nassau Suite Hotel. A boutique hotel one block from the beach, this airy retreat almost qualifies as a steal (by South Beach standards). It offers huge studio suites at a third of the price demanded by Ocean Drive properties. The original 1937 floor plan of 50 rooms gave way to 22 spacious and smart-looking suites with king beds, fully equipped kitchens, hardwood floors, white wood blinds, and free local calls. The hotel is in the heart of the action yet quiet enough to give travelers the rest they need. Note: This three-floor hotel has no elevator and no bellman. There's also very limited parking. ✉ *1414 Collins Ave., 33139,* ☎ *305/534–2354 or 866/859–4177,* FAX *305/534–3133,* WEB *www.nassausuite.com 22 suites. In-room data ports, kitchenettes, concierge. AE, D, DC, MC, V.*

$$ Kenmore. Utilitarian comfort is the theme at this place, which preserves the essence of 1930s art deco. The glass-block facade of the lobby, the courtyard bar, and patio furniture that invites you to relax all complement clean but smallish tropical-theme rooms with twin or king-size beds. On a very active street, the surprising privacy of the Kenmore is a strong selling point. A quiet pool hidden behind a low wall allows you to tan in an Adirondack chair without being the subject of voyeurs. Then again, you're only a short walk to the clubs and shops of South Beach—and you get a free breakfast, to boot. ✉ *1020–1050 Washington Ave., 33139,* ☎ *305/532–1930 or 888/424–1930,* FAX *305/972–4666,* WEB *www.parkwashingtonresort.com 60 rooms. Restaurant, bar, refrigerators, pool. AE, MC, V. CP.*

$ Banana Bungalow. This may seem like a university dormitory—indeed, some rooms have dorm-style bunk beds for about $15 a night—but the cleanliness, friendliness, and abundance of activities make this lodge worth checking into, especially for hard-core student travelers. A large pool, the bungalow's social center, is surrounded by a patio bar, game room, outdoor grills, a café, and an activity board announcing kayak rentals, scenic flights, and beach volleyball games held across the street. Some may be put off by the smell of the brackish canal nearby, but for others it's a small price to pay for a small price to stay. ✉ *2360 Collins Ave., 33139,* ☎ *305/538–1951 or 800/746–7835,* FAX *305/531–3217,* WEB *www.bananabungalow.com 60 private rooms, 25 dorm-style rooms, all with bath. Bar, café, pool, billiards, recreation room, video games, laundry service. MC, V. CP.*

$ **Bayliss Guest House.** At the Bayliss, rooms are abnormally large and surprisingly inexpensive—you may even think you've rented a house when you check into an efficiency or apartment here. Not only are the bedrooms large, so are the kitchen, the sitting room, and bath. There are also kitchenless standard rooms available. An easy three blocks west of the ocean, the Bayliss is in a residential neighborhood that's comfortably close to—but far enough away from—the din of the Art Deco District. Can't do much better than this, if you don't mind carrying your own bags. There's very limited parking. ✉ *500–504 14th St., 33139,* ☎ *305/531–3488,* FAX *305/531–4440. 12 rooms, 7 suites. Refrigerators, coin laundry. AE, D, DC, MC, V.*

$ **Cadet Hotel.** Clark Gable stayed in Room 225 when he came to Miami for Army Air Corps training in the 1940s. Although this Lincoln Road district lodging doesn't have the glamour to attract stars today, it's still a clean, friendly, and perfectly placed little hotel. Just a few minutes' walk from the Jackie Gleason Theater of the Performing Arts and the convention center and two blocks from the ocean, it's about half the cost of an Ocean Drive hotel. The other big difference is that the staff doesn't act like they're doing you a favor by letting you stay here. Bright without glitz, the Cadet features soft pastels in the lobby, blues and creams in rooms. Ordinary furniture is mixed but not necessarily matched—nor is it crummy. A complimentary breakfast is served in the lobby or on the terrace. ✉ *1701 James Ave., 33139,* ☎ *305/672–6688 or 800/432–2338,* FAX *305/532–1676,* WEB *www.cadethotel.com 44 rooms. Refrigerators. AE, D, DC, MC, V.*

$ **Days Inn Convention Center.** Nothing flashy and nothing trashy, this link in a chain is a fairly pleasant one. The lobby is bright and floral, with a fountain and gift shop. Rooms are standard hotel and include in-room safes and cable TV; deluxe rooms throw in impressive views of the ocean. If you're more concerned about your wallet than your image, this can be a good bet. Keep in mind that if you want something with character, you can find that elsewhere at these rates. Here you'll find standard style and everything you'd expect at a franchise (including a pool)—and it's all literally seconds from the beach. ✉ *100 21st St., 33139,* ☎ *305/538–6631 or 800/451–3345,* FAX *305/674–0954,* WEB *www.daysinnsouthbeach.com 172 rooms. Restaurant, bar, refrigerators, pool, beach, laundry service, parking (fee). AE, D, DC, MC, V.*

West Dade

$$$$ **Doral Golf Resort and Spa.** This 650-acre golf-and-tennis resort has put a major effort into the renovation of the eight low-slung lodges that nestle beside six golf courses. Rooms, decorated in understated tropical hues, open onto the green or the garden and have private balconies and terraces. Plantation shutters keep out the strong sun but invite in the Caribbean breezes. The famed Blue Monster has been redesigned and the other golf courses increased in size and difficulty, making them tougher on guests as well as on the pros who compete here, in the annual Genuity Championship (formerly the Doral Ryder Open). At the 148,000-square-ft spa, massages from head to foot, European facials, aroma scrubs and wraps, stress reduction, hypnotherapy, and several dozen other indulgences rejuvenate the mind, body, and soul. In 1999 Blue Lagoon, an extravagant water park, opened at the resort; golf instruction also keeps the kids busy. Dining ranges from sports-bar casual to formal. ✉ *4400 N.W. 87th Ave., 33178,* ☎ *305/592–2000 or 800/713–6725,* FAX *305/591–4682,* WEB *www.doralresort.com 693 rooms, 48 suites. 5 restaurants, 3 bars, pool, spa, five 18-hole golf courses, 11 tennis courts (5 lighted), basketball, health club, jogging, volleyball, fishing, pro shop, concierge, business services. AE, D, DC, MC, V.*

NIGHTLIFE AND THE ARTS

For information on what's happening around town, Greater Miami's English-language daily newspaper, the ***Miami Herald,*** publishes reliable reviews and comprehensive listings in its "Weekend" section on Friday and in the "IN South Florida" section on Sunday. They also publish a free tabloid, ***The Street,*** with entertainment listings. Call ahead to confirm details. ***El Nuevo Herald*** is the paper's Spanish version.

If you read Spanish, check ***Diario Las Américas,*** the area's largest independent Spanish-language paper, for information on the Spanish theater and a smattering of general performing-arts news.

The best, most complete source is the ***New Times,*** a free weekly distributed throughout Miami-Dade County each Thursday. A good source of information on the performing arts and nightspots is the calendar in ***Miami Today,*** a free weekly newspaper available each Thursday in downtown Miami, Coconut Grove, and Coral Gables. Various tabloids reporting on Deco District entertainment and the Miami social scene come and go. ***Ocean Drive*** outglosses everything else. ***Wire*** reports on the gay community.

The free ***Greater Miami Calendar of Events*** is published twice a year by the Miami-Dade County Cultural Affairs Council (✉ 111 N.W. 1st St., Suite 625, 33128, ☎ 305/375–4634).

Real Talk/WTMI (93.1 FM, ☎ 305/856–9393) provides classical concert information in on-air reports twice daily at 12:35 and 7:15. Call the station if you miss the report.

The **Greater Miami Convention & Visitors Bureau** (☎ 305/539–3000 or 800/283–2707) publishes a comprehensive list of dance venues, theaters, and museums as well as a seasonal guide to cultural events.

The Arts

Miami's performing-arts aficionados will tell you they survive quite nicely, thank you, despite the area's historic inability to support a county-based professional symphony orchestra. But in recent years this community has begun to write a new chapter in its performing-arts history.

In addition to established music groups, several churches and synagogues run classical-music series with international performers. In theater, Miami offers English-speaking audiences an assortment of professional, collegiate, and amateur productions of musicals, comedy, and drama. Spanish theater also is active.

The not-for-profit **Concert Association of Florida** (✉ 555 17th St., Miami Beach 33139, ☎ 305/532–3491), led by Judith Drucker, presents classical arts, music, and dance in venues throughout Miami-Dade and Broward counties. It boasts of presenting the world's greatest music and dance—Itzhak Perlman, Isaac Stern, Baryshnikov, Pavarotti, and the Russian National Ballet.

To order tickets for performing-arts events by telephone, call **TicketMaster** (☎ 305/358–5885). **Ticket Madness** (☎ 305/460–3188) promises half-price tickets for same-day performances.

Arts Venues

What was once a 1920s movie theater has become the 465-seat **Colony Theater** (✉ 1040 Lincoln Rd., Miami Beach 33139, ☎ 305/674–1026). The city-owned performing-arts center features dance, drama, music, and experimental cinema.

If you have the opportunity to attend a concert, ballet, or touring stage production at the **Gusman Center for the Performing Arts** (✉ 174 E. Flagler St., Miami 33131, ☎ 305/374–2444 for administration; 305/372–0925 for box office), do so. Originally a movie palace, this 1,700-plus-seat theater is as far from a mall multiplex as you can get. The stunningly beautiful hall resembles a Moorish courtyard, with twinkling stars and rolling clouds skirting across the ceiling and Roman statues guarding the wings.

Not to be confused with the ornate Gusman theater, **Gusman Concert Hall** (✉ 1314 Miller Dr., Coral Gables 33146, ☎ 305/284–2438) is a 600-seat facility on the University of Miami campus. Presenting primarily recitals and concerts by students, it has good acoustics and plenty of room, but parking is a problem when school is in session.

Acoustics and visibility are perfect for all 2,700 seats in the **Jackie Gleason Theater of the Performing Arts** (TOPA, ✉ 1700 Washington Ave., Miami Beach 33139, ☎ 305/673–7300). A pleasant walk from the heart of SoBe, TOPA hosts the Broadway Series, with five or six major productions annually; guest artists, such as David Copperfield, Stomp, and Shirley MacLaine; and classical-music concerts.

Midway between Coral Gables and downtown Miami, the **Miami-Dade County Auditorium** (✉ 2901 W. Flagler St., Miami 33135, ☎ 305/545–3395) satisfies patrons with nearly 2,500 comfortable seats, good sight lines, and acceptable acoustics. Opera, concerts, and touring musicals are usually on the schedule, and past performers have included David Helfgott and Celia Cruz.

Dance

The **Miami City Ballet** (✉ 2200 Liberty Ave., Miami Beach, ☎ 305/929–7000) has risen rapidly to international prominence since its arrival in 1985. Under the direction of Edward Villella (a principal dancer with the New York City Ballet under George Balanchine), Florida's first major, fully professional resident ballet company has become a world-class ensemble. The company re-creates the Balanchine repertoire and introduces works of its own during its September–March season. Villella also hosts children's works-in-progress programs. Performances are held at the Jackie Gleason Theater of the Performing Arts; the Broward Center for the Performing Arts; Bailey Concert Hall, also in Broward County; the Raymond F. Kravis Center for the Performing Arts; and the Naples Philharmonic Center for the Arts.

Film

Several theaters and events cater specifically to fans of fine film. In December, Florida International University sponsors the **Jewish Film Festival** (☎ 305/576–4030 ext. 14), which presents screenings of new work as well as workshops and panel discussions with filmmakers in several Miami Beach locations. Screenings of new films from all over the world—including some made here—are part of the **Miami Film Festival** (✉ 444 Brickell Ave., Suite 229, Miami, ☎ 305/377–3456). Each year more than 45,000 people descend on the eye-popping Gusman Center for the Performing Arts to watch about 25 movies over 10 days in February.

In April the **Miami Gay and Lesbian Film Festival** (☎ 305/534–9924) presents screenings at the Colony Theater on Lincoln Road and at other nearby venues. South Beach also has its own film event, the **South Beach Film Festival** (☎ 305/532–1233), traditionally held at the Colony Theater in April. This weeklong fest shows films neglected by larger festivals.

Music

From October to May, **Friends of Chamber Music** (✉ 169 E. Flagler St., Suite 1619, Miami 33130, ☎ 305/372–2975) presents a series of chamber concerts by internationally known guest ensembles, such as the Emerson and Guarneri quartets. Concerts are held at the Gusman Concert Hall at the University of Miami, with tickets averaging about $20.

Although Greater Miami has no resident symphony orchestra, the **New World Symphony** (✉ 555 Lincoln Rd., Miami Beach, ☎ 305/673–3331 or 305/673–3330), known as "America's training orchestra" because its musicians are recent graduates of the best music schools, helps fill the void. Under the direction of conductor Michael Tilson Thomas, the New World has become a widely acclaimed, artistically dazzling group that tours extensively. In a season that runs October–May, performances take place in its home venue, the acoustically perfect Lincoln Theater on Lincoln Road Mall. Guest conductors have included Leonard Bernstein and Georg Solti.

Opera

South Florida's leading company, the **Florida Grand Opera** (✉ 1200 Coral Way, Miami 33145, ☎ 305/854–1643) presents five operas each year in the Miami-Dade County Auditorium, featuring the Florida Philharmonic Orchestra (Stewart Robinson, musical director) from Ft. Lauderdale. The series brings such luminaries as Placido Domingo and Luciano Pavarotti (Pavarotti made his American debut with the company in 1965 in *Lucia di Lammermoor*). Operas are sung in the original language, with English subtitles projected above the stage.

Theater

Actor's Playhouse (✉ 280 Miracle Mile, Coral Gables, ☎ 305/444–9293), a professional Equity company, presents musicals, comedies, and dramas year-round in Coral Gables's very hip, newly renovated, 600-seat Miracle Theater. Performances of musical theater for younger audiences take place in the 300-seat Children's Balcony Theatre.

Built in 1926 as a movie theater, the **Coconut Grove Playhouse** (✉ 3500 Main Hwy., Coconut Grove 33133, ☎ 305/442–4000 or 305/442–2662) is now a serious regional theater owned by the state of Florida. The Spanish rococo Grove stages tried-and-true Broadway plays and musicals, many with Broadway actors, as well as experimental productions in its main theater and cabaret-style/black box Encore Room. The most popular recent play was the premiere of *Don't Stop the Carnival* by one-time Coconut Grove coffee bar-singer Jimmy Buffett. Parking is $5.

Adjacent to the magnificent Biltmore Hotel, the **GableStage** (✉ 1200 Anastasia Ave., Coral Gables 33134, ☎ 305/446–1116) presents classic and contemporary theater in a comfortable 154-seat hall.

The **New Theatre** (✉ 65 Almeria Ave., Coral Gables 33134, ☎ 305/443–5909) is a year-round showcase for contemporary and classical plays, with an emphasis on new works and imaginative staging.

Productions at the University of Miami's **Ring Theater** (✉ 1380 Miller Dr., Coral Gables 33124, ☎ 305/284–3355) are often as ambitious as those by its professional counterparts Broadway legend Jerry Herman is the drama school's most successful alumnus.

SPANISH THEATER

Spanish theater prospers, although many companies have short lives. About 20 Spanish companies perform light comedy, puppetry, vaudeville, and political satire. To locate them, read the Spanish newspapers. When you call, be prepared for a conversation in Spanish—few box office personnel speak English.

El Hueco (705 S.W. 17th Ave., Miami, ☎ 305/644–7272) literally translated means "the hole." But it's really an underground bilingual theater showcasing local avant-garde performances, music, and dance.

The 255-seat **Teatro de Bellas Artes** (✉ 2173 S.W. 8th St., Miami 33135, ☎ 305/325–0515), on Calle Ocho, presents eight Spanish plays and musicals a year. Midnight musical follies and female impersonators round out the showbiz lineup.

Nightlife

Bars and Lounges

COCONUT GROVE

CocoWalk presents three different but all potentially decadent drinking establishments. Classic and modern rock is on tap at the **Chili Pepper** (3300 Mary St., ☎ 305/442–2228). Drinking cold beer and gorilla-size margaritas in the middle of the Grove is part of the fun at **Fat Tuesday** (✉ 3015 Grand Ave., ☎ 305/441–2992). With more flavors than in a roll of Life Savers, the bar offers up drinks called 190 Octane (190-proof alcohol), Swampwater (also 190 proof), and Grapeshot (a meager 151-proof rum and bourbon concoction). Can you say, "designated driver"? At the Streets of Mayfair, the **Iguana Cantina and Martini Bar** (3390 Mary St., ☎ 305/443–3300) serves up salsa, merengue, and Latin music on weekends.

CORAL GABLES

What fueled the Gables's nightlife renaissance? Some think it was **The Globe** (✉ 377 Alhambra Circle, ☎ 305/445–3555). Crowds of twentysomethings spill out onto the street for live jazz on weekends. Two Irishmen missed the Emerald Isle so they opened **JohnMartin's Restaurant and Irish Pub** (✉ 253 Miracle Mile, ☎ 305/445–3777). It serves up fish-and-chips, bangers and mash, shepherd's pie, and all the accoutrements of a Dublin pub—plus the requisite pints of Guinness, Harp, Bass, and other ales. In a building that dates from 1926, **Stuart's Bar-Lounge** (✉ 162 Alcazar Ave., ☎ 305/444–1666), inside the charming Hotel Place St. Michel, is favored by locals. The style is created by beveled mirrors, mahogany paneling, French posters, pictures of old Coral Gables, and Art Nouveau lighting. Stuart's is closed Sunday.

MIAMI

Tobacco Road (✉ 626 S. Miami Ave., ☎ 305/374–1198), opened in 1912, holds Miami's oldest liquor license: Number 0001! Upstairs, in space occupied by a speakeasy during Prohibition, local and national blues bands perform nightly, accompanied by single-malt Scotch and bourbon.

MIAMI BEACH

At **The Clevelander** (✉ 1020 Ocean Dr., ☎ 305/531–3485), a giant pool-bar area attracts a young crowd of revelers for happy-hour drink specials and live music. The **Delano** (1685 Collins Ave., ☎ 305/672–2000) is dramatic and chic, with long gauzy curtains and huge pillars creating private conversation nooks around the outdoor infinity pool. Inside, the cool chic lounge area creates a glamorous setting for the modelesque crowd. **Lola** (247 23rd St., ☎ 305/695–8697) attracts savvy locals and celebs who want to keep a low profile. Offering more character than chic, the **Marlin** 1200 Collins, ☎ 305/673–8770) combines brushed steel and gray cement, Rasta and reggae, and a little bit of jazz thrown in. For South Beach fabulousness, the glass-topped bar at **The Tides** (✉ 1220 Ocean Dr., ☎ 305/604–5000) is the place to go for martinis and piano jazz. **Zeke's Road House** (✉ 625 Lincoln Rd., ☎ 305/532–0087) arrived just before Lincoln Road got its spit and polish (when it was just spit). A neighborhood bar that transcends trends, it's hidden amid revitalized buildings but keeps it simple with sandwiches and draft beers such as Chester, Harp, and Ybor Gold.

Dance Clubs

KEY BISCAYNE

Madfish House (✉ 3301 Rickenbacker Causeway, ☎ 305/365–9391) features reggae 'til the wee hours on Friday, and salsa on Saturday. The view of the skyline along the waterfront is spectacular.

MIAMI BEACH

South Beach is headquarters for nightclubs that start late and stay open until the early morning. The clientele is largely a mix of freak-show rejects, sullen male models, and sultry women.

Amnesia/Mojito Club (✉ 136 Collins Ave., ☎ 305/531–5535) has Latin-flavored dance music, with international nights on Saturdays and tea dances on Sundays. The indoor/outdoor venue is like a luxurious amphitheater in the tropics, complete with rain forest, what used to be called go-go dancers, and frenzied dancing in the rain when showers pass over the open-air ground-level club. Here since 1993, this is one of the old-timers—but still a fave. Call for hours. One look at the padded walls of this venue, and you'll think you've entered an asylum; but rest assured: you're only at **Bash** (✉ 655 Washington Ave., ☎ 305/538–2274). With two DJs spinning dance music—sometimes reggae, sometimes Latin, plenty of loud disco, and world-beat sounds—the party is always going full tilt. Inside, there are VIP seating and Euro/house/techno/trance music, while the Enchanted Garden outside features world-beat sounds. You'll see lots of Europeans, South Americans, and fashion industry folk here. The **Bermuda Bar & Grille** (✉ 3509 N.E. 163rd St., ☎ 305/945–0196) is way north of SoBe but worth the drive if you want to hang with the locals. Rock radio stations do remote broadcasts, and hard liquor and bottled beer are favored over silly drinks with umbrellas. The music is as loud as the setting is large—two floors and seven bars—and hours run 4 PM–6 AM. Male bartenders wear knee-length kilts, while female bartenders are in matching minis. The atmosphere and crowd, though, are stylish, and there's a big tropical-forest scene, booths you can hide in, and pool tables to dive into. The joint is closed from Sunday through Tuesday.

crobar (✉ 1445 Washington Ave., ☎ 305/531–5027), an import from Chicago, is the latest hot spot—the exterior is the historic Cameo Theater, while the interior is a *Blade Runner*–esque blend of high-tech marvels with some performance art thrown in. It's dazzling and lots of fun. **Krave** (1203 Washington Ave., ☎ 305/532–5632) is a high-energy dance club with a '60s feeling and the requisite VIP lounge. **Level** (1235 Washington Ave., ☎ 305/532–1525) has an impressive four dance floors, and—as its name suggests—lots of levels to search out fun.

Designed like a sultan's palace, the very classy and elegant **Living Room** (✉ 671 Washington Ave., ☎ 305/532–2340) draws A-list celebs and sheiks who drop $1,000 tips. If your bankroll hasn't risen to that level, just shoot a game of pool or have dinner before the club crowd arrives. After dinner the club hops with techno pop. There's great service all around, and the comfortable couches are a welcome addition. **Penrod's** (✉ 1 Ocean Dr., ☎ 305/538–1231) has seven bars in a beautiful beachfront location—complete with teepee cabanas—and includes the full-service Nikki Beach Club, fast becoming a celeb hangout. A truly frightening evening can be spent at the **Shadow Lounge** (✉ 1532 Washington Ave., ☎ 305/531–9411), where the club kids look like mannequins come to life. By mixing Berlin of the '30s with Havana of the

'50s and New York of the '70s, it creates a weird atmosphere that attracts Miami's crème de la creepy. If you can't take it, stay home and watch *The Twilight Zone* instead.

Blues

CORAL GABLES

Satchmo Blues Bar & Grill (60 Merrick Way, ☎ 305/774–1883), born out of the popular Coral Gables BluesFest in April, turns out live blues and jazz—including top-notch local and national talent—every night, with Cajun treats on the side.

Jazz

MIAMI BEACH

Jazid (✉ 1342 Washington Ave., ☎ 305/604–9798) is the place for blues and jazz from swing to traditional jazz. Performers change nightly, but the intimate candlelit atmosphere and no-cover policy remain constant. More restaurant than jazz club, **Van Dyke Café** (✉ 846 Lincoln Rd., ☎ 305/534–3600) serves music on the second floor seven nights a week. Its location on the Lincoln Road Mall makes it a great spot to take a break during an evening shopping excursion.

Nightclub

MIAMI BEACH

You can dine as you watch the show at the Fontainebleau Hilton's **Club Tropigala** (✉ 4441 Collins Ave., ☎ 305/672–7469), which tries to blend modern Vegas with 1950s Havana. The four-tier round room is decorated with orchids, banana leaves, and philodendrons to create an indoor tropical jungle. Some of the performances are stellar, with a Latin flavor—Ricky Martin, Julio Iglesias, and Jose Feliciano have made appearances here. Hotel guests are comped, but others pay a $20 cover. Reservations are suggested, and men should wear jackets.

OUTDOOR ACTIVITIES AND SPORTS

In addition to contacting the addresses below directly, you can get tickets to major events from **TicketMaster** (☎ 305/358–5885).

Auto Racing

Hialeah Speedway holds stock-car races on a ⅓-mi asphalt oval in a 5,000-seat stadium. Don't be fooled: the enthusiasm of the local drivers makes this as exciting as Winston Cup races. Five divisions of cars run weekly. The Marion Edwards, Jr., Memorial Race, for late-model cars, is held in November. The speedway is on U.S. 27, ¼ mi east of the Palmetto Expressway (Route 826). ✉ *3300 W. Okeechobee Rd., Hialeah,* ☎ *305/821–6644.* 🎟 *$10, special events $15.* ⏲ *Sat., gates open at 5 PM, races 7–11. Closed early Dec.–late Jan.*

For Winston Cup events, head south to the **Homestead-Miami Speedway,** which brought the NASCAR Winston Cup Series to South Florida for the first time with the 1999 Penzoil 400. The Winston Cup race highlights the annual speedway schedule and is held on the second Sunday in November in conjunction with the Miami 300, part of the NASCAR Busch series. The racing facility is home to the Infiniti Grand Prix of Miami, as well as the Grand Am Sports Car Event and a NASCAR Craftsmen Truck Series in spring. From Miami take Florida's Turnpike (Route 821) south to Exit 6, at Southwest 137th Avenue. ✉ *1 Speedway Blvd., Homestead,* ☎ *305/230–7223.* ⏲ *Weekdays 9–5.* 🎟 *Prices vary according to event.*

Baseball

Although the **Florida Marlins** (✉ 2267 N.W. 199th St., Miami 33056, ☎ 305/626–7400) team that won the 1997 World Series was split up soon afterward, games are still as exciting as baseball can be. Home games are played at Pro Player Stadium, which is 16 mi northwest of downtown.

Basketball

The **Miami Heat** are four-time defending NBA Atlantic Division champs (1996–97 through 1999–2000). They play their games at the 19,600-seat, waterfront AmericanAirlines Arena, which has a bay-front patio, a special-effects scoreboard, indoor fireworks, and restaurants. Home games are held November–April. ✉ *601 Biscayne Blvd., Miami,* ☎ *786/777–4328, ticket hot line 1-800/4NBA–TIX* 🎫 *$5–$80.*

The **Miami Sol,** a WNBA team, is coached by Ron Rothstein, the first head coach for the Miami Heat. The team plays a 32-game season from June through August at the bay-front AmericanAirlines Arena. ✉ *601 Biscayne Blvd., Miami,* ☎ *786/777–4765 (4SOL).* 🎫 *$8–$50.*

Biking

Perfect weather and flat terrain make Miami-Dade County a popular place for cyclists. A free color-coded map that points out streets best suited for bicycles, and information about bike rack–equipped buses is available from bike shops and also from the **Miami-Dade County Bicycle Coordinator** (✉ Metropolitan Planning Organization, 111 N.W. 1st St., Suite 910, Miami 33128, ☎ 305/375–1647), whose purpose is to share with you the glories of bicycling in South Florida. Information on dozens of monthly group rides is available from the **Everglades Bicycle Club** (☎ 305/598–3998). For a free map of the 10 mi of traffic-free bike trails on Key Biscayne, stop by **Mangrove Cycles** (✉ 260 Crandon Blvd., Key Biscayne, ☎ 305/361–5555), which rents bikes for $7 for two hours or $10 per day. On Miami Beach, the proximity of the **Miami Beach Bicycle Center** (MBBC; ✉ 601 5th St., Miami Beach, ☎ 305/674–0150) to Ocean Drive and the ocean itself makes it worth the $20 per day (or $5 per hour). Tours of the Deco District are offered once a month by the center.

Boating

The popular full-service **Crandon Park Marina** is a one-stop shop for all things ocean-y. You can embark on deep-sea-fishing or scuba-diving excursions, dine at a marina restaurant, or rent powerboats through Club Nautico (✉ 5420 Crandon Blvd., Key Biscayne, ☎ 305/361–9217; also ✉ 2560 Bayshore Dr., Coconut Grove, ☎ 305/858–6258), a national powerboat rental company. Half- to full-day rentals range from $229 to $699, or you can buy a membership, which costs a bundle at first but saves around 60% on future rentals. ✉ *4000 Crandon Blvd., Key Biscayne,* ☎ *305/361–1281.* ⏲ *Office daily 8–6.*

Whether you're looking to be on the water for a few hours or a few days, **Cruzan Yacht Charters** is a good choice for renting manned or unmanned sailboats and motor yachts. If you plan to captain the boat yourself, expect a three- to four-hour checkout cruise and at least a $325 daily rate (three-day minimum). ✉ *3375 Pan American Dr., Coconut Grove,* ☎ *305/858–2822 or 800/628–0785.*

Named for an island where early settlers had picnics, **Dinner Key Marina** is Greater Miami's largest, with nearly 600 moorings at nine piers. There is space for transients and a boat ramp. ✉ *3400 Pan American Dr., Coconut Grove,* ☎ *305/579–6980.* ⏲ *Daily 7 AM–11 PM.*

Haulover Marine Center is low on glamour but high on service. It offers a bait-and-tackle shop, marine gas station, and boat launch. ✉ *15000 Collins Ave., Miami Beach,* ☎ *305/945–3934.* ⏲ *Bait shop and gas station open 24 hrs.*

Although **Matheson Hammock Park** has no charter services, it does have 252 slips and boat ramps. It also has **Castle Harbor** (☎ 305/665–4994), which relocated here from Coconut Grove several years ago. In operation since 1949, it offers sailboat rentals for those with U.S. Sailing certification and classes for those without. When you're ready to rent, take your pick of boats ranging from 23 ft to 41 ft. ✉ *9610 Old Cutler Rd., Coral Gables,* ☎ *305/665–5475.* ⏲ *Daily 6–sunset.*

Near the Art Deco District, **Miami Beach Marina** has about every marine facility imaginable—restaurants, charters, boat and vehicle rentals, a complete marine-hardware store, a dive shop, excursion vendors, a large grocery store, a fuel dock, concierge services, and 400 slips accommodating vessels of up to 190 ft. There's also a U.S. Customs clearing station. One charter outfit here is the family-owned **Florida Yacht Charters** (☎ 305/532–8600 or 800/537–0050). After completing the requisite checkout cruise and paperwork, you can take off for the Keys or the Bahamas on a catamaran, sailboat, or motor yacht. Charts, lessons, and captains are available if needed. ✉ *300 Alton Rd., Miami Beach,* ☎ *305/673–6000 for marina.* ⏲ *Daily 7–6.*

Dog Racing

In the middle of Little Havana, **Flagler Greyhound Track** has dog racing during its June–November season and a poker room that's open when the track is running. Closed-circuit TV brings harness-racing action here as well. The track is five minutes east of Miami International Airport, off Dolphin Expressway (Route 836) and Douglas Road (Northwest 37th Avenue). ✉ *401 N.W. 38th Ct., Miami,* ☎ *305/649–3000.* 🎫 *Free for grandstand, $3 for clubhouse, parking free for grandstand, $2.50 for clubhouse.* ⏲ *Racing daily 8:05 PM, plus Tues.–Thurs. and Sat. 1:05 PM.*

Fishing

Before there was fashion, there was fishing. Deep-sea fishing is still a major draw, and anglers drop a line for sailfish, kingfish, dolphin, snapper, wahoo, grouper, and tuna. Small charter boats cost $450–$500 for a half day and provide everything but food and drinks. If you're on a budget, you might be better off paying around $30 for passage on a larger fishing boat—rarely are they filled to capacity. Most charters have a 50/50 plan, which allows you to take (or sell) half your catch while they do the same. Just don't let anyone sell you an individual fishing license; a blanket license for the boat should cover all passengers.

Crandon Park Marina has earned an international reputation for its knowledgeable charter-boat captains and good catches. Heading out to the edge of the Gulf Stream (about 3 to 4 mi), you're sure to wind up with something on your line (sailfish are catch-and-release). ✉ *4000 Crandon Blvd., Key Biscayne,* ☎ *305/361–1281.* 🎫 *6-passenger boats $750 full day, $500 half day (5 hrs).*

Many ocean-fishing charters sail out of **Haulover Beach Park** (✉ 10800 Collins Ave., Miami Beach), including **Blue Waters Sportfishing Charters** (☎ 305/944–4531), 🎫 6-passenger boats $750 full day, $450 half day (5 hrs); the **Kelley Fleet** (☎ 305/945–3801), 🎫 65- or 85-ft party boats $28 per person (5 hrs); ***Therapy IV*** (☎ 305/945–1578), 🎫 $85 per person for half day (5 hrs) on a 6-passenger boat; and about 10 others.

Among the charter services at **Miami Beach Marina** is the two-boat **Reward Fleet** (☎ 305/372–9470). Rates run $30 per person including bait, rod, reel, and tackle. ✉ *MacArthur Causeway, 300 Alton Rd., Miami Beach,* ☎ *305/673–6000.*

Football

Consistently ranked as one of the top teams in the NFL, the **Miami Dolphins** (☎ 305/620–2578) has one of the largest average attendance figures in the league. Fans may be secretly hoping to see a repeat of the 1972 perfect season, when the team, led by legendary coach Don Shula, compiled a 17–0 record (a record that still stands). From September through January, on home game days, the Metro Miami-Dade Transit Agency runs buses to **Pro Player Stadium,** 16 mi northwest of downtown. ✉ *2267 N.W. 199th St., Miami,* ☎ *305/626–7426.* 💵 *$20–$140, parking $20.*

Also worth checking out is the **University of Miami Hurricanes** (☎ 305/284–2263 or 800/462–2637) football team. A powerhouse within the Big East Conference, the team is regularly a Top-10 contender, with four national football championships since 1983. During the September–November season, the home-team advantage is measured in decibels, as about 45,000 fans literally rock the stadium when the team is on a roll. They play their home games at downtown's venerable **Orange Bowl Stadium.** ✉ *1145 N.W. 11th St.,* ☎ *305/575–5240.* 💵 *$20–$40, parking $8–$20.*

Golf

Greater Miami has more than 30 private and public courses. Fees at most courses are higher on weekends and in season, but you can save money by playing weekdays and after 1 PM or 3 PM (call to find out when afternoon or twilight rates go into effect). That said, costs are reasonable to play in such an appealing setting as Miami.

To get the **"Golfer's Guide for South Florida,"** which includes information on most courses in Miami and surrounding areas, call ☎ 800/864–6101. The cost is $3.

The 18-hole, par-71 championship **Biltmore Golf Course,** known for its scenic layout, has been restored to its original Donald Ross design, circa 1925. Greens fees range from $29 to $55 in season, and the gorgeous hotel makes a great backdrop. ✉ *1210 Anastasia Ave., Coral Gables,* ☎ *305/460–5364.* 💵 *Optional cart $21.*

The **California Golf Club** has an 18-hole, par-72 course, with a tight front nine and three of the area's toughest finishing holes. A round of 18 holes will set you back between $35 and $50, cart included. ✉ *20898 San Simeon Way, North Miami Beach,* ☎ *305/651–3590.*

Overlooking the bay, the **Crandon Golf Course,** formerly the Links at Key Biscayne, is a top-rated 18-hole, par-72 public course in a beautiful tropical setting. Expect to pay around $126 for a round in winter, $50 in summer, cart included. After 3, the winter rate drops to $36, cart included. The Royal Caribbean Classic is held here. ✉ *6700 Crandon Blvd., Key Biscayne,* ☎ *305/361–9129.*

Don Shula's Hotel & Golf Club has one of the longest championship courses in Miami (7,055 yards, par 72), a lighted par-3 course, and a golf school, and it hosts more than 100 tournaments a year. Weekdays you can play the championship course for $90, $125 on weekends; golf carts are included. The lighted par-3 course is $12 weekdays, $15 weekends, and $15 for an optional cart. ✉ *7601 Miami Lakes Dr., Miami Lakes,* ☎ *305/820–8106.*

Among its six courses and many annual tournaments, the **Doral Golf Resort and Spa** is best known for the par-72 Blue Monster course and the annual Genuity Classic, with $2 million in prize money. Fees range from $190 to $250—half-price after 3, carts included. ✉ *4400 N.W. 87th Ave., Miami,* ☎ *305/592–2000 or 800/713–6725.*

For a casual family outing or for beginners, the nine-hole, par-3 **Haulover Golf Course** is located right on the Intracoastal Waterway at the north end of Miami Beach. The longest hole on this walking course is 120 yards; greens fees are only $6, less weekdays for senior citizens. ✉ *10800 Collins Ave., North Miami Beach,* ☎ *305/940–6719.*

Normandy Shores Golf Course (✉ 2401 Biarritz Dr., Miami Beach, ☎ 305/868–6502) is good for seniors, with some modest slopes and average distances. The **Turnberry Isle Resort & Club** (✉ 19999 W. Country Club Dr., Aventura, ☎ 305/933–6929) has 36 holes designed by Robert Trent Jones. The South Course's 18th hole is a killer, and greens fees range from $107 to $147, but since it's private, you won't be able to play unless you're a hotel guest.

Horse Racing

The **Calder Race Course,** opened in 1971, is Florida's largest glass-enclosed, air-conditioned sports facility. It often has an unusually extended season, from late May to early January, though it's a good idea to call the track for specific starting and wrap-up dates, since Calder, Hialeah Park, and Gulfstream Park rotate their race dates. Each year between November and early January, Calder holds the Tropical Park Derby for three-year-olds. The track is on the Miami-Dade–Broward County line near Interstate 95 and the Hallandale Beach Boulevard exit, ¾ mi from Pro Player Stadium. ✉ *21001 N.W. 27th Ave., Miami,* ☎ *305/625–1311.* *$2, clubhouse $4, parking $1–$5.* *Gates open at 11, racing 12:30–5.*

A superb setting for Thoroughbred racing, **Hialeah Park** has 228 acres of meticulously landscaped grounds surrounding paddocks and a French Mediterranean–style clubhouse opened in 1925. Although Hialeah tends to get the less prestigious racing dates from March through May, it still draws crowds. The park is open year-round for free sightseeing, when you can explore the gardens and admire the park's breeding flock of Cuban flamingos. Metrorail's Hialeah Station is across the street. ✉ *2200 E. 4th Ave., Hialeah,* ☎ *305/885–8000.* *Grandstand $2, clubhouse $4, parking $1–$4.* *Gates open at 11, racing 1:15–6.*

Jai Alai

Built in 1926, the **Miami Jai Alai Fronton,** a mile east of the airport, is America's oldest fronton. It presents 13 games (14 on Friday and Saturday) daily except Tuesday—some singles, some doubles. This game, invented in the Basque region of northern Spain, is the world's fastest. Jai alai balls, called pelotas, have been clocked at speeds exceeding 170 mph. The game is played in a 176-ft-long court, and players literally climb the walls to catch the ball in a cesta (a woven basket) which has an attached glove. You can place your wager on the team you think will win or on the order in which you think the teams will finish. ✉ *3500 N.W. 37th Ave., Miami,* ☎ *305/633–6400.* *$1, reserved seats $2, Courtview Club $5.* *Mon., Wed., Thurs., Fri., Sat, noon–5; also Wed., Fri., Sat., 7–midnight; Sun. 1–6.*

Jogging

There are numerous places to run in Miami, but these recommended jogging routes are considered among the most scenic and the safest: in Coconut Grove, along the pedestrian-bicycle path on South Bayshore Drive, cutting over the causeway to Key Biscayne for a longer run; from the south shore of the Miami River, downtown, south along the sidewalks of Brickell Avenue to Bayshore Drive, where you can run alongside the bay; in Miami Beach, along Bay Road (parallel to Alton Road) or on the sidewalk skirting the Atlantic Ocean, opposite the cafés of

Ocean Drive; and in Coral Gables, around the Riviera Country Club golf course, just south of the Biltmore Country Club. A good source of running information is the **Miami Runners Club** (✉ 7920 S.W. 40th St., Miami, ☎ 305/227–1500), although the volunteer group often has an answering machine on. An even better source may be **Foot Works** (✉ 5724 Sunset Dr., South Miami, ☎ 305/667–9322), a running-shoe store that's open every day. Since 1971 it has hosted races and marathon training.

Scuba Diving and Snorkeling

Diving and snorkeling on the offshore coral wrecks and reefs can be comparable to the Caribbean, especially on a calm day. Chances are excellent you'll come face to face with a flood of tropical fish. One option is to find Fowey, Triumph, Long, and Emerald reefs in 10- to 15-ft dives that are perfect for snorkelers and beginning divers. On the edge of the continental shelf a little more than 3 mi out, these reefs are just ¼ mi away from depths greater than 100 ft. Another option is to paddle around the tangled prop roots of the mangrove trees that line the coast, peering at the fish, crabs, and other creatures hiding there.

Perhaps the most unusual diving options in Greater Miami are the artificial reefs. Since 1981, Miami-Dade County's Department of Environmental Resources Management (DERM) has sunk tons of limestone boulders and a water tower, army tanks, a 727 jet, and almost 200 boats of all descriptions to create a "wreckreational" habitat where divers can swim with yellow tang, barracudas, nurse sharks, snapper, eels, and grouper. Most dive shops sell a book listing the location of these wrecks. Information on wreck diving can be obtained from the Miami Beach Chamber of Commerce's **Water Sports Marketing Council** (✉ 1920 Meridian Ave., Miami Beach, ☎ 305/672–1270 or 888/728–2262).

Bubbles Dive Center (✉ 2671 S.W. 27th Ave., Miami, ☎ 305/856–0565), an all-purpose dive shop with PADI affiliation, runs night and wreck dives right in the center of it all. Its boat, *Divers Dream,* berths at the Miami Beach Marina on Alton Road. **Divers Paradise of Key Biscayne** (✉ 4000 Crandon Blvd., Key Biscayne, ☎ 305/361–3483), next to the full-service Crandon Park Marina, has a complete dive shop and diving-charter service. On offer are equipment rental and scuba instruction with PADI affiliation. The PADI-affiliated **Diving Locker** (✉ 223 Sunny Isles Blvd., North Miami Beach, ☎ 305/947–6025) offers full sales, service, and repairs, plus three-day and three-week international certification courses as well as more advanced certifications. The three-day accelerated course for beginners is $350. Wreck and reef sites are reached aboard fast and comfortable six-passenger dive boats.

Tennis

Greater Miami has more than a dozen tennis centers open to the public, and countywide nearly 500 public courts are open to visitors. Nonresidents are charged an hourly fee. If you're on a tight schedule, try calling in advance, as some courts take reservations on weekdays.

Biltmore Tennis Center has 10 hard courts and a view of the beautiful Biltmore Hotel. ✉ *1150 Anastasia Ave., Coral Gables,* ☎ *305/460–5360.* 💳 *Day rate $4.50 per person per hr, night rate $5.50.* ⏲ *Weekdays 7 AM–10 PM, weekends 7–8.*

Very popular with locals, **Flamingo Tennis Center** has 19 clay courts smack dab in the middle of Miami Beach. You can't get much closer to the action. ✉ *1000 12th St., Miami Beach,* ☎ *305/673–7761.* 💳 *Day rate $2.67 per person per hr, night rate $3.20.* ⏲ *Weekdays 8 AM–9 PM, weekends 8–8.*

North Shore Tennis Center, within Miami Beach's North Shore Park, has nine lighted courts, six clay courts, and three hard courts. Two additional hard courts are for daytime use only. ✉ *350 73rd St., Miami Beach,* ☎ *305/993–2022.* 💳 *Day rate $2.66 per person per hr, night rate $3.20.* ⏲ *Weekdays 8 AM–9 PM, weekends 8–7.*

Thirty-acre **Tennis Center at Crandon Park** is one of America's best. Included are 2 grass, 8 clay, and 17 hard courts. Reservations are required for night play. The only time courts are closed to the public is during the **Ericsson Open** (☎ 305/442–3367), held for 11 days each spring. Top players such as Pete Sampras, Andre Agassi, Gustavo Kuerten, Venus and Sabrina Williams, and Martina Hingis compete in a 14,000-seat stadium for more than $6 million in prize money. ✉ *7300 Crandon Blvd., Key Biscayne,* ☎ *305/365–2300.* 💳 *Laykold courts: day rate $3 per person per hr, night rate $5; clay and grass courts $6 per person per hr day rate; courts are closed at night.* ⏲ *Daily 8 AM–9 PM.*

Windsurfing

Windsurfing is more popular than ever in Miami. The safest and most popular windsurfing area is at **Hobie Beach,** sometimes called Windsurfer Beach, just off the Rickenbacker Causeway on your way to Key Biscayne. In Miami Beach, the best spots are at **1st Street** (just north of the Government Cut jetty) and at **21st Street**; you can also windsurf on the beach at 3rd, 10th, and 14th Streets.

Sailboards Miami (✉ 1 Rickenbacker Causeway, Key Biscayne, ☎ 305/361–7245), ⅓ mi past the causeway tollbooth, rents equipment and claims to teach more windsurfers each year than anyone in the United States. Rentals average $20 for one hour, $38 for two hours, and $150 for 10 hours. They promise to teach anyone to windsurf within two hours.

SHOPPING

Visitors to Greater Miami are never more than 15 minutes from a major shopping area and the familiar *ka-ching* of a cash register. Miami-Dade County has more than a dozen major malls, an international free-trade zone, and hundreds of miles of commercial streets lined with stores and small shopping centers. Latin neighborhoods contain a wealth of Latin merchants and merchandise, including children's *vestidos de fiesta* (party dresses) and men's guayaberas (a pleated, embroidered tropical shirt), conveying the feel of a South American *mercado* (market).

Malls

Aventura Mall (✉ 19501 Biscayne Blvd., Aventura) has more than 250 shops anchored by Macy's, Lord & Taylor, JCPenney, Sears, and Bloomingdale's, along with a 24-screen theater with stadium seating and a Cheesecake Factory. In a tropical garden setting, **Bal Harbour Shops** (✉ 9700 Collins Ave., Bal Harbour) is a swank collection of 100 shops, boutiques, and department stores, such as Chanel, Gucci, Cartier, Fendi, Bruno Magli, Neiman Marcus, and Florida's largest Saks Fifth Avenue. **Bayside Marketplace** (✉ 401 Biscayne Blvd., Miami), the 16-acre shopping complex on Biscayne Bay, has more than 150 specialty shops, entertainment, tour-boat docks, a food court, and a Hard Rock Cafe. It's open late (until 10 during the week, 11 on Friday and Saturday), but its restaurants stay open even later. It's a great place to browse, buy, or simply relax by the bay with a tropical drink.

A complex of clapboard, coral-rock, and stucco buildings, **Cauley Square** (✉ 22400 Old Dixie Hwy., Goulds) was erected in 1907–20 as housing for railroad workers who built and maintained the line to

Key West. Crafts, clothing, and antiques shops are well represented. The heartbeat of Coconut Grove, **CocoWalk** (✉ 3015 Grand Ave., Coconut Grove) has three floors of nearly 40 specialty shops (Victoria's Secret, the Gap, Banana Republic, among others) that stay open almost as late as the popular restaurants and clubs. Kiosks with cigars, beads, incense, herbs, and other small items are scattered around the ground level, while the restaurants and nightlife (e.g., Hooters, Fat Tuesday, an AMC theater) are upstairs. If you're ready for an evening of people-watching, this is the place.

The oldest retail mall in the county, **Dadeland** (✉ 7535 N. Kendall Dr., Miami) is always upgrading. It sits at the south side of town close to the Dadeland North and Dadeland South Metrorail stations. Retailers include Saks Fifth Avenue, JCPenney, Lord & Taylor, more than 175 specialty stores, 17 restaurants, and the largest Burdines, Limited, and Limited Express in Florida. The $250 million **Dolphin Mall** (✉ State Rd. 836 and Florida's Turnpike, Miami), 5 mi west of the airport, has plenty of less expensive shopping, including a Marshall's Megastore, Oshman's Super Sports USA, and Saks Off Fifth outlet, plus a 28-screen cinemaplex and 850-seat food court. The **Falls** (✉ 8888 S.W. 136th St., at U.S. 1, Miami), which derives its name from the several waterfalls inside, is the most upscale mall on the south side of the city. It contains a Macy's and Bloomingdale's as well as another 50 specialty stores, restaurants, and a 12-theater multiplex.

As its name suggests, **Loehmann's Fashion Island** (✉ 18701 Biscayne Blvd., Aventura) is dominated by Loehmann's, the nationwide retailer of off-price designer fashions for women and men. Fashion-conscious shoppers can also browse the International Jewelers Exchange, Ital Design, and Rochester's Big & Tall.

With a huge banyan tree to welcome visitors, **Shops at Sunset Place** (✉ U.S. 1 and Red Rd. [S.W. 57th Ave.], South Miami) is even larger than CocoWalk. The three-story, family-oriented center has upped the ante for shopping/entertainment complexes with a 24-screen cinemaplex, IMAX theater, Virgin Megastore, FAO Schwarz, NikeTown, A/X Armani Exchange, and GameWorks (a Spielberg-movie-inspired virtual-reality attraction wrapped into a restaurant). **Streets of Mayfair** (✉ 2911 Grand Ave., Coconut Grove) is an open-air promenade of shops that bustles both day and night. Thanks to its Coconut Grove setting, along with the News Café, the Limited, Borders Books Music Cafe, and a few dozen other shops and restaurants, this is a safe bet. Entertainment is provided by an improv comedy club, a 10-screen theater, and the nightclubs Iguana Cantina and Martini Bar.

Outdoor Markets

Coconut Grove Farmers Market (✉ Grand Ave., 1 block west of MacDonald Ave. [S.W. 32nd Ave.], Coconut Grove), open Saturday 8–2, originated in 1977 and was the first in the Miami area. The **Espanola Way Market** (✉ Espanola Way, Miami Beach), open Sunday noon–9, has been a city favorite since its debut in 1995. Scattered among the handcrafted items and flea market merchandise, musicians beat out Latin rhythms on bongos, conga drums, steel drums, and guitars. Food vendors sell inexpensive Latin snacks and drinks. Each Saturday morning from 8–1, mid-January to late March, some 25 produce and plant vendors sell herbs, fruits, fresh-squeezed juices, chutneys, cakes, and muffins at the **Farmers Market at Merrick Park** (✉ LeJeune Rd. [S.W. 42nd Ave.] and Biltmore Way, Coral Gables). Regular features include gardening workshops, children's activities, and cooking demonstrations offered by Coral Gables' master chefs. More than 500 vendors sell a variety of goods at the **Flagler Dog Track** (✉ 401 N.W. 38th Ct.,

Miami), every weekend 9–4. The **Lincoln Road Farmers Market** (✉ Lincoln Rd. between Meridian and Euclid Aves., Miami Beach), open Sunday 9–5:30, brings about 15 local produce vendors coupled with plant workshops and children's activities. With 1,200 dealers, **Opa-Locka/Hialeah Flea Market** (✉ 12705 N.W. 47th Ave., Miami) is one of the largest in South Florida. Although it's open daily 7–7, weekends are best. From 10 to 5 on the second and fourth Sundays of each month, locals set up the **Outdoor Antique and Collectibles Market** (✉ Lincoln and Alton Rds., Miami Beach). The eclectic goods should satisfy post-Impressionists, Deco-holics, Edwardians, Bauhausers, and Gothic, atomic, and '50s junkies.

Shopping Districts

The shopping is great on a two-block stretch of **Collins Avenue** (✉ between 6th and 8th Aves., Miami Beach). Vidal Sassoon, Nicole Miller, Nike, Kenneth Cole, Guess, Armani Exchange, and Banana Republic are among the high-profile tenants, and a parking garage is just a block away. The busy **Lincoln Road Mall** is just a few blocks from the beach and convention center, making it popular with locals and tourists. There's an energy to shopping here, especially on weekends when the pedestrian mall is filled with locals. You'll find a Brookstone's, Crate and Barrel, Gap, and a Williams-Sonoma, as well as many smaller emporiums with unique personalities. Creative merchandise, galleries, and a Sunday-morning antiques market can be found among the art galleries and cool cafés. An 18-screen movie theater anchors the west end of the street.

There are 500 garment manufacturers in Miami and Hialeah, and many sell their clothing locally in the **Miami Fashion District** (✉ 5th Ave. east of I–95, between 25th and 29th Sts., Miami), making Greater Miami the fashion marketplace for the southeastern United States, the Caribbean, and Latin America. Most of the more than 30 factory outlets and discount fashion stores are open Monday–Saturday 9–5. The **Miami International Arts and Design District** (✉ between N.E. 38th and N.E. 42nd Sts. and between Federal Hwy. and N. Miami Ave., Miami), contains some 225 wholesale stores, showrooms, and galleries specializing in interior furnishings, decorative arts, and a rich mix of exclusive and unusual merchandise. Don't expect to find a flood of shoppers here; the surrounding neighborhood keeps many tourists away. **Miracle Mile** (✉ Coral Way between 37th and 42nd Aves., Coral Gables) consists of some 160 shops along a wide, tree-lined boulevard. Shops range from posh boutiques to bargain basements, from beauty salons to chain restaurants. As you go west, the quality improves.

Specialty Stores

ANTIQUES

Alhambra Antiques Center (✉ 2850 Salzedo, Miami, ☎ 305/446–1688) is a collection of four antiques dealers that sell high-quality decorative pieces from Europe. **Architectural Antiques** (✉ 2500 S.W. 28th La., Coconut Grove, ☎ 305/285–1330) carries large and eclectic items—railroad crossing signs, statues, English roadsters—in a setting so cluttered that shopping here becomes an adventure promising hidden treasures for the determined.

Leah's Gallery (✉ 191 N.E. 40th St., Miami, ☎ 305/573–9700) is four floors of wonderful finds, including 19th-century statuary and sculpture, park benches, mannequins, stained-glass doors and panels, and a gigantic carved-wood Victorian birdcage.

BOOKS

Like others in the superstore chain, **Barnes & Noble** (✉ 152 Miracle Mile, Coral Gables, ☎ 305/446–4152) manages to preserve the essence of a neighborhood bookstore by encouraging customers to pick a book off the shelf and lounge on a couch without being hassled. A well-stocked magazine and national/international news rack and an espresso bar–café complete the effect. Greater Miami's best English-language bookstore, **Books & Books, Inc.** (✉ 296 Aragon Ave., Coral Gables, ☎ 305/442–4408; ✉ Sterling Bldg., 933 Lincoln Rd., Miami Beach, ☎ 305/532–3222) specializes in books on the arts, architecture, Florida, and contemporary and classical literature. At the Coral Gables location, a true old-fashioned bookstore, collectors enjoy browsing through the rare-book room upstairs, which doubles as a photography gallery. There are frequent poetry readings and book signings. Both locations host regular author readings. If being in the Grove prompts you to don a beret, grow a goatee, and sift through a volume of Kerouac, head to **Borders** (✉ Grand Ave. and Mary St., Coconut Grove, ☎ 305/447–1655; ✉ 9205 S. Dixie Hwy., Pinecrest, ☎ 305/665–8800; ✉ 19925 Biscayne Blvd., Aventura, ☎ 305/935–0027) at the Streets of Mayfair. Its 100,000 book titles, 70,000 CDs, 10,000 video titles, and more than 2,000 periodicals and newspapers in 10 languages from 15 countries make it seem like the southern branch of the Library of Congress.

CHILDREN'S BOOKS AND TOYS

Afro-In Books and Things (✉ 5575 N.W. 7th Ave., Miami, ☎ 305/756–6107) presents books by African-American writers for children and teen readers—it even has an impressive section of books for adults. **F.A.O. Schwarz** (✉ 9700 Collins Ave., Bal Harbour Shops, Bal Harbour, ☎ 305/865–2361; ✉ 19501 Biscayne Blvd., Aventura Mall, Aventura, ☎ 305/692–9200; ✉ 5701 Sunset Dr., Shops at Sunset Place, South Miami, ☎ 305/668–2300) has three area stores. **La Canastilla Cubana** (✉ 1300 W. 49th St., Hialeah, ☎ 305/557–5505) carries children's books and toys and specializes in elegant furnishings and designer clothing for new arrivals. The store's Spanish name means "stork's basket."

CIGARS

Although Tampa is Florida's true cigar capital, Miami's Latin population is giving it a run for its money. Smoking anything even remotely affiliated with a legendary Cuban has boosted the popularity of Miami cigar stores and the small shops where you can buy cigars straight from the press.

Bill's Pipe & Tobacco (✉ 2309 Ponce de Léon Blvd., Coral Gables, ☎ 305/444–1764) has everything for the pipe and cigar smoker, including a wide selection of pipes and pipe tobacco, cigars, accessories, and gifts. The **Cigar Connection** (✉ 534 Lincoln Road Mall, Miami Beach, ☎ 305/531–7373) is hoping to capture the trendy tastes of pedestrians strolling on Lincoln Road. Carrying such premium cigars as the Arturo Fuente Opus X and Paul Garmirians, the shop also serves coffees and cappuccino. With soft terra-cotta and ocher tones suggestive of an Italian villa, **Condal & Peñamil** (✉ 741 Lincoln Road Mall, Miami Beach, ☎ 305/604–9690) is Miami's most beautiful cigar bar. In addition to carrying the traditional ashtrays, cutters, and humidors, C&P has a "cigar cave" with a private salon, enabling you to complement your smoke with a coffee or cocktail.

In the heart of Little Havana, **El Credito** (✉ 1106 S.W. 8th St., Miami, ☎ 305/858–4162 or 800/726–9481) seems to have been transported from the Cuban capital lock, stock, and stogie. Rows of workers at wooden benches rip through giant tobacco leaves, cut them with rounded blades, wrap them tightly, and press them in vises. Dedicated smokers like Robert DeNiro, Gregory Hines, and George Hamilton have found their way here to pick up a $90 bundle or peruse the *gigantes, supremos,* panatelas, and Churchills available in natural or maduro wrappers.

It's the only cigar shop on Miracle Mile, but that's not the sole reason to drop by **Giorgio's Cigars** (✉ 210 Miracle Mile, Coral Gables, ☎ 305/448–2992). The standard lineup (Espinosa, Arturo Fuente, Macanudo, Partagas, et al.) is complemented by a large humidor, coffee bar, nice leather sofas, and a cheesy nude painting. There's added applause for the friendly staff. **Havana Ray's** (✉ 3111 Grand Ave., Coconut Grove, ☎ 305/446–4003 or 800/732–4427) continues a cigar-making dynasty that began in 1920s Cuba. The Quirantes family's devotion to cigars has resulted in this cozy Streets of Mayfair shop, where you can buy cigars and related accoutrements.

Located on South Beach, **Macabi Cigars** (✉ 1451 Ocean Dr., Miami Beach, ☎ 305/673–6167) carries cigars, cigars, and more cigars, including premium and house brands. Humidors and other accessories make great gifts. **South Beach News and Tobacco** (✉ 710 Washington Ave., No. 9, Miami Beach, ☎ 305/673–3002) has expanded beyond simple cigars to carry imported wines and beers, gourmet espresso and coffee, sandwiches, and croissants. But the real draw is cigars made on the premises or imported from the Dominican Republic, Nicaragua, and Honduras.

COLLECTIBLES

Gotta Have It! Collectibles (✉ 4231 S.W. 71st Ave., Miami, ☎ 305/446–5757) will make fans of any kind break out in a cold sweat. Autographed sports jerseys, canceled checks from the estate of Marilyn Monroe, fabulously framed album jackets signed by all four Beatles, and an elaborate autographed montage of all the *Wizard of Oz* stars are among this intriguing shop's museum-quality collectibles. Looking for an Einstein autograph? A Jack Nicklaus–signed scorecard? Look no further. And if they don't have the autograph you desire, fear not—they'll track one down.

Thomas Kinkade Gallery (✉ 401 Biscayne Blvd., Bayside Marketplace, Miami, ☎ 305/358–1893) features the popular landscape artist's work in prints and limited editions, along with other collectible items such as books, plates, and whimsical snow globes.

ESSENTIALS

Wall-to-wall merchandise is found at the **Compass Market** (✉ 860 Ocean Dr., Miami Beach, ☎ 305/673–2906), a cute and cozy basement shop that carries all the staples you'll need, especially if you're staying in an efficiency. The market stocks sandals, souvenirs, cigars, deli items, umbrellas, newspapers, and produce. If the heat of Miami gets you hot and bothered, try **Condom USA** (✉ 3066 Grand Ave., Coconut Grove, ☎ 305/445–7729) on for size. Sexually oriented games and condoms are sold by the gross. If you're easily offended, stay away. If you're easily aroused, stay the night.

FASHIONS FOR MEN & WOMEN

Look the part when you go club-hopping with help from **Ocean Drive Fashion** (✉ 840 Ocean Dr., Miami Beach, ☎ 305/538–2284), selling hip clubwear for men and women, along with accessories like bags, shoes, jewelry, and sunglasses. Miami is full of big-name boutiques, and **Polo Ralph Lauren** (✉ 9700 Collins Ave., Bal Harbour Shops, Bal Harbour, ☎ 305/861–2059) is one of them. Enhance your wardrobe with Polo for Men and Ralph Lauren for women's clothing and accessories.

JEWELRY

Beverlee Kagan (✉ 5831 Sunset Dr., S. Miami, ☎ 305/663–1937) specializes in vintage and antique jewelry, including art deco–era bangles, bracelets, and cuff links. Easily overlooked in the quick pace of downtown, the 10-story **Seybold Building** (✉ 36 N.E. 1st St., Miami, ☎ 305/374–7922) is filled from bottom to top with more than 250 independent jewelry companies. Diamonds, bracelets, necklaces, and rings are sold in a crowded, lively setting. Word is that competition makes prices flexible; it's closed Sunday.

SOUVENIRS AND GIFT ITEMS

Art Deco District Welcome Center (✉ 1001 Ocean Dr., Miami Beach, ☎ 305/531–3484) hawks the finest in Miami-inspired kitsch, from flamingo salt-and-pepper shakers to alligator-shape ashtrays, along with books and posters celebrating the Art Deco District and its recent revival.

The **Indies Company** (✉ 101 W. Flagler St., Miami, ☎ 305/375–1492), the Historical Museum of Southern Florida's gift shop, offers interesting artifacts reflecting Miami's history, including some inexpensive reproductions. The collection of books on Miami and South Florida is impressive.

SIDE TRIP

South Dade

Although the population of these suburbs southwest of Dade County's urban core was largely dislocated by Hurricane Andrew in 1992, little damage is evident today. Indeed, FEMA grants and major replanting have made the area better than ever. All attractions—many of which are especially interesting for kids—have reopened, and a complete exploration of them would probably take two days. Keep an eye open for hand-painted signs announcing agricultural attractions, such as orchid farms, fruit stands, u-pick farms, and horseback riding.

42 Aviation enthusiasts touch down at **Weeks Air Museum** to view some 15 planes of World War II vintage. Sadly, Hurricane Andrew destroyed the World War I aircraft, and those from World War II suffered damage as well. What you will find are extensive videos, a 707 cockpit you can peer into, and a nose section of a B-29 Superfortress. The museum is inside Tamiami Airport. ✉ *14710 S.W. 128th St.,* ☎ *305/233–5197,* WEB *www.weeksairmuseum.com.* *$9.95.* *Daily 10–5.*

One of the few zoos in the United States in a subtropical environment, 43 the first-class, 290-acre **Metrozoo** is state of the art. Inside the cageless zoo, some 800 animals roam on islands surrounded by moats. Take the monorail to see major attractions including the Tiger Temple, where white tigers roam, and the African Plains exhibit, where giraffes, ostriches, and zebras graze in a simulated habitat. There are also koalas, Komodo dragons, and other animals whose names begin with a *K*. The children's petting zoo is home to a meerkat exhibit, and Dr. Wilde's World is an interactive facility with changing exhibits. Kids can touch Florida animals such as alligators and possums at the Ecology Theater. ✉ *12400 Coral Reef Dr. (S.W. 152nd St.),* ☎ *305/251–0401.* *$8, 45-min tram tour $2.* *Daily 9:30–5:30, last admission at 4.*

44 Historic railroad cars on display at the **Gold Coast Railroad Museum** include a 1949 *Silver Crescent* dome car and the *Ferdinand Magellan,* the only Pullman car constructed specifically for U.S. presidents. It was used by Franklin Delano Roosevelt, Harry Truman, Dwight Eisenhower, and Ronald Reagan. On weekends, a train ride is included in the price of admission to the museum, which is next to the zoo. ✉ *12450 Coral Reef Dr. (S.W. 152nd St.),* ☎ *305/253–0063,* WEB *www.goldcoast-railroad.org.* *$5.* *Weekdays 11–3, weekends 11–4.*

45 Still a kitschy attraction for adults, **Monkey Jungle** claims to be home to more than 300 monkeys representing 25 species—including

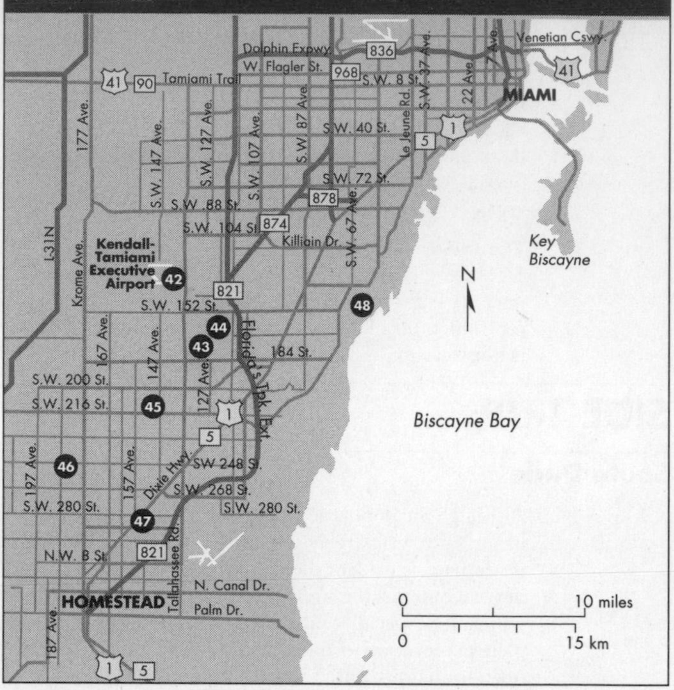

South Dade

orangutans from Borneo and Sumatra and golden lion tamarins from Brazil. New exhibits include Lemurs of Madagascar, Parrots of the Amazon, and Cameroon Jungle. Perhaps the most fun is feeding monkeys who scurry across the fences overhead, hauling up peanuts you place in a metal cup. ✉ *14805 Hainlin Mill Dr. (S.W. 216th St.),* ☎ *305/235–1611,* WEB *www.monkeyjungle.com.* 🎟 *$13.50.* ⏲ *Daily 9:30–5, last admission at 4.*

46 The 35-acre **Redland Fruit & Spice Park** has been a Dade County treasure since 1944, when it was opened as a 20-acre showcase of tropical fruits and vegetables. Plants are grouped by country of origin and include more than 500 economically important varieties of exotic fruits, herbs, spices, nuts, and poisonous plants from around the world. A sampling reveals 85 types of bananas, 40 varieties of grapes, and 100 kinds of citrus fruits. The park store offers many varieties of tropical-fruit products, jellies, seeds, aromatic teas, and reference books. ✉ *24801 Redland Rd. (S.W. 187th Ave.),* ☎ *305/247–5727,* WEB *www.co.miami-dade.fl.us/parks.* 🎟 *$3.50.* ⏲ *Daily 10–5, tours daily at 11, 1, and 2:30.*

47 **Coral Castle of Florida** was born when 26-year-old Edward Leedskalnin, a Latvian immigrant, was left at the altar by his 16-year-old fiancée. She went on with her life, while he went off the deep end and began carving a castle out of coral rock. It's hard to believe that Eddie, only 5 ft tall and 100 pounds, could maneuver tons of coral rock single-handedly. Built between 1920 and 1940, the 3-acre castle is one of South Florida's original tourist attractions. There is a 9-ton gate a child could open, an accurate working sundial, and a telescope of coral rock aimed at the North Star. ✉ *28655 S. Dixie Hwy.,* ☎ *305/248–6345,* WEB *www.coralcastle.com.* 🎟 *$7.75.* ⏲ *Mon.–Thurs. 9–6, Fri.–Sat. 9–9, Sun. 9–7.*

48 **Deering Estate at Cutler.** In 1913 Charles Deering, brother of James Deering, who built Vizcaya in Coconut Grove, bought this property for a winter residence. Nine years later he built the Mediterranean revival stone house that stands here today. This site is fascinating on several levels: historical, archaeological, and natural. Far more austere than its ornate cousin Vizcaya, the stone house has wrought-iron gates, copper doors, and a unique stone ceiling. Next door, the Richmond Cottage—fully restored after being destroyed by 1992's Hurricane Andrew—was the first inn to be built between Coconut Grove and Key West (1900), and is a fine example of South Florida frame vernacular architecture. Take a naturalist-guided tour to learn more about area's archaeology: scientists discovered human remains here and carbon-dated them to 10,000 years ago; they may belong to Paleo-Indians. A fossil pit contains the bones of dog-size horses, tapirs, jaguars, peccaries, sloths, and bison. Coastal tropical hardwood hammocks, rare orchids and trees, plus a variety of wildlife, such as gray foxes, bobcats, limpkins, peregrine falcons, and cormorants, populates the property. A huge environmental education and visitor center presents programs for children and adults. Nature tours and canoe trips to nearby Chicken Key are available. ✉ *16701 S.W. 72nd Ave.,* ☎ *305/235–1668,* WEB *www.co.miami-dade.fl.us/parks.* 🎫 *$9.* ⏲ *Daily 10–5.*

MIAMI AND MIAMI BEACH A TO Z

ADDRESSES

To research prices, get advice from other travelers, and book arrangements, visit www.fodors.com.

Greater Miami is made up of more than 30 municipalities, and tourist favorites Miami and Miami Beach are only two of the cities which make up what is actually Miami-Dade County. Within Greater Miami, addresses fall into four quadrants: NW, NE, SW, and SE. The north–south dividing line is Flagler Street, and the east–west dividing line is Miami Avenue. Numbering starts from these axes and gets higher the farther away an address is from them. Avenues run north–south and streets east–west. Some municipalities have their own street naming and numbering systems, including Miami Beach, Coral Gables, Coconut Grove, and Key Biscayne, so a map is a good idea. In South Beach, all north–south roads are named and the main drags are Ocean Drive, Collins, and Washington avenues, and Alton Road. Streets are numbered and run east–west; 1st Street is at the beach's southernmost point and numbers get higher as you head north.

AIR TRAVEL TO AND FROM MIAMI

CARRIERS

In addition to the wide range of airlines that fly into Miami International Airport (MIA), there's Pan Am Air Bridge—starting over where the original Pan Am began—with seaplane flights. Departing from Watson Island, the 30- to 60-minute rides to Bimini, Paradise Island, and Walkers Cay in the Bahamas are exciting, anachronistic, and somewhat cramped. Still, if you've got an extra $200–$250, a round-trip could be quite fun. Chalk's Ocean Airways offers daily seaplane service from Watson Island in Miami and Ft. Lauderdale International Airport to Bimini and Paradise Island.

➤ AIRLINES AND CONTACTS: **Aeroflot** (☎ 888/340–6400). **Aerolineas Argentinas** (☎ 800/333–0276). **AeroMexico** (☎ 800/237–6639). **AeroPeru** (☎ 800/777–7717). **Air Aruba** (☎ 800/882–7822). **Air Canada** (☎ 800/776–3000). **Air France** (☎ 800/237–2747). **Air Jamaica** (☎ 800/523–5585). **Alitalia** (☎ 800/223–5730). **American/Amer-**

ican Eagle (☎ 800/433–7300). **American TransAir** (☎ 800/225–2995). **Avensa** (☎ 800/428–3672). **Avianca** (☎ 800/284–2622). **Aviateca** (☎ 800/327–9832). **Bahamasair** (☎ 800/222–4262). **British Airways** (☎ 800/247–9297). **BWIA** (☎ 305/371–2942). **Cayman Airways** (☎ 800/422–9626). **Chalk's Ocean Airways** (☎ 800/424–2557). **Comair** (☎ 800/354–9822). **Continental** (☎ 800/525–0280). **Delta** (☎ 800/221–1212). **El Al** (☎ 800/223–6700). **Finnair** (☎ 800/950–5000). **Gulfstream International** (☎ 800/992–8532). **Guyana Airways** (☎ 800/242–4210). **Iberia** (☎ 800/772–4642). **LAB** (☎ 800/327–7407). **Lacsa** (☎ 800/225–2272). **Lan Chile** (☎ 800/735–5526). **Lauda Air** (☎ 800/588–8399). **LTU** (☎ 800/888–0200). **Lufthansa** (☎ 800/645–3880). **Martinair Holland** (☎ 800/366–4655). **Mexicana** (☎ 800/531–7921). **Northwest** (☎ 800/225–2525). **Pan Am Air Bridge** (✉ 1000 MacArthur Causeway, Miami, ☎ 305/373–1120 or 800/424–2557). **Paradise Island** (☎ 800/786–7202). **Saeta** (☎ 800/827–2382). **Servivensa** (☎ 800/428–3672). **South African Airways** (☎ 800/722–9675). **Taca** (☎ 800/535–8780). **Tower Air** (☎ 800/348–6937). **Transbrasil** (☎ 800/872–3153). **TWA** (☎ 800/221–2000). **United** (☎ 800/241–6522). **US Airways/US Airways Express** (☎ 800/428–4322). **Varig** (☎ 800/468–2744). **Virgin Atlantic** (☎ 800/862–8621).

AIRPORTS AND TRANSFERS

Miami International Airport, 6 mi west of downtown Miami, is the only airport in Greater Miami that provides scheduled service. With a daily average of 1,400 flights, it handled more than 35 million passengers in 1997, nearly half of them international travelers. MIA is also the nation's busiest airport for international freight. Altogether more than 120 airlines serve 200 cities and five continents with nonstop or one-stop service. MIA has 102 aircraft gates and eight concourses.

Anticipating continued growth, the airport has begun a more than $4 billion expansion program that is expected to be completed by 2005. Passengers will mainly notice rebuilt and expanded gate and public areas, which should reduce congestion.

A greatly underused convenience for passengers who have to get from one concourse to another in this long, horseshoe-shape terminal is the amazingly convenient moving walkway on the skywalk level (third floor), with access points at every concourse. MIA, the first to offer duty-free shops, now boasts 18, carrying liquors, perfumes, electronics, and various designer goods.

Heightened security at MIA has meant that it's suggested you check in 90 minutes before departure for a domestic flight, two hours for an international flight. Services for international travelers include 24-hour multilingual information and paging phones and currency conversion booths throughout the terminal. There is an information booth with a multilingual staff across from the 24-hour currency exchange at the entrance of Concourse E on the upper level.

The county's Metrobus still costs $1.25, although equipment has improved. From Concourse E on the ground level, you can take Bus 7 to downtown (weekdays 5:30 AM–9 PM every 40 minutes; weekends 6:30 AM–7:30 PM every 40 minutes), Bus 37 south to Coral Gables and South Miami (6 AM–10 PM every 30 minutes) or north to Hialeah (5:30 AM–11:30 PM every 30 minutes), Bus J south to Coral Gables (6 AM–12:30 AM every 30 minutes) or east to Miami Beach (4:30 AM–11:30 PM every 30 minutes), and Bus 42 to Coconut Grove (5:30 AM–7:20 PM hourly). Some routes change to 60-minute schedules after 7 PM and on weekends, so be prepared to wait or call the information line for exact times.

Miami has more than 100 limousine services, although they're frequently in and out of business. If you rely on the Yellow Pages, look for a company with a street address, not just a phone number. Offering 24-hour service, Club Limousine Service has shuttle vans and minibuses as well as limos. One of the oldest companies in town is Vintage Rolls Royce Limousines of Coral Gables, which operates a 24-hour reservation service and provides chauffeurs for privately owned, collectible Rolls-Royces from the 1940s.

Except for the flat-fare trips described below, cabs cost $3.25 for the first mile, $2 a mile after that, plus a $1 toll for trips originating at MIA or the Port of Miami. Approximate fares from MIA include $17 to Coral Gables or downtown Miami, $31 to Key Biscayne. In addition, Miami's regulatory commission has established flat rates for five zones of the city, four of which are listed here: $24 to between 63rd Street and the foot of Miami Beach (including South Beach); $41 to Golden Beach and Sunny Isles, north of Haulover Beach Park; $34 to between Surfside and Haulover Beach Park; and $29 to between 63rd and 87th streets. These fares are per trip, not per passenger, and include tolls and $1 airport surcharge but not tip. The approximate fare between MIA and the Port of Miami is $18.

For taxi service to destinations in the immediate vicinity, ask a uniformed county taxi dispatcher to call an ARTS (Airport Region Taxi Service) cab for you. These special blue cabs offer a short-haul flat fare in two zones. An inner-zone ride is $7; the outer-zone fare is $10. The area of service is north to 36th Street, west to the Palmetto Expressway (77th Avenue), south to Northwest 7th Street, and east to Douglas Road (37th Avenue). Maps are posted in cab windows on both sides.

SuperShuttle vans transport passengers between MIA and local hotels, the Port of Miami, and even individual residences on a 24-hour basis. At MIA the vans pick up at the ground level of each concourse (look for clerks with yellow shirts, who will flag one down). The company's service area extends from Palm Beach to Monroe County (including the Lower Keys). Drivers provide narration en route. Service from MIA is available around the clock on demand; for the return it's best to make reservations 24 hours in advance, although the firm will try to arrange pickups within Miami-Dade County on as little as four hours' notice. The cost from MIA to downtown hotels runs $9–$10; to the beaches it can be $11–$16 per passenger, depending on how far north you go. Additional members of a party pay a lower rate for many destinations, and children under three ride free with their parents. There's a pet transport fee of $10 for animals in kennels.

➤ AIRPORT INFORMATION: **Miami International Airport** (MIA, ☎ 305/876–7000). **Miami International Airport Hotel** (✉ Concourse E, upper level, ☎ 305/871–4100).

➤ TAXIS AND SHUTTLES: **Club Limousine Service** (✉ 12050 N.E. 14th Ave., Miami 33161, ☎ 305/893–9850; 800/824–4820; 800/325–9834 in FL). **Metrobus** (☎ 305/770–3131). **SuperShuttle** (☎ 305/871–2000 from MIA; 954/764–1700 from Broward [Fort Lauderdale]; 800/874–8885 from elsewhere). **Vintage Rolls Royce Limousines of Coral Gables** (✉ 4501 Monserrate St., Coral Gables 33146, ☎ 305/444–7657 or 800/888–7657).

BIKE TRAVEL

Cruise America offers Harleys, Hondas, and Suzukis with daily/weekly rentals starting at $109/$545. You must be 21 with a credit card, valid drivers license, and motorcycle endorsement.

Great weather and flat terrain make Miami perfect for cycling enthusiasts, but as a general method of transportation, it shouldn't be your first choice given traffic and limited bike paths. You can opt for Miami-Dade Transit's "Bike and Ride" program, which lets permitted cyclists take single-seat two-wheelers on Metrorail and select bus routes. Miami-Dade Bicycle/Pedestrian Coordinator has details on permits, bike maps, and lockers, and is open weekdays 8–5.

➤ BIKE RENTALS: **Cruise America** (✉ 5801 N.W. 151st St, Miami, ☎ 800/327–7799 or 305/828–1198). **Miami-Dade Bicycle/Pedestrian Coordinator** (☎ 305/375–4507).

BOAT AND FERRY TRAVEL

If you enter the United States in a private vessel along the Atlantic Coast south of Sebastian Inlet, you must call the U.S. Customs Service. Customs clears most boats of less than 5 tons by phone, but you may be directed to a marina for inspection.

The Port of Miami, in downtown Miami near Bayside Marketplace and the MacArthur Causeway, justifiably bills itself as the cruise capital of the world. Home to 18 ships and the largest year-round cruise fleet in the world, the port accommodates more than 3 million passengers a year. It has 12 air-conditioned terminals, duty-free shopping, and limousine service. Taxicabs are available at all terminals and Avis is located at the port, although other rental companies offer shuttle service to off-site locations. Parking is $10 per day and short-term parking is a flat rate of $4. From here, three-, four- and seven-day cruises depart for the Bahamas and Eastern and Western Caribbean, with longer sailings to the Far East, Europe, and South America.

➤ CRUISE LINES: **Port of Miami** (✉ 1015 North American Way, Miami, ☎ 305/347–4860 or 305/371–7678). **U.S. Customs Service** (☎ 800/432–1216 near Miami; 305/536–5263 otherwise). **Carnival Cruise Lines** (☎ 800/327–9501). **Norwegian Cruise Lines** (☎ 800/327–7030). **Royal Caribbean International** (☎ 800/255–4373).

BUS TRAVEL TO AND FROM MIAMI AND MIAMI BEACH

Regularly scheduled, interstate Greyhound buses stop at five terminals in Greater Miami; the airport terminal is 24-hour.

➤ BUS INFORMATION: **Greyhound** (☎ 800/231–2222. **Homestead:** ✉ 5 N.E. 3rd Rd., ☎ 305/247–2040. **Miami Bayside/Downtown:** ✉ 700 Biscayne Blvd., ☎ 305/374–6160. **Miami South:** ✉ 20505 S. Dixie Hwy., ☎ 305/296–9072. **Miami West/Airport:** ✉ 4111 N.W. 27th St., ☎ 305/871–1810. **North Miami:** ✉ 16560 N.E. 6th Ave., ☎ 305/945–0801.)

BUS TRAVEL WITHIN MIAMI AND MIAMI BEACH

Metrobus stops are marked by blue-and-green signs with a bus logo and route information. The frequency of service varies widely, so call in advance to obtain specific schedules. The fare is $1.25 (exact change), transfers 25¢; 60¢ with 10¢ transfers for people with disabilities, senior citizens (65 and older), and students. Some express routes carry surcharges of $1.50. Reduced-fare tokens, sold 10 for $10, are available from Metropass outlets. Lift-equipped buses for people with disabilities are available on 16 routes, including one from the airport that links up with many routes in Miami Beach as well as Coconut Grove, Coral Gables, Hialeah, and Kendall. All but four of these routes connect with Metrorail. Those unable to use regular for information on such services as curb-to-curb van pickup.

The best thing to arrive in Miami Beach since sand, the Electro-Wave is a fleet of *free* electric trolleys running every few minutes up and down Washington Avenue between 5th and 17th Streets. New service continues south of 5th Street, west to Alton Road, and over by the Miami

Beach Marina. Considering the great lengths between SoBe attractions, it'll save a lot of shoe leather. Trolleys operate Monday–Wednesday 8 AM–2 AM, Thursday–Saturday 8 AM–4 AM, and Sunday and holidays 10 AM–2 AM.

FARES AND SCHEDULES

➤ BUS INFORMATION: **Electro-Wave** (☎ 305/843–9283). **Special Transportation Services** (☎ 305/263–5400).

CAR RENTAL

The following agencies have booths near the baggage-claim area on MIA's lower level: Alamo, Avis, Budget, Dollar, Hertz, and National. Avis and Budget have offices at the Port of Miami.

If money is no object, check out Excellence Luxury Car Rental. As the name implies, you can rent some wheels (a Ferrari, perhaps?) to cruise SoBe and pretend you're Don Johnson. If you can't find the excellent car you want, you can rent a Dodge Viper, BMW, Hummer, Jag, Porsche, or Rolls from Exotic Cars. Airport pickup is provided.

CUTTING COSTS

➤ LOCAL AGENCIES: **Alamo** (☎ 800/468–2583). **Avis** (☎ 800/331–1212). **Budget** (☎ 800/527–0700). **Dollar** (☎ 800/800–4000). **Excellence Luxury Car Rental** (☎ 305/526–0000). **Exotic Cars** (☎ 888/541–1789). **Hertz** (☎ 800/654–3131). **National** (☎ 800/227–7368).

CAR TRAVEL

The main highways into Greater Miami from the north are Florida's Turnpike (a toll road) and Interstate–95. From the northwest take Interstate–75 or U.S. 27 into town. From the Everglades, to the west, use the Tamiami Trail (U.S. 41), and from the south use U.S. 1 and the Homestead Extension of Florida's Turnpike.

In general, Miami traffic is the same as in any other big city, with the same rush hours and the same likelihood that parking garages will be full at peak times. Many drivers who aren't locals and don't know their way around might turn and stop suddenly, or drop off passengers where they shouldn't. Some drivers are short-tempered and will assault those who cut them off or honk their horn.

Motorists need to be careful, even when their driving behavior is beyond censure, however, especially in rental cars. Despite the removal of identifying marks, cars piled with luggage or otherwise showing signs that a tourist is at the wheel remain prime targets for thieves. Your best bet is to "follow the sun"; major (and safer) travel routes are marked by huge sunburst logos, which connect to tourist hot spots like the Deco District. Stick with these, and you should get where you need to go fairly easily and quickly. The city has also initiated a TOP (Tourist Oriented Police) Cops program to assist tourists with directions and safety. For more safety advice on driving in Miami, *see* Car Travel *in* Smart Travel Tips A to Z.

EMERGENCIES

Dial 911 for police or ambulance. You can dial free from pay phones.

Randle Eastern Ambulance Service Inc. operates at all hours, although in an emergency they'll direct you to call 911. Dade County Medical Association is open weekdays 9–5 for medical referral. East Coast District Dental Society is open weekdays 9–4:30 for dental referral. After hours stay on the line and a recording will direct you to a dentist. Services include general dentistry, endodontics, periodontics, and oral surgery.

➤ DOCTORS AND DENTISTS: **Dade County Medical Association** (✉ 1501 N.W. North River Dr., Miami, ☎ 305/324–8717). **East Coast**

District Dental Society (✉ 420 S. Dixie Hwy., Suite 2E, Coral Gables, ☎ 305/667–3647).

➤ HOT LINES: **Randle Eastern Ambulance Service Inc.** (✉ 7255 N.W. 19th St., Suite C, Miami 33126, ☎ 305/718–6400).

➤ LATE-NIGHT PHARMACIES: **Eckerd Drug** (✉ 9031 S.W. 107th Ave., Miami, ☎ 305/274–6776). **Walgreens** (✉ 500-B W. 49th St., Palm Springs Mall, Hialeah, ☎ 305/557–5468; ✉ 2750 W. 68th St., Hialeah, ☎ 305/828–0268; ✉ 12295 Biscayne Blvd., North Miami, ☎ 305/893–6860; ✉ 5731 Bird Rd., Miami, ☎ 305/666–0757; ✉ 1845 Alton Rd., Miami Beach, ☎ 305/531–8868; ✉ 791 N.E. 167th St., North Miami Beach, ☎ 305/652–7332).

MEDIA

NEWSPAPERS AND MAGAZINES

Greater Miami's major newspaper is the ***Miami Herald.*** Your best bet for weekend happenings is the free alternative weekly, ***New Times.*** For Spanish-language news, turn to ***El Nuevo Herald.*** Regional editions of the ***Wall Street Journal*** and ***The New York Times*** can be found just about everywhere—including vending machines—and many of Europe and Latin America's major dailies and fashion glossies are available at newsstands.

RADIO AND TELEVISION

Greater Miami is served by all the major cable networks. Major broadcast television stations include **WFOR** (CBS), **WLTV** (Univision, Spanish/international), **WPBT** (PBS), **WPLG** (ABC), **WSCV** (Telemundo, Spanish/international), **WSVN** (Fox), and **WTVJ** (NBC). In the late evening, **WLRN** broadcasts BBC news.

Radio stations in Greater Miami include **WDNA/88.9FM** (jazz), **WEDR/99.1FM** (urban), **WHYI/100.7FM** (top 40), **WIOD/610AM** (news), **WKIS/99.9FM** (country), **WLRN 91.3FM** (National Public Radio), **WQAM/560AM** (sports), **WTMI/93.1FM:** (classical), and **WZTA/94.9FM** (classic rock). Near the airport, you can find basic tourist information, broadcast successively in English, French, German, Portuguese, and Spanish, on the low-wattage **WAEM/102.3FM.**

TAXIS

One cab "company" stands out immeasurably above the rest. It's actually a consortium of drivers who have banded together to provide good service, in marked contrast to some Miami cabbies, who are rude, unhelpful, unfamiliar with the city, or dishonest, taking advantage of visitors who don't know the area. To plug into this consortium—they don't have a name, simply a number—call the dispatch service, although they can be hard to understand over the phone. If you have to use another company, try to be familiar with your route and destination. For information call the Metro-Dade Passenger Transportation Regulatory Service, also known as the Hack Bureau. It takes complaints and monitors all for-hire vehicles.

Starting in 1998, fares were set at $3.25 per first mile and $2 every mile thereafter, with no additional charge for up to five passengers, luggage, and tolls. Taxis can be hailed on the street, although you may not always find one when you need one—it's better to call for a dispatch taxi or have a hotel doorman hail one for you. Some companies with dispatch service are Central Taxicab Service, Diamond Cab Company, Metro Taxicab Company, Miami-Dade Yellow Cab, Society Cab Company, Super Yellow Cab Company, Tropical Taxicab Company, and Yellow Cab Company. Many now accept credit cards; inquire when you call.

➤ TAXI COMPANIES: **Dispatch service** (☎ 305/888–4444). **Central Taxicab Service** (☎ 305/532–5555). **Diamond Cab Company** (☎ 305/

545–5555). **Metro-Dade Passenger Transportation Regulatory Service** (☎ 305/375–2460). **Metro Taxicab Company** (☎ 305/888–8888). **Miami-Dade Yellow Cab** (☎ 305/633–0503). **Society Cab Company** (☎ 305/757–5523). **Super Yellow Cab Company** (☎ 305/888–7777). **Tropical Taxicab Company** (☎ 305/945–1025). **Yellow Cab Company** (☎ 305/444–4444).

TOURS

Coconut Grove Rickshaw centers its operations at CocoWalk. Two-person rickshaws scurry along Main Highway in Coconut Grove's Village Center, nightly 7 PM–midnight. You can take a 10-minute ride through Coconut Grove or a 20-minute lovers' moonlight ride to Biscayne Bay; prices start at $5 per person, and you can pick them up curb-side.

BOAT TOURS

Island Queen, Island Lady, and *Pink Lady* are 150-passenger double-decker tour boats docked at Bayside Marketplace. They go on daily 90-minute narrated tours of the Port of Miami and Millionaires' Row, costing $14. Refreshments are available.

For something a little more private and luxe, *RA Charters* sails out of the Dinner Key Marina in Coconut Grove. Full- and half-day charters include snorkeling and even sailing lessons on the 40-ft sloop, with extended trips to the Florida Keys and Bahamas. For a romantic night, have Captain Masoud pack some gourmet fare and sail sunset to moonlight while you enjoy Biscayne Bay's spectacular skyline view of Miami. Prices range from $300 to $400 for a half day to $600–$700 for a full day, depending on the number of people aboard and refreshments provided.

➤ FEES AND SCHEDULES: ***Island Queen, Island Lady,* and *Pink Lady*** (✉ 401 Biscayne Blvd., ☎ 305/379–5119). ***RA Charters*** (☎ 305/854–7341 or 305/666–7979).

PRIVATE GUIDES

Professor Paul George, a history professor at Miami-Dade Community College and past president of the Florida Historical Society, leads a variety of walking tours as well as boat tours and tours that make use of the Metrorail and Metromover. Choose from tours covering downtown, historic neighborhoods, cemeteries, Coconut Grove, and the Miami River. They start Saturday at 10 and Sunday at 11 at various locations, depending on the tour, and generally last about 2½ hours. Call for each weekend's schedule and for additional tours by appointment. The fee is $15.

➤ CONTACTS: **Professor Paul George** (✉ 1345 S.W. 14th St., Miami, ☎ 305/858–6021).

WALKING TOURS

The Art Deco District Tour, operated by the Miami Design Preservation League, is a 90-minute guided walking tour that departs from the league's welcome center at the Oceanfront Auditorium. It costs $10 (tax-deductible) and starts at 10:30 AM Saturday and 6:30 PM Thursday. Private group tours can be arranged with advance notice. You can go at your own pace with the league's self-guided $5 audio tour, which takes roughly an hour and a half and is available in English, Spanish, French, and German.

➤ FEES AND SCHEDULES: **Art Deco District Tour** (✉ 1001 Ocean Dr., Bin L, Miami Beach 33139, ☎ 305/672–2014).

TRAIN TRAVEL

Amtrak provides service from 500 destinations to the Greater Miami area, including three trains daily from New York City. North–south service stops in the major Florida cities of Jacksonville, Orlando, Tampa, West Palm Beach, and Fort Lauderdale. For extended trips, or if you're visiting other areas in Florida, come via Auto Train from Lorton, VA, just outside of Washington, DC, to Sanford, FL, just outside of Orlando.

Tri-Rail, South Florida's commuter train system, offers daily service connecting Miami-Dade with Broward and Palm Beach counties via Metrorail (transfer at the TriRail/Metrorail Station at the Hialeah station, at 79th Street and East 11th Avenue). They also offer shuttle service to and from MIA from their airport station at 3797 Northwest 21st Street. Tri-Rail stops at 18 stations along a 71-mi route. Fares are established by zones, with prices ranging from \$3.50 to \$9.25 for a round-trip ticket.

Elevated Metrorail trains run from downtown Miami north to Hialeah and south along U.S. 1 to Dadeland, daily 5:30 AM–midnight. Trains run every five minutes in peak hours, every 15 minutes at other times. The fare is \$1.25. Transfers, which cost 25¢, must be bought at the first station entered. Parking at train stations costs \$2.

Metromover has two loops that circle downtown Miami, linking major hotels, office buildings, and shopping areas. The system spans 4½ mi, including the 1½-mi Omni Extension, with six stations to the north, and the 1-mi Brickell Extension, with six stations to the south. Quite convenient and amazingly cheap, it beats walking all around downtown. Service runs daily every 90 seconds, 6 AM–midnight. The fare is 25¢. Transfers to Metrorail are \$1.

➤ TRAIN INFORMATION: **Amtrak** (✉ 8303 N.W. 37th Ave., ☎ 305/835–1223 for recorded arrival and departure information; 800/368–8725 for shipping). **Metromover** (☎ 305/770–3131). **Metrorail** (☎ 305/770–3131). **Tri-Rail** (✉ 1 River Plaza, 305 S. Andrews Ave., Suite 200, Fort Lauderdale, ☎ 800/874–7245).

TRANSPORTATION AROUND MIAMI AND MIAMI BEACH

Greater Miami resembles Los Angeles in its urban sprawl and traffic. You'll need a car to visit many attractions and points of interest. Some are accessible via the public transportation system, run by a department of the county government—the Metro-Dade Transit Agency, which consists of 650 Metrobuses on 70 routes, the 21-mi Metrorail elevated rapid-transit system, and the Metromover, an elevated light-rail system. Free maps and schedules are available.

➤ INFORMATION: **Metro-Dade Transit Agency** (✉ Government Center Station, 111 N.W. 1st St., Miami 33128, ☎ 305/654–6586 for Maps by Mail; 305/770–3131 for route information weekdays 6 AM–10 PM and weekends 9–5).

VISITOR INFORMATION

Florida Gold Coast Chamber of Commerce serves the beach communities of Bal Harbour, Bay Harbor Islands, Golden Beach, North Bay Village, Sunny Isles, and Surfside.

➤ TOURIST INFORMATION: **Greater Miami Convention & Visitors Bureau** (✉ 701 Brickell Ave., Suite 2700, Miami 33131, ☎ 305/539–3063 or 800/283–2707). Satellite tourist information centers are at **Bayside Marketplace** (✉ 401 Biscayne Blvd., Miami 33132, ☎ 305/539–2980) and **South Dade Visitor Information Center** (✉ 160 U.S. 1, Florida City 33034, ☎ 305/245–9180 or 800/388–9669, FAX 305/247–4335).

Coconut Grove Chamber of Commerce (✉ 2820 McFarlane Rd., Coconut Grove 33133, ☎ 305/444–7270, FAX 305/444–2498). **Coral Gables Chamber of Commerce** (✉ 50 Aragon Ave., Coral Gables

33134, ☎ 305/446–1657, FAX 305/446–9900). **Florida Gold Coast Chamber of Commerce** (✉ 1100 Kane Concourse, Suite 210, Bay Harbor Islands 33154, ☎ 305/866–6020). **Greater Miami Chamber of Commerce** (✉ 1601 Biscayne Blvd., Miami 33132, ☎ 305/350–7700, FAX 305/374–6902). **Greater North Miami Chamber of Commerce** (✉ 13100 W. Dixie Hwy., North Miami 33181, ☎ 305/891–7811, FAX 305/893–8522). **Greater South Dade/South Miami Chamber of Commerce** (✉ 6410 S.W. 80th St., South Miami 33143-4602, ☎ 305/661–1621, FAX 305/666–0508). **Key Biscayne Chamber of Commerce** (✉ Key Biscayne Bank Bldg., 95 W. McIntyre St., Key Biscayne 33149, ☎ 305/361–5207). **Miami Beach Chamber of Commerce** (✉ 1920 Meridian Ave., Miami Beach 33139, ☎ 305/672–1270, FAX 305/538–4336). **Surfside Tourist Board** (✉ 9301 Collins Ave., Surfside 33154, ☎ 305/864–0722 or 800/327–4557, FAX 305/861–1302).

2 THE EVERGLADES

South Florida's wide, slow-moving "River of Grass"—the largest roadless expanse in the United States—is home to Everglades National Park and spectacular plant and animal life found no place else in the country. Nearby Biscayne National Park protects living coral reefs, mangroves, undeveloped islands, a shallow bay, and all the wild things that come with them. Both areas, within minutes of Miami's metropolis, maintain a fragile balance between humans and nature.

Updated by Diane P. Marshall

THE ONLY METROPOLITAN AREA in the United States with two national parks and a national preserve in its backyard is Miami. Everglades National Park, created in 1947, was meant to preserve the slow-moving "River of Grass"—a freshwater river 50 mi wide but only 6 inches deep, flowing from Lake Okeechobee through marshy grassland into Florida Bay. Along the Tamiami Trail (U.S. 41), marshes of cattails extend as far as the eye can see, interspersed only with hammocks or tree islands of bald cypress and mahogany, while overhead southern bald eagles make circles in the sky. A wide variety of trees and flowers, including ferns, orchids, and bromeliads, shares the brackish waters with otters, turtles, marsh rabbits, and occasionally that gentle giant, the West Indian manatee. Not so gentle, though, is the saw grass. Deceptively graceful, these tall, willowy sedges have small sharp teeth on the edges of their leaves.

Biscayne National Park, established as a national monument in 1968 and 12 years later expanded and designated a national park, is the nation's largest marine park and the largest national park within the continental United States with living coral reefs. A small portion of the park's almost 274 square mi consists of mainland coast and outlying islands, but 96% is under water, much of it in Biscayne Bay. The islands contain lush, heavily wooded forests with an abundance of ferns and native palm trees. Of particular interest are the mangroves and their tangled masses of stiltlike roots and stems that thicken the shorelines. These "walking trees," as locals sometimes call them, have striking curved prop roots, which arch down from the trunk, while aerial roots drop from branches. These trees draw freshwater from saltwater and create a coastal nursery capable of sustaining all types of marine life.

Congress established Big Cypress National Preserve in 1974 after buying up one of the least-developed watershed areas in South Florida to protect the watershed of Everglades National Park. The preserve, located on the northern edge of Everglades National Park, entails extensive tracts of prairie, marsh, pinelands, forested swamps, and sloughs. While preservation and recreation are the preserve's mainstay, hunting, off-road vehicle use, oil and gas exploration, and grazing are allowed.

Unfortunately, Miami's backyard is threatened by suburban sprawl, agriculture, and a new airport. What results is competition among environmental, agricultural, and developmental interests. The biggest issue is water. Originally, alternating floods and dry periods maintained a wildlife habitat and regulated the water flowing into Florida Bay. The brackish seasonal flux sustained a remarkably vigorous bay, including the most productive shrimp beds in American waters, with thriving mangrove thickets and coral reefs at its Atlantic edge. The system nurtured sea life and attracted anglers and divers. Starting in the 1930s, however, a giant flood-control system began diverting water to canals running to the gulf and the ocean. As you travel Florida's north–south routes, you cross this network of canals symbolized by a smiling alligator representing the South Florida Water Management District, ironically known as "Protector of the Everglades" (ironic because most people feel it's done more for the developers than the environment).

The unfortunate side effect of flood control has been devastation of the wilderness. Park visitors decry diminished bird counts (a 90% reduction over 50 years); the black bear has been eliminated; and the Florida panther is nearing extinction. Meanwhile, the loss of freshwater has made Florida Bay saltier, devastating breeding grounds and creating dead zones where pea-green algae has replaced sea grasses and sponges.

Even as the ecosystem fades, new policies, still largely on paper, hold promise. More than a score of government agencies and a host of conservation groups and industries have worked out restoration plans. The future of the natural system will be determined in the next decade.

New and Noteworthy

It's now easy to make a quick side trip from the Everglades to the Florida Keys. The new **Dade-Monroe Express** provides daily bus service from the Florida City Wal-Mart Supercenter to Mile Marker 98 in Key Largo. The bus makes several stops in Florida City, then heads for the islands for daily round-trips on the hour from 6 AM to 9 PM. The cost is $1.25 each way with senior and student discounts. For information, call 305/770–3131.

Pleasures and Pastimes

Biking and Hiking

In the Everglades there are several nice places to ride and hike. The Shark Valley Loop Road (15 mi round-trip) makes a good bike trip. Lists at the visitor centers describe others. Inquire about insect conditions before you go and plan accordingly, stocking up on insect repellent, sunscreen, and water, as necessary.

Boating and Canoeing

One of the best ways to experience the Everglades is by boat, and almost all of Biscayne National Park is accessible only by water. Boat rentals are available in both parks. Rentals are generally for half day (four hours) and full day (eight hours).

In the Everglades the 99-mi inland Wilderness Trail between Flamingo and Everglades City is open to motorboats as well as canoes, although powerboats may have trouble navigating the route above Whitewater Bay. Flat-water canoeing is best in winter, when temperatures are moderate, rainfall is minimal, and mosquitoes are tolerable. You don't need a permit for day trips, but tell someone where you're going and when you expect to return. Getting lost is easy, and spending the night without proper gear can be unpleasant, if not dangerous.

On the Gulf Coast you can explore the nooks, crannies, and mangrove islands of Chokoloskee Bay, as well as many rivers near Everglades City. The Turner River Canoe Trail, a good day trip, passes through mangrove, dwarf cypress, coastal prairie, and freshwater slough ecosystems of Everglades National Park and Big Cypress National Preserve.

Dining

With a few exceptions, dining centers on low-key mom-and-pop places that serve hearty home-style food and small eateries specializing in local fare: seafood, conch, alligator, turtle, and frogs' legs. Native American restaurants add another dimension, serving local favorites as well as catfish, Indian fry bread (a flour-and-water dough), pumpkin bread, Indian burgers (ground beef browned, rolled in fry-bread dough, and deep-fried), and tacos (fry bread with chili, lettuce, tomato, and shredded cheddar cheese on top). Restaurants in Everglades City appear to operate with a "captive audience" philosophy: prices run high, service is mediocre, and food preparation is uninspired. The closest good restaurants are in Naples, 35 mi northwest.

Although both Everglades and Biscayne national parks and Big Cypress National Preserve are wilderness areas, there are restaurants within a short drive. Most are between Miami and Shark Valley along the

Tamiami Trail (U.S. 41), in the Homestead–Florida City area, in Everglades City, and in the Florida Keys along the Overseas Highway (U.S. 1). The only food service in the preserve or in either of the parks is at Flamingo, in the Everglades, but many independent restaurants will pack picnics. You can also find fast-food establishments on the Tamiami Trail east of Krome Avenue and west of Everglades City in Naples, and along U.S. 1 in Homestead–Florida City.

Fishing

Largemouth bass are plentiful in freshwater ponds, while snapper, redfish, and sea trout are caught in Florida Bay. The mangrove shallows of the 10,000 Islands, along the gulf, yield tarpon and snook. Whitewater Bay is also a favorite spot. Note: the state has issued health advisories for sea bass, largemouth bass, and other freshwater fish, especially those caught in the canals along the Tamiami Trail, due to their high mercury content. Signs are posted throughout the park, and consumption should be limited.

Exploring the Everglades

The southern tip of the Florida peninsula is largely taken up by Everglades National Park, but land access to it is primarily by two roads. The main park road traverses the southern Everglades from the gateway towns of Homestead and Florida City to the outpost of Flamingo, on Florida Bay. In the northern Everglades you can take the Tamiami Trail (U.S. 41) from the Greater Miami area in the east to the western park entrance in Everglades City. In far southeastern Florida, Biscayne National Park lies almost completely offshore. As a result, most sports and recreational opportunities in both national parks are based on water, the study of nature, or both, so even on land, be prepared to get a bit damp on the region's marshy trails.

Although relatively compact compared to the national parks of the West, these parks still require a bit of time to see. The narrow, two-lane roads through the Everglades make for long travel, whereas it's the necessity of sightseeing by boat that takes time at Biscayne.

Numbers in the text correspond to numbers in the margin and on the Big Cypress Preserve and The Everglades and Biscayne National Parks map.

Great Itineraries

IF YOU HAVE 1 DAY

You'll have to make a choice—the Everglades, Big Cypress, or Biscayne. If you want interpretive trails and lots of exhibits, go with the Everglades. If you're interested in boating or underwater flora and fauna, Biscayne is your best bet. For quiet, wilderness canoeing, and nature, don't miss Big Cypress. Whichever you choose, you'll experience a little of what's left of the "real" Florida.

For a day in Everglades National Park, begin in **Florida City** ⑭, the southern/western gateway to the park. Head to the **Ernest F. Coe Visitor Center** ① for an overview of the park and its ecosystems, and continue to the **Royal Palm Visitor Center** ② for a look at several unique plant systems. Then go to **Flamingo** ③, where you can rent a boat or take a tour of Florida Bay.

If Biscayne is your preference, begin at **Convoy Point** ⑮ for an orientation before forsaking dry land. Sign up for a snorkel or dive trip or an outing on a glass-bottom boat, kayak, or canoe.

To spend a day in Big Cypress National Preserve, begin at the **Oasis Visitor Center** ⑨ to pick up information about canoe and walking trails and learn about the park's ecosystem. Then head to **Everglades City** ⑫, where you can rent a canoe for a tour of the Turner River.

IF YOU HAVE 3 DAYS

With three days you can explore both the northern and southern Everglades as well as Biscayne National Park. Start in the north by driving west along the Tamiami Trail, stopping at **Everglades Safari Park** ④ for an airboat ride; at **Shark Valley** ⑥ for a tram tour, walk, or bicycle trip; at the **Miccosukee Indian Village** ⑦ for lunch; at the **Big Cypress Gallery** ⑧ to see Clyde Butcher's photographs; and then at the **Ochopee post office** ⑩, before ending in **Everglades City** ⑫, home of Everglades National Park's Gulf Coast Visitor Center. From here you can visit historic Smallwood's Store on Chokoloskee Island and watch the sunset. Day two is for exploring the south. Return east on the Tamiami Trail to **Homestead** ⑬, pausing at Everglades Air Tours to take a sightseeing trip before following the one-day Everglades itinerary above and overnighting in **Florida City** ⑭. Biscayne National Park is the subject of day three. If you plan to scuba or take the glass-bottom boat, get an early start. You can explore the visitor center at **Convoy Point** ⑮ when you return and finish your day checking out sights in Florida City and Homestead. Snorkel trips leave later, giving you time to see Florida City and Homestead, have lunch, and learn about the park's ecosystem at the visitor center first. Be warned that although you can fly and then scuba dive, you can't dive and then fly within 24 hours. So if you're flying out, reverse the days' sequence accordingly.

IF YOU HAVE 5 DAYS

Follow day one above, spending the night in **Everglades City** ⑫. Begin the second day with a canoe, kayak, or boat tour of the 10,000 Islands, then make arrangements to rent a canoe for the next day's trip to Big Cypress National Preserve's Turner River. In the late afternoon take a walk on the half-mile boardwalk at **Fakahatchee Strand Preserve State Park** ⑪ to see rare epiphytic orchids or on a 2½-mi trail at the Big Cypress National Preserve. On day three, drive to the Big Cypress Oasis Visitor Center to put in for the canoe tour. If its December to April, you can join a ranger-led canoe tour. Drive east to Coopertown and take a nighttime ride with Ray Cramer's Everglades Airboat Tours. Spend the night in **Florida City** ⑭. Day four is spent at Biscayne National Park, then sightseeing in **Homestead** ⑬ and **Florida City** ⑭ as suggested above. On day five, augment your picnic lunch with goodies from the remarkable fruit stand Robert Is Here, before heading to the southern portion of Everglades National Park, as described above.

When to Tour the Everglades

Winter is the best time to visit Everglades National Park and Big Cypress National Preserve. Temperatures and mosquito activity are low to moderate, low water levels concentrate the resident wildlife around sloughs that retain water all year, and migratory birds swell the avian population. Winter is also the busiest time in the park. Make reservations and expect crowds at Flamingo, the main visitor center (known officially as the Ernest F. Coe Visitor Center), and Royal Palm.

In spring the weather turns hot and rainy, and tours and facilities are less crowded. Migratory birds depart, and you must look harder to see wildlife. Be careful with campfires and matches; this is when the wildfire-prone saw-grass prairies and pinelands are most vulnerable.

Summer brings intense sun and billowing clouds unleashing torrents of rain almost every afternoon. Start your outdoor activities early to avoid the rain and the sun's strongest rays, and use sunscreen. Water levels rise and wildlife disperses. Mosquitoes hatch, swarm, and descend on you in voracious clouds. (Carrying mosquito repellent is a good idea at any time of year, but it's a necessity in summer.) Europeans constitute 80% of the summer visitors.

Even if you're not lodging in Everglades National Park, try to stay until dusk, when dozens of bird species feed around the ponds and trails. While shining a flashlight over the water in marshy areas, look for two yellowish-red reflections above the surface—telltale alligator signs.

EVERGLADES NATIONAL PARK

11 mi southwest of Homestead, 45 mi southwest of Miami International Airport.

The best way to experience the real Everglades is to get your feet wet either by taking a walk in the muck, affectionately called a "slough slog," or by paddling a canoe into the River of Grass to stay in a backcountry campsite. Most visitors won't do that, however. Luckily, there are several ways to see the wonders of the park with dry feet. Take a boat tour in Everglades City or Flamingo, ride the tram at Shark Valley, or walk the boardwalks along the main park road. And there's more to see than natural beauty. Miccosukee Indians operate a range of attractions and restaurants worthy of a stop.

Admission to Everglades National Park is valid at all entrances for seven days. Coverage below begins in the southern Everglades, followed by the northern Everglades, starting in the east and ending in Everglades City.

The Main Park Road

The main park road (Route 9336) travels from the main visitor center to Flamingo, across a section of the park's eight distinct ecosystems: hardwood hammock, freshwater prairie, pinelands, freshwater slough, cypress, coastal prairie, mangrove, and marine-estuarine. Highlights of the trip include a dwarf cypress forest, the ecotone (transition zone) between saw grass and mangrove forest, and a wealth of wading birds at Mrazek and Coot Bay ponds. Boardwalks, looped trails, several short spurs, and observation platforms allow you to stay dry.

★ ❶ The **Ernest F. Coe Visitor Center,** at park headquarters, houses numerous interactive exhibits and films. Stand in a simulated blind and peer through a spyglass to watch birds in the wild; although it's actually a film, the quality is so good you'll think you're outside. Move on to a bank of telephones to hear differing viewpoints on the Great Water Debate. There's a 15-minute film on the park, two movies on hurricanes, and a 45-minute wildlife film for children. Computer monitors present a schedule of daily ranger-led activities park-wide as well as information on canoe rentals and boat tours. In the Everglades Discovery Shop you can browse through lots of neat nature, science, and kids' stuff and pick up the insect repellent you forgot. The center provides information on the entire park. ✉ *11 mi southwest of Homestead on Rte. 9336,* ☎ *305/242–7700.* 🎫 *Park $10 per car, $5 per pedestrian or bicyclist, $5 per motorcycle.* ⏲ *Daily 8–5.*

❷ The **Royal Palm Visitor Center** is a must for anyone who wants to experience the real Everglades. You can stroll along the Anhinga Trail boardwalk or follow the Gumbo Limbo Trail through a hardwood hammock. The visitor center has an interpretive display, a bookstore, and vending machines. ✉ *4 mi west of Ernest F. Coe Visitor Center on Rte. 9336,* ☎ *305/242–7700.* ⏲ *Daily 8–5.*

Big Cypress National Preserve and The Everglades and Biscayne National Parks

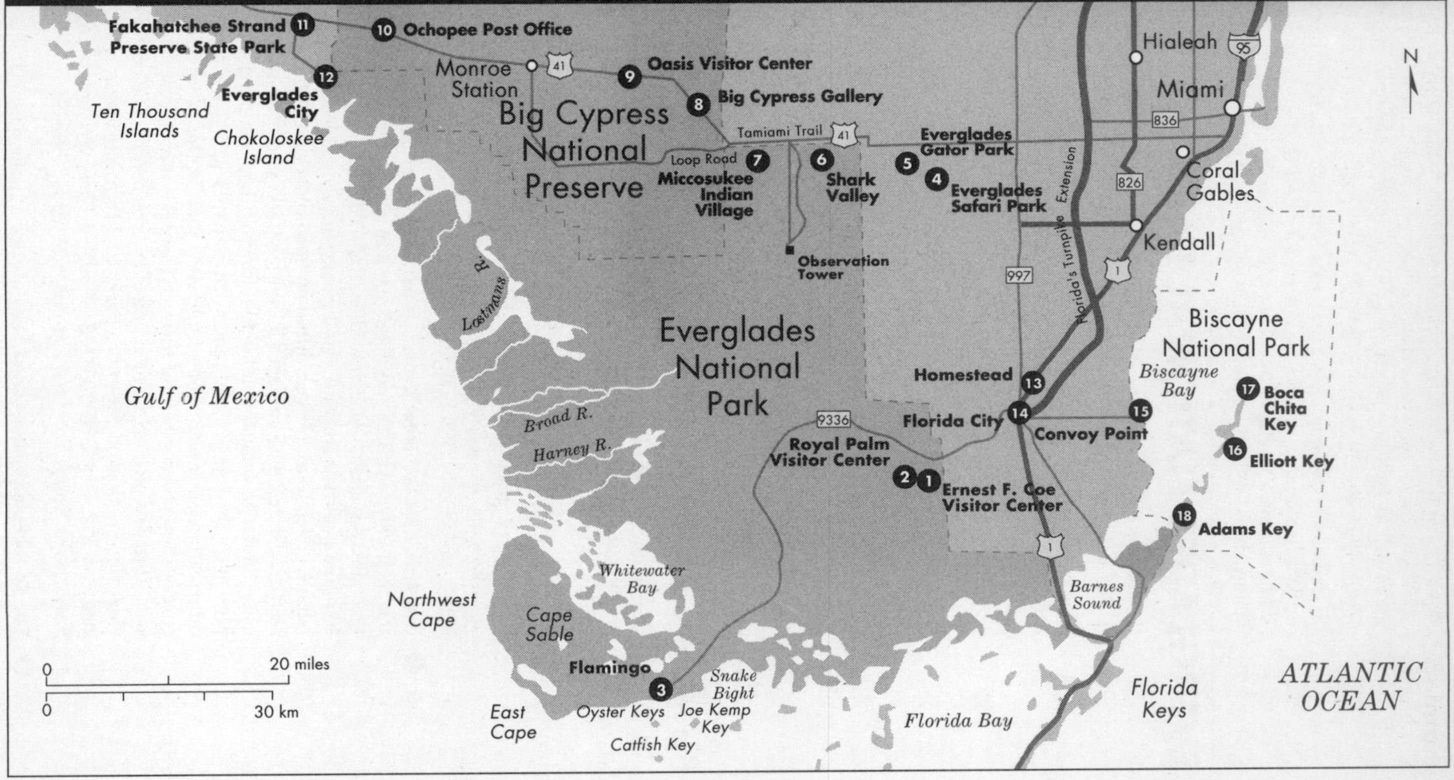

Flamingo

❸ *38 mi southwest of Ernest F. Coe Visitor Center.*

Here at the far end of the main road, you'll find a cluster of buildings where a former town of the same name was established in 1893. Today, it contains a visitor center, lodge, restaurant and lounge, gift shop, marina, and bicycle rentals, plus an adjacent campground. Tour boats narrated by interpretive guides, fishing expeditions of Florida Bay, and canoe and kayak trips all leave from here. Nearby is Eco Pond, one of the most popular wildlife observation areas.

The **Flamingo Visitor Center** provides an interactive display and has natural-history exhibits in the Florida Bay Museum. Check the schedule for ranger-led activities, such as naturalist discussions, evening programs in the campground amphitheater, and hikes along area trails. ☎ *941/695–2945.* ⏲ *Dec.–Apr., daily 7:30–5; May–Nov., hrs vary.*

Dining and Lodging

$$–$$$ ✕ **Flamingo Restaurant.** The grand view, convivial lounge, and casual style are all great reasons to visit here. Big picture windows on the visitor center's second floor overlook Florida Bay, revealing soaring eagles, gulls, pelicans, terns, and vultures. Dine at low tide to see birds flock to the sandbar just offshore. The restaurant recently upgraded its menu with the addition of more seafood and an array of local dishes such as coconut fried shrimp and chicken breast with a mango salsa. The restaurant is only open from November to April. Downstairs, the Buttonwood Patio Cafe is open year-round except November to mid-December for pizza, sandwiches, and salads. ✉ *Flamingo Lodge, 1 Flamingo Lodge Hwy.,* ☎ *941/695–3101. AE, D, DC, MC, V. Closed May–Oct.*

$$ 🏨 **Flamingo Lodge, Marina & Outpost Resort.** This simple low-rise motel is the only lodging inside the park. Accommodations are basic but well kept, and an amiable staff helps you adjust to bellowing alligators, roaming raccoons, and ibis grazing on the lawn. Rooms have contemporary furniture, floral bedspreads, and art prints of bird life. Although they face Florida Bay, they don't necessarily look out over it. Bathrooms are small. Cottages, in a wooded area on the margin of a coastal prairie, have kitchenettes (no TVs) and accommodate up to six people. Reservations are essential in winter; Continental breakfast is included from May to October. Some facilities, like the restaurant, are seasonal. ✉ *1 Flamingo Lodge Hwy., 33034,* ☎ *941/695–3101 or 800/600–3813,* FAX *941/695–3921.,* WEB *www.flamingolodge.com 102 rooms, 24 cottages, 1 suite. Restaurant, bar, snack bar, pool, coin laundry. AE, D, DC, MC, V.*

$ ⛺ **Everglades National Park.** Three developed campgrounds and group campsites have drinking water, sewage dump station, and rest rooms. Some also have picnic tables, grills, cold-water showers, and tent and trailer pads. Long Pine Key has 108 drive-up sites; Flamingo has 234 drive-up sites, 64 walk-in sites, 20 on the water, and cold showers; and Chekika, which was closed at press time following hurricane damage, has 20 sites, warm showers, and a sulfur spring where you can swim, although it's not advised. Pets are welcome in the park, but definitely should not be allowed to swim in areas where there are alligators. From late November through April, sites at Long Pine Key and Flamingo are available through a reservation system, but the rest of the year all sites are first-come, first-served. In addition, deep in the park are 48 backcountry sites, many inland with some on the beach. Three are accessible by land, the others by canoe; 16 have *chickees* (raised wooden platforms with thatched roofs). Most have chemical toilets. Several are within an easy day's canoeing of Flamingo; five are near Everglades City.

You'll need to carry your food, water, and supplies in; carry out all trash. You'll also need a site-specific permit, available on a first-come, first-served basis from the Flamingo or Gulf Coast Visitor Center. Developed sites are free June–August and $14 per night the rest of the year. Groups pay $28, and backcountry sites cost $10 or more depending on group size. ☎ *305/242–7700; 305/251–0371; 800/365–2267 for campsite reservations. 471 sites. Picnic area. D, MC, V.*

Outdoor Activities and Sports

BIKING

Flamingo Lodge, Marina & Outpost Resort (☎ 941/695–3101) rents bikes for $14 a day, $8 per half day, $3 per hour.

BOATING

The marina at **Flamingo Lodge, Marina & Outpost Resort** (☎ 941/695–3101) rents power skiffs for $90 per day, $65 per half day, and $22 per hour; four Carolina skiffs for $155 per day and $100 per half day; as well as fully furnished and outfitted houseboats that sleep up to eight. From November to April, rates (two-day minimum) run $475 without air-conditioning for two days, $575 with air-conditioning for two days. Off-season (summer) rates are lower. Several private boats are also available for charter. There are two ramps, one for Florida Bay, the other for Whitewater Bay and the backcountry. The hoist across the plug dam separating Florida Bay from the Buttonwood Canal can take boats from 16 ft to 26 ft long. A small store sells food, camping supplies, bait and tackle, propane, and fuel. A concessionaire rents rods, reels, binoculars, and coolers by the half and full day.

CANOEING AND KAYAKING

The Everglades has six well-marked canoe trails in the Flamingo area, including the south end of the 99-mi Wilderness Trail from Everglades City to Flamingo. **Flamingo Lodge, Marina & Outpost Resort** (☎ 941/695–3101) rents canoes in two sizes: small (up to two paddlers) and family size (up to four). Small canoes rent for $32 per day, $22 per half day, and $8 per hour; family-size run $40, $30, and $12, respectively. Single-person kayaks cost $43 per day, $27 per half day, and $11 per hour; doubles rent for $54, $38, and $16, respectively.

FISHING

Flamingo Lodge, Marina & Outpost Resort (☎ 941/695–3101) helps arrange charter fishing trips for two to four persons. The cost is $300 a day for up to two people, $25 each additional person.

Tamiami Trail

141 mi from Miami to Fort Myers.

In 1915, when officials decided to build an east–west highway linking Miami to Fort Myers and continuing north to Tampa, someone suggested calling it the Tamiami Trail. In 1928 the road became a reality, cutting through the Everglades and altering the natural flow of water and the lives of the Miccosukee Indians who eked out a living fishing, hunting, and frogging here.

Today the highway's traffic screams through Everglades National Park, Big Cypress National Preserve, and Fakahatchee Strand Preserve State Park. The landscape is surprisingly varied, changing from hardwood hammocks to pinelands, then abruptly to tall cypress trees dripping with Spanish moss and back to coastal prairie. Those who slow down to take in the scenery are rewarded with glimpses of alligators sunning themselves along the banks of roadside canals and in the shallow waters, and hundreds of waterbirds, especially in the dry winter season.

The man-made landscape features chickee huts, Native American villages, and airboats parked at roadside enterprises.

Businesses along the trail give their addresses either based on their distance from Krome Avenue, Florida's Turnpike, and Miami on the east coast or Fort Myers and Naples on the west coast or by mile marker. Between Miami and Fort Myers, the road goes by several names, including Tamiami Trail, U.S. 41, and, at the Miami end, Southwest 8th Street.

❹ A perennial favorite with tour bus operators, **Everglades Safari Park** has an arena that seats up to 300 people to watch an educational alligator show and wrestling demonstration. Before and after the show, you can get a closer look at the alligators, walk through a small wildlife museum, or climb aboard an airboat for a 30-minute ride through the River of Grass (included in admission). There's also a restaurant, a gift shop, and an observation platform that looks out over the Glades. ⊠ *26700 Tamiami Trail, 9 mi west of Krome Ave.,* ☎ *305/226–6923 or 305/223–3804.* 🎫 *$15.* ⏲ *Daily 8:30–5.*

❺ After visiting **Everglades Gator Park,** you can tell your friends you came face-to-face with—and even touched—an alligator, albeit a baby one. Then you can squirm in a "reptilium" of venomous and nonpoisonous native snakes or learn about Native Americans of the Everglades through a reproduction of a Miccosukee village. The park also has wildlife shows with native and exotic animals, 45-minute airboat tours, fishing charters, and RV campsites, as well as a gift shop and restaurant. ⊠ *24050 Tamiami Trail, 12 mi west of Florida's Tpk.,* ☎ *305/559–2255 or 800/559–2205.* 🎫 *Free, tours $14.* ⏲ *Daily 9–sunset.*

❻ It takes a bit of nerve to walk the paved 15-mi loop at **Shark Valley** because alligators lie on the road and alongside it, basking in the sun—most, however, do move quickly out of the way. Less fearless, or energetic, types can ride a bicycle or take a tram tour. Stop at the halfway point to climb the concrete observation tower's ramp, which spirals skyward 50 ft. From there everything as far as the eye can see is the vast River of Grass. Observe all kinds of waterbirds as well as alligators at water holes. Just behind the bike-rental area, a short boardwalk trail meanders through the saw grass. A small visitor center features rotating exhibits, a bookstore, and park rangers ready to answer questions. Shark Valley is the national park's north entrance; however, no roads here lead to other parts of the park. ⊠ *23.5 mi west of Florida's Tpk.,* ☎ *305/221–8776.* 🎫 *Park $8 per car; $4 per pedestrian, bicyclist, or motorcyclist.* ⏲ *Visitor center daily 8:30–5:30.*

❼ For more than 25 years, the cultural center at the **Miccosukee Indian Village** has showcased Miccosukee foods, crafts, skills, and lifestyle. It also presents educational alligator shows and crafts demonstrations. Narrated 30-minute airboat rides take visitors into the heart of the wilderness in which these Native Americans escaped after the Third Seminole War and Indian Removal Act during the mid-1800s. There's also a restaurant and gift shop. The Everglades Music & Craft Festival falls on a July weekend, and the weeklong Indian Arts Festival is in late December. ⊠ *West of Shark Valley entrance, 25 mi west of Florida's Tpk.,* ☎ *305/223–8380.* 🎫 *$5, rides $10.* ⏲ *Daily 9–5.*

Clyde Butcher does for the River of Grass and Big Cypress Swamp what Ansel Adams did for the West, and you can check out his stunning photographs at his ❽ **Big Cypress Gallery,** in the Big Cypress National Preserve. Working with large-format black-and-white film, Butcher captures every blade of grass, barb of feather, and flicker of light. Special exhibits, lectures, tours, photo expeditions, and slide presentations are given throughout the year. Rangers from the preserve lead special swamp walks for the gallery in the winter. ✉ *52388 Tamiami Trail, 37 mi west of Miami, 45 mi east of Naples,* ☎ *941/695–2428.* 🎫 *Free, $20 suggested donation for Big Cypress Preserve Boardwalk Fund on Labor Day weekend.* ⏲ *Wed.–Sat. 10–5.*

10 The tiny **Ochopee Post Office** is the smallest post office in North America. Buy a picture postcard of the little one-room shack and mail it to a friend, thereby helping to keep this picturesque spot in business. ✉ *75 mi west of Miami, Ochopee,* ☎ *941/695–4131.* ⏲ *Weekdays 9:30–noon and 12:30–4, Sat. 9:30–11:30.*

11 The ½-mi boardwalk at the **Fakahatchee Strand Preserve State Park** affords an opportunity to see rare plants, bald cypress, and North America's largest stand of native royal palms and largest concentration and variety of epiphytic orchids. From November to April the park's rookery, accessed down a short road 2 mi east of the boardwalk, is a birder's paradise beginning an hour before sunset. The sight of 5,000 to 7,000 wading birds returning to roost for the night is spectacular. You can launch a kayak or watch from the shore. ✉ *Boardwalk on north side of Tamiami Trail 7 mi west of Rte. 29; rookery on south side of Tamiami Trail 5 mi west of Rte. 29; ranger station ¾ mi north of Tamiami Trail on Rte. 29, Box 548, Copeland 34137,* ☎ *941/695–4593,* WEB *www.dep.state.fl.us/parks* 🎫 *Free.* ⏲ *Daily 8–sunset.*

Dining and Lodging

$$ ★ ✕ **Joanie's Blue Crab Café.** Movie set designers could not have designed a more quintessential 1950s-style swamp café and country store than this landmark restaurant diagonally across from the Ochopee post office. The decor consists of wood-plank floors, open rafters hung with cobwebs, stuffed owls, postcards from around the globe, and kitschy gator art. Joanie, the chief cook and bottle washer, came here in 1987. The staff picks fresh blue crabs—up to 372 pounds in a weekend—that they catch each day to go into sandwiches and soups. Although the steamed crabs and crab sandwich served on a kaiser roll are the stars, the fresh sautéed vegetables—not always on the menu, but ask anyway—are delicious, too. Chill out with a draft beer or glass of wine on the screened deck. ✉ *39395 Tamiami Trail, 50 mi west of Florida's Tpk., Ochopee,* ☎ *941/695–2682. D, MC, V.*

$–$$ ✕ **Coopertown Restaurant.** For more than a half century this rustic eatery just into the Everglades west of Miami has been full of Old Florida style—not to mention alligator skulls, stuffed alligator heads, and gator accessories. House specialties are frogs' legs and alligator tail prepared breaded or deep-fried, and they're available for breakfast, lunch, or dinner. You can also order more conventional selections, such as catfish, shrimp, or sandwiches. ✉ *22700 S.W. 8th St., Miami,* ☎ *305/226–6048. MC, V.*

$–$$ ✕ **Miccosukee Restaurant.** Murals depict Native American women cooking and men engaged in a powwow in this Native American restaurant at the Miccosukee Indian Village. Favorites are catfish and frogs' legs breaded and deep-fried, Indian fry bread, pumpkin bread, and Indian burgers and tacos. Breakfast is served daily. ✉ *25 mi west of Florida's Tpk.,* ☎ *305/223–8380 ext. 2374. MC, V.*

$–$$ ✕ **Pit Bar-B-Q.** On a day with a breeze, you can smell this rustic roadside eatery's barbecue and blackjack-oak smoke long before you can see it. Order at the counter, pick up your food when called, and eat at one of the indoor or outdoor picnic tables. Specialties include barbecued chicken and ribs with a tangy sauce, french fries, coleslaw, and a fried biscuit as well as catfish and frogs' legs deep-fried in vegetable oil. ✉ *16400 Tamiami Trail, Miami,* ☎ *305/226–2272. AE, D, MC, V.*

$$–$$$ **Miccosukee Resort & Convention Center.** Every few months big-name entertainers like Bill Cosby and Julio Iglesias and nationally televised boxing matches draw big crowds to this resort at the crossroads of Tamiami Trail and Krome Avenue. Like an oasis on the horizon, it's the only facility for miles and it's been situated to attract the attention of visitors going to the Everglades or Big Cypress, driving across the state, or looking for casino action. Most units have a view of Everglades saw grass and wildlife. However, a pool, an 8,500-square-ft kids' play area, a teen video center, a gaming complex, tours to Everglades National Park and the Miccosukee Indian Village, shops, live entertainment, places to eat, and shuttles to area malls are enough to distract guests from staring out the window. ✉ *500 S.W. 177th Ave., Miami 33194,* ☎ *305/925–2555 or 877/242–6464. 256 rooms, 46 suites. 3 restaurants, deli, indoor pool, hair salon, sauna, spa, exercise room, casino, nightclub, video games, nursery, convention center, meeting room, travel services, airport shuttle. AE, D, DC, MC, V.*

$ **Everglades Gator Park.** Popular with the RV set, the park has full hookups for as many as 80 vehicles, in addition to airboats, Everglades attractions, and a small store. You can rent a campsite by the night ($25), week ($100), or month ($350), or store your RV in the short-term area. ✉ *24050 S.W. 8th St., Miami,* ☎ *305/559–2255 or 800/559–2205, (13800 S.W. 8th St., Box 107, Miami, FL. 33184). 80 sites. Restaurant, lake, fishing. AE, D, MC, V.*

Outdoor Activities and Sports

Shark Valley Tram Tours (✉ Shark Valley, ☎ 305/221–8455) rents bikes daily 8:30–4 (last rental at 3) for $4.50 per hour.

Shopping

The shopping alone should lure you to the **Miccosukee Indian Village** (25 mi west of Florida's Tpk., just west of Shark Valley entrance, ☎ 305/223–8380). Wares include well-made Native American crafts including beadwork, moccasins, dolls, pottery, baskets, and patchwork fabric and clothes. There are also some fun, kitschy Florida souvenirs.

Everglades City

12 *35 mi southeast of Naples, 83 mi west of Miami.*

Ignore the Circle K and BNP gas stations on the main road into town, and the setting is perfect Old Florida. No high-rises mar the landscape at this western gateway to Everglades National Park, just off the Tamiami Trail. It was developed in the late 19th century by Barron Collier, a wealthy advertising man. When Collier built a company town to house workers for his numerous projects, including construction of the Tamiami Trail, the town grew and prospered until the Depression and World War II, and in 1953 it changed its name to Everglades City. Today it draws visitors to the park for canoeing, fishing, and bird-watching excursions. (Airboat tours, though popular with visitors, are banned within the preserve and park because of the environmental damage they cause to the mangroves. They are not recommended even outside the park in this area because operators feed wildlife dog biscuits and marshmallows to attract the alligators to the boats.) The annual Seafood Festival, held the first weekend of February, attracts 60,000–75,000 visitors to eat seafood, hear nonstop music, and buy crafts.

Dining choices are limited to a few basic eateries. For fine food drive west to Naples. In the past year, several dockside fish markets opened small restaurants inside and outside along the docks. It's best to avoid most of these due to poor food-handling practices.

There's no better place to find information about the park's watery western side than the **Gulf Coast Visitor Center.** Except during the off-season, it's filled with canoeists checking in for trips to the 10,000 Islands and 99-mi Wilderness Waterway Trail, visitors viewing interpretive exhibits about local flora and fauna while they wait for the departure of a naturalist-led boat trip, rangers answering questions, and back-country campers purchasing permits. There are no roads from here to other sections of the park. ✉ *Rte. 29,* ☎ *941/695–3311.* 🎫 *Park free.* ⏲ *Mid-Nov.–mid-Apr. daily 7:30–5; mid-Apr.–mid.-Nov 8:30–4:30.*

Through artifacts and photographs, you can meet the Native Americans, pioneers, businessmen, and fishermen who played a role in the development of southwest Florida at the **Museum of the Everglades,** which chronicles the 2,000-year history of human habitation in the southwestern Everglades. It's housed in the only remaining unaltered structure original to the town of Everglades, where it opened in 1927 as the town's laundry. In addition to the permanent displays, there are traveling exhibits, lectures, and works by local artists. ✉ *105 W. Broadway,* ☎ *941/695–0008.* 🎫 *$2.* ⏲ *Tues.–Sat. 11–4.*

OFF THE BEATEN PATH

SMALLWOOD'S STORE – Ted Smallwood pioneered this last American frontier in 1906 and built a 3,000-square-ft pine trading post raised on pilings in Chokoloskee Bay. Smallwood's granddaughter Lynn McMillin reopened it in 1989, after it had been closed several years, and installed a small gift shop and museum chock-full of original goods from the store; historic photographs; Indian clothing, furs, and hides; and area memorabilia. In March a festival celebrates the nearly 100-year relationship the store has had with local Native Americans. ✉ *360 Mamie St., Chokoloskee Island,* ☎ *941/695–2989.* 🎫 *$2.50.* ⏲ *Dec.–Apr., daily 10–5; May–Nov., daily 11–5.*

Dining and Lodging

$$–$$$ ✕ **Rod and Gun Club.** The striking polished woodwork in this historic building dates from the 1920s, when wealthy hunters, anglers, and yachting parties from all over the world came for the winter season. The main dining room primarily holds the overflow from the popular enormous screened porch that overlooks the river. Slow service is a problem; the quality of food is not. Fresh seafood dominates a menu that features stone crab claws in season, a turf-and-surf combo of steak and shrimp, a swamp-and-turf combo of frogs' legs and steak, and several seafood and pasta pairings. Dockage and ample parking allow you to come by boat or land. ✉ *200 Riverside Dr.,* ☎ *941/695–2101. No credit cards.*

$$ ✕ **Everglades Seafood Depot.** This 1928 Spanish-style stucco structure on Lake Placid has had many lives. It began as the old Everglades depot, was part of the University of Miami, appeared in the film *Winds Across the Everglades,* and has housed several restaurants. Today veteran restaurateur Billy Potter serves up well-prepared seafood—from shrimp and grouper to frogs' legs and alligator—any way you like it. The staff is slow, but eager to please. For big appetites there are generously portioned entrées of prime rib, New York steak, and fish specials that include soup or salad, potato or rice, and warm, fresh-baked biscuits. If you're not very hungry, choose the smaller "lunch-able appetites" portions. After dinner you can shoot pool in the bar. ✉ *102 Collier Ave.,* ☎ *941/695–0075. AE, D, MC, V.*

$$ ✕ **Oar House Restaurant.** Locals line up outside on Friday nights for $12.95 prime rib in this wood-paneled eatery whose picnic table–style booths and mishmash of kitschy fishing and Glades decor give it the ambience of a diner. The menu offers a blend of simple seafood and such local specialties as frogs' legs, turtle, conch, and gator. To its credit,

the service is friendly, prices are very reasonable, the food is fried in canola and corn oils, and most dishes can be grilled or broiled, if you prefer. It's popular for country-style breakfasts. ✉ *305 Collier Ave.,* ☎ *941/695–3535. AE, D, MC, V.*

$–$$ ✕ **Everglades Fish Company.** Every day during stone crab season (October–May) locals, and a growing number of visitors, stop by this fish market to buy the fresh, succulent claws. Pick up a hammer for an extra dollar and take them to the nearby city park for a picnic. There's no debate that these are the best in town. They also ship, but the cost is outrageous. It's much more affordable to have them pack some in a travel cooler to take home. When crab season is over, raw fish and raw and cooked shrimp are for sale. ✉ *208 Camellia St.,* ☎ *941/695–3241 or 888/695–2208. MC, V.*

$–$$ **Ivey House.** After half a dozen years of planning and fighting city hall, the Ivey House has finally built its new inn. The original structure, a remodeled 1928 boardinghouse for workers building the Tamiami Trail, remains a clean, friendly bed-and-breakfast bargain with shared baths. The new inn, connected by a ramp, features 17 well-priced air-conditioned rooms, each with a private bath, small refrigerator, TV, phone, and two queen beds. Most rooms surround the screen-enclosed small heated pool and landscaped courtyard. Many of the guests stay here before and after canoe and kayak trips and tours. The layout is designed to promote camaraderie, but there are several secluded patios with chairs and tables for private moments. An open-beam vaulted ceiling covers the gift shop, adventure tour desk, and spacious kitchen and dining room. There also are outside tables in screened areas for dining alfresco. The Ivey House is run by the folks who operate Everglades Rentals & Eco Adventures (formerly North American Canoe Tours), so guests save 10% on canoe, kayak, and powerboat rentals. ✉ *107 Camellia St., 34139,* ☎ *941/695–3299,* FAX *941/695–4155,* WEB *www.iveyhouse.com. 27 rooms, 17 with bath, 1 two-bedroom cottage. Restaurant, refrigerators, pool, bicycles, library, coin laundry. MC, V.*

$–$$ **On the Banks of the Everglades.** Patty Flick Richards and her father drew upon the building's former use as a bank built in 1923 to develop this pleasant bed-and-breakfast lodge. Spacious rooms, suites, and efficiencies have queen- or king-size beds and stylish coordinating linens, wall coverings, and draperies. Suites and efficiencies have private baths and kitchens (the staff does the dishes). A complimentary full breakfast with freshly baked breads and muffins is served in the bank's vault and outside deck. There is no smoking. Free use of bikes lets guests scoot around town and tennis rackets are provided for use on the public courts next door. ✉ *201 W. Broadway, Box 570, 34139,* ☎ *941/695–3151 or 888/431–1977,* FAX *941/695–3335,* WEB *www.banksoftheeverglades.com. 10 units, 5 with bath. Breakfast room, bicycles. AE, D, MC, V. Closed Dec. 23–25.*

$ **Outdoor Resorts.** This clean, amenity-rich RV resort, located on the water's edge of secluded Chokoloskee Island, has sunny, full-service sites with concrete pads and patios. Tropical flowers, shrubs, and palm trees add shade and color. All sites have a view and about a third of them are along the shore; half have dockage. Retirees escape the icy northern winters for outdoor fun here with boat rentals, tennis and shuffleboard, a marina and bait and tackle shop, swimming pools, and fishing guide service. A recreation hall and a health spa with saunas and exercise equipment help while the hours away on rainy days. There's a motel with two double-bed efficiency rooms for those who come without an RV. ✉ *Rte. 29, 6 mi south of Tamiami Trail, Box 429, Chokoloskee Island, 34138,* ☎ *941/695–3788. 283 sites. Restaurant, 3 pools, hot tub, sauna, tennis court, exercise room, shuffleboard, dock, boating, marina, fishing, recreation room, coin laundry. MC, V.*

Outdoor Activities and Sports

BIKING

Everglades Rentals & Eco Adventures (✉ Ivey House, 107 Camellia St., ☎ 941/695–4666), formerly North American Canoe Tours, rents bikes for $3 per hour, $15 per day (free for Ivey House guests).

BOATING

Everglades Rentals & Eco Adventures (✉ Ivey House, 107 Camellia St., ☎ 941/695–4666) rents 16-ft motorized skiffs with a 25-horsepower outboard, cooler, map, anchor, and safety equipment for $70 for a half day, $110 for a full day.

CANOEING AND KAYAKING

Everglades National Park Boat Tours (✉ Gulf Coast Visitor Center, ☎ 941/695–2591; 800/445–7724 in FL) rents 17-ft Grumman canoes for day and overnight use. Rates are $20 per day. Car shuttle service is provided for canoeists paddling the Wilderness Trail, and travelers with disabilities can be accommodated. **Everglades Rentals & Eco Adventures** (✉ Ivey House, 107 Camellia St., ☎ 941/695–4666) is an established source for canoes, sea kayaks, and guided Everglades trips (November–April). Canoes cost from $25 the first day, $20 for each day thereafter, and kayaks are from $35 per day. Half-day rentals are available. Car shuttles for canoeists paddling the Wilderness Trail are $135 with their canoe rental or $170 if you're using your own, plus the $10 park entrance fee. Shuttles are also available for put-ins along the Tamiami Trail.

GATEWAY TOWNS

The farm towns of Homestead and Florida City, flanked by Everglades National Park on the west and Biscayne National Park to the east, provide the closest visitor facilities to the parks. (The area's better restaurants are in Homestead, but the best lodgings are in Florida City.) The towns date from early in the 20th century, when Henry Flagler extended his railroad to Key West but soon decided that farming would do more for rail revenues than ferrying passengers.

Homestead

⓭ *30 mi southwest of Miami.*

When Hurricane Andrew tore across South Florida with winds approaching 200 mph, it ripped apart lives and the small community of Homestead. The city rebuilt itself, redefining its role as the "Gateway to the Keys" and attracting hotel chains, a shopping center, sports complex, and residential development. The historic downtown area has become a preservation-driven Main Street city. Krome Avenue (Route 997), which cuts through the city's heart, is lined with restaurants and antiques shops.

West of north–south Krome Avenue, miles of fields grow fresh fruits and vegetables. Some are harvested commercially. Others have U-PICK signs, inviting visitors to harvest their own. Stands that sell farm-fresh produce and nurseries that grow and sell orchids and tropical plants abound.

In addition to its agricultural legacy, the town has an eclectic flavor, attributable to its population mix: descendants of pioneer Crackers, Hispanic growers, and farmworkers as well as latter-day northern retirees. Until Hurricane Andrew, the military had a huge presence at Homestead Air Force Base. The economy still suffers from its loss.

With a saltwater atoll pool that's flushed by tidal action, **Homestead Bayfront Park,** adjacent to Biscayne National Park, is popular among local families as well as anglers and boaters. Highlights include a playground, ramps for people with disabilities (including a ramp that leads into the swimming area), and a picnic pavilion with grills, showers, and rest rooms. ✉ *9698 S.W. 328th St.,* ☎ *305/230–3034.* *$4 per passenger vehicle, $8 per vehicle with boat, $8 per RV.* ⏲ *Sunrise–sunset.*

Dining

$–$$ ★ ✕ **El Toro Taco.** This family-run area institution features a rustic atmosphere, good Mexican food in generous servings, homemade tortilla chips (sometimes a little greasy), and friendly service. Selections range from tasty favorites like beef or chicken fajitas, enchiladas, tamales, burritos, and tacos to more traditional Mexican dishes like *mole de pollo,* which combines cooking chocolate and spices with chicken. Desserts include *tres leches* (a cake soaked in a syrup of three types of milk—evaporated, sweetened condensed, and heavy cream) and flan. You can order spicing from mild to tongue-challenging. The restaurant is also open for breakfast. ✉ *1 S. Krome Ave.,* ☎ *305/245–8182. D, MC, V. BYOB.*

$ ✕ **Tiffany's.** What looks like a converted pioneer house with a high-pitched roof and lattice under a big banyan tree is in reality a cluster of shops and this casual restaurant. The decor is frilly nouveau Victorian, with teaberry-color tablecloths and floral place mats, and the atmosphere is quaint but noisy. Entrées include hot crabmeat au gratin and asparagus rolled in ham with hollandaise sauce. Among the homemade desserts, choose from a very tall carrot cake, strawberry whipped-cream cake, and a harvest pie that has layers of apples, cranberries, walnuts, raisins, and a caramel topping. Sunday brunch is served, too. ✉ 22 *N.E. 15th St.,* ☎ *305/246–0022. MC, V. Closed Mon. No dinner.*

Outdoor Activities and Sports

AUTO RACING

The **Miami-Dade Homestead Motorsports Complex** (✉ 1 Speedway Blvd., 33035, ☎ 305/230–7223) is a state-of-the-art facility with two tracks: a 2.21-mi continuous road course and a 1½-mi oval. There's a schedule of year-round manufacturer and race-team testing, club racing, and other national events.

BOATING

Boaters give high ratings to the facilities at **Homestead Bayfront Park.** The 174-slip marina has a ramp, dock, bait-and-tackle shop, fuel station, ice, dry storage, and boat hoist, which can handle vessels up to 25 ft long with lifting rings. The park also has a tidal swimming area. ✉ *9698 S.W. 328th St.,* ☎ *305/230–3033.* *$4 per passenger vehicle, $8 per vehicle with boat, $8 per RV, $10 hoist.* ⏲ *Sunrise–sunset.*

Shopping

In addition to Homestead Boulevard (U.S. 1) and Campbell Drive (Southwest 312th Street and Northeast 8th Street), **Krome Avenue** is popular for shopping. In the heart of old Homestead, it has a brick sidewalk and many antiques stores.

Florida City

⓮ *2 mi southwest of Homestead.*

Florida's Turnpike ends in this southernmost town on the peninsula, spilling thousands onto U.S. 1 and eventually west to Everglades National Park, east to Biscayne National Park, or south to the Florida Keys. As the last civilization before 18 mi of mangroves and water, this stretch of U.S. 1 is lined with fast-food eateries, service stations, hotels, bars, dive shops, and restaurants.

Like Homestead, Florida City has roots planted in agriculture, as shown by the hundreds of acres of farmland west of Krome Avenue and a huge farmers' market that processes produce to be shipped around the country.

Dining and Lodging

$$–$$$ ✕ **Mutineer Restaurant.** Former Sheraton Hotels builder Allan Bennett created this roadside steak and seafood restaurant with an indoor-outdoor fish and duck pond in 1980, back when Florida City was barely on the map. Etched glass divides the bi-level dining rooms, where striped-velvet chairs, stained glass, and a few portholes set the scene; in the lounge are an aquarium and nautical antiques. The big menu offers 18 seafood entrées plus another half dozen daily seafood specials, as well as game, ribs, and steaks. There's live music Friday and Saturday evenings. ✉ *11 S.E. 1st Ave. (U.S. 1 and Palm Dr.),* ☎ *305/245–3377. AE, D, DC, MC, V.*

$$ ★ ✕ **Richard Accursio's Capri Restaurant and King Richard's Room.** Locals have been dining here—one of the oldest family-run restaurants in Miami–Dade County—since 1958. Outside it's a nondescript building in the middle of a big parking lot. Inside there are dark-wood paneling and heavy wooden furniture. The tasty fare ranges from pizza with light, crunchy crusts and ample toppings to mild, meaty conch chowder. Mussels come in garlic or marinara sauce, and the yellowtail snapper *française* is a worthy selection. More than a half dozen early-bird entrées are offered 4:30–6:30 for $10.50, including soup or salad and potato or spaghetti. ✉ *935 N. Krome Ave.,* ☎ *305/247–1544. AE, MC, V. Closed Sun.*

$ ✕ **Farmers' Market Restaurant.** Although it's in the farmers' market and serves fresh vegetables, this restaurant's specialty is seafood. A family of fishermen runs the place, so fish and shellfish are only hours from the sea. Catering to the fishing and farming crowd, it opens at 5:30 AM, serving pancakes, jumbo eggs, and fluffy omelets with home fries or grits. The lunch and dinner menus have shrimp, fish, steaks, and conch baskets, as well as burgers, salads, and sandwiches. Normally the fish comes fried, but you can ask for it broiled or grilled. ✉ *300 N. Krome Ave.,* ☎ *305/242–0008. No credit cards.*

$$ 🏨 **Best Western Gateway to the Keys.** Visitors who want easy access to Everglades and Biscayne national parks as well as the Florida Keys will find themselves well situated at this two-story, no-smoking motel. All rooms are decorated in tropical colors and have coffeemakers. Standard rooms have two queen-size beds or one king-size bed. More expensive rooms also have a wet bar, refrigerator, and microwave. ✉ *1 Strano Blvd., 33034,* ☎ *305/246–5100,* FAX *305/242–0056. 114 units. Pool, coin laundry, dry cleaning. CP. AE, D, DC, MC, V.*

$$ 🏨 **Hampton Inn.** Racing fans can hear the engines roar from this two-story motel next to an outlet mall and within 15 minutes of the raceway and Everglades and Biscayne national parks. Carpeted rooms are bright and clean and have upholstered chairs, twin reading lamps, a desk and chair, coffeemaker, and an iron and ironing board. Included free are a Continental breakfast, local calls, and movie channels. ✉ *124 E. Palm Dr., 33034,* ☎ *305/247–8833 or 800/426–7866,* FAX *305/247–6456. 123 units. Pool. AE, D, DC, MC, V.*

Shopping

Prime Outlets at Florida City (✉ 250 E. Palm Dr.) has more than 50 discount stores plus a small food court. **Robert Is Here** (✉ 19200 Palm Dr. [S.W. 344th St.], ☎ 305/246–1592), a remarkable fruit stand, sells vegetables, fresh-fruit milk shakes, 10 flavors of honey, more than 100 flavors of jams and jellies, fresh juices, salad dressings, and some 40 kinds of tropical fruits, including carambola, litchi, egg fruit, monstera, sapodilla, soursop, sugar apple, and tamarind. The stand started in 1960, when six-year-old Robert sat at this spot selling his father's bumper crop of cucumbers. Now Robert ships around the world, and everything is first quality. Seconds are given to needy area families. The stand opens at 8 and never closes earlier than 7.

BISCAYNE NATIONAL PARK

Occupying 180,000 acres along the southern portion of Biscayne Bay, south of Miami and north of the Florida Keys, this national park is 96% underwater, and its altitude ranges from 4 ft above sea level to 10 fathoms, or 60 ft, below. Contained within it are four distinct zones, which from shore to sea are mangrove forest along the coast, Biscayne Bay, the undeveloped upper Florida Keys, and coral reefs.

Mangroves line the mainland shore much as they do elsewhere in South Florida. Biscayne Bay functions as a lobster sanctuary and a nursery for fish, sponges, and crabs. Manatees and sea turtles frequent its warm, shallow waters. Lamentably, the bay is under assault from forces similar to those in Florida Bay.

To the east, about 8 mi off the coast, lie 44 tiny keys, stretching 18 nautical mi north–south and accessible only by boat. There is no commercial transportation between the mainland and the islands, and only a handful can be visited: Elliott, Boca Chita, Adams, and Sands keys. The rest are either wildlife refuges or too small, or have rocky shores or waters too shallow for boats. It's best to explore the Keys between December and April, when the mosquito population is relatively quiescent. Bring repellent just in case. Diving is best in the summer, when calmer wind and smaller seas result in clearer waters.

Another 3 mi east of the Keys, in the ocean, lies the park's main attraction—the northernmost section of Florida's living tropical coral reefs. Some are the size of a student's desk, others as large as a football field. You can take a glass-bottom boat ride to see this underwater wonderland, but you really have to snorkel or scuba dive to appreciate it fully. A diverse population of colorful fish—angelfish, gobies, grunts, parrot fish, pork fish, wrasses, and many more—flits through the reefs. Shipwrecks from the 18th century are evidence of the area's international maritime heritage. A Native American midden (shell mound) dating from AD 1000 and Boca Chita Key, listed on the National Register of Historic Places for its 10 historic structures, illustrate the park's rich cultural heritage.

More than 170 species of birds have been seen around the park. Although all the Keys offer excellent birding opportunities, Jones Lagoon, south of Adams Key, between Old Rhodes Key and Totten Key, is one of the best. It's approachable only by nonmotorized craft.

Convoy Point

⓯ *9 mi east of Florida City, 30 mi south of downtown Miami.*

Reminiscent of area pioneer homes, the **Dante Fascell Visitor Center** is a wooden building with a metal roof and wide veranda from which you can look out across mangroves and Biscayne Bay and see the Miami skyline. Inside is a museum, where hands-on and historical exhibits and videos explore the park's four ecosystems. Among the facilities are a 50-seat auditorium, the park's canoe and tour concessionaire, rest rooms with showers, a ranger information area, and gift shop. The latter also sells packaged sandwiches and snacks. A short trail and boardwalk lead to a jetty and launch ramp. This is the only area of the park accessible without a boat. ✉ *9700 S.W. 328th St., Homestead,* ☎ *305/230–7275,* WEB *www.nps.gov/bisc.* 🎫 *Free.* ⏲ *Daily 8–5:30.*

Outdoor Activities and Sports

CANOEING

Biscayne National Underwater Park, Inc. (✉ Convoy Point Visitor Center, ☎ 305/230–1100), the park's official concessionaire, has half a dozen canoes and kayaks for rent on a first-come, first-served basis. Canoe prices are $8 an hour, kayaks $16 an hour. Half-day rates are also available.

SCUBA DIVING AND SNORKELING

Biscayne National Underwater Park, Inc. (✉ Convoy Point Visitor Center, Box 1270, Homestead 33090, ☎ 305/230–1100) rents equipment and conducts snorkel and dive trips aboard the 45-ft *Boca Chita.* Three-hour snorkel trips ($29.95) leave twice a day on weekdays, once a day on weekends and include mask, fins, snorkel, vest, and instruction. About half the time is spent on the reef and wrecks. Scuba divers looking for a one-tank dive can go out on the snorkel boat as long as there are two divers. Two-tank scuba trips depart at 8:30 on weekends and cost $35, tanks included. Additional trips are offered in winter. Complete gear rental and instruction are available. Even with a reservation (recommended), you should arrive one hour before departure to sign up for gear.

Elliott Key

16 *9 mi east of Convoy Point.*

This key, accessible only by boat (on your own or by special arrangement with the concessionaire), has a rebuilt boardwalk made from recycled plastic and two nature trails with tropical plant life. Take an informal, ranger-led nature walk or walk its 7-mi length on your own along a rough path through a hammock. Videos shown at the ranger station describe the island. Facilities include rest rooms, picnic tables, fresh drinking water, showers (cold), grills, and a campground. Pets are allowed on the island but not on trails.

A 30-ft-wide sandy beach about a mile north of the harbor on the west (bay) side of the key is the only one in the national park. Boaters like to anchor off it to swim. For day use only, it has picnic areas and a short trail that follows the shore and cuts through the hammock.

Boca Chita Key

17 *10 mi northeast of Convoy Point.*

This island was once owned by Mark C. Honeywell, former president of Minneapolis's Honeywell Company. A half-mile hiking trail curves around the south side of the island. Climb the 65-ft ornamental lighthouse for a panoramic view of Miami and surrounding waters. There is no fresh water, but grills, picnic tables, campsites, and saltwater rest rooms are available. Access is by private boat only. No pets are allowed.

Adams Key

18 *9 mi southeast of Convoy Point.*

This small key, a stone's throw off the western tip of Elliott Key, is open for day use and has picnic areas, rest rooms, dockage, and a short trail that runs along the shore and through a hardwood hammock. Access is by private boat.

Lodging

$ **Biscayne National Park.** Although Elliott Key's 40 campsites are listed as primitive, there are rest-room facilities nearby. Just bring plenty of insect repellent. The park charges $10-per-night for camping, $15 if you dock a private vessel. Boca Chita Key has a grassy, waterside campground with grills, picnic tables, and toilets, but no running water. There is no regular ferry service or boat rental. However, the park concessionaire's snorkel boat provides drop-off and pick-up service to campers ($24.95 round-trip).

BIG CYPRESS NATIONAL PRESERVE

Through the 1950s and early 1960s, the world's largest cypress-logging industry prospered in the Big Cypress Swamp. The industry died out in the 1960s, and the government began buying parcels. Today, 729,000 acres, or nearly half of the swamp, has become this national preserve.

The word "big" in its name refers not to the size of the trees, but to the swamp, which juts down into the north side of Everglades National Park like a piece in a jigsaw puzzle. Its size and strategic location make it an important link in the region's hydrological system, in which rainwater first flows through the preserve, then south into the park, and eventually into Florida Bay.

Its variegated pattern of wet prairies, ponds, marshes, sloughs, and strands provides a sanctuary for a variety of wildlife, and due to a politically dictated policy of balanced land use—"use without abuse"—the watery wilderness is devoted to research and recreation as well as preservation. The preserve allows—in limited areas—hunting, off-road vehicle (airboat, swamp buggy) use by permit, and cattle grazing.

Compared to Everglades National Park, the preserve is less developed and has fewer visitors. That makes it ideal for naturalists, birders, and hikers who prefer to see more wildlife than humans. Roadside picnic areas are located off the Tamiami Trail.

There are two types of trails—walking and canoeing; neither is interpretive. Both trail types are easily accessed from the Tamiami Trail near the preserve's visitor center. Equipment can be rented from outfitters in Everglades City, 24 mi west, and Naples, 40 mi west.

Projects on the drawing board for completion in the next few years include several boardwalks and interpretive trails through the preserve.

Oasis Visitor Center

24 mi east of Everglades City, 50 mi west of Miami, 20 mi west of Shark Valley.

9 The **Oasis Visitor Center** is a welcome respite along the Tamiami Trail. Drivers who speed past on their way between Miami and Naples miss out on an opportunity to learn about the surrounding Big Cypress National Preserve. Inside are a small exhibit area, an information center, a bookshop, a theater that shows a 15-minute film on the preserve and Big Cypress Swamp, and rest rooms. It also has myriad seasonal ranger-led and self-guided activities, such as campfire talks, bike hikes, slough slogs, and canoe excursions. The 8-mi Turner River Canoe Trail begins here and crosses through Everglades National Park before ending in Chokoloskee Bay, near Everglades City. Hikers can join the Florida National Scenic Trail, which runs north–south through the preserve for 31 mi. Two 5-mi trails, Concho Billy and Fire Prairie, can be ac-

cessed a few miles east off Turner River Road. Turner River Road and Birdon Road form a 17-mi gravel loop drive that is excellent for birding. All of the trails can be very wet and possibly impassable during the rainy season. Rangers at the visitor center provide road-condition information. Five primitive campsites are available on a first-come, first-served basis. ✉ *24 mi east of Everglades City, 50 mi west of Miami, 20 mi west of Shark Valley,* ☎ *941/695–4111.* 🎫 *Free.* ⏲ *Daily 8:30–4:30.*

Lodging

$ ⛺ **Big Cypress National Preserve.** There are four no-fee primitive campgrounds located within the preserve along the Tamiami Trail and Loop Road. A fifth site, Monument Lake Campground, has rest rooms, an amphitheater, and activities and seasonal programs (December–mid-April). The fee is $14 a night for tents and RVs at Monument Lake. Dona Drive Campground has a dump station ($4) and potable water. ✉ *Tamiami Trail (Hwy. 41), between Miami and Naples (HCR 61, Box 110, Ochopee, FL 34141),* ☎ *941/695–4111,* WEB *www.nps.gov/bicy.*

THE EVERGLADES A TO Z

AIRPORTS

To research prices, get advice from other travelers, and book arrangements, visit www.fodors.com.

Miami International Airport (MIA) is 34 mi from Homestead and 83 mi from Flamingo in Everglades National Park.

Airporter runs shuttle buses three times daily that stop at the Hampton Inn in Florida City on their way between MIA and the Florida Keys. Shuttle service, which takes about an hour, runs 6:10–5:20 from Florida City, 7:30–6 from the airport. Reserve in advance. Pickups can be arranged for all baggage-claim areas. The cost is $25 one-way.

Greyhound Lines buses from MIA to the Keys make a stop in Homestead four times a day. Buses leave from Concourse E, lower level, and cost from $8.50 one-way, from $16.50 round-trip.

SuperShuttle operates 11-passenger air-conditioned vans to Homestead. Service from MIA is available around the clock; booths are outside most luggage areas on the lower level. For the return to MIA, reserve 24 hours in advance. The one-way cost is $41.50 per person for the first person, $12.50 for each additional person at the same address.
➤ AIRPORT INFORMATION: **Miami International Airport** (☎ 305/876–7000). **Airporter** (☎ 800/830–3413). **Greyhound Lines** (☎ 800/231–2222; Homestead: ✉ 5 N.E. 3rd Rd., ☎ 305/247–2040). **SuperShuttle** (☎ 305/871–2000 or 800/874–8885).

BOAT TRAVEL

If you're entering the United States by pleasure boat, you must phone U.S. Customs either from a marine phone or on first arriving ashore.

Bring aboard the proper *NOAA Nautical Charts* before you cast off to explore park waters. The charts run $17 at many marine stores in South Florida, at the Convoy Point Visitor Center in Biscayne National Park, and at Flamingo Marina in the Everglades.

The annual *Waterway Guide* (southern regional edition) is widely used by boaters. Bookstores all over South Florida sell it, or you can order it directly from the publisher for $39.95 plus $5 shipping and handling.

➤ Boat Information: **U.S. Customs** (☎ 800/432–1216). ***Waterway Guide*** (✉ Intertec Publishing, Book Department, Box 12901, Overland Park, KS 66282-2901, ☎ 800/233–3359).

BUS TRAVEL

The Dade-Monroe Express provides daily bus service from the Florida City Wal-Mart Supercenter to Mile Marker 98 in Key Largo. The bus makes several stops in Florida City, then heads for the islands for daily round-trips on the hour from 6 AM to 9 PM. The cost is $1.25 each way with senior and student discounts.

➤ Bus Information: **Dade-Monroe Express** (☎ 305/770–3131).

CAR RENTAL

Agencies in the area include A&A Auto Rental, Budget, and Enterprise Rent-a-Car.

➤ Local Agencies: **A&A Auto Rental** (✉ 30005 S. Dixie Hwy., Homestead 33030, ☎ 305/246–0974). **Budget** (✉ 29949 S. Dixie Hwy., Homestead 33030, ☎ 305/248–4524 or 800/527–0700). **Enterprise Rent-a-Car** (✉ 29130 S. Dixie Hwy., Homestead 33030, ☎ 305/246–2056 or 800/736–8222).

CAR TRAVEL

From Miami the main highways to the area are U.S. 1, the Homestead Extension of Florida's Turnpike, and Krome Avenue (Route 997 [old U.S. 27]).

To reach Everglades National Park's Ernest F. Coe Visitor Center and Flamingo, head west on Route 9336 in Florida City and follow signs. From Homestead the Ernest F. Coe Visitor Center is 11 mi; Flamingo is 49 mi. The north entrance of Everglades National Park at Shark Valley is reached by taking the Tamiami Trail about 20 mi west of Krome Avenue. To reach the west entrance of Everglades National Park at the Gulf Coast Visitor Center in Everglades City, take Route 29 south from the Tamiami Trail. To reach Biscayne National Park from Homestead, take U.S. 1 or Krome Avenue to Lucy Street (Southeast 8th Street) and turn east. Lucy Street becomes North Canal Drive (Southwest 328th Street). Follow signs for about 8 mi to the park headquarters.

EMERGENCIES

Dial 911 for police, fire, or ambulance. In the national parks, rangers answer police, fire, and medical emergencies. The Florida Fish and Wildlife Conservation Commission, a division of the Florida Department of Natural Resources, maintains a 24-hour telephone service for reporting boating emergencies and natural-resource violations. The Miami Beach Coast Guard Base responds to local marine emergencies and reports of navigation hazards. The base broadcasts on VHF-FM Channel 16. The National Weather Service supplies local forecasts.

➤ Contacts: **Hospital emergency line** (☎ 305/596–6556). **Homestead Hospital** (✉ 160 N.W. 13th St., Homestead, ☎ 305/248–3232; 305/596–6557 physician referral). **Florida Fish and Wildlife Conservation Commission** (☎ 305/956–2500). **Miami Beach Coast Guard Base** (✉ 100 MacArthur Causeway, Miami Beach, ☎ 305/535–4300 or 305/535–4314). **National Parks–Biscayne unit** (☎ 305/247–7272). **National Parks–Everglades unit** (☎ 305/247–7272). **National Weather Service** (☎ 305/229–4522).

ENGLISH-LANGUAGE MEDIA

NEWSPAPERS AND MAGAZINES

The *South Dade News Leader* is published thrice weekly.

TELEVISION AND RADIO

WRLN (National Public Radio) 91.3, 92.1, or 93.5, depending on your location; WLVE (easy listening) 93.9; WFLC (pop) 97.3.

TAXIS

Action Express Taxi and South Dade Taxi have cabs that service the area.

➤ TAXI INFORMATION: **Action Express Taxi** (☎ 305/743–6800). **South Dade Taxi** (☎ 305/256–4444).

TOURS

The National Park Service organizes a variety of free programs, typically focusing on native wildlife, plants, and park history. At Biscayne National Park, for example, rangers give informal tours of Elliott and Boca Chita keys, which you can arrange in advance, depending on ranger availability. Contact the respective visitor center for details.

10,000 Islands Aero-Tours operates scenic, low-level flight tours of the 10,000 Islands, Big Cypress National Preserve, Everglades National Park, and the Gulf of Mexico in a Cessna 170. On the 20- to 60-minute flights you can see saw-grass prairies, Native American shell mounds, alligators, and wading birds. Prices start at $30. For an all-day outing, opt for the Key West or Dry Tortugas flights across the gulf in a Cessna 185.

Wooten's Everglades Airboat Tours runs airboat and swamp-buggy tours ($13.50) through the Everglades. (Swamp buggies are giant tractor-like vehicles with oversize rubber wheels.) Tours last approximately 30 minutes.

Southwest of Florida City near the entrance to Everglades National Park, Everglades Alligator Farm runs a 4-mi, 30-minute tour of the River of Grass with departures 20 minutes after the hour. The tour ($14.50) includes a free hourly alligator, snake, or wildlife show, or you can take in the show only ($9).

From the Shark Valley area, Buffalo Tiger's Florida Everglades Airboat Ride is led by a former chairman of the Miccosukee tribe. The 35- to 40-minute trip includes a stop at an old Native American camp. Tours cost $10 and operate daily except Friday 10–5. Reservations are not required. Coopertown Airboat Ride operates the oldest airboat rides in the Everglades (since 1945). The 30- to 40-minute tour ($12) visits two hammocks and alligator holes. Everglades Gator Park offers 45-minute narrated airboat tours ($14). Everglades Safari Park runs 40-minute airboat rides for $15. The price includes a show and gator tour. The Miccosukee Indian Village 30-minute narrated airboat ride stops off at a 100-year-old family camp in the Everglades to hear tales and allow passengers to walk around and explore ($10) in addition to its other attractions.

When the namesake owner sold Ray Cramer's Everglades Airboat Tours, Inc. to longtime friend Bill Barlow, with whom he had fished, frogged, and hunted in the Everglades since 1949, Bill didn't change anything but the number of trips he offered a day. His two-hour personalized excursions, on airboats accommodating only 6 to 12 passengers, venture 40 mi into the River of Grass. Daytime trips are exciting, but the tour that departs an hour before sundown lets you see birds and fish in daylight and alligators, raccoons, and other nocturnal animals when night falls. The cost is $40 per person. Half-day trips for two to five people cost $275 for the group.

Tours at Biscayne National Park are run by people-friendly Biscayne National Underwater Park, Inc. Daily trips (at 10, with a second trip at 1 during high season, depending on demand) explore the park's living coral reefs 10 mi offshore on *Reef Rover IV*, a 53-ft glass-bottom boat that carries up to 48 passengers. On days when the weather is unsuitable for reef viewing, an alternative three-hour, ranger-led interpretive tour visits Boca Chita Key. Reservations are recommended. The cost is $19.95, and you should arrive at least one hour before departure.

Everglades National Park visitors can climb aboard a six-passenger boat for the four-hour narrated Dolphin Cruise ($32) through the shallow waters of the backcountry. Everglades National Park Boat Tours is the official park concession authorized to operate tours ($16) through the 10,000 Islands region and mangrove wilderness. Boats can accommodate large numbers and wheelchairs (not electric), and one large boat has drink concessions. The 2½-hour Mangrove Wilderness tour ($25) ventures into the shallow waters of the mangrove community, where birds nest and fish have their nurseries, but only when the tide is high enough. Flamingo Lodge, Marina & Outpost Resort Boat Tours is the official concession authorized to operate sightseeing tours through Everglades National Park. The two-hour backcountry cruise ($16) is the most popular. The boat winds under a heavy canopy of mangroves, revealing abundant wildlife—from alligators, crocodiles, and turtles to herons, hawks, and egrets. A quieter option is the Sailboat Cruise ($16) into Florida Bay that runs mid-December to spring. The 90-minute Florida Bay cruise ($10) ventures into the bay to explore shallow nursery areas and encounter plentiful bird life and often dolphins, sea turtles, and sharks. To get really close to nature, adults can join a small group on the *Everglades Queen,* a replica of the *African Queen,* on a narrated three-hour cruise ($32) of the backcountry during winter and spring.

Everglades Rentals & Eco Adventures leads one-day to nine-night Everglades tours November–April. Highlights include bird and gator sightings, mangrove forests, no-man's-land beaches, relics of the hideouts of infamous and just plain reclusive characters, and spectacular sunsets. Included in the cost of extended tours ($250–$1,125) are canoes or kayaks, all necessary equipment, a guide, meals, and lodging for the first night at the Ivey House. Day trips with a naturalist by kayak, canoe, or powerboat cost $40–$95.

Starting at the Shark Valley visitor center, Shark Valley Tram Tours follows a 15-mi loop road into the interior, stopping at a 50-ft observation tower especially good for viewing gators. Two-hour narrated tours cost $10.50 and depart hourly 9–4, except May 1–Christmas, when they run every two hours. Reservations are recommended December–April.

➤ TOURS INFORMATION: **Biscayne National Underwater Park, Inc.** (✉ Convoy Point, east end of North Canal Dr. [S.W. 328th St.], Box 1270, Homestead 33090, ☎ 305/230–1100). **Buffalo Tiger's Florida Everglades Airboat Ride** (✉ 12 mi west of Krome Ave., 20 mi west of Miami city limits on Tamiami Trail, ☎ 305/559–5250). **Coopertown Airboat Ride** (✉ 5 mi west of Krome Ave. on Tamiami Trail, ☎ 305/226–6048). **Deaf Services Center** (✉ 2182 McGreggor Blvd., Fort Myers, FL 33901, ☎ 941/461–0334 or 813/939–9977 TDD). **Everglades Alligator Farm** (✉ 40351 S.W. 192nd Ave., ☎ 305/247–2628 or 800/644–9711). **Everglades Gator Park** (✉ 12 mi west of Florida's Tpk. on Tamiami Trail, ☎ 305/559–2255 or 800/559–2205). **Everglades National Park Boat Tours** (✉ Gulf Coast Visitor Center, Everglades

City, ☎ 941/695–2591; 800/445–7724 in FL). **Everglades Rentals & Eco Adventures** (✉ Ivey House, 107 Camellia St., Box 5038, Everglades City 34139, ☎ 941/695–3299). **Everglades Safari Park** (✉ 26700 Tamiami Trail, 9 mi west of Krome Ave., ☎ 305/226–6923 or 305/223–3804). **Flamingo Lodge, Marina & Outpost Resort Boat Tours** (✉ 1 Flamingo Lodge Hwy., Flamingo, ☎ 941/695–3101 ext. 286 or 180). **Miccosukee Indian Village** (✉ 25 mi west of Florida's Tpk. on Tamiami Trail, ☎ 305/223–8380). **Ray Cramer's Everglades Airboat Tours, Inc.** (✉ Coopertown, ☎ 305/852–5339 or 305/221–9888; ✉ mailing address: Box 940082, Miami 33194). **Shark Valley Tram Tours** (✉ Box 1739, Tamiami Station, Miami 33144, ☎ 305/221–8455). **10,000 Islands Aero-Tours** (✉ Everglades Airport, 650 Everglades City Airpark Rd., Box 482, Everglades City, 34139, ☎ 941/695–3296). **Wooten's Everglades Airboat Tours** (✉ Wooten's Alligator Farm, 1½ mi east of Rte. 29 on Tamiami Trail, ☎ 941/695–2781 or 800/282–2781).

VISITOR INFORMATION

➤ TOURIST INFORMATION: **Big Cypress National Preserve** (✉ HCR61, Box 11, Ochopee 34141, ☎ 941/695–4111). **Biscayne National Park** Dante Fascell Visitor Center (✉ 9700 S.W. 328th St., Box 1369, Homestead 33090-1369, ☎ 305/230–7275). **Everglades City Chamber of Commerce** (✉ Rte. 29 and Tamiami Trail, Box 130, Everglades City 34139, ☎ 941/695–3941). **Everglades National Park** Ernest F. Coe Visitor Center (✉ 40001 Rte. 9336, Homestead 33034-6733, ☎ 305/242–7700). **Flamingo Visitor Center** (✉ 1 Flamingo Lodge Hwy., Flamingo 33034-6798, ☎ 941/695–2945). **Gulf Coast Visitor Center** (✉ Rte. 29, Everglades City 34139, ☎ 941/695–3311). **Greater Homestead–Florida City Chamber of Commerce** (✉ 43 N. Krome Ave., Homestead 33030, ☎ 305/247–2332 or 888/352–4891). **Tropical Everglades Visitor Association** (✉ 160 U.S. 1, Florida City 33034, ☎ 305/245–9180 or 800/388–9669).

3 FORT LAUDERDALE AND BROWARD COUNTY

From Hollywood north to Fort Lauderdale and beyond, the county's famous beaches are just one of the attractions. Downtowns are being spruced up, and Fort Lauderdale's Arts and Science District draws the culturally minded.

Updated by Alan Macher

A **COLLEGE STUDENT FROM THE 1960S** returning to Fort Lauderdale for a vacation today wouldn't recognize the place. Back then, the Fort Lauderdale beachfront was lined with bars, T-shirt shops, souvenir stores, and fast-food stands, and the downtown area consisted of a single office tower and some government buildings. Now, following an enormous renovation program, the beach is home to upscale shops and restaurants, including the popular Beach Place retail and dining complex, while downtown growth continues at a rapid pace. The movie and entertainment complex, Las Olas Riverfront, is complete; several new office towers have been built; and a major airport expansion is entering its final phases.

In the years following World War II, sleepy Fort Lauderdale—with miles of inland waterways—promoted itself as the "Venice of America" and the nation's yachting capital. But in 1960 the film *Where the Boys Are* changed everything. The movie described how college students—upward of 20,000—were beginning to swarm to the city for spring break. By 1985 the 20,000 had mushroomed to 350,000. Hotel owners complained of 12 students to a room, the beachfront was littered with tacky bars, and drug trafficking and petty theft were major problems. So city leaders put in place policies and restrictions designed to encourage students to go elsewhere. They did, and no one seems to miss them.

A major beneficiary is Las Olas Boulevard, whose emergence has been credited with creating a new identity for Fort Lauderdale. Although it was already famous for its trendy shops, now the sidewalks aren't rolled up when the sun goes down. Dozens of restaurants have sprung up, and on weekend evenings strollers tour the boulevard, taking in the food, the jazz bands, and the scene. On-street parking on weekends has slowed traffic, and the street has a village atmosphere.

Farther west, along New River, is evidence of Fort Lauderdale's cultural renaissance: the arts and entertainment district and its crown jewel, the Broward Center for the Performing Arts. Still farther west, is the county's major-league sports venue, the arena for the National Hockey League's Florida Panthers, in Sunrise.

Of course, what makes Fort Lauderdale and Broward County a major draw for visitors is the beaches. Fort Lauderdale's 2-mi stretch of unobstructed beachfront has been enhanced even further with a sparkling promenade designed for the pleasure of pedestrians rather than cars.

Tying this all together is a transportation system that is relatively hassle free, unusual in congested South Florida. A new expressway system, including the widening of Interstate 95, connects the city and suburbs and even provides a direct route to the airport and Port Everglades. For a slower and more scenic ride to really see this canal-laced city, cruise aboard the water taxi.

None of this was envisioned by Napoleon Bonaparte Broward, Florida's governor from 1905 to 1909, for whom the county was named. His drainage schemes opened much of the marshy Everglades region for farming, ranching, and settling (in retrospect, an environmental disaster). Fort Lauderdale's first known white settler, Charles Lewis, established a plantation along the New River in 1793. But it was for Major William Lauderdale, who built a fort at the river's mouth in 1838 during the Seminole Indian wars, that the city was named.

Incorporated in 1911 with just 175 residents, Fort Lauderdale grew rapidly during the Florida boom of the 1920s. Today its population is 170,000, and its suburbs keep growing—1.5 million live in the county.

New homes, offices, and shopping centers have filled in the gaps between older communities along the coastal ridge. Now they're marching west along Interstate 75, Interstate 595, and Route 869 (the Sawgrass Expressway). Broward County is blessed with near-ideal weather, with some 3,000 hours of sunshine a year. The average temperature is 66°F–77°F in winter, 84°F in summer. Once a home for retirees, the county today attracts younger, working-age families, many living in such new communities as Weston, southwest of Fort Lauderdale. With a revitalized downtown, many young professionals also are buying aging beachside condominiums as they come on the market, and remodeling them. The area has always been a sane and pleasant place to live. Now it's also becoming one of Florida's most diverse and dynamic places to vacation.

New and Noteworthy

The time you spend in the airport is certainly not the high point of your vacation. But **Fort Lauderdale–Hollywood International Airport** is easing the experience somewhat. The airport completed a fourth terminal in 2001 that nearly doubled the number of gates. It's all part of the airport's $334 million expansion and renovation program. With discount airlines picking the Broward destination as their South Florida hub, passenger traffic has risen steadily, and a number of carriers have announced plans to increase service

Pleasures and Pastimes

Beaches

Broward County's beachfront extends for miles without interruption, although the character of the communities behind the beach changes. For example, in Hallandale the beach is backed by towering condominiums; in Hollywood, by motels and the Broadwalk; and just north of there—blessedly—there's nothing at all.

Dining

Food critics in dining and travel magazines agree that the Greater Fort Lauderdale area offers some of the finest and most varied dining of any U.S. city its size. You can choose from the cuisines of Asia, Europe, or Central and South America—and, of course, good ol' America—and enjoy more than just the food. The ambience, wine, service, and decor can be as varied as the language spoken, and as memorable, too.

Fishing

Four main types of fishing are available in Broward County: bottom or drift-boat fishing from party boats, deep-sea fishing for large sport fish on charters, angling for freshwater game fish, and dropping a line off a pier. For bottom fishing, party boats typically charge between $20 and $22 per person for up to four hours, including rod, reel, and bait. For charters, a half day for as many as six people runs up to $325, six-hour charters up to $495, and full-day charters (eight hours) up to $595. Skipper and crew plus bait and tackle are included. Split parties can be arranged at a cost of about $85 per person for a full day.

Several Broward towns—Dania Beach, Lauderdale-by-the-Sea, Pompano Beach, and Deerfield Beach—have fishing piers that draw anglers for pompano, amberjack, bluefish, snapper, blue runners, snook, mackerel, and Florida lobster.

Golf

More than 50 courses green the landscape in Greater Fort Lauderdale, including famous championship links. Most area courses are inland, in the suburbs west of the city, and there are some great bargains. Off-season (May–October) greens fees start at $15; peak-season (November–April) charges run from $35 to more than $100. Fees can be trimmed by working through Next Day Golf, a local service, and many hotels offer golf packages.

Scuba Diving

Good diving can be enjoyed within 20 minutes of shore. Among the most popular of the county's 80 dive sites is the 2-mi-wide, 23-mi-long Fort Lauderdale Reef, the product of Florida's most successful artificial reef–building program. More than a dozen houseboats, ships, and oil platforms have been sunk in depths of from 10 to 150 ft to provide a habitat for fish and other marine life, as well as to help stabilize beaches. The most famous sunken ship is the 200-ft German freighter *Mercedes,* which was blown onto Palm Beach socialite Mollie Wilmot's pool terrace in a violent Thanksgiving storm in 1984; the ship is now underwater a mile off Fort Lauderdale beach.

Exploring Fort Lauderdale and Broward County

Although most activity centers on Fort Lauderdale, there's plenty to see in other parts of Broward County, to the north, south, and, increasingly, west.

The metro area is laid out in a basic grid system, and only the hundreds of canals and waterways interrupt the straight-line path of the streets and roads. Nomenclature is important here. Streets, roads, courts, and drives run east–west. Avenues, terraces, and ways run north–south. Boulevards can run any which way. Las Olas Boulevard is one of the most important east–west thoroughfares, whereas Route A1A—referred to as Atlantic Boulevard and Ocean Boulevard along some stretches—runs along the north–south oceanfront. These names can be confusing to visitors, as there are separate streets called Atlantic and Ocean in Hollywood and Pompano Beach.

The boulevards, those that are paved and those made of water, give Fort Lauderdale its distinct character. Honeycombed with more than 260 mi of navigable waterways, the city is home port for about 44,000 privately owned boats. You won't see the gondolas you'd find in Venice, but you will see just about every other type of craft imaginable docked beside the thousands of homes and businesses that each have a little piece of waterfront, such as you'll see on Gordon Drive. Visitors can tour the canals via the city's water-taxi system, made up of small motor launches that provide transportation and quick, narrated tours. Larger, multideck touring vessels and motorboat rentals for self-guided tours are other options. The Intracoastal Waterway, a massive canal that parallels Route A1A, is the nautical equivalent of an interstate highway. It runs north–south through the metro area and provides easy access to neighboring beach communities; Deerfield Beach and Pompano Beach lie to the north and Dania and Hollywood lie to the south. All are within a 15-mi radius of the city center.

Great Itineraries

Since most Broward County sights are relatively close to one another, it's easy to pack a lot into very little time, but you will probably need a car. You can catch a lot of the history, the museums, and the shops and bistros in Fort Lauderdale's downtown area and along Las Olas Boulevard, and then if you feel like hitting the beach, just take a 10-minute drive east to the intersection of Las Olas and A1A and you're there. Many of the neighboring suburbs, with attractions of their own, are just north or south of Fort Lauderdale. As a result, you can hit most of the high points in three days, and with seven to 10 days, you can see virtually all of Broward's mainstream charms.

Numbers in the text correspond to numbers in the margin and on the Broward County and Fort Lauderdale maps.

IF YOU HAVE 3 DAYS

With a bigger concentration of hotels, restaurants, and sights to see than its suburban neighbors, **Fort Lauderdale** ①–⑪ makes a logical base of operations for any visit. On your first day there see the downtown area, especially Las Olas Boulevard between Southeast 6th and Southeast 11th avenues. After enjoying lunch at a sidewalk café, head for the nearby Arts and Science District and the downtown **Riverwalk** ⑤, which you can see at a leisurely pace in half a day. On your second day spend at least some time at the beach, shopping when the hot sun drives you off the sand. Tour the canals on the third day, either on a rented boat from one of the various marinas along Route A1A, or via the water taxi or a sightseeing boat, both of which can be boarded all along the Intracoastal Waterway.

IF YOU HAVE 5 DAYS

With additional time you can see more of the beach and the arts district and still work in some outdoor sports—and you'll be more able to rearrange your plans depending on the weather. On the first day visit the Arts and Science District and the downtown **Riverwalk** ⑤. Set aside the next day for an offshore adventure, perhaps a deep-sea fishing charter or a dive trip to the Fort Lauderdale Reef. On the third day shop, dine, and relax along the **Fort Lauderdale beachfront** ⑨, and at the end of the day, sneak a peak at the Hillsboro Light, at **Lighthouse Point** ⑱. Another good day can be spent at the **Hugh Taylor Birch State Recreation Area** ⑩. Enjoy your fifth day in **Hollywood** ⑳, perhaps combining time on the Broadwalk with a visit to the Anne Kolb Nature Center, at West Lake Park.

IF YOU HAVE 7 DAYS

With a full week you have time for a wider variety of attractions, fitting in beach time around other activities. In fact, enjoy any of the county's public beach areas on your first day. The second day can be spent in another favorite pastime—shopping, either at chic shops or at one of the malls. On the next day tour the canals on a sightseeing boat or water taxi. Then shop and dine along Las Olas Boulevard. The fourth day might be devoted to the many museums in downtown Fort Lauderdale and the fifth to an airboat ride at **Sawgrass Recreation Park** ⑭, at the edge of the Everglades. Fort Lauderdale offers plenty of facilities for outdoor recreation; spend the sixth day fishing and picnicking on one of the area's many piers or playing a round at a top golf course. Set aside the seventh day for **Hollywood** ⑳, where you can stroll along the scenic Broadwalk or walk through the aviary at Flamingo Gardens, in **Davie** ㉒, before relaxing in peaceful Hollywood North Beach Park.

When to Tour Fort Lauderdale and Broward County

Tourists visit the area all year long, choosing to come in winter or summer depending on interests, hobbies, and the climate where they live. The winter season, about Thanksgiving through March, still sees the biggest influx of visitors and "snowbirds"—seasonal residents who show up when the snow starts to fly up north. Concert, art, and show seasons are at their height then, and restaurants and highways all show the stress of crowds, Americans, Canadians, and Europeans alike.

Summer has its own fans. Waits at even the most popular restaurants are likely to be reasonable or even nonexistent, but although few services close in the summer, some may establish slightly shorter hours than during the peak season. Summer is the rainy season; the tropics-style rain arrives about mid-afternoon and is usually gone in an hour. When downpours hit, however, driving can be treacherous.

For golfers, almost anytime is great for playing. As everywhere else, waits for tee times are longer on weekends year-round.

Remember that sun can cause scorching burns all year long, especially at midday, marking the tourist from the experienced resident or vacationer. And when the sun is the strongest, if you jump in the water to cool off, the sun reflecting off the water can substantially increase your chance of burning. You might want to plan your beach time for morning and late afternoon and go sightseeing or shopping in between.

FORT LAUDERDALE

Like some southeast Florida neighbors, Fort Lauderdale has been revitalizing itself for several years. What's unusual in a state where gaudy tourist zones stand aloof from workaday downtowns is that the city exhibits consistency at both ends of the 2-mi Las Olas corridor. The sparkling look results from a decision to thoroughly improve both beachfront and downtown, as opposed to focusing design attention in town and letting the beach fall prey to development solely by T-shirt retailers. Matching the downtown's new arts district, cafés, and boutiques is an equally inventive beach area with its own share of cafés and shops facing an undeveloped shoreline.

Downtown

The jewel of the downtown area along the New River is the arts and entertainment district. Pricey tickets are available for Broadway shows at the riverfront Broward Center for the Performing Arts. Clustered within a five-minute walk are the Museum of Discovery and Science, the expanding Fort Lauderdale Historical Museum, and the Museum of Art. Restaurants, sidewalk cafés, delis, and blues, folk, jazz, reggae, and rock clubs flourish. The latest gem is Las Olas Riverfront, a multistory entertainment, dining, and retail complex along several blocks once owned by pioneers William and Mary Brickell.

Tying this district together is the Riverwalk, which extends 2 mi along the New River's north and south banks. Tropical gardens with benches and interpretive displays fringe the walk on one side, boat landings on the other. East along Riverwalk is Stranahan House, and a block away Las Olas attractions begin. Tropical landscaping and trees separate the traffic lanes in some blocks, setting off fine shops, restaurants, and popular nightspots. From here it's five minutes by car or 30 minutes by water taxi back to the beach.

A Good Tour

Start on Southeast 6th Avenue at Las Olas Boulevard, where you'll find **Stranahan House** ①, a turn-of-the-last-century structure that's now a museum. Between Southeast 6th and 11th avenues, Las Olas has Spanish colonial buildings housing high-fashion boutiques, jewelry shops, and art galleries. If you drive east, you'll cross into the Isles, Fort Lauderdale's most prestigious neighborhood, where homes line canals with large yachts beside the seawalls.

Return west on Las Olas to Andrews Avenue, turn right, and park in one of the municipal garages so you can walk around downtown Fort Lauderdale. First stop is the **Museum of Art** ②, which has a major collection of works from the CoBrA (Copenhagen, Brussels, and Amsterdam) movement. Walk one block north to the **Broward County Main Library** ③ to see works from Broward's Art in Public Places program.

Broward County

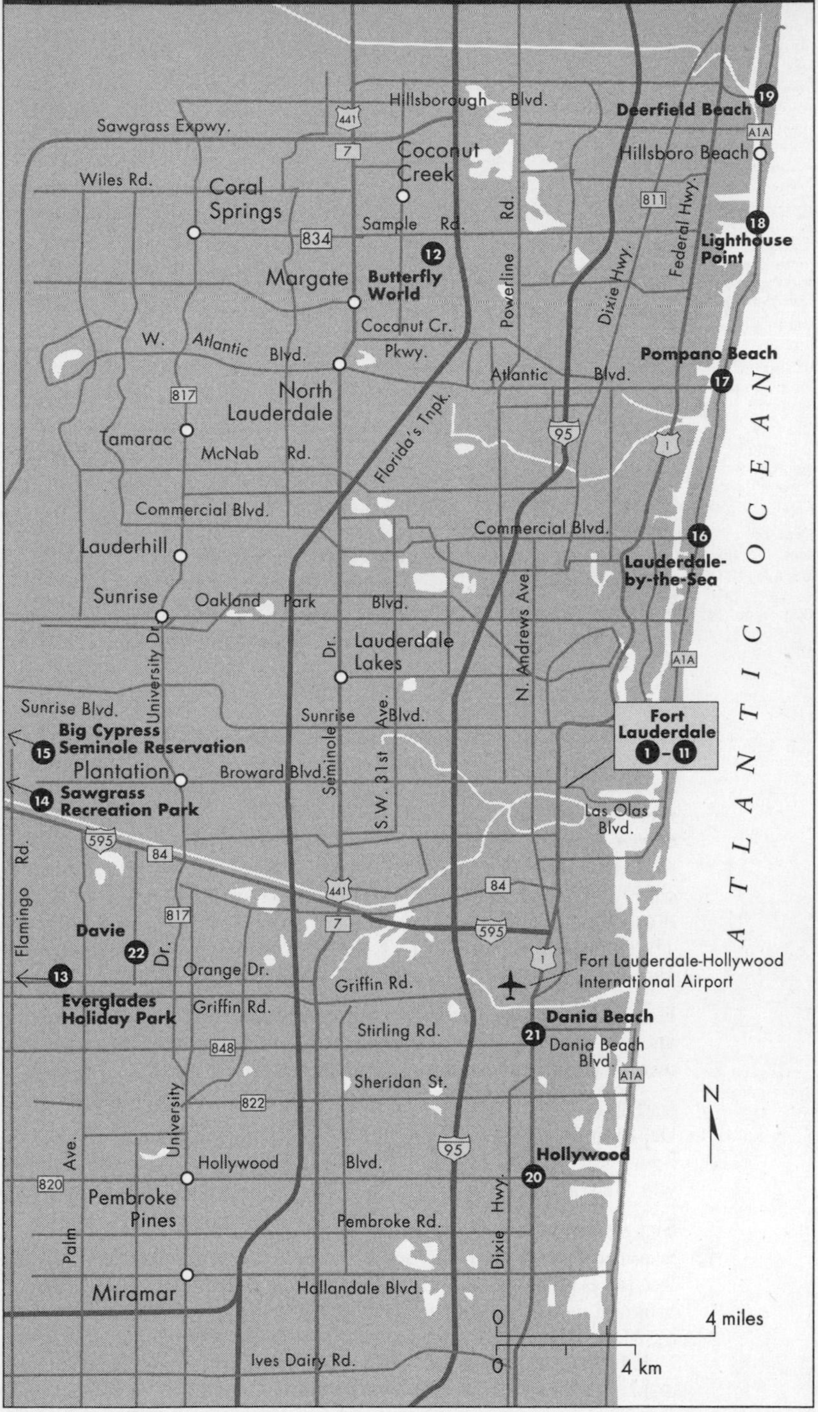

Bonnet House 11
Broward County Main Library 3
Fort Lauderdale Beachfront . . .9
Hugh Taylor Birch State Recreation Area 10
International Swimming Hall of Fame Museum and Aquatic Complex 8
Museum of Art 2
Museum of Discovery and Science 6
Old Fort Lauderdale Museum of History 4
Riverwalk 5
Sailboat Bend 7
Stranahan House 1

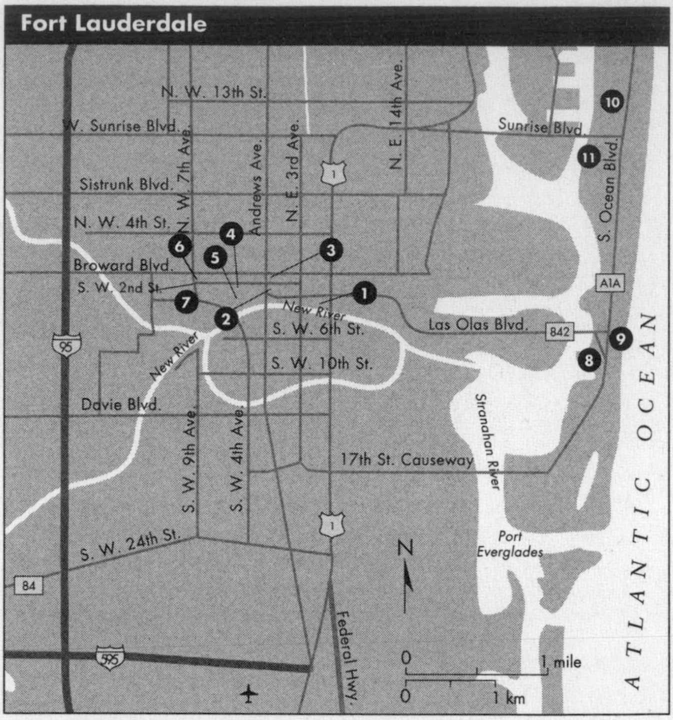

Go west on Southeast 2nd Street to Southwest 2nd Avenue, turn left, and stop at the **Old Fort Lauderdale Museum of History** ④, which surveys the city's not-so-recent history. Just to the south is the palm-lined **Riverwalk** ⑤, a good place for a leisurely stroll. Head north toward a cluster of new facilities collectively known as the Arts and Science District. The district contains the outdoor Esplanade, whose exhibits include a hands-on display of the science and history of navigation, and the major science attraction, the **Museum of Discovery and Science** ⑥. The adjacent Broward Center for the Performing Arts, a massive glass-and-concrete structure by the river, opened in 1991.

Finally, go west along Las Olas Boulevard to Southwest 7th Avenue and the entrance to **Sailboat Bend** ⑦. You can return to the start of the tour by traveling east along Las Olas Boulevard.

TIMING

Depending on how long you like to linger in museums and how many hours you want to spend in the quaint shops on Las Olas Boulevard, you can spend anything from half a day to an entire day on this tour.

Sights to See

3 **Broward County Main Library.** This distinctive building was designed by Marcel Breuer. Works on display from Broward's Art in Public Places program include a painting by Yaacov Agam, a wooden construction by Marc Beauregard, an outdoor aluminum-and-steel sculpture by Dale Eldred, and ceramic tile by Ivan Chermayeff. (Art in Public Places displays more than 200 works—painting, sculpture, photographs, weaving—by nationally renowned and Florida artists. Pieces can be found at 13 major sites, including the main bus terminal and the airport.) A community technology center offers personal computers for public use and assistant/adaptive devices for persons with special learn-

ing and physical disabilities. Productions from theater to poetry readings are presented in a 300-seat auditorium. And don't miss La Charcuterie, a cozy cafeteria set amid the books on the second floor, with wonderful homemade breakfast and lunch treats. ✉ *100 S. Andrews Ave.,* ☎ *954/357–7444; 954/357–7457 for self-guided Art in Public Places walking tour brochure.* 🎫 *Free.* ⏲ *Mon.–Thurs. 9–9, Fri.–Sat. 9–5, Sun. noon–5:30.*

★ ❷ **Museum of Art.** Housed in an Edward Larrabee Barnes–designed building that's considered an architectural masterpiece, this museum has Florida's largest art exhibition space. The impressive permanent collection features 20th-century European and American art, including works by Picasso, Calder, Moore, Dalí, Rivers, Warhol, and Stella, as well as a notable collection of works by celebrated Ashcan School artist William Glackens. Opened in 1986, the museum launched a revitalization of the downtown district and nearby Riverwalk area. ✉ *1 E. Las Olas Blvd.,* ☎ *954/763–6464.* 🎫 *$10.* ⏲ *Tues.–Thurs. and Sat. 10–5, Fri. 10–8, Sun. noon–5.*

★ ❻ **Museum of Discovery and Science.** Like other similar museums, the aim here is to show children—*and* adults—the wonders of science in an entertaining fashion. And as soon as visitors see the 52-ft-tall Great Gravity Clock in the courtyard entrance, they know they're in for a cool experience. Inside, exhibits include Choose Health, about making healthy lifestyle choices; Kidscience, which encourages youngsters to explore the world around them; and Gizmo City, a look at how gadgets work. Florida Ecoscapes has a living coral reef and also features live bees, bats, frogs, turtles, and alligators. An IMAX theater, part of the complex, shows changing films (some 3-D) on a five-story screen. More than 700,000 visit the museum annually, making it downtown's most popular attraction. ✉ *401 S.W. 2nd St.,* ☎ *954/467–6637 for museum; 954/463–4629 for IMAX,* WEB *www.mods.org.* 🎫 *Museum $6, IMAX $9, both $12.50.* ⏲ *Mon.–Sat. 10–5, Sun. noon–6.*

❹ **Old Fort Lauderdale Museum of History.** The museum surveys city history from the Seminole era to more recent times. A model in the lobby depicts old Fort Lauderdale. In recent years the museum has expanded into several adjacent historic buildings, including the King-Cromartie House, the Historical Society's research center, and the New River Inn, the home of the museum. ✉ *231 S.W. 2nd Ave.,* ☎ *954/463–4431,* WEB *www.oldfortlauderdale.org.* 🎫 *$4.* ⏲ *Tues.–Fri. 10–4.*

★ ❺ **Riverwalk.** This lovely, paved promenade on the north bank of the New River is great for entertainment as well as views. On the first Sunday of every month a jazz brunch attracts visitors. The walk has been extended 2 mi on both sides of the beautiful urban stream, connecting the facilities of the Arts and Science District.

❼ **Sailboat Bend.** Between Las Olas and the river, as well as just across the river, lies a neighborhood with much of the character of Old Town in Key West and historic Coconut Grove in Miami. No shops or services are located here.

❶ **Stranahan House.** The oldest standing structure in the city was once the home of pioneer businessman Frank Stranahan. Stranahan arrived in 1892 and, with his wife, Ivy, befriended the Seminole Indians, traded with them, and taught them "new ways." In 1901 he built a store and later made it his home. Now it's a museum with many of his original furnishings on display. ✉ *335 S.E. 6th Ave. (at Las Olas Blvd.),* ☎ *954/524–4736,* WEB *www.stranahanhouse.com.* 🎫 *$5.* ⏲ *Wed.–Sat. 10–4, Sun. 1–4.*

Close-Up

CRUISING FOR A TAXI

SHOUT "TAXI! TAXI!" IN FORT LAUDERDALE, and your ship may have just come in.

Actually, it's a water taxi–boat, a floating "cab" that you can hail from one of the many docks along the Intracoastal Waterway.

The venture was started by longtime resident Bob Bekoff, who decided to combine the need for transportation with one of the area's most appealing features: its miles of waterways that make the city known as the Venice of America. The water taxis may not have crooning gondoliers like their Italian counterparts, but they do provide a delightful and surprisingly efficient way to get from one place to another.

For a day of sightseeing, the taxi will pick you up at one of a number of hotels along the waterway, and you can stop off at attractions like the Museum of Science and Discovery or the John Lloyd State Park. For lunch, you can enjoy a restaurant on Las Olas Boulevard or Las Olas Riverfront. In the evening, it's a great way to go bar hopping (no worry about a designated driver) or a fun way to go out to dinner.

The best way to use the water taxi is by calling 954/467–6677 about 20 minutes ahead of the desired pick-up. A one-way ticket is $7.50, round-trip is $14, and an all-day pass is $16 (the best deal). The water taxi will go anywhere within the nearly 7 mi of Intracoastal Waterway, between Port Everglades and Commercial Boulevard, and up the New River to downtown Fort Lauderdale.

— Alan Macher

Along the Beach

Fort Lauderdale's beachfront offers the best of all possible worlds, with easy access to restaurants and shops. For 2 mi beginning at the Bahia Mar yacht basin, strollers and café patrons along Route A1A enjoy clear views, typically across rows of colorful beach umbrellas, to the sea and ships passing in and out of nearby Port Everglades. Those on the beach can look back on an exceptionally graceful promenade.

Pedestrians rank ahead of cars in Fort Lauderdale. Broad walkways line both sides of the beach road, and traffic has been trimmed to two gently curving northbound lanes, where in-line skaters dance alongside slow-moving cars. On the beach side, a low masonry wall, which serves as an extended bench, extends the promenade. At night the wall is wrapped in ribbons of fiber-optic color. The most crowded portion of beach is between Las Olas and Sunrise boulevards. The tackiness of this onetime strip—famous for the springtime madness spawned by the film *Where the Boys Are*—is now but a memory.

North of the redesigned beachfront is another 2 mi of open and natural coastal landscape. Much of the way parallels the Hugh Taylor Birch State Recreation Area, which preserves a patch of primeval Florida.

A Good Tour

Go east on Southeast 17th Street across the Brooks Memorial Causeway over the Intracoastal Waterway and bear left onto Seabreeze

Boulevard (Route A1A). You will pass through a neighborhood of older homes set in lush vegetation before emerging at the south end of Fort Lauderdale's beachfront strip. On your left is the Radisson Bahia Mar Beach Resort, where novelist John McDonald's fictional hero from his series of mystery novels, Travis McGee, is honored with a plaque at marina slip F-18, where he docked his houseboat. Three blocks north, visit the **International Swimming Hall of Fame Museum and Aquatic Complex** ⑧. As you approach Las Olas Boulevard, you will see the lyrical styling that has given a distinctly European flavor to the **Fort Lauderdale beachfront** ⑨. Plan to break for lunch and perhaps a bit of shopping at Beach Place, the 100,000-square-ft entertainment, retail, and dining complex just north of Las Olas.

Turn left off Route A1A at Sunrise Boulevard, then right into **Hugh Taylor Birch State Recreation Area** ⑩, where many outdoor activities can be enjoyed amid vivid flora and fauna. Cross Sunrise Boulevard and visit the **Bonnet House** ⑪ to marvel at both the mansion and the surrounding subtropical 35-acre estate.

TIMING

The beach is all about recreation and leisure. To enjoy it as it's meant to be, allow at least a day to loll about, or rent a fishing boat.

Sights to See

★ ⓫ **Bonnet House.** A 35-acre oasis in the heart of the beach area, this subtropical estate is a tribute to the history of Old South Florida. The charming mansion was the winter residence of Frederic and Evelyn Bartlett, artists whose personal touches and small surprises are evident throughout. Whether you're interested in architecture, artwork, or the natural environment, this is a special place. ✉ *900 N. Birch Rd.,* ☎ *954/563–5393,* WEB *www.bonnethouse.com.* 🎟 *$9.* ⏲ *Wed.–Fri. 10–1:30, weekends noon–2:30.*

★ ❾ **Fort Lauderdale Beachfront.** A wave theme unifies the setting—from the low, white wave wall between the beach and widened beachfront promenade to the widened and bricked inner promenade in front of shops, restaurants, and hotels. Alone among Florida's major beachfront communities, Fort Lauderdale's beach remains open and uncluttered. More than ever, the boulevard is worth promenading.

❿ **Hugh Taylor Birch State Recreation Area.** Amid the tropical greenery of this 180-acre park you can stroll along a nature trail, visit the Birch House Museum, picnic, play volleyball, pitch horseshoes, and paddle a rented canoe. Since parking is limited on A1A, beachgoers can park here and take a walkway underpass to the beach (between 9 and 5). ✉ *3109 E. Sunrise Blvd.,* ☎ *954/564–4521,* WEB *www.abfla.com/parks.* 🎟 *$3.25 per vehicle with up to 8 people.* ⏲ *Daily 8–sunset; ranger-guided nature walks Fri. at 10:30.*

★ ❽ **International Swimming Hall of Fame Museum and Aquatic Complex.** This monument to underwater accomplishments has two 10-lane, 50-meter pools and an exhibition building with photos, medals, and other souvenirs from major swimming events around the world, as well as a theater that shows films of onetime swimming and film stars Johnny Weissmuller and Esther Williams. ✉ *1 Hall of Fame Dr.,* ☎ *954/462–6536 for museum; 954/468–1580 for pool,* WEB *www.ishof.org.* 🎟 *Museum $3, pool $3.* ⏲ *Museum and pro shop daily 9–7; pool weekdays 8–4 and 6–8, weekends 8–4; closed late Dec.–mid-Jan.*

Dining

American

$$–$$$$ ✕ **Burt & Jack's.** At the far end and most scenic lookout of Port Everglades, this local favorite has been operated by veteran restaurateur Jack Jackson and actor Burt Reynolds since 1984. Behind the heavy mission doors and bougainvillea, you can dine on Maine lobster, steaks, and chops, and the waitstaff displays the main ingredients in the raw before orders are taken. The two-story gallery of haciendalike dining rooms surrounded by glass has views of both Port Everglades and John U. Lloyd Beach State Recreation Area. Come for cocktails in early evening on Saturday or Sunday and watch the cruise ships steam out. ✉ *Berth 23, Port Everglades,* ☎ *954/522–2878 or 954/525–5225. Jacket required. AE, D, DC, MC, V. No lunch.*

$$–$$$$ ✕ **Shula's on the Beach.** With all the sports figures attaching their names to restaurants, it's only fitting that Don Shula, a legendary coach in the rough-and-tough world of pro football, should have a steak house. The good news for steak—and sports—fans is that the staff here turns out winners. The meat is cut thick and grilled over a superhot fire (for quick charring). This is a pure steak house, so don't look for many other menu choices. Appetizers are adequate although unexciting; you'll probably want to go straight to the porterhouse. Outside tables give you a delightful view of sand and ocean. Inside, a spacious bar is decorated with sports memorabilia and large-screen TVs so you can watch your favorite game. ✉ *Sheraton Yankee Trader, 321 N. Atlantic Blvd.,* ☎ *954/355–4000. AE, D, DC, MC, V.*

$$ ✕ **Tropical Acres.** This popular family-owned restaurant has been serving up sizzling steaks from a fireplace grill since 1949—a millennium by South Florida standards. There are more than 40 other entrée items to choose from, including excellent seafood dishes. Scrod is the best choice for fish. The waitstaff has been here for many years, and it shows in its friendly service. Locals and visitors are drawn to some of the best early-bird specials around. The wine list is slim, but the prices are moderate. ✉ *2500 Griffin Rd.,* ☎ *954/989–2500. AE, D, DC, MC, V.*

$–$$ ✕ **Floridian.** This Las Olas landmark has been around for as long as anyone can remember, and it still serves up one of the best breakfasts in the downtown area. People flock here on weekend mornings for oversize omelets, sausage, bacon, and biscuits. Servers can be a bit brusque, but it's all part of the atmosphere. Open 24 hours, the restaurant also serves sandwiches and hot platters for lunch and dinner. ✉ *1410 E. Las Olas Blvd.,* ☎ *954/463–4041. AE, D, DC, MC, V.*

Asian

$–$$ ✕ **Siam Cuisine.** Locals say this restaurant, tucked away in a small storefront in Wilton Manors, serves up the best Thai in the Ft. Lauderdale area, and they may be right. The waitstaff is attentive and efficient, and the family-run kitchen consistently turns out appealing and flavorful delights. Thai curry dishes with chicken or shrimp are favorites, along with appetizers of steamed dumplings. Another speciality is roast duck. ✉ *2010 Wilton Dr.,* ☎ *954/564–3411. AE, MC, V.*

Contemporary

$$–$$$$ ★ ✕ **By Word of Mouth.** This unassuming but outstanding restaurant never advertises, hence its name. But word has gotten around, because locals consistently put it at the top of "reader's choice" restaurant polls. There is no menu. Patrons are shown the day's specials and then make their choice. There's usually a good selection of fish, fowl, beef, pasta, and vegetarian entrées. A salad is served with each entrée. There's also a good selection of appetizers and desserts. ✉ *3200 N. E. 12th Ave.,* ☎ *954/564–3663. AE, MC, V.*

$$–$$$$ ★ ✕ **Mark's Las Olas.** Mark Militello, a star among South Florida chefs, is in command at this popular restaurant, where metallic finishes bounce the hubbub around the room. Militello's loyal following is enchanted with his Florida-style cuisine, which blends flavors from Caribbean, southwestern, and Mediterranean traditions. Entrées change daily, but typical choices include gulf shrimp, dolphinfish, yellowtail snapper, grouper, swordfish, Florida lobster, and callaloo (a West Indian spinach), chayote (cho-cho on Mark's menu), ginger, jicama, and plantain, all brilliantly presented and combined in sauces that tend to be low fat. Pastas and full-size dinner pizzas are thoughtful offerings. ✉ *1032 E. Las Olas Blvd.,* ☎ *954/463–1000. AE, DC, MC, V. No lunch weekends.*

Continental

$$$–$$$$ ✕ **Grill Room.** With all of the trendy eateries sprouting up along Las Olas Boulevard, you may be ready to take a break and try some of the excellent Continental cuisine served up at this historic Riverside Hotel. The room is accented in the grand style of a colonial British officers club and the menu features traditional favorites such as grilled steaks and chateaubriand and rack of lamb—both prepared for two. Other choices include roasted duck with thyme, and baked snapper served with a spicy shrimp sauce. Many dishes are prepared tableside, including a grand Caesar salad. An extensive wine list is available. The adjacent Golden Lyon Bar has the feeling of a pub somewhere in India. ✉ *Riverside Hotel, 620 E. Las Olas Blvd.,* ☎ *954/467–0671. AE, MC, V.*

French

$$–$$$$ ✕ **La Coquille.** Although this French restaurant sits at the edge of busy Sunrise Boulevard, it seems worlds away thanks to an art deco look, along with paintings of the sea and a tropical garden. The friendly and helpful service comes with a delightful French accent, and the cuisine is equally authentic: Dubonnet and vermouth cassis aperitifs are a prelude to seared sea scallops with spring vegetables, honey-glazed duckling with lingonberry sauce and wild rice, sweetbreads in a morel and truffle sauce, or veal with shallots and sweet bell peppers. There's always a soufflé among the desserts as well as a multicourse dinner special most nights. Chef-owner Jean Bert has been serving up his popular dishes for almost 20 years, so he must be doing something right. ✉ *1619 E. Sunrise Blvd.,* ☎ *954/467–3030. AE, MC, V. Closed Mon. No lunch Sat.–Thurs.*

$$$ ✕ **Left Bank.** Just off busy Las Olas Boulevard, this quiet oasis has been drawing a loyal following for more than two decades. Now chef-owner Jean-Pierre Brehier has lightened the decor—light beige walls decorated with paintings to create a Renoir-like appearance—and also the menu. Gone are the heavy cream sauces that once typified French dishes, replaced by many low-fat choices such as seared rare tuna with mushrooms, Cajun-spiced mahimahi, and grilled salmon with rum and vanilla sauce. Two menus are offered, one à la carte, and another providing a complete dinner with three choices of appetizers, four entrées, and dessert. ✉ *214 S.E. 6th Ave.,* ☎ *954/462–5376. AE, D, DC, MC, V.*

$$–$$$ ✕ **French Quarter.** This 1920 building, formerly a Red Cross headquarters, sits on a quiet street, just off bustling Las Olas Boulevard. The French-style architecture has a touch of New Orleans, and the food captures both creole and traditional French elements. Interior rooms are small and intimate, watched over by the friendly, excellent waitstaff. Among the favorites are shrimp *maison* (large shrimp sautéed with carrots and mushrooms in beurre blanc), bouillabaisse, crab cakes, and escargot appetizers. French baking is done on site, and delicious fresh bread and all pastry desserts are made daily. A prix-fixe three-course

pre-theater dinner is served until 6:30. ✉ *215 S.E. 8th Ave.,* ☎ *954/463–8000. AE, MC, V. Closed Sun. No lunch Sat.*

Italian

$$–$$$$ ✕ **Louie, Louie.** Some of the best pasta dishes on Las Olas are served at this friendly, tavern-style establishment. The menu is varied: you can order individual pizza, sandwiches, or complete dinners. Fresh fish specials are offered daily. Sea bass, for example, is cooked to perfection. Prices are reasonable, and while waiting for a table you can sample one of the large selection of beers on tap. ✉ *1103 E. Las Olas Blvd.,* ☎ *954/524–5200. AE, D, DC, MC, V.*

$$–$$$ ✕ **Primavera.** Northern Italian food is the specialty at this lovely find in the middle of an ordinary shopping plaza. Elegant floral arrangements enhance the fine dining experience. In addition to interesting pasta and risotto entrées, there is a wide variety of creative fish, poultry, veal, and beef dinners. One of chef-owner Giacomo Dresseno's favorites is veal chop Boscaiola (with shallots, wild mushrooms, and bordelaise sauce). Primavera is renowned for its spectacular assortment of both appetizers and desserts. ✉ *830 E. Oakland Park Blvd.,* ☎ *954/564–6363. AE, D, DC, MC, V. No lunch.*

$$ ✕ **Casa D'Angelo.** Owner-chef Angelo Elia has re-created his former Café D'Angelo into a gem of a Tuscan-style restaurant. Almost everything is created from scratch, and the oak oven turns out some marvelous seafood and beef dishes. The pappardelle with porcini mushrooms takes pasta to a new level. Another favorite from the pasta menu is linguine with arugula, shrimp, and scallops. Be sure to ask about the oven-roasted fish of the day. ✉ *1201 N. Federal Hwy.,* ☎ *954/564–1234. AE, D, DC, MC, V. No lunch.*

Mexican

$$–$$$$ ✕ **Eduardo de San Angel.** Forget tacos and burritos, which aren't even available here, and try the classic dishes served in true Mexican style. Authentic chilies, spices, and herbs enhance an array of seafood, meat, and poultry dishes. Typical specialties are beef tenderloin tips sautéed with Portobello mushrooms and onions with a chipotle chili sauce, and a marvelous mesquite-grilled red snapper flavored with jalapeños and mango salsa. The gourmet dishes are matched by a sophisticated setting. ✉ *2822 E. Commercial Blvd.,* ☎ *954/772–4731. AE, MC, V. Closed Sun.*

Seafood

$$$–$$$$ ★ ✕ **Blue Moon Fish Company.** The setting, on the Intracoastal Waterway, is superb; virtually every table has a lovely water view. But the real magic is in the kitchen, where chefs Baron Skorish and Bryce Statham create some of the region's best seafood dishes. Favorites include pan-seared snapper with asparagus, sea bass fillet crusted with macadamia nuts, and rare-charred tuna. Appetizers feature choices from the raw bar, including a sushi sampler, plus tasty crab and crawfish cakes and charred Portobello mushrooms. On Saturday night, a blues band performs. ✉ *4405 W. Tradewinds Ave.,* ☎ *954/267–9888. AE, MC, V.*

$$–$$$ ✕ **15th Street Fisheries.** An impressive view of the Intracoastal Waterway is only the beginning at this seafood spot. A variety of satisfying dishes include a cold seafood salad and a spicy conch chowder for starters. Homemade breads, a specialty, are accompanied by a cold onion spread. More than 65 entrées range from the traditional, such as grilled mahimahi, to the exotic, such as alligator. The fresh key lime pie has an Oreo crust. ✉ *1900 SE 15th St.,* ☎ *954/763–2777. AE, D, DC, MC, V.*

$–$$$ ✕ **Rustic Inn Crabhouse.** Wayne McDonald started with a cozy one-room roadhouse in 1955, when this stretch was a remote service road just west of the little airport. Now, the plain, rustic place is huge. Steamed crabs seasoned with garlic and herbs, spices, and oil are opened with mallets on tables covered with newspapers; peel-and-eat shrimp are served either with garlic and butter or spiced and steamed with Old Bay seasoning. The big menu includes other seafood items as well. Pies and cheesecakes are offered for dessert. ✉ *4331 Ravenswood Rd.,* ☎ *954/584–1637. AE, D, DC, MC, V.*

Southwestern

$$–$$$ ★ ✕ **Canyon.** Adventurous southwestern cuisine helps you escape the ordinary at this small but very popular spot. Take, for example, the ostrich skewers, smoked salmon tostada, Brie and wild-mushroom quesadilla, and marvelous Chilean sea bass. Free-range chicken and brook trout are served with a tempting crabmeat salsa. Many guests like to start off with Canyon's famous prickly-pear margaritas, or choose from a well-rounded wine list or selection of beers, including many microbrews. ✉ *1818 E. Sunrise Blvd.,* ☎ *954/765–1950. AE, MC, V. No lunch.*

Lodging

On the Beach

$$$$ **Marriott's Harbor Beach Resort.** If you look down from the upper stories (14 in all) at night, this 16-acre property south of the big public beach shimmers like a jewel. Spacious guest rooms are done in tropical colors, lively floral prints, rattan, wicker, and wood. Each has a balcony facing the ocean or the Intracoastal Waterway. No other hotel on the beach gives you so many activity options. ✉ *3030 Holiday Dr., 33316,* ☎ *954/525–4000 or 800/222–6543,* FAX *954/766–6152,* WEB *www.marriotthotels.com. 588 rooms, 36 suites. 5 restaurants, 3 bars, minibars, pool, massage, sauna, 5 tennis courts, health club, beach, windsurfing, boating, parasailing, children's program (ages 5–12). AE, DC, MC, V.*

$$$–$$$$ ★ **Lago Mar Resort Hotel & Club.** The sprawling Lago Mar has been owned by the Banks family since the early 1950s and after a round of renovations in recent years, it's better than ever. Most accommodations are suites, making it an ideal choice for family vacations. Suite highlights include a king-size bed, pull-out sofa, and full kitchens. Allamanda trellises and bougainvillea plantings edge the swimming lagoon, and guests have use of the broadest beach in the city. Lago Mar is less a big resort than a small town—and, in its way, a slice of Old Florida. ✉ *1700 S. Ocean La., 33316,* ☎ *954/523–6511 or 800/524–6627,* FAX *954/524–6627,* WEB *www.lagomar.com. 52 rooms, 143 one-bedroom suites, 17 two-bedroom suites. 4 restaurants, 2 pools, miniature golf, 2 tennis courts, shuffleboard, volleyball, video games, playground. AE, DC, MC, V.*

$$–$$$ **The Pillars.** Described as Fort Lauderdale's "small secret," this property at New River Sound is one block in from the beach. Its design recalls the colorful architecture of British colonial plantations found in the Caribbean in the 18th century. Most rooms yield views of the Intracoastal Waterway, with French doors opening to the patio. Rooms have rattan and mahogany headboards, period desks and nightstands, and lush draperies. Poolside rooms have French doors opening to a courtyard with a tropical garden. Suites include wet bars with refrigerators and microwaves and a sitting area. ✉ *111 North Birch Rd., 33304,* ☎ *954/467–9639,* FAX *954/763–2845. 19 rooms, 4 suites. Pool. AE, D, DC, MC, V.*

$–$$ **Nina Lee/Imperial House.** Although adjacent to one another, the Nina Lee and the Imperial House operate as one property. The Nina Lee is typical of the modest, affordable 1950s-style lodgings that can be found within a block or two of the ocean along the beach. Rooms are homey and clean, and not tiny. Efficiencies have gas kitchens, large closets, and tub-showers. The pool is set in a garden, and the entire property is just removed enough from the beach causeway to be quiet. The Imperial House has apartment-style accommodations consisting of a living room, kitchen, and bedroom. Guests may use the facilities at the nearby beachfront Sheraton Yankee Clipper hotel. ✉ *3048 Harbor Dr., 33316,* ☎ *954/524–1568. 26 units. 2 pools. MC, V.*

Downtown and Beach Causeways

$$$$ ★ **Hyatt Regency Pier Sixty-Six.** The trademark of this high-rise resort on the Intracoastal Waterway is its rooftop Pier Top Lounge. Overlooking the resort's marina, it revolves every 66 minutes and is reached by an exterior elevator. The 17-story tower dominates a 22-acre spread that includes the Spa LXVI. Tower and lanai lodgings are top choices. Each room has a balcony with views of the 142-slip marina, the ocean, and Intracoastal Waterway. Lush landscaping, and convenience to the beach, shopping, and restaurants add to this resort's appeal. When you want to swim in the ocean, hail the water taxi at the resort's dock for a three-minute trip to the beach. ✉ *2301 S. 17th St., 33316,* ☎ *954/525–6666 or 800/233–1234,* FAX *954/728–3541,* WEB *www.hyatt.com. 380 rooms, 8 suites. 3 restaurants, 3 bars, pool, hot tub, spa, 2 tennis courts, snorkeling, boating, marina, parasailing, waterskiing, fishing. AE, D, MC, V.*

$$$–$$$$ **Riverside Hotel.** On Las Olas Boulevard, just steps from boutiques, restaurants, and art galleries, this six-story hotel was built in 1936 and has been steadily upgraded. A sidewalk café fronts Bob Jenny's tropical murals, one of which is a New Orleans–style work that stretches across 725 square ft of the hotel's facade. Old Fort Lauderdale photos grace the hallways, and rooms are outfitted distinctively, with antique oak furnishings, framed French prints, and European-style baths. The poolside bar in back offers a great view of the New River, as do the best guest rooms. An attentive staff includes many who have been with the hotel for two decades or more. You can enjoy afternoon tea in the lobby, and fine dining at Indigo, which has Southeast Asian cooking, or the elegant Grill Room. ✉ *620 E. Las Olas Blvd., 33301,* ☎ *954/467–0671 or 800/325–3280,* FAX *954/462–2148,* WEB *www.riversidehotel.com. 109 rooms, 7 suites. 2 restaurants, bar, no-smoking room, pool, dock. AE, DC, MC, V.*

$$–$$$ ★ **Banyan Marina Apartments.** These outstanding waterfront apartments, on a residential island just off Las Olas Boulevard, are set amid imaginative landscaping that includes a walkway through the upper branches of a banyan tree. With leather sofas, springy carpets, live potted plants, sheer curtains, custom drapes, high-quality art, French doors, and jalousies for sweeping the breeze in, the luxurious units are as comfortable as any first-class hotel—but for half the price. Also included are a full kitchen, dining area, beautiful gardens, dockage for eight yachts, and exemplary housekeeping. ✉ *111 Isle of Venice, 33301,* ☎ *954/524–4430 or 800/524–4431,* FAX *954/764–4870. 10 rooms, 1 efficiency, 4 one-bedroom apartments, 2 two-bedroom apartments. Dining room, pool, dock. MC, V.*

Nightlife and the Arts

For the most complete weekly listing of events, read the **"Showtime!"** entertainment insert and events calendar in the Friday *Fort Lauderdale Sun Sentinel.* **"Weekend,"** in the Friday Broward edition of the *Miami Herald,* also carries listings of area happenings. The weekly ***City Link*** is principally an entertainment and dining paper with a relic "underground" look. A 24-hour **Arts & Entertainment Hotline** (☎ 954/357–5700) provides updates on art, attractions, children's events, dance, festivals, films, literature, museums, music, opera, and theater.

Tickets are sold at individual box offices and through **Ticketmaster** (☎ 954/523–3309); there is a service charge.

The Arts

Broward Center for the Performing Arts (✉ 201 S.W. 5th Ave., ☎ 954/462–0222) is the waterfront centerpiece of Fort Lauderdale's cultural arts district. More than 500 events a year are scheduled at the 2,700-seat architectural masterpiece, including Broadway musicals, plays, dance, symphony and opera, rock, film, lectures, comedy, and children's theater.

Nightlife

BARS AND LOUNGES

Bahia Cabana (✉ 3001 Harbor Dr., ☎ 954/524–1555) features pop groups and a DJ in a setting that includes a biergarten and a view of the harbor. **Café Iguana** (✉ Beach Place, 17 S. Atlantic Blvd., ☎ 954/763–7222) has a nightly DJ to keep the dance floor hopping. **Cheers** (✉ 941 E. Cypress Creek Rd., ☎ 954/771–6337) is an action-filled nightspot with a wide variety of rock bands, two bars, and a dance floor. **Chili Pepper** (✉ 200 W. Broward Blvd., ☎ 954/525–0094) brings hot current rock bands to the stage. **Howl at the Moon** (✉ Beach Place, 17 S. Atlantic Blvd., ☎ 954/522–5054) has dueling piano players and sing-alongs nightly. **Kitty Ryan's O'Hara's Pub** (✉ 722 E. Las Olas Blvd., ☎ 954/524–1764) has live jazz and blues nightly. It's packed for TGIF, although usually by the end of each day the trendy crowd spills onto this prettiest of downtown streets. **Maguire's Hill 16** (✉ 535 N. Andrews Ave., ☎ 954/764–4453) highlights excellent bands in a classic Irish pub setting. **Tavern 213** (✉ 213 S.W. 2nd St., ☎ 954/463–6213) is a small, no-frills club that highlights jazz and blues.

Outdoor Activities and Sports

Baseball

From mid-February to the end of March, the **Baltimore Orioles** (✉ Fort Lauderdale Stadium, N.W. 12th Ave., ☎ 954/776–1921) are in spring training.

Biking

Some of the most popular routes are Route A1A and Bayview Drive, especially early in the morning before traffic builds, and a 7-mi bike path that parallels Route 84 and the New River and leads to Markham Park, which has mountain-bike trails. Most area bike shops also have cycling maps.

Fishing

If you're interested in a saltwater charter, check out the **Radisson Bahia Mar Beach Resort** (✉ 801 Seabreeze Blvd., ☎ 954/627–6357). Both sportfishing and drift-fishing bookings can be arranged.

Scuba Diving and Snorkeling

Lauderdale Diver (✉ 1334 S.E. 17th St. Causeway, ☎ 954/467–2822 or 800/654–2073), which is PADI affiliated, arranges dive charters throughout the county. Dive trips typically last four hours. Nonpackage reef trips are open to divers for $42; scuba gear is extra.

Pro Dive (✉ 515 Seabreeze Blvd., ☎ 954/761–3413 or 800/772–3483), a PADI five-star facility, is the area's oldest diving operation and offers packages with Radisson Bahia Mar Beach Resort, from where its 60-ft boat departs. Snorkelers can go out for $24 on a two-hour snorkeling trip, which includes equipment. Scuba divers pay $39 using their own gear or $79 with all rentals included.

Soccer

South Florida's major-league soccer team, the **Miami Fusion** (✉ 5301 N.W. 12th Ave., ☎ 954/717–2200), plays its home schedule at 20,000-seat Lockhart Stadium in Ft. Lauderdale.

Tennis

With 21 courts, 18 of them lighted clay courts, the **Jimmy Evert Tennis Center at Holiday Park** is Fort Lauderdale's largest public tennis facility. Chris Evert, one of the game's greatest players, learned the sport here under the watchful eye of her father, Jimmy, who retired after 37 years as the center's tennis professional. ✉ *701 N.E. 12th Ave.,* ☎ *954/761–5378.* *$4.50 per person per hr.* *Weekdays 8 AM–9:15 PM, weekends 8–7.*

Shopping

Malls

Just north of Las Olas Boulevard on Route A1A is the happening **Beach Place** (✉ 17 S. Atlantic Blvd.). Here you can browse through such shops as the Gap, Bath & Body Works, and Banana Republic; have lunch or dinner at an array of restaurants, from casual Caribbean to elegant American; or carouse at a selection of nightspots—all open late. By and large, eateries on the lower level are more upscale, whereas on the upper level the prices are lower and the ocean view is better.

With a convenient in-town location just west of the Intracoastal Waterway, the split-level **Galleria Mall** (✉ 2414 E. Sunrise Blvd.) contains more than 1 million square ft of space. It's anchored by Neiman-Marcus, Lord & Taylor, Dillards, and Saks Fifth Avenue and features 150 world-class specialty stores with an emphasis on fashion and sporting goods.

Shopping Districts

When you're downtown, check out the **Las Olas Riverfront** (✉ 1 block west of Andrews Ave. on the New River), a shopping, dining, and entertainment complex. If only for a stroll and some window-shopping, don't miss the **Shops of Las Olas** (✉ 1 block off New River east of U.S. 1). The city's best boutiques plus top restaurants (many affordable) and art galleries line a beautifully landscaped street.

Side Trips

The Western Suburbs and Beyond

West of Fort Lauderdale is an ever-growing mass of suburbs flowing one into the other. They're home to most of the city's golf courses as well as some attractions and large malls. As you head farther west, the terrain becomes more Evergladeslike, and you'll occasionally see an alligator sunning itself on a canal bank. No matter how dedicated developers are to building over this natural resource, the Everglades keeps trying to assert itself. Waterbirds, fish, and other creatures are found in canals and lakes, even man-made ones, throughout the western areas.

As many as 80 butterfly species from South and Central America, the Philippines, Malaysia, Taiwan, and other Asian nations are typically
12 found within **Butterfly World,** a 3-acre site inside Tradewinds Park. A screened aviary called North American Butterflies is reserved for native species. The Tropical Rain Forest Aviary is a 30-ft-high construction, with observation decks, waterfalls, ponds, and tunnels where thousands of colorful butterflies flit and fly about. ✉ *3600 W. Sample Rd., Coconut Creek,* ☎ *954/977–4400,* WEB *www.butterflyworld.com.* *$12.95.* *Mon.–Sat. 9–5, Sun. 1–5.*

13 The 30-acre **Everglades Holiday Park** provides a good glimpse of the Everglades. Here you can take an airboat tour, look at an 18th-century-style Native American village, or watch an alligator-wrestling show. A souvenir shop, TJ's Grill, a convenience store, and a campground with RV hookups and tent sites are all here as well. ✉ *21940 Griffin Rd.,* ☎ *954/434–8111,* WEB *www.evergladesholidaypark.com.* *Free, airboat tour $14.50.* ⏲ *Daily 9–5.*

14 To understand and enjoy the Everglades, take an airboat ride at **Sawgrass Recreation Park.** You'll see all sorts of plants and wildlife, such as birds, alligators, turtles, snakes, and fish. Included in the entrance fee along with the airboat ride is admission to an Everglades nature exhibit, a native Seminole Indian village, and exhibits about alligators, other reptiles, and birds of prey. A souvenir and gift shop, food service, and an RV park with hookups are also at the park. ✉ *U.S. 27 north of I–595,* ☎ *954/426–2474,* WEB *www.evergladestours.com.* *$14.68.* ⏲ *Daily 6–6, airboat rides 8–5.*

Some distance from Fort Lauderdale's tranquil beaches, but worth the
15 one-hour drive, is the **Big Cypress Seminole Reservation** and its two very different attractions. At the **Billie Swamp Safari,** you can experience the majesty of the Everglades firsthand. Daily tours of the wetlands and hammocks, where wildlife abound, yield sightings of deer, water buffalo, bison, wild hogs, hawks, eagles, alligators, and even the rare Florida panther. Tours are provided aboard swamp buggies—customized motor vehicles specially designed to provide you with an elevated view of the frontier. ✉ *Snake Rd., 19 mi north of I–75 Exit 14,* ☎ *941/983–6101 or 800/949–6101,* WEB *www.nps.gov/bicy.* *Free, swamp buggy ecotour/alligator and snake education show/airboat ride package $38.* ⏲ *Daily 8–5.*

Not far away from the Billie Swamp Safari is the **Ah-Tha-Thi-Ki Museum,** whose name means "a place to learn, a place to remember." It is just that. The museum honors the culture and tradition of the Seminoles through artifacts and reenactments of rituals and ceremonies. The site includes a living Seminole village, nature trails, and a boardwalk through a cypress swamp. ✉ *Snake Rd., 17 mi north of I–75 Exit 14,* ☎ *954/792–0745.* *$6.* ⏲ *Tues.–Sun. 9–5.*

DINING AND LODGING

$–$$$ ✕ **Wolfgang Puck Café.** Just in case you were lacking an excuse, here's another reason to go the mall. Food celebrity Wolfgang Puck picked the Oasis section of Sawgrass Mills, the giant outlet mall, for one of his signature cafés that are now springing up around the nation. Beginning in California, Puck helped pioneer open kitchens, wood-burning ovens, and gourmet pizzas, all on display here. Amid their shopping bags, patrons here are treated to excellent service and quality dishes. Plate-size pizzas are crispy and offer tasty toppings, including spicy shrimp with peppers, vegetable combinations, and smoked salmon. One of the unusual but flavorful pasta dishes include roasted pumpkin ravioli. All-American entrées include rosemary chicken and a very good meat loaf with garlic mashed potatoes. ✉ *Sawgrass Mills, 2610 Sawgrass Mills Circle, Sunrise,* ☎ *954/846–8668. AE, D, MC, V.*

$$–$$$$ **Radisson Resort Coral Springs.** The resort is adjacent to the Tournament Players Club golf course in Heron Bay, home of the Honda Golf Classic. Its location near the Sawgrass Expressway also makes it convenient to area attractions. Spacious rooms are furnished with oak and cherrywood and have data ports for those with laptops in tow. The property also has a conference center, an outdoor terrace, and a gameroom. ✉ *11775 Heron Bay Blvd., 33076,* ☎ *954/753–5598,*

FAX 954/753–2888. 224 rooms, 6 suites. Restaurant, bar, pool, sauna, exercise room. AE, D, MC, V.

$$–$$$$ **Wyndham Resort & Spa Fort Lauderdale.** As its name suggests, this resort offers the luxury, amenities, and facilities of a resort with the health-consciousness of a spa. Spacious guest rooms and suites are done in tropical colors with rattan seating and overlook a lake or golf course. Oversize baths have dressing areas. In the morning complimentary caffeine-free herbal teas are offered; in the afternoon it's fresh fruit. The staff nutritionist follows American Heart Association and American Cancer Society guidelines and can accommodate macrobiotic and vegetarian diets. Also on site and open to the public is a full-service beauty salon. The resort offers combination spa-tennis and spa-golf packages. ✉ *250 Racquet Club Rd., 33316,* ☎ *954/389–3300 or 800/327–8090,* FAX *954/384–0563,* WEB *www.wyndham.com. 496 units. 4 restaurants, 2 bars, 5 pools, hair salon, spa, 2 18-hole golf courses, 24 tennis courts, bowling, horseback riding, roller-skating rink, shops. AE, D, MC, V.*

NIGHTLIFE AND THE ARTS

Sunrise Musical Theatre (✉ 5555 N.W. 95th Ave., Sunrise, ☎ 954/741–7300) is a 4,000-seat theater presenting everything from ballet to top-name pop, rock, and country artists.

OUTDOOR ACTIVITIES AND SPORTS

Fishing. The marina at **Everglades Holiday Park** (✉ 21940 Griffin Rd., ☎ 954/434–8111) caters to freshwater fishing. For $67.50 for five hours, you can rent a 14-ft johnboat (with a 9.9-horsepower Yamaha outboard) that carries up to four people. A rod and reel rent for $9 a day, and bait is extra. For two people, a fishing guide for a half day (four hours) is $170; for a full day (eight hours), $220. A third person adds $35 for a half day, $70 for a full day. You can also buy a freshwater fishing license (mandatory) here; a seven-day nonresident license is $17. Freshwater fishing with a guide out of **Sawgrass Recreation Park** (✉ U.S. 27 north of I–595, ☎ 954/426–2474) costs $175 for two people for a half day, $225 for a full day. Resident and nonresident fishing licenses and live bait are available.

Golf. Next Day Golf (☎ 954/772–2582) provides access at no extra fee to private courses normally limited to members and arranges bookings up to 12 months in advance—a big advantage for golfers planning trips during the busy winter months. They also offer last-minute discount tee times (call 12 hours in advance). **Bonaventure Country Club** (✉ 200 Bonaventure Blvd., ☎ 954/389–2100) has 36 holes. **Broken Woods Country Club** (✉ 9000 Sample Rd., Coral Springs, ☎ 954/752–2140) has 18 holes. **Colony West Country Club** (✉ 6800 N.W. 88th Ave., Tamarac, ☎ 954/726–8430) offers play on 36 holes. Just west of Florida's Turnpike, the **Inverrary Country Club** (✉ 3840 Inverrary Blvd., Lauderhill, ☎ 954/733–7550) has three 18-hole courses. **Jacaranda Golf Club** (✉ 9200 W. Broward Blvd., Plantation, ☎ 954/472–5855) has 18 holes to play. **Sabal Palms Golf Course** (✉ 5101 W. Commercial Blvd., Tamarac, ☎ 954/731–2600) has 18 holes. **Sunrise Country Club** (✉ 7400 N.W. 24th Pl., Sunrise, ☎ 954/742–4333) provides 18 holes.

Ice Hockey. National Car Rental Center is the home of the National Hockey League's **Florida Panthers** (✉ 2555 N.W. 137th Way, Sunrise, ☎ 954/523–3309).

SHOPPING

Broward's shopping extravaganza, **Fashion Mall at Plantation** (✉ University Dr. north of Broward Blvd., Plantation) is a jewel of a mall. The three-level complex includes such department stores as Macy's, Lord

& Taylor, and Burdines; a Sheraton Suites Hotel; and more than 100 specialty shops. In addition to a diverse food court, the Brasserie Max restaurant offers gourmet dining.

Travel industry surveys reveal that shopping is vacationers' number one activity. With 25 million visitors annually, **Sawgrass Mills Mall** (✉ 12801 W. Sunrise Blvd., at Flamingo Rd., Sunrise), 9 mi west of downtown Fort Lauderdale, proves the point, ranking as the second-biggest tourist attraction in Florida, behind Disney. This so-called world's largest retail outlet mall is one of the first places visitors ask about. The complex itself is alligator shape, and walking every nook and cranny is about 2 mi. (If the 800-member Mall Walkers Club—mostly seniors—can do it, so can you.) Shops, many of them manufacturer's outlets, retail outlets, and name-brand discounters, include Neiman-Marcus, Loehmann's, Ann Taylor, Levi's, Donna Karan, Saks Fifth Avenue, and Kenneth Cole. At the Oasis, a Hard Rock Cafe, Legal Seafood from Boston, and 24-screen movieplex are joined by Wolfgang Puck's first South Florida eatery.

NORTH ON SCENIC A1A

North of Fort Lauderdale's Birch Recreation Area, Route A1A edges back from the beach through the section known as the Galt Ocean Mile, and a succession of ocean-side communities lines up against the sea. Traffic can line up, too, as it passes through a changing pattern of beach-blocking high-rises and modest family vacation towns and back again. Here and there a scenic lighthouse or park punctuates the landscape, while other attractions and recreational opportunities are found inland.

Lauderdale-by-the-Sea

16 *5 mi north of Fort Lauderdale.*

Tucked just north of Fort Lauderdale's northern boundary, this low-rise family resort town bans construction of more than three stories. You can drive along lawn-divided El Mar Drive, lined with garden-style motels a block east of Route A1A. However, you don't actually need a car in Lauderdale-by-the-Sea. Dozens of good restaurants and shops are in close proximity to hotels and the beach.

Where Commercial Boulevard meets the ocean, you can walk out onto **Anglin's Fishing Pier,** stretching 875 ft into the Atlantic. Here you can fish, stop in at any of the popular restaurants clustered around the seafront plaza, or just soak up the scene.

Dining and Lodging

$$ ✕ **Sea Watch.** It's set back from the road and easy to miss, but after more than 25 years this nautical-theme restaurant right on Lauderdale-by-the-Sea's beach stays packed during lunch and dinner. Waits can be as long as 30 minutes, but time passes quickly in the sumptuous upstairs lounge with comfy sofas and high-back rattan chairs. The menu has all the right appetizers: oysters Rockefeller, gulf shrimp, clams casino, and Bahamian conch fritters. Typical daily specials might be oat-crusted sautéed yellowtail snapper with roasted red bell pepper sauce and basil, or a charbroiled dolphinfish fillet marinated with soy sauce, garlic, black pepper, and lemon juice. Desserts include a cappuccino brownie and strawberries Romanoff. Good early-bird specials are offered off-season. ✉ *6002 N. Ocean Blvd. (Rte. A1A), Fort Lauderdale,* ☎ *954/781–2200. AE, MC, V.*

$–$$ ✕ **Aruba Beach Café.** This is your best bet at the pier. A big beachside barn of a place—very casual, always crowded, always fun—it serves large portions of Caribbean conch chowder, Cuban black-bean soup, fresh tropical salads, burgers, sandwiches, and seafood. A reggae/jazz band performs Friday and Sunday 2 to 7. ✉ *1 E. Commercial Blvd.,* ☎ *954/776–0001. AE, D, DC, MC, V.*

$$–$$$ **A Little Inn by the Sea.** French, German, and English are spoken at this inn, which caters to a very international clientele. Innkeeper Uli Brandt and his family maintain tropical charm and bed-and-breakfast style. Since taking over the property in 1994, they have continued to make upgrades, including remodeled kitchens in efficiencies and one- and two-bedroom suites, and new bamboo and rattan furniture throughout. Adding to the flavor are fountains and classical background music at breakfast. The inn is directly on the ocean, and rooms have nice views from private balconies. ✉ *4546 El Mar Dr., 33308,* ☎ *954/772–2450 or 800/492–0311,* FAX *954/938–9354,* WEB *www.alittleinn.com. 10 rooms, 7 suites, 12 efficiencies. Pool, beach, bicycles. AE, D, DC, MC, V.*

$$ **Tropic Seas Resort Inn.** It's only a block off A1A, but it's a million-dollar location—directly on the beach and two blocks from municipal tennis courts. Built in the 1950s, units are plain but clean and comfortable, with tropical rattan furniture and ceiling fans. The complimentary Sunday brunch and weekly wiener roast and rum swizzle party are good opportunities to mingle with other guests. ✉ *4616 El Mar Dr., 33308,* ☎ *954/772–2555 or 800/952–9581,* FAX *954/771–5711. 16 rooms, 6 efficiencies, 7 apartments. Pool, beach. AE, D, DC, MC, V.*

$–$$ **Blue Seas Courtyard.** Bubbly innkeeper Cristie Furth, with her husband Marc, runs this small one- and two-story motel—in a quiet resort area just a block from the beach. Lattice fencing and gardens of cactus and impatiens were added in front for more privacy around the brick patio and pool. Guest quarters have a Mexican hacienda look with hand-painted/stenciled decor, and have kitchenettes, terra-cotta tiles, and bright artwork. Handmade painted shutters and indoor plants add to the atmosphere. ✉ *4525 El Mar Dr., 33308,* ☎ *954/772–3336,* FAX *954/772–6337,* WEB *www.blueseascourtyard.com. 12 units. Pool, coin laundry. MC, V.*

Outdoor Activities and Sports

Anglin's Fishing Pier (☎ 954/491–9403) is open for fishing 24 hours a day. Fishing costs $4, tackle rental is an additional $5 (plus $10 deposit), and bait averages $2.

Pompano Beach

17 *3 mi north of Lauderdale-by-the-Sea.*

As Route A1A enters this town directly north of Lauderdale-by-the-Sea, the high-rise procession begins again. Sportfishing is big in Pompano Beach, as its name implies, but there's more to beachside attractions than the popular Fisherman's Wharf. Behind a low coral-rock wall, Alsdorf Park extends north and south of the wharf along the road and beach.

Dining and Lodging

$$$–$$$$ ★ ✕ **Cafe Maxx.** New-wave epicurean dining had its South Florida start here in the early 1980s, and Cafe Maxx remains popular among regional food lovers. The setting is ordinary, in a little strip of stores, but inside there's a holiday glow year-round. Chef Oliver Saucy demonstrates ritual devotion to the preparation of fine cuisine. The menu changes nightly but always showcases foods from the tropics: jumbo stone-crab claws with honey-lime mustard sauce and black-bean and banana-pepper chili with Florida avocado. Appetizer favorites include duck and smoked mozzarella ravioli with brown butter, basil, and sun-dried tomatoes—a pure delight. Desserts also reflect a tropical theme, from praline macadamia mousse over chocolate cake with butterscotch sauce to candied ginger with pears poached in muscatel and sun-

dried cherry ice cream. More than 200 wines are offered by the bottle, another 20 by the glass. ✉ *2601 E. Atlantic Blvd.,* ☎ *954/782–0606. AE, D, DC, MC, V. No lunch.*

$$$–$$$$ 🏨 **Palm-Aire Spa Resort.** This 750-acre health, fitness, and stress-reduction spa offers exercise activities, personal treatments, and calorie-controlled meals. Separate men's and women's pavilions have private sunken Roman baths, Swiss showers, and some of the most experienced hands in the massage business. There are 166 spacious rooms and 18 golf villas with private terraces. All have separate dressing rooms, and some have two baths. You can have use of the spa for $96 for a half day or $220 for the whole day, including lunch, massage, facial, and fitness classes. ✉ *2601 Palm-Aire Dr. N, 33069,* ☎ *954/972–3300. 184 units. Restaurant, pool, hot tub, massage, sauna, spa, steam room, 94-hole golf course, 37 tennis courts, aerobics, exercise room, racquetball, squash. AE, D, MC, V.*

$$$ 🏨 **Beachcomber.** This Best Western property's beach location is central to most Broward County attractions. Ocean views are everywhere, from the oversize guest-room balconies to the dining rooms. Although there are also villas and penthouse suites atop the eight-story structure, standard rooms are spacious. The multilingual staff is attentive to guest requests. ✉ *1200 S. Ocean Blvd., 33062,* ☎ *954/941–7830 or 800/231–2423,* WEB *www.beachcomber-ftlaud.com. 134 rooms, 9 villas, 4 suites. Restaurant, bar, 2 pools, beach. AE, D, MC, V.*

Outdoor Activities and Sports

FISHING

Pompano Pier (☎ 954/943–1488) extends 1,080 ft into the Atlantic. The cost is $2.65; rod-and-reel rental is $10.18 (including admission and initial bait).

For drift fishing try ***Fish City Pride*** (✉ Fish City Marina, 2621 N. Riverside Dr., ☎ 954/781–1211). Morning, afternoon, and evening trips cost $28 and include fishing gear. You can arrange for a saltwater charter boat through the **Hillsboro Inlet Marina** (✉ 2629 N. Riverside Dr., ☎ 954/943–8222). The 10-boat fleet offers half-day charters for $325, including gear, for up to six people.

GOLF

Crystal Lake South Course (✉ 3800 Crystal Lake Dr., ☎ 954/943–2902) has 18 holes. **Palm-Aire Country Club & Resort** (✉ 3701 Oaks Clubhouse Dr., ☎ 954/978–1737; 954/975–6244 for tee line), part of the Palm-Aire Spa Resort, has 94 holes of golf, including a course with an extra four holes.

HORSE RACING

Pompano Harness Track, Florida's only harness track features world-class trotters and pacers during its October–August meet. The Top o' the Park restaurant overlooks the finish line. The track also has simulcast betting and a poker room. ✉ *1800 S.W. 3rd St.,* ☎ *954/972–2000.* 🎟 *Grandstand free, clubhouse $2.* ⏲ *Racing Mon., Wed., Fri., and Sat. 7:30.*

ICE-SKATING

Visitors from the North who miss ice and cold can skate at the **Gold Coast Ice Arena** during morning, afternoon, or evening sessions. ✉ *4601 N. Federal Hwy.,* ☎ *954/943–1437.* 🎟 *Sessions $6, skate rental $2.* ⏲ *Sun.–Thurs. 8:30–4 (Tues. 8:15 PM–10 PM), Fri.–Sat. 8:15 AM–11 PM.*

Shopping

Bargain hunters head to the **Festival Flea Market** (✉ 2900 W. Sample Rd.), where more than 600 vendors sell merchandise in a 400,000-square-ft building. There are also a games section for youngsters and an 18-screen cinema. The old Pompano Fashion Square has been reborn as

Pompano Square (✉ 2001 N. Federal Hwy.) and now features a tropical motif. This comfortably sized city mall has 60 shops, three department stores, and a few places for food.

Lighthouse Point

18 *2 mi north of Pompano Beach.*

The big attraction here is the view across Hillsboro Inlet to **Hillsboro Light,** the brightest lighthouse in the Southeast. Mariners have used this landmark for decades. From the ocean you can see the light almost halfway to the Bahamas. Although the lighthouse is on private property and is inaccessible to the public, it's well worth a peek.

Dining

$$–$$$ ★ ✕ **Cap's Place.** On an island that was once a bootlegger's haunt, this seafood restaurant is reached by launch and has served such luminaries as Winston Churchill, FDR, and John F. Kennedy. Cap was Captain Theodore Knight, born in 1871, who, with partner-in-crime Al Hasis, floated a derelict barge to the area in the 1920s. Today the rustic restaurant, built on the barge, is run by descendants of Hasis. Baked wahoo steaks are lightly glazed and meaty, the long-cut french fries arouse gluttony, hot and flaky rolls are baked fresh several times a night, and tangy lime pie is a great finishing touch. Turn east off Federal Highway onto Northeast 24th Street (two blocks north of Pompano Square); follow the double yellow line to the launch. ✉ *Cap's Dock, 2765 N.E. 28th Ct.,* ☎ *954/941–0418. AE, MC, V. No lunch.*

En Route To the north, Route A1A traverses the so-called Hillsboro Mile (actually more than 2 mi), a millionaire's row of some of the most beautiful and expensive homes in Broward County. The road runs along a narrow strip of land between the Intracoastal Waterway and the ocean, with bougainvillea and oleanders edging the way and yachts docked along both banks. In winter the traffic often creeps at a snail's pace, as vacationers and retirees gawk at the views.

Deerfield Beach

19 *3½ mi north of Lighthouse Point.*

The name **Quiet Waters Park** belies what's in store for kids here. Splash Adventure is a high-tech water-play system with swings, slides, and tunnels, among other activities. There's also cable waterskiing and boating on the park's lake. ✉ *401 S. Powerline Rd.,* ☎ *954/360–1315.* *$1 weekends, free weekdays; Splash Adventure $3.* ⏲ *Daily 8–6.*

Deerfield Island Park, an 8½-acre island that can only be reached by boat, is a paradise of coastal hammock, or tree islands. Officially designated an urban wilderness area along the Intracoastal Waterway, it contains a mangrove swamp that provides a critical habitat for gopher tortoises, gray foxes, raccoons, and armadillos. Boat shuttles run on the hour Wednesday 10–noon and Sunday 10–3; space is limited, so call for reservations. Call also for special events. ✉ *1 Deerfield Island; boat landing at Riverview Restaurant, Riverview Rd.,* ☎ *954/360–1320.* *Free.*

Dining and Lodging

$$–$$$$ ★ ✕ **Brooks.** This is one of the area's better restaurants, thanks to a French perfectionist, Bernard Perron. Meals are served in a series of rooms filled with replicas of old masters, cut glass, antiques, and tapestrylike floral wallpapers, although the shedlike dining room still feels very Florida. Fresh ingredients go into distinctly Floridian cuisine. Main courses include red snapper in papillote, broiled fillet of pompano with seasoned root vegetables, and a sweet lemongrass linguine with bok

choy and julienned crisp vegetables. ✉ *500 S. Federal Hwy.,* ☎ *954/427–9302. AE, D, MC, V.*

$$ ★ ✕ **Whale's Rib.** If you're looking for a casual, almost funky, nautical setting near the beach, look no farther. For more than 20 years the Williams family has been serving up excellent seafood and good cheer. Fish specials are offered daily, along with whale fries—thinly sliced potatoes that look like hot potato chips. Those with smaller appetites can choose from a good selection of salads and fish sandwiches. Other favorites are specials from the raw bar and a popular fish dip for starters. The place is crowded on weekends, and parking is limited. ✉ *2031 N.E. 2nd St.,* ☎ *954/421–8880. AE, MC, V.*

$$–$$$$ **Ocean Terrace Suites.** This four-story motel is in one of the quieter sections of north Broward, just south of the Palm Beach county line, across the narrow shore road from the beach. Large units—efficiencies and one- and three-bedroom apartments—all have big balconies overlooking the sea. Colors vary from shore-washed to bright; pink and green pastels tint the bedrooms. The furniture is rattan, and units are clean and neat. Art is throwaway, flowers are artificial, and materials are bargain quality. Still, for size, location, and price, this is a good buy. An outdoor barbecue grill is available. ✉ *2080 E. Hillsboro Blvd., 33441,* ☎ *954/427–8400,* FAX *954/427–0555,* WEB *www.ocean-terracesuites.com. 30 units. Pool. AE, D, DC, MC, V.*

$$–$$$ **Royal Flamingo Villas.** A small community of houselike villas built in the 1970s reaches from the Intracoastal Waterway to the ocean. The roomy and comfortable one- and two-bedroom villas are all condominium owned, so they're fully furnished the way owners want them. All are so quiet that you hear only the soft click of the ceiling fans. The development is wisely set back a bit from the beach, which is being restored. If you don't need lavish public facilities, this is your upscale choice at a reasonable price. ✉ *1225 Hillsboro Mile (Rte. A1A), Hillsboro Beach 33062,* ☎ *954/427–0669, 954/427–0660, or 800/241–2477,* FAX *954/427–6110. 41 villas. Pool, putting green, shuffleboard, beach, dock, boating, coin laundry. D, MC, V.*

$–$$ **Carriage House Resort Motel.** This clean and tidy motel sits one block from the ocean. Run by a French-German couple, the white, two-story colonial-style motel with black shutters is actually two buildings connected by a second-story sundeck. Steady improvements have been made to the facility, including the addition of Bahama beds that feel and look like sofas. Kitchenettes are equipped with good-quality utensils. Rooms are self-contained and quiet and have walk-in closets and room safes. ✉ *250 S. Ocean Blvd., 33441,* ☎ *954/427–7670,* FAX *954/428–4790,* WEB *www.carriagehouseresort.com. 6 rooms, 14 efficiencies, 10 apartments. Pool, shuffleboard, coin laundry. AE, MC, V.*

Outdoor Activities and Sports

FISHING

The **Cove Marina** (✉ Hillsboro Blvd. and the Intracoastal Waterway, ☎ 954/360–9343) is home to a deep-sea charter fleet. During the winter season there are excellent runs of sailfish, kingfish, dolphinfish, and tuna. A half-day charter costs about $325 for six people. Enter the marina through the Cove Shopping Center.

GOLF

Off Hillsboro Boulevard west of Interstate 95, **Deer Creek Golf Club** (✉ 2801 Country Club Blvd., ☎ 954/421–5550) has 18 holes.

SCUBA DIVING

One of the area's most popular dive boats, the 43-ft ***Lady Go-Diver*** (✉ Cove Marina, Hillsboro Blvd. and the Intracoastal Waterway, ☎ 954/942–7333) has morning and afternoon dives, plus evening dives on weekends. Divers can explore the marine life of nearby reefs and shipwrecks. The cost is $40, plus $8 for each tank. Riders are welcome for $25.

SOUTH BROWARD

From Hollywood's Broadwalk, a 27-ft-wide thoroughfare paralleling 2 mi of palm-fringed beach, to the western reaches of Old West–flavored Davie, this region has a personality all its own. South Broward's roots are in early Florida settlements. Thus far it has avoided some of the glitz and glamour of its neighbors to the north and south, and folks here like it that way. Still, there's plenty to see and do—excellent restaurants in every price range, world-class pari-mutuels, and a new focus on the arts.

Hollywood

20 *7 mi south of Fort Lauderdale.*

Hollywood is a city undergoing a revival. New shops, restaurants, and art galleries are opening at a rate that rivals that of Miami's South Beach. The city recently spiffed up its Broadwalk, a wide pedestrian walkway along the beach, where Rollerbladers are as common as visitors from the North. Trendy sidewalk cafés have opened, vying for space with mom-and-pop T-shirt shops. Downtown, along Harrison Street, jazz clubs and still more fashionable restaurants are drawing young professionals to the scene.

In 1921 Joseph W. Young, a California real-estate developer, began developing the community of Hollywood from the woody flatlands. It quickly became a major tourist magnet, home to casino gambling and everything else that made Florida hot. Reminders of the glory days of the Young era remain in places like Young Circle (the junction of U.S. 1 and Hollywood Boulevard) and the stately old homes that line east Hollywood streets.

The **Art and Culture Center of Hollywood** is a visual and performing-arts center with an art reference library, outdoor sculpture garden, arts school, and museum store. It's just east of Young Circle. ✉ *1650 Harrison St.,* ☎ *954/921–3274.* 🎫 *Wed.–Sat. $3, Sun. $8 (including classical or jazz concert); donation welcome Tues.* ⏲ *Tues.–Sat. 10–4, Sun. 1–4.*

With the Intracoastal Waterway to its west and the beach and ocean to the east, the 2.2-mi paved promenade known as the **Broadwalk** has been popular with pedestrians and cyclists since 1924. Expect to hear French spoken along this scenic stretch, especially during the winter; Hollywood Beach has been a favorite winter getaway for Québecois ever since Joseph Young hired French-Canadians to work here in the 1920s.

Hollywood North Beach Park is at the north end of the Broadwalk. No high-rises overpower the scene, nothing hip or chic, just a laid-back, old-fashioned place for enjoying the sun, sand, and sea. ✉ *Rte. A1A and Sheridan St.,* ☎ *954/926–2444.* 🎫 *Free; parking $4 until 2, $2 after.* ⏲ *Daily 8–6.*

Comprising 1,500 acres at the Intracoastal Waterway, **West Lake Park** is one of Florida's largest urban nature facilities, providing a wide range of recreational activities. You can rent a canoe, kayak, or boat with an electric motor (no fossil fuels are allowed in the park) or take the 40-minute environmental boat tour. Extensive boardwalks traverse a mangrove community, where endangered and threatened species abound. A 65-ft observation tower allows views of the entire park. More than $1 million in exhibits are on display at the **Anne Kolb Nature Cen-**

ter, named after the late county commissioner who was a leading environmental advocate. A great place to take youngsters, the center's exhibit hall features 27 interactive displays, an ecology room, and a trilevel aquarium. ✉ *1200 Sheridan St.,* ☎ *954/926–2410.* 🎫 *Weekends $1, weekdays free; exhibit hall $3.* ⏲ *Daily 8–6.*

At the edge of Hollywood lies **Seminole Native Village,** a reservation where you can pet a cougar, hold a baby alligator, and watch other wildlife demonstrations. The Seminole Indians also sell their arts and crafts. ✉ *3551 N. Rte. 7,* ☎ *954/961–4519.* 🎫 *Self-guided tour $5, guided tour including alligator wrestling and snake demonstrations $10.* ⏲ *Daily 9–5.*

Across the street from the Seminole Native Village, **Hollywood Seminole Gaming** has high-stakes bingo, low-stakes poker, and more than 500 gaming machines. ✉ *4150 N. Rte. 7,* ☎ *954/961–3220.* 🎫 *Free.* ⏲ *Daily 24 hrs.*

In addition to displaying a collection of artifacts from the Seminoles and other tribes, Joe Dan and Virginia Osceola sell contemporary Native American arts and crafts at the **Anhinga Indian Museum and Art Gallery.** It's also across the street from the Seminole Native Village, although that technically puts it over the Fort Lauderdale border. ✉ *5791 S. Rte. 7, Fort Lauderdale,* ☎ *954/581–0416.* ⏲ *Daily 9–5.*

Dining and Lodging

$$$–$$$$ ✕ **Martha's.** Guests have two choices of dining location, both providing impressive views of the Intracoastal Waterway. Martha's Tropical Grille, on the upper deck, is more informal. Martha's Supper Club, on the lower level, is dressier—tables adorned with orchid buds, fanned napery, etched-glass dividers, brass, rosewood, and an outdoor patio surrounded by a floral mural. Piano music accompanies dinner downstairs, and later a band plays for dancing, setting a supper-club mood. Both floors offer similar menus, however—chiefly Florida seafood: flaky dolphinfish in a court bouillon; shrimp dipped in a piña colada batter, rolled in coconut, and panfried with orange mustard sauce; and snapper prepared 17 ways. For dessert try sorbet and vanilla and chocolate ice cream topped with meringue and hot fudge brandy sauce. Complimentary dock space is provided for those arriving by boat. ✉ *6024 N. Ocean Dr.,* ☎ *954/923–5444. Reservations essential. AE, D, DC, MC, V.*

$$–$$$ ✕ **Giorgio's Grill.** Good food and service are hallmarks of this large, 400-seat restaurant overlooking the Intracoastal Waterway. Seafood is a specialty on the self-described "Mediterranean-inspired" menu, but you'll also find a nice selection of pasta and meat dishes. A great water view and friendly staff add to the experience. A surprisingly extensive wine list is reasonably priced. ✉ *606 N. Ocean Dr.,* ☎ *954/929–7030. AE, MC, V.*

$$–$$$ ✕ **Las Brisas.** There's a wonderful bistro atmosphere at this small and cozy restaurant with Mexican tiles and blue-and-white check tablecloths beneath paddle fans. Right next to the beach, Las Brisas offers seating inside or out, and the food is Argentine with an Italian flair. Antipasto salads are prepared for two; the roasted vegetables are crunchy and flavorful. A small pot sits on each table filled with *chimichurri* (a paste made of oregano, parsley, olive oil, salt, garlic, and crushed pepper), for spreading on steaks. Grilled or deep-fried fish is a favorite, as are pork chops, chicken, and pasta entrées. Desserts include a rum cake, a flan like *mamacita* used to make, and a *dulce con leche* (a sweet milk pudding). The wine list is predominantly Argentine. ✉ *600 N. Surf Rd.,* ☎ *954/923–1500. AE, MC, V. Closed Mon. No lunch.*

$$–$$$ ✕ **Sushi Blues Café.** First-class Japanese food is served up in a cubicle setting that's so jammed you wonder where this hip group goes by day.

Japanese chefs prepare conventional and macrobiotic-influenced dishes that range from a variety of sushi and rolls (California, tuna, and the Yozo roll, with snapper, flying-fish eggs, asparagus, and Japanese mayonnaise) to steamed veggies with tofu and steamed snapper with miso sauce. Also available are a few wines by the glass or bottle, a selection of Japanese beers, and some very un-Japanese desserts—fried bananas and Swiss chocolate mousse cake. The house band, the Sushi Blues Band, performs on Friday and Saturday; guest musicians often sit in. ✉ *1836 S. Young Circle,* ☎ *954/929–9560. AE, MC, V. Closed Sun. No lunch.*

$–$$ ✕ **Le Tub.** Formerly a Sunoco gas station, this place is now a quirky waterside saloon with a seeming affection for claw-foot bathtubs. Hand-painted tubs are everywhere—under ficus, sea grape, and palm trees. The eatery is highly favored by locals for affordable food: mostly shrimp, burgers, and barbecue. ✉ *1100 N. Ocean Dr.,* ☎ *954/921–9425. No credit cards.*

$$$–$$$$ ★ **Diplomat Resort Country Club & Spa.** This new Diplomat, on the site of the original hotel of the same name, evokes memories of one of South Florida's grandest resorts of the 1960s and '70s. Back then, celebrities, presidents, and entertainers frequented the original ocean-side Diplomat. The original was imploded to make way for the new 39-story, twin-tower, 1,000-room property. Built at a cost of $600 million, the hotel has a lobby/atrium area with ceilings soaring to 60 ft in height, accented with nearly 50 42-ft-tall palm trees. The Florida theme carries to the guest rooms and suites, where clean lines and sweeping curves highlight the art deco style. More than 70% of the rooms have spacious balconies with an ocean or Intracoastal Waterway view. The top four floors make up the concierge levels, with added services and more stylish features. A signature of the resort is its 120-ft bridged pool, extending from the lobby to the beachfront. It includes a see-through bottom and two waterfalls flowing to the lagoon pool below. The Country Club portion of the Resort is ½ mi from the beach part of the hotel and contains the tennis and golf facilities. Shuttle service is provided between the properties. ✉ *1995 E. Hallandale Beach Blvd., 33309,* ☎ *954/457–2000 or 800/327–1212,* WEB *www.diplomatresort.com. 900 rooms, 100 one- or two-bedroom suites. 3 restaurants, pool, spa, 18-hole golf course, 10 tennis courts, health club, spa, marina, convention center. AE, DC, MC, V.*

$$–$$$ **Driftwood on the Ocean.** This attractive late-1950s-era resort motel faces the beach at the secluded south end of Surf Road. The setting is what draws guests, but attention to maintenance and frequent refurbishing are what make it a value. Accommodations range from a standard hotel room to a deluxe two-bedroom, two-bath suite. Most units have a kitchen, one-bedroom apartments have a daybed, and standard rooms have a queen-size Murphy bed. All have balconies. ✉ *2101 S. Surf Rd., 33019,* ☎ *954/923–9528 or 800/944–3148,* FAX *954/922–1062,* WEB *www.driftwoodontheocean.com. 6 rooms, 4 suites, 39 efficiencies. Pool, shuffleboard, beach, bicycles, coin laundry. AE, MC, V.*

$$–$$$ **Greenbriar Beach Club.** In a neighborhood of Hollywood Beach known for its flowered streets, this oceanfront all-suites hotel retains its 1950s style outside, but inside the rooms have been renovated and feature full kitchens. The staff is multilingual, and the TVs even have four Spanish and two French channels. Fronting on a 200-ft stretch of beach, the hotel bills itself as "Florida's best-kept secret," and it just could be. ✉ *1900 S. Surf Rd., 33019,* ☎ *954/922–2606 or 800/861–4873,* FAX *954/923–0897,* WEB *www.greenbriarbc.com. 47 suites. Pool, volleyball, beach, coin laundry. AE, MC, V.*

$$ ★ **Manta Ray Inn.** Canadians Donna and Dwayne Boucher run this exemplary two-story lodging on the beach and have kept the place immaculate and the rates affordable. Dating from the 1940s, the inn of-

fers the casual, comfortable beachfront for which vacations in Hollywood are famous. Nothing's fussy—white spaces with burgundy trim and rattan furniture—and everything's included. Kitchens are equipped with pots, pans, and mini-appliances that make housekeeping convenient. All apartments have full closets, and all except for two-bedroom units with stalls have tub-showers. Grills are available. ✉ *1715 S. Surf Rd., 33019,* ☎ *954/921–9666 or 800/255–0595,* FAX *954/929–8220,* WEB *www.mantarayinn.com. 12 units. Beach. No credit cards.*

$–$$ **Sea Downs.** This three-story lodging directly on the Broadwalk is a good choice for efficiency or apartment living (one-bedroom apartments can be joined to make two-bedroom units). All but two units have ocean views, and all are comfortably done in chintz, but with blinds, not drapes. Kitchens are fully equipped, and most units have tub-showers and closets. Housekeeping is provided once a week. In between, guests receive fresh towels daily and sheets on request, but they make their own beds. Sea Downs's sister property, Bougainvillea, is a few paces off the beach, so rates are slightly lower. However, Bougainvillea's guests can use the Sea Downs pool, while those at Sea Downs can enjoy Bougainvillea's gardens. ✉ *2900 N. Surf Rd., 33019-3704,* ☎ *954/923–4968,* FAX *954/923–8747,* WEB *www.seadowns.com. 6 efficiencies, 8 one-bedroom apartments. Pool. No credit cards.*

Outdoor Activities and Sports

BIKING

The 2-mi **Broadwalk,** which has its own bike path, is popular with cyclists.

DOG RACING

Hollywood Greyhound Track has dog-racing action during its December–May season. There is a clubhouse dining room. ✉ *831 N. Federal Hwy., Hallandale,* ☎ *954/454–9400.* *Grandstand $1, clubhouse $3, parking free.* ⏲ *Racing Tues., Thurs., and Sat. at 12:30 and 7:30; Sun.–Mon., Wed., and Fri. at 7:30.*

FISHING

Sea Leg's III (✉ 5400 N. Ocean Dr., ☎ 954/923–2109) runs drift-fishing trips from 8 AM to 12:30 PM and 1:30 to 6 and bottom-fishing trips from 7 PM to midnight. Trips cost $27 to $30, and include fishing gear.

GOLF

The **Diplomat Country Club** (✉ 501 Diplomat Pkwy., Hallandale, ☎ 954/457–2000), with 18 holes, is south of town. The course at **Emerald Hills** (✉ 4100 Hills Dr., ☎ 954/961–4000) has 18 holes.

HORSE RACING

Gulfstream Park Race Track is the winter home of some of the nation's top thoroughbreds, trainers, and jockeys. New owners have upgraded facilities, added family days with attractions for kids, and scheduled concerts with name performers. The season is capped by the $1 million Florida Derby, which features Kentucky Derby hopefuls. Racing is held from January through mid-March. ✉ *901 S. Federal Hwy., Hallandale,* ☎ *954/454–7000.* *Grandstand $3, clubhouse $5.* ⏲ *Racing Wed.–Mon. at 1.*

Dania Beach

21 *3 mi north of Hollywood, 4 mi south of Fort Lauderdale.*

This town at the south edge of Fort Lauderdale is probably best known for its antiques dealers, but there are other attractions as well.

★ The **Graves Museum of Archaeology & Natural History** has an extensive dinosaur exhibit that includes a recent discovery, bambiraptor, better known as "Bambi"—the missing link in the dinosaur-bird evolution. This hidden treasure of a museum also has a wide-ranging permanent collection ranging from pre-Columbian art and Greco-Roman materials to artifacts from early Florida. Also on display are a 3-ton quartz crystal and dioramas on Tequesta Indian life and a jaguar habitat. Monthly lectures, conferences, field trips, and a summer archaeological camp are offered. The museum bookstore is one of the best in Florida. ✉ *481 S. Federal Hwy.,* ☎ *954/925–7770,* WEB *www.gravesmuseum.org.* 🎟 *$9.95.* ⏲ *Tues.–Fri. 10–4, Sat. 10–6, Sun. noon–6.*

★ The **John U. Lloyd Beach State Recreation Area** is a pleasant plot of land with a pine-shaded beach, a jetty pier where you can fish, a marina, nature trails, and canoeing on Whiskey Creek. This is a great spot to watch cruise ships entering and departing Port Everglades, to the west across the waterway. ✉ *6503 N. Ocean Dr.,* ☎ *954/923–2833.* 🎟 *$4 per vehicle with up to 8 people.* ⏲ *Daily 8–sunset.*

IGFA Fishing Hall of Fame and Museum is a shrine to the sport of fishing. Near the Fort Lauderdale airport at Interstate 95 and Griffin Rd., the center is the creation of the International Game Fishing Association. In addition to checking out the World Fishing Hall of Fame, a marina, and an extensive museum and research library, you can visit seven galleries with virtual-reality fishing and other interactive displays. And in the Catch Gallery, you can cast off via virtual reality and try to reel in a marlin, sailfish, or bass. ✉ *300 Gulfstream Way, Dania Beach,* ☎ *954/922–4212,* WEB *www.igfa.org/museum.* 🎟 *$4.99.* ⏲ *Daily 10–6.*

Outdoor Activities and Sports

FISHING

The 920-ft **Dania Pier** (☎ 954/927–0640) is open around the clock. Fishing is $3 (including parking), tackle rental is $6, bait is about $2, and spectators pay $1.

JAI ALAI

Dania Jai-Alai Palace has one of the fastest games on the planet, scheduled year-round. Added features include simulcast wagering from other tracks, and a poker room. ✉ *301 E. Dania Beach Blvd.,* ☎ *954/428–7766.* 🎟 *$1.50; reserved seats $2–$7, including parking and program.* ⏲ *Games Tues. and Sat. at noon and 7:15, Wed.–Fri. at 7:15, Sun. at 1; closed Wed. in June.*

ROLLER COASTER

The Hurricane roller coaster isn't the highest, fastest, or longest coaster in the world, but it's near the top in all those categories and it is the tallest wooden roller coaster south of Atlanta. Best yet, even though it's brand new, it doesn't feel like a clone of the antiseptic modern steel coaster that whips you through 360° loops. This is a retro-feeling ride—a wooden coaster that creaks like an old staircase while you travel its 3,200 ft of track and plummet from 100 ft high. ✉ *1760 N.W. First St.,* ☎ *954/921–7433.* 🎟 *$6.25.* ⏲ *Sun.–Thurs. 10 AM–11 PM, Fri. and Sat. 10 AM–2 AM.*

Shopping

More than 75 **antiques dealers** line Federal Highway (U.S. 1), ½ mi south of the Fort Lauderdale airport and ½ mi north of Hollywood. Take the Stirling Road or Griffin Road East exit off Interstate 95.

Davie

22 *4 mi west of Dania.*

This town's horse farms and estates are the closest thing to the Old West in South Florida. Folks in Western wear ride their fine horses through downtown—where they have the same right of way as motorists—and order up takeout at "ride-through" windows. With 70,000 residents, the town has doubled in size in 15 years, and gated communities are now found alongside ranches. A monthly rodeo is Davie's most famous activity.

Gators, crocodiles, river otters, and birds of prey can be seen at **Flamingo Gardens,** as can a 23,000-square-ft walk-through aviary, a plant house, and an Everglades museum in the pioneer Wray Home. A half-hour guided tram ride winds through a citrus grove and wetlands area. ✉ *3750 Flamingo Rd.,* ☎ *954/473–2955,* WEB *www.flamingogardens.org.* *$12, tram ride $2.* *Daily 9:30–5:30; Closed Mon. June–Sept.*

At the **Young at Art Children's Museum,** kids can work with paint, graphics, sculpture, and crafts according to themes that change three times a year. Then they take their masterpieces home with them. ✉ *11584 Rte. 84, in the Plaza,* ☎ *954/424–0085,* WEB *www.youngatartmuseum.org.* *$4.* *Mon.–Sat. 10–5, Sun. noon–5.*

Dining

$$–$$$ ★ ✕ **Armadillo Cafe.** Chefs Eve Montella and Kevin McCarthy have created a restaurant whose southwestern theme, casual decor, and inspired food have made it popular with visitors from around the world for more than a decade. Seafood is the mainstay of the menu, but other specialties include boneless duck and marinated leg of lamb. ✉ *3400 S. University,* ☎ *954/791–5104. AE, D, DC, MC, V.*

Nightlife and the Arts

THE ARTS

Bailey Concert Hall (✉ Central Campus of Broward Community College, 3501 S.W. Davie Rd., ☎ 954/475–6884) is a popular place for classical music concerts, dance, drama, and other performing-arts activities, especially October–April.

NIGHTLIFE

Davie Junction (✉ 6311 Orange Dr., ☎ 954/581–1132), South Florida's hottest location for country music, is in the heart of Broward's horse country. Local and national performers are featured. There are dance lessons, and the club is open until 4 AM daily.

Uncle Funny's Comedy Club (✉ 9160 Rte. 84, Pine Island Plaza, ☎ 954/474–5653) showcases national and local comics Wednesday–Sunday at 8:30 plus Friday and Saturday at 11.

Outdoor Activities and Sports

BIKING

Bicycle enthusiasts can ride at the **Brian Piccolo Park velodrome** (✉ Sheridan St. and N.W. 101st Ave., Cooper City), south of Davie.

GOLF

Rolling Hills (✉ 3501 Rolling Hills Circle, ☎ 954/475–3010) has 18 holes.

RODEO

The local **rodeo** (✉ 6591 S.W. 45th St., ☎ 954/475–9787) is held the fourth weekend of every month. Special national rodeos come to town some weekends.

FORT LAUDERDALE AND BROWARD COUNTY A TO Z

AIR TRAVEL

CARRIERS

To research prices, get advice from other travelers, and book arrangements, visit www.fodors.com.

The following airlines serve Ft. Lauderdale/Hollywood International Airport.

➤ AIRLINES AND CONTACTS: **Air Canada** (☎ 800/776–3000). **Air Jamaica** (☎ 800/523–5585). **AirTran** (☎ 800/825–8538). **America West** (☎ 800/235–9282). **American** (☎ 800/433–7300). **Comair** (☎ 800/354–9822). **Continental** (☎ 800/525–0280). **Delta** (☎ 800/221–1212). **Island Express** (☎ 954/359–0380). **Laker** (☎ 888/525–3724). **Midway** (☎ 800/446–4392). **Northwest** (☎ 800/225–2525). **Southwest** (☎ 800/435–9792). **Spirit** (☎ 800/772–7117). **TWA** (☎ 800/221–2000). **United** (☎ 800/241–6522). **US Airways** (☎ 800/428–4322).

AIRPORTS

Fort Lauderdale–Hollywood International Airport, 4 mi south of downtown Fort Lauderdale and just off U.S. 1, is one of Florida's busiest, serving more than 14 million passengers a year. A major airport expansion added a new terminal and access roads.

Broward Transit operates bus route No. 1 between the airport and its main terminal at Broward Boulevard and Northwest 1st Avenue, in the center of Fort Lauderdale. Service from the airport is every 20 minutes and begins daily at 5:30 AM; the last bus from the downtown terminal to the airport leaves at 9:50 PM. The fare is $1 (50¢ for senior citizens). Airport Express provides limousine service to all parts of Broward County. Fares to most Fort Lauderdale beach hotels are in the $8–$12 range.

➤ AIRPORT INFORMATION: **Fort Lauderdale–Hollywood International Airport** (☎ 954/359–6100). **Airport Express** (☎ 954/561–8888). **Broward Transit** (☎ 954/357–8400).

BOAT AND FERRY TRAVEL

Water Taxi provides service along the Intracoastal Waterway in Fort Lauderdale between the 17th Street Causeway and Commercial Boulevard 10 AM–1 AM. *See* Close-Up: Cruising for a Taxi, *below.*

➤ BOAT AND FERRY INFORMATION: **Water Taxi** (☎ 954/467–6677).

BUS TRAVEL

Greyhound Lines buses stop in Fort Lauderdale.

Broward County Mass Transit bus service covers the entire county. The fare is $1 plus 15¢ for a transfer. Service on all beach routes starts before 6 AM and continues past 10 PM except on Sunday. Call for route information.

Fort Lauderdale has replaced its motorized trolley service with expanded, free TMAX bus service. Routes cover both the downtown loop and on weekends, the beach area, with the Las Olas/Beach Line connecting major tourist sites in both places. Buses run every 10 minutes, weekdays 11:30–2:30, Friday night 5 PM–2 AM, and Saturday nights 7 PM–2 AM.

CUTTING COSTS

Broward County Mass Transit offers special seven-day tourist passes that cost $9 and are good for unlimited use on all county buses. These are available at some hotels, at Broward County libraries, and at the main bus terminal.

➤ BUS INFORMATION: **Broward County Mass Transit** (☎ 954/357–8400; Main Bus Terminal: ✉ Broward Blvd. at N.W. 1st Ave., Fort Lauderdale). **Greyhound Lines** (☎ 800/231–2222; Fort Lauderdale: ✉ 515 N.E. 3rd St., ☎ 954/764–6551). **TMAX** (☎ 954/761–3543).

CAR RENTAL

Agencies in the airport include Avis, Budget, Dollar, Hertz, and National. In addition, Alamo and Enterprise offer shuttle services to nearby rental centers.

➤ LOCAL AGENCIES: **Alamo** (☎ 954/525–4713). **Avis** (☎ 954/359–3255). **Budget** (☎ 954/359–4700). **Dollar** (☎ 954/359–7800). **Enterprise** (☎ 954/760–9888). **Hertz** (☎ 954/359–5281). **National** (☎ 954/359–8303).

CAR TRAVEL

Access to Broward County from north or south is via Florida's Turnpike, Interstate 95, U.S. 1, or U.S. 441. Interstate 75 (Alligator Alley) connects Broward with Florida's west coast and runs parallel to Route 84 within the county.

Except during rush hour, Broward County is a fairly easy place in which to drive. East–west Interstate 595 runs from westernmost Broward County and links Interstate 75 with Interstate 95 and U.S. 1, providing handy access to the airport. The scenic but slow Route A1A generally parallels the beach. Another road less traveled is the Sawgrass Expressway (Route 869), a toll road that's a handy link to Sawgrass Mills shopping and the ice-hockey arena, both in Sunrise.

EMERGENCIES

Dial 911 for police or ambulance.

➤ 24-HOUR PHARMACIES: **Eckerd Drug** (✉ 1385 S.E. 17th St., Fort Lauderdale, ☎ 954/525–8173; ✉ 1701 E. Commercial Blvd., Fort Lauderdale, ☎ 954/771–0660; ✉ 154 University Dr., Pembroke Pines, ☎ 954/432–5510). **Walgreens** (✉ 2855 Stirling Rd., Fort Lauderdale, ☎ 954/981–1104; ✉ 5001 N. Dixie Hwy., Oakland Park, ☎ 954/772–4206; ✉ 289 S. Federal Hwy., Deerfield Beach, ☎ 954/481–2993; ✉ 3210 S. University Dr., Davie, ☎ 954/475–9375).

ENGLISH-LANGUAGE MEDIA

NEWSPAPERS AND MAGAZINES

The*Fort Lauderdale Sun-Sentinel* is published daily.

RADIO

FM: 93.1 WTMI, classical; 105.9 WBGG, classic rock; 102.7 WMXJ, oldies; 101.5 WLIF, adult contemporary; 99.9 WKIS, country. AM: 560 WQAM, sports; 610 WIOD, news.

TAXIS

It's difficult to hail a cab on the street. Sometimes you can pick one up at a major hotel. Otherwise, phone ahead. Fares are not cheap; meters run at a rate of $2.75 for the first mile and $2 for each additional mile; waiting time is 25¢ per minute. The major company serving the area is Yellow Cab.

➤ TAXI INFORMATION: **Yellow Cab** (☎ 954/565–5400).

TOURS

Carrie B., a 300-passenger day cruiser, gives 90-minute tours up the New River and Intracoastal Waterway. Cruises depart at 11, 1, and 3 each day and cost $11.95.

Jungle Queen III and *IV* are 175-passenger and 527-passenger tour boats that take day and night cruises up the New River through the heart of Fort Lauderdale. The sightseeing cruises at 10 and 2 cost $12.50, while the evening dinner cruise costs $26.95. You can also take a daylong trip to Miami's Bayside Marketplace ($15.50), on Biscayne Bay, for shopping and sightseeing on Wednesday and Saturday, departing at 9:15.

Hannah Glover offers leisurely narrated tours along the Intracoastal Waterway. There are two options: cruise only ($9.50), which departs at 12:20, and 2:50, and a cruise/meal combination ($28.50), which leaves at 10 and features lunch at the dockside Charley's Crab restaurant.

Professional Diving Charters operates the 60-ft glass-bottom boat *Pro Diver II*. On Tuesday through Saturday mornings and Sunday afternoon, two-hour sightseeing trips costing $18 take in offshore reefs; snorkeling can be arranged at $24 per person.

National Audubon Society Education Dept., a not-for-profit organization, conducts dry-land field trips throughout South Florida and one-day, overnight, and longer boat tours as part of its program. Call in advance for availability.

Cosponsored by the Fort Lauderdale Historical Society, Walking Tours traces the New River by foot during the winter and spring.
➤ TOURS INFORMATION: ***Carrie B.*** (✉ Riverwalk at S.E. 5th Ave., Fort Lauderdale, ☎ 954/768–9920). ***Hannah Glover*** (✉ Cove Shopping Center, Hillsboro Blvd. at Intracoastal Waterway, Deerfield Beach, ☎ 954/428–4026). ***Jungle Queen III* and *IV*** (✉ Radisson Bahia Mar Beach Resort, 801 Seabreeze Blvd., Fort Lauderdale, ☎ 954/462–5596). **National Audubon Society Education Dept.** (✉ 444 Brickell Ave., Suite 850, Miami 33131, ☎ 305/371–6399 or 800/498–8129). **Professional Diving Charters** (✉ 515 Seabreeze Blvd., Fort Lauderdale, ☎ 954/761–3413). **Walking Tours** (✉ 219 S.W. 2nd Ave., Fort Lauderdale, ☎ 954/463–4431).

TRAIN TRAVEL

Amtrak provides daily service to the Fort Lauderdale station as well as other Broward County stops at Hollywood and Deerfield Beach.

Tri-Rail operates train service daily 5 AM–11 PM (more limited on weekends) through Broward, Miami-Dade, and Palm Beach counties. There are six Broward stations west of Interstate 95: Hillsboro Boulevard in Deerfield Beach, Cypress Creek, Fort Lauderdale, Fort Lauderdale Airport, Sheridan Street in Hollywood, and Hollywood Boulevard.
➤ TRAIN INFORMATION: **Amtrak** (☎ 800/872–7245; Fort Lauderdale: ✉ 200 S.W. 21st Terr., ☎ 954/463–8251). **Tri-Rail** (☎ 954/728–8445).

VISITOR INFORMATION

➤ TOURIST INFORMATION: **Chamber of Commerce of Greater Fort Lauderdale** (✉ 512 N.E. 3rd Ave., Fort Lauderdale 33301, ☎ 954/462–6000). **Davie/Cooper City Chamber of Commerce** (✉ 4185 S.W. 64th Ave., Davie 33314, ☎ 954/581–0790). **Greater Deerfield Beach Chamber of Commerce** (✉ 1601 E. Hillsboro Blvd., Deerfield Beach 33441, ☎ 954/427–1050). **Greater Fort Lauderdale Convention & Visitors Bureau** (✉ 1850 Eller Dr., Suite 303, Fort Lauderdale 33301, ☎ 954/765–4466). **Hollywood Chamber of Commerce** (✉ 330 N. Federal Hwy., Hollywood 33019, ☎ 954/923–4000). **Lauderdale-by-the-Sea Chamber of Commerce** (✉ 4201 N. Ocean Dr., Lauderdale-by-the-Sea 33308, ☎ 954/776–1000). **Pompano Beach Chamber of Commerce** (✉ 2200 E. Atlantic Blvd., Pompano Beach 33062, ☎ 954/941–2940).

4 PALM BEACH AND THE TREASURE COAST

Long stretches of golden beaches are the unifying theme along this part of the Florida coast. The southern end is anchored by the sophisticated beach towns of Boca Raton and Delray Beach. Just north is wealthy and glitzy Palm Beach, internationally known for power shopping and pricey dining. Then comes the Treasure Coast, an appealing mix of quaint, rustic, and upscale beach towns set between peaceful nature preserves.

Updated by Pamela Acheson and Richard B. Myers

THIS SECTION OF ATLANTIC COAST defies categorization. Although it's easy to affix labels—the stretch from Palm Beach to Boca Raton is considered the northern reaches of the Gold Coast (which in its entirety extends all the way to Miami), while north of Palm Beach is called the Treasure Coast—the individual communities along this section of the Florida coastline all have their own personalities. Here you'll find everything from the center-stage glitziness of Palm Beach to the low-key quiet of Hutchinson Island. The unifying attraction is compelling—golden beaches bordered by luxuriant palms. The arts also flourish here. In town after town you will find a profusion of museums, galleries, theaters, and groups committed to historic preservation.

The focus of the region is indisputably Palm Beach. Although tourists may go to Delray Beach or Jupiter Island or scores of other towns to catch some rays and feel sand between their toes, most stop in Palm Beach for a completely different pastime: gawking. The gold on this stretch of coast is the kind you put in a vault, and for more than a century now the island town has been a hotbed of conspicuous consumption. Palm Beach is the richest city in Florida and would easily compete for honors with places like Monaco and Malibu as the most affluent community in the world. It has long been the winter address for families with names such as Rockefeller, Vanderbilt, Kennedy, and Trump.

It all started with Henry Morrison Flagler, cofounder of Standard Oil, who, in addition to bringing the railroad to Florida in the 1890s, brought his own view of civilization. The poor and middle-class fishermen and laborers who inhabited the place in the pre-Flagler era were moved a mile west or so to West Palm Beach. Today West Palm is a bustling community in its own right; but, it still can't compete with the glitz of Flagler's luxe Palm Beach legacy.

The town of Palm Beach represents only 1% of the land area in Palm Beach County, however. The rest is given over to sprawling West Palm Beach, classic Florida beach towns, malls, and to the west, citrus farms, the Arthur R. Marshall–Loxahatchee National Wildlife Refuge, and Lake Okeechobee, the largest lake in Florida and one of the country's hot spots for bass-fishing devotees.

Also worth exploring is the Treasure Coast, which encompasses the northernmost part of Palm Beach County plus Martin, St. Lucie, and Indian River counties. Although late to develop, the Treasure Coast now has its share of malls and beachfront condominiums, and yet much of its shoreline is laid-back and peaceful. Inland is largely devoted to citrus and sugar production and cattle ranching in rangelands of pine and palmetto scrub.

Along the coast, the broad tidal lagoon called the Indian River separates the barrier islands from the mainland. In addition to sheltering boaters on the Intracoastal Waterway and playing nursery for many saltwater game fish, it's a natural radiator, keeping frost away from the tender orange and grapefruit trees that grow near its banks. Sea turtles come ashore at night from late April to September to lay their eggs on the beaches.

Pleasures and Pastimes

Beaches

Half the towns in the area include the word *beach* in their name, and for good reason. Here are miles of golden strands—some relatively remote and uncrowded, some buzzing with activity, and all blessed with the kind of blue-green waters you just won't find farther north. Among the least crowded are those at Hobe Sound National Wildlife Refuge and Fort Pierce Inlet State Recreation Area. Boca Raton's three beaches and Delray Beach's broad stretch of sand are among the most popular.

Dining

Not surprisingly, numerous elegant establishments offer upscale Continental and contemporary cuisine, but the area also has many good, casual waterfront watering holes that serve up a mean fried or blackened grouper, a local delicacy. Just an hour west, on Lake Okeechobee, you can dine on panfried catfish a few hundred yards from where it was caught. Most restaurants have early-bird menus, a Florida hallmark, which usually offer most or all dinner entrées at a reduced price if ordered during certain hours.

Fishing

Within a 50-mi radius of Palm Beach, you'll find virtually every form of fishing except, of course, ice fishing. If it involves a hook and a line, you can do it here—year-round. Charter a boat for deep-sea fishing out of towns from Boca Raton to Sebastian Inlet. West of Vero Beach, there's tremendous marsh fishing for catfish, bass, and perch. Lake Okeechobee is one of the world's bass-fishing capitals.

Golf

Palm Beach County is to golf what Saudi Arabia is to oil. For openers, there's the Professional Golfing Association (PGA) headquarters at the PGA National Resort & Spa in Palm Beach Gardens (a mere five golf courses). In all, there are approximately 150 public, private, and semiprivate golf courses in Palm Beach County. A Golf-A-Round program, in which more than 100 hotels participate, lets you play at one of 10 courses each day, with no greens fees.

Shopping

Some of the most expensive stores in the United States cluster on Palm Beach's Worth Avenue, which is comparable to Rodeo Drive in Beverly Hills as an upscale shopper's nirvana. But there's also plenty of reasonable shopping nearby, including the likes of the Palm Beach Mall, the Manufacturers Outlet Center, and the impressive new Palladium at CityPlace, all in West Palm Beach, and Mizner Park in Boca Raton. You can browse in art galleries and antique shops in Vero Beach and Delray Beach.

Exploring Palm Beach and the Treasure Coast

The center of most any visit to the area is Palm Beach proper. Not only is it within an hour's drive of most of the region, but its Gatsby-era architecture, stunning mansions, and highbrow shopping make it unlike any other place in Florida. From there you can head in any of three directions: south along the Gold Coast toward Boca Raton, back to the mainland and north to the barrier-island treasures of the Treasure Coast, or west for some inland delights.

Great Itineraries

Tucked into an island 12 mi long and about ¼ mi wide, Palm Beach is easy to cover thoroughly in just a day or two. If you have several days, you can take in a lot of varied sights, exploring everything from galleries to subtropical wildlife preserves, and with a week you'll easily be able to see the whole area, from Boca Raton all the way north to Sebastian. Of course you could just do what a lot of visitors prefer—laze around soaking up the rays and the atmosphere.

Numbers in the text correspond to numbers in the margin and on the Gold Coast and Treasure Coast and the Palm Beach and West Palm Beach maps.

IF YOU HAVE 3 DAYS

With a short amount of time, make **Palm Beach** ①–⑪ your base. On the first day, start in the middle of downtown, **Worth Avenue** ⑦, to do some window-shopping and gallery browsing. After you've refreshed yourself with a *très* chic bistro lunch, head for that other must-see on even the shortest itinerary: the **Henry Morrison Flagler Museum** ②. Your second day is for the beach; two good options are Lantana Public Beach, which has great food concessions, and Oceanfront Park, in **Boynton Beach** ㉔. Spend the better part of your last day exploring attractions you wouldn't expect to find in South Florida, such as the Morikami Museum and Japanese Gardens in nearby **Delray Beach** ㉖. Trite as it may sound, it's like a one-day visit to Japan.

IF YOU HAVE 5 DAYS

With five days you can be more contemplative at the galleries and museums, more leisurely at the beaches, and have time for more serendipitous exploring. Stay in **Palm Beach** ①–⑪ for two nights. The first day visit the **Henry Morrison Flagler Museum** ② and the luxury hotel known as **The Breakers** ④, another Flagler legacy. Then head to **Worth Avenue** ⑦ for a leisurely lunch and an afternoon of window-shopping. On the second day drive over to **West Palm Beach** ⑫–㉑ and the **Norton Museum of Art** ⑬, which has an extensive collection of 19th-century French Impressionists. On day three, choose between making an overnight visit to **Lake Okeechobee,** the bass-fishing capital of the world, and staying in Palm Beach another night and driving a half hour to explore the Arthur R. Marshall–Loxahatchee National Wildlife Refuge. Head south to **Boca Raton** ㉗ on the fourth day, and check into a hotel near the beach before spending the rest of the afternoon wandering through Mizner Park's shops. On your fifth day, meander through the Boca Raton Museum of Art in the morning and get some sun at South Beach Park after lunch.

IF YOU HAVE 7 DAYS

With an entire week you can see the Gold and Treasure coasts thoroughly, with time left to fit in such recreational pursuits as taking sailboard or croquet lessons, catching a polo match, or going deep-sea fishing or jet skiing. Stay two nights in **Palm Beach** ①–⑪, spending your first day taking in its best sights, mentioned above. On day two, rent a bicycle and follow the 10-mi path along Lake Worth, providing a great look at the backyards of many of Palm Beach's big mansions. Drive north on day three, going first to the mainland and then across Jerry Thomas Bridge to Singer Island and John D. MacArthur Beach State Park. Spend the third night farther north, on **Hutchinson Island** ㉝, and relax the next morning on the beach in front of your hotel. On your way back south, explore **Stuart** ㉜ and its tiny but interesting historic downtown area, and pause at the Arthur R. Marshall–Loxahatchee National Wildlife Refuge before ending up in **Boca Raton** ㉗, for three nights at a hotel near the beach. Split day five between shopping at Mizner Park and beaching it at South Beach Park. Day six is for cultural attractions: the Boca Raton Museum of Art followed by the galleries and interesting Japanese museum in **Delray Beach** ㉖. If you have time on your last day, take in one of Boca Raton's other two beaches, Spanish River and Red Reef parks.

When to Tour Palm Beach and the Treasure Coast

The weather is optimum November–May, but the trade-off is that facilities are more crowded and prices somewhat higher. In summer you'll need a tolerance for heat and humidity if you want to spend time outside; also watch for frequent afternoon downpours. If you're set on watching the sea turtles come ashore to nest, make sure to visit between mid-May and early August, which is when most of the turtles lay their eggs, and remember that nesting occurs at night. No matter when you visit, bring insect repellent if you plan outdoor activities.

PALM BEACH

78 mi north of Miami.

Setting the tone in this incredibly wealthy town is the ornate architecture of developer Addison Mizner, who began building homes, stores, and public buildings here in the 1920s and whose Moorish-Gothic style has influenced virtually all the landmarks of the community. Thanks to Mizner and those influenced by him, Palm Beach looks like a kind of neo-Camelot, the perfect backdrop for a playground of the rich and famous.

Exploring Palm Beach

You can get a taste of what this town is all about when you squeeze into a parking place on Worth Avenue, among the Mercedes and Bentleys, and head to its boutiques to rub Versace-covered shoulders with shoppers whose credit-card limits likely exceed the gross national product of Liechtenstein. Away from downtown, along County Road and Ocean Boulevard (the shore road, also designated as Route A1A), are Palm Beach's other defining landmarks: mansions. In some parts they're fronted by thick 20-ft hedgerows and topped by the seemingly de rigueur barrel-tile roofs. The low wall that separates the dune-top shore road from the sea hides a badly eroded beach in many places. Here and there, where the strand deepens a bit, homes are built directly on the beach.

A Good Tour

Start on the north end of the island with a quick drive through the sandstone and limestone minicanyon that is the **Canyon of Palm Beach** ①, on Lake Way Road. Drive south, across Royal Poinciana Way, to the **Henry Morrison Flagler Museum** ②, in a 73-room palace that was once Flagler's home. đFrom here, backtrack to Royal Poinciana Way, turn right, and follow the road until it ends at North County Road and the Spanish-style **Palm Beach Post Office** ③. Here County Road changes from north to south designations. Take it southbound and look for the long, stately driveway on the left that leads to **The Breakers** ④, a famous hotel built in the style of an Italian Renaissance palace. Continue south on South County Road about ¼ mi farther to **Bethesda-by-the-Sea** ⑤, a Spanish Gothic Episcopal church. Keep driving south on South County Road until you reach Royal Palm Way; turn right, then right again on Cocoanut Row. In just a few blocks you'll see the gardens of the **Society of the Four Arts** ⑥.

Head south on Cocoanut Row until you reach famed **Worth Avenue** ⑦, where you can park and walk around and ogle the designer goods available for high-end shoppers. After taking in the sights, drive south on South County Road for a peek at some magnificent estates, including **El Solano** ⑧, built by Addison Mizner, and **Mar-A-Lago** ⑨, now owned by Donald Trump. At this point you might want to get out of the car for some sun and fresh air, so continue south on South County Road until you reach **Phipps Ocean Park** ⑩ and its stretch of sandy beach, or head back toward town along South Ocean Boulevard to the popular **Mid-Town Beach** ⑪.

TIMING

You'll need half a day, minimum, to see these sights. A few of the destinations are closed Sunday or Monday. In the winter, traffic can be very heavy and usually gets worse as the day wears on. Consider doing your exploring in the morning, when sights are less crowded and roads are less congested.

Sights to See

5 **Bethesda-by-the-Sea.** This Spanish Gothic Episcopal church, with stunning stained-glass windows, was built in 1925 by the first Protestant congregation in southeast Florida. Next to it are the formal, ornamental **Cluett Memorial Gardens.** ✉ *141 S. County Rd.,* ☎ *561/655–4554,* WEB *www.bbts.org.* ⏲ *Church and gardens daily 8–5; services Sept.–May, Sun. at 8, 9, and 11, Tues. at 8, Wed. at 12:05, Fri. at 12:05; June–Aug., Sun. at 8 and 10. Times are subject to change, call to confirm.*

★ 4 **The Breakers.** Originally built by Henry Flagler in 1895 and rebuilt by his descendants after a fire in 1925, this luxury hotel was one of the starting points of Florida tourism. It resembles an ornate Italian Renaissance palace and was renovated to the tune of $100 million not long ago. Walk into the lobby and take a look at the painted arched ceilings hung with crystal chandeliers, and peek into the ornate Florentine Dining Room with its 15th-century Flemish tapestries. ✉ *1 S. County Rd.,* ☎ *561/655–6611,* WEB *www.thebreakers.com.*

1 **Canyon of Palm Beach.** A road runs through a ridge of reddish-brown sandstone and oolite limestone and gives you the brief sensation of being in the desert Southwest. It's the remains of an ancient coral reef and the walls of the canyon rise straight up about 15 ft on both sides of the road. ✉ *Lake Way Rd.*

8 **El Solano.** Perhaps no Palm Beach mansion represents the town's ongoing generations of flashbulb fame better than this one. The Spanish-style home was built by Addison Mizner as his personal residence in 1925. Mizner then sold it to Harold Vanderbilt, and the property made the rounds of socialites, photo shoots, and expansions until it was bought by John Lennon and Yoko Ono 10 months before Lennon's death. Now owned by a banking executive, El Solano is not open to the public. ✉ *721 S. County Rd.*

★ 2 **Henry Morrison Flagler Museum.** The opulence of Florida's Gilded Age is still apparent at Whitehall, the palatial 73-room mansion Henry Flagler had built in 1901 for his third wife, Mary Lily Kenan, that is now a museum. Then-famous architects John Carrère and Thomas Hastings were instructed to spare no expense in creating the finest home they could imagine. They did as they were told, and Whitehall rivals some of the fine palaces of Europe. In 1960 Flagler's granddaughter, Jean Flagler Matthews, bought the building, which had been the Whitehall Hotel from 1929 to 1959, and made it a museum. On display are many of the original furnishings, an art collection, a 1,200-pipe organ, and exhibits on the history of the Florida East Coast Railway. Flagler's personal railroad car, the *Rambler,* is parked behind the building. A tour with well-informed guides takes about an hour. ✉ *1 Whitehall Way,* ☎ *561/655–2833,* WEB *www.flagler.org.* 🎫 *$8.* ⏲ *Tues.–Sat. 10–5, Sun. noon–5.*

9 **Mar-A-Lago.** Still one of the grandest of homes along Ocean Boulevard, the former estate of breakfast-food heiress Marjorie Meriweather Post has Italianate towers silhouetted against the sky. It's currently owned by real-estate magnate Donald Trump, who has turned it into a private membership club. ✉ *1100 S. Ocean Blvd.*

Gold Coast and Treasure Coast

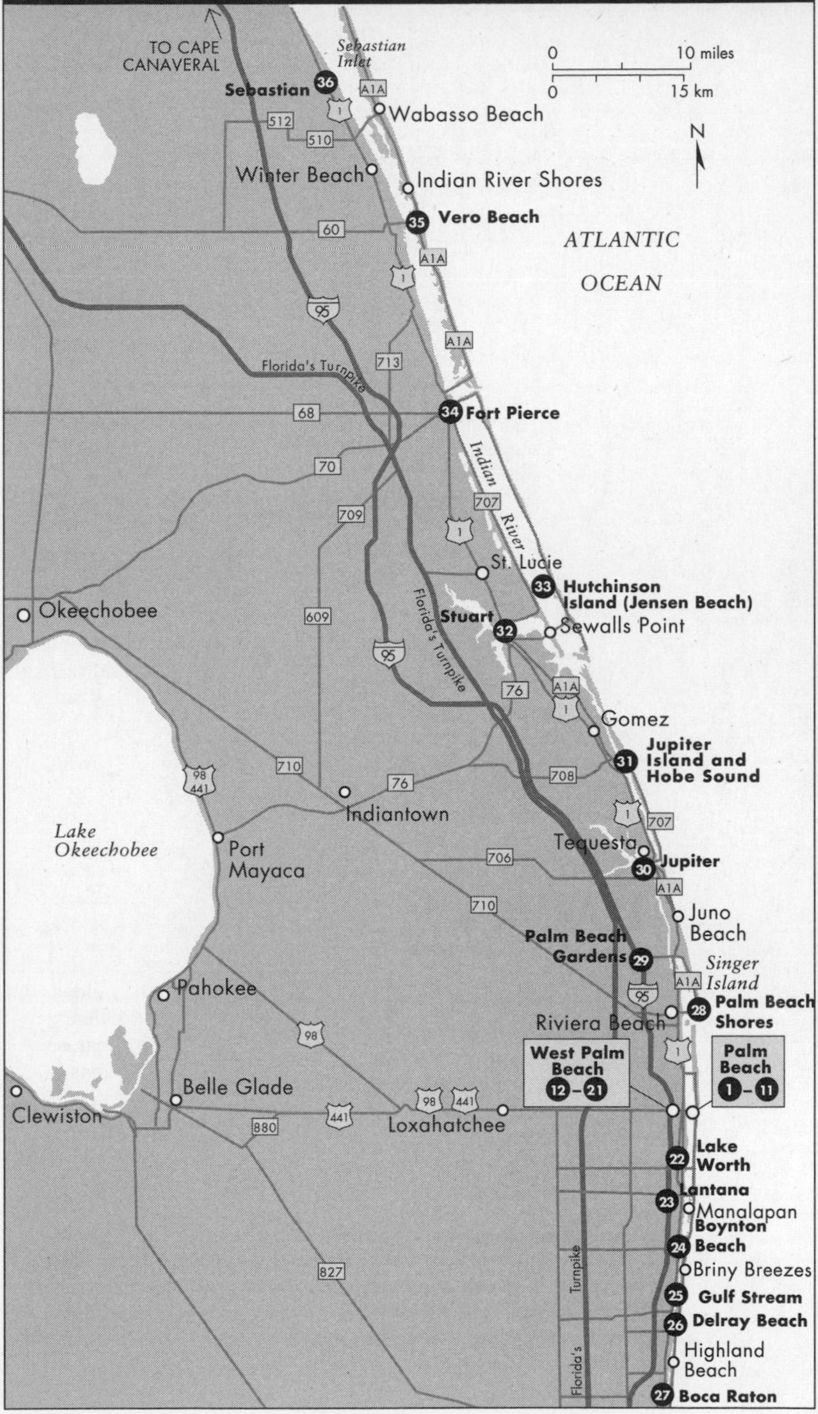

Palm Beach and West Palm Beach

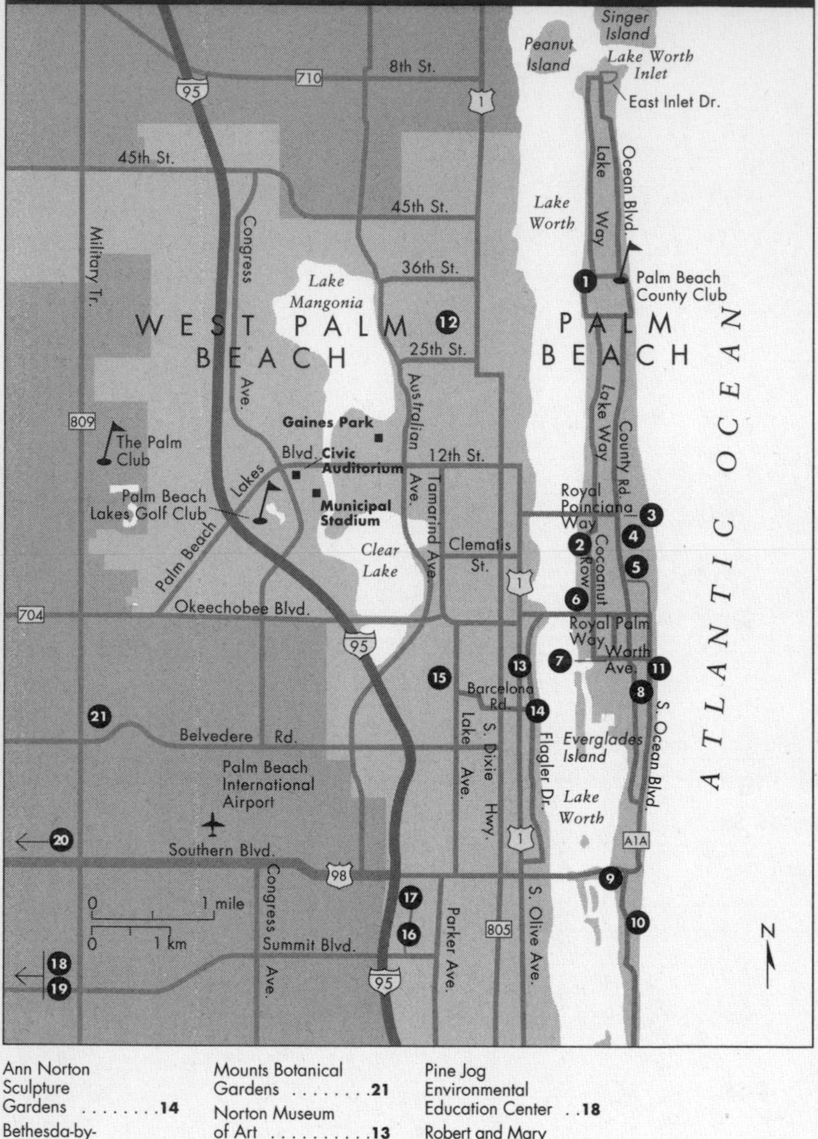

Ann Norton Sculpture Gardens 14
Bethesda-by-the-Sea 5
The Breakers 4
Canyon of Palm Beach 1
El Solano 8
Henry Morrison Flagler Museum 2
Lion Country Safari 20
Mar-A-Lago 9
Mid-Town Beach . . . 11
Mounts Botanical Gardens 21
Norton Museum of Art 13
Okeeheelee Nature Center 19
Old Northwood Historic District 12
Palm Beach Post Office 3
Palm Beach Zoo at Dreher Park 16
Phipps Ocean Park 10
Pine Jog Environmental Education Center . . 18
Robert and Mary Montgomery Armory Arts Center 15
Society of the Four Arts 6
South Florida Science Museum, Planetarium, and Aquarium 17
Worth Avenue 7

11 **Mid-Town Beach.** This small beach directly east of Worth Avenue is especially popular because it's so close to town. But be warned: the only parking meters along Ocean Boulevard—ergo, the only convenient public beach access—are found between Worth Avenue and Royal Palm Way. ✉ *400 S. Ocean Blvd.,* ☎ *no phone.* 🎫 *Parking 25¢ for 15 mins.* ⏲ *Daily 8–8.*

3 **Palm Beach Post Office.** Spanish-style architecture defines the exterior of this 1932 National Historic Site building. Inside, murals depict Seminole Indians in the Everglades and stately royal and coconut palms. ✉ *95 N. County Rd.,* ☎ *800/275–8777.*

10 **Phipps Ocean Park.** Besides the ubiquitous beautiful beach, some picnic tables, and grills, this park contains a Palm Beach County landmark in the **Little Red Schoolhouse.** Dating from 1886, it was the first schoolhouse in what was then Dade County. Tours are given weekday mornings. ✉ *2145 S. Ocean Blvd.,* ☎ *561/832–0731.* 🎫 *Free.*

6 **Society of the Four Arts.** In addition to presenting cultural events, this privately endowed arts and educational institution incorporates an exhibition hall, library, 13 distinct gardens, and the Philip Hulitar Sculpture Garden. ✉ *Four Arts Plaza,* ☎ *561/655–7226,* WEB *www.fourarts.org.* 🎫 *$4.* ⏲ *Galleries Jan.–mid-Apr., Mon.–Sat. 10–5, Sun. 2–5; library, children's library, and gardens Nov.–May, weekdays 10–5, Sat. 9–1.*

★ **7** **Worth Avenue.** This ¼-mi-long street is synonymous with posh, pricey shopping. A stroll amid the Moorish architecture of its scores of top-drawer shops—Cartier, Charles Jourdan, and Giorgio Armani, to name a few—gives you a taste of the elegance of the area. ✉ *Between Cocoanut Row and S. Ocean Blvd.*

Dining and Lodging

$$$–$$$$ ✕ **Bice Ristorante.** The atmosphere here is so thoroughly Italian that it's easy to be disappointed when the parking attendant speaks to you in English. Brilliant flower arrangements and lots of brass accent the interior's beige-and-ocher color scheme. Tables outside on the terrace are sheltered by umbrellas and shade trees. The aroma of basil, chives, and oregano fills the air as waiters bring out the divine home-baked focaccia that accompanies such house favorites as *Robespierre alla moda della Bice* (sliced steak topped with arugula salad) and *costoletta di vitello impanata alla milanese* (breaded veal cutlet with a tomato salad). ✉ *313¼ Worth Ave.,* ☎ *561/835–1600. AE, DC, MC, V.*

$$$–$$$$ ★ ✕ **Café L'Europe.** This is one of the most popular, elegant, and expensive, restaurants in Palm Beach. Sumptuous oak paneling, dim lighting, and elaborate flower bouquets set the mood. Ladies-who-lunch can enjoy spa cuisine, while evening guests select from seasonally changing menus that might include specialty pastas such as *cappelacci Trestavarina,* envelopes of pasta stuffed with spinach, ricotta cheese, walnuts, and basil tomato sauce; seafood dishes such as pan-seared pompano with shiitake mushrooms or jumbo lump crabmeat risotto, or a sliced loin of venison prepared with grilled black plums. There's also a page of enticing appetizers, including a choice of select caviars with prices to match. ✉ *331 S. County Rd.,* ☎ *561/655–4020. Reservations essential. Jacket required. AE, DC, MC, V. No lunch Sun.–Mon.*

$$$–$$$$ ✕ **Echo.** A slinky sushi bar snakes along one side of this austere and dramatic newcomer. The decor is a mix of glistening stainless steel and polished wood and walls are hung with striking abstract artwork. A wall of floor-to-ceiling glass doors separates the inside diners from those eating on the popular terrace. Bucking the fusion trend, the chef creates dishes that are distinctly Chinese, Thai, Japanese, and Vietnamese. Chinese hot and sour soup, Thai shrimp soup, Vietnamese spring rolls, and ginger chicken are a sampling of the small plate starters. Shanghai barbecued duck, Vietnamese roasted chicken, sweet-and-sour pork tenderloin, and pad Thai are among the entrées offered. There are also sharing menus, a sushi and sashimi menu, and a selection of Asian beers and sakes in addition to the full bar. ✉ *230 Sunrise Ave.,* ☎ *561/802–4222. Reservations essential. AE, D, MC, V. Closed Mon. No lunch.*

$$$–$$$$ ★ ✕ **Janeiro.** Versace-designed Rosenthal china and Riedel crystal on black-on-black tablecloths provide the setting for a spectacularly elegant contemporary French dining experience. Wild mushrooms sautéed with garlic, lobster and crayfish cakes with a champagne lobster sauce, and baked goat cheese with tomatoes in a pastry shell are some of the appetizers. Entrées, brought to the table under silver domes, include Mediterranean bouillabaisse, grilled Chilean sea bass with red mullet caviar, boneless rack of lamb stuffed with spinach and wild mushrooms wrapped in puff pastry, and a beef fillet with green peppercorn sauce. Save room for the chocolate soufflé dessert; it's topped with edible 24-carat gold leaf. ✉ *191 Bradley Pl.,* ☎ *561/659–5223. Reservations essential. Jacket required. AE, DC, MC, V. No lunch.*

$$$–$$$$ ★ ✕ **Leopard Lounge and Restaurant.** The sleek and exotic leopard inspired the decor for this elegant, intimate restaurant located in the Chesterfield hotel. Fabrics, carpeting, and wall treatments in the stunning, dimly lit dining room mimic the leopard's spotted skin and are dramatically enhanced by a background of black and lacquer red. Choose a romantic banquette against the wall or a table near the open kitchen. The eclectic menu draws on a global array of cuisines. You might start with an order of lobster ravioli with sauternes-ginger sauce, a carpaccio of beef, or the restaurant's signature starter of Stilton soufflé over a bed of baby field greens. Then move on to nori-wrapped, sesame-seared ahi tuna over buckwheat soba noodles or rosemary rack of lamb with potato rösti or a grilled New York strip. This is an elegant stop for lunch or breakfast, too. ✉ *363 Cocoanut Row,* ☎ *561/659–5800. AE, DC, MC, V.*

$$–$$$$ ✕ **Amici.** Night after night, a steady stream of six-figure automobiles pulls into the valet parking spot of this trendy eatery. Inside, the lighting is dim, and tables are close together but never empty. The northern Italian menu features such house specialties as antipasti of cold marinated and grilled vegetables, rigatoni with spicy tomato sauce and roasted eggplant, potato gnocchi with grilled chicken and roasted peppers, grilled veal chops, risottos, and a long list of pizzas cooked in the wood-burning oven. There are nightly pasta and fresh-fish specials as well. If you want to avoid the crowds, stop by for a late lunch. ✉ *228 S. County Rd.,* ☎ *561/832–0201. Reservations essential. AE, D, DC, MC, V. No lunch Sun.*

$$–$$$ ✕ **Chuck & Harold's.** Ivana Trump, Larry Holmes, Brooke Shields, and Michael Bolton are among the celebrities who have eaten at this combination power-lunch bar, sidewalk café, and jazz–big band hot spot, which is popular day and night, as well as for breakfast. Locals who want to be part of the scenery and tourists hot to people-watch catch a seat and linger in the outdoor café, next to pots of red and white begonias mounted on the sidewalk rail. Specialties include conch chowder, terrific hamburgers, an onion-crunchy gazpacho, grilled steaks, and tangy key lime pie. A big blackboard lists daily specials and celebrity birthdays. ✉ *207 Royal Poinciana Way,* ☎ *561/659–1440. AE, DC, MC, V.*

$$–$$$ ★ ✕ **Ta-boó.** Dressed in gorgeous pinks, greens, and florals, the spaces of this Worth Avenue landmark are divided into discreet dining rooms: one resembles a courtyard, another an elegant living room with a fireplace, and a third a skylighted gazebo. The Tiki Tiki bar makes an el-

egant salon for the neighborhood crowd. Appetizers range from a very proletarian nachos grande with chili to Beluga caviar; entrées include chicken and arugula from the grill, prime rib, steaks, frogs' legs, and main-course salads. White pizza with goat and mozzarella cheeses, pesto, and sweet roasted red peppers is a favorite. Drop in late at night during the winter high season, and you're bound to spot a famous face or two. ✉ *221 Worth Ave.,* ☎ *561/835–3500. AE, DC, MC, V.*

$–$$ ✕ **TooJay's.** New York deli food served in a bright California-style setting—what could be more Florida? The menu at this spot, one of nine TooJay's in the Sunshine State, includes matzo-ball soup, corned beef on rye, and a killer cake made with five kinds of chocolate and topped with whipped cream. A salami-on-rye sandwich layered with onions, Muenster cheese, coleslaw, and Russian dressing is a house favorite. During the Jewish High Holidays in the fall look for carrot *tzimmes* (a sweet vegetable compote), brisket, and roast chicken. Wisecracking waitresses keep the pace fast. ✉ *313 Royal Poinciana Way,* ☎ *561/659–7232. AE, DC, MC, V.*

$$$$ ★ **The Breakers.** Dating from 1926 and enlarged in 1969, this opulent seven-story Italian Renaissance–style resort sprawls over 140 splendidly manicured acres. Cupids frolic in the Florentine fountain at the main entrance, while majestic ceiling vaults and frescoes grace the lobby and the long hallways that lead to restaurants and ballrooms. A recent $120 million renovation included the construction of a fabulous spa and beach club, a renovation of the historic Ocean Course and a new golf and tennis clubhouse, plus a complete modernization of the rooms and bathrooms. Although the resort's elegance has been enhanced, a relaxed atmosphere has replaced the old-world formality that prevailed for three-quarters of a century. For example, men are no longer *required* to wear jackets and ties everywhere after 7 PM. ✉ *1 S. County Rd., 33480,* ☎ *561/655–6611 or 888/273–2537,* FAX *561/659–8403,* WEB *www.thebreakers.com. 569 rooms, 49 suites. 9 restaurants, 5 bars, 5 pools, sauna, spa, 36 holes of golf, putting green, 10 tennis courts, croquet, health club, jogging, shuffleboard, beach, boating, children's programs. AE, D, DC, MC, V.*

$$$$ **The Colony.** What distinguishes this legendary pale yellow Georgian-style hotel only steps from Worth Avenue is its attentive staff; youthful yet experienced, they demonstrate a buzz of competence and a true desire to please. Cool and classical guest rooms have fluted blond cabinetry and matching draperies and bedcovers in pastel floral prints. As in many older hotels, bathrooms are small. The "scene" for glitterati after charity balls at the Breakers, this is where Roxanne Pulitzer retreated after her infamous seven-week marriage in 1992. ✉ *155 Hammon Ave., 33480,* ☎ *561/655–5430 or 800/521–5525,* FAX *561/832–7318,* WEB *www.thecolonypalmbeach.com. 68 rooms, 19 suites and apartments, 7 villas. Restaurant, bar, pool, spa. AE, DC, MC, V.*

$$$$ ★ **Four Seasons Ocean Grand.** This 6-acre property at the south end of town is coolly elegant but warm in detail. Marble, art, fanlight windows, swagged drapes, chintz, and palms create a serene atmosphere. Rooms are spacious, with a separate seating area and private balcony, and many have gorgeous ocean views. On weekend evenings year-round, piano music accompanies cocktails in the Living Room lounge. On some weekend nights in season, jazz groups perform, and there are classical recitals on Sunday afternoon. Although its name suggests grandeur, this four-story hotel with a long beach is more like a small jewel. ✉ *2800 S. Ocean Blvd., 33480,* ☎ *561/582–2800 or 800/432–2335,* FAX *561/547–1557,* WEB *www.fourseasons/palmbeach.com. 200 rooms, 10 suites. 3 restaurants, 2 bars, pool, sauna, 3 tennis courts, health club, beach. AE, D, DC, MC, V.*

$$$–$$$$ ★ **Brazilian Court.** Spread out over half a block, the yellow stucco Spanish-style facade with a red-tile roof reminds you of this hotel's Roaring '20s origins. Rooms and spacious suites look out to gardens and are decorated in soft, muted tones. Original art hangs on the walls. Remodeled bathrooms are marble and completely modernized. Outside, stone fountains and private courtyards (one with a wishing well) offer peaceful oases. Not only are pets welcome, there's a pet room-service menu, with items like Chancellor Chow and Chicken Meow Mein. ✉ *301 Australian Ave., 33480,* ☎ *561/655–7740; 800/552–0335; 800/228–6852 in Canada;* FAX *561/655–0801,* WEB *www.braziliancourt.com. 63 rooms, 34 one-bedroom suites, 6 two-bedroom suites. Restaurant, bar, kitchenettes, pool, hair salon, exercise room, library. AE, D, DC, MC, V.*

$$–$$$$ **Palm Beach Historic Inn.** This delightfully unexpected inn is in the heart of downtown, tucked between Town Hall and a seaside residential block. B&B touches include flowers, wine and fruit, snacks, seasonal turndown, tea and cookies in rooms, bath towels as thick as parkas, and a generous Continental breakfast. Guest rooms tend to the frilly with lots of lace, ribbons, and scalloped edges. Most are furnished with Victorian antiques and reproductions (some out of old mansions, others more secondhand than authentic) and chiffon wall drapings above the bed. ✉ *365 S. County Rd., 33480,* ☎ *561/832–4009,* FAX *561/832–6255,* WEB *www.palmbeachhistoricinn.com. 9 rooms, 4 suites. Library. AE, D, DC, MC, V.*

$–$$$$ ★ **The Chesterfield.** Just two blocks north of famous Worth Avenue, you'll find this elegant four-story, white stucco, European-style, luxury hotel. Inviting rooms range in size from small to spacious, but all are individually and richly decorated with print bedspreads and draperies, plush upholstered chairs, antique desks, paintings, and marble bathrooms. Service is exceptional. Settle into a leather couch in front of the cozy library's fireplace with the latest newspapers from around the world or with a book selected from the floor-to-ceiling shelves. A quiet courtyard surrounds a large pool. The Leopard restaurant is exceptional. Ongoing but unobtrusive renovation and redecoration keeps this hotel in tip-top shape. ✉ *363 Cocoanut Row, 33480,* ☎ *561/659–5800 or 800/243–7871,* FAX *561/659–6707,* WEB *www.redcarnationhotels.com. 44 rooms, 11 suites. Restaurant, bar, pool, library. AE, D, DC, MC, V.*

$$$ ★ **Plaza Inn.** This three-story hotel, deco-designed from the 1930s, operates B&B style; a full breakfast is included. The pool, gardens, and piano bar have the intimate charm of a trysting place for the likes of Cary Grant and Katharine Hepburn. Inn owner Ajit Asrani is a retired Indian army officer who raises show horses and polo ponies. The courteous staff and location in the heart of Palm Beach are pluses, and the uncluttered, individually decorated rooms with phone and refrigerator provide a welcome change from other B&Bs. So, too, does the appealing courtyard with waterfalls and a pool. ✉ *215 Brazilian Ave., 33480,* ☎ *561/832–8666 or 800/233–2632,* FAX *561/835–8776,* WEB *www.plazainnpalmbeach.com. 47 rooms and 5 suites. Bar, pool, hot tub. AE, MC, V.*

$$–$$$ **Palm Beach Hawaiian Ocean Inn.** Families gravitate to this casual, two-story resort that is reasonably priced and right on the beach. Large rooms and spacious suites face tropical gardens or look out to the ocean. They are simply but adequately furnished and have bedspreads and draperies in colorful stripe pastels. The real draw here is the beachfront location. A wide wooden sunning deck surrounds the free-form pool, and both look out to the beach and the Atlantic Ocean. The informal restaurant and outdoor bar also overlook the water. ✉ *3550 S. Ocean Blvd., 33480,* ☎ FAX *561/582–5631,* WEB *www.palmbeachhawaiian.com. 50 rooms, 8 suites. Restaurant, bar, refrigerator, pool, beach. D, MC, V.*

Nightlife and the Arts

The Arts

The **Royal Poinciana Playhouse** (✉ 70 Royal Poinciana Plaza, ☎ 561/659–3310) presents seven productions each year between December and April. **Society of the Four Arts** (✉ Four Arts Plaza, ☎ 561/655–7226) has concerts, lectures, and Friday films December–March. Movie tickets can be purchased at time of showing; other tickets may be obtained a week in advance.

Nightlife

Cheek-to-cheek dancers head to the **Colony** (✉ 155 Hammon Ave., ☎ 561/655–5430) for a spin around the dance floor. A duo plays Thursday, Friday, and Saturday nights. Young professionals gather at the **Leopard Lounge** (✉ 363 Cocoanut Row, ☎ 561/659–6767) in the Chesterfield Hotel to listen to piano music during cocktail hour and return later to dance to a duo until the wee hours. As the weekend dinner crowd thins out, late-night party seekers fill up **Ta-boó** (✉ 221 Worth Ave., ☎ 561/835–3500), where a DJ keeps people on their feet.

Outdoor Activities and Sports

Biking

Bicycling is an excellent way to get a good look at Palm Beach, which is as small and flat as the top of a billiard table (and just as green). The wonderful 10-mi, palm-fringed **Palm Beach Bicycle Trail** (parallel to Lake Way) skirts the backyards of many palatial mansions and the edge of Lake Worth. Just a block from the bike trail, the **Palm Beach Trail Bicycle Shop** (✉ 223 Sunrise Ave., ☎ 561/659–4583) rents bikes by the hour or day. They provide free maps of all the bike trails.

Dog Racing

Since 1932 the hounds have been racing year-round at the 4,300-seat **Palm Beach Kennel Club.** There are also simulcasts of jai alai and horse racing, as well as wagering on live and televised sports. ✉ *1111 N. Congress Ave.,* ☎ *561/683–2222.* 🎫 *50¢, terrace level $1, parking free.* ⏲ *Racing Mon., Wed., Fri., Sat. at 12:40, Wed.–Sat. also at 7:30, Sun. at 1; simulcasts Thurs.–Tues. at 12:30, Mon., Wed., Fri. at 7:35.*

Golf

Breakers Hotel Golf Club (✉ 1 S. County Rd., ☎ 561/655–6611 or 800/833–3141) has 36 holes. The **Palm Beach Golf Club** (✉ 2345 S. Ocean Blvd., ☎ 561/547–0598) has 18 holes, including four on the Atlantic and three on the inland waterway.

Shopping

One of the world's showcases for high-quality shopping, **Worth Avenue** runs ¼ mi east–west across Palm Beach, from the beach to Lake Worth. The street has more than 250 shops, and many upscale stores (Gucci, Hermès, Pierre Deux, Saks Fifth Avenue, and Van Cleef & Arpels) are represented, their merchandise appealing to the discerning tastes of the Palm Beach clientele. The six blocks of **South County Road** north of Worth Avenue have interesting (and somewhat less expensive) stores. For specialty items (out-of-town newspapers, health foods, and books), try the shops along the north side of **Royal Poinciana Way.**

WEST PALM BEACH

2 mi west of Palm Beach.

Long considered Palm Beach's impoverished cousin, West Palm is now economically vibrant in its own right. Far larger in area than its upper-crust neighbor to the east, it has become the cultural, entertainment, and business center of the county and of the region to the north. Sparkling government buildings like the mammoth $124 million Palm Beach County Judicial Center and Courthouse and the State Administrative Building exemplify the health of the city's corporate life, and facilities such as the $60 million Kravis Center for the Performing Arts attest to the strength of the arts and entertainment community.

Downtown

The heart of revived West Palm Beach is a small but attractive downtown area, which has been spurred on by an active historic preservation movement. Along beautifully landscaped Clematis Street, you'll find boutiques and restaurants in charmingly restored buildings and exuberant nightlife that, at least in a small way, mimics that of South Beach. Even at the downtown's fringes, you'll encounter sights of cultural interest. There's a free downtown shuttle by day and free on-street parking at night and on weekends.

A Good Tour

From a geographical perspective, the best place to start is at the north end of the city with a walk through the **Old Northwood Historic District** ⑫, on the National Register of Historic Places. Drive south on U.S. 1, take a left onto 12th Street, and then a right onto South Olive Avenue to view the exceptional art collection at the **Norton Museum of Art** ⑬. From here it is just a few blocks farther south to the peaceful **Ann Norton Sculpture Gardens** ⑭. Finally, drive west across Barcelona Road to the **Robert and Mary Montgomery Armory Arts Center** ⑮ and check out the current exhibit.

TIMING

Late morning is a good time to start this tour, so you can walk through the historic neighborhood before having lunch on Clematis Street. In the afternoon you'll need about three hours at the various arts-oriented sights. It's important to take this tour during daytime business hours.

Sights to See

⓮ **Ann Norton Sculpture Gardens.** This monument to the late American sculptor Ann Weaver Norton, second wife of Norton Museum founder Ralph H. Norton, consists of charming 3-acre grounds displaying seven granite figures and six brick megaliths. The plantings were designed by Norton, an environmentalist, to attract native bird life. ✉ *253 Barcelona Rd.,* ☎ *561/832–5328.* 🎫 *$5.* ⏲ *Wed.–Sun. 11–4 (call ahead; schedule is not always observed) or by appointment.*

★ ⓭ **Norton Museum of Art.** Constructed in 1941 by steel magnate Ralph H. Norton, this museum boasts an extensive permanent collection of 19th- and 20th-century American and European paintings with special emphasis on 19th-century French Impressionists. There are also Chinese bronze and jade sculptures, a sublime outdoor patio with sculptures on display in a tropical garden, and a library housing more than 3,000 art books and periodicals. Nine galleries showcase traveling exhibits as well as art from the permanent collection. ✉ *1451 S. Olive Ave.,* ☎ *561/832–5194,* WEB *www.museum@norton.org.* 🎫 *$6.* ⏲ *Tues.–Sat. 10–5, Sun. 1–5.*

⓬ **Old Northwood Historic District.** This 1920s-era neighborhood, on the National Register of Historic Places, hosts special events and Sunday walking tours. ✉ *West of Flagler Dr. between 26th and 35th Sts.*

⓯ **Robert and Mary Montgomery Armory Arts Center.** Built by the WPA in 1939, the facility is now a complete visual-arts center. Its gallery hosts rotating exhibitions, and art classes are held throughout the year. ✉ *1703 S. Lake Ave.,* ☎ *561/832–1776.* 🎫 *Free.* ⏲ *Weekdays 9–5:30, Sat. 9:30–2:30, Sun. 10–2.*

Away from Downtown

At its outskirts, West Palm Beach sprawls. Flat, straight stretches lined with fast-food outlets and car dealerships may not be pretty to drive past, but it's worth it to reach some of the interesting attractions scattered around the southern and western reaches of the city. Several are especially rewarding for children and other animal and nature lovers.

A Good Tour

Head south from downtown and turn right on Southern Boulevard, left onto Parker Avenue, and right onto Summit Boulevard to reach the **Palm Beach Zoo at Dreher Park** ⑯. In the same area (just turn right onto Dreher Trail) and also appealing to kids, the **South Florida Science Museum, Planetarium, and Aquarium** ⑰ is full of hands-on exhibits.

Backtrack to Summit Boulevard and go west to the 150-acre **Pine Jog Environmental Education Center** ⑱. For more natural adventure, head farther west on Summit until you reach Forest Hills Boulevard, where you turn right to reach the **Okeeheelee Nature Center** ⑲ and its miles of wooded trails.

Now retrace your steps to Summit Boulevard, drive east until you reach Military Trail, and take a left. Drive north to Southern Boulevard and turn west to reach **Lion Country Safari** ⑳, a 500-acre cageless zoo. For the last stop on this tour, backtrack to Military Trail and travel north to the gardens of the **Mounts Botanical Gardens** ㉑.

TIMING

You could easily spend most of a day at some of these sights, so you'll want to pick and choose based on your interests, creating your own subtour. During morning and afternoon rush hours and in the winter, be prepared for heavy traffic; sightseeing in the morning (not *too* early) will be somewhat less trafficked.

Sights to See

⓴ **Lion Country Safari.** Drive your own car (with windows closed) on 8 mi of paved roads through a 500-acre cageless zoo where 1,300 wild animals roam. Lions, elephants, white rhinoceroses, giraffes, zebras, antelopes, chimpanzees, and ostriches are among those in residence. Special exhibits include the Kalahari Bushvelt, designed after a South African plateau and containing water buffalo and Nilgai (the largest type of Asian antelope), and the Gir Forest, modeled after a game forest in India and showcasing a pride of lions. Stop by the petting zoo, or take a ride on the *Safari Queen* cruise. No convertibles or pets are allowed. ✉ *Southern Blvd. W,* ☎ *561/793–1084,* WEB *www.lioncountrysafari.com.* 🎫 *$15.50, van rental $6 per hr.* ⏲ *Daily 9:30–5:30, last vehicle in by 4:30.*

㉑ **Mounts Botanical Gardens.** Take advantage of balmy weather by walking among the tropical and subtropical plants here. Free tours are given. ✉ *531 N. Military Trail,* ☎ *561/233–1749.* 🎫 *Free.* ⏲ *Mon.–Sat. 8:30–4:30, Sun. 1–5; tours Sat. 11, Sun. 2:30.*

19 **Okeeheelee Nature Center.** At this popular spot, you can explore 5 mi of trails through 90 acres of native pine-flat woods and wetlands. A spacious visitor center/gift shop features hands-on exhibits. ✉ *7715 Forest Hill Blvd.,* ☎ *561/233–1400.* *Free.* *Visitor center Tues.–Fri. 1–4:45, Sat. 8:15–4:45; trails open daily sunrise–sunset.*

16 **Palm Beach Zoo at Dreher Park.** This wild kingdom is a 23-acre complex with more than 500 animals representing more than 100 species, including Florida panthers, red kangaroos, and Bengal tigers. The Tropics of America exhibit has 6 acres of tropical rain forest plus Mayan ruins, an Amazon river village, and an aviary. Also of note are a nature trail, an Australian Outback exhibit, and a children's zoo. ✉ *1301 Summit Blvd.,* ☎ *561/533–0887 or 561/547–9453,* WEB *www.palmbeachzoo.com.* *$6.* *Daily 9–5 (until 7 on spring and summer weekends).*

18 **Pine Jog Environmental Education Center.** The draw here is 150 acres of mostly undisturbed Florida pine-flat woods with one self-guided ½-mi trail. Formal landscaping around the five one-story buildings features an array of native plants, and dioramas and displays show native ecosystems. School groups use the trails during the week but the public is also welcome. Call for a schedule of special events and periodic open houses. ✉ *6301 Summit Blvd.,* ☎ *561/686–6600.* *Free.* *Weekdays 9–5.*

17 **South Florida Science Museum, Planetarium, and Aquarium.** Here you'll find hands-on exhibits, aquarium displays with touch tanks, planetarium shows, and a chance to observe the heavens Friday nights through the most powerful telescope in South Florida (weather permitting). ✉ *4801 Dreher Trail N,* ☎ *561/832–1988.* *$5, planetarium $2 extra, laser show $4 extra.* *Mon.–Thurs. 10–5, Fri. 10–10, Sat. 10–6, Sun. noon–6.*

Dining and Lodging

$$–$$$$ ✕ **Raindancer Steak House.** Since 1975, steak lovers have been stopping by this dark and cozy establishment to indulge in exceptional steaks: thick and juicy filet mignons, giant 24-ounce porterhouse steaks, sizzling sirloins for two, New York strips prepared au poivre, and grilled lean flank steaks. But if beef isn't your entrée of choice, there are lamb chops, chicken breasts prepared four ways, lobster, shrimp scampi, baked scallops, stuffed shrimp, and a bountiful salad bar. ✉ *2300 Palm Beach Lakes Blvd.,* ☎ *561/684–2811. AE, MC, V. No lunch.*

$$–$$$ ✕ **Café Protégé.** As this restaurant of the Florida Culinary Institute, you can sample superb cuisine at less than astronomical prices. The contemporary Continental menu changes frequently, and patrons can watch students at work slicing, dicing, and sautéing in the unique observation kitchen. ✉ *2400 Metrocentre Blvd.,* ☎ *561/687–2433. AE, MC, V. No lunch weekends; no dinner Sun.–Mon.*

$$ ✕ **Pescatore Seafood and Oyster Bar.** When you want to rest your feet after wandering around Clematis Street, slip through the handsome French doors of this trendy spot for a light lunch, an afternoon snack, or a leisurely dinner. Tables are close together, and there's a sophisticated bustle. Naturally, fresh oysters and clams are on the menu, but you'll also find a variety of grilled fish, including mahimahi, tuna, and salmon; steamed Maine lobster; grilled shrimp; assorted pasta dishes; and a grilled Black Angus burger. ✉ *200 Clematis St.,* ☎ *561/837–6633. AE, DC, MC, V.*

$–$$ ✕ **Aleyda's Tex-Mex Restaurant.** Since 1981, this casual, family-friendly eatery has been showing up as a favorite on local popularity polls. Fajitas, the house specialty, are brought to the table sizzling in the pan, and enchiladas, chili con queso, and quesadillas are just a few more examples of the classic Mexican offerings. The bar claims to make the best margaritas in town. ✉ *1890 Okeechobee Blvd.,* ☎ *561/688–9033. AE, DC, MC, V. No lunch weekends.*

$$–$$$ ★ **Hibiscus House.** Few Florida B&B hosts work harder at hospitality and at looking after their neighborhood than Raleigh Hill and Colin Rayner. As proof, since the inn opened in the late 1980s, 11 sets of guests have bought houses in Old Northwood, which is listed on the National Register of Historic Places thanks to Hill and Rayner's efforts. Their Cape Cod–style B&B is full of the antiques Hill has collected during decades of in-demand interior designing: a 150-year-old four-square piano, a gorgeous green cane planter chair, and Louis XV pieces in the living room. Guest rooms are individually decorated and furnished in a mix of antiques and reproductions. Outstanding, too, is the landscaped, tropical pool-patio area. Both Hill and Rayner are informed about the best—and most affordable—dining in the area. ✉ *501 30th St., 33407,* ☎ *561/863–5633 or 800/203–4927,* WEB *www.hibiscushouse.com. 8 rooms. Pool. BP. AE, DC, MC, V.*

$–$$ **Royal Palm House Bed & Breakfast.** Located in the Old Northwood Historic District, this charming two-story frame house was built in 1925. Three guest rooms and a suite are in the main house and close by is a one-bedroom cottage with a kitchenette. All rooms are individually decorated in a tasteful, uncluttered fashion and have pretty gardens views. Morning breakfast and cocktail hour wine and cordials are included in the rate. A swimming pool surrounded by a brick courtyard offers a spot for reading and relaxing. ✉ *3215 Spruce Ave., 33407,* ☎ *561/863–9836 or 800/655–3196,* FAX *561/848–7350,* WEB *www.royalpalmhouse.com. 3 rooms, 1 suite, 1 cottage. Pool. BP. AE, MC, V.*

Nightlife and the Arts

The Arts

Part of the treasury of arts attractions is the **Raymond F. Kravis Center for the Performing Arts** (✉ 701 Okeechobee Blvd., ☎ 561/832–7469), a $60 million, 2,200-seat glass, copper, and marble showcase occupying the highest ground in West Palm Beach. Its 250-seat Rinker Playhouse includes a space for children's programming, family productions, and other special events. Some 300 performances of drama, dance, and music—everything from gospel and bluegrass to jazz and classical—are scheduled each year.

Palm Beach Opera (✉ 415 S. Olive Ave., ☎ 561/833–7888) stages four productions each winter at the Kravis Center. The **Carefree Theatre** (✉ 2000 S. Dixie Hwy., ☎ 561/833–7305) is Palm Beach County's premier showcase of foreign and art films.

Nightlife

Young professionals gather at **E. R. Bradley's Saloon** (✉ 104 Clematis St., ☎ 561/833–3520) to trade stories of the day and to try their hand at 3-D video golf. You'll find full-size palm trees and trellises bright with bougainvillea blossoms plus a state-of-the-art light and laser sound system and a 7,500-square-ft dance floor at the Caribbean-themed **Monkeyclub** (✉ 219 Clematis St., ☎ 561/833–6500). Music is 1970s, '80s, and '90s. The **Respectable Street Café** (✉ 518 Clematis St., ☎ 561/832–9999) explodes in high energy like an indoor Woodstock. It's open until 4 AM Wednesday–Saturday and features the best in underground alternative sound, new wave, and retro. Call for schedules and for special concerts held other days. **Underground Coffeeworks** (✉ 105 S. Narcissus Ave., ☎ 561/835–4792), a retro '60s spot, has "something different going on" (but always live music) Tuesday–Saturday. The cover charge varies, depending on the performers.

Outdoor Activities and Sports

Picturesque **Binks Forest Golf Club** (✉ 400 Binks Forest Dr., Wellington, ☎ 561/795–0595) has an 18-hole layout. The plush **Emerald Dunes** (✉ 2100 Emerald Dunes Dr., ☎ 561/684–4653) offers 18 holes of golf. **Palm Beach Polo and Country Club** (✉ 13198 Forest Hill Blvd., Wellington, ☎ 561/798–7000 or 800/327–4204) features 45 holes with an excellent overall layout. The **West Palm Beach Country Club** (✉ 7001 Parker Ave., ☎ 561/582–2019) offers 18 holes with no water hazards, unusual for Florida.

Shopping

As good as the malls are, they're sterile compared to the in-the-midst-of-things excitement—the mix of food, art, performance, landscaping, and retailing—that has renewed downtown West Palm around **Clematis Street.** Water-view parks, outdoor performing areas, and attractive plantings and lighting—including fanciful palm tree sculptures—add to the pleasure of browsing, window-shopping, and resting at an outdoor café. For those single-mindedly bent on mall shopping, the **Palm Beach Mall** (✉ Palm Beach Lakes Blvd. at I–95) has a Burdines, JCPenney, Lord & Taylor, and Sears Roebuck.

The 55-acre, $550 million **CityPlace** (✉ 700 S. Rosemary Ave.) is a shopping and entertainment complex with 78 national and regional stores including Macy's, FAO Schwarz, and Restoration Hardware.

Side Trip

Lake Okeechobee

40 mi west of West Palm Beach.

Rimming the western edge of Palm Beach and Martin counties, the second-largest freshwater lake in the United States is girdled by 120 mi of roads; yet for almost its entire circumference it remains hidden from sight. The Seminole's Big Water and the heart of the great Everglades watershed, Lake Okeechobee measures 730 square mi—roughly 33 mi north–south and 30 mi east–west—with an average natural depth of only 10 ft (flood control brings the figure up to 12 ft and deeper). Six major lock systems and 32 separate water-control structures manage the water.

Encircling the lake is a 30-ft-high grassy levee, known locally as "the wall," and the Lake Okeechobee Scenic Trail, a coarse track that has been integrated into the Florida National Scenic Trail. Inside the wall, on the big lake itself, fisherfolk come from everywhere for reputedly the best bass fishing in North America.

Small towns dot the lakeshore in an area that's still largely agricultural. To the southeast is Belle Glade, whose motto—"Her soil is her fortune"—results from the town's role as the eastern hub of the 700,000-acre Everglades Agricultural Area, the crescent of farmlands lying south and east of the lake. To the southwest lies Clewiston, the most prosperous lake town. It's known as "the sweetest town in America" thanks to the resident headquarters of the United States Sugar Corporation. At the north end of the lake, around Okeechobee, citrus production has outgrown cattle ranching as the principal economy, while dairying, although still important, is diminishing as the state acquires land in its efforts to reduce water pollution. Somewhat set back from the lake, Indiantown is the western hub of Martin County, noteworthy for citrus production, cattle ranching, and timbering. The town reached its apex in 1927, when the Seaboard Airline Railroad briefly established its southern headquarters and a model town here.

Grouped together in Belle Glade's **Municipal Complex** are the public library and the **Lawrence E. Will Museum,** both with materials on the town's history. On the front lawn is a Ferenc Verga sculpture of a family fleeing the wall of water that rose from the lake during the catastrophic hurricane of 1928. More than 2,000 people lost their lives and 15,000 families were left homeless by the torrential flood. ✉ *530 Main St., Belle Glade,* ☎ *561/996–3453.* 🎫 *Free.* ⏲ *Mon.–Wed. 10–8, Thurs.–Sat. 10–5.*

The **Clewiston Museum** details the history of the city, with stories not only of sugar and of the Herbert Hoover Dike construction, but also of a ramie crop grown here to make rayon, of World War II RAF pilots who trained at the Clewiston airfield, and of a German POW camp. ✉ *112 S. Commercio St., Clewiston,* ☎ *863/983–2870.* 🎫 *Free.* ⏲ *Tues.–Fri. 10–4.*

The Florida Power and Light Company's Martin Power Plant maintains the **Barley Barber Swamp,** a 400-acre freshwater cypress swamp preserve. A 5,800-ft-long boardwalk enables you to walk through this vestige of what near-coastal Florida was largely like before vast water-control efforts began in the 19th century. Dozens of birds, reptiles, and mammals inhabit these wetlands and lowlands, with an outstanding reserve of bald cypress trees, land and swamp growth, and slow-flowing coffee-color water. Reservations are required at least one week in advance for tours, which are held weekdays from October to May. In January and February there are manatee walks and in June and July there are turtle walks. Call for specific schedules. ✉ *Rte. 710, Indiantown,* ☎ *800/552–8440.* 🎫 *Free.* ⏲ *Tours Fri.–Wed. 8:30 and 12:30.*

DINING AND LODGING

$–$$ ✕ **Colonial Dining Room.** The Clewiston Inn's restaurant has ladder-back chairs, chandeliers, and fanlight windows, and although the food is good, the attitude's not fancy. Southern regional and Continental dishes—chicken, pork, steak, and the ubiquitous catfish—are served. ✉ *108 Royal Palm Ave., at U.S. 27, Clewiston,* ☎ *863/983–8151. MC, V.*

$–$$ ✕ **Lightsey's.** The pick of the lake, this beautiful lodgelike restaurant at the Okee-Tantie Recreation Area started closer to town as a fish company with four tables in a corner. Now everybody comes out here. You can get most items fried, steamed, broiled, or grilled. The freshest are the catfish, cooter (freshwater turtle), frogs' legs, and gator. ✉ *10430 Rte. 78W, Okeechobee,* ☎ *863/763–4276. MC, V. Beer and wine only.*

$–$$ ★ 🏨 **Seminole Country Inn.** This two-story, Mediterranean revival inn, once the southern headquarters of the Seaboard Airline Railroad, was restored by longtime Indiantown patriarch, the late Holman Wall. It's now being run by his daughter, Jonnie Wall Williams, a fifth-generation native, who is devoted to the inn's restoration. Rooms are done in country ruffles and prints, with full carpeting and comfy beds. There are rocking chairs on the porch, Indiantown memorabilia in the lobby, a sitting area on the second floor, and good local art throughout. ✉ *15885 S.W. Warfield Blvd., Indiantown 34956,* ☎ *561/597–3777,* WEB *www.seminoleinn.com. 28 rooms. 2 restaurants, pool. AE, D, MC, V.*

$ ⛺ **Belle Glade Marina Campground.** A few miles north of downtown Belle Glade, just offshore in Lake Okeechobee, is Torry Island. Campsites have water and electrical hookups; some have sewer hookups and docking facilities. ✉ *Torry Island 33493,* ☎ *561/996–6322. 370 campsites. Picnic area, horseshoes, shuffleboard, dock, boating, fishing. MC, V.*

$ **Clewiston Inn.** A classic antebellum-style country hotel in the heart of town, this inn was built in 1938. The cypress-panel lobby, wood-burning fireplace, colonial dining room, and Everglades lounge with a wraparound Everglades mural are standouts. Rooms are pleasant but basic, with reproduction furniture. Still it's worth a stay to soak up the lore and take advantage of the excellent value. A pool is across the street in the park. ✉ *108 Royal Palm Ave., at U.S. 27, Clewiston 33440,* ☎ *863/983–8151 or 800/749–4466,* FAX *863/983–4602,* WEB *www.clewistoninn.com. 48 rooms, 5 suites. Restaurant, bar, 6 tennis courts, jogging. AE, MC, V. BP.*

$ **Okeechobee Inn.** Rooms in this simple, two-story L-shape motel, 2 mi west of Belle Glade, are furnished in green floral prints. Large windows let in plenty of light. All rooms have balconies that overlook the pool, and fishing and boat ramps are just a mile away. ✉ *265 N. U.S. 27, South Bay 33493,* ☎ *561/996–6517. 115 rooms. Pool, playground. MC, V.*

$ **Okee-Tantie Recreation Area.** In addition to its recreational facilities, the park offers 215 RV sites, 38 tent sites, picnic spots, rest rooms, showers, Lightsey's restaurant, and a shop at which you can buy groceries and sandwiches. ✉ *10430 Rte. 78W, Okeechobee 34974,* ☎ *863/763–2622. Restaurant, grocery, picnic area, dock, boating, fishing, playground. MC, V.*

$ ★ **Pier II Resort.** This modern two-story motel on the rim canal has a five-story observation tower for looking over the levee to the lake. Large, clean, motel-plain rooms are well maintained. Out back there are a 600-ft fishing pier and the Oyster Bar, one of the best hangouts on the lake for shooting a game of pool or watching a game on TV. It attracts a good mix of locals and out-of-towners. ✉ *2200 S.E. U.S. 441, Okeechobee 34974,* ☎ *863/763–8003 or 800/874–3744,* FAX *863/763–2245. 89 rooms. Bar, fishing. AE, D, DC, MC, V.*

OUTDOOR ACTIVITIES AND SPORTS

Fishing. J-Mark Fish Camp (✉ Torry Island, ☎ 561/996–5357) provides fully equipped bass boats, airboat rides, fishing guides, tackle, bait, and licenses. Since the **Okee-Tantie Recreation Area** (✉ 10430 Rte. 78W, Okeechobee, ☎ 863/763–2622) has direct access to the lake, it's a popular place for fishing. There are two public boat ramps, fish-cleaning stations, a marina, picnic areas and a restaurant, a playground, rest rooms, showers, and a **bait shop** (☎ 863/763–9645) that stocks groceries. In addition to operating the bridge to Torry Island (the last remaining swing bridge in Florida, it is cranked open and closed by hand, swinging at right angles to the road), brothers Charles and Gordon Corbin run **Slim's Fish Camp** (✉ Torry Island, ☎ 561/996–3844). Here you'll find a complete tackle shop, guides, camping facilities, fully equipped bass boats, and even the name of a good taxidermist to mount your trophy.

Golf. Belle Glade Municipal Country Club (✉ Torry Island Rd., Belle Glade, ☎ 561/996–6605) has an 18-hole golf course and restaurant open to the public.

SOUTH TO BOCA RATON

Strung together by Route A1A, the towns between Palm Beach and Boca Raton are notable for their variety. Although the glamour of Palm Beach has rubbed off on many towns, there are pockets of modesty and unpretentiousness alongside the well-established high and mighty. In one town you might find a cluster of sophisticated art galleries and fancy eateries, while the very next town could have a few hamburger stands and mom-and-pop "everything" stores.

Lake Worth

22 *2 mi south of West Palm Beach.*

For years, tourists were mainly interested in this town for its inexpensive lodging and close proximity to Palm Beach since a bridge leads from the mainland to a barrier island that is home to Lake Worth's beach, and to the north, Palm Beach. However, there are now several blocks here with interesting restaurants and art galleries making this a good place for a stroll.

Lake Worth Municipal Park, also known as Casino Park, has a beach, Olympic-size swimming pool, fishing pier, picnic areas, shuffleboard, restaurants, and shops. ✉ *Rte. A1A at end of Lake Worth Bridge,* ☎ *561/533–7367.* 🎫 *Pool $3, parking 25¢ for 15 min.* ⏲ *Daily 9–4:45.*

The Arts

Klein Dance Company (✉ 3208 2nd Ave. N, No. 10, 33461, ☎ 561/586–1889) is a nationally acclaimed, world-touring professional troupe that also gives local performances.

Dining and Lodging

$$–$$$$ ✕ **Paradiso.** The aroma of garlic is overwhelming as you step into this noisy, popular, and sophisticated Italian eatery. Two walls show off a mural of the Italian countryside. Tables are spaced close together but are elegantly set with white linens. Begin with the pasta *y fagiole* (with white beans) soup, the polenta with porcini mushrooms, or the fresh mozzarella with tomatoes. The numerous pasta offerings, which can be served as appetizer portion or entrées, include linguine tossed with clams, penne arrabiata, tagliolini with pesto, and orecchiette with broccoli rabe. Veal scallopini with prosciutto, chicken breast stuffed with goat cheese, grilled scampi, and several risotto specials make excellent main course choices. ✉ *625 Lucerne Ave.,* ☎ *561/547–2500. AE, MC, V. No lunch Sun.*

$–$$ ✕ **John G's.** About the only time the line lets up is when the restaurant closes at 3 PM. The menu is as big as the crowd: big fruit platters, sandwich-board superstars, grilled burgers, seafood, and eggs every which way, including a United Nations of omelets. Breakfast is served until 11. ✉ *Lake Worth Casino,* ☎ *561/585–9860. No credit cards. No dinner.*

$ ✕ **TooJay's.** There's not much elbow room here as locals fill the tables all day long to sample the giant sandwiches. Try the corned beef on rye, the roast beef and onion on pumpernickel, the tuna melt, or the tasty Reuben. Overstuffed wraps, hot dogs, chili, matzo-ball soup, meat loaf, lox, bagels, and everything else you would expect a New York deli to offer is right here in Lake Worth. The menu at this spot, one of nine in the Sunshine State, also includes killer desserts. ✉ *5030 Champion Blvd.,* ☎ *561/241–5903. AE, DC, MC, V.*

$–$$$ 🏨 **Mango Inn.** It's just a 10-minute walk to the beach from this white frame B&B that was built as a private house in 1915. Each of the seven rooms is individually decorated and all have bouquets of fresh flowers from the gardens. The two first-floor rooms have elegant French doors that open out onto a patio and overlook the pool. Some rooms are furnished with four-poster beds and all have private baths. The poolside cottage comes with its own kitchenette. Breakfast can be enjoyed in the dining room, on the veranda overlooking the heated pool, or in the peaceful courtyard. ✉ *128 N. Lakeside Dr., 33460,* ☎ *561/533–6900,* FAX *561/533–6992,* WEB *www.mangoinn.com. 7 rooms, 1 cottage. Pool. AE, MC, V.*

$–$$$ 🏨 **Sabal Palm House.** Built in 1936, this historic two-story frame bed-and-breakfast is just a short walk from the Intracoastal Waterway. Three rooms and a suite are in the main house and three rooms are across a brick courtyard in the carriage house. The decor in each room is inspired by a different artist: Renoir, Dalí, Norman Rockwell, Chagall, Michelangelo, Lautrec, and Degas. All have oak floors and private balconies and are furnished with antiques. Two units have Jacuzzi tubs. Fresh flowers and nightly turndown service are provided. A gourmet breakfast is served in the two indoor dining rooms and also outside in the courtyard, under the palms. There is an inviting parlor in which to read or meet other guests. ✉ *109 N. Golfview Rd., 33460,* ☎ *561/582–1090,* FAX *561/582–0933,* WEB *www.sabalpalmhouse.com. 6 rooms, 1 suite. AE, MC, V. BP.*

Outdoor Activities and Sports

The **Gulfstream Polo Club,** the oldest club in the Palm Beach area, began in the 1920s and plays medium-goal polo (for teams with handicaps of 8–16 goals). There are six polo fields. ✉ *4550 Polo Rd.,* ☎ *561/965–2057.* *Free.* *Games Dec.–Apr.*

Nightlife

Some nights its free concerts by local and regional artists and other nights the headliners are nationally known professionals, but every night, Tuesday through Saturday, you'll find traditional blues at the **Bamboo Room** (✉ 25 S. J St., ☎ 561/585–2583).

Lantana

23 *2 mi south of Lake Worth.*

Like Lake Worth, Lantana has inexpensive lodging and a bridge connecting the town to its own beach on Palm Beach's barrier island. It's just a bit farther away from Palm Beach. A closer island neighbor is **Manalapan**, a tiny residential community with a luxury beach resort.

Lantana Public Beach has one of the best food concessions around, the **Dune Deck Cafe**. You'll find fresh fish on weekends and breakfast and lunch specials every day outdoors under beach umbrellas. ✉ *100 N. Ocean Ave.,* ☎ *no phone.* *Parking 25¢ for 15 min.* *Daily 9–4:45.*

Dining and Lodging

$$–$$$ ✕ **Old Key Lime House.** Overlooking the Intracoastal Waterway, the 1889 Lyman House has grown in spurts over the years and is now a patchwork of shedlike spaces, an informal Old Florida seafood house that serves not only local seafood but also, Key lime pie—the specialty. Although there's air-conditioning, dining is still open-air most evenings and in cooler weather. ✉ *300 E. Ocean Ave.,* ☎ *561/533–5220. AE, MC, V.*

$$$$ ★ **Ritz-Carlton, Palm Beach.** Despite its name, this hotel is actually in Manalapan, halfway between Palm Beach and Delray. The bisque-color, triple-tower landmark may look like the work of Addison Mizner, but in fact it was built in 1991. Dominating the lobby is a huge double-side marble fireplace, foreshadowing the luxury of the guest rooms' marble tubs and upholstered furniture. Most rooms have ocean views, and all rooms have balconies. Not to be outdone by the fabulous beaches, a large pool and courtyard area has more than 100 coconut palms. Bikes and scuba and snorkeling equipment can be rented. ✉ *100 S. Ocean Blvd., Manalapan 33462,* ☎ *561/533–6000 or 800/241–3333,* FAX *561/588–4555,* WEB *www.ritz-carlton.com. 257 rooms, 13 suites. 4 restaurants, 2 bars, pool, hair salon, massage, sauna, spa, steam room, 5 tennis courts, basketball, beach, bicycles. AE, D, DC, MC, V.*

$ **Super 8 Motel.** There's nothing special about this sprawling one-story motel except the price—a real bargain, considering the proximity to Palm Beach. Efficiencies and rooms are clean but basically furnished. ✉ *1255 Hypoluxo Rd., 33462,* ☎ *561/585–3970,* FAX *561/586–3028. 129 rooms, 8 efficiencies. Refrigerators, pool, coin laundry. AE, DC, MC, V.*

Outdoor Activities and Sports

B-Love Fleet (✉ 314 E. Ocean Ave., ☎ 561/588–7612) offers three deep-sea fishing excursions daily: 8–noon, 1–5, and 7–11. No reservations are needed; just show up 30 minutes before the boat is scheduled to leave. The cost is $24 per person.

Boynton Beach

24 *3 mi south of Lantana.*

This town is far enough from Palm Beach to have kept its laid-back, low-key atmosphere. Its two parts, on the mainland and the barrier island, are connected by a causeway.

Knollwood Groves dates from the 1930s, when it was planted by the partners of the *Amos & Andy* radio show. You can take a 30-minute, 30-acre tram tour through the orange groves and a processing plant and visit the **Hallpatee Seminole Indian Village,** where there are an alligator exhibit and crafts shop. During the high season, special guest Martin Twofeather gives a weekly one-hour alligator-handling show. ✉ *8053 Lawrence Rd.,* ☎ *561/734–4800,* WEB *www.knollwoodgroves.com.* *Tour $1, show $5.* ⏲ *Daily 8:30–5:30, show Sat. 2. Closed Sun. May and Oct.*

The **Puppetry Arts Center** provides shows and educational programs from the home of the Gold Coast Puppet Guild. ✉ *3633 S. Federal Hwy.,* ☎ *561/737–3334.* *Shows $2.50.* ⏲ *Call for schedule.*

Oceanbeach Park has a beach, boardwalk, concessions, grills, a jogging trail, and playground. Parking is expensive if you're not a Boynton resident. ✉ *Ocean Ave. at Rte. A1A,* ☎ *no phone.* *Parking $10 per day in winter, $5 per day rest of year.* ⏲ *Daily 9 AM–midnight.*

OFF THE BEATEN PATH

ARTHUR R. MARSHALL–LOXAHATCHEE NATIONAL WILDLIFE REFUGE – The most robust part of the Everglades, this 221-square-mi refuge is one of three huge water-retention areas that account for much of the Everglades outside the national park. These areas are managed less to protect natural resources, however, than to prevent flooding to the south. Start from the visitor center, where there are two walking trails: a boardwalk through a dense cypress swamp and a marsh trail to a 20-ft-high observation tower overlooking a pond. There is also a 5½-mi canoe trail, recommended for more experienced canoeists because it's rather overgrown. Wildlife viewing is good year-round, and you can fish for bass and panfish. ✉ *10119 Lee Rd., off U.S. 441 between Boynton Beach Blvd. (Rte. 804) and Atlantic Ave. (Rte. 806), west of Boynton Beach,* ☎ *561/734–8303.* *$5 per vehicle, $1 per pedestrian.* ⏲ *Daily 6 AM–sunset; visitor center weekdays 9–4, weekends 9–4:30.*

Dining and Lodging

$–$$ ✗ **Mama Jennie's.** Tucked at the end of a strip mall, this inviting, casual Italian restaurant attracts families, who come here to share large, traditional pizza pies topped with mozzarella, mushrooms, and anchovies. Spaghetti with meatballs, eggplant parmigiana, and stuffed shells are also fine choices, and all dishes are homemade. ✉ *706 W. Boynton Beach Blvd.,* ☎ *561/737–2407. AE, MC, V. No lunch.*

$$ **Holiday Inn Express.** Conveniently located right off Interstate 95, this four-story hotel contains large rooms with purple and green fabrics, blond-wood furniture, and a small sitting area. The heated pool is surrounded by a large sundeck. Complimentary breakfast is served in the morning, and complimentary beverages are available at the end of the day. ✉ *480*

W. Boynton Beach Blvd., 33435, ☎ 561/734–9100, FAX 561/738–7193. 105 rooms, 6 suites. Pool, coin laundry. AE, DC, MC, V.

Outdoor Activities and Sports

FISHING

You can fish the canal at the **Arthur R. Marshall–Loxahatchee National Wildlife Refuge** (☎ 561/734–8303). There's a boat ramp, and the waters are decently productive, but bring your own equipment.

GOLF

Boynton Beach Municipal Golf Course (✉ 8020 Jog Rd., ☎ 561/742–6500) offers 27 holes.

Gulf Stream

25 *2 mi south of Boynton Beach.*

This beautiful little beachfront community was also touched by Mizner. As you pass the bougainvillea-topped walls of the Gulf Stream Club, a private police officer may stop traffic for a golfer to cross.

Lodging

$ **Riviera Palms Motel.** Hans and Herter Grannemann have owned this small, quaint two-story motel dating from the 1950s since 1978. It has two primary virtues: it's clean, and it's well located. It's across Route A1A from mid-rise apartment houses on the ocean. Three wings with green awnings surround a grassy front yard and heated pool. Rooms are done in Danish modern and a blue, brown, and tan color scheme; all have at least a refrigerator but no phone. ✉ *3960 N. Ocean Blvd., 33483,* ☎ *561/276–3032. 17 rooms, suites, and efficiencies. Pool. No credit cards.*

Delray Beach

26 *2 mi south of Gulf Stream.*

What began as an artists' retreat and a small settlement of Japanese farmers is now a sophisticated beach town with a successful local historic preservation movement. Atlantic Avenue, the main drag, has been transformed into a 1-mi stretch of palm-dotted brick sidewalks, almost entirely lined with stores, art galleries, and dining establishments. Running east–west and ending at the beach, it's a pleasant place for a stroll, day or night. Another active pedestrian way begins at the edge of town, across Northeast 8th Street (George Bush Boulevard), along the big broad swimming beach that extends north and south of Atlantic Avenue.

Municipal Beach (✉ Atlantic Ave. at Rte. A1A) has a boat ramp and volleyball court.

The chief landmark along Atlantic Avenue is the Mediterranean revival **Colony Hotel** (✉ 525 E. Atlantic Ave., ☎ 561/276–4123), still open only for the winter season as it has been almost every year since 1926.

Cason Cottage, a restored Victorian-style home that dates from about 1915, now serves as offices of the Delray Beach Historical Society. The house is filled with relics of the Victorian era, including an old pipe organ donated by descendants of one of the original families to settle Delray Beach. Periodic displays celebrate the town's architectural evolution. The cottage is a block north of the cultural center. ✉ *5 N.E. 1st St.,* ☎ *561/243–0223. Free.* ⏲ *Tues.–Fri. 11–4.*

The **Old School Square Cultural Arts Center,** just off Atlantic Avenue, houses several museums in restored school buildings dating from 1913 and 1926. The **Cornell Museum of Art & History** offers an ever-changing array of art exhibits. ✉ *51 N. Swinton Ave.,* ☎ *561/243–7922.* 🎫 *$6.* ⏲ *Tues.–Sat. 11–4, Sun. 1–4.*

★ Florida seems to be an odd place for the **Morikami Museum and Japanese Gardens.** At this 200-acre cultural and recreational facility, there is a beautiful Japanese imperial-style villa with a display that recalls the Yamato Colony, an agricultural community of Japanese settlers who came to Florida in 1905. Gardens include the only known collection of bonsai Florida plants. There are also programs and exhibits in a lakeside museum and theater, as well as a nature trail, picnic pavilions, a library and audiovisual center, and a snack bar. The on-site Cornell Café is a pleasant retreat serving light Asian fare. ✉ *4000 Morikami Park Rd.,* ☎ *561/495–0233.* 🎫 *Park and museum $5.25, free Sun. 10–noon.* ⏲ *Park daily sunrise–sunset; museum Tues.–Sun. 10–5; café Tues.–Sun. 10–5.*

Dining and Lodging

$$–$$$ ✕ **Splendid Blendeds Café.** Dine outside on the sidewalk terrace or inside in the dining room decorated with large primitive art originals. The café is a popular gathering spot both day and night, and the cuisine is an eclectic blend of Italian, Mexican, Asian, and contemporary. Come for the tasty starters such as duck and wild-mushroom quesadilla, shrimp and mascarpone ravioli, grilled Thai duck satay, or radicchio and apple-walnut salad. Entrées include pasta dishes like spinach linguine with Brie, angel hair pomodoro, as well as grilled yellowfin tuna, shrimp scampi, a filet mignon stuffed with roasted garlic, and chicken with a black-bean sauce or marinated with Jamaican jerk spices. ✉ *432 E. Atlantic Ave.,* ☎ *561/265–1035. AE, MC, V. Closed Sun.*

$–$$ ★ ✕ **Blue Anchor.** Unbelievably, this pub was actually shipped from England, where it stood for 150 years as the Blue Anchor Pub in London's historic Chancery Lane. There it was a regular watering hole for many famous Englishmen, including Winston Churchill. The Delray Beach incarnation still cooks up authentic British pub fare: ploughman's lunch (a chunk of cheddar or Stilton cheese, a hunk of bread, and pickled onions), steak-and-kidney pie, fish-and-chips, and bangers and mash (sausages with mashed potatoes), to name just a few. You can also get delicious hamburgers, sandwiches, and salads. The dessert menu includes an English sherry trifle and a Bailey's Irish Cream pie. English beers and ales are available on tap and by the bottle. ✉ *804 E. Atlantic Ave.,* ☎ *561/272–7272. AE, MC, V.*

$–$$ ★ ✕ **Boston's on the Beach.** Often a restaurant that's facing a beach relies on its location to fill the place up and doesn't worry enough about the food. Not so with Boston's. As you might expect from the name, you'll find good New England clam chowder and several lobster dishes, as well as fresh fish grilled, fried, or prepared just about any other way. All this is presented in an ultra-informal setting. Tables are old and wooden, and walls are decorated with traffic signs and other conversation starters, most notably paraphernalia from the Boston Bruins, New England Patriots, and Boston Red Sox, including a veritable shrine to Ted Williams. An outdoor deck upstairs is a terrific place to catch ocean breezes. After dark the place becomes a casual club with live music. ✉ *40 S. Ocean Blvd. (Rte. A1A),* ☎ *561/278–3364. AE, MC, V.*

$$$–$$$$ 🏨 **Delray Beach Marriott.** A bright Caribbean pink five-story hotel, it's by far the largest in Delray and with one of the best locations. It's at the east end of Atlantic Avenue and within easy walking distance of restaurants, shops, and art galleries and right across the road from the beach. Rooms and suites are spacious and come with the amenities one expects from a Marriott: data ports, in-room movies, and minibars. Fabrics are in Caribbean pastels. Many rooms have stunning ocean views;

rates vary depending on your view. The giant, free-form pool looks across the street to the ocean and is surrounded by a comfortable deck for sunning. ✉ *10 N. Ocean Blvd., 33483,* ☎ *561/274–3200,* FAX *561/274–3202,* WEB *www.marriotthotels.com. 244 rooms, 68 suites. 3 restaurants, 2 bars, pool, health club. AE, DC, MC, V.*

$$$–$$$$ ★ **Seagate Hotel & Beach Club.** One of the best garden hotels in Palm Beach County, this property offers value, comfort, style, and personal attention. All units have at least kitchenettes. The less expensive studios have compact facilities behind foldaway doors, while more expensive units have a separate living room and a larger kitchen. The one- and two-bedroom suites are all chintz and rattan, with many upholstered pieces. You can dress up and dine in a smart little mahogany- and lattice-trimmed beachfront salon or have the same Continental fare in casual attire in the equally stylish bar. Guests enjoy privileges at the private beach club. ✉ *400 S. Ocean Blvd., 33483,* ☎ *561/276–2421 or 800/233–3581. 70 suites. Restaurant, bar, saltwater pool, beach. AE, DC, MC, V.*

Nightlife and the Arts

THE ARTS

The **Crest Theater** (✉ 51 N. Swinton Ave., ☎ 561/243–7922), in the Old School Square Cultural Arts Center, presents productions in dance, music, and theater.

NIGHTLIFE

The **Back Room Blues Lounge** (✉ 909 W. Atlantic Ave., ☎ 561/243–9110), behind Westside Liquors, has a D.J. Wednesday through Saturday. **Boston's on the Beach** (✉ 40 S. Ocean Blvd., ☎ 561/278–3364) presents live reggae music Monday and rock and roll Tuesday through Sunday. **The Colony Hotel** (✉ 525 E. Atlantic Ave., ☎ 561/276–4123) has a convivial bar and live music most nights.

Outdoor Activities and Sports

BIKING

There is a bicycle path in Barwick Park and a special oceanfront lane along Route A1A. **Rich Wagen's Cycles** (✉ 217 E. Atlantic Ave., ☎ 561/276–4234) rents bikes by the hour or day. Free maps showing nearby bicycle routes are available.

SCUBA DIVING AND SNORKELING

Scuba and snorkeling equipment can be rented from longtime family-owned **Force E** (✉ 660 Linton Blvd., ☎ 561/276–0666). It has PADI affiliation, provides instruction at all levels, and offers charters.

TENNIS

Each winter the **Delray Beach Tennis Center** (✉ 201 W. Atlantic Ave., ☎ 561/243–7380) hosts a professional women's tournament that attracts players like the Williams sisters. The center is also a great place to practice or learn; it has 14 clay courts and five hard courts and offers individual lessons and clinics.

WATERSKIING

Lake Ida Park (✉ 2929 Lake Ida Rd., ☎ 561/964–4420) is an excellent place to water-ski, whether you're a beginner or a veteran. The park has a boat ramp, a slalom course, and a trick ski course.

Shopping

Street-scaped **Atlantic Avenue** is a showcase for art galleries, shops, and restaurants. In addition to serving lunch and a traditional afternoon tea, the charming **Sundy House** (✉ 106 S. Swinton Ave., ☎ 561/272–5678) sells antiques and gifts in the former home of the first Delray mayor, John Shaw Sundy. The structure's beautiful gardens and five gingerbread gables complement Delray's finest wraparound porch.

Boca Raton

27 *6 mi south of Delray Beach.*

This upscale town at the south end of Palm Beach County, 30 minutes south of Palm Beach, has a lot in common with its ritzy cousin. For one thing, both reflect the unmistakable architectural presence of Addison Mizner, their principal developer in the mid-1920s. Mizner Park, an important Boca Raton shopping district, bears his name.

Built in 1925 as the headquarters of the Mizner Development Corporation, the structure at **2 East El Camino Real** is a good example of Mizner's characteristic Spanish revival architectural style, with its wrought-iron grilles and handmade tiles.

Championed by *Beetle Bailey* cartoonist Mort Walker, the **International Museum of Cartoon Art** showcases more than 160,000 pieces of art created over two centuries by more than 1,000 artists from more than 50 countries—everything from turn-of-the-last-century Buster Brown cartoons to the *Road Runner* to Charles Schulz's *Peanuts.* ✉ *201 Plaza Real,* ☎ *561/391–2200,* WEB *www.museumofcartoonart.com.* *$6.* ⏲ *Tues.–Sat. 10–6, Sun. noon–6.*

The **Boca Raton Museum of Art,** in a spectacular building in Mizner Park, is a must. First-floor highlights include an interactive children's gallery and changing exhibition galleries showcasing internationally known artists. Upstairs galleries feature the museum's permanent collection and include works by Picasso, Degas, Matisse, Klee, and Modigliani as well as notable pre-Columbian art. ✉ *501 Plaza Real,* ☎ *561/392–2500,* WEB *www.bocamuseum.com.* *$6.* ⏲ *Tues., Thurs., Sat., 10–5, Wed. and Fri. 10-9, Sun. noon–5.*

The residential area behind the Boca Raton Museum of Art is known as **Old Floresta.** Developed by Addison Mizner starting in 1925 and landscaped with many varieties of palms and cycads, it includes houses that are mainly in a Mediterranean style, many with upper balconies supported by exposed wood columns.

Hands-on interactive exhibits make the **Children's Science Explorium** a definite kid pleaser. Children can create their own laser-light shows, explore a 3-D kiosk that illustrates wave motion, and try all kinds of electrifying experiments. There are also wind tunnels, microscopes, and microwave and radiation experiment stations. ✉ *300 S. Military Trail,* ☎ *561/347–3913.* *Free.* ⏲ *Weekdays 8 AM–10:30 PM, Sat. 8–5, Sun. 10–5.*

A big draw for kids, the **Gumbo Limbo Nature Center** has four huge saltwater sea tanks containing all sorts of sea life—from coral to stingrays—and a long boardwalk through dense forest with a 50-ft tower you can climb to overlook the tree canopy. In the spring and early summer, staff members lead nighttime turtle walks to see nesting females come ashore and lay their eggs. ✉ *1801 N. Ocean Blvd.,* ☎ *561/338–1473,* WEB *www.fauedu/gumbo.com.* *Donation welcome; turtle tours $4 (tickets must be obtained in advance).* ⏲ *Mon.–Sat. 9–4, Sun. noon–4; turtle tours late May–mid-July, Mon.–Thurs. 9 PM–midnight.*

Red Reef Park(✉ 1400 N. Rte. A1A) has a beach and playground plus picnic tables and grills. In addition to its beach, **Spanish River Park** (✉ 3001 N. Rte. A1A) has picnic tables, grills, and a large playground. Popular **South Beach Park** (✉ 400 N. Rte. A1A) has a concession stand along with its sand and ocean.

Close-Up

FLORIDA'S SEA TURTLES: THE NESTING SEASON

FROM MAY TO OCTOBER it's turtle nesting season all along the Florida coast. Female loggerhead, Kemp's ridley, and other species of turtles that live way out in the Atlantic Ocean or Gulf of Mexico swim as many as 2,000 mi to the Florida shore. They arrive in the dark of night and drag their 100- to 400-pound bodies up the beach to the dune line. Once there, they arduously dig a hole with their flippers, drop in about 100 eggs, cover up the hole, and return to sea.

About 60 days later, generally in the middle of the night, the baby turtles hatch. It can take them several days just to make it up to the surface. However, once they burst out of the ground, the little hatchlings must get to the sea as fast as possible, or they will be caught by crabs or birds or become dehydrated by the morning sun.

Instinctively the baby turtles head to the brightest light. It's believed they do this because for millions of years starlight or moonlight reflected on the waves was the brightest light around, and it guided the hatchlings right to water. These days, however, light from buildings along the beach can disorient the baby turtles and cause them to go in the wrong direction. Every year many turtle hatchings are killed because they run to the street rather than to the water and are crushed by cars. To prevent this, many coastal towns have lighting restrictions during nesting months. These are seriously enforced, and more than one homeowner has been surprised by a police officer at the door requesting that lights be dimmed.

At night volunteers walk the beaches, searching for signs of turtle nests. When they find the telltale scratches in the sand, they cordon off the site, so daytime beachgoers will leave the spots undisturbed. These same volunteers keep an eye on the nests when babies are about to hatch and provide assistance if the hatchlings do get disoriented.

IT'S A HAZARDOUS WORLD for baby turtles. They can die after eating tar balls or plastic garbage or can get eaten by sharks, large fish, or circling birds. Only about one in 1,000 survives to adulthood. Once the baby turtles reach the water, they make their way to warm currents. East coast hatchlings drift into the Gulf Stream and spend several years floating around the Atlantic.

Males never, ever return to land, but when females attain maturity, which takes 15–20 years, they come back to shore to lay their eggs. Remarkably, even though they migrate hundreds and even thousands of miles out at sea, most return to the very beach where they were born to deposit their eggs. Sea turtles nest at least twice a season—sometimes as many as 10 times—and then skip a year or two. Each time they nest, they come back to the same tiny stretch of beach. In fact, the more they nest, the more accurate they get, until eventually they return time and again to within a few feet of where they last laid their eggs. Although scientists have studied these incredible navigation skills for some time, they remain a complete mystery. If you want to find out more about sea turtles, check out the Sea Turtle Survival League's and Caribbean Conservation Corporation's Web site at www.cccturtle.org.

— Pam Acheson

The Arts

Caldwell Theatre Company (✉ 7873 N. Federal Hwy., ☏ 561/241–7432), an Equity regional theater, hosts the multimedia Mizner Festival each April and May and stages four productions each winter. **Jan McArt's Royal Palm Dinner Theatre** (✉ 303 S. E. Mizner Blvd., Royal Palm Plaza, ☏ 561/392–3755 or 800/841–6765), an Equity theater, presents five or six musicals a year.

Dining and Lodging

$$–$$$$ ★ ✕ **La Vieille Maison.** Considered to be one of the temples of haute cuisine along the Gold Coast, the restaurant has a stunning courtyard and occupies a 1920s-era dwelling believed to be an Addison Mizner design. Closets and cubbyholes have been transformed into intimate private dining rooms. Both the prix-fixe and à la carte menus showcase Provençal dishes such as *soupe au pistou* (vegetable soup with basil and Parmesan cheese) and venison chop with red currant–pepper sauce and roasted chestnuts. Health-conscious selections are available on all menus. Dessert choices include French sponge cake with lemon cream and strawberries, French apple tart, and a chocolate lover's delight called *L'Indulgence de Chocolat. ✉ 770 E. Palmetto Park Rd., ☏ 561/391–6701 or 561/737–5677. AE, D, DC, MC, V. Closed early July–Aug.*

$$–$$$$ ✕ **Mark's at the Park.** Exotic cars pour into valet parking at this Mark Militello creation, where the decor—a whimsical 21st-century interpretation of retro and art deco—is as exciting as the food. On the outside terrace, furnishings are metal, but wood and fabric reign indoors, where asymmetrical columns and banquettes with immense backs and fabric inserts create cozy but noisy dining spaces. If you can tear your eyes away to focus on the dazzling menu, consider the chopped Sicilian salad, calamari cakes, or pizza with Maine lobster or onion, bacon, Gorgonzola, and walnuts. For an entrée, try the fusilli with a roasted eggplant and tomato ragout or the braised lamb shank with almond and raisin couscous. Desserts are deliciously old-fashioned. *✉ 344 Plaza Real, Mizner Park, ☏ 561/395–0770. AE, D, MC, V.*

$$–$$$$ ★ ✕ **Ristorante La Finestra.** Belle Epoque lithographs decorate the walls, and although the formal interior is just this side of austere, the cuisine itself is an extravaganza of taste treats. Start with the Portobello mushroom with garlic or the Corsican baby sardines in olive oil. For a main course try a pasta dish, such as ricotta ravioli with vodka or rigatoni *Bolognese* (with ground veal, marinara sauce, and Parmesan). Or order the scallopini of veal stuffed with crabmeat, lobster, and Gorgonzola; the Tuscan fish stew; or the mignonettes of pork and chicken in a Barola wine sauce. *✉ 171 E. Palmetto Rd., ☏ 561/392–1838. AE, DC, MC, V. No lunch.*

$$–$$$ ✕ **Crab House Seafood Restaurant.** Crowds come here day and night to dine on fresh Florida seafood and the restaurant's well-known crab specials. Landlubbers will find chicken, steaks, and salads to satisfy their fancies. There's a nautical theme to the decor, a wide deck for outside dining, a raw bar, and a cocktail lounge. *✉ 6909 S.W. 18th St., ☏ 561/750–0498. AE, D, MC, V.*

$$–$$$ ✕ **Uncle Tai's.** People flock here for some of the best Szechuan cuisine on Florida's east coast. House specialties include sliced duck with snow peas and water chestnuts in a tangy plum sauce, sliced fillet of snapper stir-fried and sautéed in a rice-wine sauce, and Uncle Tai's famous Orange Beef Delight—flank steak stir-fried until crispy and then sautéed with pepper sauce, garlic, and orange peel. Szechuan-style cooking is extremely hot and spicy, so remember to specify if you want the chef to go easy on you. *✉ 5250 Town Center Circle, ☏ 561/368–8806. AE, MC, V. No lunch.*

$–$$ ✕ **Draft House.** Sports aficionados will love this place. It's decorated with sports equipment and memorabilia and photos of famous coaches, players, and moments in sports and a dozen televisions show the night's top games. Regulars order the homemade chili wings, the fried chicken tenders, and the juicy burgers. The hungrier crowd digs into a char-grilled New York strip or a full rack of baby back ribs. Draft beers are just 99¢. *✉ 22191 Powerline Rd., ☎ 561/394–6699. AE, MC, V.*

$–$$ ★ ✕ **Tom's Place.** "This place is a blessing from God," says the sign over the fireplace, and after braving the long lines and sampling the superb menu, you will add, "Amen!" That's in between mouthfuls of Tom Wright's soul food—sauce-slathered ribs, pork-chop sandwiches, chicken cooked in peppery mustard sauce over hickory and oak, and sweet-potato pie. Buy a bottle or two of Tom's barbecue sauce ($2.25 a pint) just as Lou Rawls, Ben Vereen, Sugar Ray Leonard, and a rush of NFL players have before you. *✉ 7251 N. Federal Hwy., ☎ 561/997–0920. MC, V. Closed Sun., Mon.*

$$$–$$$$ ★ **Boca Raton Resort & Club.** Addison Mizner built the Mediterranean-style Cloister Inn here in 1926; it has been added to several times since to create this sprawling resort with a beach accessible by shuttle. Rooms in the Cloister are small and warmly traditional, those in the 27-story Tower are similar in style but larger, and rooms in the Beach Club are light, airy, and contemporary. Golf villas are, naturally, near the golf course. The concierge staff speaks at least 12 languages. Winter rates don't include meals, but you can pay extra for MAP (including breakfast and dinner). Rooms have been refurbished, the main golf course has been redesigned and there's now a new and spacious two-story golf clubhouse and a $10 million Tennis & Fitness Center that guests use for free. *✉ 501 E. Camino Real, 33431-0825, ☎ 561/395–3000 or 800/327–0101, FAX 561/447–5888, WEB www.bocaresort.com. 840 rooms, 63 suites, 60 golf villas. 7 restaurants, 3 bars, 5 pools, 36-hole golf course, 40 tennis courts, basketball, 3 health clubs, beach, boating, fishing. AE, DC, MC, V.*

$$ **Inn at Boca Teeca.** If golf is your game, this is an excellent place to stay. Inn guests can play the outstanding golf course at the adjoining Boca Teeca Country Club, otherwise available only to club members. Guest rooms are in a three-story building, and most have a patio or balcony. Although the inn is nearly 30 years old, the interior was recently refurbished, and rooms are small but comfortable and contemporary. *✉ 5800 N.W. 2nd Ave., 33487, ☎ 561/994–0400, FAX 561/998–8279. 46 rooms. Restaurant, 27-hole golf course, 6 tennis courts. AE, DC, MC, V.*

$$ **Ocean Lodge.** The price is right at this small motel because instead of being directly on the beach, it's just across the street. Rooms are in a simple two-story building, and all have refrigerators. Eleven rooms also have small kitchenettes with a two-burner stove top. Restaurants are within easy walking distance. *✉ 531 N. Ocean Blvd., 33432, ☎ 561/395–7772, FAX 561/395–0554. 18 rooms. Pool, coin laundry. AE, DC, MC, V.*

Nightlife and the Arts

Drop by the **Ambience Bar & Bistro** (✉ 5500 N. Federal Hwy., ☎ 561/988–8820) any night of the week for live bands. Sounds range from new wave and alternative to 1970s through '90s.

Outdoor Activities and Sports

BIKING

Plenty of bike trails and quiet streets make for pleasant pedaling in the area; for current information contact the city of Boca Raton's **Bicycle Coordinator** (☎ 561/346–3410). You can rent bikes and Rollerblades at **International Bicycle** (✉ 17 E. Palmetto Park Rd., ☎ 561/394–

0404) by the hour and by the day. Free bike maps show off the trails in the area.

BOATING

If you ever wanted the thrill of blasting across the water at up to 80 mph, check out **Air and Sea Charters** (✉ 490 E. Palmetto Park Rd., Suite 330, ☎ 561/368–3566). For $50 per person (three-person minimum), you can spend a wild-eyed half hour holding on to your life vest aboard a 1,000-horsepower offshore racing boat. For a more leisurely trip go for Air and Sea's two 55-ft catamarans or 45-ft sailboat.

GOLF

Two championship courses and golf programs run by Dave Pelz and Nicklaus/Flick are available at **Boca Raton Resort & Club.**

POLO

Royal Palm Polo Sports Club (✉ 6300 Old Clint Moore Rd., ☎ 561/994–1876), founded in 1959 by Oklahoma oilman John T. Oxley and now home to the $100,000 International Gold Cup Tournament, has seven polo fields within two stadiums. Games are held January through April, Sunday at 1 and 3. Admission is $8 to $15 for seats, $15 per car.

SCUBA DIVING AND SNORKELING

Information about dive trips, as well as rental scuba and snorkeling equipment, can be obtained at **Force E** (✉ 877 E. Palmetto Park Rd., ☎ 561/368–0555).

Shopping

Mizner Park (✉ Federal Hwy. between Palmetto Park Rd. and Glades Rd.) is a distinctive 30-acre shopping center with apartments and town houses among its gardenlike spaces. Some three dozen retail stores include the excellent Liberties Fine Books & Music, a Jacobson's specialty department store, seven restaurants with sidewalk cafés, and 12 movie screens. **Town Center** (✉ 6000 W. Glades Rd.) combines a business park with ritzy shopping and great dining. Major retailers include Bloomingdale's, Burdines, Lord & Taylor, Saks Fifth Avenue, and Sears Roebuck—201 stores and restaurants in all.

THE TREASURE COAST

From south to north, the Treasure Coast encompasses the top end of Palm Beach County plus Martin, St. Lucie, and Indian River counties. Although dotted with destinations, this section of coastline is one of Florida's quietest. Most towns are small and laid-back, and there's lots of undeveloped land between them. Vero is the region's most sophisticated area and the one place you'll find clusters of fine-dining establishments and upscale shops. The beaches along here are sought out by nesting sea turtles; you can join locally organized watches that go out to view the turtles laying their eggs in the sand between late April and August. Remember that you must not touch or disturb the turtles or their nests in any way.

Palm Beach Shores

28 *7 mi north of Palm Beach.*

This residential town rimmed by mom-and-pop motels is at the southern tip of Singer Island, across Lake Worth Inlet from Palm Beach. To get between the two, however, you must cross over to the mainland before returning to the beach. The main attraction of this unpretentious middle-class community is its affordable beachfront lodging and its proximity to several nature parks.

Peanut Island, a 79-acre island in the Intracoastal Waterway between Palm Beach Shores and Riviera Beach, opened in 1999 as a recreational park. The $2.75 million project includes a 20-ft-wide walking path surrounding the entire island, a 19-slip boat dock, a 170-ft T-shape fishing pier, six picnic pavilions, a visitor center, and 20 overnight campsites. The small **Palm Beach Maritime Museum** (☎ 561-842-8202) is open Friday and Saturday and showcases the "Kennedy Bunker," a bomb shelter prepared for President John F. Kennedy (call for exact visiting hours.) To get to the island, you'll have to drive your own boat or catch a water taxi (call for schedules and pickup locations). ✉ *6500 Peanut Island Rd., Riviera Beach,* ☎ *561/845–4445,* WEB *www.pbmm.org.* *Free.* ⏲ *Sunrise–sunset for noncampers.*

OFF THE BEATEN PATH

JOHN D. MACARTHUR BEACH STATE PARK – Almost 2 mi of beach, good fishing and shelling, and one of the finest examples of subtropical coastal habitat remaining in southeast Florida can be found here. To learn about what you see, take an interpretive walk to a mangrove estuary along the upper reaches of Lake Worth. Or visit the **William T. Kirby Nature Center** (☎ 561/624–6952), open Wednesday–Monday from 9 to 5, which has exhibits on the coastal environment. ✉ *10900 Rte. A1A, North Palm Beach,* ☎ *561/624–6950,* WEB *www.macbeach.org.* *$3.25 per vehicle with up to 8 people.* ⏲ *8–5:30.*

LOGGERHEAD PARK MARINE LIFE CENTER OF JUNO BEACH – Established by Eleanor N. Fletcher, "the turtle lady of Juno Beach," the center focuses on the natural history of sea turtles. Also on view are displays of coastal natural history, sharks, whales, and shells. ✉ *1200 U.S. 1 (entrance on west side of park), Juno Beach,* ☎ *561/627–8280,* WEB *www.marinelife.org.* *Donation welcome.* ⏲ *Tues.–Sat. 10–4, Sun. noon–3.*

Dining and Lodging

$$–$$$ ✕ **Sailfish Marina Restaurant.** Formerly known as The Galley, this old-time favorite may have changed names, but not cuisine. After a hot day of mansion gawking or beach bumming, there's no better place to chill out than this waterfront restaurant that looks out to Peanut Island. Choose a seat inside or out. The blender seems to run nonstop, churning out tropical drinks like piña coladas and Goombay Smashes. Old Florida favorites such as grouper, brought in fresh daily from the Bahamas, and conch chowder are mainstays, but there are also a few highbrow entrées—this is Palm Beach County, after all—such as lobster tail or baby sea scallops sautéed in garlic and lemon butter as well as old-fashioned staples like meat loaf with Portobello mushrooms. This is also a good spot for breakfast. ✉ *98 Lake Dr.,* ☎ *561/842–8449. MC, V. No dinner Mon.*

$$$–$$$$ ★ **Radisson Palm Beach Shores Resort.** Sitting at the edge of a long stretch of sandy beach is this large, pink, six-story resort with a red tile roof. Suites are furnished in natural rattan and tropical prints and walls are painted white or a pale pastel. Each suite has a separate bedroom, a living room with a sofa bed, plus a refrigerator, microwave, and dining area. The oceanfront pool is surrounded by a brick courtyard. The resort is a superb family destination. The Beach Buddies Kids Club has a wide array of programs for children ages 2 to 12 (for a fee) that include field trips, arts and crafts, seashell hunts, and water sports. Teenagers are invited to participate as counselors-in-training. ✉ *181 Ocean Ave., 33404,* ☎ *561/863–4000,* FAX *561/863–9502,* WEB *www.radisson.com. 257 suites. Restaurant, bar, pool, spa, health club, beach, children's programs (ages 2–12). AE, D, DC, MC, V.*

$$ ★ **Sailfish Marina and Sportfishing Resort.** This long-established one-story motel has a marina with 94 deep-water slips and 30 rooms and efficiencies that open to landscaped grounds. None are directly on the water, but Units 9–11 have ocean views across the blacktop drive. Rooms have peaked ceilings, carpeting, king-size or twin beds, and stall showers; all have ceiling fans. From the seawall you can see fish through the clear inlet water. The motel's staff is informed and helpful. ✉ *98 Lake Dr., 33404,* ☎ *561/844–1724 or 800/446–4577,* FAX *561/848–9684,* WEB *www.sailfishmarina.com. 30 units. Restaurant, bar, grocery, pool, dock. AE, MC, V.*

Outdoor Activities and Sports

Biking

To rent bikes by the hour or by the day, stop by the **Sailfish Marina and Resort** (✉ 98 Lake Dr., ☎ 561/844–1724). They provide free maps of all the bike trails.

Fishing

The **Sailfish Marina and Resort** (✉ 98 Lake Dr., ☎ 561/844–1724) has a large sportfishing fleet, with 28 ft to 60 ft boats and seasoned captains. They offer full- or half-day deep-sea fishing with a maximum of six people.

Palm Beach Gardens

29 *5 mi north of West Palm Beach.*

About 15 minutes northwest of Palm Beach is this relaxed, upscale residential community widely known for its high-profile golf complex, the PGA National Resort & Spa. Although the town is not on the beach, the ocean is just a 15-minute drive away.

Dining and Lodging

$$–$$$ ★ ✕ **Arezzo.** The pungent smell of fresh garlic tips you off that the food's the thing at this outstanding Tuscan grill at the PGA National Resort & Spa. In this unusually relaxed, upscale resort setting, you can dine in shorts or in jacket and tie. Families are attracted by the affordable prices (as well as by the food), so romantics might be tempted to pass Arezzo up, but that would be a mistake. Dishes include the usual variety of chicken, veal, fish, and steaks, but there are a dozen pastas, including rigatoni Bolognese and penne *alla puttanesca,* and almost as many pizzas. The decor, too, has the right idea: an herb garden in the center of the room, slate floors, upholstered banquettes to satisfy the upscale mood, and butcher paper over yellow table covers to establish the light side. ✉ *400 Ave. of the Champions,* ☎ *561/627–2000. AE, MC, V. No lunch.*

$$ ✕ **River House.** People keep returning to this waterfront restaurant for the large portions of straightforward American fare; the big salad bar and fresh, slice-it-yourself breads; the competent service; and, thanks to the animated buzz of a rewarded local clientele, the feeling that you've come to the right place. Choices include seafood (always with a daily catch), steaks, chops, and seafood-steak combo platters. Booths and freestanding tables are surrounded by blond wood, high ceilings, and nautical art. The wait on Saturday night in season can be 45 minutes. Reserve one of the 20 upstairs tables, available weekends only; the upstairs is a little more formal and doesn't have a salad bar (bread comes from below), but it does have a lovely cathedral ceiling. ✉ *2373 PGA Blvd.,* ☎ *561/694–1188. AE, MC, V. No lunch.*

$$$$ 🏨 **PGA National Resort & Spa.** Outstanding mission-style rooms are decorated in deep, almost somber florals, and the rest of the resort is equally richly detailed, from lavish landscaping to limitless sports facilities to excellent dining. The spa is housed in a building styled after a Mediterranean fishing village. Its six outdoor therapy pools, dubbed "Waters of the World," are joined by a collection of imported mineral salt pools; there are 22 private treatments. Golf courses and croquet courts are adorned with 25,000 flowering plants amid a 240-acre nature preserve. Two-bedroom, two-bath cottages with fully equipped kitchens and no-smoking rooms are available, too. Among the dining options here is a Don Shula's Steakhouse. ✉ *400 Ave. of the Champions, 33418,* ☎ *561/627–2000 or 800/633–9150,* FAX *561/622–0261,* WEB *www.pga-resort.com. 279 rooms, 60 suites, 80 cottages. 5 restaurants, 4 bars, 9 pools, lake, hot tub, sauna, spa, 90-hole golf course, 19 tennis courts, croquet, health club, boating. AE, D, DC, MC, V.*

Nightlife

For DJ Top 40s, try the **Club Safari** (✉ 4000 RCA Blvd., ☎ 561/622–8888), except on Thursday, when the focus is on oldies.

Outdoor Activities and Sports

AUTO RACING

Weekly ¼-mi drag racing; monthly 2¼-mi, 10-turn road racing; and monthly AMA motorcycle road racing take place year-round at the **Moroso Motorsports Park** (✉ 17047 Beeline Hwy., ☎ 561/622–1400).

GOLF

PGA National Resort & Spa (✉ 1000 Ave. of the Champions, ☎ 561/627–1800) offers a reputedly tough 90 holes.

Shopping

The Gardens Mall (✉ 3101 PGA Blvd.) contains the standards if you want to make sure you're not missing out on anything at home: Bloomingdale's, Burdines, Macy's, Saks Fifth Avenue, and Sears Roebuck.

Jupiter

30 *12 mi north of Palm Beach Shores.*

This little town is on one of the few parts of the east coast of Florida that do not have an island in front of them. Beaches here are part of the mainland, and Route A1A runs for almost 4 mi along the beachfront dunes.

Take a look at how life once was in the **Dubois Home,** a modest pioneer home dating from 1898. Sitting atop an ancient Jeaga Indian mound 20 ft high and looking onto Jupiter Inlet, it features Cape Cod as well as Cracker (old Florida) design. Even if you arrive when the house is closed, surrounding Dubois Park is worth the visit for its lovely beaches and swimming lagoons. ✉ *Dubois Rd.,* ☎ *no phone.* 🎫 *Donation welcome.* ⏲ *Wed. 1–4.*

Permanent exhibits at the **Florida History Center and Museum** review not only modern-day development along the Loxahatchee River but also shipwrecks, railroads, and Seminole, steamboat-era, and pioneer history. ✉ *805 N. U.S. 1, Burt Reynolds Park,* ☎ *561/747–6639.* 🎫 *$5.* ⏲ *Tues.–Fri. 10–5, weekends noon–5.*

The **Jupiter Inlet Lighthouse,** a redbrick Coast Guard navigational beacon designed by Civil War hero General George Meade, has operated here since 1860. Tours of the 105-ft-tall local landmark are given every half hour, and there is also a small museum. Those familiar with the lighthouse may notice a significant change, courtesy of an $858,000 federal grant: the lighthouse has been transformed from bright red to natural brick, which is how it looked from 1860 to 1918. ✉ *Off U.S. 1,* ☎ *561/747–8380,* WEB *www.jupiterinletlighthouse.com.* 🎫 *Tour $6.* ⏲ *Sun.–Wed. 10–4, last tour 3:15.*

Carlin Park (✉ 400 Rte. A1A) has beachfront picnic pavilions, hiking trails, a baseball diamond, playground, six tennis courts, fishing sites, and, naturally, a beach. The Park Galley, serving snacks and burgers, is usually open daily 9–5.

Dining and Lodging

$$–$$$$ ★ ✕ **Charley's Crab.** The grand view across the Jupiter River complements the soaring ceiling and striking interior architecture of this marina-side restaurant. Tables are arranged so that many have great water views, and if you eat after dark, you can watch the searching beam of the historic Jupiter Inlet Lighthouse. Come here for expertly prepared seafood, such as black grouper, Florida pompano, red snapper, or Gulf Stream yellowfin tuna. There are also outstanding pasta choices: *pagliara* with scallops, fish, shrimp, mussels, spinach, garlic, and olive oil; fettuccine *verde* with lobster, sun-dried tomatoes, fresh basil, and goat cheese; and shrimp and tortellini Boursin with cream sauce and tomatoes. Other branches of Charley's are in Boca Raton, Deerfield Beach, Fort Lauderdale, Palm Beach, and Stuart. ✉ *1000 N. U.S. 1,* ☎ *561/744–4710. AE, D, DC, MC, V.*

$$–$$$ ✕ **Sinclairs Ocean Grill & Rotisserie.** This popular spot in the Jupiter Beach Resort has tall French doors that look out to the pool and tropical greenery. The menu features a daily selection of fresh locally caught fish, such as cashew-encrusted Florida grouper, Cajun-spiced tuna, and mahimahi with pistachio sauce. Landlubbers can choose thick juicy steaks (filet mignon is the house specialty) and a variety of chicken and veal dishes. Sunday brunch is a big draw. ✉ *5 N. Rte. A1A,* ☎ *561/745–7120. AE, MC, V.*

$–$$ ✕ **Lighthouse Restaurant.** Low prices match the plain decor in this coffee shop–style building, but the menu and cuisine are a delightful surprise. You can get chicken breast stuffed with sausage and fresh vegetables, burgundy beef stew, and king-crab cakes, and a full-time pastry chef is at work, too. The same people-pleasing formula has been employed since 1936: round-the-clock service (except 10 PM Sunday–6 AM Monday) and a menu that changes daily to take advantage of the best market buys. Those looking for something less stick-to-the-ribs can order one of the affordable "lite dinners." ✉ *1510 U.S. 1,* ☎ *561/746–4811. D, DC, MC, V.*

$$$–$$$$ 🏨 **Jupiter Beach Resort.** This unpretentious resort has undergone a multimillion dollar refurbishment and it shows. Rooms, which are painted in pastel colors and decorated in floral prints and rattan, are in an eight-story tower. Most rooms have balconies, and higher rooms have excellent ocean views. Taking further advantage of its location, the resort offers turtle watches in season (May to October), during which you can see newly hatched turtles make their way to the water for the first time. Plentiful activities and a casual atmosphere draw families here. Snorkeling and scuba equipment and Jet Skis are available for rent, and the restaurant is worth staying in for. ✉ *5 N. Rte. A1A, 33477,* ☎ *561/746–2511 or 800/228–8810,* FAX *561/747–3304,* WEB *www.jupiterbeachresort.com. 187 rooms, 28 suites. 2 restaurants, 2 bars, pool, tennis court, beach, dive shop, recreation room, children's programs, coin laundry, business services. AE, D, MC, V.*

Outdoor Activities and Sports

BASEBALL

Both the **St. Louis Cardinals and Montreal Expos** (✉ 4751 Main St., ☎ 561/684–6801) train at the $28 million Roger Dean Stadium, which has seating for 7,000 fans and 12 practice fields.

CANOEING

Canoe Outfitters of Florida (✉ 4100 W. Indiantown Rd., ☎ 561/746–7053) runs trips along 8 mi of the Loxahatchee River, Florida's only designated Wild and Scenic River. Canoe rental for two people, with drop-off and pickup, costs $35 for the first two hours (two hour minimum) and then $4 per additional hour plus tax.

GOLF

The **Golf Club of Jupiter at Indian Creek** (✉ 1800 Central Blvd., ☎ 561/747–6262) offers 18 holes of varying difficulty. **Jupiter Dunes Golf Club** (✉ 401 Rte. A1A, ☎ 561/746–6654) features 18 holes and a putting green.

Jupiter Island and Hobe Sound

31 *5 mi north of Jupiter.*

Northeast across the Jupiter Inlet from Jupiter is the southern tip of Jupiter Island, which includes a carefully planned community of the same name. Here estates often retreat from the road behind screens of vegetation, while at the north end of the island, turtles come to nest in a wildlife refuge. To the west, on the mainland, is the little community of Hobe Sound.

Within **Blowing Rocks Preserve,** a 73-acre Nature Conservancy holding, you'll find plant communities native to beachfront dune, coastal strand (the landward side of the dunes), mangrove, and hammock (tropical hardwood forests). The best time to visit is when high tides and strong offshore winds coincide, causing the sea to blow spectacularly through holes in the eroded outcropping. Park in the lot; police ticket cars parked along the road. ✉ *Rte. 707, Jupiter Island,* ☎ *561/744–6668.* *$4 donation.* *Daily 9–4:30.*

The **Hobe Sound National Wildlife Refuge** actually consists of two tracts: 232 acres of sand-pine and scrub-oak forest in Hobe Sound and 735 acres of coastal sand dune and mangrove swamp on Jupiter Island. Trails are open to the public in both places. Turtles nest and shells wash ashore on the 3½-mi beach, which has been severely eroded by winter high tides and strong winds. ✉ *13640 S.E. Federal Hwy., Hobe Sound,* ☎ *561/546–6141;* ✉ *Beach Rd. off Rte. 707, Jupiter Island.* *$5 per vehicle.* *Daily sunrise–sunset.*

Although on the Hobe Sound National Wildlife Refuge, the appealing **Hobe Sound Nature Center** is an independent organization. Its museum, which has baby alligators and crocodiles, and a scary-looking tarantula, is a child's delight. Interpretive exhibits focus on the environment, and a ½-mi trail winds through a forest of sand pine and scrub oak—one of Florida's most unusual and endangered plant communities. A classroom program on environmental issues is for preschool-age children to adults. ✉ *13640 S.E. Federal Hwy., Hobe Sound,* ☎ *561/546–2067.* *Free.* *Trail daily sunrise–sunset; nature center weekdays 9–11 and 1–3, call for Sat. hrs, group tours by appointment.*

Once you've gotten to the **Jonathan Dickinson State Park,** follow signs to Hobe Mountain. An ancient dune topped with a tower, it yields a panoramic view across the park's 10,285 acres of varied terrain, as well as the Intracoastal Waterway. The Loxahatchee River, part of the federal government's Wild and Scenic Rivers program, cuts through the park and harbors manatees in winter and alligators year-round. Two-hour boat tours of the river leave four times daily. Among amenities here are bicycle and hiking trails, a campground, and a snack bar. ✉ *16450 S.E. Federal Hwy., Hobe Sound,* ☎ *561/546–2771 or 561/746–5804.* *$3.25 per vehicle with up to 8 people, boat tours $12.* *Daily 8–sunset.*

Outdoor Activities and Sports

Jonathan Dickinson's River Tours (✉ Jonathan Dickinson State Park, ☎ 561/746–1466) rents canoes for use around the park.

Stuart

32 *7 mi north of Hobe Sound.*

This compact little town on a peninsula that juts out into the St. Lucie River has a remarkable amount of river shoreline for its size as well as a charming historic district. The ocean is about 5 mi east.

Strict architectural and zoning standards guide civic renewal projects ★ in **Historic Downtown Stuart,** which now claims eight antiques shops, six restaurants, and more than 50 specialty shops within a two-block area. The old courthouse has become the **Cultural Court House Center** (✉ 80 E. Ocean Blvd., ☎ 561/288–2542), which features art exhibits. The George W. Parks General Store is now the **Stuart Heritage Museum** (✉ 101 S.W. Flagler Ave., ☎ 561/220–4600). On the National Register of Historic Places, the **Lyric Theatre** (✉ 59 S.W. Flagler Ave., ☎ 561/220–1942) has been revived for performing and community events; a gazebo has free music performances. For information on downtown, contact the **Stuart Main Street Office** (✉ 151 S.W. Flagler Ave., 34994, ☎ 561/286–2848).

Dining and Lodging

$$ ✕ **Jolly Sailor Pub.** In an old historic-district bank building, this eatery is owned by a 27-year British Merchant Navy veteran, which may account for the endless ship paraphernalia. A veritable Cunard museum, it has a model of the *Britannia,* prints of 19th-century side-wheelers, and a big bar painting of the *QE2.* There is a wonderful brass-railed wood bar, complete with dartboard, and such pub grub as fish-and-chips, cottage pie, and bangers and mash, with Guinness and Double Diamond ales on tap. You can also get hamburgers and salads. ✉ *1 S.W. Osceola St.,* ☎ *561/221–1111. AE, MC, V.*

$–$$ ✕ **The Ashley.** Although plants hang from the ceiling and art decorates the walls, this restaurant still has elements of the old bank that was robbed three times early in the 20th century by the Ashley Gang (hence the name). The big outdoor mural in the French Impressionist style was paid for by downtown revivalists, whose names are duly inscribed on wall plaques inside. The Continental menu is appealing, with lots of salads, fresh fish, and pastas. Crowds head to the lounge for a popular happy hour. ✉ *61 S.W. Osceola St.,* ☎ *561/221–9476. AE, MC, V. Closed Mon. in off-season.*

$–$$$ ★ 🏨 **HarborFront.** On a quiet site that slopes to the St. Lucie River, this B&B combines an unusual mix of accommodations and imaginative extras, including picnic baskets and concierge-like custom planning. Units are cozy and eclectic, ranging from a spacious chintz-covered suite to a cozy apartment with full kitchen, from rooms that are tweedy and dark to those that are airy and bright with a private deck. Furnishings mix wicker and antiques. You can relax in hammocks in the yard or in the hot tub, or take a full- or half-day sail on the 33-ft sailboat that's tied up to the dock. ✉ *310 Atlanta Ave., 34994,* ☎ *561/288–7289. 6 rooms, 2 suites, 1 cottage, 2 apartments. Hot tub, dock, boating. MC, V.*

Outdoor Activities and Sports

Deep-sea charters are available at the **Sailfish Marina** (✉ 3565 S.E. St. Lucie Blvd., ☎ 561/283–1122).

Shopping

More than 60 restaurants and shops featuring antiques, art, and fashions have opened along **Osceola Street** in the restored downtown area.

Hutchinson Island (Jensen Beach)

33 *5 mi northeast of Stuart.*

Unusual care limits development here and prevents the commercial crowding found to the north and south, although there are some high-rises here and there along the shore. The small town of Jensen Beach, part of which is in the central part of the island, actually stretches across both sides of the Indian River. Citrus farmers and fishermen still play a big role in the community, giving the area a down-to-earth feel. Its most notable population is that of the sea turtles; between late April and August more than 600 turtles come to nest along the town's Atlantic beach.

Built in 1875, the **House of Refuge Museum** is the only remaining building of nine such structures erected by the U.S. Life Saving Service (a predecessor of the Coast Guard) to aid stranded sailors. Exhibits include antique lifesaving equipment, maps, artifacts from nearby wrecks, and boatmaking tools. ✉ *301 S.E. Mac Blvd.,* ☎ *561/225–1875,* WEB *www.goodnature.org.* *$4.* *Tues.–Sun. 11–4.*

Run by the Florida Oceanographic Society, the **Coastal Science Center** consists of a coastal hardwood hammock and mangrove forest. Expansion has yielded a visitor center, a science center with interpretive exhibits on coastal science and environmental issues, and a ½-mi interpretive boardwalk. Guided nature walks are offered. ✉ *890 N.E. Ocean Blvd.,* ☎ *561/225–0505,* WEB *www.fosusa.org.* *$6.* *Mon.–Sat. 10–5, nature walks Mon.–Sat. 10:30 and by request.*

The pastel-pink **Elliott Museum** was built in 1961 in honor of Sterling Elliott, inventor of an early automated addressing machine and a four-wheel cycle. The museum displays antique automobiles, dolls and toys, and fixtures from an early general store, blacksmith shop, and apothecary shop. ✉ *825 N.E. Ocean Blvd.,* ☎ *561/225–1961,* WEB *www.goodnature.org.* *$6.* *Daily 10–4.*

Bathtub Beach (✉ MacArthur Blvd. off Rte. A1A), at the north end of the Indian River Plantation, is ideal for children because the waters are shallow for about 300 ft offshore and usually calm. At low tide bathers can walk to the reef. Facilities include rest rooms and showers.

Dining and Lodging

$$–$$$ ★ ✕ **11 Maple Street.** This 16-table restaurant is as good as it gets on the Treasure Coast. Run by Margee and Mike Perrin, it offers a Continental menu that changes nightly. The soft recorded jazz and the earnest, friendly staff satisfy as fully as the brilliant food served in ample portions. Appetizers might include roasted garlic focaccia with duck leg confit, panfried conch with balsamic vinegar, or a warm salad of spinach and crispy calamari. For entrées you may find pan-seared rainbow trout, wood-grilled venison with onion potato hash, and an oak-grilled beef tenderloin with white truffle and chive butter. For dessert look for cherry *clafouti* (similar to a bread pudding) and white-chocolate custard with blackberry sauce. ✉ *3224 Maple Ave.,* ☎ *561/334–7714. Reservations essential. MC, V. Closed Mon.–Tues. No lunch.*

$$–$$$ ✕ **Scalawags.** The look is plantation tropical—coach lanterns, gingerbread molding, wicker, slow-motion paddle fans—but the top-notch buffets are aimed at today's resort guests. Standouts are the prime rib buffet on Friday night and the all-you-can-eat Wednesday evening Seafood Extravaganza, with jumbo shrimp, Alaskan crab legs, clams on the half shell, marinated salmon, and fresh catch. A regular menu with a big selection of fish, shellfish, and grills plus a big salad bar is also offered. The main dining room in this second-floor restaurant at

the Indian River Plantation Marriott Beach Resort overlooks the Indian River; there is also a private 20-seat wine room and a terrace that looks out on the marina. ✉ *555 N.E. Ocean Blvd.,* ☎ *561/225–6818. AE, DC, MC, V.*

$$ ✕ **Conchy Joe's.** This classic Florida stilt house full of antique fish mounts, gator hides, and snakeskins dates from the late 1920s—but Conchy Joe's, like a hermit crab sliding into a new shell, only moved up from West Palm Beach in 1983. Under a huge Seminole-built *chickee* (raised wood platform) with a palm through the roof, you'll find a supercasual atmosphere and the freshest Florida seafood from a menu that changes daily. Staples, however, are the grouper marsala, broiled sea scallop, and fried cracked conch. Try the rum drinks with names like Goombay Smash and Bahama Mama, while listening to live music Thursday, Friday, and Saturday evenings. Happy hour is 3–6 daily and during all NFL games. ✉ *3945 N. Indian River Dr.,* ☎ *561/334–1130. AE, D, MC, V.*

$ ✕ **The Emporium.** Indian River Plantation Marriott Beach Resort's coffee shop is an old-fashioned soda fountain and grill that also serves hearty breakfasts. Specialties include eggs Benedict, omelets, deli sandwiches, and salads. ✉ *555 N.E. Ocean Blvd.,* ☎ *561/225–3700. AE, DC, MC, V.*

$$$–$$$$ **Hutchinson Island Marriott Beach Resort and Marina.** With a wealth of recreational activities and facilities as well as many restaurants and bars, this 200-acre sprawling yet self-contained resort is an excellent choice for families. Reception, some of the restaurants, and many rooms are in three yellow four-story buildings that form an open courtyard with a large swimming pool. Additional rooms and apartments with kitchens are in numerous other buildings spread around the property. Some overlook the Intracoastal Waterway and the resort's 77-slip marina, while other rooms look out to the ocean or onto tropical gardens. Complimentary tram service runs to key points around the property day and night. ✉ *555 N.E. Ocean Blvd., Hutchinson Island, Stuart 34996,* ☎ *561/225–3700 or 800/775–5936,* FAX *561/225–0033,* WEB *www.flatreasures.com. 299 rooms, 27 suites, 150 condominiums. 5 restaurants, 4 bars, 4 pools, spa, golf privileges, 13 tennis courts, beach, dock, boating. AE, DC, MC, V.*

$$–$$$ **Hutchinson Inn.** Sandwiched among the high-rises, this modest and affordable two-story motel from the mid-1970s has the feel of a B&B thanks to pretty canopies at the entrance and management's friendly attitude. An expanded Continental breakfast is served in the well-appointed lobby or on little tables outside, and you can borrow a book or a stack of magazines to take to your room, where homemade cookies are delivered in the evenings. On Saturday there's a noon barbecue. Motel-style rooms range from small but comfortable to fully equipped efficiencies and two seafront suites with private balconies. ✉ *9750 S. Ocean Dr., 34957,* ☎ *561/229–2000,* FAX *561/229–8875,* WEB *www.hutchinsoninn.com. 21 rooms, 2 suites. Pool, tennis court, beach. MC, V.*

Outdoor Activities and Sports

BASEBALL

The **New York Mets** (✉ 525 N.W. Peacock Blvd., Port St. Lucie, ☎ 561/871–2115) train at the St. Lucie County Sport Complex.

GOLF

Indian River Plantation Marriott Beach Resort (✉ 555 N.E. Ocean Blvd., ☎ 561/225–3700 or 800/444–3389) offers 18 holes. The PGA-operated **PGA Golf Club at the Reserve** (✉ 1916 Perfect Dr., Port St. Lucie, ☎ 561/467–1300 or 800/800–4653) is a public facility which opened its third 18-hole course in early 2000.

Fort Pierce

34 *11 mi north of Stuart.*

This community, about an hour north of Palm Beach, has a distinctive rural feel, focusing on ranching and citrus farming rather than tourism. It has several worthwhile stops for visitors, including those easily seen while following Route 707.

Once a reservoir, 550-acre **Savannahs Recreation Area** has been returned to its natural state. Today the semiwilderness area has campsites, a petting zoo, botanical garden, boat ramps, and trails. ⊠ *1400 E. Midway Rd.,* ☎ *561/464–7855.* 🎟 *$1 per vehicle.* ⏲ *Daily 8–6.*

At the **Heathcote Botanical Gardens,** a self-guided tour takes in a palm walk, Japanese garden, and subtropical foliage. ⊠ *210 Savannah Rd.,* ☎ *561/464–4672.* 🎟 *$3.* ⏲ *Tues.–Sat. 9–5, also Sun. 1–5 Nov.–Apr.*

As the home of the Treasure Coast Art Association, the **A. E. "Bean" Backus Gallery** displays the works of one of Florida's foremost landscape artists. The gallery also mounts changing exhibits and offers exceptional buys on work by local artists. ⊠ *500 N. Indian River Dr.,* ☎ *561/465–0630.* 🎟 *Donation welcome.* ⏲ *Tues.–Sun. 1–5.*

Highlights at the **St. Lucie County Historical Museum** include historic photos, early 20th-century memorabilia, vintage farm tools, a restored 1919 American La France fire engine, replicas of a general store and the old Fort Pierce railroad station, and the restored 1905 Gardner House. ⊠ *414 Seaway Dr.,* ☎ *561/462–1795.* 🎟 *$3.* ⏲ *Tues.–Sat. 10–4, Sun. noon–4.*

The 340-acre **Fort Pierce Inlet State Recreation Area** contains sand dunes and a coastal hammock. The park offers swimming, surfing, picnicking, hiking, and walking along a self-guided nature trail. ⊠ *905 Shorewinds Dr.,* ☎ *561/468–3985.* 🎟 *$3.25 per vehicle with up to 8 people.* ⏲ *Daily 8–sunset.*

The **UDT-Seal Museum** commemorates the site where more than 3,000 navy frogmen trained during World War II. Weapons and equipment are on view, and exhibits depict the history of the UDTs (Underwater Demolition Teams). Numerous patrol boats and vehicles are displayed outdoors. ⊠ *3300 N. Rte. A1A,* ☎ *561/595–5845.* 🎟 *$4.* ⏲ *Tues.–Sat. 10–4, Sun. noon–4.*

Accessible only by footbridge, the **Jack Island Wildlife Refuge** contains 4⅓ mi of trails. The 1½-mi Marsh Rabbit Trail across the island traverses a mangrove swamp to a 30-ft observation tower overlooking the Indian River. ⊠ *Rte. A1A,* ☎ *561/468–3985.* 🎟 *Free.* ⏲ *Daily 8–sunset.*

The **Harbor Branch Oceanographic Institution** is an internationally recognized diversified research and teaching facility that offers a glimpse into the high-tech world of marine research. Its fleet of research vessels—particularly its two submersibles—operates around the world for NASA, NOAA, and NATO, among other contractors. Visitors can take a 90-minute tour of the 500-acre facility, including aquariums of sea life indigenous to the Indian River Lagoon, exhibits of marine technology, and other learning facilities. There are also lifelike and whimsical bronze sculptures created by founder J. Seward Johnson, Jr., and a gift shop with imaginative sea-related items. ⊠ *5600 Old Dixie Hwy.,* ☎ *561/465–2400,* WEB *www.hboi.com.* 🎟 *$10.* ⏲ *Tours Mon.–Sat. at 10, noon, and 2.*

Dining and Lodging

$$–$$$ ✕ **Mangrove Mattie's.** Since its opening in the late 1980s, this upscale but rustic spot on Fort Pierce Inlet has provided dazzling waterfront views and imaginative nautical decor with delicious seafood. Dine outdoors on the terrace or inside in the cool air-conditioning, and try the coconut-fried shrimp or the chicken and scampi. Or come by during happy hour (weekdays 5–8) for a free buffet of snacks. ✉ *1640 Seaway Dr.,* ☎ *561/466–1044. AE, D, DC, MC, V.*

$$ ✕ **Theo Thudpucker's Raw Bar.** Businesspeople dressed for work mingle here with people fresh from the beach wearing shorts. On squally days everyone piles in off the jetty. Specialties include oyster stew, smoked fish spread, conch salad and conch fritters, fresh catfish, and alligator tail. ✉ *2025 Seaway Dr. (South Jetty),* ☎ *561/465–1078. MC, V.*

$–$$ 🏨 **Dockside Harbor Light Resort.** Formerly two adjacent motels, this expanded resort is the pick of the pack of lodgings lining the Fort Pierce Inlet along Seaway Drive. Spacious units on two floors feature a kitchen or wet bar and routine but well-cared-for furnishings. Some rooms have a waterfront porch or balcony. In addition to the motel units there is a set of four apartments across the street (off the water), where in-season weekly rates are $360. ✉ *1156–1160 Seaway Dr., 34949,* ☎ *561/468–3555 or 800/433–0004,* WEB *www.docksideinn.com. 60 rooms, 4 apartments. Pool, fishing, coin laundry. AE, D, DC, MC, V.*

$–$$ 🏨 **Mellon Patch Inn.** This appealing B&B has an excellent location—across the shore road from a beach park, at the end of a canal leading to the Indian River Lagoon. One side of the canal has a bank of attractive new homes; the other has the Jack Island Wildlife Refuge. Andrea and Arthur Mellon built this B&B in 1994, and images of split-open melons (note the pun) permeate the house—on pillows, crafts, and candies on night tables. All guest rooms face the finger canal behind the inn and each room is decorated with imaginative accessories, art, and upholstery appropriate to its individual theme. The cathedral-ceiling living room has a wood-burning fireplace. ✉ *3601 N. Rte. A1A, North Hutchinson Island 34949,* ☎ *561/461–5231 or 800/656–7824,* WEB *www.mellonpatchinn.com. 4 rooms. Hot tub, dock, boating, fishing. BP. AE, MC, V.*

Outdoor Activities and Sports

FISHING

For charter boats and fishing guides, try the **Dockside Harbor Light Resort** (✉ 1152 Seaway Dr., ☎ 561/461–4824).

JAI ALAI

Fort Pierce Jai Alai (✉ 1750 S. Kings Hwy., off Okeechobee Rd., ☎ 561/464–7500 or 800/524–2524) operates seasonally for live jai alai and year-round for off-track betting on horse-racing simulcasts. Admission is $1, and live games are played January through April, Wednesday and Saturday at noon and 7, Friday at 7, and Sunday at 1. Call to double-check schedule.

SCUBA DIVING

Some 200 yards from shore and ¼ mi north of the UDT-Seal Museum on North Hutchinson Island, the **Urca de Lima Underwater Archaeological Preserve** features the remains of a flat-bottom, round-bellied storeship. Once part of a treasure fleet bound for Spain, it was destroyed by a hurricane. Dive boats can be chartered through the **Dockside Harbor Light Resort** (✉ 1152 Seaway Dr., ☎ 561/461–4824).

En Route To reach Vero Beach, you have two options—Route A1A, along the coast, or Route 605 (often called Old Dixie Highway), on the mainland. As you approach Vero on the latter, you'll pass through an unfussied landscape of small farms and residential areas. On the beach route, part of the drive is through an unusually undeveloped section of the Florida coast. Both trips are very relaxing.

Vero Beach

35 *12 mi north of Fort Pierce.*

There's a tranquility to this Indian River County seat, an affluent town with a strong commitment to the environment and the arts. Retirees make up about half the winter population. In the exclusive Riomar Bay area of town, "canopy roads" are shaded by massive live oaks, and a popular cluster of restaurants and shops is just off the beach.

At the **Indian River Citrus Museum,** photos, farm tools, and videos tell about a time when oxen hauled the citrus crop to the railroads, when family fruit stands dotted the roadsides, and when gorgeous packing labels made every crate arriving up north an enticement to visit the Sunshine State. You can also book free citrus tours of actual groves. ✉ *2140 14th Ave.,* ☎ *561/770–2263.* *Donation welcome.* ⏲ *Tues.–Sat. 10–4, Sun. 1–4.*

In Riverside Park's Civic Arts Center, the **Center for the Arts** presents a full schedule of exhibitions, art movies, lectures, workshops, and other events, with a focus on Florida artists. ✉ *3001 Riverside Park Dr.,* ☎ *561/231–0707,* WEB *www.verocfta.org.* *Free.* ⏲ *Fri.–Wed. 10–4:30, Thurs. 10–8.*

In addition to a wet lab containing aquariums filled with Indian River Lagoon life, the outstanding 51-acre **Environmental Learning Center** has a 600-ft boardwalk through mangrove shoreline and a 1-mi canoe trail. The center is on the north edge of Vero Beach, on Wabasso Island, but it's a pretty drive and worth the trip. ✉ *255 Live Oak Dr.,* ☎ *561/589–5050,* WEB *www.elcweb.org.* *Free.* ⏲ *Sun.–Fri. and Sun. 10–4, Sat. 9–12.*

Humiston Park is just one of the beach-access parks along the east edge of town that have boardwalks and steps bridging the foredune. It has a large children's play area and picnic tables and is across the street from shops. ✉ *Ocean Dr. below Beachland Blvd.,* ☎ *no phone.* *Free.* ⏲ *Daily 7 AM–10 PM.*

The Arts

The **Civic Arts Center** (✉ Riverside Park), a cluster of cultural facilities, includes the **Riverside Theatre** (✉ 3250 Riverside Park Dr., ☎ 561/231–6990), which stages six productions each season in its 633-seat performance hall; the **Agnes Wahlstrom Youth Playhouse** (✉ 3280 Riverside Park Dr., ☎ 561/234–8052), which mounts children's productions; and the **Center for the Arts** (✉ 3001 Riverside Park Dr., ☎ 561/231–0707), which presents art movies and lectures in addition to its other offerings. **Riverside Children's Theatre** (✉ 3280 Riverside Park Dr., ☎ 561/234–8052) offers a series of professional touring and local productions, as well as acting workshops at the Agnes Wahlstrom Youth Playhouse.

Dining and Lodging

$$–$$$ ✕ **Black Pearl Riverfront.** This intimate and sophisticated restaurant, one of Vero's trendiest dining picks, has a stunning riverfront location, and peaceful water views accompanying the superb cuisine. The menu emphasizes fresh local ingredients. Appetizers include chilled leek-and-asparagus soup; spinach, walnut, and goat cheese fritters; fresh-baked oysters; and the house specialty, fish chowder. For entrées, onion-crusted grouper, mesquite-grilled dolphin, roasted duckling with apples and cashew sauce, and a veal chop stuffed with baby spinach are popular choices. ✉ *4455 N. Rte. A1A,* ☎ *561/234–4426. AE, MC, V. No lunch weekends.*

$$–$$$ ★ ✕ **Ocean Grill.** Opened by Waldo Sexton as a hamburger shack in 1938, the oceanfront Ocean Grill is now furnished with Tiffany lamps, wrought-iron chandeliers, and Beanie Backus paintings of pirates and Seminole Indians. The menu includes black-bean soup, jumbo lump-crabmeat salad, and at least three kinds of fish every day. The house drink, the Leaping Limey, a curious blend of vodka, blue curaçao, and lemon, commemorates the 1894 wreck of the *Breconshire,* which occurred just offshore and from which 34 British sailors escaped. The bar and some tables look over the water. ✉ *1050 Sexton Plaza (Beachland Blvd. east of Ocean Dr.),* ☎ *561/231–5409. AE, D, DC, MC, V. Closed 2 wks following Labor Day. No lunch weekends.*

$$ ✕ **Pearl's Bistro.** Island-style cuisine is the draw at this laid-back and less expensive sister restaurant to the Black Pearl. For starters try the pasta Rasta (pasta with seafood in a creole sauce), roasted shrimp with guacamole, Bahamian conch fritters, or the Jamaican jerk shrimp. Then move on to a Caesar salad topped with mesquite grilled chicken, crispy fried shrimp, baby back barbecued pork ribs, Bahamian shrimp and grouper pepper pot, or blackened New York strip with peppery rum sauce. ✉ *56 Royal Palm Blvd.,* ☎ *561/778–2950. AE, MC, V. No lunch weekends.*

$$$–$$$$ 🏨 **Disney's Vero Beach Resort.** Built on 71 oceanfront acres, this sprawling vacation getaway, which operates both as a time-share and a hotel, is the classiest resort in Vero Beach. The main four-story building, three freestanding villas, and six beach cottages are nestled among tropical greenery. Buildings are painted in pale pastels and sport steeply pitched gables, and many units have balconies. Bright interiors have rattan furniture and tile floors. ✉ *9235 Rte. A1A, 32963,* ☎ *561/234–2000,* WEB *www.dvc.com. 161 rooms, 14 suites, 6 cottages. 2 restaurants, bar, pool, wading pool, 6 tennis courts, basketball, bicycles, video games. AE, D, DC, MC, V.*

$$$–$$$$ 🏨 **DoubleTree Guest Suites.** This five-story rose-color stucco hotel is conveniently located—right on the beach and near restaurants, specialty shops, and boutiques. One- and two-bedroom suites have patios opening onto a pool or balconies and excellent ocean views. ✉ *3500 Ocean Dr., 32963,* ☎ *561/231–5666. 55 suites. Bar, 2 pools, wading pool, hot tub. AE, D, DC, MC, V.*

$$–$$$ 🏨 **Palm Court Resort.** The views from this resort are outstanding. The white, five-story building is tucked among palm trees and right on the beach. Oceanfront units look out to the water across private balconies. Most other units have partial ocean views. Fabrics in restful pastels and rattan furniture give the comfortable rooms a warm, tropical feel. The rectangular pool looks out over the water and pink shade umbrellas and blue-and-white stripe cabanas line the beach. Efficiencies and suites have kitchens. ✉ *3244 Ocean Dr., 32963,* ☎ *561/231–2800 or 800/245–3297,* WEB *www.palmcourtvero.com. 1,110 rooms, 4 efficiencies, 2 suites. Restaurant, pool, beach. AE, DC, MC, V.*

$$ 🏨 **Captain Hiram's Islander Motel.** Across from the beach, the aqua-and-white trim Islander has a snoozy Key West style that contrasts stylishly with the smart shops it's tucked between. Jigsaw-cut brackets and balusters and beach umbrellas dress up the pool. All rooms have white wicker, paddle fans hung from vaulted ceilings, and fresh flowers. It's just right for beachside Vero. ✉ *3101 Ocean Dr., 32963,* ☎ *561/231–4431 or 800/952–5886. 16 rooms, 1 efficiency. Pool. AE, DC, MC, V.*

Outdoor Activities and Sports

The **Los Angeles Dodgers** (✉ 4101 26th St., ☎ 561/569–4900) train at Dodgertown, actually in Vero Beach.

Shopping

Along **Ocean Drive** near Beachland Boulevard, a specialty shopping area includes art galleries, antiques shops, and upscale clothing stores.

Sebastian

36 *14 mi north of Vero Beach.*

One of only a few sparsely populated areas on Florida's east coast, this little fishing village has as remote a feeling as you'll find anywhere between Jacksonville and Miami Beach. That remoteness adds to the appeal of the recreation area around Sebastian Inlet, where you can walk for miles along quiet beaches.

The **McLarty Treasure Museum,** designated a National Historical Landmark, has displays dedicated to the 1715 hurricane that sank a fleet of Spanish treasure ships. ✉ *13180 N. Rte. A1A,* ☎ *561/589–2147.* *$2.* ⏲ *Daily 10–4:30.*

You've really come upon hidden loot when you step into **Mel Fisher's Treasure Museum.** Here you can view some of what was recovered in 1985 from the Spanish treasure ship *Atocha* and its sister ships of the 1715 fleet. Fisher operates a similar museum in Key West. ✉ *1322 U.S. 1,* ☎ *561/589–9875,* WEB *www.melfisher.com.* *$5.* ⏲ *Mon.–Sat. 10–5, Sun. noon–5.*

Because of the highly productive fishing waters of Sebastian Inlet, at the north end of Orchid Island, the 578-acre **Sebastian Inlet State Recreation Area** is one of the best-attended parks in the Florida state system. On both sides of the high bridge that spans the inlet—from which the views are spectacular—the recreation area attracts plenty of anglers as well as those eager to enjoy the fine sandy beaches (both within the recreation area and outside it), which are known for having the best waves in the state. A concession stand on the north side of the inlet sells short-order food, rents various craft, and has an apparel and surf shop. A boat ramp is available. Not far away along the sea is a dune area that's part of the **Archie Carr National Wildlife Refuge,** a haven for sea turtles and other protected Florida wildlife. ✉ *9700 S. Rte. A1A, Melbourne Beach,* ☎ *407/984–4852; 1300 Rte. A1A, Melbourne Beach,* ☎ *561/589–9659,* WEB *www.dep.state.fl.us/parks.* *$3.25.* ⏲ *Daily 24 hrs, bait and tackle shop daily 7:30–6, concession stand daily 8–5.*

Dining and Lodging

$$–$$$ ✕ **Hurricane Harbor.** Built in 1927 as a garage and used during Prohibition as a smugglers' den, Hurricane Harbor now draws a year-round crowd of retirees and locals. Guests love the waterfront window seats on stormy nights, when sizable waves break outside in the Indian River Lagoon. The menu has seafood, steaks, and grills, along with lighter fare. Take a peek into the Antique Dining Room with linen, stained glass, and a huge antique breakfront. It's used only for special occasions. There's also live music nightly. ✉ *1540 Indian River Dr.,* ☎ *561/589–1773. AE, D, MC, V. Closed Mon.*

$–$$ ✕ **Capt. Hiram's.** This family-friendly restaurant on the Indian River Lagoon is easygoing, fanciful, and fun—as the sign says, NECKTIES ARE PROHIBITED. The place is "real"—full of wooden booths, stained glass, umbrellas on the open deck, and ceiling fans. Don't miss Capt. Hiram's Sandbar, where kids can play while parents enjoy a drink at stools set in an outdoor shower or a beached boat. Choose from among seafood brochette, New York strip steak, the fresh catch, crab cakes, stuffed shrimp, and lots of other seafood dishes as well as raw-bar items. The full bar has a weekday happy hour and free hot hors d'oeuvres Friday

5–6. There's nightly entertainment in season. ✉ *1606 N. Indian River Dr.,* ☎ *561/589–4345. AE, D, MC, V.*

$–$$ 🏨 **Captain's Quarters Riverfront Motel.** Five units—four overlooking the Indian River Lagoon and the marina at Capt. Hiram's restaurant and one two-room suite—are all Key West–cute. Painted in bright colors with matching fabrics, the rooms have pine and white-wicker furniture and pine-plank floors with grass rugs. The adequate bathrooms have large stall showers. Glass doors open to a plank porch, but the porches are all within sight of each other. ✉ *1606 Indian River Dr., 32958,* ☎ *561/589–4345,* FAX *561/589–4346,* WEB *www.hirams.com. 4 rooms, 1 suite. Restaurant. AE, D, MC, V.*

$ 🏨 **Davis House Inn.** Vero native Steve Wild modeled his two-story inn after the clubhouse at Augusta National, and, perhaps surprisingly, it fits right in with Sebastian's fishing-town look. Wide overhung roofs shade wraparound porches. In a companion house that Steve calls the Gathering Room, he serves a complimentary expanded Continental breakfast. Rooms are huge—virtual suites, with large sitting areas—although somewhat underfurnished. Guests congregate at the self-serve Tiki Bar, which is also the site of periodic barbecues. Overall, it's a terrific value. ✉ *607 Davis St., 32958,* ☎ *561/589–4114,* WEB *www.davishouseinn.com. 12 rooms. Bicycles. MC, V.*

Outdoor Activities and Sports

CANOEING AND KAYAKING

The concession stand at **Sebastian Inlet State Recreation Area** (✉ 9700 S. Rte. A1A, Melbourne Beach, ☎ 321/984–4852) rents canoes, kayaks, and paddleboats.

FISHING

The best inlet fishing in the region is at **Sebastian Inlet State Recreation Area** (✉ 9700 S. Rte. A1A, Melbourne Beach), where the catch includes bluefish, flounder, jack, redfish, sea trout, snapper, snook, and Spanish mackerel. For deep-sea fishing, try ***Miss Sebastian*** (✉ Sembler Dock, ½ block north of Capt. Hiram's restaurant, ☎ 561/589–3275); $25 for a half day covers rod, reel, and bait. **Sebastian Inlet Marina at Capt. Hiram's** (✉ 1606 Indian River Dr., ☎ 561/589–4345) offers half- and full-day fishing charters.

PALM BEACH AND THE TREASURE COAST A TO Z

AIR TRAVEL

CARRIERS

To research prices, get advice from other travelers, and book arrangements, visit www.fodors.com.

Palm Beach International Airport (PBIA) is served by Air Canada, American/American Eagle, American TransAir, Carnival Airlines, Comair, Continental, Delta, KIWI International Airlines, Northwest, Paradise Island, Republic Air Travel, Southwest Airlines, Spirit Airlines, TWA, United, US Airways/US Airways Express, and World of Vacations.

➤ AIRLINES AND CONTACTS: **Air Canada** (☎ 800/776–3000). **American/American Eagle** (☎ 800/433–7300). **American TransAir** (☎ 800/225–2995). **Carnival Airlines** (☎ 800/824–7386). **Comair** (☎ 800/354–9822). **Continental** (☎ 800/525–0280). **Delta** (☎ 800/221–1212). **KIWI International Airlines** (☎ 800/538–5494). **Northwest** (☎ 800/225–2525). **Paradise Island** (☎ 800/432–8807). **Republic Air Travel** (☎ 800/233–0225). **Southwest Airlines** (☎ 800/435–9792). **Spirit Airlines** (☎ 561/471–7467). **TWA** (☎ 800/221–2000). **United** (☎ 800/

241–6522). US Airways/US Airways Express (☎ 800/428–4322). World of Vacations (☎ 800/661–8881).

AIRPORT INFORMATION

Route 10 of Tri-Rail Commuter Bus Service runs from the airport to Tri-Rail's nearby Palm Beach airport station daily.

Palm Beach Transportation provides taxi and limousine service from PBIA. Reserve at least a day in advance for a limousine. The lowest fares are $1.75 per mile, with the meter starting at $1.25. Depending on your destination, a flat rate (from PBIA only) may save money. Wheelchair-accessible vehicles are available.

➤ AIRPORT INFORMATION: **Palm Beach International Airport (PBIA)** (✉ Congress Ave. and Belvedere Rd., West Palm Beach, ☎ 561/471–7400). **Palm Beach Transportation** (☎ 561/689–4222). **Tri-Rail Commuter Bus Service** (☎ 800/874–7245).

BUS TRAVEL

Greyhound Lines buses arrive at the station in West Palm Beach.

Palmtran buses, which run between Worth Avenue and Royal Palm Way in Palm Beach and major areas of West Palm Beach, require exact change. The cost is $1.25 or 50¢ for students, senior citizens, and people with disabilities (with reduced-fare ID). Service operates from 5:25 AM to 8:55 PM. Call for schedules, routes, and rates for multiple-ride punch cards.

➤ BUS INFORMATION: **Greyhound Lines** (☎ 800/231–2222) West Palm Beach (✉ 100 Banyan Blvd., ☎ 561/833–8534). **Palmtran** (☎ 561/233–4287).

CAR TRAVEL

Interstate 95 runs north–south, linking West Palm Beach with Miami and Fort Lauderdale to the south and with Daytona, Jacksonville, and the rest of the Atlantic coast to the north. To get to central Palm Beach, exit at Belvedere Road or Okeechobee Boulevard. Florida's Turnpike runs up from Miami through West Palm Beach before angling northwest to reach Orlando.

U.S. 1 threads north–south along the coast, connecting most coastal communities, while the more scenic Route A1A ventures out onto the barrier islands. Interstate 95 runs parallel to U.S. 1 but a bit farther inland.

A nonstop four-lane route, Okeechobee Boulevard carries traffic from west of downtown West Palm Beach, near the Amtrak station in the airport district, directly to the Flagler Memorial Bridge and into Palm Beach. Plans are in the works to turn Flagler Drive over to pedestrian use sometime in the next several years.

The best way to get to Lake Okeechobee from West Palm is to drive west on Southern Boulevard from Interstate 95 past the cutoff road to Lion Country Safari. From there the boulevard is designated U.S. 98/441.

EMERGENCIES

Dial 911 for police or ambulance.

➤ LATE-NIGHT PHARMACIES: **Eckerd Drug** (✉ 3343 S. Congress Ave., Palm Springs, ☎ 561/965–3367). **Walgreens** (✉ 1688 S. Congress Ave., Palm Springs, ☎ 561/968–8211; ✉ 7561 N. Federal Hwy., Boca Raton, ☎ 561/241–9802; ✉ 1634 S. Federal Hwy., Boynton Beach, ☎ 561/737–1260; ✉ 1208 Royal Palm Beach Blvd., Royal Palm Beach, ☎ 561/798–9048; ✉ 6370 Indiantown Rd., Jupiter, ☎ 561/744–6822; ✉ 20 E. 30th St., Riviera Beach, ☎ 561/848–6464).

ENGLISH-LANGUAGE MEDIA

NEWSPAPERS AND MAGAZINES

The *Palm Beach Post* and the *Vero Press Journal* are published daily.

RADIO

LOVE 93.9 FM easy listening, WDBF 1420 AM jazz, WDDO 93.1 FM classical.

TAXIS

Palm Beach Transportation has a single number serving several cab companies. Meters start at $1.25, and the charge is $1.75 per mile within West Palm Beach city limits; if the trip at any point leaves the city limits, the fare is $2 per mile. Some cabs may charge more. Waiting time is 50¢ per minute.

➤ TAXIS INFORMATION: **Palm Beach Transportation** (☎ 561/689–4222).

BY TRAIN

Amtrak (☎ 800/872–7245) connects West Palm Beach (✉ 201 S. Tamarind Ave., ☎ 561/832–6169) with cities along Florida's east coast and the Northeast daily and via the *Sunset Limited* to New Orleans and Los Angeles three times weekly. Included in Amtrak's service is transport from West Palm Beach to Okeechobee (✉ 801 N. Parrott Ave.); the station is unmanned.

GETTING AROUND

The **Downtown Transfer Facility** (✉ Banyan Blvd. and Clearlake Dr., West Palm Beach), off Australian Avenue at the west entrance to downtown, links the downtown shuttle, Amtrak, Tri-Rail (the commuter line of Miami-Dade, Broward, and Palm Beach counties), CoTran (the county bus system), Greyhound, and taxis.

TOURS

Capt. Doug's offers three-hour lunch and dinner cruises along the Indian River on board a 35-ft sloop. Cost is $100 per couple, including meal, tips, beer, and wine. J-Mark Fish Camp has 45- to 60-minute airboat rides for $30 per person, with a minimum of two people and a maximum of six. Jonathan Dickinson's River Tours runs two-hour guided riverboat cruises daily at 9, 11, 1, and 3. The cost is $12. Loxahatchee Everglades Tours operates airboat tours year-round from west of Boca Raton through the marshes between the built-up coast and Lake Okeechobee. The *Manatee Queen,* a 49-passenger catamaran, offers day and evening cruises November–May on the Intracoastal Waterway and into the park's cypress swamps.

Ramblin' Rose Riverboat operates luncheon, dinner-dance, and Sunday brunch cruises along the Intracoastal Waterway. Water Taxi Scenic Cruises offers several different daily sightseeing tours in a 16-person launch. Two are designed to let you get a close-up look at the mansions of the rich and famous. The southern tour passes Peanut, Singer, and Munyan islands as well as many mansions of Palm Beach. A second tour just runs along the shore of Palm Beach mansions. A third tour takes you past the Craig Norman estate and goes into Lake Worth and Sawgrass Creek.

Contact the Audubon Society of the Everglades for field trips and nature walks.

The Boca Raton Historical Society offers afternoon tours of the Boca Raton Resort & Club on Tuesday year-round and to other South Florida sites. Main Street Fort Pierce gives walking tours of the town's historic section, past buildings built by early settlers. The Indian River County

Historical Society conducts walking tours of downtown Vero on Wednesday at 11 and 1 (by reservation). Old Northwood Historic District Tours leads two-hour walking tours that include visits to historic home interiors. They leave Sunday at 2, and a $5 donation is requested. Tours for groups of six or more can be scheduled almost any day.

➤ TOURS INFORMATION: **Audubon Society of the Everglades** (✉ Box 16914, West Palm Beach 33461, ☎ 561/588–6908). **Boca Raton Historical Society** (✉ 71 N. Federal Hwy., Boca Raton, ☎ 561/395–6766). **Capt. Doug's** (✉ Sebastian Marina, Sebastian, ☎ 561/589–2329). The **Indian River County Historical Society** (✉ 2336 14th Ave., Vero Beach, ☎ 561/778–3435). **J-Mark Fish Camp** (✉ Torry Island, ☎ 561/996–5357). **Jonathan Dickinson's River Tours** (✉ Jonathan Dickinson State Park, 16450 S.E. Federal Hwy., Hobe Sound, ☎ 561/746–1466). **Loxahatchee Everglades Tours** (✉ 10400 Loxahatchee Rd., ☎ 561/482–6107). **Main Street Fort Pierce** (✉ 131 Main St., Fort Pierce, ☎ 561/466–3880). ***Manatee Queen*** (✉ Jonathan Dickinson State Park, 16450 S.E. Federal Hwy., Hobe Sound, ☎ 561/744–2191). **Old Northwood Historic District Tours** (✉ 501 30th St., West Palm Beach, ☎ 561/863–5633). ***Ramblin' Rose Riverboat*** (✉ 1 N.E. 1st St., Delray Beach, ☎ 561/243–0686). **Water Taxi Scenic Cruises** (✉ Sailfish Marina and Riviera Beach Marina, Palm Beach, ☎ 561/775–2628).

TRAIN TRAVEL

Amtrak connects West Palm Beach with cities along Florida's east coast and the Northeast daily and via the *Sunset Limited* to New Orleans and Los Angeles three times weekly. Included in Amtrak's service is transport from West Palm Beach to Okeechobee; the station is unmanned.

Tri-Rail, the commuter rail system, has six stations in Palm Beach County (13 stops altogether between West Palm Beach and Miami). The round-trip fare is $5, $2.50 for students and senior citizens.

➤ TRAIN INFORMATION: **Amtrak** (☎ 800/872–7245; West Palm Beach: ✉ 201 S. Tamarind Ave., ☎ 561/832–6169; Okeechobee: ✉ 801 N. Parrott Ave.). **Tri-Rail** (☎ 800/874–7245).

VISITOR INFORMATION

➤ TOURIST INFORMATION: **Belle Glade Chamber of Commerce** (✉ 540 S. Main St., Belle Glade 33430, ☎ 561/996–2745). **Chamber of Commerce of the Palm Beaches** (✉ 401 N. Flagler Dr., West Palm Beach 33401, ☎ 561/833–3711). **Clewiston Chamber of Commerce** (✉ 544 W. Sugarland Hwy., Clewiston 33440, ☎ 863/983–7979). **Glades County Chamber of Commerce** (✉ U.S. 27 and 10th St., Moore Haven 33471, ☎ 863/946–0440). **Indian River County Tourist Council** (✉ 1216 21st St., Box 2947, Vero Beach 32961, ☎ 561/567–3491). **Indiantown and Western Martin County Chamber of Commerce** (✉ 15518 S.W. Osceola St., Indiantown 34956, ☎ 561/597–2184). **Okeechobee County Chamber of Commerce** (✉ 55 S. Parrott Ave., Okeechobee 34974, ☎ 863/763–6464). **Pahokee Chamber of Commerce** (✉ 115 E. Main St., Pahokee 33476, ☎ 561/924–5579). **Palm Beach County Convention & Visitors Bureau** (✉ 1555 Palm Beach Lakes Blvd., Suite 204, West Palm Beach 33401, ☎ 561/471–3995). **St. Lucie County Tourist Development Council** (✉ 2300 Virginia Ave., Fort Pierce 34982, ☎ 561/462–1535). **Stuart/Martin County Chamber of Commerce** (✉ 1650 S. Kanner Hwy., Stuart 34994, ☎ 561/287–1088). **Town of Palm Beach Chamber of Commerce** (✉ 45 Cocoanut Row, Palm Beach 33480, ☎ 561/655–3282). **U.S. Army Corps of Engineers (Okeechobee area information)** (✉ South Florida Operations Office, 525 Ridgelawn Rd., Clewiston 33440-5399, ☎ 863/983–8101).

5 THE FLORIDA KEYS

The Keys are some of America's last frontiers. Here both humans and nature seek refuge in a verdant island chain that stretches raggedly west-southwest across a deep blue-green seascape at the base of the Florida peninsula.

Revised by Diane P. Marshall

THE FLORIDA KEYS ARE A WILDERNESS of flowering jungles and shimmering seas, a jade necklace of mangrove-fringed islands dangling toward the tropics. The Florida Keys are also, at the same time and in direct contrast to this, a string of narrow islands overburdened by a growing population and booming tourism that have created sewage contamination at beaches and a 110-mi traffic jam lined with garish billboards, hamburger stands, shopping centers, motels, and trailer courts. Unfortunately, in the Keys you can't have one without the other.

The river of visitor traffic gushes along U.S. 1 (also called the Overseas Highway), the main artery linking the inhabited islands. Residents of Monroe County live by diverting the river's flow of green dollars to their own pockets. In the process, the fragile beauty of the Keys—or at least the 45 that are inhabited and linked to the mainland by 43 bridges—is paying an environmental price. At the top, nearest the mainland, is Key Largo, becoming more and more congested as it evolves into a bedroom community and weekend hideaway for escaping residents of Miami and Fort Lauderdale. At the bottom, 106 mi southwest, is Key West, where for several years now the effluent of the overburdened island has washed into the near-shore waters and closed the island's major beaches for months and where local opposition is erupting against increasing tourism pressures.

Despite designation as "an area of critical state concern" in 1975 and a subsequent state-mandated development slowdown, growth has continued, and the Keys' natural resources remain imperiled. In 1990, Congress established the Florida Keys National Marine Sanctuary, covering 2,800 square nautical mi of coastal waters. Adjacent to the Keys landmass are spectacular, unique, and nationally significant marine environments, including sea-grass meadows, mangrove islands, and extensive living coral reefs. These fragile environments support rich and diverse biological communities possessing extensive conservation, recreational, commercial, ecological, historical, research, educational, and aesthetic values.

The sanctuary protects the coral reefs and water quality, but problems continue. Increased salinity in Florida Bay causes large areas of sea grass to die and drift in mats out of the bay. These mats then block sunlight from reaching the reefs, stifling their growth and threatening both the Keys' recreational diving economy and tourism in general.

Other threats to the Keys' charm also loom. Debate continues on the expansion of U.S. 1 to the mainland to four lanes, opening the floodgates to increased traffic, population, and tourism. Observers wonder if the four-laning of the rest of U.S. 1 throughout the Keys can be far away and if a trip to paradise will then be worth it.

The solutions are not easy. Keys residents struggle with the issues at home, in social settings and in the voting booths. In 1998, 1999, and 2000 local communities dissatisfied with the county's handling of the impacts of tourism and development went to the polls to determine their own destinies as independent municipalities. Others are waiting for state permission to do the same.

For now, however, take pleasure as you drive down U.S. 1 along the islands. Gaze over the silvery blue and green Atlantic and its still-living reef, with Florida Bay, the Gulf of Mexico, and the backcountry on your right (the Keys extend east–west from the mainland). At a few points the ocean and gulf are as much as 10 mi apart. In most places, however, they are from 1 to 4 mi apart, and on the narrowest landfill islands, they are separated only by the road. First, remind yourself to get off the highway. Once you do, rent a boat, anchor and then fish, swim, or marvel at the sun, sea, and sky. In the Atlantic you can dive spectacular coral reefs or pursue grouper, blue marlin, and other deep-water game fish. Along Florida Bay's coastline you can kayak and canoe to secluded islands and bays or seek out the bonefish, snapper, snook, and tarpon that lurk in the grass flats and in the shallow, winding channels of the backcountry.

More than 600 kinds of fish populate the reefs and islands. Diminutive deer and pale raccoons, related to but distinct from their mainland cousins, inhabit the Lower Keys. And throughout the islands you'll find such exotic West Indian plants as Jamaica dogwood, pigeon plum, poisonwood, satin leaf, and silver and thatch palms, as well as tropical birds, including the great white heron, mangrove cuckoo, roseate spoonbill, and white-crowned pigeon. Mangroves, with their gracefully bowed prop roots, appear to march out to sea. Day by day they busily add more keys to the archipelago.

With virtually no distracting air pollution or obstructive high-rises, sunsets are a pure, unadulterated spectacle that each evening attracts thousands of visitors and locals to waterfront parks, piers, restaurants, bars, and resorts throughout the Keys.

Weather is another attraction: Winter is typically 10°F warmer than on the mainland; summer is usually 10°F cooler. The Keys also get substantially less rain, around 30 inches annually, compared to an average 55–60 inches in Miami and the Everglades. Most rain falls in quick downpours on summer afternoons, except in June, September, and October, when tropical storms can dump rain for two to four days. Winter continental cold fronts occasionally stall over the Keys, dragging overnight temperatures down to the high 40s.

The Keys were only sparsely populated until the early 20th century. In 1905, however, railroad magnate Henry Flagler began building the extension of his Florida railroad south from Homestead to Key West. His goal was to establish a rail link to his steamships that sailed between Key West and Havana, just 90 mi across the Straits of Florida. The railroad arrived at Key West in 1912 and remained a lifeline of commerce until the Labor Day hurricane of 1935 washed out much of its roadbed. The Overseas Highway, built over the railroad's old roadbeds and bridges, was completed in 1938.

New and Noteworthy

It's now easy to make a quick side trip from the Florida Keys to Florida City shops and restaurants. The **Dade–Monroe Express** provides daily bus service from the Mile Marker 98 in Key Largo to the Florida City Wal-Mart Supercenter. In other transportation news, **American Airlines** began nonstop service on American Eagle between Key West and Orlando.

The **National Key Deer Refuge** on Big Pine Key is increasing the size of its visitor center and adding more displays on Keys biology and ecology. Through the refuge's efforts, the tiny Key deer has made a comeback from a population low of fewer than 50 to more than 800.

Pleasures and Pastimes

Biking

Cyclists are able to ride all but a tiny portion of the bike path that runs along the Overseas Highway from MM 106 south to the Seven Mile Bridge. The state plans to extend the route throughout the Keys. Some areas have lots of cross traffic, however, so ride with care.

Boating

If it floats, local marinas rent it. For up-close exploration of the mangroves and near-shore islands in Florida Bay, nothing beats a kayak or canoe. You can paddle within a few feet of a flock of birds without disturbing them, and on days when the ocean is too rough for diving or fishing, the rivers that course through the bay-side mangroves are tranquil. Visiting the backcountry islands and inlets of Everglades National Park requires a shallow-draft boat: a 14- to 17-ft skiff with a 40- to 50-horsepower outboard is sufficient. For diving the reef or fishing on the open ocean, you'll need a larger boat with greater horsepower. Houseboats are ideal for cruising the Keys.

Only experienced sailors should attempt to navigate the shallow waters surrounding the Keys with deep-keeled sailboats. On the other hand, small shallow-draft, single-hull sailboats and catamarans are ideal. Personal water vehicles, such as Wave Runners and Jet Skis, can be rented by the half hour or hour but are banned in many areas. Flat, stable pontoon boats are a good choice for anyone with seasickness. Those interested in experiencing the reef without getting wet can take a glass-bottom boat trip.

Dining

A number of talented young chefs have settled in the Keys—especially Key West—contributing to the area's image as one of the nation's points of culinary interest. Restaurants' menus, rum-based fruit beverages, and music reflect the Keys' tropical climate and their proximity to Cuba and other Caribbean islands. Better restaurants serve imaginative and tantalizing fusion cuisine that draws on traditions from all over the world.

Florida citrus, seafood, and tropical fruits figure prominently, and Florida lobster and stone crab should be local and fresh from August to March. Also keep an eye out for authentic key lime pie. The real McCoy has a yellow custard in a graham-cracker crust and tastes like nothing else.

Restaurants may close for a two- to four-week vacation during the slow season—between mid-September and mid-November. Check local newspapers or call ahead, especially if driving any distance.

Fishing

These sun-bathed waters are home to 100 species of game fish as well as to lobster, shrimp, and crabs. Flats fishing and backcountry fishing are Keys specialties. In flats fishing, a guide poles a shallow-draft outboard boat through the shallow, sandy-bottom waters while sighting for bonefish and snook to be caught on light tackle, spin, and fly. Backcountry fishing may include flats fishing or fishing in the channels and basins around islands in Florida Bay. Charter boats fish the reef and Gulf Stream for deep-sea fish. Party boats, which can be crowded, carry up to 50 people to fish the reefs for grouper, kingfish, and snapper. Some operators boast a guarantee, or "no fish, no pay" policy.

Scuba Diving and Snorkeling

Diving in the Keys is spectacular. In shallow and deep water with visibility up to 120 ft, you can explore sea canyons and mountains covered with waving sea plumes, brain and star coral, historic shipwrecks, and sunken submarines. The colors of the coral are surpassed only by the brilliance of the fish that live around it. There's no best season for diving, but occasional storms in June, September, and October cloud the waters and make seas rough.

You can dive the reefs with scuba, snuba (a cross between scuba and snorkeling), or snorkeling gear, using your own boat, a rented boat, or by booking a tour with a dive shop. Tours depart two or three times a day, stopping at two sites on each trip. The first trip of the day is usually the best. It's less crowded—vacationers like to sleep in—and visibility is better before the wind picks up in the afternoon. There's also night diving.

If you want to scuba dive but are not certified, take an introductory resort course. Although it doesn't result in certification, it allows you to dive with an instructor in the afternoon following morning classroom and pool instruction.

Nearly all the waters surrounding the Keys are part of the Florida Keys National Marine Sanctuary and thus are protected. Signs, brochures, tour guides, and marine enforcement agents remind visitors that the reef is fragile and shouldn't be touched.

Exploring the Florida Keys

Finding your way around the Keys isn't hard once you understand the unique address system. Many addresses are simply given as a mile marker (MM) number. The markers themselves are small, green rectangular signs along the side of the Overseas Highway (U.S. 1). They begin with MM 126 a mile south of Florida City and end with MM 0, in Key West. Keys residents use the abbreviation BS for the bay side of U.S. 1 and OS for the ocean side. From Marathon to Key West, residents may refer to the bay side as the gulf side.

The Keys are divided into four areas: the Upper Keys, from Key Largo to the Long Key Channel (MM 106–65) and Ocean Reef and North Key Largo, off Card Sound Road and Route 905, respectively; the Middle Keys, from Conch (pronounced *konk*) Key through Marathon to the south side of the Seven Mile Bridge, including Pigeon Key (MM 65–40); the Lower Keys, from Little Duck Key south through Big Coppitt Key (MM 40–9); and Key West, from Stock Island through Key West (MM 9–0). The Keys don't end with the highway, however; they stretch another 70 mi west of Key West to the Dry Tortugas.

Numbers in the text correspond to numbers in the margin and on the Florida Keys and Key West maps.

Great Itineraries

IF YOU HAVE 3 DAYS

You can fly and then dive; but if you dive, you can't fly for 24 hours, so spend your first morning diving or snorkeling at John Pennekamp Coral Reef State Park in **Key Largo** ②. If you aren't certified, take a resort course, and you'll be exploring the reefs by afternoon. Afterward, breeze through the park's visitor center. The rest of the afternoon can be whiled away either lounging around a pool or beach or visiting the Maritime Museum of the Florida Keys. Dinner or cocktails at a bay-side restaurant or bar will give you your first look at a fabulous Keys sunset. On day two, get an early start to savor the breathtaking views on the two-hour drive to Key West. Along the way make stops at the natural-history museum that's part of the Museums and Nature Center of Crane Point Hammock, in **Marathon** ⑧, and Bahia Honda State Park, on **Bahia Honda Key** ⑨, where you can stretch your legs on a forest trail or snorkel on an offshore reef. Once in **Key West** ⑫–㉞, you can watch the sunset before dining at one of the island's first-class restaurants. Spend the next morning exploring beaches, visiting any of the myriad museums, or taking a walking or trolley tour of Old Town before driving back to the mainland.

IF YOU HAVE 4 DAYS

Spend the first day as you would above, overnighting in **Key Largo** ②. Start the second day by renting a kayak and exploring the mangroves and small islands of Florida Bay or take an eco-tour of the islands in Everglades National Park. In the afternoon stop by the Florida Keys Wild Bird Rehabilitation Center before driving down to **Islamorada** ④. Pause to read the inscription on the Hurricane Monument, and before day's end, make plans for the next day's fishing. After a late lunch on day three—perhaps at one of the many restaurants that will prepare your catch for you—set off for **Key West** ⑫–㉞. Catch the sunset celebration at Mallory Square, and spend the last day as you would above.

IF YOU HAVE 7 DAYS

Spend your first three days as you would in the four-day itinerary, but stay the third night in **Islamorada** ④. In the morning catch a boat, or rent a kayak to paddle, to Lignumvitae Key State Botanical Site, before making the one-hour drive to **Marathon** ⑧, where you can visit the natural-history museum that's part of the Museums and Nature Center of Crane Point Hammock and walk or take a train across the Old Seven Mile Bridge to Pigeon Key. The next stop is just 10 mi away at Bahia Honda State Park, on **Bahia Honda Key** ⑨. Take a walk on a wilderness trail, go snorkeling on an offshore reef, wriggle your toes in the beach's soft sand, and spend the night in a waterfront cabin, letting the waves lull you to sleep. Your sixth day starts with either a half day of fabulous snorkeling or diving at Looe Key Reef or a visit to the National Key Deer Refuge, on **Big Pine Key** ⑩. Then continue on to **Key West** ⑫–㉞, and get in a little sightseeing before watching the sunset. The next morning take a walking, bicycling, or trolley tour of town or catch a ferry or seaplane to Dry Tortugas National Park before heading home.

When to Tour the Florida Keys

High season in the Keys is mid-December through March, and traffic on the Overseas Highway is inevitably heavy. đFrom November to the middle of December, crowds are thinner, the weather is superlative, and hotels and shops drastically reduce their prices. Summer, which is hot and humid, is becoming a second high season, especially among families and Europeans. Key West's annual Fantasy Fest is the last week in October; if you plan to attend this popular event, reserve at least six months in advance. Rooms are also scarce the first few weekends of lobster season, which starts in August.

THE UPPER KEYS

The tropical coral reef tract that runs a few miles off the seaward coast accounts for most of the Upper Keys' reputation. This is a diving heaven, thanks to scores of diving options, accessible islands and dive sites, and an established tourism infrastructure.

Yet although diving is king here, fishing, kayaking, and nature touring draw an enviable number of tourists. Within 1½ mi of the bay coast lie the islands of Everglades National Park; here naturalists lead eco-tours to see one of the world's few saltwater forests, endangered manatees, dolphins, roseate spoonbills, and tropical-bird rookeries. Although the number of birds has dwindled since John James Audubon captured their beauty on a visit to the Keys, bird-watchers won't be disappointed. At sunset flocks take to the skies, and in spring and autumn migrating birds add their numbers. Tarpon and bonefish teem in the shallow waters surrounding the islands, providing food for birds and a challenge to light-tackle fishermen. These same crystal-clear waters attract windsurfers, sailors, and powerboaters.

With few exceptions, dining in the Upper Keys tends toward the casual in food, service, and dress. Wherever you go, you'll find a pleasant mix of locals, visitors, snowbirds (in season), and South Floridian weekenders.

Accommodations are as varied as they are plentiful. The majority are in small waterfront resorts, whose efficiency and one- or two-bedroom units are decorated in tropical colors. They offer dockage and either provide or will arrange boating, diving, and fishing excursions. Depending on which way the wind blows and how close the property is to the highway, noise from U.S. 1 can be bothersome. In high season, expect to pay $85–$165 for an efficiency (in low season, $65–$145). Campground and RV park rates with electricity and water run $25–$55. Some properties require two- or three-day minimum stays during holidays and on weekends in high season. Conversely, discounts are given for midweek, weekly, and monthly stays, and rates can drop 20%–40% April–June and October–mid-December. Keep in mind that salty winds and soil play havoc with anything man-made, and constant maintenance is a must; inspect your accommodations before checking in.

Key Largo

56 mi south of Miami International Airport.

The first Key reachable by car, 30-mi-long Key Largo—named Cayo Largo (long key) by the Spanish—is also the largest island in the chain. Comprising three areas—North Key Largo, Key Largo, and Tavernier—it runs northeast–southwest between Lake Surprise and Tavernier Creek, at MM 95. Most businesses are on the four-lane divided highway (U.S. 1) that runs down the middle, but away from the overdevelopment and generally suburban landscape you can find many areas of pristine wilderness.

❶ One such area is **North Key Largo,** which still contains a wide tract of virgin hardwood hammock and mangroves as well as a crocodile sanctuary (not open to the public). To reach North Key Largo, take Card Sound Road just south of Florida City, or from within the Keys, take Route 905 north.

Rest rooms, information kiosks, and picnic tables make the 2,400-acre **Key Largo Hammocks State Botanical Site** user-friendly and a terrific place to explore the largest remaining stand of the vast West Indian tropical hardwood hammock and mangrove wetland that once covered most of the Keys' upland areas. Nearly 100 species of protected plants and animals coexist here, including the endangered American crocodile, Key Largo wood rat, Key Largo cotton mouse, and Schaus swallowtail butterfly. Interpretive signs describe many of the tropical tree species along a 1¼-mi paved road (2½ mi round-trip) that invites walking, rollerblading, and biking. On guided tours, rangers point out rare species, tell humorous nature stories, and encourage visitors to taste the fruits of native plants. Pets are welcome if on a 6-ft leash. ✉ *1 mi north of U.S. 1 on Rte. 905, OS, North Key Largo,* ☎ *305/451–1202.* 🎟 *Free.* 🕗 *Daily 8–5, tours Thurs. and Sun. 10.*

Taking the Overseas Highway from the mainland lands you closer to ❷ **Key Largo** proper, abounding with shopping centers, chain restaurants, and, of course, dive shops.

★ Whenever people talk about the best diving sites in the world, **John Pennekamp Coral Reef State Park** is on the short list. The park is home

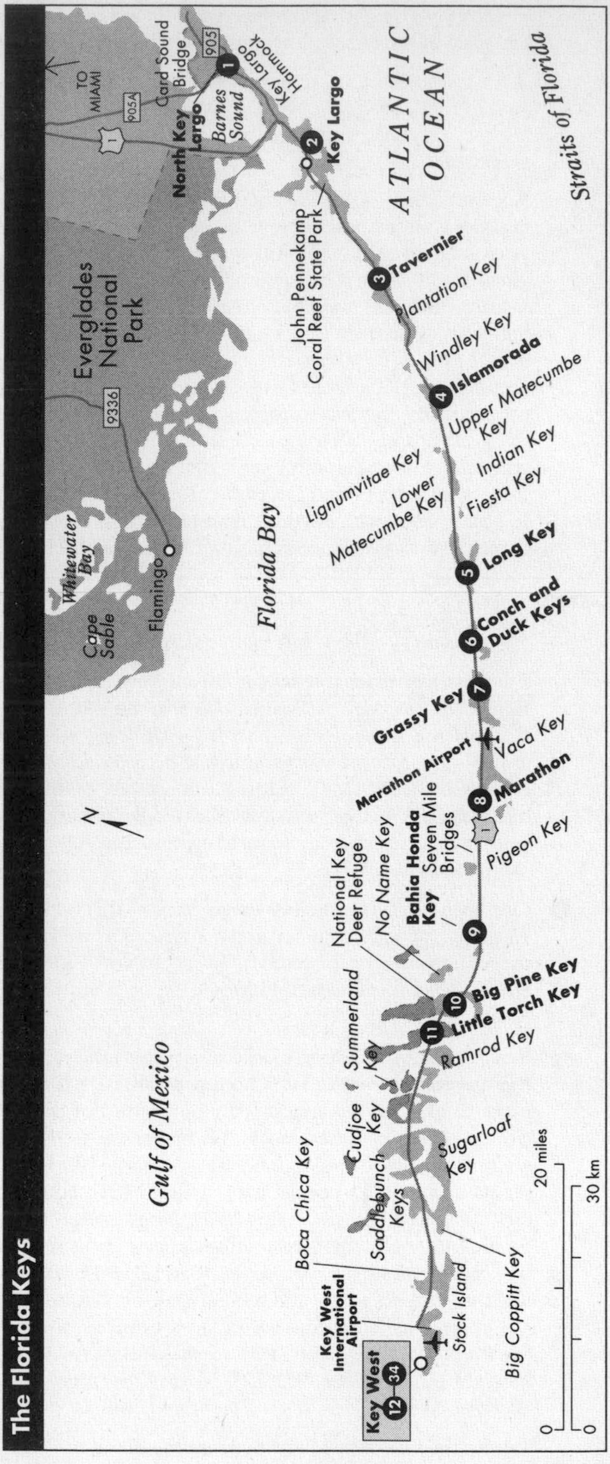

The Florida Keys

to 78 square mi of coral reefs, sea-grass beds, and mangrove swamps. Its reefs contain 40 of the 52 species of coral in the Atlantic Reef System and more than 650 varieties of fish. Its revamped visitor center/aquarium features a large center floor-to-ceiling aquarium surrounded by numerous smaller tanks, a video room, and exhibits. A concessionaire rents canoes and powerboats and offers snorkel, dive, and glass-bottom boat trips to the reef. The park also includes short nature trails, two man-made beaches, picnic shelters, a snack bar, and a campground. No pets are allowed for visitors who are camping or going out on a boat trip. ✉ *MM 102.5, OS, Box 487, 33037,* ☎ *305/451–1202,* WEB *www.dep.state.fl.us/parks.* 🎫 *$4 per vehicle plus 50¢ per person, $1.50 per pedestrian or bicyclist.* ⏲ *Daily 8–sunset.*

Few images conjure up more romance than the *African Queen*—the steam-powered boat on which Katharine Hepburn and Humphrey Bogart rode in the movie of the same name. This 20th-century icon is moored at the **Key Largo Harbor Marina,** from which you depart on an hour-long ride. Also on display is the *Thayer IV,* a 22-ft mahogany Chris-Craft used by Hepburn and Henry Fonda in *On Golden Pond.* Both vessels are in demand at boat shows and occasionally vacate their moorings. ✉ *MM 99.7, OS, next to the Holiday Inn Key Largo Resort,* ☎ *305/451–4655.* 🎫 *Boat ride $15.* ⏲ *Boat ride by appointment.*

❸ The southernmost part of Key Largo is **Tavernier.** Here, at the **Florida Keys Wild Bird Rehabilitation Center,** injured and recovering ospreys, hawks, pelicans, cormorants, terns, and herons of various types rest undisturbed in large, screened enclosures lining a winding boardwalk on some of the best waterfront real estate in the Keys. Wood-carver and teacher Laura Quinn opened the center in 1991. Rehabilitated birds are set free, others become permanent residents. A short nature trail runs into the mangrove forest (bring bug spray May–October), and a video explains the center's mission. ✉ *MM 93.6, BS, Tavernier,* ☎ *305/852–4486.* 🎫 *Donation welcome.* ⏲ *Daily sunrise–sunset.*

Weekends are crowded at **Harry Harris County Park,** which has play equipment, a small swimming lagoon, a boat ramp, ball fields, barbecue grills, and rest rooms. Although the turnoff is clearly marked on the Overseas Highway, the road to the ocean is circuitous. ✉ *MM 93, OS, Burton Dr., Tavernier,* ☎ *305/852–7161 or 888/227–8136.* 🎫 *Weekdays free, weekends $5.* ⏲ *Daily 7:30 AM–sunset.*

Dining and Lodging

$$–$$$ ★ ✕ **The Fish House.** A nautical, Keys-y casual decor and friendly, diligent servers at this perennial favorite create the feeling of dining in the home of a friend, albeit a friend who knows how to prepare fresh seafood like a world-class chef. Fish is prepared any way you like—from charbroiled or fried to Jamaican jerked or pan-sautéed. Nightly specials like shrimp and lobster creole in a spicy tomato sauce served over rice are another reason why locals and visitors keep coming back. The key lime pie is homemade. Their next-door annex, the Gift House, has coffees, fabulous desserts, and souvenirs. ✉ *MM 102.4, OS,* ☎ *305/451–4665. AE, D, MC, V. Closed early Sept.–early Oct.*

$–$$$ ★ ✕ **Frank Keys Café.** Hundreds of little white twinkling lights visible from the porch and windows of the wooden Victorian-style house create a romantic setting for dinner. Equally enticing is the cuisine skillfully prepared by chef-owner Frank Graves III and executive chef Ralph Salvatore. Locals favor the fresh-fish dishes like yellowtail *tropicale,* a pan-sautéed yellowtail snapper topped with fresh tropical fruit in a Malibu rum sauce. There's a different dessert soufflé each night. Salvatore enthusiastically welcomes special requests. If he has the ingredients, he'll make it, whatever it is. The downside to this otherwise lovely restaurant is that smoking is allowed in the small indoor space. ✉ *MM 100, OS,* ☎ *305/453–0310. AE, MC, V. Closed Tues., plus Mon. Easter–Christmas.*

$–$$ ★ ✕ **Café Largo.** You're on vacation and someone in your group wants Italian, someone else craves seafood. This bistro-style eatery prepares both quite well. The penne with shrimp and broccoli has tender shrimp, al dente broccoli, and a hint of garlic. There's lobster and shrimp scampi, too. A more than ample wine list, international beers, Italian bottled waters, focaccia, garlic rolls, and, of course, espresso and cappuccino are offered, and the dessert list is short but sweet. ✉ *MM 99.5, BS,* ☎ *305/451–4885. AE, MC, V. No lunch.*

$–$$ ✕ **Calypso's.** Much of what you find on the menu here was created by self-taught chef Todd Lollis. For example, his special Nuts for Snapper, a local yellowtail snapper encrusted in macadamia nuts and served in an orange Frangelica coulis. Lollis consistently takes away a panful of prizes at local cook-offs thanks to his innovative seafood dishes. A select wine list shows he knows his wines, too, but there are no desserts. The setting is Keys casual; plastic outdoor furniture is complemented by paper napkins and plastic cutlery. ✉ *MM 99.5, OS, 1 Seagate Blvd.,* ☎ *305/451–0600. D, MC, V. Closed Tues.*

$–$$ ✕ **Mrs. Mac's Kitchen.** Fortunately, some things never change. The architecture, atmosphere, and decor of this rustic wood-paneled, screened, open-air restaurant harken back to the 1950s, when the Keys had more fishermen than well-heeled visitors. The cooks still serve up traditional American sandwiches, burgers, barbecue, and seafood like the popular TJ Dolphin, a mahimahi fillet with a spicy tomato salsa served with black beans and rice. At breakfast and lunch, the counter and booths fill up early with locals. Regular nightly specials are worth the stop. The chili is always good, and the beer of the month is still $1.50 a bottle. ✉ *MM 99.4, BS,* ☎ *305/451–3722. No credit cards. Closed Sun.*

$ ✕ **Alabama Jack's.** While some people might come to this nearly 50-year-old eatery for the food, most come for the ambience. The weathered open-air seafood restaurant floats on two roadside barges in an old fishing community 13 mi southeast of Homestead. Regular customers include Keys characters, Sunday cyclists, local retirees, and boaters, who come to admire tropical birds in nearby mangroves, the occasional crocodile in the canal, or the live band on weekends. The place closes by 7 or 7:30, when the skeeters come out. ✉ *58000 Card Sound Rd., Card Sound,* ☎ *305/248–8741. MC, V.*

$ ✕ **Chad's Deli & Bakery.** "This sandwich is huge," is the frequent cry of first-timers to this small four-table establishment that specializes in attractively priced ($5.25–$6.25) sandwiches made on a choice of eight kinds of fresh-baked bread. If you're not in the mood for one of the regular sandwiches, ranging from certified Angus roast beef to veggie, try the daily special. The menu also includes salads, sides, soft drinks, and a choice of two cookies—white-chocolate macadamia nut and chocolate chip—with a whopping 8-inch diameter (75¢–$1). Most orders are takeout. ✉ *MM 92.3, BS,* ☎ *305/853–5566. No credit cards. No dinner.*

$ ✕ **Harriette's Restaurant.** If you're looking for comfort food in a cozy Keys setting, come to this refreshing throwback. Little has changed here over the years except for a recent mural and bright, island-style paint job. Owner Harriette Mattson still personally welcomes her guests, and the regulars—many of whom have been coming here since it opened—still come for breakfast: steak and eggs with hash browns or grits and toast and jelly for $7.95 or old-fashioned hot cakes with butter and syrup and sausage or bacon for $4.25. ✉ *MM 95.7, BS,* ☎ *305/852–8689. No credit cards. No dinner.*

$$$$ **Jules' Undersea Lodge.** Had he been a time traveler to this century, the 19th-century namesake French writer might have enjoyed staying in this hotel, a former underwater research lab, at 5 fathoms (30 ft) below the surface. The only way to gain access to the lodge is by diving, and guests must either be certified divers or take the hotel's three-hour introductory course (an additional $75). Rooms have a shower, telephone, VCR and stereo (no TV reception), and galley. Rates include breakfast, dinner, snacks, beverages, and unlimited dives and diving gear. Because of the length of stay underwater, once back on terra firma, you can't fly for 24 hours. ✉ *MM 103.2, OS, 51 Shoreland Dr., 33037,* ☎ *305/451–2353,* FAX *305/451–4789,* WEB *www.jul.com. 2 bedrooms, sleeps up to 6. Dining room. AE, D, MC, V.*

$$$$ **Marriott's Key Largo Bay Beach Resort.** The Upper Keys are best known for small, mom-and-pop-style accommodations. One of the exceptions is this 17-acre bay-side resort whose five lemon-yellow, grill-balconied, and spire-topped stories slice between highway and bay and exude an air of warm, indolent days. There are diversions galore. Guests while away the days on the sandy beach or poolside or take an adventurous parasail or personal watercraft ride. Rooms and suites feature rattan furnishings, paddle fans, and balconies. From some you can watch the sunset sweep across the bay. ✉ *MM 103.8, BS, 103800 Overseas Hwy., 33037,* ☎ *305/453–0000 or 800/932–9332,* FAX *305/453–0093,* WEB *www.marriotthotels.com. 153 rooms, 20 two-bedroom suites, 6 three-bedroom suites, 1 penthouse suite. Restaurant, 3 bars, pool, hair salon, hot tub, massage, miniature golf, tennis court, volleyball, beach, dive shop, fishing, meeting room. AE, D, DC, MC, V.*

$$$–$$$$ ★ **Kona Kai Resort.** The owners of these beautifully landscaped cottages have created an escape. That's probably why there's so much repeat business. Cottages have video and CD players with CDs by local artists, tropical furnishings, toiletries made from fruits and flowers, and Noritake china. Studios and one- and two-bedroom suites—with full kitchens and original art—are spacious and light filled. Beachfront hammocks and a heated pool make it easy to while away the day, but there's also plenty to do. Try a paddleboat or kayak, visit the expanded art gallery with works by major South Florida and European artists, or view the shade house's 250 orchids. There are no room phones, but there's Internet access on the premises. The staff is there only when needed. Maid service is every third morning. Guests trade in their fluffy towels at a linen cabinet as they please. Smoking is not permitted, nor are guests under age 16. ✉ *MM 97.8, BS, 97802 Overseas Hwy., 33037,* ☎ *305/852–7200 or 800/365–7829,* WEB *www.konakairesort.com. 11 units. Pool, tennis court, basketball, volleyball, boating, beach, dock. AE, D, MC, V.*

$$$–$$$$ ★ **Westin Beach Resort, Key Largo.** Rather than destroy the vegetation and clutter the roadside landscape with yet another building, the original owners ensconced this compact resort off the road in a bay-front hardwood hammock. Most rooms overlook the water or woods, others face the lushly landscaped parking lot. The spacious, comfortable rooms have tropical decor. Rate includes buffet breakfast and two drink coupons. Lighted nature trails and boardwalks wind through the woods to a small beach. Two small pools are separated by a coral rock wall and waterfall. Both restaurants, one very casual, overlook the water. ✉ *MM 96.9, BS, 97000 Overseas Hwy., 33037,* ☎ *305/852–5553 or 800/826–1006,* FAX *305/852–8669,* WEB *www.keylargoresort.com. 190 rooms, 10 suites. 2 restaurants, 2 bars, 2 pools, hot tub, 2 tennis courts, beach, dock, windsurfing, boating, fishing. AE, D, DC, MC, V.*

$$–$$$ **Frank's Key Haven Resort.** If you weren't looking for it, you'd probably miss this small, tidy waterfront lodge in a residential neighborhood. Even so, the owners rarely advertise. Word-of-mouth and repeat guests keep them busy. Towering gumbo-limbo and buttonwood trees shelter

the lodge, which was built in the 1930s to withstand hurricanes. The original owner ran bird-watching tours. Later, racks for dive equipment were added to cater to divers. Although the facilities still offer dive packages—the owners help arrange fishing, diving, kayaking, and ecotours—the lodge attracts guests with many interests, including those who just want to read on the screened porch. Rooms vary from one-room efficiencies to one- and two-bedroom apartments and family units. An indoor public area has a TV, half kitchen, and cozy seating. ✉ *MM 92, BS, 198 Harborview Dr., Tavernier 33070,* ☎ *305/852–3017 or 800/765–5397,* FAX *305/852–3880,* WEB *www.fkeyhaven.com. 14 units. Pool, dock, coin laundry. MC, V.*

$$ ★ **Largo Lodge.** A palpable calm hangs over the 1950s-vintage adults-only guest cottages hidden in a tropical garden of palms, sea grapes, and orchids. Accommodations are cozy and fully equipped with kitchens, rattan furniture, and screened porches but no phones. There's 200 ft of bay frontage. Late in the day, wild ducks, pelicans, herons, and other birds come looking for a handout from longtime owner Harriet "Hat" Stokes, who sets the tone at this laid-back, top-value tropical hideaway not too far down the Keys. ✉ *MM 101.5, BS, 101740 Overseas Hwy., 33037,* ☎ *305/451–0424 or 800/468–4378,* WEB *www.largolodge.com. 6 apartments, 1 efficiency. Beach, dock. MC, V.*

$$ **Popp's Motel.** A high wall with stylized metal white herons marks the entrance to this 50-year-old family-run motel. It's roomy, homey, breezy, and ideal for families whose kids can safely play on swings and a sandy beach just yards from their rooms. Clean, well-maintained bedroom units and efficiencies have a kitchen, dark-wood paneling, and terrazzo floors. It's simple, but a gem of a resort. ✉ *MM 95.5, BS, 95500 Overseas Hwy., 33037,* ☎ *305/852–5201,* FAX *305/852–5200,* WEB *www.popps.com. 9 units. Picnic area, beach, dock, playground. AE, MC, V.*

$ **America Outdoors.** This friendly waterfront campground has a heavily wooded setting. It fills up with repeat campers, especially snowbirds from January to mid-March, and South Floridians, who crowd the place on weekends and holidays. Security is tight and amenities are plentiful. There are boat ramps and rentals, a sandy beach, store, bait shop, two air-conditioned bathhouses, modem hookups, and a recreation center. It's also family oriented, very clean, orderly, and well managed. Sites are on the smallish side. Rates for tents and RVs vary depending on season, day of week, location, and services. ✉ *MM 97.5, BS, 97450 Overseas Hwy., 33037,* ☎ *305/852–8054,* WEB *www.aokl.com. 154 sites. Restaurant, grocery, beach, dock, boating, marina, fishing, coin laundry, recreation room. AE, D, MC, V.*

Nightlife

The semiweekly *Keynoter* (Wednesday and Saturday), weekly *Reporter* (Thursday), and Friday to Sunday editions of the *Miami Herald* are the best sources of information on entertainment and nightlife.

Local movers and shakers mingle with visitors over cocktails and sunsets at **Breezers Tiki Bar** (✉ MM 103.8, BS, ☎ 305/453–0000), in Marriott's Key Largo Bay Beach Resort. Walls plastered with Bogart memorabilia remind customers that the classic 1948 Bogart-Bacall flick *Key Largo* was shot in the **Caribbean Club** (✉ MM 104, BS, ☎ 305/451–9970). An archetype of a laid-back Keys bar, it draws a hairy-faced, down-home group to shoot the breeze while shooting pool, but is friendlier than you might imagine. It also has postcard-perfect sunsets and live entertainment that's good enough to draw late-night crowds on Friday and Saturday and at 6 on Sunday evenings. **Coconuts** (✉ MM 100, OS, 528 Caribbean Dr., ☎ 305/453–9794), in Marina Del Mar Resort, has nightly entertainment year-round, except Sunday and Monday during football season. The crowd is primarily thirty- and fortysomething, sprinkled with a few grizzled locals. **Zappie's Bar and Tackle** (✉ MM 99.2, BS, ☎ 305/451–0531) goes by the slogan "Live Bait & Live Music." Sorry, this isn't the ultimate pickup spot. The bait refers to fishing bait that's sold in the adjoining shop, Bill's Bait, which has been here for years. New owners have thrown lots of money at it and promise to develop a tradition of good, live music on weekends and on other nights in high season. They've added picnic tables and a barbecue grill out back to feed the hungry crowds.

Outdoor Activities and Sports

BIKING

Equipment Locker Sport & Cycle (✉ Tradewinds Plaza, MM 101, OS, ☎ 305/453–0140) rents single-speed adult and children's bikes. Cruisers go for $10 a day, $50 a week. No helmets are available.

FISHING

Sailors Choice (✉ MM 99.7, OS, ☎ 305/451–1802 or 305/451–0041) runs a party boat twice daily plus a night trip on Friday and Saturday. The ultramodern 60-ft, 49-passenger boat with air-conditioned cabin costs $28 and leaves from the Holiday Inn docks.

SCUBA DIVING AND SNORKELING

American Diving Headquarters (✉ MM 105.5, BS, ☎ 305/451–0037 or 877/451–0037) is a good choice for first-time divers. Along with a Water-Tight Guarantee that you'll get your money's worth, the dives start off with a reef ecology and fish identification course so you'll know what you're looking at when you take the plunge. The cost is $60 for a two-tank reef dive with tank and weight rental, $85 if you need everything; $97 includes a wet suit, suggested in winter.

Amy Slate's Amoray Dive Resort (✉ MM 104.2, BS, ☎ 305/451–3595 or 800/426–6729) makes diving easy. You get out of bed, walk out your room and into a full-service dive shop (NAUI, PADI, TDI, and British BSAC certified), then onto a 45-ft catamaran. They provide multidive discounts and accommodations packages and perform underwater weddings.

Coral Reef Park Co. (✉ John Pennekamp Coral Reef State Park, MM 102.5, OS, ☎ 305/451–6322) offers scuba and snorkeling tours of the park aboard sailing and motorized boats.

Divers City, USA (✉ MM 104, OS, ☎ 305/451–4554 or 800/649–4659) keeps convenient hours—daily 8 to 7—for divers who need to purchase or have their equipment repaired. It also offers some of the best prices on equipment in town and runs two-tank, two-location dives for $49.95, tanks and weights included.

Quiescence Diving Service, Inc. (✉ MM 103.5, BS, ☎ 305/451–2440) sets itself apart in two ways: it limits groups to six to ensure personal attention and offers day, night, and twilight (in summer) dives an hour before sundown, the time when sea creatures are most active.

WATER SPORTS

Coral Reef Park Co. (✉ John Pennekamp Coral Reef State Park, MM 102.5, OS, ☎ 305/451–1621) frequently renews its fleet of canoes, kayaks, and Spyaks (personal glass-bottom boats) for scooting around the mangrove trails or the sea. You can rent a canoe, a one- or two-person sea kayak, or even camping equipment from **Florida Bay Outfitters** (✉ MM 104, BS, ☎ 305/451–3018). Real pros; they help with trip planning and match the equipment to the skill level, so even novices feel confident paddling off. Rentals are by the half day or full day. They also run myriad tours and sell camping and outdoor accessories, kayaks, and canoes.

Shopping

Original works by major international artists—including American photographer Clyde Butcher and French painter Jalinepol W and French sculptor Polles—are shown at **The Gallery at Kona Kai** (✉ MM 97.8, BS, 97802 Overseas Hwy., ☎ 305/852–7200). It's in the Kona Kai Resort. There are lots of shops in the Keys that carry fun souvenirs. The **Gift House** (✉ MM 102.3, OS, 102341 Overseas Hwy., ☎ 305/451–0650) stands out because along with the usual kitschy magnets, wind chimes, and shell flowers, it also carries handcrafted gift items and home furnishings by Caribbean and local artists. There's also a dessert and coffee bar with wonderfully decadent desserts. It's adjacent to the Fish House restaurant.

Islamorada

❹ *MM 90.5–70.*

Early settlers named Islamorada after their schooner, the *Island Home,* but to make the name more romantic, they translated it into Spanish—*isla morada.* The local chamber of commerce prefers to say it means "the purple isles." Early maps show Islamorada as only Upper Matecumbe Key. Historians refer to it as the group of islands between Tavernier Creek at MM 90 and Fiesta Key at MM 70, including Plantation Key, Windley Key, Upper Matecumbe Key, Lower Matecumbe Key, Craig Key, and Fiesta Key. In addition, two islands—Indian Key, in the Atlantic Ocean, and Lignumvitae Key, in Florida Bay—belong to the group.

Officially called the Village of Islands, Islamorada is one of the world's most renowned sportfishing areas. For nearly 100 years, seasoned anglers have recognized these clear, warm waters as home to a huge variety of game fish as well as lobster, shrimp, and crabs. The rich, the famous, and the powerful have all fished here, including Lou Gehrig, Ted Williams, Zane Grey, and presidents Hoover, Truman, Carter, and Bush Sr. More than 150 backcountry guides and 400 offshore captains operate out of this 20-mi stretch.

Activities range from fishing tournaments to historic reenactments. During September and October, Heritage Days feature free lectures on Islamorada history, a golf tournament, and the Indian Key Festival. Holiday Isle Resort sponsors boating, fishing, car, and golf tournaments, as well as bikini and body-building contests.

Between 1885 and 1915, settlers earned good livings growing pineapples on **Plantation Key** (✉ MM 90.5–86), using black Bahamian workers to plant and harvest their crops. The plantations are gone, replaced by a dense concentration of homes and businesses.

At 16 ft above sea level, **Windley Key** (✉ MM 86–84) is the highest point in the Keys. Originally two islets, the area was first inhabited by Native Americans, who left middens and other remains, and then by settlers, who farmed and fished in the mid-1800s and called the islets the Umbrella Keys. The Florida East Coast Railway bought the land from homesteaders in 1908, filled in the inlet between the two islands, and changed the name. They quarried rock for the rail bed and bridge approaches in the Keys—the same rock used in many historic South Florida structures, including Miami's Vizcaya and the Hurricane Monument on Upper Matecumbe. Although the Quarry Station stop was destroyed by the 1935 hurricane, quarrying continued until the 1960s. Today a few resorts and attractions occupy the island.

The once-living fossilized coral reef that was laid down about 125,000 years ago shows that the Florida Keys were at some time underwater.

When the Florida East Coast Railway excavated Windley Key's limestone bed, it exposed the petrified reef. The **Windley Key Fossil Reef State Geologic Site** has a museum called the Alison Fahrer Environmental Education Center, which contains historic, biological, and geological displays about the area. There also are guided and self-guided tours along trails that lead to the railway's old quarrying equipment and cutting pits, where you can take rubbings of beautifully fossilized brain coral and sea ferns from the quarry walls. There's an annual festival in February. ✉ *MM 85.5, BS,* ☎ *305/664–2540.* 🎫 *Education center free, quarry trails $1.50.* ⏲ *Education center Thurs.–Mon. 8–5; inquire about quarry tour schedule.*

The lush, tropical 17-acre **Theater of the Sea** is the second-oldest marine mammal facility in the world. Entertaining and educational shows provide insight into conservation issues, natural history, and mammal anatomy, physiology, and husbandry. Shows run continuously. Visitors can ride a glass-bottom boat and take a four-hour Dolphin Adventure Snorkel Cruise or guided tours to view marine life, raptors, and reptiles. They can visit dolphins and sea lions and participate in animal interaction programs such as Swim with the Dolphins ($110), Swim with Sea Lions ($75), Stingray Reef Swim ($35), and Trainer for a Day ($75). Reservations are recommended for interaction programs. ✉ *MM 84.5, OS, 84721 Overseas Hwy, 33036,* ☎ *305/664–2431,* WEB *www.theaterofthesea.com.* 🎫 *$17.25 (included for participants of interaction programs).* ⏲ *Daily 9:30–4.*

Upper Matecumbe Key (✉ MM 84–79) was one of the earliest in the Upper Keys to be permanently settled. Homesteaders were so successful at growing pineapples as well as limes in the rocky soil that at one time the island had the largest U.S. pineapple crop; however, Cuban pineapples and the hurricane of 1935 killed the industry. Today life centers on fishing and tourism, and the island is lively with homes, charter fishing boats, bait shops, restaurants, stores, nightclubs, marinas, nurseries, and offices.

With so many folks stopping by, what started out as a jewelry store decorated with the owner's collection of nautical treasures became the **Somewhere in Time** museum. It still sells jewelry, but the crowd pleasers are the hundreds of interesting artifacts salvaged from merchant and slave ships that once plied Florida's waters. There are coins from the *Atocha,* rare ceramic containers, original 18th-century maps, cannons, silver bars, slave artifacts, religious medallions, rare bottles, and a corny diorama of two infamous English women pirates. The owner tells marvelous stories about the objects. ✉ *MM 82.3, OS, 82255 Overseas Hwy.,* ☎ *305/664–9699.* 🎫 *Free.* ⏲ *Daily 9–5.*

Home to the local chamber of commerce, a **red train caboose** sits at the site where the Florida East Coast Railway had a station and living quarters, before they washed away with the hurricane of 1935. ✉ *MM 82.5, BS.* 🎫 *Free.* ⏲ *Weekdays 9–5, Sat. 9–4.*

While the possibility of a hurricane is something Keys residents live with, few hurricanes actually make landfall here. One major exception was the 1935 Labor Day hurricane, in which 423 people died. Beside the highway, the 65-ft-by-20-ft art deco–style **Hurricane Monument** (✉ MM 81.6, OS) marks their mass grave. Many of those who perished were World War I veterans who had been working on the Overseas Highway. The monument, built of Keys coral limestone with a ceramic map of the Keys, depicts wind-driven waves and palms bowing before the storm's fury.

Tucked away behind the Islamorada library is a small beach on a creek at **Islamorada County Park** (✉ MM 81.5, BS). The water isn't very deep, but it is crystal clear. Currents are swift, making swimming unsuitable for young children, but they can enjoy the playground as well as picnic tables, grassy areas, and rest rooms. Formerly part of a commercial resort, **Islamorada Founder's Park,** formerly Plantation Yacht Harbor (✉ MM 87, BS, ☎ 305/852–2381) is now a public village park with a beach, water-sports equipment rentals, a dog park, and, soon, an Olympic-size pool.

OFF THE BEATEN PATH

INDIAN KEY STATE HISTORIC SITE – Murder, mystery, and misfortune surround 10½-acre Indian Key on the ocean side of the Matecumbe islands. Before it became one of the first European settlements outside of Key West, it was inhabited by Native Americans for several thousand years. The islet served as a county seat and base for 19th-century shipwreck salvagers until an Indian attack wiped out the settlement in 1840. Dr. Henry Perrine, a noted botanist, was killed in the raid. Today his plants overgrow the town's ruins. In October the Indian Key Festival celebrates the key's heritage. Guided tours were suspended due to damage to the docks from recent hurricanes, but you can roam among the marked trails and sites. The island is reachable by boat—your own, a rental, or a ferry. Robbie's Marina, the official concessioner, rents kayaks and boats and operates twice-daily ferry service. For information, contact Long Key State Recreation Area. Locals kayak out from **Indian Key Fill** (✉ MM 78.5, BS). Rentals are available from Florida Keys Kayak and Sail. ✉ *MM 78.5, OS,* ☎ *305/664–9814 for ferry service; 305/664–4815 for Long Key State Recreation Area.* *Ferry (includes tour) $15, $25 with Lignumvitae Key.* *Daily sunrise–sunset.*

LIGNUMVITAE KEY STATE BOTANICAL SITE – On the National Register of Historic Places, this 280-acre bay-side island is the site of a virgin hardwood forest and home and gardens that chemical magnate William Matheson built as a private retreat in 1919. Access is by boat—your own, a rental, or a ferry operated by the official concessionaire, Robbie's Marina, which also rents kayaks and boats. (Kayaking out from Indian Key Fill, at MM 78.5, is a popular pastime.) On the key you can take a tour with the resident ranger and request a list of native and well-naturalized plants. As a courtesy, you should arrange for a tour in advance with Long Key State Recreation Area if you're using your own or a rental boat. On the first weekend in December, the Park Service holds an annual Lignumvitae Christmas Celebration. ✉ *MM 78.5, BS,* ☎ *305/664–9814 for ferry service; 305/664–4815 for Long Key State Recreation Area.* *Free; tour $1; ferry (includes tour) $15, $25 with Indian Key.* *Tours Thurs.–Mon. 10 and 2.*

Tarpon, large prehistoric-looking denizens of the not-so-deep, congregate around the docks at **Robbie's Marina,** on Lower Matecumbe Key, where children—and lots of adults—buy a $2 bucket of bait fish to feed them. ✉ *MM 77.5, BS,* ☎ *305/664–9814 or 877/664–8498.* *Dock access $1.* *Daily 8–5:30.*

Although recent hurricanes uprooted trees and dramatically changed the shoreline, **Anne's Beach,** on Lower Matecumbe Key, remains a popular village park whose beach is best enjoyed at low tide. It also has a ½-mi elevated wooden boardwalk that meanders through a natural wetland hammock. Covered picnic areas along the boardwalk provide a place to rest and enjoy the view. Rest rooms are at the north end. ✉ *MM 73.5, OS,* ☎ *305/852–2381.*

Dining and Lodging

$$–$$$$ ★ ✕ **Morada Bay.** In the Upper Keys, this bay-front restaurant stands out among the other eateries and elbow-to-elbow resorts. First, there's the spectacular water view. Then, there's the traditional wooden Conch architecture decorated with Clyde Butcher's black-and-white Everglades photos. Best of all is the contemporary menu featuring tapas and innovative small dishes, mostly from the sea. Meals start with a basket of fresh rolls and a plate of tapenade, white-bean dip, and garlic-infused olive oil. You can dine indoors (noisy) or outdoors on the porch overlooking a sandy beach dotted with Adirondack chairs. There's frequently live entertainment, especially on weekends. ✉ *MM 81, BS,* ☎ *305/664–0604. AE, MC, V.*

$$–$$$$ ★ ✕ **Pierre's.** First came the tony Moorings resort on the ocean. Then French windsurfer-turned-Keys-entrepreneur Hubert Baudoin opened his first restaurant, the popular Morada Bay, on the bay. Now, he's outdone himself with this two-story showpiece that marries British colonial decadence with South Florida trendiness. The place is loaded with dark wood, rattan, French doors, Indian and Asian architectural artifacts, and a wide, wicker-chair–strewn veranda that overlooks the beach and bay. Dishes, heavily inspired by those same Asian and Indian accents, are complex: layered, colorful, and beautifully presented. Weather permitting, dine outside. Even if you don't come for dinner upstairs, stop in at the wonderfully sophisticated downstairs bar where wicker chairs and buttery leather sofas provide a perfect vantage point from which to watch the sun set over the palm trees. Reservations are recommended. ✉ *MM 81.5, BS,,* ☎ *305/664–3225. AE, MC, V.*

$$ ✕ **Manny & Isa's.** This Keys institution has no frills, fancy decor, or pretense. Instead, it has friendly waitresses who serve consistently delicious Cuban and Spanish food in a simple room crowded with a dozen tables. The regular menu is split between traditional Cuban dishes and local seafood, and there are daily fish, chicken, and pork-chop specials, all served with salad and Cuban bread. The large-portion paella, loaded with fresh seafood, must be ordered the day before for at least two people ($17.95 each). Manny's sweet-tart key lime pies are legendary. Order them by the slice or by the pie. There's always a wait for dinner on weekends and during the winter high season. Avoid the line by calling for takeout. ✉ *MM 81.6, OS, 81610 Old Hwy.,* ☎ *305/664–5019. AE, D, MC, V. Closed Tues. and mid-Oct.–mid.-Nov.*

$$ ★ ✕ **Squid Row.** The food is so fresh and good at this roadside seafood eatery that no gimmicks are needed to lure customers. That doesn't prevent the affable staff from offering a playful challenge. Along with local fish—grilled and divinely flaky, or breaded and sautéed—they offer a nightly special bouillabaisse ($26.95), thick with fish and shellfish—even stone crab claws—that is simply wonderful. If you can eat it all by yourself, they'll give you a free slice of key lime pie. End the meal with a cup of coffee and a slice of the banana bread that comes at the start of the meal but is best as dessert. ✉ *MM 81.9, OS,* ☎ *305/664–9865. AE, D, DC, MC, V.*

$$$$ 🏨 **Cheeca Lodge.** This classy, classic resort combines a sense of luxury with a sense of familiarity. Complexes of buildings, gardens, a sandy beach, and fish-filled lagoons stretch across 27 acres along the ocean. Tropically decorated units and screened balconies (on suites) encourage you to linger, but the beach, pools, golf course, and water sports beckon. Suites have kitchens; fourth-floor rooms in the main lodge have ocean or bay views. The resort is the local leader in green activism with everything from recycling programs to eco-tours. Camp Cheeca for kids is fun and educational. ✉ *MM 82, OS, Box 527, 33036,* ☎ *305/664–4651 or 800/327–2888,* FAX *305/664–2893,* WEB *www.cheeca.com. 139 rooms, 64 suites. 2 restaurants, lobby lounge, 2 pools, 9-hole golf course,*

6 tennis courts, boating, parasailing, fishing, children's programs (ages 6–12), playground. AE, D, DC, MC, V.

$$$–$$$$ **Casa Morada.** Once a plain-Jane budget hotel, new owners are turning it into something you'd find on the Mexican Riviera. Clean, cool tile and terrazo floors invite you to kick off your shoes. Cool white bedding tempts you to stay indoors, but lounge chairs on your private patio overlooking the gardens and bay beckon. If you like the furnishings—mahogany and wrought-iron mixed with French and Italian artifacts and lamps—you can buy them, or at least identical pieces. The furniture is made to order in Mexico for the resort and its guests. Suites feature in-room safes, hair dryers, and direct-dial and modem phone lines. The pool's built on a small concrete island in the bay. Since there's no beach, a ladder lets you climb into the bay from the island for a dip or a swim to a small floating dock. There's free weekend Continental breakfast and room-service delivery from local eateries. For other dining, walk to nearby restaurants or use the spotless communal kitchen to prepare meals that you can eat on the adjoining terrace. ✉ *MM 82, BS, 136 Madeira Rd., 33036,* ☎ *305/664–0044 or 888/881–3030,* FAX *305/664–0674,* WEB *www.casamorada.com. 16 suites. Pool, massage, boccie, dock, marina. AE, MC, V.*

$$$–$$$$ ★ **The Moorings.** When you think of a tropical retreat, visions of palm trees, ocean views, sandy beaches, and wooden houses with porches and wicker furniture come to mind. That's exactly what you'll find here at one of the Keys' finest hostelries. Tucked in a tropical forest along one of the finest beaches in the Keys are one-, two-, and three-bedroom cottages and two-story houses outfitted with wicker and artistic African fabrics and pristine white kitchens. There are many exquisite touches, from thick towels to extra-deep, cushiony bedcovers. The beach has a scattering of Adirondack chairs and hammocks, complimentary windsurfing and kayaking, and a swimming dock. There's a two-night minimum on one-bedrooms and a one-week minimum on other lodgings. ✉ *MM 81.6, OS, 123 Beach Rd., 33036,* ☎ *305/664–4708,* FAX *305/664–4242,* WEB *www.themooringsvillage.com. 18 cottages and houses. Pool, tennis court, beach, windsurfing. MC, V.*

$$–$$$ ★ **Sea Isle Resort and Marina.** You can't tell a resort by its sign. Behind a nondescript sign and fence, this picturesque resort on 8.5 acres has a beautiful natural sandy beach, two long docks, complimentary marina facilities, and two types of accommodations. On one side, old concrete duplex "villas" were modernized with very tasteful island furnishings, tile floors, full kitchens, and a private deck or patio. You can smell the sea from all of them. Next door are the resort's gilded lilies: Caribbean-style one- and two-bedroom houses with open-beam ceilings, wraparound porches with ceiling fans, grills, laundry, the works. The decor is light, breezy, and oh so tropical. They sleep 4 to 10 people and start at $225. Public areas are equally appealing. The large walk-in, beach-entry-style pool has a "sandy" bottom and is surrounded by palm trees, lounge chairs, and two wooden gazebos. ✉ *MM 82, OS, 109 E. Carroll St., Box 1298., 33036,* ☎ *305/664–2235 or 800/799–9175,* FAX *305/664–2093,* WEB *www.seaisleres.com. 21 units, 9 villas, 12 houses. Pool, outdoor hot tub, beach, dock, marina, fishing. AE, MC, V.*

$$ **White Gate Court.** This well-run inn on the edge of Florida Bay comprises five restored wooden 1940s cottages laid out on 3 pretty landscaped acres along 200 ft of white-sand beach. Resident owner Susanne Orias de Cargnelli created this intimate escape, where everyone in the family, including the dog, is welcome. All the units, which sleep either two or four, have a full kitchen, cable TV, direct phone lines, and air-conditioning. Barbecue grills, umbrella-shaded tables, and big old palm and native trees create a relaxing mood. ✉ *MM 76, BS, 76010 Over-*

seas Hwy., 33036, ☏ 305/664–4136, WEB www.whitegatecourt.com. 7 units. Picnic area, beach, dock, coin laundry. MC, V.

$ **Ragged Edge Resort.** Smack on the water's edge, this no frills, laid-back getaway has simple, clean rooms with pine paneling, chintz, and a tile bath suite, and most have kitchens with irons. Many downstairs units have screened porches, while upper units have large decks, more windows, and beam ceilings. It's affordable due to a lack of staff and things like in-room phones. Amenities take the form of a thatch-roof observation tower, picnic areas, barbecue pits, and free bikes. There's not much of a beach, but you can swim off the dock. *✉ MM 86.5, OS, 243 Treasure Harbor Rd., 33036, ☏ 305/852–5389, WEB www.ragged-edge.com. 10 units. Picnic area, pool, shuffleboard, dock, bicycles. MC, V.*

Nightlife

Holiday Isle Beach Resorts & Marina (✉ MM 84, OS, ☏ 305/664–2321) is the liveliest spot in the Upper Keys. On weekends, especially during spring break and holidays, the resort's three entertainment areas are mobbed, primarily with the under-30 set. Live bands play everything from reggae to heavy metal. Behind the larger-than-life mermaid is the Keys-easy, over-the-water cabana bar the **Lorelei** (✉ MM 82, BS, ☏ 305/664–4656). Live nightly sounds are mostly reggae and light rock. **Zane Grey Long Key Lounge** (✉ MM 81.5, BS, ☏ 305/664–4244) above the World Wide Sportsman was created to honor Zane Grey, one of South Florida's greatest legends in fishing and writing and one of the most famous members of the Long Key Fishing Club. The lounge features the author's photographs, books, and memorabilia, as well as live music on weekends, and a wide veranda that invites sunset watching.

Outdoor Activities and Sports

BOATING

Wildlife in the Keys is most active at sunrise and sunset. Be there comfortably at both times with **Houseboat Vacations of the Florida Keys** (✉ MM 85.9, BS, 85944 Overseas Hwy., 33036, ☏ 305/664–4009), which rents a fleet of 40- to 44-ft boats that accommodate from six to eight people and come fully outfitted with safety equipment and necessities—except food. The three-day minimum starts at $660; a week costs $1,140. Kayaks, canoes, and 16-ft skiffs are also for hire. **Robbie's Boat Rentals & Charters** (✉ MM 77.5, BS, 77520 Overseas Hwy., 33036, ☏ 305/664–9814) rents a 15-ft skiff with a 25-horsepower outboard (the smallest you can charter) for $25 an hour, $70 for four hours, and $90 for the day. Boats up to 27 ft are also available, but there's a two-hour minimum, as are pontoon boats, with a half-day minimum. When you're in the Keys, do as the locals do. Get out on the water, preferably for a few days. Captains Pam and Pete Anderson of **Treasure Harbor Marine** (✉ MM 86.5, OS, 200 Treasure Harbor Dr., 33036, ☏ 305/852–2458 or 800/352–2628) provide everything you'll need for a vacation at sea: linens, safety gear, and, best of all, advice on where to find the best beaches, marinas, and lobster sites. You can rent a vessel bareboat or crewed, with sail or with power. Boats range from a 19-ft Cape Dory to a 41-ft custom-built ketch. A 47-ft Tradewind comes with a captain. Rates start at $95 a day, $395 a week. Marina facilities are basic—water, electric, ice machine, laundry, picnic tables, and shower/rest rooms—and dockage is only $1 a foot.

FISHING

Long before fly-fishing became a trendy sport, Sandy Moret was fishing the Keys for bonefish, tarpon, and redfish. Now he operates **Florida Keys Outfitters** (✉ MM 82, BS, ☏ 305/664–5423), home to a store and the Florida Keys Fly Fishing School, which attracts anglers from around the world. Two-day weekend fly-fishing classes, which include classroom instruction, equipment, arrival cocktails, and daily breakfast and lunch, cost $895. Add another $900 for two days of fishing. Guided fishing trips cost $310 for a half day, $450 for a full day. Fishing and accommodations packages (at Cheeca Lodge) are available. The 65-ft party boat ***Gulf Lady*** (✉ Whale Harbor Marina, MM 83.5, OS, ☎ 305/664–2628 or 305/664–2461) offers full-day ($50; $55 with rod and reel) and night trips. The boat can be crowded, so call about loads in advance. Captain Ken Knudsen of the ***Hubba Hubba*** (✉ MM 79.8, OS, ☎ 305/664–9281) quietly poles his flats boat through the shallow water, barely making a ripple. Then he points and his client casts. Five seconds later there's a zing, and the excitement of bringing in a snook, redfish, trout, or tarpon begins. Knudsen has fished Keys waters since he was 12. Now a licensed backcountry guide, he's ranked among the top 10 guides in Florida by national fishing magazines. He offers four-hour sunset trips for tarpon ($325) and two-hour sunset trips for bonefish ($175), as well as half- ($275) and full-day ($400) outings. Prices are for one or two anglers. Tackle and bait are included.

SCUBA DIVING AND SNORKELING

Florida Keys Dive Center (✉ MM 90.5, OS, Box 391, Tavernier 33070, ☎ 305/852–4599 or 800/433–8946) organizes dives from John Pennekamp Coral Reef State Park to Alligator Light. The center has two Coast Guard–approved dive boats, offers scuba training, and is one of the few Keys dive centers to offer Nitrox (mixed gas) diving. Since 1980, **Lady Cyana Divers** (✉ MM 85.9, BS, Box 1157, 33036, ☎ 305/664–8717 or 800/221–8717), a PADI five-star training resort, has operated dives on deep and shallow wrecks and reefs between Molasses and Alligator reefs. The 40- and 55-ft boats provide everything a diver needs, including full bathrooms.

TENNIS

Not all Keys recreation is on the water. You can play tennis year-round at the **Islamorada Tennis Club** (✉ MM 76.8, BS, ☎ 305/664–5340). It's a well-run facility with four clay and two hard courts, same-day racket stringing, ball machines, private lessons, a full-service pro shop, night games, and partner pairing. Rates are from $12 an hour.

WATER SPORTS

Florida Keys Kayak and Sail (✉ MM 77.5, BS, 77522 Overseas Hwy, ☎ 305/664–4878) rents kayaks within a 20- to 30-minute paddle of Indian and Lignumvitae keys, two favorite destinations for kayakers. Rates are $10 per hour, $25 per half day.

Shopping

Whether you're looking to learn more about Keys history, flora and fauna, or fishing, you'll find it in a large selection of books, cards, and maps on Florida and the region at **Cover to Cover Books** (✉ Tavernier Towne Shopping Center, MM 91.2, BS, 91272 Overseas Hwy., ☎ 305/852–1415). At **Down to Earth** (✉ MM 82.2, OS, 82229 Overseas Hwy., ☎ 305/664–9828), you can indulge your passion for *objets* that are at once practical and fanciful. Take the salad tongs carved from polished coconut shells and the Italian dishes painted with palm trees. Prices are reasonable, too. When locals need a one-of-a-kind gift, they head for the **Gallery at Morada Bay** (✉ MM 81.6, BS, ☎ 305/664–3650), stocked with blown glass and glassware, and home furnishings, original paintings and lithographs, sculptures, and hand-painted scarves and earrings by top South Florida artists. Among the best buys in town are the used best-sellers and hardbacks that sell for less than $5 after locals trade them in for store credit at **Hooked on Books** (✉ MM 82.6, OS, 82681 Overseas Hwy, ☎ 305/517–2602). They also carry new titles, audio books, cards, and CDs. **Island Silver & Spice** (✉ MM 82, OS, ☎ 305/664–2714) bills itself as a "tropical department store." To that end, it sells women's and men's resort wear, a large jewelry selection with high-end Swiss watches and marine-theme jewelry, tropical housewares, cards, toys and games, bedding, and bath goods.

Former U.S. presidents, celebs, and record holders beam alongside their catches in black-and-white photos on the walls at **World Wide Sportsman** (✉ MM 81.5, BS, ☎ 305/664–4615), a two-level attraction and retail center that sells upscale fishing equipment, art, resort clothing, and gifts. There's also a marina and the Zane Grey Long Key Lounge.

ART GALLERIES

The **Rain Barrel** (✉ MM 86.7, BS, ☎ 305/852–3084) is a natural and unhurried shopping showplace. Set in a tropical garden of shady trees, native shrubs, and orchids, the 1977 crafts village is comprised of shops with works by local and national artists and eight resident artists in studios, including John Hawver, noted for Florida landscapes and seascapes. In March it hosts the largest arts show in the Keys; some 20,000 visitors, 100 artists, and live jazz. Their Garden Café offers a primarily vegetarian menu. The **Redbone Gallery** (✉ MM 81, OS, 200 Industrial Dr., ☎ 305/664–2002), the largest sporting-art gallery in Florida, recently expanded, adding hand-stitched clothing and giftware to its collection of wood and bronze sculptors such as Kendall Van Sant; watercolorists Chet Reneson, Jeanne Dobie, and Kathleen Denis; and painters C. D. Clarke and Tim Borski. One of the most-photographed subjects in the Upper Keys is the enormous fabricated lobster by artist Richard Blaes that stands in front of **Treasure Village** (✉ MM 86.7, OS, 86729 Old Hwy., ☎ 305/852–0511), a former 1950s treasure museum that houses a dozen crafts and specialty shops such as **Art Lovers Gallery** (☎ 305/852–1120), featuring noted Florida artists. It's also home to an excellent little Made to Order eat-in and carryout restaurant.

Long Key

5 *MM 70–65.5.*

Long Key is steeped in cultural and ecological history. Among its attributes is **Long Key State Recreation Area.** On the ocean side, the Golden Orb Trail leads onto a boardwalk through a mangrove swamp alongside a lagoon, where waterbirds congregate. The park has a campground, picnic area, rest rooms and showers, a canoe trail through a tidal lagoon, and a not-very-sandy beach fronting a broad expanse of shallow grass flats. Bring a mask and snorkel to observe the marine life in this rich nursery area. Repairs and replantings following hurricanes have left the park with improved facilities, but with a lot less shade. Replanting efforts continue. Across the road, near a historical marker partially obscured by foliage, is the **Layton Nature Trail** (✉ MM 67.7, BS), which takes 20–30 minutes to walk and leads through tropical hardwood forest to a rocky Florida Bay shoreline overlooking shallow grass flats. A marker relates the history of the Long Key Viaduct, the first major bridge on the rail line, and the exclusive Long Key Fishing Camp, which Henry Flagler established nearby in 1906 and which attracted sportsman Zane Grey, the noted Western novelist and conservationist, who served as its first president. The camp was washed away in the 1935 hurricane and never rebuilt. For Grey's efforts, the creek running near the recreation area was named for him. ✉ *MM 67.5, OS, Box 776, 33001,* ☎ *305/664–4815,* WEB *www.dep.state.fl.us/parks.* 🎟 *$3.25 for 1 person, plus 50¢ each additional person; canoe rental $4 per hr, $10 per day; Layton Nature Trail free.* ⏲ *Daily 8–sunset.*

Dining and Lodging

$–$$ ✕ **Little Italy.** Good news. A longtime employee purchased this traditional family-style Italian and seafood restaurant and vowed not to change it. The food is still good, and prices are still low. Lunch favorites include Caesar salad, chicken marsala, stone crabs, and stuffed snapper for $3.95–$7.95. Dinner selections are equally tasty and well priced—pasta, chicken, seafood, veal, and steak for $8.50–$13.95. Don't miss the rich, dreamy hot chocolate-pecan pie. Breakfast, too, is served, and a light-bites menu features smaller portions for kids and calorie-watchers. ✉ *MM 68.5, BS,* ☎ *305/664–4472. AE, D, MC, V.*

$$ **Lime Tree Bay Resort Motel.** This popular 2½-acre resort is directly on Florida Bay and far from the hubbub of other hotels and businesses. An on-site water-sports concession encourages activity, but a beach, pool, hammocks, pleasantly landscaped setting, and wicker- and rattan-furnished guest rooms invite you to do nothing more energetic than to turn the pages of a book. The best units are the cottages out back (no bay views) and four deluxe rooms upstairs, which have cathedral ceilings and skylights. The best bet for two couples traveling together is the upstairs Tree House. ✉ *MM 68.5, BS, Box 839, Layton 33001,* ☎ *305/664–4740 or 800/723–4519,* FAX *305/664–0750,* WEB *www.limetreebayresort.com. 30 rooms. Restaurant, picnic area, pool, hot tub, tennis court, horseshoes, shuffleboard, beach, dive shop, snorkeling, windsurfing, boating, jet skiing. AE, D, DC, MC, V.*

$ **Long Key State Recreation Area.** Although upgrades and repairs have been completed following two hurricanes, tent and RV sites remain relatively exposed, while rangers and volunteers continue the hard work of recreating the narrow semi-sandy beach and replanting the lost vegetation that once shaded the sites. Fishing for bonefish, permit, and tarpon remains good in the near-shore flats. All sites have water and electricity and campground hostesses are available to help out. You can reserve up to 11 months in advance by phone or in person. Sites cost $19, plus $2 for electricity. ✉ *MM 67.5, OS, Box 776, 33001,* ☎ *305/664–4815. 60 sites. Picnic area, hiking, beach, fishing. D, MC, V.*

Outdoor Activities and Sports

At **Lime Tree Water Sports** (✉ MM 68.5, BS, Lime Tree Bay Resort Motel, ☎ 305/664–0052) you can sign up for sunset cruises, backcountry fishing trips, and snorkeling and scuba excursions or rent a sailboat, powerboat, kayak, sailboard, or Wave Runner. They also offer PADI diving certification and windsurfing and sailing lessons.

En Route As you cross Long Key Channel, look beside you at the old **Long Key Viaduct.** The second-longest bridge on the former rail line, this 2-mi-long structure has 222 reinforced-concrete arches.

THE MIDDLE KEYS

Stretching from Conch Key to the far side of the Seven Mile Bridge, the Middle Keys contain U.S. 1's most impressive stretch, MM 65–40, bracketed by the Keys' two longest bridges—Long Key Viaduct and Seven Mile Bridge, both historic landmarks. Activity centers on the town of Marathon, the Keys' third-largest metropolitan area.

Fishing and diving are the main attractions. In both bay and ocean, the deep-water fishing is superb at places like the Marathon West Hump, whose depth ranges from 500 to more than 1,000 ft. Anglers successfully fish from a half dozen bridges, including Long Key Bridge, the Old Seven Mile Bridge, and both ends of Toms Harbor. There are also many beaches and natural areas to enjoy in the Middle Keys.

Conch and Duck Keys

❻ *MM 63–61.*

This stretch of islands is rustic. Fishing dominates the economy, and many residents are descendants of immigrants from the mainland South. Across a causeway from Conch Key, a tiny fishing and retirement village, lies Duck Key, an upscale community and resort.

Dining and Lodging

$$–$$$$ ✕ **Waters Edge.** This plush, yet relaxed restaurant at the Hawk's Cay Resort gathers flavors and techniques from around the world to present a menu that emphasizes seafood with traces of tropical Caribbean and Florida and European sensibility. Favorites include St. Thomas, a land-and-sea combo of jumbo shrimp and tournedos of beef, chicken Key West (stuffed with crab, shrimp, and scallops), and Florida stone crab claws (in season), and for dessert mud pie and coconut ice cream. Soup and a 40-item salad bar are included with dinners. You can dine indoors or outdoors under the dockside canopy. A collection of historic photos on the walls recalls the regional history of the island and the notables who have visited. ✉ *MM 61, OS, Duck Key,* ☏ *305/743–7000. AE, D, DC, MC, V. No lunch mid-Dec.–mid-Apr.*

$$$$ ★ **Hawk's Cay Resort.** This rambling Caribbean-style retreat, which opened in 1959, is popular with vacationing families and people looking for a little piece of a tropical paradise. New two-bedroom villas and upgrades improved the tony resort, which has spacious rooms decorated in a light, casual style of wicker and earthy colors. Sports and recreational facilities are extensive, such as a sailing school, dive and snorkel trips, volleyball overlooking the Atlantic, a saltwater lagoon and pool, a fitness center with state-of-the-art equipment, and a whirlpool spa. There is also a wide range of supervised programs for kids and teens. The Dolphin Connection provides three educational experiences with dolphins, including the in-the-water Dolphin Discovery program that lets you get up-close and personal with the intelligent mammals. ✉ *MM 61, OS, 33050,* ☏ *305/743–7000 or 800/432–2242,* FAX *305/743–5215,* WEB *www.hawkscay.com. 160 rooms, 16 suites, 170 two-bedroom villas. 4 restaurants, 2 bars, 5 pools, golf privileges, 8 tennis courts, basketball, health club, volleyball, dive shop, boating, fishing, video games, children's programs (ages 5–12). AE, D, DC, MC, V.*

$$ **Conch Key Cottages.** Shrubs covered with brightly colored flowers, palm trees, hammocks, a beach, and ocean breezes evoke the spirit of the tropics at this small, secluded resort comprising a four-plex motel efficiency and lattice-trimmed pastel-color cottages furnished in reed, rattan, and wicker. One- and two-bedroom cottages have kitchens. Three cottages face the beach. Although not on the water, the small honeymoon cottage is very charming. On rare days when the wind shifts, highway noise can be distracting. Complimentary use of a double kayak is included. ✉ *MM 62.3, OS, R.R. 1, Box 424, Marathon 33050,* ☏ *305/289–1377 or 800/330–1577,* FAX *305/743–8207,* WEB *www.conchkeycottages.com. 12 units. Pool, beach. D, MC, V.*

Grassy Key

❼ *MM 60–57.*

Local lore has it that this sleepy little key was named not for its vegetation—mostly native trees and shrubs—but for an early settler with the name Grassy. It's primarily inhabited by a few families who operate small fishing camps and motels.

The original *Flipper* movie popularized the notion of dolphins interacting with humans. The film's creator, Milton Santini, also created

Close-Up

CLOSE ENCOUNTERS OF THE FLIPPER KIND

HERE IN THE FLORIDA KEYS, where Milton Santini created the original 1963 *Flipper* movie, close encounters of the Flipper kind are an everyday occurrence at a handful of facilities that allow you to commune with trained dolphins.

There are in-water and waterside programs. The former are the most sought-after and require advance reservations. All of the programs emphasize education and consist of three parts: first, you learn about dolphin physiology and behavior from a marine biologist or researcher; then you go waterside for an orientation on dos and don'ts (for example, don't talk with your hands—you might, literally, send the wrong signal); finally, you interact with the dolphins—into the water you go.

For the in-water programs, the dolphins swim around you and cuddle up next to you. If you lie on your back with your feet out, they use their snouts to push you around; or, you can grab onto a dorsal fin and hang on for an exciting ride. The in-water encounter lasts about 10 to 25 minutes, depending on the program.

On waterside-interaction programs, participants feed, shake hands, kiss, and do tricks with the dolphins from a submerged platform.The programs vary from facility to facility, but share a few rules and the entire program, from registration to departure, takes about two hours. The best time to go is when it's warm, from March through December. You spend a lot of time near or in and out the water, and even with a wetsuit on you can get cold on a chilly day.

Call ahead to get information on restrictions (there are often age or height requirements) and other relevant details. Also, be wary of programs not listed below. Some industrious types have made a business of chartering boats, chumming the waters, and then letting wild dolphins swim with you—this is very dangerous and can lead to serious injury.

Dolphin Cove. The educational part of the DolphinEncounter program takes place on a 30-minute boat ride on adjoining Florida Bay. Then it's back to the facilities lagoon for a get-acquainted session from a platform. Then you slip into the water for the program's highlight: swimming and playing with your new dolphin pals. ✉ *101900 Overseas Hwy., MM 101.9, BS, Key Largo,* ☎ *305/451–4060,* *Cost: $150.*

Dolphins Plus, Inc. Programs here emphasize education and therapy. Natural Swim begins with a one-hour briefing, then you don snorkel gear and enter the water to become totally immersed in the dolphins' world. ✉ *31 Corrine Pl., MM 99, Key Largo,* ☎ *305/451–1993 or 866/860–7946.* *Cost: $100.*

Theater of the Sea. The Dolphin Swim program at this marine park starts with a 30-minute classroom session and orientation. Then, through a variety of trained behaviors, including kisses, dorsal tows, and jumps, dolphins interact with swimmers in a 15-ft-deep salt-water lagoon. ✉ *84721 Overseas Hwy., MM 84.7, Islamorada,* ☎ *305/664–2431.* *Cost: $110.*

Dolphin Connection at Hawk's Cay Resort. Marine biologists at the Dolphin Connection inspire awareness and promote conservation through programs at this stylish mid-Keys resort. Dolphin Discovery is an in-water, non-swim program that lasts about 45 minutes and lets you kiss, touch, and feed the dolphins. ✉ *MM 61 OS, 61 Hawks Cay Blvd., Duck Key,* ☎ *888/814–9174.* *Cost: $90 resort guests/$100 non-guests.*

Dolphin Research Center. This not-for-profit organization that is home to a colony of Atlantic bottlenose dolphins and California sea lions. Dolphin Encounter is a swim-interaction program, and in Dolphin Splash you stand on a submerged platform rather than swim. ✉ *MM 59, Marathon Shores,* ☎ *305/289–1121 or 305/289–0002.* *Cost: Dolphin Encounter $125, Dolphin Splash $70.*

— Diane Marshall

the **Dolphin Research Center,** now home to a colony of dolphins and sea lions. This not-for-profit organization offers tours and several programs that allow participants to interact with dolphins in the water (Dolphin Encounter) or from a submerged platform (Dolphin Splash). Some programs have age or height restrictions and some require 30-day advance reservations. ✉ *MM 59, BS, Box 522875, Marathon Shores 33052,* ☎ *305/289–1121 general information; 305/289–0002 interactive program information,* WEB *www.dolphins.org.* 🎟 *Tours $12.50, Dolphin Splash $70, Dolphin Encounter $110.* ⏲ *Daily 9–4, walking tours daily 10, 11, 12:30, 2, and 3:30.*

OFF THE BEATEN PATH

CURRY HAMMOCK STATE PARK – This littoral park covers 260 acres of upland hammock, wetlands, and mangroves on the ocean and bay sides of U.S. Hwy 1. On the bay side, there's a trail through thick hardwoods to a rocky shoreline. The ocean side is more developed, with a sandy beach, a clean bathhouse, picnic tables, and a parking lot. Brown park signs mark the entrance. Plans for a campground and entrance fees are still undecided. Locals consider the trails that meander under canopies of arching mangroves one of the best areas for kayaking in the Keys. Manatees frequent the area, and it's a birding paradise. Information is provided by Long Key State Recreation Area. ✉ *MM 57, OS, Crawl Key,* ☎ *305/664–4815.* 🎟 *Free.* ⏲ *Daily 8–sunset.*

Dining and Lodging

$–$$ ✕ **Grassy Key Dairy Bar.** A casual island menu that's strong on seafood has earned this friendly, family-owned, 1959 restaurant a loyal following of locals and returning visitors. Despite the name, the only ice cream served is a delicious ice cream pie. The sign reads Grassy Key DB to avoid confusion. The popular broiled dolphinfish with black beans and rice and cheese sauce is recommended. There's also broiled or grilled fish with wasabi, homemade bread, and fresh-cut beef. On Tuesday night they add Mexican dishes to the menu, and in fall their OctoberFest features German foods, beers, and music. ✉ *MM 56.3 OS,* ☎ *305/743–3816. MC, V. Closed Sun.–Mon.*

$ 🏨 **Valhalla Beach Motel.** Just steps from the water, this simple motel has clean rooms with small refrigerators and efficiencies with kitchens. Both have TVs but no telephones. Guests can lounge on the beach or read in the Adirondack chairs, grill dinner on a barbecue, or paddle a canoe through mangrove trails in the neighboring state park. Rates are for two. There's a charge for additional children or adults. ✉ *MM 56.3, OS, 56243 Ocean Dr., Crawl Key 33050,* ☎ *305/289–0616. 4 rooms, 1 suite, 5 efficiencies. Beach, dock, boating. No credit cards.*

$ 🏨 **Valhalla Point.** This unpretentious Crawl Key motel with a to-die-for waterfront location changed its name three times in as many years. That's all been a product of family and politics and in no way reflects any change in the quality of the place. In the late 1990s the property was split into two resorts, Valhalla Beach Motel and Valhalla Point, with a fence dividing the property. This half has the feel of a friend's simple beach house. There's a very good beach with hammocks and chaises, a dock from which manatees are frequently sighted, picnic tables, barbecue grills, and kayaks and canoes, a nice touch since the property borders Curry Hammock State Park. Family-oriented snorkeling trips to the reefs are offered. There are no phones in rooms, but there's an outdoor phone station. ✉ *MM 56.2, OS, 56223 Ocean Dr., Crawl Key 33050,* ☎ *305/289–0614,* WEB *www.keysresort.com. 1 room, 4 efficiencies. Picnic area, beach, dock, boating. MC, V.*

Marathon

8 *MM 53–47.5.*

A few years ago Marathon become an independent municipality. Now, this commercial hub of the Middle Keys is carving out a more visible piece of the local tourist pie. Commercial fishing—still a big local industry—began here in the early 1800s. Pirates, salvagers, fishermen, spongers, and, later, farmers eked out a living, traveling by boat between islands. About half the population were blacks who stoked charcoal furnaces for a living. According to local lore, Marathon was renamed when a worker commented that it was a marathon task to rebuild the railway across the 6-mi island after a 1906 hurricane.

The railroad brought businesses and a hotel, and today Marathon is a bustling town by Keys standards. Fishing, diving, and boating are the primary attractions.

Tucked away from the highway behind a stand of trees, the **Museums and Nature Center of Crane Point Hammock**—part of a 63-acre tract that includes the last-known undisturbed thatch-palm hammock—is an undeveloped oasis of greenery. The complex comprises the **Museum of Natural History of the Florida Keys,** inside of which are a few dioramas, a shell exhibit, and displays on Keys geology, wildlife, and cultural history. Also here is the **Florida Keys Children's Museum,** which has iguanas, fish, and a replica of a 17th-century Spanish galleon and pirate dress-up room in which children can play as swashbucklers. Outside, on the 1-mi indigenous loop trail, you can visit the remnants of a Bahamian village, site of the restored **George Adderly House,** the oldest surviving example of Bahamian tabby (a cement-type material created from sand and seashells) construction outside of Key West. A new boardwalk crosses wetlands, a river, and mangroves before ending at Adderly Village. From November to Easter, docent-led tours, included in the price, are available; bring good walking shoes and bug repellent during warm weather months. ✉ *MM 50.5, BS, 5550 Overseas Hwy., Box 536, 33050,* ☎ *305/743–9100.* *$7.50.* *Mon.–Sat. 9–5, Sun. noon–5; call to arrange trail tours.*

Pleasant, shaded picnic kiosks overlook a grassy stretch and the Atlantic Ocean at **Sombrero Beach.** Separate areas allow swimmers, jet boats, and windsurfers to share the beach. There are lots of facilities, as well as a grassy park with barbecue grills, picnic kiosks, showers, rest rooms, plus a baseball diamond, a large playground, and a volleyball court. The park is accessible for travelers with disabilities and allows leashed pets. Turn left at the traffic light in Marathon and follow signs to the end. ✉ *MM 50, OS, Sombrero Rd.,* ☎ *305/289–3000.* *Free.* *Daily 7:30–sunset.*

OFF THE BEATEN PATH

PIGEON KEY – There's a lot to like about this 5 acre island under the Old Seven Mile Bridge. It's reached by walking or riding a tram across a 2.2-mi section of the old bridge. Once there, you can tour the island on your own with a brochure or join a guided tour. The tour explores the buildings that formed the early 20th-century work camp for the Overseas Railroad, which linked the mainland to Key West. Later, their uses changed as the island became a fish camp, then a park, and then government administration headquarters. Today, the focus is on Florida Keys culture, environmental education, and marine research. Exhibits in a museum and a video recall the history of the railroad, the Keys, and railroad baron Henry M. Flagler. Pick up the shuttle at the depot on Knight's Key (✉ MM 47, OS). ✉ *MM 45, OS, Box 500130, Pigeon Key 33050,* ☎ *305/289–0025 general information; 305/743–7655 eco-tour information,* WEB *www.pigeonkey.org.* *$7.50.* *Daily 9–5.*

Dining and Lodging

$$–$$$$ ★ ✕ **Barracuda Grill.** For those who think Keys food is limited to grilled dolphinfish and coconut shrimp, Barracuda Grill will be a revelation. Lance and Jan Hill present an eclectic menu that capitalizes on the local bounty—fresh fish—but is equally represented by tender, aged Angus beef; rack of lamb; and even meat loaf. Innovation is in everything but not at the expense of good, solid cooking. Thai Money Bags, a delicate pastry pouch filled with shrimp and veggies, suggests an Asian influence. Ribbiting Frog's Legs, with butter, garlic, and a touch of tomato sauce, screams South Florida. You can't miss on either. Decadent desserts include a sensationally rich key lime cheesecake. The well-thought-out wine list is heavily Californian. ✉ *MM 49.5, BS,* ☎ *305/743–3314. AE, MC, V. Closed Sun. No lunch.*

$–$$$ ✕ **Hurricane Grille.** This roadside restaurant has an attractively priced menu with generous portions of rib-sticking seafood, chicken, and steaks, as well as shellfish, which comes steamed (clams, crabs, oysters, shrimp, lobster) or raw (clams only) from the moment the doors open until the bar closes, as late as 4 AM. Nightly blues and rock bands also enliven the place. Satellite TV broadcasts sports, keeping the bar, which takes up half the building, humming. Alas, they have not yet spruced up the kitschy decor. ✉ *MM 49.5, BS, 4650 Overseas Hwy.,* ☎ *305/743–2220. AE, MC, V.*

$–$$ ✕ **Island City Fish Market and Eatery.** Nothing about this restaurant in a weathered gray building says "eat here" as you drive past on U.S. Highway 1, but business is brisk thanks to local word-of-mouth recommendations. Half the place is glass cases filled with fresh-from-the-boat seafood that you can buy to take home or order to be served at one of the few inside tables or outside picnic tables. Try the barbecue shrimp or fish of the day prepared Provençale style, sautéed with mushrooms, tomatoes, red peppers, and scallions in garlic wine sauce. For those who aren't seafood fans, there's chicken Parmesan or a chicken breast sandwich. Kids can eat hot dogs and fish and chicken fingers. They offer takeout service and nationwide overnight shipping, and will cook your catch. ✉ *MM 53, OS, 11711 Overseas Hwy.,* ☎ *305/743–9196 or 888/662–4822. AE, MC, V. Closed Tues.*

$–$$ ✕ **Key Colony Inn.** The inviting aroma of an Italian kitchen pervades this popular family-owned restaurant. The menu has well-prepared chicken, steak, pasta, and veal dishes, and the service is friendly and attentive. For lunch there are fish and steak entrées served with fries, salad, and bread. At dinner you can't miss with traditional Continental dishes like veal Oscar and New York strip or such Italian specialties as seafood Italiano, a light dish of scallops and shrimp sautéed in garlic butter over a bed of linguine with a hint of marinara sauce. ✉ *MM 54, OS, 700 W. Ocean Dr., Key Colony Beach,* ☎ *305/743–0100. AE, MC, V.*

$ ★ ✕ **7 Mile Grill.** This nearly 50-year-old, weatherworn open-air restaurant easily could serve as a movie set for a 1950s-era black-and-white movie based in the tropics. Situated at the Marathon end of the Seven Mile Bridge, it serves up friendly service that rivals the casual food at breakfast, lunch, and dinner. Favorites on the mostly seafood menu include fresh-squeezed orange juice, creamy shrimp bisque, and fresh grouper and dolphinfish grilled, broiled, or fried. Don't pass up the authentic key lime pie, which won the local paper's "Best in the Keys" award three years in a row. ✉ *MM 47, BS,* ☎ *305/743–4481. MC, V. Closed Wed., plus Thurs. mid-Apr.–mid-Nov., and at owner's discretion Aug.–Sept.*

$$–$$$ ★ **Seascape Ocean Resort.** The charming lobby filled with soothing sea colors and original artwork gives way to nine pastel-color guest rooms—three with kitchens—decorated with more original artwork, hand-painted headboards, and fresh flowers and fruit. Transforming the 5-acre

oceanfront property with a large, two-story bay-front house into an exclusive, yet unsnobbish retreat was the inspiration of painter Sara Stites and her husband, Bill, a magazine photographer. Guests can swim, paddle a kayak, or simply relax around the pool, at the beach, or under a shade tree. Continental breakfast and afternoon cocktails and hors d'oeuvres are set out for guests. Rooms are no-smoking and have no phones. ✉ *MM 50.5, OS, 1075 75th St., 33050,* ☎ *305/743–6455 or 800/332–7327,* FAX *305/743–8469,* WEB *www.floridakeys.net/seascape. 9 rooms. Pool, beach, dock. AE, MC, V.*

$–$$ **Coral Lagoon.** Private sundecks with lazy hammocks provide calming views of a deep-water canal and pretty landscaping. Cheerfully painted duplex cottages have kitchens, ceiling fans, king or twin beds, and sofa beds. Extras not usually available at this rate include videocassette players ($1 tape rental), wall safes, hair dryers, and morning coffee. To ensure that your stay is fun, the inn provides tennis rackets, fishing equipment, dockage, and barbecues. For a fee you can use a private beach club, rent bikes, charter a fishing trip, and go on scuba and snorkel trips arranged through the Diving Site, a dive shop that also offers certification. ✉ *MM 53.5, OS, 12399 Overseas Hwy., 33050,* ☎ *305/289–0121,* FAX *305/289–0195,* WEB *www.corallagoonresort.com, 18 units. Pool, tennis court, dive shop, dock, library. AE, D, MC, V.*

Outdoor Activities and Sports

BIKING

Tooling around on two wheels is a good way to see Marathon. There are paved paths along Aviation Boulevard on the bay side of Marathon Airport, the four-lane section of the Overseas Highway through Marathon, Sadowski Causeway to Key Colony Beach, Sombrero Beach Road to the beach, and the roads on Boot Key (across a bridge on 20th Street, OS). There's easy cycling on a 1-mi off-road path that connects to the 2 mi of the Old Seven Mile Bridge that go to Pigeon Key.

Equipment Locker Sport & Cycle (✉ MM 53, BS, ☎ 305/289–1670) rents cruisers for $10 per day, $50 per week, and mountain bikes for adults and children. It's open weekdays 9 to 6.

BOATING

Fish 'n' Fun (✉ MM 53.5, OS, ☎ 305/743–2275), next to the Boat House Marina, lets you get out on the water on 18- to 25-ft boats starting at $95 for a half day, $135–$205 for a full day. You also can pick up bait, tackle, licenses, and snorkel gear.

FISHING

Morning and afternoon, you can fish for dolphinfish, grouper, and other deep-sea game aboard the 75-ft ***Marathon Lady*** and the 65-ft *Marathon Lady III* (✉ MM 53.5, OS, at 117th St., 33050, ☎ 305/743–5580), two party boats that depart on half-day ($27 or $25) excursions from the Vaca Cut Bridge, north of Marathon. Captain Jim Purcell, a deep-sea specialist for ESPN's *The Outdoorsman,* provides one of the best values in fishing in the Keys. His **Sea Dog Charters** (✉ MM 47.5, BS, ☎ 305/743–8255), next to the 7 Mile Grill, give personalized half- and full-day offshore, reef and wreck, tarpon, and backcountry fishing trips as well as combination fishing and snorkeling trips on the 32-ft *Bad Dog* for up to six people. The cost is $59.99 per person for a half day, regardless of whether your group fills the boat, and includes bait, light tackle, licensing, ice, and coolers. If you prefer an all-day private charter on a 37-ft boat, he offers those too, for $550 to $600.

GOLF

Key Colony Golf & Tennis (✉ MM 53.5, OS, 8th St., Key Colony Beach, ☎ 305/289–1533), a nine-hole course near Marathon, charges

$7.50 for the course, $2 per person for club rental, and $1 for a pull cart. There are no tee times and there's no rush. Play from 7:30 to dusk. A little golf shop meets basic golf needs. They have two lighted tennis courts open from 7:30 to 10. Rates are $4 for singles, $6 for doubles.

SCUBA DIVING AND SNORKELING

There's more to diving in the Keys than beautiful reefs. So **Hall's Diving Center and Career Institute** (✉ MM 48.5, BS, 1994 Overseas Hwy., 33050, ☎ 305/743–5929 or 800/331–4255), next to Faro Blanco Resort, runs two trips a day to Looe Key, a few other reefs, and several wrecks, including *Thunderbolt,* and the *Adolphus Busch.*

En Route The **Seven Mile Bridge** is one of the most-photographed images in the Keys. Actually measuring 6.79 mi long, it bridges the Middle and Lower keys and is believed to be the world's longest segmental bridge. It has 39 expansion joints separating its cement sections. Each April, runners gather in Marathon for the annual Seven Mile Bridge Run. The expanse running parallel to it is what remains of the **Old Seven Mile Bridge,** an engineering marvel in its day that's now on the National Register of Historic Places. It rested on a record 546 concrete piers. No cars are allowed on the bridge today, but a 2.2-mi segment is open for biking, walking, and rollerblading with a terminus at historic Pigeon Key.

THE LOWER KEYS

In truth, the Lower Keys include Key West, but since it's covered in its own section and is as different from the rest of the Lower Keys as peanut butter is from jelly, this section comprises just the limestone keys between MM 37 and MM 9. From Bahia Honda Key south, islands are clustered, smaller, and more numerous, a result of ancient tidal waters flowing between the Florida Straits and the gulf. Here you're likely to see more birds and mangroves than other tourists, and more refuges, beaches, and campgrounds than museums, restaurants, and hotels.

The islands are made up of two types of limestone, both more dense than the highly permeable Key Largo limestone of the Upper Keys. As a result, freshwater forms pools rather than percolating, creating watering holes that support Key deer, alligators, fish, snakes, Lower Keys rabbits, raccoons, migratory ducks, Key cotton and silver rice rats, pines, saw palmettos, silver palms, grasses, and ferns. (Many of these animals and plants can be seen in the National Key Deer Refuge on Big Pine Key.)

Nature was generous with her beauty in the Lower Keys. They're home to both Looe Key Reef, arguably the Keys' most beautiful coral reef tract, and Bahia Honda State Park, considered one of the best beaches in the world for its fine sand dunes, clear warm waters, and panoramic vista of bridges, hammocks, and azure sky and sea.

Bahia Honda Key

❾ *MM 38–36.*

★ **Bahia Honda State Park.** This 524-acre sun-soaked, state-owned park sprawls across both sides of the highway, giving it beautiful sandy beaches—the best in the Keys—on both the Atlantic Ocean and the Gulf of Mexico. Although swimming, kayaking, fishing, and boating are the main reasons to come, there are many other activities, including walks on the Silver Palm Trail, where you can see rare West Indian plants and several species found nowhere else in the Keys, and seasonal ranger-led nature programs, including illustrated talks on the history of the Overseas Railroad and birding outings. There are rental cabins, a campground, a snack bar, a marina, and a concessioner for snorkeling. You can get a panoramic view of the island from what's left of the railroad—the Bahia Honda Bridge. ✉ *MM 37, OS, 36850 Overseas Hwy., 33043,* ☎ *305/872–2353,* WEB *www.dep.state.fl.us/parks.* *$2 for 1 person, $4 per vehicle for 2–8 people plus 50¢ per person county surcharge; $2 per vehicle an hr before closing.* ⏲ *Daily 8–sunset.*

Lodging

$$ **Bahia Honda State Park.** You usually have to pay big bucks for the caliber of water views afforded from the cabins here. Each is completely furnished (although there's no television, radio, or phone); has two bedrooms, full kitchen, and bath; and sleeps six. The park also has 80 popular campsites, suitable for motor homes and tents. Cabins and campsites are very popular, so reserve up to 11 months before your planned visit. ✉ *MM 37, OS, 36850 Overseas Hwy., 33043,* ☎ *305/872–2353,* WEB *www.dep.state.fl.us/parks. 3 duplex cabins. Picnic area, beach, boating, fishing. AE, D, MC, V.*

Outdoor Activities and Sports

Bahia Honda Dive Shop (✉ MM 37, OS, ☎ 305/872–3210), the concessionaire at Bahia Honda State Park, manages a 19-slip marina, rents wet suits, snorkel equipment, and corrective masks, and operates twice-a-day offshore-reef snorkel trips ($26 plus $5 for equipment) that run almost three hours (with 90 minutes on the reef). Park visitors looking for other fun can rent kayaks ($10 per hour single, $18 double), bicycles, fishing rods, and beach chairs.

Big Pine Key

10 *MM 32–30.*

In the Florida Keys, more than 20 animals and plants are endangered or threatened. Among them is the Key deer, which stands about 30 inches at the shoulders and is a subspecies of the Virginia white-tailed deer. The 8,354-acre **National Key Deer Refuge** was established in 1957 to protect the dwindling population of Key deer. Following the first comprehensive estimate since 1969, reports show that under the refuge's aegis the deer have made a comeback, more than doubling their numbers to around 800. These deer once ranged throughout the Lower and Middle keys, but hunting, habitat destruction, and a growing human population had caused their numbers to decline to fewer than 50. The best place to see Key deer in the refuge is at the end of Key Deer Boulevard (Route 940), off U.S. 1, and on No Name Key, a sparsely populated island just east of Big Pine Key. Deer may turn up along the road at any time of day, so drive slowly. Feeding them is against the law. The **Blue Hole,** a quarry left over from railroad days, is the largest body of freshwater in the Keys. From the observation platform and nearby walking trail, you might see alligators, birds, turtles, Key deer, and other wildlife. There are two well-marked trails: the Jack Watson Nature Trail (⅔ mi), named after an environmentalist and the refuge's first warden; and the Fred Mannillo Nature Trail, one of the most wheelchair accessible places to see an unspoiled pine rockland forest. The visitor center has exhibits on Keys biology and ecology. The refuge also provides information on the Key West National Wildlife Refuge and the Great White Heron National Wildlife Refuge. Both, accessible only by water, are popular with kayak outfitters. ✉ *Visitor Center/Headquarters, Big Pine Shopping Center, MM 30.5, BS,* ☎ *305/872–0774.* *Free.* ⏲ *Daily sunrise–sunset; headquarters weekdays 8–5.*

Dining and Lodging

$ ✕ **No Name Pub.** Those who don't like change will be delighted by this ramshackle American-casual establishment in existence since 1936.

Locals come for the cold beer, excellent pizza, and sometimes questionable companionship. The owners have conceded to the times by introducing a full menu, adding "city food" like pasta and chicken wings. (Real Keys men don't eat chicken wings.) The lighting is poor, the furnishings are rough, and the jukebox doesn't play Ricky Martin. It's hard to find but worth the search if you want to experience the Keys as old-timers say they once were; turn north at Big Pine Key traffic light, right at the fork, left at the four-way stop, and then over a humpback bridge. It's on the left, before the No Name Bridge. ✉ *MM 30, BS, N. Watson Blvd.,* ☎ *305/872–9115. D, MC, V.*

$$–$$$ **Deer Run.** You don't have to go to a park or a preserve to enjoy Florida wildlife. At this 2-acre beachfront B&B, the wildlife comes to you. A herd of Key deer regularly forages along the beach a few feet from the back door. Innkeeper Sue Abbott also keeps a variety of cats and caged tropical birds. She is caring and informed, well settled and hospitable. Two large oceanfront rooms are furnished with whitewashed wicker and king-size beds. An upstairs unit looks out on the sea through trees. Guests have use of a living room, a 52-ft veranda cooled by paddle fans, hammocks, a large barbecue grill, a hot tub on a deck overlooking the ocean, and water toys. Smoking and children are prohibited. ✉ *MM 33, OS, 1985 Long Beach Dr., Box 430431, 33043,* ☎ *305/872–2015,* FAX *305/872–2842,* WEB *www.floridakeys.net/deer. 3 rooms. Hot tub, beach, bicycles. No credit cards.*

$$ ★ **The Barnacle.** With very little air pollution in the area, the star-flecked moonlit nights seen from this B&B's atrium are as romantic as the sunny days spent lazing on the beach. Owners Tim and Jane Marquis offer two second-floor rooms in the main house; one in a cottage with a kitchen; another, below the house, that opens to the beach; and a smaller fifth room with skylights on the roof. Guest rooms are large. Full breakfast is included, as is use of paddleboats and kayaks. As former owners of a diving business, Tim and Jane offer personalized snorkel and dive charters and certifications, as well as fishing excursions. ✉ *MM 33, OS, 1557 Long Beach Dr., 33043,* ☎ *305/872–3298 or 800/465–9100,* FAX *305/872–3863,* WEB *www.thebarnacle.net. 5 rooms. Hot tub, beach, dock, boating, bicycles. D, MC, V.*

$$ ★ **Casa Grande.** Beautifully located on a white-sand beach abutting a rocky shoreline, this adults-only three-guest-room B&B affords a gracious island stay under the proprietorship of Kathleen Threlkeld. Her warm personality pervades the Mediterranean-style house with a massive Spanish door and mainly contemporary furnishings. There are a screened porch and rich Berber carpeting in the spacious guest rooms. Rooms have small refrigerators, air-conditioning, and high open-beam ceilings with paddle fans. A screened, second-story waterfront atrium provides you the opportunity to gaze out across the soothing sea. Then on cool nights, you can cozy up to the sitting-room fireplace or watch TV. ✉ *MM 33, OS, 1619 Long Beach Dr., Box 430378, 33043,* ☎ *305/872–2878,* WEB *www.floridakeys.net/casagrande. 3 rooms. Hot tub, beach, dock, boating, bicycles. No credit cards.*

$–$$ ★ **Big Pine Key Fishing Lodge.** It's a family affair at this 30-year-old combination lodge and campground. Rooms and sites ($29–$39 per site, including satellite TV hookup) are attractively priced and have tile floors, wicker furniture, doors that allow sea breezes to blow through, queen-size beds, a second-bedroom loft, vaulted ceilings, and minikitchens. A skywalk joins them with a pool and deck. The lodge is slowly replacing its older units—either spic-and-span mobile homes or efficiencies—with more modern facilities. Immaculately clean tile lines the spacious bathhouse for campers. Separate game and recreation rooms house TVs, organized family-oriented activities, and other amusements, and there is dockage along a 735-ft canal. A three-day minimum is required. No dogs are allowed. ✉ *MM 33, OS, Box 430513, 33043,* ☎ *305/872–2351,* FAX *305/872–3868. 16 rooms, 158 campsites, 102 with full hookups, 56 without hookups. Pool, Ping-Pong, shuffleboard, dock, billiards, recreation room, video games. D, MC, V.*

Outdoor Activities and Sports

BIKING

A good 10 mi of paved and unpaved roads run from MM 30.3, BS, along Wilder Road, across the bridge to No Name Key, and along Key Deer Boulevard into the National Key Deer Refuge. You might see some Key deer. Stay off the trails that lead into wetlands, where fat tires can do damage.

Marty Baird, owner of **Big Pine Bicycle Center** (✉ MM 30.9, BS, ☎ 305/872–0130), is an avid rider and enjoys sharing his knowledge of great places to ride. He's also skilled in repairing and selecting the right bike for customers to rent or purchase. His old-fashioned single-speed, fat-tire cruisers for adults rent for $6 per half day, $9 for a full day, and $34 a week, second week $17; children for $5, $7, $26, and $13. Helmets, baskets, and locks are included. Join him at the shop Sunday mornings at 8 for a free off-road fun ride.

FISHING

You can fish with pros year-round in air-conditioned comfort with **Strike Zone Charters** (✉ MM 29.6, BS, 29675 Overseas Hwy., 33043, ☎ 305/872–9863 or 800/654–9560). Charter rates are $450 for a half day, $590 for a full day.

Little Torch Key

⑪ *MM 28–29.*

With a few exceptions, this key and its neighbor islands are more jumping-off points for divers headed for Looe Key Reef, a few miles offshore, than destinations themselves.

NEED A BREAK? The intoxicating aroma of rich, roasting coffee beans at **Baby's Coffee** (MM 15, OS, Saddlebunch Keys, ☎ 305/744–9866 or 800/523–2326) arrests you at the door of "the Southernmost Coffee Roaster." Buy it by the pound or by the cup along with fresh-baked goods. While sipping your warm joe, browse through the art gallery, Burning Bread at Baby's Coffee, which spotlights the work of local talented artists.

The undeveloped backcountry is at your door, making this an ideal location for fishing and kayaking, too. Nearby **Ramrod Key,** which also caters to divers bound for Looe Key, derives its name from a ship that wrecked on nearby reefs in the early 1800s.

Dining and Lodging

$–$$ ✕ **Montes Restaurant & Fish Market.** In this gray wood-frame building with screened sides, a canvas roof, wood-plank floors, a tropical mural, and picnic tables, they serve a traditional Keys-style fish sandwich, either grilled dolphinfish or fried grouper depending on what's fresh, along with a flavorful variation stuffed with crabmeat. Casually clad, experienced waitresses provide good service. The menu also has crabs and shrimp that are steamed, broiled, stuffed, or fried. ✉ *MM 25, BS, Summerland Key,* ☎ *305/745–3731. No credit cards.*

$$$$ ★ 🏨 **Little Palm Island.** *Haute tropical* best describes this luxury retreat on a 5-acre palm-fringed island 3 mi offshore. The decor of the 28 oceanfront one-bedroom, thatch-roof bungalow suites is laid-back luxe, with Mexican-tile baths, Jacuzzis, mosquito netting–draped king beds, and wicker and rattan furniture. Other comforts include an indoor and outdoor shower, private veranda, ceiling fans, a separate living room, minisafe, and robes and slippers. Two Island Grand Suites are twice the size of the others and offer his and her bathrooms, an outdoor hot tub, and uncompromising ocean views. There are no in-room phones or TVs, and cellular phones are *verboten* in public areas. Indulge in a fountain-fed pool, an indoor or outdoor massage, or some terrific snorkeling, kayaking, windsurfing, sailing, diving, and fishing. Chef Adam Votaw has recrafted the resort's cuisine with contemporary menus that reflect a mix of Caribbean, French, and Asian tastes. ✉ *MM 28.5, OS, 28500 Overseas Hwy., 33042,* ☎ *305/872–2524 or 800/343–8567,* FAX *305/872–4843,* WEB *www.littlepalmisland.com. 30 suites. Restaurant, bar, in-room data ports, minibars, pool, hair salon, massage, sauna, exercise room, beach, dive shop, dock, snorkeling, windsurfing, boating, marina, fishing, shops, library, concierge, airport shuttle. AE, D, DC, MC, V.*

$ **Parmer's Place.** This is the perfect spot for a family getaway in the Lower Keys in three respects. Guests stay in family-style waterfront cottages with a deck or balcony, cable TV, a half or full kitchen, and no telephones. It's spread out on 5 landscaped acres, so the kids have room to play. And the price is right. Lots of families agree. Many are repeat guests and recommend it. The proprietors treat them all like family, right down to sending out nearly 12,000 holiday cards every December. For couples, the motel rooms are comfortable for two people and the best buy. There are activities such as swimming, kayaking, and bicycling. ✉ *MM 29, BS, 565 Barry Ave., 33042,* ☎ *305/872–2157,* FAX *305/872–2014,* WEB *www.parmersplace.com. 43 units, 18 rooms, 12 efficiencies, 13 apartments. Pool, dock, boating, bicycles. AE, D, MC, V. CP.*

Outdoor Activities and Sports

FISHING

The only thing grouchy about Captain Mark André of **The Grouch Charters** (✉ Summerland Key Cove Marina, MM 24.5, OS, Summerland Key, ☎ 305/745–1172 or 305/304–0039) is his original boat's name, derived from his father's nickname. This knowledgeable captain takes up to six passengers on offshore fishing trips ($450 for a half day, $550 for a full day). He provides oceanfront vacation rentals for $725–$850 a week and can package accommodations, fishing, snorkeling, and sightseeing for better deals.

SCUBA DIVING AND SNORKELING

In 1744, the HMS *Looe,* a British warship, ran aground and sank on one of the most beautiful and diverse coral reefs in the Keys. Today, **Looe Key Reef** owes its name to the ill-fated ship. The 5.3-square-nautical-mi reef, part of the **Florida Keys National Marine Sanctuary** (✉ MM 27.5, OS, 216 Ann St., Key West 33040, ☎ 305/292–0311), has stands of elk-horn coral on its eastern margin, purple sea fans, and abundant sponges and sea urchins. On its seaward side, it drops almost vertically 50–90 ft. Snorkelers and divers will find the sanctuary a quiet place to observe reef life, except in July, when the annual Underwater Music Festival pays homage to Looe Key's beauty and promotes reef awareness with six hours of music broadcast via underwater speakers. Dive shops and private charters transport hundreds of divers to hear the spectacle, which includes Caribbean, classical, jazz, new age, and, of course, Jimmy Buffett.

Rather than the customary morning and afternoon two-tank, two-location trips offered by most dive shops, **Looe Key Dive Center** (✉ MM 27.5, OS, Box 509, Ramrod Key 33042, ☎ 305/872–2215 ext. 2 or 800/942–5397), the closest dive shop to Looe Key Reef, runs a single three-tank, three-location dive from 10 AM to 3 PM. The maximum depth is 30 ft, so snorkelers and divers go on the same boat. On Saturday and Wednesday, they run a 3/3 dive on wrecks in the area. It's part of the full-service Looe Key Reef Resort, which, not surprisingly, caters to divers. The dive boat, a 45-ft Corinthian catamaran, is docked outside the hotel, whose guests have free use of tanks, weights, and snorkeling equipment. **Strike Zone Charters** (✉ MM 29.6, BS, 29675 Overseas Hwy., Big Pine Key 33043, ☎ 305/872–9863 or 800/654–9560) offers dive trips to two sites on Looe Key, resort courses, and various certifications. The outfit uses glass-bottom boats, so nondivers can experience the reef, too.

En Route The huge object that looks like a white whale floating over Cudjoe Key (✉ MM 23–21) is not a figment of your imagination. It's Fat Albert, a radar balloon that monitors local air and water traffic.

KEY WEST

MM 4–0.

Situated 150 mi from Miami and just 90 mi from Havana, this tropical island city has always maintained a strong sense of detachment, even after it was connected to the rest of the United States—by the railroad in 1912 and by the Overseas Highway in 1938.

The U.S. government acquired Key West from Spain in 1821 along with the rest of Florida. The Spanish had named the island Cayo Hueso (Bone Key) after the Native American skeletons they found on its shores. In 1823 Uncle Sam sent Commodore David S. Porter to chase pirates away.

For three decades, the primary industry in Key West was wrecking—rescuing people and salvaging cargo from ships that foundered on the nearby reefs. According to some reports, when pickings were lean, the wreckers hung out lights to lure ships aground. Their business declined after 1849, when the federal government began building lighthouses.

In 1845 the army started construction of Fort Taylor, which held Key West for the Union during the Civil War. After the war, an influx of Cuban dissidents unhappy with Spain's rule brought the cigar industry here. Fishing, shrimping, and sponge-gathering became important industries, and a pineapple-canning factory opened. Major military installations were established during the Spanish-American War and World War I. Through much of the 19th century and into the second decade of the 20th, Key West was Florida's wealthiest city in per-capita terms.

In 1929 the local economy began to unravel. Modern ships no longer needed to provision in Key West, cigar making moved to Tampa, Hawaii dominated the pineapple industry, and the sponges succumbed to a blight. Then the Depression hit, and the military moved out. By 1934 half the population was on relief. The city defaulted on its bond payments, and the Federal Emergency Relief Administration took over the city and county governments.

By promoting Key West as a tourist destination, federal officials attracted 40,000 visitors during the 1934–35 winter season, but when the 1935 Labor Day hurricane struck the Middle Keys, it wiped out the railroad and the tourist trade.

An important naval center during World War II and the Korean conflict, the island remains a strategic listening post on the doorstep of Fidel Castro's Cuba. It was during the 1960s that the fringes of society began moving here and in the mid-'70s that gay guest houses began opening in rapid succession.

In April 1982 the U.S. Border Patrol threw a roadblock across the Overseas Highway just south of Florida City to catch drug runners and illegal aliens. Traffic backed up for miles as Border Patrol agents searched vehicles and demanded that the occupants prove U.S. citizenship. City officials in Key West, outraged at being treated like foreigners by the federal government, staged a mock secession and formed their own "nation," the so-called Conch Republic. They hoisted a flag and distributed mock border passes, visas, and Conch currency. The embarrassed Border Patrol dismantled its roadblock, and now an annual festival recalls the secessionists' victory.

Key West reflects a diverse population: native "Conchs" (white Key Westers, many of whom trace their ancestry to the Bahamas), freshwater Conchs (longtime residents who migrated from somewhere else years ago), gays (who now make up at least 20% of Key West's citizenry), black Bahamians (descendants of those who worked the railroads and burned charcoal), Hispanics (primarily Cuban immigrants), recent refugees from the urban sprawl of mainland Florida, navy and air force personnel, and an assortment of vagabonds, drifters, and dropouts in search of refuge.

Although the rest of the Keys are more oriented to nature and the outdoors, Key West has more of a city feel. Few open spaces remain, as promoters continue to foster fine restaurants, galleries, shops, and museums to interpret the city's intriguing past. As a tourist destination, Key West has a lot to sell—an average temperature of 79°F, quaint 19th-century architecture, and a laid-back lifestyle. There's also a growing calendar of festivals and artistic and cultural events—including the Conch Republic Celebration in April and a Halloween Fantasy Fest. Few cities of its size—a mere 2 mi by 4 mi—offer the joie de vivre of this one.

Yet, as elsewhere, when preservation has successfully revived once-tired towns, next have come those unmindful of style and eager for a buck. Duval Street is becoming showbiz—an open-air mall of T-shirt shops and tour shills. Mass marketers directing the town's tourism have attracted cruise ships, which dwarf the town's skyline, and Duval Street floods with day-trippers who gawk at the earringed hippies with dogs in their bike baskets and the otherwise oddball lot of locals.

Old Town

The heart of Key West, this historic area runs from White Street west to the waterfront. Beginning in 1822, wharves, warehouses, chandleries, ship-repair facilities, and eventually in 1891 the U.S. Custom House sprang up around the deep harbor to accommodate the navy's large ships and other sailing vessels. Wealthy wreckers, merchants, and sea captains built lavish houses near the bustling waterfront. A remarkable number of these fine Victorian and pre-Victorian structures have been restored to their original grandeur and now serve as homes, guest houses, and museums. These, along with the dwellings of famous writers, artists, and politicians who've come to Key West over the past 175 years, are among the area's approximately 3,000 historic structures. Old Town also has the city's finest restaurants and hotels, lively street life, and popular nightspots.

A Good Tour

To cover a lot of sights, take the Old Town Trolley, which lets you get off and reboard a later trolley, or the Conch Tour Train. Old Town is also very manageable on foot, bicycle, or moped, but be warned the tour below covers a lot of ground. You'll want either to pick and choose from it or break it into two days. Or pick up a copy of one of several self-guided tours on the area.

Start on Whitehead Street at the **Hemingway House** ⑫, the author's former home, and then cross the street and climb to the top of the **Lighthouse Museum** ⑬ for a spectacular view. Exit through the museum's parking lot and cross Truman Avenue to the **Lofton B. Sands African-Bahamian Museum** ⑭ to learn about nearly two centuries of black history in Key West. Return to Whitehead Street and follow it north to Angela Street, then turn right. At Margaret Street, the **City Cemetery** ⑮ has above-ground vaults and unusual headstone inscriptions. Head north on Margaret to Southard Street, turn left, then right onto Simonton Street. Halfway up the block, Free School Lane is occupied by **Nancy Forrester's Secret Garden** ⑯. After touring this tropical haven, return west on Southard to Duval Street and turn right, where you can view the lovely tiles and woodwork in the **San Carlos Institute** ⑰. Return again to Southard Street, turn right, and follow it through Truman Annex to **Ft. Zachary Taylor State Historic Site** ⑱; after viewing the fort, you can take a dip at the beach.

Go back to Simonton Street and walk north, then turn left on Caroline Street, where you can climb to the widow's walk on top of **Curry Mansion** ⑲. A left on Duval Street puts you in front of the **Duval Street Wreckers Museum** ⑳, Key West's oldest house. Continue west into Truman Annex to see the **Harry S Truman Little White House Museum** ㉑, President Truman's vacation residence. Return east on Caroline and turn left on Whitehead to visit the **Audubon House and Gardens** ㉒, honoring the artist-naturalist. Follow Whitehead north to Greene Street and turn left to see the salvaged sea treasures of the **Mel Fisher Maritime Heritage Society Museum** ㉓. At Whitehead's north end are the **Key West Aquarium** ㉔ and the **Key West Museum of Art and History** ㉕, the former historic U.S. Custom House.

By late afternoon you should be ready to cool off with a dip or catch a few rays at the beach. (Heed signs about the water's condition.) From the aquarium, head east two blocks to the end of Simonton Street, where you'll find the appropriately named **Simonton Street Beach** ㉖. On the Atlantic side of Old Town is **South Beach** ㉗, named for its location at the southern end of Duval Street. If you've brought your pet, stroll a few blocks east to **Dog Beach** ㉘, at the corner of Vernon and Waddell streets. A little farther east is **Higgs Beach** ㉙, on Atlantic Boulevard between White and Reynolds streets. As the sun starts to sink, return to the north end of Old Town and follow the crowds to Mallory Square, behind the aquarium, to watch Key West's nightly sunset spectacle. For dinner, head east on Caroline Street to **Historic Seaport at Key West Bight** ㉚ (formerly known simply as Key West Bight), a renovated area where there are numerous restaurants and bars.

TIMING

Allow two full days to see all the Old Town museums and homes, especially with a little shopping thrown in. For a narrated trip on the tour train or trolley, budget 1½ hours to ride the loop without getting off, an entire day if you plan to get off and on at some of the sights and restaurants.

Sights to See

㉒ **Audubon House and Gardens.** If you've ever seen an engraving by ornithologist John James Audubon, you'll understand why his name is synonymous with birds. You can see his work in this three-story house, which was built in the 1840s for Captain John Geiger, but now commemorates Audubon's 1832 stop in Key West while he was traveling

Key West

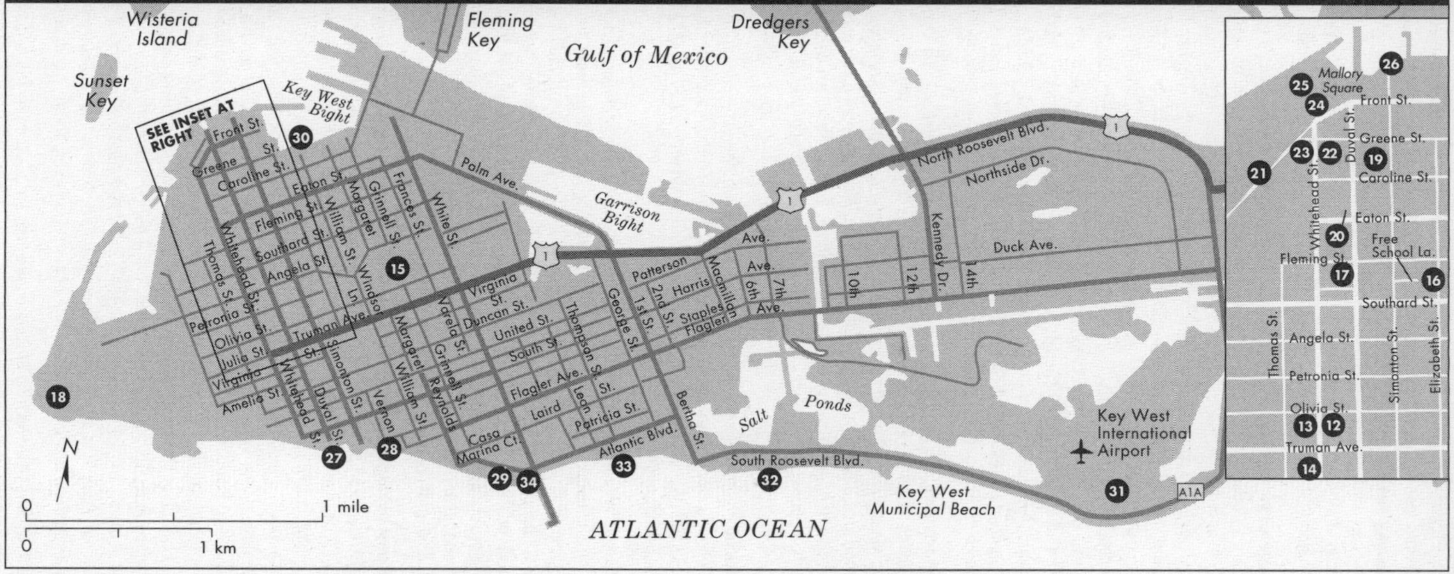

Audubon House and Gardens 22
C.B. Harvey Rest Beach 33
City Cemetery 15
Curry Mansion 19
Dog Beach 28
Duval Street Wreckers Museum 20
East Martello Tower 31
Ft. Zachary Taylor State Historic Site 18
Harry S Truman Little White House Museum 21
Hemingway House 12
Higgs Beach 29
Historic Seaport at Key West Bight 30
Key West Aquarium 24
Key West Museum of Art & History 25
Lighthouse Museum 13
Lofton Sands House 14
Mel Fisher Maritime Heritage Society Museum 23
Nancy Forrester's Secret Garden 16
San Carlos Institute 17
Simonton Street Beach 26
Smathers Beach . . .32
South Beach 27
West Martello Tower 34

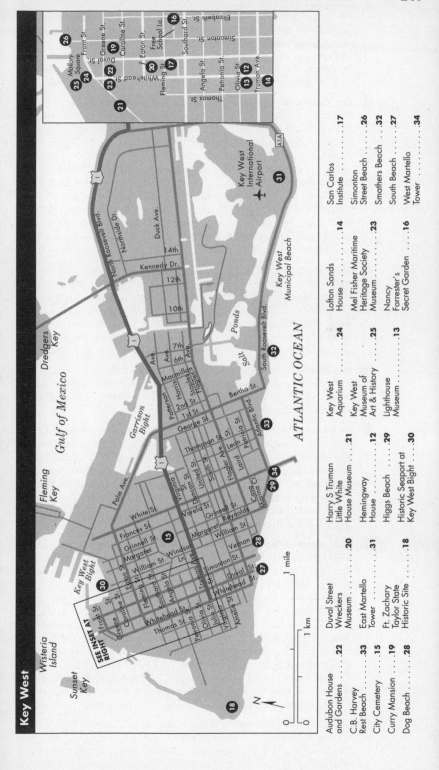

through Florida to study birds. Several rooms of period antiques and a children's room are also of interest. Admission includes an audiotape (in English, French, German, or Spanish) for the self-guided tour of the house and tropical gardens, complemented by an informational booklet and signs that identify the rare indigenous plants and trees. ⊠ *205 Whitehead St.,* ☎ *305/294–2116.* 🎫 *$8.50.* ⏲ *Daily 9:30–5.*

★ ⑮ **City Cemetery.** You can learn almost as much about a town's history through its cemetery as through its historic houses. Key West's celebrated 20-acre burial place is no exception. Among the interesting plots are a memorial to the sailors killed in the sinking of the battleship U.S.S. *Maine,* carved angels and lambs marking graves of children, and grand above-ground crypts. There are separate plots for Catholics, Jews, and martyrs of Cuba. Although you can walk around the cemetery on your own, the best way to take it in is on a 60-minute tour given by the staff and volunteers of the Historic Florida Keys Foundation. Tours leave from the main gate, and reservations are requested. ⊠ *Margaret and Angela Sts.,* ☎ *305/292–6718.* 🎫 *$10.* ⏲ *Sunrise–6, tours Tues. and Thurs. 9:30; call for additional times.*

⑲ **Curry Mansion.** See the opulence enjoyed by Key West's 19th-century millionaires in this well-preserved 22-room house. It was begun by William Curry, a ship salvager and Key West's first millionaire, and completed in 1899 by his son, Milton Curry. The owners have restored most of the house and turned it into a plush B&B. Take an unhurried self-guided tour; a brochure describes the home's history and contents. ⊠ *511 Caroline St.,* ☎ *305/294–5349.* 🎫 *$5.* ⏲ *Daily 10–5.*

㉘ **Dog Beach.** Next to Louie's Backyard, this small beach—the only one in Key West where dogs are allowed—has a shore that's a mix of sand and rocks. ⊠ *Vernon and Waddell Sts.,* ☎ *no phone.* 🎫 *Free.* ⏲ *Daily sunrise–sunset.*

⑳ **Duval Street Wreckers Museum.** Most of Key West's early wealthy residents made their fortunes from the sea. Among them was Francis Watlington, a sea captain and wrecker, who in 1829 built this house, alleged to be the oldest house in South Florida. Six rooms are open, furnished with 18th- and 19th-century antiques and providing exhibits on the island's wrecking industry of the 1800s, which made Key West one of the most affluent towns in the country. ⊠ *322 Duval St.,* ☎ *305/294–9502.* 🎫 *$5.* ⏲ *Daily 10–4.*

★ ⑱ **Ft. Zachary Taylor State Historic Site.** Construction of the fort began in 1845, and in 1861, even though Florida seceded from the Union during the Civil War, Yankee forces used the fort as a base to block Confederate shipping (more than 1,500 Confederate vessels were detained in Key West's harbor). The fort, finally completed in 1866, was also used in the Spanish-American War. Visitors can take a 30-minute tour of this National Historic Landmark. In February, a weekend celebration called Civil War Days includes costumed reenactments and demonstrations. Its uncrowded beach is the best in Key West. There is an adjoining picnic area with barbecue grills and shade trees. ⊠ *End of Southard St., through Truman Annex,* ☎ *305/292–6713.* 🎫 *$2.50 per person for first 2 people in vehicle plus 50¢ each additional up to $8, then $1 each additional; $1.50 per pedestrian or bicyclist.* ⏲ *Daily 8–sunset, tours noon and 2.*

㉑ **Harry S Truman Little White House Museum.** In a letter to his wife during one of his visits, President Harry S Truman wrote, "Dear Bess, you should see the house. The place is all redecorated, new furniture and everything." If he visited today, he'd write something similar. There are a photographic review of visiting dignitaries and permanent audiovisual and artifact exhibits on the Florida Keys as a presidential retreat, starting with Ulysses Grant in 1880 and ending with George Bush in the 1990s. Located on the grounds of **Truman Annex,** a 103-acre former military parade grounds and barracks, the home served as a winter White House for Presidents Truman, Eisenhower, and Kennedy. The two-bedroom Presidential Suite with a veranda and sundeck is available for guest stays. ✉ *111 Front St.,* ☎ *305/294–9911.* 🎫 *$8.* ⏲ *Daily 9–5, grounds 8–sunset.*

★ ⓬ **Hemingway House.** Infuriated that the local visitor bureau had added his home to a tourist brochure, Ernest Hemingway built the surrounding tall brick wall in 1935. Four years earlier he had moved in with his wife, Pauline, and two sons. While living here, he wrote about 70% of his life's work, including *For Whom the Bell Tolls.* It is now a museum dedicated to the novelist's life and work. The museum staff gives guided tours rich with anecdotes about Hemingway and his family and feeds the feline descendants of Hemingway's cats. Tours begin every 10 minutes and take 25–30 minutes; then you're free to explore on your own. ✉ *907 Whitehead St.,* ☎ *305/294–1575,* WEB *www.hemingwayhome.com.* 🎫 *$8.* ⏲ *Daily 9–5.*

㉙ **Higgs Beach.** This Monroe County park is a popular sunbathing spot. A nearby grove of Australian pines provides shade, and the West Martello Tower provides shelter should a storm suddenly sweep in. ✉ *Atlantic Blvd. between White and Reynolds Sts.,* ☎ *no phone.* 🎫 *Free.* ⏲ *Daily 7 AM–11 PM.*

㉚ **Historic Seaport at Key West Bight.** What used to be a funky—in some places even seedy—part of town, is now an 8.5-acre historic restoration project of 100 businesses, including waterfront restaurants, open-air people- and dog-friendly bars, museums, clothing stores, bait shops, docks, a marina, a wedding chapel, the Waterfront Market, the Key West Rowing Club, and dive shops. It's all linked by the 2-mi waterfront Harborwalk, which runs between Front and Grinnell streets, passing big ships, schooners, sunset cruises, fishing charters, and glass-bottom boats. Additional construction continues on outlying projects.

㉔ **Key West Aquarium.** Explore the fascinating underwater realm of the Keys without getting wet at this kid-friendly aquarium. Hundreds of brightly colored tropical fish and sea creatures live here. A touch tank enables you to handle starfish, sea cucumbers, horseshoe and hermit crabs, even horse and queen conchs—living totems of the Conch Republic. Built in 1934 by the Works Progress Administration as the world's first open-air aquarium, most of the building has been enclosed for all-weather viewing. Guided tours include shark feedings. ✉ *1 Whitehead St.,* ☎ *305/296–2051.* 🎫 *$8.* ⏲ *Daily 10–6, tours at 11, 1, 3, and 4:30.*

㉕ **Key West Museum of Art and History.** When Key West was designated a U.S. port of entry in the early 1820s, a customs house was established. Salvaged cargoes from ships wrecked on the reefs could legally enter here, thus setting the stage for Key West to become the richest city in Florida. Following an $8 million restoration, the imposing redbrick and terra-cotta Richardsonian Romanesque–style U.S. Custom House reopened as a museum. Its main gallery displays major rotating exhibits. Smaller galleries feature long-term and changing exhibits about the history of Key West, such as *Remember the Maine.* ✉ *281 Front St.,* ☎ *305/295–6616.* 🎫 *$6.* ⏲ *Daily 9–6.*

⓭ **Lighthouse Museum.** For the best view in town and a history lesson at the same time, climb the 88 steps to the top of this 92-ft lighthouse. It was built in 1847. About 15 years later, a Fresnel lens was installed at a cost of $1 million. The keeper lived in the adjacent 1887 clapboard house, which now exhibits vintage photographs, ship models, nautical

Close-Up

HEMINGWAY WAS HERE

IN A TOWN WHERE Pulitzer Prize–winning writers are almost as common as coconuts, Ernest Hemingway stands out. Bars and restaurants around the island boast that he ate or drank there, and though he may not have been at all of them, like all legends his larger-than-life image continues to grow.

Hemingway came to Key West in 1928 at the urging of writer John dos Passos and rented a house with wife number two, Pauline Pfeiffer. They spent winters in the Keys and summers in Europe and Wyoming, occasionally taking African safaris. Along the way they had two sons, Patrick and Gregory. In 1931 Pauline's wealthy uncle Gus gave the couple the house at 907 Whitehead Street, now known as Hemingway House and Key West's number one tourist attraction. They renovated the palatial home, added a swimming pool, and put in a tropical garden with peacocks.

In 1935, when the visitor bureau included the house in a tourist brochure, Hemingway promptly built the high brick wall that surrounds it today. He wrote of the visitor bureau's offense in a 1935 essay for *Esquire,* stating, "The house at present occupied by your correspondent is listed as number eighteen in a compilation of the forty-eight things for a tourist to see in Key West. So there will be no difficulty in a tourist finding it or any other of the sights of the city, a map has been prepared by the local F.E.R.A. authorities to be presented to each arriving visitor . . . This is all very flattering to the easily bloated ego of your correspondent but very hard on production."

During his time in Key West, Hemingway penned some of his most important works, including *A Farewell to Arms, To Have and Have Not, Green Hills of Africa,* and *Death in the Afternoon.* His rigorous schedule consisted of writing almost every morning in his second-story studio above the pool, then promptly descending the stairs at midday. By afternoon and evening he was ready for drinking, fishing, swimming, boxing, and hanging around with the boys.

One close friend was Joe Russell, a craggy fisherman and owner of the rugged bar Sloppy Joe's, originally at 428 Greene Street but now at 201 Duval Street. Russell was the only one in town who would cash Hemingway's $1,000 royalty check. Russell and Charles Thompson introduced him to deep-sea fishing, which became fodder for his writing. Another of Hemingway's loves was boxing. He set up a ring in his yard and paid local fighters to box with him as well as refereeing matches at Blue Heaven, then a saloon but now a restaurant, at 729 Thomas Street.

FEELING AT HOME among Key West's characters, Hemingway honed his macho image dressed in cutoffs and old shirts and took on the name Papa. In turn, he gave his friends new names and used them as characters in his stories. Joe Russell became Freddy, captain of the *Queen Conch* charter boat in *To Have and Have Not.*

Hemingway stayed in Key West for 11 years before leaving Pauline for wife number three. A foreign correspondent, Martha Gellhorn, arrived in town and headed for Sloppy Joe's, intent on meeting him. When the always restless Hemingway packed up to cover the Spanish Civil War, so did she. Though he returned to Pauline occasionally, he finally left her and Key West to be with Martha in 1939. They married a year later and moved to Cuba, and he seldom returned to Key West after that. Pauline and the boys stayed on in the house, which sold in 1951 for $80,000, 10 times its original cost.

— Diane Marshall

charts, and lighthouse artifacts from all along the Key reefs. ✉ *938 Whitehead St.,* ☎ *305/294–0012.* 🎫 *$8.* ⏲ *Daily 9:30–5, last admission 4:30.*

14 **Lofton B. Sands African-Bahamian Museum.** Vintage photographs and memorabilia chronicle the nearly 200-year history of Key West's black community in this modest 1928 house on the edge of Bahama Village. The house was built by the namesake owner, a master electrician, in the mid-1920s in what was then called Black Town or Africa Town. There are photographs of graduations and dances at the segregated high school, photos of funeral parades, candids of people at social clubs and balls, and posed wedding pictures. Crafts and demonstrations of traditional Afro-Caribbean arts are scheduled periodically. ✉ *324 Truman Ave.,* ☎ *305/295–7337, 305/293–9692.* 🎫 *Donation suggested.* ⏲ *Daily 10–6. Tours by appointment.*

23 **Mel Fisher Maritime Heritage Society Museum.** In 1622, two Spanish galleons loaded with riches from South America foundered in a hurricane 40 mi west of the Keys. In 1985, Mel Fisher recovered the treasures from the lost ships, the *Nuestra Señora de Atocha* and the *Santa Margarita.* In this museum, you can see, touch, and learn about some of the artifacts, including a gold bar weighing 6.3 troy pounds and a 77.76-carat natural emerald crystal worth almost $250,000. Exhibits on the second floor rotate and might cover slave ships or the evolution of Florida maritime history. Captain's Corne offers dive expeditions to the *Atocha.* ✉ *200 Greene St.,* ☎ *305/294–2633.* 🎫 *$6.50.* ⏲ *Daily 9:30–5:30.*

16 **Nancy Forrester's Secret Garden.** It's hard to believe that this green escape exists in the middle of Old Town Key West. Despite damage by hurricanes and pressures from developers, Nancy Forrester has maintained her more than 30-year-old naturalized garden. Growing in harmony are rare palms and cycads, ferns, bromeliads, bright gingers and heliconias, gumbo-limbos strewn with orchids and vines, and a few surprises. The gardens are popular for weddings. Afterwards, the bride and groom can stay in the garden's cottage ($140–$175, two-day minimum). There are picnic tables where you can sit and have lunch. An art gallery has botanical prints and environmental art. ✉ *1 Free School La.,* ☎ *305/294–0015.* 🎫 *$6.* ⏲ *Daily 10–5.*

17 **San Carlos Institute.** South Florida's Cuban connection began long before Fidel Castro was born. The institute was founded in 1871 by Cuban immigrants. Now it houses a research library and museum rich with the history of Key West and 19th- and 20th-century Cuban exiles. Cuban patriot Jose Martí delivered speeches from the balcony of the auditorium, and opera star Enrico Caruso sang in the Opera House, which reportedly has exceptional acoustics. ✉ *516 Duval St.,* ☎ *305/294–3887.* 🎫 *$3.* ⏲ *Tues.–Fri. 11–5, Sat. 11–9, Sun. 11–4.*

26 **Simonton Street Beach.** This beach facing the gulf is a great place to watch boat traffic in the harbor. Parking, however, is difficult. ✉ *North end of Simonton St.,* ☎ *no phone.* 🎫 *Free.* ⏲ *Daily 7 AM–11 PM.*

27 **South Beach.** On the Atlantic, this stretch of sand, also known as City Beach, is popular with travelers staying at nearby motels. It has limited parking and a nearby buffet-type restaurant, the South Beach Seafood and Raw Bar. ✉ *Foot of Duval St.,* ☎ *no phone.* 🎫 *Free.* ⏲ *Daily 7 AM–11 PM.*

New Town

The Overseas Highway splits as it enters Key West, the two forks rejoining to encircle New Town, the area east of White Street to Cow

Key Channel. The southern fork runs along the shore as South Roosevelt Boulevard (Route A1A), past municipal beaches, salt ponds, and Key West International Airport. Along the north shore, North Roosevelt Boulevard (U.S. 1) passes the Key West Welcome Center, shopping centers, chain hotels, and fast-food eateries. Part of New Town was created with dredged fill. The island would have continued growing this way had the Army Corps of Engineers not determined in the early 1970s that it was detrimental to the nearby reef.

A Good Tour

Attractions are few in New Town. The best way to take in the sights is by car or moped. Take South Roosevelt Boulevard from the island's entrance to **East Martello Tower** ㉛, near the airport. Continue past the Riggs Wildlife Refuge salt ponds and stop at **Smathers Beach** ㉜ for a dip, or continue west onto Atlantic Boulevard to **C. B. Harvey Rest Beach** ㉝. A little farther along, at the end of White Street, is the **West Martello Tower** ㉞.

TIMING

Allow one to two hours for brief stops at each attraction. If your interests lie in art, gardens, or Civil War history, you'll need three or four hours. Throw in time at the beach, and you can make it a half-day affair.

Sights to See

33 **C. B. Harvey Rest Beach.** This beach and park were named after former Key West mayor and commissioner Cornelius Bradford Harvey. It has half a dozen picnic areas, dunes, and a wheelchair and bike path. ✉ *East side of White Street Pier,* ☎ *no phone.* *Free.* *Daily 7 AM–11 PM.*

★ 31 **East Martello Tower.** This Civil War citadel never saw any action. Today, it serves as a museum with historical exhibits of the 19th to 20th century. Among the latter are relics of the U.S.S. *Maine,* a Cuban refugee raft, and books by famous writers—including seven Pulitzer Prize winners—who have lived in Key West. The tower, operated by the Key West Art and Historical Society, also has a collection of Stanley Papio's "junk art" sculptures and Cuban folk artist Mario Sanchez's chiseled and painted wooden carvings of historic Key West street scenes. ✉ *3501 S. Roosevelt Blvd.,* ☎ *305/296–3913.* *$6.* *Daily 9:30–5, last admission 4.*

32 **Smathers Beach.** This beach has nearly 2 mi of sand. Trucks along the road rent rafts, Windsurfers, and other beach "toys." ✉ *S. Roosevelt Blvd.,* ☎ *no phone.* *Free.* *Daily 7 AM–11 PM.*

34 **West Martello Tower.** The ruins of this Civil War–era fort are home to the Key West Garden Club, which maintains lovely gardens of native and tropical plants. It also holds art, orchid, and flower shows in March and November and leads private garden tours in March. ✉ *Atlantic Blvd. and White St.,* ☎ *305/294–3210.* *Donation welcome.* *Tues.–Sat. 9:30–3.*

Dining

American

$–$$ ✕ **Pepe's Café and Steak House.** Pepe's is a Key West institution. It was established downtown in 1909 (making it the oldest eating house in the Keys) and moved here in 1962. With few exceptions, it's been serving three squares a day with the same nightly specials for years such as meat loaf on Monday, seafood on Tuesday, and traditional Thanksgiving every Thursday. Dine indoors or on the garden patio under the trees. The walls are plastered with local color. Service is fast and friendly. It's worth coming back. ✉ *806 Caroline St.,* ☎ *305/294–7192. D, MC, V.*

Caribbean

$$–$$$ ★ ✕ **Caribe Soul.** A lesser restaurant would have gone out of business. It's a testament to the quality of the food and creativity of co-founders Kevin Robinson and Michael Weston that despite three locations in three years, they're still in business with a loyal following. The sophisticated menu here is influenced by home-style Caribbean and Southern soul food cooking as reflected in such dishes as grilled mango chicken and Voodoo ribs grilled in their own spicy/sweet Voodoo Sauce. The new location has three themed rooms, ranging from British colonial to the quirky, late-night Bamboo Room, that has a bar, pool table, videos, and a separate tapas menu. Many of the sauces and relishes used in the restaurant are on sale as are cookbooks, including their own, *Using What You've Got.* ✉ *1202 Simonton St.,* ☎ *305/296–0094. AE, D, DC, MC, V. No lunch Mon.*

Contemporary

$$$–$$$$ ★ ✕ **Café des Artistes.** The food here is superb, reflecting Chef Andrew Berman's French interpretation of tropical cuisine, using fresh local seafood and produce and light sauces. The best choices are the featured items of the day such as Atlantic salmon prepared in a light curry ginger butter or venison with a black currant sauce. There's been an improvement in the wine list, with better quality and value and a stronger focus on exceptional domestic vintages. Dining is in two indoor rooms or on a rooftop deck beneath a sapodilla tree and the stars. ✉ *1007 Simonton St.,* ☎ *305/294–7100. AE, MC, V. No lunch.*

$$$–$$$$ ✕ **Louie's Backyard.** Often if a restaurant has a steal-your-breath view, it lets its clientele feast their eyes, rather than their palates. Not here. Executive chef Doug Shook consistently offers an enticing menu that changes seasonally. The winter menu might include roast rack of lamb with mint sauce and roasted garlic or grilled sour orange–rubbed grouper with black beans and mango salsa. Louie's key lime pie has a pistachio crust and is served with a raspberry coulis. Dine outside under a mahoe tree. Come for lunch if you're on a budget; the menu is less expensive and the view is still just as fantastic. For night owls, the Afterdeck Bar serves cocktails on the water until the wee hours. ✉ *700 Waddell Ave.,* ☎ *305/294–1061. AE, DC, MC, V.*

$$–$$$$ ★ ✕ **Café Marquesa.** The hospitality machine is well oiled at this refined restaurant adjoining the intimate Marquesa Hotel. Chef Susan Ferry, who trained with Norman Van Aken (of Norman's restaurant in Coral Gables), presents 10 or so entrées each night. Although every dish she makes is memorable, frequent guests favor the sesame-crusted yellowtail snapper that comes with a sake-miso broth, udon noodles, sautéed spinach, and pineapple-chili salsa. Some low-fat options like grilled meats are featured, but desserts are quite the contrary. There are also a fine selection of wines and a choice of microbrewery beers. ✉ *600 Fleming St.,* ☎ *305/292–1244. AE, DC, MC, V. No lunch.*

$$–$$$ ★ ✕ **Alice's at La Te Da.** Chef-owner Alice Weingarten, a very popular local chef, serves breakfast, brunch, lunch, and dinner poolside with live evening entertainment. Her talent shows in her exemplary selection of wines that complement the creative mix of seafood, game, beef, pork, and poultry dishes. A sizzling Key West yellowtail features an aromatic blend of Thai red curry and Asian vegetables served over coconut basmati rice. The bar is as popular as the dining room. ✉ *1125 Duval St.,* ☎ *305/296–6706. AE, D, MC, V. Closed Mon.*

$$ ★ ✕ **Rick's Blue Heaven.** There is so much to like about this historic restaurant where Hemingway once refereed boxing matches and customers watched cockfights. Upstairs is an art gallery (check out the zebra-stripe bikes), and downstairs are affordable fresh eats, in both the house and the big leafy yard. Business is booming with nightly specials and a good

mix of natural and West Indian foods. All of the desserts, breads, torts, buns, and rolls are baked on-site. Three meals are served six days a week; Sunday there's a to-die-for brunch. The water tower hauled here in the 1920s recently gave its name to the restaurant's all-day Water Tower Bar. Expect a line—everybody knows how good this is. ✉ *729 Thomas St.,* ☏ *305/296–8666. Reservations not accepted. D, MC, V.*

Cuban

$–$$ ✕ **El Siboney.** Dining at this sprawling three-room, family-style restaurant is like going to mom's for Sunday dinner; that is, if your mother is Cuban. It's noisy—everyone talks as though they're at home—and the food is traditional, including a well-seasoned black-bean soup. Specials include beef stew Monday, chicken fricassee Wednesday, chicken and rice Friday, and oxtail stew on Saturday. Always available are roast pork, cassava, paella, and *palomilla* steak. Popular with locals, but enough visitors pass through that you'll fit right in. ✉ *900 Catherine St.,* ☏ *305/296–4184. No credit cards. Closed 2 wks in June.*

French

$$–$$$ ★ ✕ **Café Solé.** This little piece of France is concealed behind a high wall and a gate in a residential neighborhood. Inside, chef John Correa shows his considerable culinary talents. Marrying his French training with local foods and produce, he creates some delicious takes on classics like *moules marinaires* (mussels served in garlic, butter, and white wine), and some of the best bouillabaisse that you'll find outside of Marseille. From the land, there is exotic grilled ostrich served with a béarnaise sauce. His salads are lightly kissed with balsamic vinegar. The chef welcomes requests on pasta preparations. ✉ *1029 Southard St.,* ☏ *305/294–0230. D, MC, V. Closed Wed. No lunch.*

Italian

$$–$$$ ★ ✕ **Salute Ristorante Sul Mare.** This funky wooden indoor and open-air restaurant is right on Higgs Beach, giving it one of the island's best lunch views (and a bit of sand and salt spray on a windy day). The dinner menu is a medley of Italian pastas, antipasto, soups, and traditional dishes like *quaglia spiedine* (skewered quails with wilted greens) and *petto di pollo marsala* (sautéed chicken breast with Portobello mushrooms and marsala). At lunch there are bruschetta, panini, and mussels and calamari marinara, as well as a fresh local fish sandwich. The wine list shows a knowledgeable palate. Dining here is light and fun. ✉ *1000 Atlantic Blvd, Higgs Beach.,* ☏ *305/292–1117. AE, MC, V. Closed Sun.*

$–$$ ★ ✕ **Mangia Mangia.** Elliot and Naomi Baron, ex-Chicago restaurateurs, serve large, flavorful portions of homemade pasta. Diners select a fresh pasta from the daily selection and match it with one of the homemade sauces. Tables are arranged in a twinkly brick garden with specimen palms and in a nicely dressed-up old-house dining room. It's one of the best restaurants in Key West—and one of the best values. Everything that comes out of the open kitchen is outstanding, including the Mississippi mud pie and key lime pie. The wine list, with more than 350 selections, the largest in Monroe County, contains a good selection under $20. ✉ *900 Southard St.,* ☏ *305/294–2469. AE, MC, V. No lunch.*

Pan-Asian

$$–$$$ ★ ✕ **Dim Sum's Far East.** This charming little restaurant succeeds by making your experience memorable from the moment you are greeted at the door to the moment you are wished good night. Service is exemplary and the food, Pan-Asian cuisine and a fusion of classical French and Asian cooking, is outstanding in artistic presentation and taste. The menu features such favorite aromatic dishes as crisp deep-fried whole yellowtail snapper enveloped in a pepper and basil sauce. Nightly spe-

cials range from chicken and shrimp in a green Thai curry with essence of cilantro root, lemongrass, and galangal to duck in a red Thai curry sauce. The setting is authentic-feeling Far East, and the selection of beer and wine is good. ✉ *613½ Duval St. (rear),* ☎ *305/294–6230. AE, D, DC, MC, V. No lunch May–late Dec.*

Steak/Seafood

$$–$$$$ ✕ **Michael's Restaurant.** White tablecloths, carpet, heavy drapes, subdued lighting, a few oil paintings, and light jazz give Michael's the feel of a favorite restaurant in a comfortable urban neighborhood. To give it that Key West touch, there's also seating outside in the garden surrounded by a tall fence and lush vegetation. A soothing waterfall hushes the street traffic. Even the dishes are familiar, but with creative touches. There's *filet al forno* (tenderloin of beef rubbed with roasted garlic and Roquefort), as well as macadamia-crusted grouper, a huge portion of fish spiced with wasabi and served with crisp snow peas and lightly flavored rice. If you're a chocolate lover, don't miss the volcano, a hot Ghirardelli chocolate cake with a molten chocolate center that erupts when the cake is broken open. ✉ *532 Margaret St.,* ☎ *305/295–1300. AE, D, MC, V. No lunch.*

Lodging

Lodging opportunities rival those found in mainland cities. You'll find historic cottages, restored turn-of-the-last-century Conch houses, and large resorts. Rates are the highest in the Keys, with a few properties as low as $65, but the majority from $100 to $300 a night. Most properties raise prices during October's Fantasy Fest week and other events. Guest houses and inns often do not welcome children under 16. In addition, some guest houses and inns do not permit smoking.

Guest Houses

$$$$ ★ **Paradise Inn.** Gloriously chic best describes this romantic palm-shaded inn. Renovated cigar makers' cottages and authentically reproduced Bahamian-style houses with sundecks and balconies stand amid lush gardens with a heated pool, lily pond, and whirlpool, light-years in feeling from the hubbub of Key West. Suites are stylish, spacious, and filled with gracious appointments such as French doors, sensuous fabrics, phones and whirlpools in marble bathrooms, plush robes, polished oak floors, armoires, and complimentary fresh breakfast pastries. Suite 205 and the Poinciana Cottage are gilded lilies. ✉ *819 Simonton St., 33040,* ☎ *305/293–8007 or 800/888–9648,* FAX *305/293–0807,* WEB *www.theparadiseinn.com. 3 cottages, 15 suites. In-room safes, minibars, pool, hot tub, concierge. AE, D, DC, MC, V.*

$$$–$$$$ ★ **Heron House.** If your idea of the perfect place to stay is a vernacular-style hotel loaded with amenities, Heron House will suit you well. A high coral fence, brilliantly splashed with spotlights at night, surrounds the compound of four Key West–style buildings centered on a pool. Most units feature a complete wall of exquisitely laid wood, entries with French doors, and bathrooms of polished granite. Some have floor-to-ceiling panels of mirrored glass and/or an oversize whirlpool. Complementing the superb interior detailing are full concierge service, daily newspapers, and bathrobes. An expanded Continental breakfast and complimentary wine and cheese are included. ✉ *512 Simonton St., 33040,* ☎ *305/294–9227,* FAX *305/294–5692 or 888/861–9066,* WEB *www.heronhouse.com. 23 rooms. Pool, concierge. AE, DC, MC, V.*

$$$–$$$$ **Island City House.** There's a real sense of conviviality at this guest house comprised of three buildings, each with a unique style (and price). The vintage-1880s Island City House, with a widow's walk and Victorian flavor expressed through antiques, pine floors, and ceiling

fans. Arch House, a former carriage house, has a dramatic carriage entry that opens into a lush courtyard. Although all its suites front on busy Eaton Street, only Nos. 5 and 6 actually face it. A 1970s reconstruction of a cigar factory has become the Cigar House, with porches and decks and plantation-style teak and wicker furnishings. Guests share a private tropical garden. Children are welcome—a rarity in Old Town guest houses. There are also VCR rentals with free movies. ✉ *411 William St., 33040,* ☎ *305/294–5702 or 800/634–8230,* FAX *305/294–1289,* WEB *www.islandcityhouse.com. 24 suites. Pool, hot tub, bicycles. AE, D, DC, MC, V. CP.*

$$–$$$$ ★ **Popular House/Key West Bed & Breakfast.** Key West embodies the arts, the tropics, and the finer things in life, as well as a laissez-faire attitude. Jody Carlson's B&B is a model of Key West. Local art—large splashy canvases, a mural in the style of Gauguin—hangs on the walls, and tropical gardens and music set the mood. Jody offers both inexpensive rooms with shared bath (whose rates haven't been raised in more than 10 years) and luxury rooms, reasoning that budget travelers deserve the same good local style (and lavish Continental breakfast) as the rich. Less-expensive rooms burst with bright colors; the hand-painted dressers will make you laugh. Spacious third-floor rooms are best (and most expensive), decorated with a paler palette and brilliantly original furniture. Jody also keeps two friendly dogs. ✉ *415 William St., 33040,* ☎ *305/296–7274 or 800/438–6155,* FAX *305/293–0306,* WEB *www.keywestbandb.com. 9 rooms, 4 with bath. Hot tub, sauna. AE, D, DC, MC, V.*

$$$ ★ **Ambrosia House.** If you enjoy interesting art and architecture or if you simply like personal attention and a casual atmosphere with a dollop of style, stay at these twin inns comprising pool-view rooms, suites, town houses, and cottages spread out on nearly 2 acres. On one side of the street is Ambrosia, Kate Miano's original bed-and-breakfast, with a more intimate setting. On the other side is Ambrosia Too, the former Fleming Street Inn that Kate bought and is turning into a delightful art-filled hideaway with a larger pool. Rooms are distinctly decorated with original artwork by Keys artists, wicker or wood furniture, ceiling fans, and spacious bathrooms. They all have a private entrance and a deck, patio, or porch with a table and chairs, lounge chairs, a hammock, or swings. Phones are portable so you can take calls poolside. ✉ *615, 618, 622 Fleming St., 33040,* ☎ *305/296–9838 or 800/535–9838,* FAX *305/296–2425,* WEB *www.ambrosiakeywest.com. 19 rooms, 6 rooms, 3 town houses, 1 cottage, 9 suites. In-room data ports, refrigerators, 3 pools, bicycles, concierge. AE, D, MC, V. BP.*

$$$ ★ **Key Lime Inn.** This inn, an 1854 grand Bahama-style house on the National Register of Historic Places with adjacent cottages and cabanas succeeds by offering amiable service, good value, a tropical ambience, and pretty, light-filled rooms furnished with natural wood and white dressers and tables. The inn derives most of its character from the gardens shaded by fruit and palm trees, tin-roof buildings with clapboard siding, classic white picket fences, and breezy porches. The least expensive Cabana rooms, some with a patio, surround the pool. The Garden Cottages have one room, some include a porch. All rooms in the historic Maloney House have a porch or patio. The Maloney House and Garden Cottages rooms also have a VCR, small refrigerator, coffee machine, and morning paper delivered with juice and croissants. ✉ *725 Truman Ave., 33040,* ☎ *305/294–5229 or 800/549–4430,* FAX *305/294–9623,* WEB *www.keylimeinn.com. 37 rooms. Pool, concierge, parking. AE, D, MC, V.*

$$$ ★ **Mermaid & The Alligator.** Each room in this restored circa-1904 Victorian house is uniquely decorated with period furnishings that harken to colonial Caribbean. Rooms are painted in colors so luscious that

guests frequently request paint chips. The color is offset by rich wood floors, furniture, window trim, French doors, and ceiling fans. Some downstairs rooms open onto the deck, pool, and lovely gardens designed by one of the resident owners, a landscape designer. Upstairs rooms have balconies overlooking the house gardens. The Caribbean Queen honeymoon suite has a large soaking tub, four-poster queen bed, and wraparound veranda, but its street-side location makes it noisy and it has a tiny shower. Even if you're on your honeymoon, opt for the Garden Room or Audubon Room. A full breakfast is served poolside. The owners and their two retrievers make this a delightful place to stay. ✉ *729 Truman Ave., 33040,* ☎ *305/294–1894 or 800/773–1894,* FAX *305/295–9925,* WEB *www.kwmermaid.com. 6 rooms. Pool. AE, D, DC, MC, V.*

$$–$$$ **Center Court Historic Inn & Cottages.** This lodging is delightful. Duval is half a block away, but when you're here, you're enveloped in calm and quiet. Units range from spacious rooms with a queen bed to efficiency cottages, each with a deck and spa (sleeping two to eight) to studios and fully equipped three-bedroom, two-bath house-size cottages (they sleep six). There's even a two-bedroom, 2½-bathhouse with its own pool. All units are decorated in relaxed tropical style and both breakfast and happy-hour beverages are included. The heated pools are surrounded by lush foliage, whirlpools, a sundeck, and exercise pavilion. The restoration work to the historic houses that the inn comprises here earned an award from the Key West Historical Preservation Society. An annex called Center Court Hideaways has two-bedroom, two-bath units on Duval Square and on the waterfront with dockage. Some units have laundry facilities. ✉ *915 Center St., 33040,* ☎ *305/296–9292 or 800/797–8787,* FAX *305/294–4104,* WEB *www.centercourtkw.com. 5 rooms, 5 suites, 2 efficiencies, 10 cottages, 1 house. 2 pools, hot tub, exercise room. AE, D, MC, V.*

$$–$$$ **Eden House.** This 1920s art deco guest house is one of the best values in town. Two levels of accommodations surround a lush garden courtyard with a pool bordered by lounges and umbrella-covered tables. Rooms range from small, simple spaces with a double or two twin beds with a bathroom shared by two rooms to large spaces with a queen bed, kitchenette, refrigerator, and private porch. No matter the size, they all have pleasant furnishings and tropical colors. Shared baths are squeaky clean. Spacious suites come in two sizes and feature paler decors. The staff is genuinely helpful and friendly. There's a daily complimentary happy hour. ✉ *1015 Fleming St., 33040,* ☎ *305/296–6868 or 800/533–5397,* FAX *305/294–1221,* WEB *www.edenhouse.com. 4 rooms with shared bath, 17 rooms, 9 suites, 1 two-bedroom unit. Restaurant, pool, hot tub, bicycles, shops, concierge, parking. AE, MC, V.*

$$–$$$ ★ **Merlinn Inn.** Key West guest houses don't usually welcome families. The Merlinn Inn is a pleasant exception. It was originally a boardinghouse, then a bordello, before becoming a legitimate inn. It was revived with colorful rooms, suites, and cottages connected by brick walkways that curve through a courtyard, pool area, and profuse tropical plantings. Rooms in the 1930s Simonton House are most suitable for couples. They have ceiling fans, queen four-poster beds, and front or garden porches. Suites are individually designed and decorated and can accommodate two to four people. Wooden floors, French doors, area rugs, small refrigerators, four-poster beds, sundecks or porches, and queen sleeper sofas are some of their features. Bright, roomy cottages are equally well appointed, and sleep up to six people. The inn has no parking facilities—a drawback, since it's just one block off busy Duval Street. ✉ *811 Simonton St., 33040,* ☎ *305/296–3336 or 800/642–4753,* FAX *305/296–3524,* WEB *www.merlinnkeywest.com. 10 rooms, 6 suites, 4 cottages. Pool. AE, D, MC, V.*

$$–$$$ **Speakeasy Inn.** This inn's notorious history began during Prohibition, when Raul Vasquez smuggled liquor from Cuba and taxi drivers pulled up in front to fill suitcases with the bootleg. Today, it's an attractively priced inn. Spacious studios, suites, and two-bedroom units have bright white walls offset by bursts of color in throw rugs, pillows, and seat cushions; queen-size beds and tables made from 1876 salvaged pine; Saltillo tiles in the bathrooms; kitchenettes; oak floors; and claw-foot tubs in some baths. Maid and concierge service are provided on request. Ironically, although the inn is adjacent to owner Thomas Favelli's other pride and joy, the Key West Havana Cigar Co., there is no smoking in the rooms. Casa 325 Suites, an upscale all-suites property at the opposite end of Duval, is under the same ownership. ✉ *1117 Duval St., 33040,* ☎ *305/296–2680 or 800/217–4884,* FAX *305/296–2608,* WEB *www.keywestcigar.com. 4 suites, 4 studios, 2 two-bedroom units. Pool, massage, concierge. AE, D, MC, V.*

$–$$ **Angelina Guest House.** Just two blocks off Duval Street, in the heart of Old Town Key West, this gambling hall and bordello–turned–guest house could command top dollar for its rooms, but that's not what the owners have in mind. They prefer to provide simple, clean accommodations at an attractive price. Rooms are basic: a bed, ceiling fan, pretty curtains, a chair and shared bath in the plainest rooms; a bed, sleeper sofa, refrigerator and microwave or full kitchen in others. That's not to say that the Angelina is without charm. Built in the 1920s, this rambling, white, wooden building has second-floor porches, gabled roofs, and a white picket fence. It also has a pool and fountain surrounded by old bricks and a lovely garden. Breakfast of homemade baked goods is included. Rooms don't have phones or TV. ✉ *302 Angela St., 33040,* ☎ *305/294–4480,* WEB *www.angelinaguesthouse.com. 13 rooms. Pool. D, MC, V.*

Hostel

$ ★ **Hostelling International–Key West.** Yes, you can afford to stay in Key West. This financial refuge in a sea of expensive hotels gets high marks for location, comfort, friendliness, amenities, and good value. It's two blocks from the beach in Old Town, yet costs only $18.50 for members of Hostelling International–American Youth Hostels, $21.50 for nonmembers. There's a communal kitchen. When you're not snorkeling ($20) or scuba diving ($55, gear included), you can rent bicycles, write letters in the outdoor courtyard, or enjoy a barbecue. ✉ *718 South St., 33040,* ☎ *305/296–5719,* FAX *305/296–0672,* WEB *www.hiayh.org. 96 beds in dorm-style rooms without baths. Bicycles, billiards, recreation room, library. MC, V.*

Hotels

$$$$ ★ **Ocean Key Resort.** You can't get any closer to the water or the pulse of Key West than Ocean Key Resort set on a pier where locals and visitors alike find their way nightly to watch the sun as it sets seemingly just offshore. Live music, good food and drinks from the Sunset Pier Bar & Grill, fantasy colors, and that fantastic sunset view make the Sunset Pier the place to be. Even in the morning, some guests foresake breakfast in bed for breakfast on the pier. The pier isn't the only reason to stay here. The resort exudes casual elegance. Large, colorful, beautifully decorated rooms and suites with oversize hot tubs, ceiling fans, and balconies that overlook gardens or water are other reasons. Rooms have all the requisite extras—hair dryers, coffeemakers, irons, modems, and direct-dial phones. The concierge can set up off-site fishing, parasailing, diving, snorkeling, Wave Runner rentals, and island tours or you can loll around the heated pool or buy Keys-made arts and crafts in the extensive gift shop. After sunset, you can dance into the wee hours with guests and locals. ✉ *Zero Duval St., 33040,* ☎ *305/296–7701 or 800/*

328–9815, FAX *305/292–7685,* WEB *www.oceankey.com. 100 rooms and suites. 2 restaurants, 2 bars, pool, massage, spa, health club, dock, marina, bicycles, shops, dance club, dry cleaning, concierge, business services, meeting rooms, free parking. AE, D, DC, MC, V.*

$$$$ ★ **Pier House Resort & Caribbean Spa.** If any resort typifies Key West, it is this convivial, sprawling pleasure dome at the end of Duval and Front streets. One of the first modern resorts, the complex of weathered gray buildings, including an original Conch house, flanks a courtyard of tall coconut palms and hibiscus blossoms. All rooms are light filled, cozy, and bursting with color and have either a water, pool, or garden view. Most rooms are smaller than in newer hotels, except in the more expensive Caribbean Spa section, which has hardwood floors, two-poster plantation beds, CD and video players, and some baths that convert to steam rooms or have whirlpools. The best lodgings in the house are in the Harbor Front, whose name accurately describes the vantage point from each large room's private balcony. It's also one of those pampering places where you can get a massage, manicure, and body treatments. Sunset on the Havana Docks is an everyday special occasion. Rooms nearest the public areas can be noisy. ✉ *1 Duval St., 33040,* ☎ *305/296–4600 or 800/327–8340,* FAX *305/296–7569,* WEB *www.pierhouse.com. 128 rooms, 16 suites. 3 restaurants, 4 bars, pool, massage, health club, beach. AE, D, DC, MC, V.*

$$$$ ★ **Sunset Key Guest Cottages at Hilton Key West Resort.** It's as if they polled people on their vision of a tropical getaway to create this resort. Guests check in at the Hilton in Key West, then board a 10-minute launch to their quiet Key West–style two- and three-bedroom cottages on Sunset Key. Sandy beaches, swaying palm trees, flowering gardens, a delicious sense of privacy—it's all here. Ask for a sea view (as opposed to the garden view) so you can sit on your shaded porch and gaze across the water. The decor is handsome; the plush creature comforts reflect first-class accommodations, including CD, stereo, and VCR; multiple bathrooms; full kitchen; two-line phone; and pantry bar. And then there are the little extras: a private chef on request; grocery delivery; and a CD, video, board-game, and book library. You can go between the island and Key West around the clock at no extra charge or remain at Sunset Key, where you can dine, swim, play tennis or basketball, and relax on a lounge at the very civilized beach, complete with attendants and cabanas. ✉ *245 Front St., 33040,* ☎ *305/292–5300,* FAX *305/292–5395,* WEB *www.hilton.com. 37 cottages. Restaurant, in-room safes, pool, massage, putting green, tennis, basketball, exercise room, beach, jet skiing, marina, fishing, shops, billiards, library, baby-sitting, concierge. AE, D, DC, MC, V.*

$$$$ **Wyndham's Casa Marina Resort.** This historic resort is like something out of a Gatsby novel. It revolves around an outdoor patio and lawn facing the ocean. At any moment, you expect the landed gentry to walk across that manicured lawn, just as they did during the 1920s when Henry Flagler's heirs built the 13-acre resort at the end of the Florida East Coast Railway line. It has the same rich, luxurious lobby with a beamed ceiling, polished Dade County pine floor, artwork, and island French Provincial furniture. Guest rooms are stylishly decorated and armoires and wicker chairs with thick cushions lend a warm touch. All the amenity-packed rooms are equally luxurious, but if you have a choice, stay in the two-bedroom loft suites with balconies facing the ocean or the main building's lanai rooms on the ground floor, whose French doors open onto the lawn. There are myriad recreational and spa facilities. ✉ *1500 Reynolds St., 33040,* ☎ *305/296–3535, 800/442–3727,* FAX *305/296–9960,* WEB *www.casamarinakeywest.com. 311 rooms, 63 suites. 2 restaurants, 2 bars, 2 pools, barbershop, hair salon, massage, sauna, 3*

tennis courts, exercise room, health club, volleyball, boating, jet skiing, fishing, bicycles, baby-sitting, children's programs (ages 4–12), concierge, airport shuttle. AE, D, DC, MC, V.

$$$–$$$$ ★ **Marquesa Hotel.** In a town that prides itself on its laid-back luxe, this restored 1884 house stands out. Guests—typically shoeless in Marquesa robes—relax among richly landscaped pools and gardens against a backdrop of brick steps rising to the villalike suites on the property's perimeter. Elegant rooms contain eclectic antique and reproduction furnishings, dotted Swiss curtains, botanical-print fabrics, and marble baths. Turndown service includes a Godiva chocolate on your pillow. The lobby resembles a Victorian parlor, with antique furniture, Audubon prints, flowers, and wonderful photos of early Key West, including one of Harry Truman in a convertible. Although the clientele is mostly straight, the hotel is very gay-friendly. ✉ *600 Fleming St., 33040,* ☎ *305/292–1919 or 800/869–4631,* FAX *305/294–2121,* WEB *www.marquesa.com. 27 rooms. Restaurant, 2 pools. AE, DC, MC, V.*

$$$ ★ **Best Western Key Ambassador Inn.** Every room in this well-maintained 7-acre property has a screened balcony, most with a view of the ocean or pool. Accommodations are roomy and cheerful, with Caribbean-style light-color furniture and linens in coordinated tropical colors. A deck-rimmed, palm-shaded pool that looks over the Atlantic and a covered picnic area with barbecue grills encourage socializing. There is a par course for exercising. The outdoor bar serves drinks and light dishes. A complimentary Continental breakfast and free weekday newspaper are included. ✉ *3755 S. Roosevelt Blvd., New Town, 33040,* ☎ *305/296–3500 or 800/432–4315,* FAX *305/296–9961,* WEB *www.keyambassador.com. 100 rooms. Bar, picnic area, refrigerator, pool, shuffleboard, coin laundry, airport shuttle. AE, D, DC, MC, V.*

Motels

$$ **Harborside Motel & Marina.** This simple little motel neatly packages three appealing characteristics—affordability, safety, and a pleasant location between a quiet street and Garrison Bight (the charter-boat harbor), at the border of Old Town and New Town. Units are boxy, clean, and basic, with little patios, ceramic-tile floors, phones, and basic color cable TV. Four stationary houseboats each sleep four. Barbecue grills are available for cookouts. ✉ *903 Eisenhower Dr., 33040,* ☎ *305/294–2780,* FAX *305/292–1473,* WEB *www.keywestharborside.com. 14 efficiencies. Pool, coin laundry. AE, D, DC, MC, V.*

$$ **Southwinds.** If you're looking for a practical, affordable place to stay that's just a short walk from Old Town, consider this friendly lodging run by the same folks who operate Harborside Motel & Marina. The pastel 1940s-style motel has mature tropical plantings, all nicely set back from the street a block from the beach. Rooms have basic furnishings. It's as good as you'll find at the price, and although rates have gone up, they drop if demand gets slack. ✉ *1321 Simonton St., 33040,* ☎ *305/296–2215,* WEB *www.keywestsouthwinds.com. 13 rooms, 5 efficiencies. Pool, coin laundry, free parking. AE, D, DC, MC, V.*

Nightlife and the Arts

The Arts

With more than 20 years' experience, the **Red Barn Theater** (✉ 319 Duval St. [rear], ☎ 305/296–9911), a professional small theater, performs dramas, comedies, and musicals, including works by new playwrights. The **Tennessee Williams Fine Arts Center** (✉ Florida Keys Community College, 5901 College Rd., ☎ 305/296–9081 ext. 5), on Stock Island, presents chamber music, dance, jazz concerts, and dramatic and musical plays with major stars, as well as other performing arts events, November–April. The **Waterfront Playhouse** (✉ Mallory Sq., ☎ 305/294–5015) is a mid-1850s wrecker's warehouse that was converted into a 180-seat, non-Equity regional theater presenting comedy and drama December–June.

Nightlife

BARS AND LOUNGES

In its earliest incarnation, back in 1851, **Capt. Tony's Saloon** (✉ 428 Greene St., ☎ 305/294–1838) was a morgue and icehouse, then Key West's first telegraph station. It became the original Sloppy Joe's in the mid-1930s, when Hemingway was a regular. Later, a young Jimmy Buffett sang here. Live bands play nightly. Pause for a libation at the open-air **Green Parrot Bar** (✉ 601 Whitehead St., at Southard St., ☎ 305/294–6133). Built in 1890, the bar is said to be Key West's oldest, a sometimes-rowdy saloon where locals outnumber out-of-towners, especially on weekends when bands play. It opened a smokehouse, Meteor, behind it that serves up smoked shrimp, pork, chicken, and beef. A youngish crowd sprinkled with aging hippies frequents **Margaritaville Café** (✉ 500 Duval St., ☎ 305/292–1435), owned by former Key West resident and recording star Jimmy Buffett, who has been known to perform here. The drink of choice is, of course, a margarita. There's live music nightly, as well as lunch and dinner.

The **Schooner Wharf Bar** (✉ 202 William St., ☎ 305/292–9520), an open-air waterfront bar and grill in the historic seaport district, retains its funky Key West charm. There's live music all day, plus happy hour, and special events. There's more history and good times at **Sloppy Joe's** (✉ 201 Duval St., ☎ 305/294–5717), the successor to a famous 1937 speakeasy named for its founder, Captain Joe Russell. Ernest Hemingway came here to gamble and tell stories. Decorated with Hemingway memorabilia and marine flags, the bar is popular with travelers and is full and noisy all the time. Live entertainment plays daily, noon–2 AM. The **Top Lounge** (✉ 430 Duval St., ☎ 305/296–2991) is on the seventh floor of the La Concha Holiday Inn and is one of the best places to view the sunset. (Celebrities, on the ground floor, has nightly entertainment and serves food.)

DANCE CLUBS

Originally built as the Monroe Theater in 1912 with a large dance floor, garden bar, and smaller upstairs bars, **Club Epoch** (✉ 623 Duval St., ☎ 305/296–8521) is a 22,000-square-ft dance club with a garden bar, open-air terrace bar above Duval Street, and a DJ pumping music from the 1970s through today. There's even a teen night, complete with a breakdance competition. In the Pier House, **Havana Docks Lounge** (✉ 1 Duval St., ☎ 305/296–4600) has live music nightly in season and live dance music Friday and Saturday nights year-round, as well as a nightly sunset celebration with a band.

Outdoor Activities and Sports

Biking

Key West is a cycling town, but ride carefully: narrow and one-way streets along with car traffic result in several bike accidents a year. Some hotels rent or loan bikes to guests; others will refer you to a nearby shop and reserve a bike for you.

Keys Moped & Scooter (✉ 523 Truman Ave., ☎ 305/294–0399) rents beach cruisers with large baskets as well as scooters. Rates start at $12 for three hours. Look for the huge American flag on the roof. **Moped Hospital** (✉ 601 Truman Ave., ☎ 305/296–3344) supplies balloon-tire bikes with yellow safety baskets for adults and kids, as well as mopeds and double-seater scooters for adults. There's no charge for helmets, but lights cost $4.

Fishing

Captain Steven Impallomeni works as a flats-fishing guide, specializing in ultralight and fly-fishing for tarpon, permit, and bonefish, as well as near-shore and light-tackle fishing. Charters on the ***Gallopin' Ghost*** leave from Murray's Marina (✉ MM 5, Stock Island, ☎ 305/292–9837). **Key West Bait and Tackle** (✉ 241 Margaret St., ☎ 305/292–1961) carries live bait, frozen rigged and unrigged bait, and fishing and rigging equipment. It also has the Live Bait Lounge, where you can unwind and sip ice-cold beer while telling tall tales after fishing. Be sure to ask why the marlin on the roof is red.

Golf

Key West Resort Golf Course (✉ 6450 E. College Rd., ☎ 305/294–5232) is an 18-hole course on the bay side of Stock Island. Nonresident fees are $125 for 18 holes (cart included) in season, $70 off-season.

Scuba Diving and Snorkeling

Adventure Charters & Tours (✉ 6810 Front St., Stock Island 33040, ☎ 305/296–0362 or 888/817–0841) offers sail-and-snorkel coral reef adventure tours ($25) aboard the 42-ft trimaran sailboat *Fantasea,* with a maximum of 16 people. There are two daily departures and sometimes one at sunset. In 1999, **Captain's Corner** (✉ 125 Ann St., 33040, ☎ 305/296–8865), a PADI five star–rated shop, began offering exclusive dives to Mel Fisher's famous *Nuestra Señora de Atocha* wreck, whose treasures are in the Mel Fisher Maritime Heritage Society Museum, and the neighboring reef on which the galleon originally struck. The full-day dive expeditions run March to October or November, cost $250, include lunch, and require six people to sign up. Call for dates. Captain's Corner also provides dive classes in several languages. All captains are licensed dive masters and/or instructors. A 60-ft dive boat, *Sea Eagle,* and the 48-ft *Sea Hawk* depart twice daily. Reservations are accepted for regular reef and wreck diving.

Shopping

Key West contains dozens of characterless T-shirt shops, as well as art galleries and curiosity shops with lots worth toting home.

Arts and Crafts

The **Gallery on Greene** (✉ 606 Greene St., ☎ 305/294–1669) showcases politically incorrect art by Jeff McNally and three-dimensional paintings by local artist Mario Sanchez, among others, in a large space. The oldest private art gallery in Key West, **Gingerbread Square Gallery** (✉ 1207 Duval St., ☎ 305/296–8900), represents mainly Keys artists who have attained national and international prominence in media ranging from graphics to art glass. **Haitian Art Co.** (✉ 600 Frances St., ☎ 305/296–8932), containing 4,000 paintings and spirit flags, claims the largest collection of Haitian art outside Haiti, representing a range of artists working in wood, stone, metal, and papier-mâché. **Lucky Street Gallery** (✉ 1120 White St., ☎ 305/294–3973) sells high-end contemporary paintings, watercolors, and jewelry by internationally recognized Key West–based artists. It's part of the White Street Gallery District, where you'll also find Three-Legged Dog Gallery, Harrison Gallery, and The Wave Gallery, the domain of Barbara Grob, the doyenne of outrageous gecko and animal sculptures. **Pelican Poop** (✉ 314 Simonton St., ☎ 305/296–3887) sells Caribbean art in a gorgeous setting around a lush, tropical courtyard garden with a fountain and pool. The owners buy direct from Caribbean artisans every year, so prices are very attractive. (Hemingway wrote *A Farewell to Arms* while living in the complex's apartment.) Potters Charles Pearson and Timothy Roeder *are* **Whitehead St. Pottery** (✉ 1011 Whitehead St., ☎ 305/294–5067), where they display their porcelain stoneware and raku-fired vessels. They also have a photo gallery where they exhibit Polaroid image transfers and black-and-white photos. In the not-to-be-missed category is the **Woodenhead Gallery** (✉ 907 Caroline St., ☎ 305/294–3935), where the artists-owners create avant-garde works from recycled materials and *objets* found in and around Key West. Their coffee bar is a favorite meeting spot for artists, friends, and clients.

Books

Flaming Maggie's (✉ 830 Fleming St., ☎ 305/294–3931) specializes in books and magazines for and about gays and lesbians and also carries books—and artwork—by or about local authors. It contains a popular coffee bar, too. They expanded the **Key West Island Bookstore** (✉ 513 Fleming St., ☎ 305/294–2904), the literary bookstore of the large Key West writers' community. It carries new, used, and rare titles and specializes in Hemingway, Tennessee Williams, and South Florida mystery writers.

Clothes and Fabrics

Since 1964, **Key West Hand Print Fashions and Fabrics** (✉ 201 Simonton St., ☎ 305/294–9535 or 800/866–0333) has been noted for its vibrant tropical prints, yard goods, and resort wear for men and women. It's in the Curry Warehouse, a brick building erected in 1878 to store tobacco. **Tikal Trading Co.** (✉ 129 Duval St. and 910 Duval St., ☎ 305/296–4463) sells its own line of women's clothing of handwoven Guatemalan cotton and knit tropical prints.

Food and Drink

The air outside **Cole'z Peace Artisan Breads** (✉ 930A Eaton St., ☎ 305/292–6511), an old-world–style bakery, is deliciously redolent of warm breads. Each loaf of hand-kneaded unbleached, unbromated flour, organic flour, or organic grain bread is hand-shaped, then baked in a hearth stone oven. The crusts are hard and thick; the insides light and flavorful. **Fausto's Food Palace** (✉ 522 Fleming St., ☎ 305/296–5663; ✉ 1105 White St., ☎ 305/294–5221) may be under a roof, but it's a market in the traditional town-square sense. Since 1926, Fausto's has been the spot to catch up on the week's gossip and to chill out in summer—it has gourmet groceries, organic foods, marvelous wines, a sushi chef on duty from 8 AM to 6 PM, and box lunches to go. You'll spend the first five minutes at the **Waterfront Market** (✉ 201 William St., ☎ 305/296–0778) wondering how to franchise one of these great markets in your hometown. Along with health and gourmet foods, they sell savory deli items from around the world, produce, salads, cold beer, and wine. Don't miss the fish market, bakery, deli, juice bar, and a new sushi bar fresh from the Origami Restaurant.

Gifts and Souvenirs

Like a parody of Duval Street T-shirt shops, the hole-in-the-wall **Art Attack** (✉ 606 Duval St., ☎ 305/294–7131) throws in every icon and trinket anyone nostalgic for the days of peace and love might fancy: beads, necklaces, harmony bells, and of course Grateful Dead and psychedelic T-shirts. **Fast Buck Freddie's** (✉ 500 Duval St., ☎ 305/294–2007) sells such imaginative items as a noise-activated rat in a trap and a raccoon tail in a bag. There are also crystal, furniture, tropical clothing, and every flamingo item imaginable. The ambiance in **Kindred Spirit** (✉ 1204 Simonton St., ☎ 305/296–1515) is very New Age, but in addition to aromatherapy candles, inspirational music, and scented soaps there are jewelry made by Keys artists, delicate picture frames, and tea—tea leaves, tea bags, and formal tea, complete with freshly baked scones, fruitbread, and cake and confections. In a town with a gazillion T-shirt shops, **Last Flight Out** (✉ 706A Duval St., ☎ 305/294–8008) stands out for its selection of classic namesake Ts, specialty clothing, and gifts that appeal to aviation types as well as those reaching for the stars. A survivor of Key West's seafaring days, **Perkins & Son Chandlery** (✉ 901 Fleming St., ☎ 305/294–7635), redolent of pine tar and kerosene, offers one of the largest selections of used marine gear in the Keys, as well as nautical antiques, books, outdoor clothing, and collectibles.

Health and Beauty

Key West Aloe (✉ 524 Front St., ☎ 305/294–5592 or 800/445–2563) was founded in a garage in 1971; today it produces some 300 perfume, sunscreen, and skin-care products for men and women. You can also visit the factory store (✉ Greene and Simonton Sts.).

Side Trip

Dry Tortugas National Park

This sanctuary for thousands of birds, 70 mi off the shores of Key West, consists of seven small islands. Its main facility is the long-deactivated Fort Jefferson, where Dr. Samuel Mudd was imprisoned for his alleged role in Lincoln's assassination. You can tour the fort, then lay out your blanket on the sunny beach for a picnic before you head out to snorkel on the protected reef. Many people like to camp here, but note that there's no freshwater supply and you must carry off whatever you bring on to the island. For information and a list of authorized charter boats, seaplanes, and water taxis, contact **Everglades National Park** (✉ 40001 Rte. 9336, Homestead 33034-6733, ☎ 305/242–7700).

The fast, sleek 100-ft catamaran, the *Yankee Freedom II,* of the **Yankee Fleet Dry Tortugas National Park Ferry,** cuts the travel time to the Dry Tortugas to 2¼ hours. The time passes quickly on the roomy vessel equipped with three rest rooms, two freshwater showers, and two bars. You can stretch out on two decks, one air-conditioned salon with cushioned seating, the other an open sundeck with sunny and shaded seating. Breakfast and lunch are included. On arrival, a naturalist leads a 45-minute guided tour, followed by lunch and a free afternoon for swimming, snorkeling (gear included), and exploring. ✉ *Lands End Marina, 240 Margaret St., Key West 33040,* ☎ *305/294–7009 or 877/327–8228.* 🎫 *$95.* ⏲ *Trips daily 8* AM.

THE FLORIDA KEYS A TO Z

AIR TRAVEL

To research prices, get advice from other travelers, and book arrangements, visit www.fodors.com.

Service between Key West International Airport and Miami, Fort Lauderdale/Hollywood, Naples, Orlando, and Tampa is provided by American Eagle, Cape Air, Comair/Delta Connection, Gulfstream/Continental Connection, and US Airways/US Airways Express.

The Airporter operates scheduled van and bus pickup service from all Miami International Airport (MIA) baggage areas to wherever you want to go in Key Largo ($35) and Islamorada ($38). A group discount is given for three or more passengers. Reservations are required. The Super Shuttle charges $78.50 for the first passenger ($15.50 each additional) for trips to the Upper Keys. To go farther into the Keys, you must book an entire van (up to 11 passengers), which costs $250 to Marathon, $350 to Key West. Super Shuttle requests 24-hour advance notice for transportation back to the airport.

CARRIERS

➤ AIRLINES AND CONTACTS: **American Eagle** (☎ 800/433–7300). **Cape Air** (☎ 305/293–0603). **Comair/Delta Connection** (☎ 800/354–9822).

Gulfstream/Continental Connection (☎ 800/525–0280). **US Airways/US Airways Express** (☎ 800/428–4322).

➤ AIRPORT INFORMATION: **Key West International Airport** (✉ S. Roosevelt Blvd., Key West, ☎ 305/296–5439). **Miami International Airport** (☎ 305/876–7000). **Airporter** (☎ 305/852–3413 or 800/830–3413). **Super Shuttle** (☎ 305/871–2000).

BOAT AND FERRY TRAVEL

Boaters can travel to and along the Keys either along the Intracoastal Waterway (5-ft draft limitation) through Card, Barnes, and Blackwater sounds and into Florida Bay or along the deeper Atlantic Ocean route through Hawk Channel, a buoyed passage. Refer to NOAA Nautical Charts Numbers 11451, 11445, and 11441. The Keys are full of marinas that welcome transient visitors, but they don't have enough slips for everyone. Make reservations in advance and ask about channel and dockage depth—many marinas are quite shallow.

For non-emergency information contact Coast Guard Group Key West; VHF-FM Channel 16. Safety and weather information is broadcast at 7 AM and 5 PM Eastern Standard Time on VHF-FM Channels 16 and 22A. There are stations in Islamorada and Marathon.

Key West Water Express operates a 225-passenger catamaran ferry between Key West and Marco Island, on the mainland's southwest coast. The trip takes three hours each way. A $114 day-trip departs Marco Island at 9 AM and leaves Key West at 5 PM. For travelers returning on another day, the fare is $65 each way. A galley is available for non-inclusive full breakfast, light lunch, and full bar service. Advance reservations are recommended.

Chambers of commerce, marinas, and dive shops offer Teall's Guides, land and nautical charts that pinpoint popular fishing and diving areas. A complete set can also be purchased for $7.95.

➤ BOAT AND FERRY INFORMATION: **Coast Guard Group Key West** (✉ Key West 33040, ☎ 305/292–8779). Islamorada (☎ 306/664–8077 for information; 305/664–4404 for emergencies). Marathon (☎ 305/743–6778 for information; 305/743–6388 for emergencies). **Key West Water Express** (☎ 800/650–5397 or 941/394–0014). **Teall's Guides** (✉ 111 Saguaro La., Marathon 33050, ☎ 305/743–3942).

BUS TRAVEL

Greyhound Lines runs a special Keys shuttle three or four times a day (depending on the day of the week) between MIA (departing from Concourse E, lower level) and stops throughout the Keys. Fares run from $12.50/$14.50 one-way weekday/weekend and $25/$28 round-trip for Key Largo (Howard Johnson, MM 102) to $31/$34 one-way and $59.50/$65.50 round-trip for Key West (3535 S. Roosevelt, Key West Airport).

City of Key West Department of Transportation has four color-coded bus routes covering the island from 6:30 AM to 11:30 PM. Stops have signs with the international symbol for bus. Schedules are available on buses and at hotels, visitor centers, and shops. The fare is 75¢ (exact change).

Bone Island Shuttle circles the island from 9 AM to 10 PM, stopping at attractions, hotels, and restaurants. Passengers pay $5 per day for unlimited riding. You can park at the city's Park 'n' Ride 24-hour garage at the corner of Caroline and Grinnell streets and catch a city bus to Old Town at no extra cost. The shuttle runs 10 AM to 6:30 PM and costs 50¢ each way. Parking runs $1 an hour/$6 a day if you use the shuttle, $1.25 an hour/$8 a day if you don't.

The Dade–Monroe Express provides daily bus service from the Mile Marker 98 in Key Largo to the Florida City Wal-Mart Supercenter. The bus makes several stops in Key Largo, then heads for the islands for daily round-trips on the hour from 6:55 AM to 9:55 PM. The cost is $1.25 each way.

➤ BUS INFORMATION: **Bone Island Shuttle** (☎ 305/293–8710). **City of Key West Department of Transportation** (☎ 305/292–8160). **Dade–Monroe Express** (☎ 305/770–3131). **Greyhound Lines** (☎ 800/410–5397 or 800/231–2222). **Park 'n' Ride** (✉ 300 Grinnell St., ☎ 305/293–6426).

CAR RENTAL

Two- and four-passenger open-air electric cars that travel about 25 mph are an environmentally friendly way to get around the island. Rent them from Key West Cruisers for $89/$129 a half day for the two-/four-seater or $119/$169 a day.

Avis and Budget serve Marathon Airport. Key West's airport has booths for Alamo, Avis, Budget, Dollar, and Hertz. Tropical Rent-A-Car is based in the city center. Enterprise Rent-A-Car has offices in Key Largo, Marathon, and Key West. Thrifty Car Rental has an office in Tavernier.

CUTTING COSTS

Avoid flying into Key West and driving back to Miami; there are substantial drop-off charges for leaving a Key West car in Miami.

➤ LOCAL AGENCIES: **Alamo** (☎ 305/294–6675 or 800/327–9633). **Avis** (✉ Key West Airport, ☎ 305/294–4846; Marathon Airport, ☎ 305/743–5428 or 800/831–2847). **Budget** (✉ Key West Airport, ☎ 305/294–8868; Marathon Airport, ☎ 305/743–3998 or 800/527–0700). **Dollar** (☎ 305/296–9921 or 800/800–4000). **Enterprise Rent-A-Car** (☎ 800/325–8007). **Hertz** (☎ 305/294–1039 or 800/654–3131). **Key West Cruisers** (✉ Truman Ave. at Duval St., ☎ 305/294–4724 or 888/800–8802). **Thrifty Car Rental** has an office in Tavernier (✉ MM 91.8, OS, ☎ 305/852–6088). **Tropical Rent-A-Car** (✉ 1300 Duval St., Key West, ☎ 305/294–8136).

CAR TRAVEL

From MIA follow signs to Coral Gables and Key West, which put you on Lejeune Road, then Route 836 west. Take the Homestead Extension of Florida's Turnpike south (toll road), which ends at Florida City and connects to U.S. 1. Tolls from the airport run approximately $1.25. The alternative from Florida City is Card Sound Road (Route 905A), which has a bridge toll of $1.75. Continue to the only stop sign and turn right on Route 905, which rejoins U.S. 1 31 mi south of Florida City. Avoid flying into Key West and driving back to Miami; there are substantial drop-off charges for leaving a Key West car in Miami.

In Key West's Old Town, parking is scarce and costly ($1.50 per hour at Mallory Square). It's better to take a taxi, rent a bicycle or moped, walk, or take a shuttle to get around.

Elsewhere in the Keys, a car is crucial. Gas costs more than on the mainland, so fill your tank in Miami and top it off in Florida City.

Most of the Overseas Highway is narrow and crowded (especially weekends and in high season). Expect delays behind RVs, trucks, cars towing boats, and rubbernecking tourists.

The best Keys road map, published by the Homestead/Florida City Chamber of Commerce, can be obtained for $3.25 from the Tropical Everglades Visitor Center.

➤ CONTACTS: **Tropical Everglades Visitor Center** (✉ 160 U.S. 1, Florida City 33034, ☎ 305/245–9180 or 800/388–9669).

EMERGENCIES

Dial 911 for police, fire, or ambulance. Keys Hotline provides information and emergency assistance in six languages. Florida Marine Patrol maintains a 24-hour telephone service to handle reports of boating emergencies and natural-resource violations. Coast Guard Group Key West responds to local marine emergencies and reports of navigation hazards.

The Keys have no 24-hour pharmacies. Hospital pharmacists will help with emergencies after regular retail business hours.

The following hospitals have 24-hour emergency rooms: Fishermen's Hospital, Lower Florida Keys Health System, and Mariners Hospital.
➤ CONTACTS: **Coast Guard Group Key West** (☎ 305/295–9700). **Fishermen's Hospital** (✉ MM 48.7, OS, Marathon, ☎ 305/743–5533). **Florida Marine Patrol** (✉ MM 48, BS, 2796 Overseas Hwy., Suite 100, State Regional Service Center, Marathon 33050, ☎ 305/289–2320; 800/342–5367 after 5 PM). **Keys Hotline** (☎ 800/771–5397). **Lower Florida Keys Health System** (✉ MM 5, BS, 5900 College Rd., Stock Island, ☎ 305/294–5531). **Mariners Hospital** (✉ MM 88.5, BS, 50 High Point Rd., Plantation Key, ☎ 305/852–4418).

ENGLISH-LANGUAGE MEDIA

NEWSPAPERS AND MAGAZINES

The best of the publications covering Key West is weekly *Solares Hill.* The best weekday source of information on Key West is the *Key West Citizen,* which also publishes a Sunday edition. For the Upper and Middle Keys, turn to the semiweekly *Keynoter.* The *Free Press, Reporter,* and *Upper Keys Independent* cover the same area once a week. The *Miami Herald* publishes a Keys edition with good daily listings of local events. The monthly *Celebrate Key West* is a good source for gay and lesbian travelers.

TELEVISION AND RADIO

WLRN (National Public Radio) is 91.3, 92.1, and 93.5, depending on where you are in the Keys; WKLG 102.1 bilingual (English and Spanish) adult contemporary; WCTH 100.3 country; WFKZ 103.1 adult contemporary; WKEZ 96.9 easy listening; WFFG AM 1300 Keys talk radio, sports, and news; WKYZ 101.3 classic rock.

LODGING

Brenda Donnelly represents more than 60 guest houses, B&Bs, and inns in prices ranging from $60–$545 a night through Inn Touch in Key West. Key West Vacation Rentals lists historic cottages, homes, and condominiums for rent. Although it prefers to handle reservations for all types of accommodations in advance, the Key West Welcome Center gets a lot of walk-in business because of its location on U.S. 1 at the entrance to Key West. Property Management of Key West, Inc. offers lease and rental service for condominiums, town houses, and private homes. Rent Key West Vacations specializes in renting vacation houses. Vacation Key West lists all kinds of properties throughout Key West.

APARTMENT AND VILLA RENTALS

➤ LOCAL AGENTS: **Inn Touch in Key West** (✉ 1214 Laird St., #1, Key West 33040, ☎ 305/296–2953 or 800/492–1911, FAX 305/292–1621). **Key West Vacation Rentals** (✉ 525 Simonton St., Key West 33040, ☎ 305/292–7997 or 800/621–9405, FAX 305/294–7501). **Key West Welcome Center** (✉ 3840 N. Roosevelt Blvd., Key West 33040, ☎ 305/296–4444 or 800/284–4482). **Property Management of Key West,**

Inc. (✉ 1213 Truman Ave., Key West 33040, ☎ 305/296–7744). **Rent Key West Vacations** (✉ 1107 Truman Ave., Key West 33040, ☎ 305/294–0990 or 800/833–7368, WEB www.rentkeywest.com). **Vacation Key West** (✉ 513 Fleming St., Key West 33040, ☎ 305/295–9500 or 800/595–5397).

TAXIS

Serving the Keys from Ocean Reef to Key West, Luxury Limousine has luxury sedans and limos that seat up to 10 passengers.

In the Upper Keys (MM 94–74), Village Taxi charges $2 per mile for vans that hold six. It also makes airport runs. In the Middle Keys, Cheapo Taxi rates are $1 for pickup and $1 per mile. Drops beyond MM 61 and MM 40 are $1.50 a mile. Florida Keys Taxi Dispatch operates around the clock in Key West. The fare for two or more from the Key West airport to New Town is $5 per person with a cap of $15; to Old Town it's $7 and $30, respectively. Otherwise meters register $1.75 to start, 45¢ for each ⅕ mi, and 45¢ for every 50 seconds of waiting time.
➤ TAXI INFORMATION: **Cheapo Taxi** (☎ 305/743–7420). **Florida Keys Taxi Dispatch** (☎ 305/296–1800). **Luxury Limousine** (☎ 305/664–0601, 305/367–2329, or 800/664–0124). **Village Taxi** (☎ 305/664–8181).

TOURS

Island Aeroplane Tours flies up to two passengers in a 1941 Waco, an open-cockpit biplane. Tours range from a quick six- to eight-minute overview of Key West ($50 for two) to a 50-minute look at the offshore reefs ($245 for two). Seaplanes of Key West offers half-day trips to the Dry Tortugas, where you can explore Fort Jefferson, built in 1846, and snorkel on the beautiful protected reef. A cooler of drinks and snorkel equipment is included in the $159 per person fee.

Key West Nature Bike Tour explores the natural, noncommercial side of Key West at a leisurely pace, stopping on back streets and in backyards of private homes to sample native fruits and view indigenous plants and trees. The tours run 90–120 minutes and cost $20, including a bike.

Coral Reef Park Co. runs sailing trips on a 38-ft catamaran as well as glass-bottom boat tours. Captain Sterling's Everglades Eco-Tours operates Everglades and Florida Bay ecology tours ($35 per person), sunset cruises ($25 per person), and a private charter evening crocodile tour ($199 for up to four passengers). Bob and Gale Dumouchel have run low-impact eco-tours through Gale Force Charters since 1988. Tours leave from Sugarloaf Marina and venture into the channels and islands of the Great White Heron National Wildlife Refuge aboard the *Gale Force,* a 24-ft Carolina skiff whose shallow draft allows the boat to get really close to nature. It also has a viewing tower. Half-day tours cost $200 for two, $25 each additional person up to six people. A Seagrass Awareness excursion shows seahorses and other inhabitants of the grass beds. All tours include snorkel gear, instruction, narration walking tours, and beach time. Fishing, snorkel, and kayak tours are also offered. They also run guided kayak tours.

Key Largo Princess offers two-hour glass-bottom boat trips ($18) and sunset cruises on a luxury 70-ft motor yacht with a 280-square-ft glass viewing area, departing from the Holiday Inn docks. M/V *Discovery* and the 65-ft *Pride of Key West* are glass-bottom boats. Strike Zone Charters offers glass-bottom boat excursions into the backcountry and to Looe Key. The five-hour Island Excursion ($45) emphasizes nature and Keys history. Besides close encounters with birds, sea life, and vegetation, there's a fish cookout on an island. Snorkel and fishing equipment, food, and drinks are included. This is one of the few nature outings in the Keys with wheelchair access.

Victoria Impallomeni, noted wilderness guide and authority on the ecology of Florida Bay, invites nature lovers—and especially children—aboard the *Imp II,* a 24-ft Aquasport, for four-hour half-day ($400) and seven-hour full-day ($550) eco-tours that frequently include encounters with wild dolphins. While island-hopping, you visit underwater gardens, natural shoreline, and mangrove habitats. Everything is supplied except the picnic. Tours leave from Murray's Marina. *Wolf* is Key West's tall ship and the flagship of the Conch Republic. The 74-ft, 44-passenger topsail schooner operates day cruises as well as sunset and starlight cruises with live music.

The Conch Tour Train is a 90-minute narrated tour of Key West, traveling 14 mi through Old Town and around the island. Board at Mallory Square and Roosevelt Boulevard (just north of the Quality Inn) every half hour (9–4:30 from Mallory Square, later at other stops). The cost is $19. Old Town Trolley operates 12 trackless trolley-style buses, departing from the Mallory Square and Roosevelt Boulevard depots every 30 minutes (9:30–4:30 from Mallory Square, later at other stops), for 75-minute narrated tours of Key West. The smaller trolleys go places the train won't fit. You may disembark at any of nine stops and reboard a later trolley. The cost is $19.

Adventure Charters & Tours loads kayaks onto the 42-ft catamaran *Island Fantasea* and heads out to the Great White Heron National Wildlife Refuge for guided kayak nature tours with a maximum of 14 passengers. Half-day trips ($30) last 2½ hours and depart at 9 and 2. Full-day trips ($100) include snorkeling, fishing, a grilled lunch, drinks, and a sunset. The folks at Florida Bay Outfitters know Upper Keys and Everglades waters well. You can take a one- to seven-day canoe or kayak tour to the Everglades or Lignumvitae or Indian Key, or a night trip to neighboring islands. Trips run $45–$800. Highly recommended lost World Kayaking leads personalized guided kayak nature tours ($45 half day) through the Lower Keys and Key West, with stops at nearby refuges. A 16-ft motorized skiff takes two kayakers and their kayaks deep into the backcountry. Then they anchor and explore the remote area by kayak. Half-day trips run $90 per person, up to two people. Mosquito Coast Island Outfitters and Kayak Guides runs full-day guided sea-kayak natural-history tours around the mangrove islands just east of Key West. The $45-a-day charge covers transportation, bottled water, a snack, and supplies, including snorkeling gear. Under Emily Graves' ownership, Reflections Nature Tours operates daily custom and group kayak trips into the Great White Heron National Wildlife Refuge and Everglades National Park to explore mangrove hammocks, shallow water, islands, creeks, and sponge and grass flats. Three-hour tours start at $49.

In addition to publishing several good guides on Key West, the Historic Florida Keys Foundation conducts tours of the City Cemetery Tuesday and Thursday at 9:30. As the former state historian in Key West and the current owner of a historic-preservation consulting firm, Sharon Wells of Island City Strolls knows plenty about Key West. She's authored many works, including the "The Walking and Biking Guide to Historic Key West," which features 10 self-guided tours of the historic district. It's available free at guest houses, hotels, and Key West bookstores. If that whets your appetite, sign on for one of her walking tours, including Architectural Strolls, Literary Landmarks, and Historic 1847 Cemetery Stroll, which cost $25.

"Pelican Path" is a free walking guide to Key West published by the Old Island Restoration Foundation. The tour discusses the history and architecture of 43 structures along 25 blocks of 12 Old Town streets. Pick up a copy at the chamber of commerce.

➤ TOURS INFORMATION: **Adventure Charters & Tours** (✉ 6810 Front St., Stock Island 33040, ☎ 305/296–0362). **Conch Tour Train** (☎ 305/294–5161). **Coral Reef Park Co.** (✉ John Pennekamp Coral Reef State Park, MM 102.5, OS, Key Largo 33037, ☎ 305/451–1621). **Everglades Eco-Tours** (✉ Dolphin's Cove, MM 102, BS, Key Largo 33037, ☎ 305/853–5161 or 888/224–6044). **Florida Bay Outfitters** (✉ MM 104, BS, 104050 Overseas Hwy., Key Largo 33037, ☎ 305/451–3018). **Gale Force Charters** (✉ 27960 Porgie Path, Little Torch Key 33042, ☎ 305/745–2868). **Historic Florida Keys Foundation** (✉ 510 Greene St., Old City Hall, Key West 33040, ☎ 305/292–6718). **Island Aeroplane Tours** (✉ Key West Airport, 3469 S. Roosevelt Blvd., ☎ 305/294–8687). **Island City Strolls** (☎ 305/294–8380). ***Key Largo Princess*** (✉ MM 99.7, OS, 99701 Overseas Hwy., Key Largo 33037, ☎ 305/451–4655). **Key West Nature Bike Tour** (✉ Truman Ave. and Simonton St., Key West, ☎ 305/294–1882). **Lost World Kayaking** (✉ Box 431311, Big Pine Key 33043, ☎ 305/872–8950, 305/395–0930, or 877/595–2925). **Mosquito Coast Island Outfitters and Kayak Guides** (✉ 1107 Duval St., Key West 33040, ☎ 305/294–7178). **Murray's Marina** (✉ MM 5, Stock Island). **M/V *Discovery*** (✉ Land's End Marina, 251 Margaret St., Key West 33040, ☎ 305/293–0099). **Old Town Trolley** (✉ 6631 Maloney Ave., Key West, ☎ 305/296–6688). ***Pride of Key West*** (✉ 2 Duval St., Key West 33040, ☎ 305/296–6293). **Reflections Nature Tours** (✉ Big Pine Key, ☎ 305/872–2896). **Seaplanes of Key West** (✉ Key West Airport, 3471 S. Roosevelt Blvd., ☎ 305/294–0709). **Strike Zone Charters** (✉ MM 29.6, BS, 29675 Overseas Hwy., Big Pine Key 33043, ☎ 305/872–9863 or 800/654–9560). **Sugarloaf Marina** (✉ MM 17, BS, Sugarloaf Key). **Victoria Impallomeni** (✉ 5710 U.S. 1, Key West 33040, ☎ 305/294–9731 or 888/822–7366). ***Wolf*** (✉ Schooner Wharf, Key West Seaport, end of Greene St., Key West 33040, ☎ 305/296–9653).

VISITOR INFORMATION

➤ TOURIST INFORMATION: **Big Pine and the Lower Keys Chamber of Commerce** (✉ MM 31, OS, Box 430511, Big Pine Key 33043, ☎ 305/872–2411 or 800/872–3722, FAX 305/872–0752). **Florida Keys & Key West Visitors Bureau** (✉ 402 Wall St., Key West 33040, ☎ 800/352–5397, WEB www.fla-keys.com). **Greater Key West Chamber of Commerce (mainstream)** (✉ 402 Wall St., Key West 33040, ☎ 305/294–2587 or 800/527–8539, FAX 305/294–7806). **Greater Marathon Chamber of Commerce & Visitor Center** (✉ MM 53.5, BS, 12222 Overseas Hwy., Marathon 33050, ☎ 305/743–5417 or 800/842–9580). **Islamorada Chamber of Commerce** (✉ MM 82.5, BS, Box 915, Islamorada 33036, ☎ 305/664–4503 or 800/322–5397). **Key Largo Chamber of Commerce** (✉ MM 106, BS, 106000 Overseas Hwy., Key Largo 33037, ☎ 305/451–1414 or 800/822–1088, FAX 305/451–4726). **Key West Business Guild (gay)** (✉ 728 Duval St, Box 1208, Key West 33041, ☎ 305/294–4603 or 800/535–7797, WEB www.gaykeywestfl.com). **Monroe Council of the Arts** (✉ 5100 College Rd, Box 717, Key West 33040, ☎ 305/294–4406 Key West; 305/743–0079 Middle Keys; 305/852–1469 Upper Keys, WEB www.keysarts.org). **Reef Relief Environmental Center & Store** (✉ 201 William St., Key West 33041, ☎ 305/294–3100).

6 BACKGROUND AND ESSENTIALS

WHAT TO READ AND WATCH BEFORE YOU GO

Books

Fiction

Steamy nights, sultry breezes, palm-dotted beaches, the heady whiff of frangipani in the air—all this idyllic setting needs is some seedy characters, a femme (or homme) fatale and a hard-boiled detective. South Florida's colorful scenery, both natural and human, is the canvas used by a whole posse of detective, mystery, and crime writers.

Interestingly, some of the finest fiction writers come from the *Miami Herald*, the city's top-notch daily newspaper. At the top of the list is Carl Hiaasen, who brilliantly skewers the pack of corrupt politicians, big-business phonies, land developers, and tourism interests every week in his *Herald* column. But it is his satirical fiction that manages to encompass everything that makes up Florida, for better and for worse. Populated by con artists, plastic surgeons, crooked cops, rednecks, bass fishermen, strippers, the Mafia, theme-park developers, backwoods hermits, and lottery winners, Hiaasen's hilarious novels will tell you all you need to know about South Florida. Read *Lucky You, Stormy Weather, Tourist Season, Skin Tight, Double Whammy, Native Tongue, Sick Puppy,* and *Strip Tease,* and you will be educated and entertained.

Pulitzer Prize–winner Edna Buchanan's two nonfiction books, *The Corpse Had a Familiar Face* and *Never Let Them See You Cry,* related the unbelievable and absolutely true crime stories she covered as a *Miami Herald* reporter. She later turned to fiction with a series of mysteries featuring Britt Montero, a Cuban-American reporter, including *Margin of Error*; *Contents Under Pressure*; *Miami, It's Murder*; and *Suitable for Framing*.

Additional suspense novels that are rich in details about South Florida include Elmore Leonard's *La Brava* and Palm Beach–based *Maximum Bob*; Paul Levine's Jake Lassiter series, featuring a pro football player turned lawyer, including *Night Vision* and *False Dawn*; Les Standiford's *Deal on Ice,* one in a series of books featuring contractor-sleuth John Deal; former prosecuting attorney Barbara Parker's *Suspicion of Innocence*; John D. MacDonald's *The Empty Copper Sea*; and Charles Willeford's *Miami Blues*. James W. Hall features Florida in many of his big sellers, such as *Mean High Tide,* the chilling *Bones of Coral,* and *Hard Aground.* Another Miami-based mystery is *The Informant,* James M. Grippando's thriller about an FBI hunt for a serial killer. South Florida native Carl Hiaasen has turned out lots of Florida-based books, including *Double Whammy, Lucky You,* and *Sick Puppy.*

Peter Matthiessen's *Killing Mister Watson* re-creates turn-of-the-last-century lower southwest Florida. *Princess of the Everglades,* by Charles Mink, is a novel about the 1926 hurricane. A more recent look at Florida's past is in Bill Belleville's *River of Lakes: A Journey on Florida's St. Johns River,* which shows there are still traces of wilderness here.

Other recommended titles include Roxanne Pulitzer's *Facade,* set against a backdrop of Palm Beach; Pat Booth's *Miami*; Sam Harrison's *Bones of Blue Coral* and *Birdsong Ascending*; T. D. Allman's *Miami*; Joan Didion's *Miami*; David Rieff's *Going to Miami*; and *Florida Straits,* by Laurence Shames; *To Have and Have Not,* by Ernest Hemingway; and *Their Eyes Were Watching God,* by Zora Neale Hurston.

For a peek into Cuban-American society, check out Christina Garcia's

The Agüero Sisters, the story of two long-estranged Cuban sisters, one in Cuba, the other in Florida. *Miami Herald* columnist Ana Veciana-Suarez chronicles the lives of three generations of Cuban-American women in *The Chin Kiss King.* Although they are not set in South Florida, the novels of young Haitian author Edwidge Danticat—*Breath, Eyes, Memory*; *The Farming of Bones: A Novel*; and *Krik? Krak!*—offer insight into Haitian life and culture.

Nonfiction

Among recommended nonfiction books are *The Commodore's Story,* by Ralph Munroe and Vincent Gilpin, a luminous reminiscence about the golden years (pre-railroad) of Coconut Grove; *Key West Writers and Their Homes,* by Lynn Kaufelt; and *The Everglades: River of Grass,* by Marjory S. Douglas—a must-read for those interested in capturing the essence of those unique wetlands. *Some Kind of Paradise,* by Mark Derr reviews Florida's environmental follies. John Rothchild's *Up for Grabs* is about the state's commercial lunacy. *The Florida Reader* (Maurice O'Sullivan and Jack Lane, editors) is a good anthology.

A good introduction to greater Miami is *Miami, the Magic City,* by historian Arva Moore Parks, one of the best-known chroniclers of local lore. Also check out the well-documented *Miami Beach: A History,* by Howard Kleinberg. For more on Miami's questionable politics and weird culture, pick up *Kick Ass,* a collection of Haissen's newspaper columns.

Pictures tell photogenic greater Miami's story well. With 400 color photos, *Miami: Hot and Cool,* by Laura Cerwinske, takes a sophisticated look at Miami as the capital of American chic. *Miami,* by Santi Visalli, is one of a series of large-format photographic books on great American cities. Another good coffee-table book is *Miami: City of Dreams,* by Les Standiford and photographer Alan S. Maltz.

How Miami deals with its unique cultural diversity and influx of immigrants has been a hot topic for social observation. *City on the Edge: The Transformation of Miami,* by Alejandro Portes documents the development of Miami's ethnic communities. Other titles include T. D. Allman's *Miami, City of the Future*; David Rieff's *Going to Miami: Exiles, Tourists and Refugees in the New America*; and Joan Didion's *Miami,* an exploration of the influential Cuban community.

The chronicles of South Beach's Art Deco District are told by one of the key players in the preservation movement, the late Barbara Baer Capitman, in *Deco Delights: Preserving the Beauty* and *Joy of Miami Beach Architecture.* For more Deco pick up *Tropical Deco: The Architecture and Design of Old Miami Beach,* by Laura Cerwinske and David Kaminsky, photographer.

A good way to whet your appetite for South Florida's distinctive cuisine—dubbed Floribbean or New World by foodies—is to check out *Mmmmiami: Tempting Tropical Tastes for Home Cooks Everywhere,* by cooking teacher Carole Kotkin and *Miami Herald* food editor Kathy Martin. Another good choice is Steven Raichlen's *Miami Spice: The New Florida Cuisine,* 200 recipes that use native ingredients to capture the convergence of Latin, Caribbean and Cuban cultures.

The country's most gleefully sophomoric humor columnist, Dave Barry, is on staff at the *Miami Herald,* and his many weekly columns and books deal with living in South Florida. One of his latest is *Dave Barry Turns 50.*

Film and Video

There's a great misconception that California is the center of the motion picture industry. Never heard of 'em. Florida is the *true* film capital, and we have the recount to prove it. Greater Miami's ever-growing film business is visible as movie, fashion, and video shoots take over the streets of South Beach, locations such as the Venetian Pool, or lush lots in Coconut Grove. Locals have come to take the street closings and detours in stride, but celebrity sightings are duly reported the next day in the *Miami Herald*.

Certainly Greater Miami's moviemaking industry has increased in stature since 1967, when Elvis Presley's *Clambake* was shot here (despite the appearance of mountains in some of the Miami scenes), and 1972, when Linda Lovelace's infamous *Deep Throat* gained notoriety. Recent movies at least partially filmed in South Florida include *Random Hearts,* with Harrison Ford; *Primary Colors,* with John Travolta and Emma Thompson; *Donnie Brasco,* with Johnny Depp and Anne Heche; *The Birdcage,* with Robin Williams and Nathan Lane; *Up Close and Personal,* with Robert Redford and Michelle Pfeiffer; and *Wrestling Ernest Hemingway,* with Robert Duvall and Shirley MacLaine.

The blockbuster gross-out comedy *There's Something About Mary,* with Cameron Diaz and Ben Stiller, was filmed at several South Florida locations. So was Jim Carrey's popular *Ace Ventura: Pet Detective. True Lies,* one of James Cameron's pre-*Titanic* megaeffects extravaganzas, captivated downtown Miami for days during filming of a helicopter mounted on a high-rise. Key scenes for critical dud *The Specialist,* with sometime Miami resident Sylvester Stallone and Sharon Stone, were shot at the Biltmore in Coral Gables.

Other films—panned by critics but sometimes providing escapist fun—include *Wild Things,* with Kevin Bacon and Neve Campbell; *Big City Blues,* with Burt Reynolds and Vivian Wu; *Fair Game,* with William Baldwin and Cindy Crawford; *Blood and Wine,* with Jack Nicholson and Jennifer Lopez; and the unfortunate film version of Carl Hiaasen's very funny novel *Strip Tease,* starring Demi Moore and Burt Reynolds.

ESSENTIAL INFORMATION

AIR TRAVEL

BOOKING

When you book **look for nonstop flights** and **remember that "direct" flights stop at least once.** Try to avoid connecting flights, which require a change of plane. For more booking tips and to check prices and make online flight reservations, log on to www.fodors.com.

CARRIERS

➤ MAJOR AIRLINES: **American** (☎ 800/433–7300). **Continental** (☎ 800/525–0280). **Delta** (☎ 800/221–1212). **Midway** (☎ 800/446–4392). **Northwest** (☎ 800/225–2525). **Spirit** (☎ 800/772–7117). **TWA** (☎ 800/221–2000). **United** (☎ 800/241–6522). **US Airways** (☎ 800/428–4322).

➤ REGIONAL AIRLINES: **AirTran** (☎ 800/247–8726) to Miami and Fort Lauderdale. **Jet Blue** (☎ 800/538–2583) to Fort Lauderdale. **Midwest Express** (☎ 800/452–2022) to Fort Lauderdale. **Southwest** (☎ 800/435–9792) to Fort Lauderdale.

➤ FROM THE U.K.: **American** (☎ 0345/789–789). **British Airways** (☎ 0345/222–111). **Continental** (☎ 0800/776–464) via Newark. **Delta** (☎ 0800/414–767). **Northwest** (☎ 0990/561–000) via Detroit or Minneapolis. **TWA** (☎ 0800/222–222) via St. Louis. **United** (☎ 0800/888–555). **Virgin Atlantic** (☎ 01293/747–747).

CHECK-IN & BOARDING

Assuming that not everyone with a ticket will show up, airlines routinely overbook planes. When everyone does, airlines ask for volunteers to give up their seats. In return, these volunteers usually get a certificate for a free flight and are rebooked on the next flight out. If there are not enough volunteers, the airline must choose who will be denied boarding. The first to get bumped are passengers who checked in late and those flying on discounted tickets, so **get to the gate and check in as early as possible,** especially during peak periods.

Always **bring a government-issued photo I.D. to the airport;** a passport is best. You may be asked to show it before you are allowed to check in.

CUTTING COSTS

The least expensive airfares to Florida must usually be purchased in advance and are nonrefundable. It's smart to **call a number of airlines, and when you are quoted a good price, book it on the spot**—the same fare may not be available the next day. Always **check different routings** and look into using different airports. Travel agents, especially low-fare specialists (☞ Discounts & Deals), are helpful.

Consolidators are another good source. They buy tickets for scheduled international flights at reduced rates from the airlines, then sell them at prices that beat the best fare available directly from the airlines, usually without restrictions. Sometimes you can even get your money back if you need to return the ticket. Carefully read the fine print detailing penalties for changes and cancellations, and **confirm your consolidator reservation with the airline.**

➤ CONSOLIDATORS: **Cheap Tickets** (☎ 800/377–1000). **Discount Airline Ticket Service** (☎ 800/576–1600). **Unitravel** (☎ 800/325–2222). **Up & Away Travel** (☎ 212/889–2345). **World Travel Network** (☎ 800/409–6753).

➤ CHEAP RATES FROM THE U.K.: **Flight Express Travel** (✉ 77 New Bond St., London W1Y 9DB, U.K., ☎ 0171/409–3311). **Trailfinders**

(✉ 42–50 Earls Court Rd., London W8 6FT, U.K., ☎ 0171/937–5400). **Travel Cuts** (✉ 295A Regent St., London W1R 7YA, U.K., ☎ 0171/637–3161).

ENJOYING THE FLIGHT

For more legroom, **request an emergency-aisle seat.** Don't sit in the row in front of the emergency aisle or in front of a bulkhead, where seats may not recline. If you have dietary concerns, **ask for special meals when booking.** These can be vegetarian, low-cholesterol, or kosher, for example. On long flights, try to maintain a normal routine, to help fight jet lag. At night, **get some sleep.** By day, **eat light meals, drink water** (not alcohol), and **move around the cabin** to stretch your legs. For additional jet-lag tips consult *Fodor's FYI: Tarvel Fit & Healthy* (available at bookstores everywhere).

FLYING TIMES

Flying times to Florida vary based on the city you're flying to, but typical times are 3 hours from New York, 4 hours from Chicago, 2¾ hours from Dallas, 4½–5½ hours from Los Angeles, and 8–8½ hours from London.

HOW TO COMPLAIN

If your baggage goes astray or your flight goes awry, complain right away. Most carriers require that you **file a claim immediately.**

➤ AIRLINE COMPLAINTS: U.S. Department of Transportation **Aviation Consumer Protection Division** (✉ C-75, Room 4107, Washington, DC 20590, ☎ 202/366–2220, WEB www.dot.gov/airconsumer). **Federal Aviation Administration Consumer Hotline** (☎ 800/322–7873).

AIRPORTS

If you're destined for the north side of Miami-Dade County (metro Miami), or are renting a car at the airport, **consider flying into Fort Lauderdale–Hollywood International**; it's much easier to use than Miami International, and often—if not always—cheaper. The airports are only 40 minutes apart by car.

➤ AIRPORT INFORMATION: **Fort Lauderdale–Hollywood International (FLL)** (☎ 954/359–1200). **Miami International Airport (MIA)** (☎ 305/876–7000). **Palm Beach International (PBI)** (☎ 561/471–7420).

BIKE TRAVEL

Florida statutes require that bikers under 16 wear a helmet. Bicycle passengers under 4 years old must be in a sling or child seat. All bikes must have lamps or reflectors—white in the front, and red in the back, visible from 500 ft—between sunset and sunrise.

BIKES IN FLIGHT

Most airlines accommodate bikes as luggage, provided they are dismantled and boxed. Airlines sell bike boxes, which are often free at bike shops, for about $5 (it's at least $100 for bike bags). International travelers can sometimes substitute a bike for a piece of checked luggage at no charge; otherwise, the cost is about $100. Domestic and Canadian airlines charge $25–$50.

BUS TRAVEL

Greyhound passes through practically every major city in Florida. For schedules and fares, **contact your local Greyhound Information Center.**

➤ BUS INFORMATION: **Greyhound Lines** (☎ 800/231–2222).

BUSINESS HOURS

MUSEUMS & SIGHTS

Many museums in South Florida are closed Mondays and are open 10–5 Tuesday through Friday and noon–5 on Sundays.

CAMERAS & PHOTOGRAPHY

EQUIPMENT PRECAUTIONS

Don't pack film and equipment in checked luggage, where it is much more susceptible to damage. X-ray machines used to view checked luggage are becoming much more powerful and therefore are much more likely to ruin your film. Always **keep film and tape out of the sun.** Carry an extra supply of batteries, and **be prepared to turn on your camera or camcorder** to prove to security personnel that the device is real. Always **ask for hand inspection of film,** which becomes clouded after repeated exposure to airport X-ray machines, and **keep videotapes away from metal detectors.** The *Kodak Guide to Shooting Great Travel Pictures* (available at bookstores everywhere) is loaded with tips.

CAR RENTAL

In-season rates in Miami begin at $36 a day and $170 a week for an economy car with air-conditioning, an automatic transmission, and unlimited mileage. Rates in Fort Lauderdale begin at $36 a day and $159 a week. This does not include tax on car rentals, which is 6%. Bear in mind that rates fluctuate tremendously—both above and below these quoted figures—depending on demand and the season. Rental cars are more expensive (and harder to find) during peak holidays and in season.

It used to be that major rental agencies were located at the airport whereas cheaper firms weren't. Now however, even the majors might be off airport property. It varies firm to firm and airport to airport. Speedy check-in and frequent shuttle buses make off-airport rentals almost as convenient as on-site service. However, it's wise to allow a little extra time for bus travel between the rental agency and the airport.

➤ Major Agencies: **Alamo** (☎ 800/327–9633; 020/8759–6200 in the U.K.). **Avis** (☎ 800/331–1212; 800/879–2847 in Canada; 02/9353–9000 in Australia; 09/525–1982 in New Zealand; 0870/606–0100 in the U.K.). **Budget** (☎ 800/527–0700; 0144/227–6266 in the U.K., through affiliate Europcar). **Dollar** (☎ 800/800–4000; 0124/622–0111 in the U.K., where it is known as Sixt Kenning; 02/9223–1444 in Australia). **Hertz** (☎ 800/654–3131; 800/263–0600 in Canada; 020/8897–2072 in the U.K.; 02/9669–2444 in Australia; 09/256–8690 in New Zealand). **National Car Rental** (☎ 800/227–7368; 0845/722–2525 in the U.K., where it is known as National Europe).

CUTTING COSTS

To get the best deal, **book through a travel agent who will shop around.** Also **price local car-rental companies,** although the service and maintenance may not be as good as those of a major player. Remember to ask about required deposits, cancellation penalties, and drop-off charges if you're planning to pick up the car in one city and leave it in another. If you're traveling during a holiday period, also make sure that a confirmed reservation guarantees you a car.

➤ Local Agencies: **Apex Rent A Car** (☎ 954/782–3400) in Fort Lauderdale. **Continental Florida Auto Rental** (☎ 954/764–1008 or 800/327–3791) in Fort Lauderdale. **InterAmerican Car Rental** (☎ 305/871–3030 or 800/327–1278) in Fort Lauderdale, Miami, and Miami Beach. **Tropical Rent-A-Car** (☎ 305/294–8136) in Key West.

INSURANCE

When driving a rented car you are generally responsible for any damage to or loss of the vehicle as well as for any property damage or personal injury that you may cause. Before you rent, see what coverage your personal auto-insurance policy and credit cards provide.

For about $15 to $20 per day, rental companies sell protection, known as a collision- or loss-damage waiver (CDW or LDW), that eliminates your liability for damage to the car.

In most states you don't need a CDW if you have personal auto insurance or other liability insurance. However, **make sure you have enough coverage to pay for the car.** If you do not have auto insurance or an umbrella policy that covers damage to third parties, purchasing liability insurance and a CDW or LDW is highly recommended.

REQUIREMENTS & RESTRICTIONS

In Florida you must be 21 to rent a car, and rates may be higher if you're under 25. You'll pay extra for child seats (about $3 a day), which are compulsory for children under five, and for additional drivers (about $2 per day). Non-U.S. residents need a reservation voucher (for prepaid reservations that were made in the traveler's home country), a passport, a driver's license, and a travel policy that covers each driver, when picking up a car.

SURCHARGES

Before you pick up a car in one city and leave it in another, **ask about drop-off charges or one-way service fees,** which can be substantial. Note, too, that some rental agencies charge extra if you return the car before the time specified in your contract. To avoid a hefty refueling fee, **fill the tank just before you turn in the car,** but be aware that gas stations near the rental outlet may overcharge.

CAR TRAVEL

Two major interstates lead to South Florida. Interstate 95 begins in Maine, runs south through the Mid-Atlantic states, and enters Florida just north of Jacksonville. It continues south past Daytona Beach, the Space Coast, Vero Beach, Palm Beach, and Fort Lauderdale, eventually ending in Miami.

Interstate 75 begins in Michigan at the Canadian border and runs south through Ohio, Kentucky, Tennessee, and Georgia, then moves south through the center of the state before veering west into Tampa. It follows the west coast south to Naples, then crosses the state through the northern section of the Everglades, and ends in Fort Lauderdale.

ROAD CONDITIONS

Florida has its share of traffic problems. Downtown areas of such major cities as Miami, Orlando, and Tampa can be extremely congested during rush hours, usually 7 to 9 AM and 4 to 6 PM on weekdays. When you drive the interstate system in Florida, try to **plan your trip so that you are not entering, leaving, or passing through a large city during rush hour,** when traffic can slow to 10 mph for 10 mi or more. In addition, snowbirds usually rent in Florida for a month at a time, which means they all arrive on the first of the month and leave on the 31st. Believe it or not, from November to March, when the end and beginning of a month occur on a weekend, north–south routes like Interstate 75 and Interstate 95 almost come to a standstill during daylight hours. It's best to avoid traveling on these days if possible.

RULES OF THE ROAD

Speed limits are 55 mph on state highways, 30 mph within city limits and residential areas, and 55–70 mph on interstates and Florida's Turnpike. Be alert for signs announcing exceptions.

All passengers are required to wear seat belts; **children under 16 are required to ride in the rear seat.** Florida's Alcohol/Controlled Substance DUI Law is one of the toughest in the United States. A blood alcohol level of.08 or higher can have serious repercussions even for the first-time offender.

Always **secure children under age five into an approved child-restraint device.**

SAFETY

Before setting off on any drive, **make sure you know where you're going** and carry a map. At the car-rental agency or at your hotel **ask if there are any areas that you should avoid.** Always **keep your doors locked,** and ask questions only at toll booths, gas stations, or other obviously safe locations. Also, **don't stop if your car is bumped from behind** or if you're asked for directions. One hesitates to foster rude behavior, but at least for now the roads are too risky to stop any place you're not familiar with (other than as traffic laws require). If you'll be renting a car and won't have a cellular phone with you, **ask the car-rental agency for a cellular phone.** Alamo, Avis, and Hertz are among the companies with in-car phones.

CHILDREN IN FLORIDA

If you are renting a car, don't forget to **arrange for a car seat** when you reserve. *Fodor's Around Miami with Kids* (available in bookstores everywhere) can help you plan your days together. For general advice about travelling with children, consult *Fodor's FYI: Travel with your Baby* (available at bookstores everywhere).

FLYING

If your children are two or older, **ask about children's airfares.** As a general rule, infants under two not occupying a seat fly at greatly reduced fares or even for free.

Experts agree that it's a good idea to use safety seats aloft for children weighing less than 40 pounds. Airlines set their own policies: U.S. carriers usually require that the child be ticketed, even if he or she is young enough to ride free, since the seats must be strapped into regular seats. Do **check your airline's policy about using safety seats during takeoff and landing.** And since safety seats are not allowed everywhere in the plane, get your seat assignments early.

When reserving, **request children's meals or a freestanding bassinet** if you need them. But note that bulkhead seats, where you must sit to use the bassinet, may lack an overhead bin or storage space on the floor.

LODGING

Florida may have the highest concentration of hotels with organized children's programs in the United States. Activities range from simple fun and recreation to learning about the Keys' environment from marine-science counselors at Cheeca Lodge. Sometimes kids' programs are complimentary; sometimes there's a charge. Not all accept children in diapers, and some offer programs when their central reservations services say they don't. Some programs are only offered during peak seasons or restrict hours in less-busy times. It always pays to **confirm details with the hotel in advance.** And **reserve space as soon as possible**; programs are often full by the morning or evening you need them.

Most hotels in Florida allow children under a certain age to stay in their parents' room at no extra charge, but others charge for them as extra adults; be sure to **find out the cutoff age for children's discounts.**

➤ FORT LAUDERDALE: **Marriott's Harbor Beach Resort's Beachside Buddies** (✉ 3030 Holiday Dr., Fort Lauderdale, FL 33316, ☎ 954/525–4000 or 800/228–9290), ages 5–12.

➤ THE KEYS: **Cheeca Lodge's Camp Cheeca** (✉ MM 82, OS, Box 527, Islamorada, FL 33036, ☎ 800/327–2888), ages 4–12. **Hawks Cay Resort's Island Adventure Club** (✉ MM 61, Duck Key, FL 33050, ☎ 800/432–2242), ages 5–12. **Westin Beach Resort's Westin Kids Club** (✉ MM 96.9, BS, 97000 Overseas Hwy., Key Largo, FL 33037, ☎ 305/852–5553 or 800/325–3535), ages 5–12.

➤ MIAMI AREA: **Sonesta Beach Resort's Just Us Kids** (✉ 350 Ocean Dr., Key Biscayne, FL 33149, ☎ 305/361–2021 or 800/766–3782), ages 5–13.

➤ PALM BEACH AND THE TREASURE COAST: **Club Med's Sandpiper** (✉ 3500 SE Morningside Blvd., Port St. Lucie, FL 34952, ☎ 561/398–5100 or 800/258–2633), Baby Club ages 4–24 months, Mini Club ages 2–11. **Hutchinson Island Marriott Resort's Pineapple Bunch Children's Camp** (✉ 555 N.E. Ocean Blvd., Hutchinson Island, Stuart, FL 34996, ☎ 561/225–3700), ages 4–12, plus a teen program.

SIGHTS & ATTRACTIONS

Places that are especially appealing to children are indicated by a rubber-duckie icon (🐤) in the margin.

TRANSPORTATION

Florida law requires that all children three years old or younger ride in a federally approved child safety seat when in any motor vehicle, regardless of the vehicle's registration state. Children four and five years of age must be restrained in either a child safety seat, booster seat, or safety belt.

CONSUMER PROTECTION

Whenever shopping or buying travel services in Florida, **pay with a major credit card,** if possible, so you can cancel payment or get reimbursed if there's a problem. If you're doing business with a particular company for the first time, **contact your local Better Business Bureau and the attorney general's offices** in your state and (for U.S. businesses) the company's home state as well. Have any complaints been filed? Finally, if you're buying a package or tour, always **consider travel insurance** that includes default coverage (☞ Insurance).

➤ BBBs: **Council of Better Business Bureaus** (✉ 4200 Wilson Blvd., Suite 800, Arlington, VA 22203, ☎ 703/276–0100, FAX 703/525–8277, WEB www.bbb.org).

CRUISE TRAVEL

The port of Miami is the cruise capital of the world, with the world's largest year-round fleet. It also handles more megaships—vessels capable of transporting more than 2,000 people at a time—than any other port in the world. Port Everglades, located 23 mi north of Miami, is the world's second-busiest cruise ship terminal. Seven-day eastern and western Caribbean cruises are the most popular type of cruise leaving from Miami-area ports. To learn how to plan, choose, and book a cruise-ship voyage, check out Cruise How-to's on www.fodors.com.

➤ CRUISE LINES: **Carnival Cruise Lines** (☎ 800/398–9819), **Celebrity Cruises** (☎ 800/437–3111), **Costa Cruises Lines** (☎ 800/462–6782), **Crystal Cruises** (☎ 800/446–6620), **Cunard Cruise Line** (☎ 800/728–6273), **Discovery Cruises** (☎ 800/866–8687), **Holland America Cruises** (☎ 800/628–4855), **Imperial Majesty Cruise Lines** (☎ 800/511–5737), **Norwegian Cruises** (☎ 800/327–7030 ext. 111), **Premier Cruises** (☎ 800/990–7770), **Princess** (☎ 800/774–6237), **Sea Escape Cruises** (☎ 800/327–2005), **SilverSea Cruises** (☎ 800/722–9955), **Windjammer** (☎ 800/327–2601).

DINING

The restaurants we list are the cream of the crop in each price category.

CATEGORY	COST*
$$$$	over $30
$$$	$20–$30
$$	$10–$20
$	under $10

**per person for one main course at dinner*

One cautionary word: Raw oysters have been identified as a problem for people with chronic illness of the liver, stomach, or blood, or who have immune disorders. Since 1993, all Florida restaurants serving raw oysters are required to post a notice in plain view of all patrons warning of the risks associated with consuming them.

RESERVATIONS & DRESS

Reservations are always a good idea at fancier restaurants: we mention them only when they're essential or not accepted. Book as far ahead as you can, and reconfirm as soon as you arrive. We mention dress only when men are required to wear a jacket or a jacket and tie.

SPECIALTIES

A trip to South Florida is incomplete without a taste of Cuban food. The cuisine is heavy, with pork dishes like *lechon asado,* served in garlic-based sauces. The two most typical dishes are *arroz con frijoles,* the staple side dish of rice and black beans, and *arroz con pollo,* chicken in a sticky yellow rice. Though available elsewhere in Florida, Key West is a mecca for lovers of key lime pie. Stands in Key West also serve up conch fritters. Stone crab claws, another South Florida delicacy, can be savored November through May.

DISABILITIES & ACCESSIBILITY

➤ LOCAL RESOURCES: **Metro-Dade Disability Services** (✉ 1335 NW 14th St., Miami, FL 33125, ☎ 305/547–5445, 305/545–3575 TDD) publishes a guidebook on the accessibility of Florida's hotels and motels, entitled *Access Florida,* and a *Directory of*

Services for the Physically Disabled in Dade County, both free.

Deaf Services Center (✉ 2182 McGreggor Blvd., Fort Myers, FL 33901, ☎ 941/461–0334 or 813/939–9977 TDD). **Florida Relay Service** (☎ 800/955–8770).

RESERVATIONS

When discussing accessibility with an operator or reservations agent, **ask hard questions.** Are there any stairs, inside *or* out? Are there grab bars next to the toilet *and* in the shower/tub? How wide is the doorway to the room? To the bathroom? For the most extensive facilities meeting the latest legal specifications, **opt for newer accommodations.**

➤ COMPLAINTS: **Aviation Consumer Protection Division** (☞ Air Travel) for airline-related problems. **Civil Rights Office** (✉ U.S. Department of Transportation, Departmental Office of Civil Rights, S-30, 400 7th St. SW, Room 10215, Washington, DC 20590, ☎ 202/366–4648, FAX 202/366–9371, WEB www.dot.gov/ost/docr/index.htm) for problems with surface transportation. **Disability Rights Section** (✉ U.S. Department of Justice, Civil Rights Division, Box 66738, Washington, DC 20035-6738, ☎ 202/514–0301 or 800/514–0301; 202/514–0383 TTY; 800/514–0383 TTY, FAX 202/307–1198, WEB www.usdoj.gov/crt/ada/adahom1.htm) for general complaints.

TRAVEL AGENCIES

In the United States, the Americans with Disabilities Act requires that travel firms serve the needs of all travelers. Some agencies specialize in working with people with disabilities.

➤ TRAVELERS WITH MOBILITY PROBLEMS: **Access Adventures** (✉ 206 Chestnut Ridge Rd., Scottsville, NY 14624, ☎ 716/889–9096, dltravel@prodigy.net), run by a former physical-rehabilitation counselor. **Accessible Vans of America** (✉ 9 Spielman Rd., Fairfield, NJ 07004, ☎ 877/282–8267, FAX 973/808–9713, WEB www.accessiblevans.com). **CareVacations** (✉ 5-5110 50th Ave., Leduc, Alberta T9E 6V4, Canada, ☎ 780/986–6404 or 877/478–7827, FAX 780/986–8332, WEB www.carevacations.com), for group tours and cruise vacations. **Flying Wheels Travel** (✉ 143 W. Bridge St., Box 382, Owatonna, MN 55060, ☎ 507/451–5005 or 800/535–6790, FAX 507/451–1685, WEB www.flyingwheelstravel.com).

➤ TRAVELERS WITH DEVELOPMENTAL DISABILITIES: **New Directions** (✉ 5276 Hollister Ave., Suite 207, Santa Barbara, CA 93111, ☎ 805/967–2841 or 888/967–2841, FAX 805/964–7344, WEB www.newdirectionstravel.com). **Sprout** (✉ 893 Amsterdam Ave., New York, NY 10025, ☎ 212/222–9575 or 888/222–9575, FAX 212/222–9768, WEB www.gosprout.org).

DISCOUNTS & DEALS

Be a smart shopper and **compare all your options** before making decisions. A plane ticket bought with a promotional coupon from travel clubs, coupon books, and direct-mail offers or on the Internet may not be cheaper than the least expensive fare from a discount ticket agency. And always keep in mind that what you get is just as important as what you save.

DISCOUNT RESERVATIONS

To save money, **look into discount reservations services** with toll-free numbers, which use their buying power to get a better price on hotels, airline tickets, even car rentals. When booking a room, always **call the hotel's local toll-free number** (if one is available) rather than the central reservations number—you'll often get a better price. Always ask about special packages or corporate rates.

➤ AIRLINE TICKETS: ☎ **800/FLY-ASAP.**

➤ HOTEL ROOMS: **Accommodations Express** (☎ 800/444–7666, WEB www.accommodationsexpress.com). **Central Reservation Service (CRS)** (☎ 800/548–3311). **Hotel Reservations Network** (☎ 800/964–6835, WEB www.hoteldiscount.com). **Players Express Vacations** (☎ 800/458–6161, WEB www.playersexpress.com). **Quikbook** (☎ 800/789–9887, WEB www.quikbook.com). **RMC Travel** (☎ 800/245–5738, WEB www.rmcwebtravel.com). **Steigenberger Reservation Service** (☎ 800/

223–5652, WEB www.srs-worldhotels.com). **Turbotrip.com** (☎ 800/473–7829, WEB www.turbotrip.com).

PACKAGE DEALS

Don't confuse packages and guided tours. When you buy a package, you travel on your own, just as though you had planned the trip yourself. Fly/drive packages, which combine airfare and car rental, are often a good deal.

ECOTOURISM

South Florida's environment is one of its chief draws; it's also very fragile. If you're out in nature, follow the basic rules of environmental responsibility: take nothing but pictures; leave nothing but footprints. Most important, **be extremely careful around the tenuous dunes.** Picking the sea grasses that hold the dunes in place can carry stiff fines, as can walking or playing or digging in the dunes. So stay on the beach, gaze at the beautiful dunes, but don't go on them. An afternoon of roughhousing can completely destroy a dune that could take years for nature to rebuild. Ecotours (☞ Tours *in* each chapter's A to Z section) operate throughout South Florida.

GAY & LESBIAN TRAVEL

South Beach and Key West have a reputation for being especially gay and lesbian friendly.

Fodor's *Gay Guide to the USA, 3rd Edition,* provides information on travel throughout South Florida. It's available in bookstores everywhere.

➤ GAY- & LESBIAN-FRIENDLY TRAVEL AGENCIES: **Different Roads Travel** (✉ 8383 Wilshire Blvd., Suite 902, Beverly Hills, CA 90211, ☎ 323/651–5557 or 800/429–8747, FAX 323/651–3678, lgernert@tzell.com). **Kennedy Travel** (✉ 314 Jericho Turnpike, Floral Park, NY 11001, ☎ 516/352–4888 or 800/237–7433, FAX 516/354–8849, WEB www.kennedytravel.com). **Now Voyager** (✉ 4406 18th St., San Francisco, CA 94114, ☎ 415/626–1169 or 800/255–6951, FAX 415/626–8626, WEB www.nowvoyager.com). **Skylink Travel and Tour** (✉ 1006 Mendocino Ave., Santa Rosa, CA 95401, ☎ 707/546–9888 or 800/225–5759, FAX 707/546–9891, WEB www.skylinktravel.com), serving lesbian travelers.

HEALTH

If you are unaccustomed to strong subtropical sun, you run a risk of sunburn and heat prostration, even in winter. So hit the beach or play tennis, golf, or another outdoor sport before 10 or after 3. If you must be out **at midday, limit strenuous exercise, drink plenty of liquids, and wear a hat.** If you begin to feel faint, get out of the sun immediately and sip water slowly. Even on overcast days, ultraviolet rays shine through the haze, so **use a sunscreen with an SPF of at least 15,** and have children wear a waterproof SPF 30 or better.

While you're frolicking on the beach, **steer clear of what look like blue bubbles on the sand.** These are Portuguese man-of-wars, and their tentacles can cause an allergic reaction. Also be careful of other large jellyfish, some of which can sting.

If you walk across a grassy area on the way to the beach, you'll probably encounter sand spurs. They are quite tiny, light brown, and remarkably prickly. You'll feel them before you see them; if you get stuck with one, just pull it out.

DIVERS' ALERT

Do not fly within 24 hours of scuba diving.

HOLIDAYS

Major national holidays include New Year's Day (Jan. 1); Martin Luther King, Jr., Day (3rd Mon. in Jan.); President's Day (3rd Mon. in Feb.); Memorial Day (last Mon. in May); Independence Day (July 4); Labor Day (1st Mon. in Sept.); Thanksgiving Day (4th Thurs. in Nov.); Christmas Eve and Christmas Day (Dec. 24 and 25); and New Year's Eve (Dec. 31).

INSURANCE

The most useful travel-insurance plan is a comprehensive policy that includes coverage for trip cancellation and interruption, default, trip delay, and medical expenses (with a waiver for preexisting conditions).

Without insurance you will lose all or most of your money if you cancel your trip, regardless of the reason. Default insurance covers you if your tour operator, airline, or cruise line goes out of business. Trip-delay covers expenses that arise because of bad weather or mechanical delays. Study the fine print when comparing policies.

Always **buy travel policies directly from the insurance company**; if you buy them from a cruise line, airline, or tour operator that goes out of business you probably will not be covered for the agency or operator's default, a major risk. Before making any purchase, **review your existing health and home-owner's policies** to find what they cover away from home.

➤ TRAVEL INSURERS: In the U.S.: **Access America** (✉ 6600 W. Broad St., Richmond, VA 23230, ☎ 804/285–3300 or 800/284–8300, FAX 804/673–1586, WEB www.previewtravel.com), **Travel Guard International** (✉ 1145 Clark St., Stevens Point, WI 54481, ☎ 715/345–0505 or 800/826–1300, FAX 800/955–8785, WEB www.noelgroup.com).

FOR INTERNATIONAL TRAVELERS

CAR TRAVEL

In South Florida gasoline was $1.41–$1.60 a gallon at press time. Stations are plentiful. Most stay open late (24 hours along large highways and in big cities), except in rural areas, where Sunday hours are limited and where you may drive long stretches without a refueling opportunity. Highways are well paved. Interstate highways—limited-access, multilane highways whose numbers are prefixed by "I–"—are the fastest routes. Interstates with three-digit numbers encircle urban areas, which may have other limited-access expressways, freeways, and parkways as well. Tolls may be levied on limited-access highways. So-called U.S. highways and state highways are not necessarily limited-access but may have several lanes.

Along larger highways, roadside stops with rest rooms, fast-food restaurants, and sundries stores are well spaced. State police and tow trucks patrol major highways and lend assistance. If your car breaks down on an interstate, pull onto the shoulder and wait for help, or have your passengers wait while you walk to an emergency phone. If you carry a cell phone, dial *55 or *FHP, noting your location on the small green roadside mileage markers.

Driving in the United States is on the right. Do **obey speed limits** posted along roads and highways. Watch for lower limits in small towns and on back roads. Florida law requires all passengers to wear seat belts. On weekdays between 6 and 10 AM and again between 4 and 7 PM **expect heavy traffic.** To encourage carpooling, some freeways have special lanes for so-called high-occupancy vehicles (HOV)—cars carrying more than one passenger.

Book stores, gas stations, convenience stores, and rest stops sell maps (about $3) and multiregion road atlases (about $10).

CURRENCY

The dollar is the basic unit of U.S. currency. It has 100 cents. Coins include the copper penny (1¢); the silvery nickel (5¢), dime (10¢), quarter (25¢), and half-dollar (50¢); and the golden $1 coin, replacing a now-rare silver dollar. Bills are denominated $1, $5, $10, $20, $50, and $100, all green and identical in size; designs vary. The exchange rate at press time was US $1.44 per British pound, $.64 per Canadian dollar, $.51 per Australian dollar, and $.41 per New Zealand dollar.

ELECTRICITY

The U.S. standard is AC, 110 volts/60 cycles. Plugs have two flat pins set parallel to each other.

EMERGENCIES

For police, fire, or ambulance, **dial 911** (0 in rural areas).

INSURANCE

Britons and Australians need extra medical coverage when traveling overseas.

➤ INSURANCE INFORMATION: In the U.K.: **Association of British Insurers** (✉ 51–55 Gresham St., London EC2V 7HQ, U.K., ☎ 020/7600–3333, FAX 020/7696–8999, WEB www.abi.org.uk). In Australia: **Insurance Council of Australia** (✉ Level 3, 56 Pitt St., Sydney NSW 2000, ☎ 03/9614–1077, FAX 03/9614–7924). In Canada: **RBC Insurance** (✉ 6880 Financial Dr., Mississauga, Ontario L5N 7Y5, Canada, ☎ 905/816–2400 or 800/668–4342 in Canada, FAX 905/816–2498, WEB www.royalbank.com). In New Zealand: **Insurance Council of New Zealand** (✉ Box 474, Wellington, New Zealand, ☎ 04/472–5230, FAX 04/473–3011, WEB www.icnz.org.nz).

MAIL & SHIPPING

You can buy stamps and aerograms and send letters and parcels in post offices. Stamp-dispensing machines can occasionally be found in airports, bus and train stations, office buildings, drugstores, and the like. You can also deposit mail in the stout, dark blue, steel bins at strategic locations everywhere and in the mail chutes of large buildings; pickup schedules are posted.

For mail sent within the United States, you need a 34¢ stamp for first-class letters weighing up to 1 ounce (21¢ for each additional ounce) and 20¢ for domestic postcards. For overseas mail, you pay 80¢ for 1-ounce airmail letters, 70¢ for airmail postcards, and 35¢ for surface-rate postcards. For Canada and Mexico you need a 60¢ stamp for a 1-ounce letter and 50¢ for a postcard. For 70¢ you can buy an aerogram—a single sheet of lightweight blue paper that folds into its own envelope, stamped for overseas airmail.

To receive mail on the road, have it sent c/o General Delivery at your destination's main post office (use the correct five-digit zip code). You must pick up mail in person within 30 days and show a driver's license or passport.

PASSPORTS & VISAS

When traveling internationally, **carry your passport** even if you don't need one (it's always the best form of I.D.) and **make two photocopies of the data page** (one for someone at home and another for you, carried separately from your passport). If you lose your passport, promptly call the nearest embassy or consulate and the local police.

Visitor visas are not necessary for Canadian citizens, or for citizens of Australia and the United Kingdom who are staying fewer than 90 days.

➤ AUSTRALIAN CITIZENS: **Australian Passport Office** (☎ 131–232). **U.S. Office of Australia Affairs** (✉ MLC Centre, 19-29 Martin Pl., 59th floor, Sydney NSW 2000, Australia).

➤ CANADIAN CITIZENS: **Passport Office** (☎ 819/994–3500; 800/567–6868 in Canada).

➤ NEW ZEALAND CITIZENS: **New Zealand Passport Office** (☎ 04/494–0700 for application procedures; 0800/225–050 in New Zealand for application-status updates). **U.S. Office of New Zealand Affairs** (✉ 29 Fitzherbert Terr., Thorndon, Wellington, New Zealand).

➤ U.K. CITIZENS: **London Passport Office** (☎ 0870/521–0410) for application procedures and emergency passports. **U.S. Embassy Visa Information Line** (☎ 01891/200–290). **U.S. Embassy Visa Branch** (✉ 5 Upper Grosvenor Sq., London W1A 1AE, U.K.); send a self-addressed, stamped envelope. **U.S. Consulate General** (✉ Queen's House, Queen St., Belfast BTI 6EO, Northern Ireland).

TELEPHONES

All U.S. telephone numbers consist of a three-digit area code and a seven-digit local number. Within most local calling areas, dial only the seven-digit number (except in the Miami and Orlando areas, where you will need all 10 digits). Within the same area code, dial "1" first. To call between area-code regions, dial "1" then all 10 digits; the same goes for calls to numbers prefixed by "800," "888," and "877"—all toll-free. For calls to numbers preceded by "900" you must pay—usually dearly.

For international calls, dial "011" followed by the country code and the local number. For help, dial "0" and ask for an overseas operator. The country code is 61 for Australia, 64 for New Zealand, 44 for the United Kingdom. Calling Canada is the same as calling within the United States. Most local phone books list country codes and U.S. area codes. The country code for the United States is 1.

For operator assistance, dial "0". To obtain someone's phone number, call directory assistance, 555–1212 or occasionally 411 (free at public phones). To have the person you're calling foot the bill, phone collect; dial "0" instead of "1" before the 10-digit number.

At pay phones, instructions are usually posted. Usually you insert coins in a slot (10¢–35¢ for local calls) and wait for a steady tone before dialing. When you call long-distance, the operator will tell you how much to insert; prepaid phone cards, widely available in various denominations, are easier. Call the number on the back, punch in the card's personal identification number when prompted, then dial your number.

LANGUAGE

Spanish can be quite useful to know in South Florida, especially in Miami-Dade county, where Hispanics make up more than half the population. A good percentage of Miami tourism comes from Latin America, so Spanish can be heard quite frequently in hotels, stores, and restaurants.

LODGING

South Florida has every conceivable type of lodging—from tree houses to penthouses, mansions for hire to hostels. Even with occupancy rates inching above 70%, there are almost always rooms available, except maybe at Christmas and other holidays. Affordable lodgings can be found in even the most glittery resort towns, typically motel rooms that may cost as little as $50–$60 a night; they may not be in the best part of town, mind you, but they won't be in the worst, either (perhaps along busy highways where you'll need the roar of the air-conditioning to drown out the traffic). Since beachfront properties tend to be more expensive, **look for properties a little off the beach.** Still, many beachfront properties are surprisingly affordable, too.

Children are welcome generally everywhere in Florida. Pets are another matter, so **inquire ahead of time if you're bringing an animal with you.**

In the busy seasons—over Christmas, from late January through Easter, and during holiday weekends in summer—always **reserve ahead for the top properties.** Fall is the slowest season: Rates are low and availability is high, but this is also the prime time for hurricanes. Key West is jam-packed for Fantasy Fest at Halloween. If you're not booking through a travel agent, call the visitors bureau or the chamber of commerce in the area where you're going to check whether any special event is scheduled for when you plan to arrive. If demand isn't especially high for the time you have in mind, you can often **save by showing up at a lodging in mid- to late afternoon**—desk clerks are typically willing to negotiate with travelers in order to fill those rooms late in the day. In addition, **check with chambers of commerce for discount coupons for selected properties.**

The lodgings we list are the cream of the crop in each price category. We always list the facilities that are available—but we don't specify whether they cost extra: When pricing accommodations, always ask what's included and what costs extra.

CATEGORY	COST*
$$$$	over $220
$$$	$140–$220
$$	$80–$140
$	under $80

**All prices are for a standard double room, excluding 6% sales tax (more in some counties) and 1%–4% tourist tax.*

Assume that hotels operate on the **European Plan** (EP, with no meals), unless we specify that they use the **Continental Plan** (CP, with a Continental breakfast), **Breakfast Plan** (BP, with a full breakfast), **Modified American Plan** (MAP, with breakfast and dinner), or the **Full American Plan** (FAP, with all meals).

APARTMENT & VILLA RENTALS

If you want a home base that's roomy enough for a family and comes with cooking facilities, **consider a furnished rental.** These can save you money, especially if you're traveling with a group. Home-exchange directories sometimes list rentals as well as exchanges.

➤ INTERNATIONAL AGENTS: **Hideaways International** (✉ 767 Islington St., Portsmouth, NH 03801, ☎ 603/430–4433 or 800/843–4433, FAX 603/430–4444, WEB www.hideaways.com; membership $129). **Hometours International** (✉ Box 11503, Knoxville, TN 37939, ☎ 865/690–8484 or 800/367–4668, WEB thor.he.net/~hometour/). **Interhome** (✉ 1990 N.E. 163rd St., Suite 110, N. Miami Beach, FL 33162, ☎ 305/940–2299 or 800/882–6864, FAX 305/940–2911, WEB www.interhome.com). **Vacation Home Rentals Worldwide** (✉ 235 Kensington Ave., Norwood, NJ 07648, ☎ 201/767–9393 or 800/633–3284, FAX 201/767–5510, WEB www.vhrww.com).

➤ LOCAL AGENTS: **American Realty** (✉ Box 1133, Captiva, FL 33924 ☎ 800/547–0127). **Beachside Realty** (✉ S. Atlantic Ave., New Smyrna Beach, FL 32169, ☎ 800/345–8635 or 904/426–5684). **Fairfield Communities** (✉ 5353 Del Verde Way, Orlando, FL 32819, ☎ 407/397–4494). **Florida Sunbreak** (✉ 828 Washington Ave., Miami Beach, FL 33139, ☎ 800/786–2732 or 305/532–1516). **Freewheeler Vacations** (✉ Box 1634 [MM 86], Islamorada, FL 33036, ☎ 305/664–2075). **Marr Properties** (✉ 101925 Overseas Hwy., Key Largo, FL 33037, ☎ 800/277–3728 or 305/451–4321). **Resort Quest** (✉ 26201 Hickory Blvd., Naples, FL 34134, ☎ 941/992–6620). **Sand Key Realty** (✉ 2701 Gulf Blvd., Clearwater, FL 33785, ☎ 800/257–7332 or 727/595–5441).

B&BS

Small inns and guest houses are increasingly numerous in South Florida, but they vary tremendously, ranging from economical places that are plain but serve a good home-style breakfast to elegantly furnished Victorian houses with four-course gourmet morning meals and rates to match. Many offer a homelike setting. In fact, many are in private homes with owners who treat you almost like family, while others are more businesslike. It's a good idea to **make specific inquiries of B&Bs you're interested in.** The association listed below offers descriptions and suggestions for bed-and-breakfasts throughout Florida.

➤ BED AND BREAKFAST ASSOCIATION: **Florida Bed and Breakfast Inn** (✉ Box 6187, Palm Harbor, FL 34684, ☎ 281/499–1374 or 800/524–1880).

CAMPING

Camping is popular throughout the state. Camping on nondesignated beach sites is not allowed. For information on camping facilities, contact the national and state parks and forests you plan to visit and the Florida Department of Environmental Protection (☞ National Parks).

To find a commercial campground, **pick up a copy of the free annual "Official Florida Camping Directory,"** which lists 305 campgrounds, with over 55,000 sites. It's available at Florida welcome centers, from the Florida Tourism Industry Marketing Corporation (☞ Visitor Information), and from the Florida Association of RV Parks & Campgrounds.

➤ CAMPING ASSOCIATION: **Florida Association of RV Parks & Camp-**

grounds (✉ 1340 Vickers Dr., Tallahassee, FL 32303-3041, ☎ 850/562–7151, FAX 850/562–7179).

CONDOS

➤ CONDO GUIDE: ***The Condo Lux Vacationer's Guide to Condominium Rentals in the Southeast*** (Vintage Books/Random House, New York; $9.95), by Jill Little.

HOME EXCHANGES

If you would like to exchange your home for someone else's, **join a home-exchange organization,** which will send you its updated listings of available exchanges for a year and will include your own listing in at least one of them. It's up to you to make specific arrangements.

➤ EXCHANGE CLUBS: **HomeLink International** (✉ Box 47747, Tampa, FL 33647, ☎ 813/975–9825 or 800/638–3841, FAX 813/910–8144, WEB www.homelink.org; $98 per year). **Intervac U.S.** (✉ Box 590504, San Francisco, CA 94159, ☎ 800/756–4663, FAX 415/435–7440, WEB www.intervacus.com; $93 yearly fee includes one catalog and on-line access).

HOSTELS

No matter what your age, you can **save on lodging costs by staying at hostels.** In some 5,000 locations in more than 70 countries around the world, Hostelling International (HI), the umbrella group for a number of national youth-hostel associations, offers single-sex, dorm-style beds and, at many hostels, rooms for couples and family accommodations. Membership in any HI national hostel association, open to travelers of all ages, allows you to stay in HI-affiliated hostels at member rates; one-year membership is about $25 for adults (C$26.75 in Canada, £9.30 in the United Kingdom, $30 in Australia, and $30 in New Zealand); hostels run about $10–$25 per night. Members have priority if the hostel is full; they're also eligible for discounts around the world, even on rail and bus travel in some countries.

➤ ORGANIZATIONS: **Hostelling International—American Youth Hostels** (✉ 733 15th St. NW, Suite 840, Washington, DC 20005, ☎ 202/783–6161, FAX 202/783–6171, WEB www.hiayh.org). **Hostelling International—Canada** (✉ 400–205 Catherine St., Ottawa, Ontario K2P 1C3, Canada, ☎ 613/237–7884, FAX 613/237–7868, WEB www.hostellingintl.ca). **Youth Hostel Association of England and Wales** (✉ Trevelyan House, 8 St. Stephen's Hill, St. Albans, Hertfordshire AL1 2DY, U.K., ☎ 0870/870–8808, FAX 01727/844126, WEB www.yha.org.uk). **Australian Youth Hostel Association** (✉ 10 Mallett St., Camperdown, NSW 2050, Australia, ☎ 02/9565–1699, FAX 02/9565–1325, WEB www.yha.com.au). **Youth Hostels Association of New Zealand** (✉ Box 436, Christchurch, New Zealand, ☎ 03/379–9970, FAX 03/365–4476, WEB www.yha.org.nz).

HOTELS

Wherever you look in South Florida, it seems, you'll find lots of plain, inexpensive motels and luxurious resorts, independents alongside national chains, and an ever-growing number of modern properties as well as quite a few timeless classics.

All hotels listed have private bath unless otherwise noted.

➤ HOTEL AND MOTEL ASSOCIATION: **Florida Hotel & Motel Association** (✉ 200 W. College Ave., Box 1529, Tallahassee, FL 32301-1529, ☎ 850/224–2888).

➤ RESERVATION SERVICES: **Accommodations Express** (☎ 800/663–7666, FAX 609/525–0111). **Florida Hotel Network** (☎ 800/538–3616). **Florida Sunbreak** (✉ 169 Lincoln Rd., Miami Beach, FL 33139, ☎ 305/532–1516, FAX 305/532–0564).

VACATION OWNERSHIP RESORTS

Vacation ownership resorts sell hotel rooms, condominium apartments, and villas in weekly, monthly, or quarterly increments. The weekly arrangement is most popular; it's often referred to as "interval ownership" or "time sharing." Nonowners can rent at many of these resorts by contacting the individual property or a real-estate broker in the area.

MONEY MATTERS

Prices throughout this guide are given for adults. Reduced fees are almost always available for children, students, and senior citizens. For information on taxes, *see* Taxes.

ATMS

Automatic Teller Machines (ATMs) are ubiquitous in South Florida. In addition to banks, you will find them at grocery store chains like Publix and Winn Dixie, in shopping malls big and small, and, increasingly, at gas stations.

CREDIT CARDS

Throughout this guide, the following abbreviations are used: **AE,** American Express; **D,** Discover; **DC,** Diners Club; **MC,** MasterCard; and **V,** Visa.

➤ REPORTING LOST CARDS: **American Express** (☎ 800/528–4800). **Diners Club** (☎ 800/525–9135). **Discover** (☎ 800/347–2683). **MasterCard** (☎ 800/843–0777). **Visa** (☎ 800/336–8472).

NATIONAL PARKS

Look into discount passes to save money on park entrance fees. The National Parks Pass ($50) gets you and your companions free admission to all parks for one year. (Camping and parking are extra.) A percentage of the proceeds from sales of the pass will fund National Parks projects. Both the Golden Age Passport ($10), for those 62 and older, and the Golden Access Passport (free), for travelers with disabilities, entitle holders to free entry to all national parks, plus 50% off fees for the use of many park facilities and services. You must show proof of age and of U.S. citizenship or permanent residency (such as a U.S. passport, driver's license, or birth certificate) and, if requesting Golden Access, proof of disability. The Golden Age and Golden Access passes are available at all national parks wherever entrance fees are charged. The National Parks Pass is available by mail or through the Internet.

➤ PASSES BY MAIL: **National Park Service** (✉ National Park Service/Department of Interior, 1849 C St. NW, Washington, DC 20240, ☎ 202/208–4747, WEB www.nps.gov). **National Parks Pass** (✉ 27540 Ave. Mentry, Valencia, CA 91355, ☎ 888/GO–PARKS, WEB www.nationalparks.org).

PRIVATE PRESERVES

➤ FLORIDA SANCTUARY INFORMATION: **National Audubon Society** (✉ Sanctuary Director, Miles Wildlife Sanctuary, R.R. 1, Box 294, W. Cornwall Rd., Sharon, CT 06069, ☎ 860/364–0048). **Nature Conservancy:** Blowing Rocks Preserve (✉ 574 South Beach Rd., Hobe Sound, FL 33455, ☎ 561/744–6668). Offices: SE Division (333 Fleming St., Key West, FL, FL 33040, ☎ 305/296–3880; Comeau Bldg., 319 Clematis St., Suite 611, West Palm Beach, FL 33401, ☎ 561/833–4226).

STATE PARKS

Florida's Department of Environmental Protection (DEP) is responsible for hundreds of historic buildings, landmarks, nature preserves, and parks. When requesting a free *Florida State Park Guide,* mention which parts of the state you plan to visit. For information on camping facilities at the state parks, ask for the free "Florida State Parks, Fees and Facilities" and "Florida State Parks Camping Reservation Procedures" brochures. Responding to cutbacks in its budget, the DEP established Friends of Florida State Parks, a citizen support organization open to all.

➤ STATE PARKS INFORMATION: **Florida Department of Environmental Protection** (✉ Marjory Stoneman Douglas Bldg., MS 536, 3900 Commonwealth Blvd., Tallahassee, FL 32399-3000, ☎ 850/488–2850, FAX 850/922–4923); **Friends of Florida State Parks** (☎ 850/488–8243).

OUTDOORS & SPORTS

Recreational opportunities abound in South Florida. The Governor's Council on Physical Fitness and Sports puts on the Sunshine State Games each July in a different part of the state.

➤ GENERAL INFORMATION: **Florida Department of Environmental Protection** (✉ Office of Greenways, MS 585,

3900 Commonwealth Blvd., Tallahassee, FL 32399-3000, ☎ 850/487–4784) for information on bicycling, canoeing, kayaking, and hiking trails.

➤ MARINE CHARTS: **Tealls Guides** (✉ 111 Saguaro La., Marathon, FL 33050, ☎ 305/743–3942, FAX 305/743–3943; $7.95 set, $3.60 each individual chart).

BIKING

Biking is a popular Florida sport. **Rails to Trails** (☎ 850/942–2379), a nationwide group that turns unused railroad rights-of-way into bicycle and walking paths, has made great inroads in Florida. For bike information, **check with Florida's Department of Transportation (DOT),** which publishes free bicycle trail guides, dispenses free touring information packets, and provides names of bike coordinators around the state.

➤ BICYCLE INFORMATION: **DOT state bicycle-pedestrian coordinator** (✉ 605 Suwannee St., MS 82, Tallahassee, FL 32399-0450, ☎ 850/487–1200).

CANOEING & KAYAKING

Both the DEP and outfitter associations provide information on canoeing and kayaking trails and their conditions, events, and contacts for trips and equipment rental.

➤ OUTFITTERS AND OUTFITTING ASSOCIATIONS: **Canoe Outpost System** (✉ 2816 N.W. Rte. 661, Arcadia, FL 33821, ☎ 863/494–1215 or 800/268–0083), comprising five outfitters. **Florida Professional Paddlesports Association** (✉ Box 1764, Arcadia, FL 34265, ☎ no phone).

FISHING

Fishing seasons and other regulations vary by location and species. You will need to **buy one license for freshwater fishing and another license for saltwater fishing.** Nonresident fees for a saltwater license are $31.50. Nonresidents can purchase freshwater licenses good for three days ($6.50), seven days ($16.50), or for one year ($31.50). Typically, you'll pay a $1.50 surcharge at most any marina, bait shop, Kmart, Wal-Mart, or other license vendor.

➤ FISHING INFORMATION: **Florida Fish and Wildlife Conservation Commission** (✉ 620 S. Meridian St., Tallahassee, FL 32399-1600, ☎ 850/488–1960) for the free *Florida Fishing Handbook* with license vendors, regional fishing guides, and educational bulletins.

HORSEBACK RIDING

Horseback riding is a popular sport outside of South Florida's metropolitan areas. There are even beaches on which you can ride.

➤ HORSEBACK RIDING INFORMATION: **Horse & Pony** (✉ 6225 Virginia La., Seffner, FL 33584, ☎ 813/621–2510).

JOGGING, RUNNING, & WALKING

Many towns have walking and running trails, and most of South Florida's beaches stretch on for miles, testing the limits of even the most stalwart runners and walkers. Many local running clubs sponsor weekly public events.

➤ CLUBS & EVENTS: **Miami Runners Club** (✉ 7920 S.W. 40th St., Miami, FL 33155, ☎ 305/227–1500, FAX 305/220–2450) for South Florida events.

PARI-MUTUEL SPORTS

Jai-alai frontons and greyhound-racing tracks are in most major Florida cities. Patrons can bet on the teams or dogs or on televised horse races.

➤ SCHEDULES: Department of Business & Professional Regulations **Division of Pari-Mutuel Wagering** (✉ 8405 N.W. 53rd St., Suite C-250, Miami, FL 33166, ☎ 305/470–5675, FAX 305/470–5683).

TENNIS

Tennis is extremely popular in Florida, and virtually every town has well-maintained public courts. In addition, many tennis tournaments are held in the state.

➤ TOURNAMENT AND EVENT SCHEDULES: **United States Tennis Association Florida Section** (✉ 1280 S.W. 36th Ave., Suite 305, Pompano Beach, FL 33069, ☎ 954/968–3434,

FAX 954/968–3986; tournament book and yearbook $11).

WILDERNESS & RECREATION AREAS

South Florida is studded with trails, rivers, and parks that are ideal for hiking, bird-watching, canoeing, bicycling, and horseback riding.

➤ PUBLICATIONS: **"Florida Trails: A Guide to Florida's Natural Habitats,"** available from Florida Tourism Industry Marketing Corporation (☞ Visitor Information), for bicycling, canoeing, horseback riding, and walking trails; camping; snorkeling and scuba diving; and Florida ecosystems. **Florida Wildlife Viewing Guide,** available from Falcon Press (✉ Box 1718, Helena, MT 59624, ☎ 800/582–2665); $10.95 plus $4 shipping, by Susan Cerulean and Ann Morrow, for marked wildlife-watching sites. **"Recreation Guide to District Lands,"** available from St. Johns River Water Management District (✉ Box 1429, Palatka, FL 32178-1429); free for marine, wetland, and upland recreational areas.

PACKING

South Florida is warm year-round and often extremely humid in summer months. Be prepared for sudden summer storms in the summer months, but keep in mind that plastic raincoats are uncomfortable in the high humidity.

Dress is casual throughout the state, with sundresses, jeans, or walking shorts appropriate during the day; **bring comfortable walking shoes or sneakers** for theme parks. A few restaurants request that men wear jackets and ties, but most do not. Be prepared for air-conditioning working in overdrive.

You can generally swim year-round in South Florida. Be sure to **take a sun hat and sunscreen** because the sun can be fierce, even in winter and even if it is chilly or overcast.

In your carry-on luggage, **pack an extra pair of eyeglasses or contact lenses** and **enough of any medication you take** to last the entire trip. You may also ask your doctor to write a spare prescription using the drug's generic name, since brand names may vary from country to country. In luggage to be checked, **never pack prescription drugs or valuables.** To avoid customs delays, carry medications in their original packaging. And don't forget to carry with you the addresses of offices that handle refunds of lost traveler's checks. Check *Fodor's How to Pack* (available in bookstores everywhere) for more tips.

CHECKING LUGGAGE

How many carry-on bags you can bring with you is up to the airline. Most allow two, but not always, so make sure that everything you carry aboard will fit under your seat or in the overhead bin, and get to the gate early. Note that if you have a seat at the back of the plane, you'll probably board first, while the overhead bins are still empty.

If you are flying internationally, note that baggage allowances may be determined not by piece but by weight—generally 88 pounds (40 kilograms) in first class, 66 pounds (30 kilograms) in business class, and 44 pounds (20 kilograms) in economy.

Airline liability for baggage is limited to $1,250 per person on flights within the United States. On international flights it amounts to $9.07 per pound or $20 per kilogram for checked baggage (roughly $640 per 70-pound bag) and $400 per passenger for unchecked baggage. You can buy additional coverage at check-in for about $10 per $1,000 of coverage, but it excludes a rather extensive list of items, shown on your airline ticket.

Before departure, **itemize your bags' contents** and their worth, and label the bags with your name, address, and phone number. (If you use your home address, cover it so potential thieves can't see it readily.) Inside each bag, **pack a copy of your itinerary.** At check-in, **make sure that each bag is correctly tagged** with the destination airport's three-letter code. If your bags arrive damaged or fail to arrive at all, file a written report with the airline before leaving the airport.

SAFETY

Stepped-up policing of thieves who prey on tourists in rental cars has helped address what was a serious issue in the early '90s. Still, visitors should be especially wary when driving in strange neighborhoods and leaving the airport, especially in the Miami area. Don't assume that valuables are safe in your hotel room; use in-room safes or the hotel's safety deposit boxes. Try to use ATMs only during the day or in brightly lit, well-traveled locales.

BEACH SAFETY

Before swimming, **make sure there's no undertow.** Rip currents, caused when the tide rushes out through a narrow break in the water, can overpower even the strongest swimmer. If you do get caught in one, resist the urge to swim straight back to shore—you'll tire before you make it. Instead, stay calm. Swim parallel to the shore line until you are outside the current's pull, then work your way in to shore.

SENIOR-CITIZEN TRAVEL

Since Florida has a significant retired population, senior-citizen discounts are ubiquitous. To qualify for age-related discounts, **mention your senior-citizen status up front** when booking hotel reservations (not when checking out) and before you're seated in restaurants (not when paying the bill). When renting a car, ask about promotional car-rental discounts, which can be cheaper than senior-citizen rates.

➤ EDUCATIONAL PROGRAMS: **Elderhostel** (✉ 11 Ave. de Lafayette, Boston, MA 02111-1746, ☎ 877/426–8056, FAX 877/426–2166, WEB www.elderhostel.org). **Interhostel** (✉ University of New Hampshire, 6 Garrison Ave., Durham, NH 03824, ☎ 603/862–1147 or 800/733–9753, FAX 603/862–1113, WEB www.learn.unh.edu).

STUDENTS IN SOUTH FLORIDA

Students flock to the beaches of South Florida during spring break, but there are also special tours for students year-round. Students presenting identification qualify for discounts at most movie theaters and art museums.

➤ I.D.S & SERVICES: **Council Travel** (CIEE; ✉ 205 E. 42nd St., 15th floor, New York, NY 10017, ☎ 212/822–2700 or 888/268–6245, FAX 212/822–2699, WEB www.councilexchanges.org) for mail orders only, in the U.S. **Travel Cuts** (✉ 187 College St., Toronto, Ontario M5T 1P7, Canada, ☎ 416/979–2406 or 800/667–2887 [only available in Canada], FAX 416/979–8167, WEB www.travelcuts.com).

TAXES

SALES TAX

Florida's sales tax is currently 6%, but local sales and tourist taxes can raise that number considerably, especially for certain items, such as lodging. Miami hoteliers, for example, collect roughly 12.5% for city and resort taxes. It's best to **ask about additional costs up front,** to avoid a rude awakening.

TELEPHONES

To make local calls within the 305 (Miami area) calling area, **begin calls with the local area code,** dialing a total of 10 digits.

TIME

South Florida is in the Eastern Time Zone.

TIPPING

Whether they carry bags, open doors, deliver food, or clean rooms, hospitality employees work to receive a portion of your travel budget. In deciding how much to give, **base your tip on what the service is and how well it's performed.**

In transit, tip an airport valet $1–$3 per bag, a taxi driver 15%–20% of the fare.

For hotel staff, recommended amounts are $1–$3 per bag for a bellhop, $1–$2 per night per guest for chambermaids, $5–$10 for special concierge service, $1–$3 for a doorman who hails a cab or parks a car, 15% of the greens fee for a caddy, 15%–20% of the bill for a massage, and 15% of a room service bill (bear in mind that sometimes 15%–18% is automatically added to room service bills so don't add it twice).

In a restaurant, give 15%–20% of your bill before tax to the server, 5%–10% to the maître d', 15% to a bartender, and 15% of the wine bill for a wine steward who makes a special effort in selecting and serving wine.

TOURS & PACKAGES

Because everything is prearranged on a prepackaged tour or independent vacation, you'll spend less time planning—and often get it all at a good price.

BOOKING WITH AN AGENT

Travel agents are excellent resources. But it's a good idea to collect brochures from several agencies as some agents' suggestions may be influenced by relationships with tour and package firms that reward them for volume sales. If you have a special interest, **find an agent with expertise in that area**; ASTA (☞ Travel Agencies) has a database of specialists worldwide.

Make sure your travel agent knows the accommodations and other services of the place they're recommending. Ask about the hotel's location, room size, beds, and whether it has a pool, room service, or programs for children, if you care about these. Has your agent been there in person or sent others whom you can contact?

Do some homework on your own, too: local tourism boards can provide information about lesser-known and small-niche operators, some of which may sell only direct.

BUYER BEWARE

Each year consumers are stranded or lose their money when tour operators—even large ones with excellent reputations—go out of business. So **check out the operator.** Ask several travel agents about its reputation, and try to **book with a company that has a consumer-protection program.** (Look for information in the company's brochure.) In the United States, members of the National Tour Association and the United States Tour Operators Association are required to set aside funds to cover your payments and travel arrangements in the event that the company defaults. It's also a good idea to choose a company that participates in the American Society of Travel Agents' Tour Operator Program (TOP); ASTA will act as mediator in any disputes between you and your tour operator.

Remember that the more your package or tour includes the better you can predict the ultimate cost of your vacation. Make sure you know exactly what is covered, and **beware of hidden costs.** Are taxes, tips, and transfers included? Entertainment and excursions? These can add up.

➤ TOUR-OPERATOR RECOMMENDATIONS: **American Society of Travel Agents** (ASTA; ☎ 800/965–2782 24-hr hot line, FAX 703/739–7642, WEB www.astanet.com). **National Tour Association** (NTA; ✉ 546 E. Main St., Lexington, KY 40508, ☎ 859/226–4444 or 800/682–8886, WEB www.ntaonline.com). **United States Tour Operators Association** (USTOA; ✉ 342 Madison Ave., Suite 1522, New York, NY 10173, ☎ 212/599–6599 or 800/468–7862, FAX 212/599–6744, WEB www.ustoa.com).

TRAIN TRAVEL

Amtrak provides north–south service on two routes to the major cities of West Palm Beach, Fort Lauderdale, and Miami, with many stops in between on all routes.

➤ TRAIN INFORMATION: **Amtrak** (☎ 800/872–7245).

TRAVEL AGENCIES

A good travel agent puts your needs first. Look for an agency that has been in business at least five years, emphasizes customer service, and has someone on staff who specializes in your destination. In addition, **make sure the agency belongs to a professional trade organization.** The American Society of Travel Agents (ASTA), with more than 26,000 members in some 170 countries, is the largest and most influential in the field. Operating under the motto "Without a travel agent, you're on your own," it maintains and enforces a strict code of ethics and will step in to help mediate any agent-client disputes if necessary. ASTA also maintains a Web site that includes a directory of agents. (If a travel agency is also acting as your tour operator, *see* Buyer Beware *in* Tours & Packages.)

➤ LOCAL AGENT REFERRALS: **American Society of Travel Agents** (ASTA; ☎ 800/965–2782 24-hr hot line, FAX 703/739–7642, WEB www.astanet.com). **Association of British Travel Agents** (✉ 68–71 Newman St., London W1T 3AH, U.K., ☎ 020/7637–2444, FAX 020/7637–0713, WEB www.abtanet.com). **Association of Canadian Travel Agents** (✉ 130 Albert St., Ste. 1705, Ottawa, Ontario K1P 5G4, Canada, ☎ 613/237–3657, FAX 613/237–7502, WEB www.acta.net). **Australian Federation of Travel Agents** (✉ Level 3, 309 Pitt St., Sydney NSW 2000, Australia, ☎ 02/9264–3299, FAX 02/9264–1085, WEB www.afta.com.au). **Travel Agents' Association of New Zealand** (✉ Box 1888, Wellington 10033, New Zealand, ☎ 04/499–0104, FAX 04/499–0827, WEB www.taanz.org.nz).

VISITOR INFORMATION

For general information about South Florida's attractions, contact the office below. For regional tourist bureaus and chambers of commerce see individual chapters.

➤ STATE: **Florida Tourism Industry Marketing Corporation** (✉ Box 1100, 661 E. Jefferson St., Suite 300, Tallahassee, FL 32302, ☎ 850/487–1462, FAX 850/224–2938).

➤ IN THE U.K.: **ABC Florida** (✉ Box 35, Abingdon, Oxon OX14 4TB, U.K., ☎ 0891/600–555, 50p per minute; send £2 for vacation pack).

WEB SITES

Do check out the World Wide Web when you're planning your trip. You'll find everything from current weather forecasts to virtual tours of famous cities. Be sure to **visit Fodors.com** (www.fodors.com), a complete travel-planning site. You can research prices and book plane tickets, hotel rooms, rental cars, vacation packages, and more. In addition, you can post your pressing questions in the Travel Talk section and, in the site's Rants & Raves section, read comments about some of the restaurants and hotels in this book—and chime in yourself. Other planning tools include a currency converter and weather repotrs, and there are loads of links to other travel resources.The state of Florida is very visitor-oriented and has created a terrific Web site—www.flausa.com—with superb links to help you find out all you want to know. It's a wonderful place to learn about everything from fancy resorts to camping trips to car routes to beach towns.

WHEN TO GO

South Florida is a destination for all seasons, although most visitors prefer October–April.

Winter remains the height of the tourist season, when South Florida is crowded with "snowbirds" fleeing cold weather in the north. (It did snow in Miami once in the 1970s, but since then the average snowfall has been exactly 00.00 inches.) Hotels, bars, discos, restaurants, shops, and attractions are all crowded. Hollywood and Broadway celebrities appear in sophisticated supper clubs, and other performing artists hold the stage at ballets, operas, concerts, and theaters.

For the college crowd, spring vacation is still the time to congregate; Fort Lauderdale, where city officials have refashioned the beachfront more as a family resort, no longer indulges young revelers, so it's much less popular with college students than it once was.

Summer in South Florida, as smart budget-minded visitors have discovered, is often hot and very humid, but along the coast, ocean breezes make the season quite bearable and many hotels lower their prices considerably.

CLIMATE

What follows are average daily maximum and minimum temperatures for major cities in South Florida.

➤ FORECASTS: **Weather Channel Connection** (☎ 900/932–8437), 95¢ per minute from a Touch-Tone phone.

KEY WEST (THE KEYS)

Jan.	76F	24C	May	85F	29C	Sept.	90F	32C
	65	18		74	23		77	25
Feb.	76F	24C	June	88F	31C	Oct.	83F	28C
	67	19		77	25		76	24
Mar.	79F	26C	July	90F	32C	Nov.	79F	26C
	68	20		79	26		70	21
Apr.	81F	27C	Aug.	90F	32C	Dec.	76F	24C
	72	22		79	26		67	19

MIAMI

Jan.	74F	23C	May	83F	28C	Sept.	86F	30C
	63	17		72	22		76	24
Feb.	76F	24C	June	85F	29C	Oct.	83F	28C
	63	17		76	24		72	22
Mar.	77F	25C	July	88F	31C	Nov.	79F	26C
	65	18		76	24		67	19
Apr.	79F	26C	Aug.	88F	31C	Dec.	76F	26C
	68	20		77	25		63	17

FESTIVALS AND SEASONAL EVENTS

➤ DEC.: In mid-December, the **Winterfest Boat Parade** lights up the Intracoastal Waterway in Fort Lauderdale (☎ 954/767–0686). The **Coconut Grove King Mango Strut** toward year's end in Miami is a parody of the King Orange Parade (☎ 305/445–1865).

➤ LATE DEC.–EARLY JAN.: The **Orange Bowl and Junior Orange Bowl Festival,** in the Miami area, are best known for the downtown King Orange Jamboree Parade on December 31 and the Orange Bowl Football Classic at Pro Player Stadium but also include more than 20 youth-oriented events (☎ 305/371–4600). The **Micron PC Bowl,** at Miami's Pro Player Stadium, usually takes place on the final days of December (☎ 954/564–5000).

➤ JAN.: The weekend nearest to January 6 is Miami's **Three Kings Parade** along Southwest Eight Street, a tradition nearly as old as the city's Latin population. Mid-month, **Art Deco Weekend** spotlights Miami Beach's historic district with an art deco street fair along Ocean Drive, a 1930s-style Moon Over Miami Ball, and live entertainment (☎ 305/672–2014). **Taste of the Grove Food and Music Festival** is a popular fund-raiser put on in Coconut Grove's Peacock Park by area restaurants (☎ 305/444–7270). Early in the month, **Polo Season** opens at the Palm Beach Polo and Country Club in West Palm Beach (☎ 561/793–1440).

➤ FEB.: The **Coconut Grove Art Festival,** mid-month, is the state's largest (☎ 305/447–0401). The **Miami Film Festival,** sponsored by the Film Society of America, is 10 days of international, domestic, and local films (☎ 305/377–3456).

➤ MAR.: The self-proclaimed world's largest street party, **Calle Ocho** packs one million people onto Miami's Southwest Eighth Street for a frenetic day of live Latin music, ethnic food, and massive corporate product give-aways (☎ 305/644–8888). The 80-acre **Miami-Dade County Fair and Exposition** is the largest fair in Florida, and one of the biggest in the country. It runs 18 days beginning the third Thursday in March and features 50,000 adult and youth exhibits from woodwork to financial investing (☎ 305/223–7060). The **Lauderdale-by-the-Sea Craft Festival** features crafts vendors and live entertainment on the beachfront along Commercial Boulevard and A1A ☎ 954/472–3755); there's a second festival held in October.

➤ APR.: The **Delray Affair,** held the weekend following Easter, is the biggest event in the area and features arts, crafts, and food (☎ 561/279–

1380). The **Cedar Key Sidewalk Arts Festival** is celebrated in one of the state's most historic towns mid-month (☎ 352/543–5600).

➤ LATE APR.–EARLY MAY: The **Conch Republic Celebration** honors the founding fathers of the Conch Republic, "the small island nation of Key West" (☎ 305/296–0123).

➤ MAY: The **Air & Sea Show** draws more than 2 million people to the Fort Lauderdale beachfront for performances by big names in aviation, such as the navy's Blue Angels and the air force's Thunderbirds (☎ 954/527–5600 ext. 88). The first weekend in May, the **Arabian Nights Festival,** in Opa-locka, is a mix of contemporary and fantasy-inspired entertainment (☎ 305/758–4166).

➤ JUNE: The **Miami-Bahamas Goombay Festival,** in Miami's Coconut Grove, celebrates the city's Bahamian heritage the first weekend of the month (☎ 305/443–7928 or 305/372–9966) with food, crafts, and street music all day.

➤ JUNE–JULY: **Beethoven by the Beach,** in Fort Lauderdale, features Beethoven's symphonies, chamber pieces, and piano concertos performed by the Florida Philharmonic (☎ 954/561–2997).

➤ JULY: **Summer Family Fun Film Fest,** run by the Fort Lauderdale Film Festival, offers games for kids and family movies on Fort Lauderdale's South Beach beginning at sunset (☎ 800/245–4621).

➤ OCT.: The **Fort Lauderdale International Boat Show,** the world's largest show based on exhibit size, displays boats of every size, price, and description at the Bahia Mar marina and four other venues (☎ 954/764–7642). **Fantasy Fest,** in Key West, is a no-holds-barred Halloween costume party, parade, and town fair (☎ 305/296–1817).

➤ OCT.–NOV.: The **Fort Lauderdale International Film Festival** showcases three weeks of independent cinema from around the world beginning in late October (☎ 954/760–9898).

➤ NOV.: The **Miami Book Fair International,** the largest book fair in the United States, is held on the Wolfson campus of Miami-Dade Community College (☎ 305/237–3032). The **Broward County Fair,** the county's largest family event, features lots of carnival rides, concerts, and food mid-month (☎ 954/450–1234).

Florida Peninsula

INDEX

Icons and Symbols

★ Our special recommendations
✕ Restaurant
🏨 Lodging establishment
✕🏨 Lodging establishment whose restaurant warrants a special trip
🦆 Good for kids (rubber duck)
☞ Sends you to another section of the guide for more information
✉ Address
☎ Telephone number
⏲ Opening and closing times
🎟 Admission prices

Numbers in white and black circles ③ ❸ that appear on the maps, in the margins, and within the tours correspond to one another.

A

B

NOTES

NOTES

NOTES

NOTES

NOTES

NOTES

FODOR'S SOUTH FLORIDA 2002

EDITORS: Shannon Kelly, Melissa Klurman

Editorial Contributors: Pamela Acheson, Kathy Foster, Jennie Hess, Jen Karetnick, Martha Limner, Alan Macher, Tiffany Madera, Diane Marshall, Gary McKechnie, Richard Myers, Laura Randolph, Gretchen Schmidt, Lisa Simundson, Rowland Stiteler, Matthew Windsor

Editorial Production: Taryn Luciani

Maps: David Lindroth, *cartographer*; Rebecca Baer, *map editor*

Design: Fabrizio La Rocca, *creative director*; Guido Caroti, *art director*; Jolie Novak, *senior picture editor*; Melanie Marin, *photo editor*

Cover Design: Pentagram

Production/Manufacturing: Colleen Ziemba

COPYRIGHT

ISBN 0-679-00871-3

ISSN 1526-2219

SPECIAL SALES

Fodor's Travel Publications are available at special discounts for bulk purchases for sales promotions or premiums. Special editions, including personalized covers, excerpts of existing guides, and corporate imprints, can be created in large quantities for special needs. For more information, contact your local bookseller or write to Special Markets, Fodor's Travel Publications, 280 Park Avenue, New York, NY 10017. Inquiries from Canada should be directed to your local Canadian bookseller or sent to Random House of Canada, Ltd., Marketing Department, 2775 Matheson Boulevard East, Mississauga, Ontario L4W 4P7. Inquiries from the United Kingdom should be sent to Fodor's Travel Publications, 20 Vauxhall Bridge Road, London SW1V 2SA, England.

PRINTED IN THE UNITED STATES OF AMERICA

10 9 8 7 6 5 4 3 2 1

IMPORTANT TIP

Although all prices, opening times, and other details in this book are based on information supplied to us at press time, changes occur all the time in the travel world, and Fodor's cannot accept responsibility for facts that become outdated or for inadvertent errors or omissions. So always confirm information when it matters, especially if you're making a detour to visit a specific place.

PHOTOGRAPHY

Jack Hollingsworth, *cover. (South Beach, Miami).*

Biscayne National Park: *Steven Frink, 8A.*

The Breakers, *3 bottom right.*

Corbis: *Tony Arruza, 1, 10B. Morton Beebe, 16. Richard Bickel, 4–5. Richard Cummins, 11C.*

Delano Hotel, *14J.*

Fotoconcept, Inc., *14E.*

John Gillan, *9D.*

Greater Fort Lauderdale Convention and Visitors Bureau, *2 top left, 3 center, 10 top right.*

Greater Miami Convention and Visitors Bureau, *2 top right, 2 bottom left, 2 bottom center, 2 bottom right.*

Gumbo Limbo Nature Center, *p. 11B.*

The Image Bank: *Luis Castañeda, p. 7E, 8B. Angelo Cavalli, 6B, 7F, 13D. Gary Crallé, 10A, 11A. Grant V. Faint, 6C. Robert Holland, 9E. Jeff Hunter, 13E. Walter Iooss Jr., 12A. Michael Melford, 12B. Marvin E. Newman, 9C. Guido Alberto Rossi, 14I. Nicholas Russell, 7D.*

Impressions Unlimited, *14B.*

Little Palm Island, *14C.*

The Morikami Museum of Japanese Gardens, *14H.*

Museum of Discovery and Science, *14F.*

National Park Service, *3 top right.*

Norman's Restaurant, *14G.*

Visit Florida Tourism,. *3 top left, 3 bottom left, 6A, 12C, 13 top, 14D.*

Vizcaya Museum & Gardens, *14A*

ABOUT OUR WRITERS

The more you know before you go, the better your trip will be. The area's most secluded beach, finest Cuban restaurant, or best key lime pie could be just around the corner from your hotel, but if you don't know it's there, it might as well be on the other side of the globe. That's where this book comes in. It's a great step toward making sure your next trip lives up to your expectations. As you plan, check out the Web as well. Guidebooks have been helping smart travelers find the special places for years; the Web is one more tool. Whatever reference you consult, be savvy about what you read, and always consider the source. Images and language can be massaged to make places appear better than they are. And one traveler's quaint is another's grimy. Here at Fodor's, and at our on-line arm, Fodors.com, our focus is on providing you with information that's not only useful but accurate and on target. Every day Fodor's editors put enormous effort into getting things right, beginning with the search for the right contributors—people who have objective judgment, broad travel experience, and the writing ability to put their insights into words. There's no substitute for advice from a like-minded friend who has just come back from where you're going, but our writers, having seen all corners of South Florida, are the next best thing. They're the kind of people you'd poll for tips yourself if you knew them.

After almost two decades in New York City, husband and wife team **Pamela Acheson** and **Richard Myers** decided one snowy winter to make a change in latitude and head south. Now these regular Fodor's contributors divide their time between Florida and the Caribbean. Together they are the co–authors of *The Best Romantic Escapes in Florida* and *More of the Best Romantic Escapes in Florida*. Pam and Dick also contribute to *Fodor's Florida* and *Fodor's Caribbean*.

Starting behind an old manual typewriter at his hometown newspaper, **Alan Macher** has written everything from human-interest stories to speeches. He makes his home in Boca Raton, where he can play tennis and bike along Route A1A year-round.

Intrepid traveler and intrepid shopper **Diane Marshall** was formerly editor and publisher of the newsletter "The Savvy Shopper: The Traveler's Guide to Shopping Around the World." From her home in the Keys, she has written for numerous travel guides, newspapers, magazines, and on-line services.

Florida native and Elvis fan **Gary McKechnie** has written humor and travel articles for newspapers and magazines nationwide and has produced award-winning training films and resort videos.

Don't Forget to Write

Your experiences—positive and negative—matter to us. If we have missed or misstated something, we want to hear about it. We follow up on all suggestions. Contact the South Florida editor at editors@fodors.com or c/o Fodor's, 280 Park Avenue, New York, New York 10017. And have a fabulous trip!

Karen Cure
Editorial Director